P9-CEA-986

Police Operations

Theory and Practice | Fifth Edition

Kären Matison Hess, Ph.D.
Normandale Community College

Christine Hess Orthmann, MS
Orthmann Writing and Research, Inc.

With Contributions by **Sgt. Henry Lim Cho**

DELMAR
CENGAGE Learning

Australia • Brazil • Japan • Korea • Mexico • Singapore • Spain • United Kingdom • United States

Police Operations: Theory and Practice, 5th edition

Author(s): Kären Matison Hess, Christine Hess Orthmann

Vice President, Career and Professional Editorial: Dave Garza

Director of Learning Solutions: Sandy Clark

Senior Acquisitions Editor: Shelley Esposito

Managing Editor: Larry Main

Product Manager: Anne Orgren

Editorial Assistant: Danielle Klahr

Vice President, Career and Professional Marketing: Jennifer Baker

Marketing Director: Deborah S. Yarnell

Marketing Manager: Erin Brennan

Marketing Coordinator: Jonathan Sheehan

Production Director: Wendy Troeger

Production Manager: Mark Bernard

Senior Content Project Manager: Betty Dickson

Senior Art Director: Joy Kocsis

Photo Research: Terri Wright, www.terriwright.com

Library of Congress Control Number: 2009942333

ISBN-13: 978-1-4354-8866-3

ISBN-10: 1-4354-8866-0

Delmar
5 Maxwell Drive
Clifton Park, NY 12065-2919
USA

Cengage Learning is a leading provider of customized learning solutions with office locations around the globe, including Singapore, the United Kingdom, Australia, Mexico, Brazil, and Japan. Locate your local office at: international.cengage.com/region

Cengage Learning products are represented in Canada by Nelson Education, Ltd.

To learn more about Delmar, visit www.cengage.com/delmar

Purchase any of our products at your local college store or at our preferred online store **www.CengageBrain.com**

Printed in the United States of America
3 4 5 6 7 12 11

DEDICATION

Dedicated to the hundreds of thousands of uniformed law enforcement officers, past and present, whose accomplishments have made such a difference in the quality of life in communities throughout the United States, and to those who are about to join them.

BRIEF CONTENTS

SECTION I
The Basics behind Effective Police Operations

SECTION II
Getting the Job Done: Basic Police Operations

SECTION III
Specialized Police Operations

SECTION IV
The Personal Side of Police Operations

CONTENTS

FOREWORD

Donald J. Clough,
Bloomington Police Department

Police Operations is a well-researched, comprehensive and up-to-date text that covers all major aspects of policing. It deals with what law enforcement leaders and researchers feel are the most critical issues facing law enforcement in the 21st century. A theme running throughout *Police Operations* is that the motivated, professional uniformed officer can make a tremendous difference in how citizens are "served and protected."

The authors focus attention on what could be rather than on what has been in the past. They emphasize what the police responsibility is, the constitutional and statutory constraints under which police function and how the tasks to be performed can be accomplished responsibly and humanely within these constraints. Relevant landmark Supreme Court cases affecting police operations are presented throughout the text, giving students an understanding of case law and police procedures under varying circumstances.

Students are challenged to apply the information contained in each chapter to application exercises, critical thinking problems, Gale Emergency Services Database assignments, and discussion questions. These exercises, problems and questions underscore the complexity of policing and the need for knowledge, skill and common sense in carrying out police operations. With such a base, police officers of the future will be able to find new ways to deliver police services fairly, equitably and effectively. They can, indeed, reshape approaches to some of the critical problems confronting law enforcement and may become the change agents of the future. The authors are to be congratulated on writing a text that not only covers all the basics of police operations, but does so in a way that students should find both interesting and challenging.

PREFACE

PURPOSE

Welcome to ***Police Operations, Fifth Edition.*** This text is *not* an introduction to law enforcement and the criminal justice system. It is intended to describe what police officers do and why. Therefore, it is short on theory and long on practical application, presenting the fundamentals of what policing is all about.

The basic reason modern society has police departments is summarized in the classic statement of police sociologist Egon Bittner*: "Something-ought-not-to-be-happening—about-which-something-ought-to-be-done-NOW!" This text goes beyond this reactive approach (which will always be an important and unavoidable part of policing), however, by also incorporating the techniques of proactive policing. Proactive policing is perhaps best illustrated in *community policing*, in which law enforcement partners with the citizens and organizations in a community to make the community safer for all. For such partnerships to work, law enforcement agencies must have carefully thought-through policies and procedures for dealing with crime and violence, both reactively and proactively. Community policing also emphasizes the need for individual officers on the street to be creative in their approaches to problems and to work with citizens as they solve these problems.

ORGANIZATION OF THE TEXT

The first section of *Police Operations* discusses the basics behind effective police operations, including the context in which services are provided and the skills required to provide these services (Chapter 1). Law enforcement officers must be thoroughly familiar with the citizens they are sworn to "serve and protect" (Chapter 2) as well as with the constitutional restraints within which they must operate (Chapter 3). They must be proficient in communication skills as well as in the numerous profession-specific skills required in law enforcement: conducting stops and frisks, making arrests, searching crime scenes and suspects, investigating crimes and assisting victims.

Section II discusses basic police operations, including patrol (Chapter 4); traffic (Chapter 5); crime, disorder and quality-of-life issues (Chapter 6); violence—domestic, school and workplace (Chapter 7); emergencies (Chapter 8); and homeland security (Chapter 9). The third section presents specialized police operations such as those performed by detectives in investigating crimes (Chapter 10), juvenile officers (Chapter 11) and officers who deal with gangs and drugs (Chapter 12). The final section discusses the personal side of law enforcement—what officers need to know about maintaining their physical and emotional well-being so they can continue in their chosen profession (Chapter 13) and what they need to know about protecting themselves from being sued and about acting legally and ethically (Chapter 14).

---

*From "Florence Nightingale in Pursuit of Willie Sutton: A Theory of Police," in ***The Potential for Reform of Criminal Justice,*** edited by H. Jacob. Beverly Hills, CA: Sage, 1974, p.30.

NEW TO THIS EDITION

The Fifth Edition has updated all statistics and references, with most of the more than 500 new references having been published after 2006. New to this edition is inclusion of selected relevant standards from the Commission for the Accreditation of Law Enforcement Agencies (CALEA). Also new throughout the revised edition are insights from Sgt. Henry Cho, a Rosemount (Minnesota) police officer, reflecting practical, applied information. In addition, the following changes have been made:

Chapter 1 • Police Operations in Context

- An introduction to the Commission for Law Enforcement Agencies (CALEA)
- An overview of contemporary police operations
- Characteristics of the four generations of officers now found in many departments
- Advances in technology in police operations
- Geo-policing
- The impact of the economic downturn and abandoned homes

Chapter 2 • Communication

- Updated content on wireless communications technology
- Added material on law enforcement databases
- Expanded discussion on interoperability issues
- Increased coverage of NG9-1-1
- New content on language barriers and challenges (translators, cultural views of police, etc.)
- Expanded content on effective interviewing/interrogating
- Building rapport
- New section: The Certified Forensic Interviewer Program
- More thorough discussion of interrogating without *Mirandizing* and the issue of beachheading, or questioning first *(Missouri v. Seibert, 2004)*
- New content on detecting deception

Chapter 3 • Operational Skills: Performing within the Law

- New cases on arrests/seizures: *Brendlin v. California* (2007), *Georgia v. Randolph* (2006), *Hudson v. Michigan* (2006), *Scott v. Harris* (2007), *Virginia v. Moore* (2008).
- Expanded discussion on Exclusionary Rule
- New content on Verbal Judo
- New material on use-of-force continuums
- Increased discussion on knock and announce laws
- More detailed coverage of handcuffing
- Expanded discussion on less-lethal weapons
- Importance of written reports on use of force
- 10-point quiz on excessive force

Chapter 4 • Patrol

- Although the organizational contradiction of the status of patrol was discussed in previous editions, the realization of patrol's importance has overcome the supposed hierarchical barriers of the past. It is now commonly accepted in the law enforcement culture that patrol is the most important part of a police agency and is its backbone.
- Expanded discussion on foot patrol
- New data on assigned versus pooled vehicles
- Updated content on GPS/GIS

Chapter 5 • Traffic

- Added content on uniform visibility for traffic detail
- Expanded content on automated license plate recognition (ALPR) technology
- Updated material on seat belt laws
- Updated discussion of speeding and traffic calming measures
- New material on illegal street racing
- New and updated material on DUI/DWI stops
- New data on automated citations and e-ticketing
- Expanded discussion regarding racial profiling and the Racial Profiling Data Collection Center
- New coverage of foot pursuits and vehicle pursuits
- Updated information on pursuit policies and national data
- Discussed new case: *Scott v. Harris* (2007) and pursuit liability
- Discussed Electronic Emergency Response Management System (E2RMS)
- Updated discussion on crash management, response and investigation/reconstruction
- New material on the National Highway Traffic Safety Administration (NHTSA)'s Safe Communities program, sponsored by the U.S. Department of Transportation
- New material on the Area Traffic Officer (ATO) Program

Chapter 6 • Crime, Disorder and Quality-of-Life Issues

- New and expanded content on technology to assist crime analysis: crime mapping, hot spot enforcement, geographic information systems (GIS), global positioning systems (GPS), CompStat
- Added discussion on issues related to disseminating crime information to the public
- Updated material on responding to crime-related calls: theft, identity theft, patrolling motels, drive-by shootings
- New content on challenges posed by immigration and the relationship to crime
- New discussion on responding to calls involving disorder and quality-of-life issues: panhandling, prostitution, problem bars, homeless, mentally ill
- New coverage on responding to civil disobedience: protests, demonstrations, mass gatherings
- Expanded discussion on responding to crisis situations: hostage situations, suicidal persons, including suicide by cop (SBC) and officer suicides

Chapter 7 • Violence

- Expanded discussion on risk factors for domestic violence victimization
- Expanded content on intimate partner violence (IPV)
- Inserted material on theories about why men batter
- New content on teen dating violence
- Expanded coverage on enhancing police response to domestic violence
- New content regarding mandatory versus discretionary arrest laws
- GPS tracking of abusers
- Moved bulk of content on child abuse/maltreatment and Internet crimes against children to Chapter 11
- Updated and revised content on elder abuse: warning signs, research findings, risk factors and the police response
- Expanded discussion on school resource officers (SROs) and campus police, including Clery Act requirements
- New and expanded material on bullying
- Updated statistics on workplace violence, types of workplace violence and the law enforcement response to such violence

Chapter 8 • Emergency Situations

- New material on the Department of Homeland Security (DHS)'s recommendations for emergency planning and preparedness
- Added information on the Federal Emergency Management Agency (FEMA) and the Emergency Management Assistance Compact (EMAC)
- Expanded discussion of the National Incident Management System (NIMS)
- Updated content on how to deal with the media during emergencies
- Added content on dealing with hazmat incidents, critical infrastructure failure (e.g., bridge collapses) and pandemics

Chapter 9 • Terrorism: Homeland Security

- Thoroughly updated throughout—new statistics, new stories of attacks and attempts, new technologies and techniques to combat terrorism
- Renewal of the USA PATRIOT Act
- Key lessons learned from the attacks in Mumbai, India
- New figure and tables: National Infrastructure Protection Plan (NIPP) Risk Management Framework

Chapter 10 • Criminal Investigation

- New material on classification of evidence (four types)
- New discussion on the state of the national forensic science system and the need for changes and upgrades to the system and process
- Expanded content on crime analysis
- New material on digital and electronic evidence
- New material on microstamping (gun identification technology)
- Added criminal vehicular homicide

- Added myths and truths about serial killers
- Added to and updated discussion on fraud and white-collar crime

Chapter 11 • Responding to Children and Juveniles

- Moved content on child abuse/maltreatment from Chapter 7 to here
- Expanded discussion on Internet crimes against children, including coverage of Innocent Images National Initiative (IINI)
- New material on Child Abduction Response Team (CART)
- Added to discussion on truancy
- New content regarding confidentiality versus openness of juvenile cases, records and proceedings

Chapter 12 • Gangs and Drugs

- Added to discussions on female and hybrid gangs
- New figure on gang signs and symbols
- Enhanced table on criminal organizations to reflect emerging gangs in the United States: MS-13, Sureños, Norteños, Hmong gangs, Somali gangs, and so on.
- Expanded discussions on identifying gang members, gang units and gang task forces
- New content on the Office of Juvenile Justice and Delinquency Prevention (OJJDP)'s Comprehensive Gang Model and Gang Reduction Program, the G.R.E.A.T. Program, and combating the "Stop Snitching Code of Silence"
- Greatly enhanced section on the growing threat of Mexican Drug Trafficking Organizations (DTOs) crossing our borders
- New material on field testing of drugs and investigative/technological aids
- Updated information on undercover drug operations
- Modified discussion on dealing with meth labs
- New content on asset forfeitures
- New section on what the research says regarding effective drug interventions

Chapter 13 • Physical and Mental Health Issues

- Updated information about fitness for duty
- New content about the threat of methicillin-resistant *Staphylococcus aureus* (MRSA) infection
- New inclusion of the FBI's *Handbook of Forensic Services* precautions for infection control
- Expanded discussion on guarding against mental stress and balancing the job with other aspects of officer life
- New discussion on fatigue and the effects of sleep deprivation on officer safety
- Added content to posttraumatic stress disorder (PTSD) discussion on post-event memory loss

Chapter 14 • Liability and Ethics

- Expanded discussion on use-of-force reports, also called subject management or response-to-resistance reports
- Expanded content on ethics and discretion in police decision making
- Added the International Association of Chiefs of Police (IACP) oath of honor
- Added research findings on the prevalence of a police code of silence
- New discussion on the ethical issues involved in professional courtesy

HOW TO USE THIS TEXT (PEDAGOGICAL AIDS)

Police Operations is more than a text. It is a learning experience requiring *your* active participation to obtain the best results. You will get the most out of the text if you first familiarize yourself with the total scope of law enforcement: read and think about the subjects listed in the Contents. Then follow five steps for each chapter to get *triple-strength learning.*

Triple-Strength Learning

1. Read the objectives at the beginning of each chapter, stated in the form of "Do You Know" questions. This is your *first* exposure to the key concepts of the text. The following is an example of this format:
   - What police operations are and what they include?
2. Review the key terms and think about their meaning in the context of law enforcement.
3. Read the chapter, underlining or taking notes if that is your preferred study style. Pay special attention to all information within the highlighted areas. This is your *second* exposure to the chapter's key concepts. The following is an example of this format:

Police operations refers to activities conducted in the field by law enforcement officers as they "serve and protect," including patrol, traffic, investigation and general calls for service.

   The key concepts of each chapter are emphasized in this manner. Also pay attention to all words in bold print. All key terms will be in bold print when they are first defined.

4. Read the summary carefully. This will be your *third* exposure to the key concepts. By now, you should have internalized the information.
5. To make sure you have learned the information, when you have finished reading a chapter, reread the list of objectives given at the beginning of that chapter to make certain you can answer each question. If you find yourself stumped, find the appropriate material in the chapter and review it. Often these questions will be used as essay questions during testing.
6. Review the key terms to be certain you can define each. These also are frequently used as test items.

A Note: This text is designed to give you *triple-strength* learning *if* you (1) think about the questions at the beginning of the chapter before you read, (2) read the chapter thoughtfully for in-depth answers to these questions and then (3) read and reread the summary. Do not misinterpret triple-strength learning to mean you need only focus on three elements—the "Do You Know" items, highlighted boxes and summaries—to master the chapter. You are also responsible for reading and understanding the material that surrounds these basics—the "meat" around the bones, so to speak. The summaries are intended as a *review*, not as shortcuts or replacements to reading the entire chapter. If you read only the summaries, or focus only on the highlighted key concepts, you are not likely to understand or recall the content. Remember, your livelihood and your life is on the line in this demanding and rewarding profession. Begin your habits of self-discipline now.

EXPLORING FURTHER

The text also provides an opportunity for you to apply what you have learned or to go into specific areas in greater depth. To further strengthen your learning experience, the text includes discussion questions, application exercises in which you create policies and procedures related to the content of each chapter, and critical thinking exercises. Professional law enforcement officers should be able to create reasonable, legal, ethical and effective policies and procedures for the most common situations encountered in law enforcement. In addition, they should be able to approach each situation as a unique experience, perhaps requiring a more creative approach. Law enforcement officers must have good critical thinking skills. It is the intent of this text to provide a balance of both.

Finally, each chapter contains Gale Emergency Services database assignments allowing you to go into greater depth in areas of interest to you. Do as many of these assignments as your time permits.

Good reading and learning!

ANCILLARIES

To further enhance your study of law enforcement and criminal justice, several supplements are available:

Instructor Support Materials:

- The Instructor's Resource Manual to accompany this text includes detailed chapter outlines, chapter summaries, key terms reviews, class activity suggestions, and a test bank with a full answer key
- Instructor materials available on the companion Web site include *new* PowerPoint® lecture slides, a computerized test bank and an electronic version of the Instructor's Resource manual.

Student Materials:

- The **companion website** for this text provides students with access to chapter-by-chapter critical thinking questions. **New to this edition** are Internet exercises, tutorial chapter quizzes and Web links.
- **The Criminal Justice Resource Center** http://cj.wadsworth.com—This Web site's "Discipline Resources" section contains links to popular criminal justice sites, Supreme Court updates, and more.

Additional Resources Available:

- **Careers in Criminal Justice Website** academic.cengage.com/criminaljustice/careers—This unique Web site helps students investigate the criminal justice career choices that are right for them with the help of several important tools.
- **Cengage Learning Video Library**—This library includes compelling videos from *Court TV* and *A&E* featuring provocative one-hour court cases to illustrate seminal and high-profile cases in depth. Contact your Cengage Learning representative for a complete listing of videos.
- **Crime Scenes 2.0: Interactive Criminal Justice CD-ROM**—An interactive CD-ROM featuring six vignettes allowing you to play various roles as you explore all aspects of the criminal justice system.
- **Careers in Criminal Justice and Related Fields: From Internship to Promotion, Sixth Edition**—This book provides specific information on many criminal justice professions, helpful tips on resumes and cover letters, and practical advice on interview techniques.

ACKNOWLEDGMENTS

First, we would like to acknowledge Henry M. Wrobleski (1922–2007), the original lead author for the first two editions of this text. Henry was the coordinator of the Law Enforcement Program at Normandale Community College as well as a respected author, lecturer, consultant and expert witness with 30 years of experience in law enforcement and security. He was also the Dean of Instruction for the Institute for Professional Development and a graduate of the FBI Academy. Other Cengage texts Wrobleski contributed to were *Introduction to Law Enforcement and Criminal Justice* and *Private Security*. He is very much missed.

We would also like to thank Waldo Asp for creating the *Exercises in Critical Thinking* found at the end of each chapter. We would like to thank the reviewers for the Fifth Edition: Irl R. (Chris) Carmean, Houston Community College; Steven B. Carter, Kaplan College; Richard H. Martin, Auburn University–Montgomery; and Jay Zumbrun, Community College of Baltimore County. Thanks are also due to the reviewers of the original manuscript and previous editions for their careful reading and constructive suggestions: James S. Albritton, Marquette University; Becky Allen, Minot State University; David Barlow, University of Wisconsin–Milwaukee; Michael B. Blankenship, Memphis State University; William D. Braddock, Boise State University; Laura Brooks, University of Maryland; David L. Carter, Michigan State University; Robert Ives, Rock Valley College (Illinois); David A. Kramer, Bergen Community College; Floyd W. Liley, Jr., Mansfield University; Neal W. Lippold, Waubonsee Community College; Steven Livernois, SUNY–Canton; Jeff Magers, Stephen F. Austin State University; James Malcolm, College of Lake County; James L. Massey, Northern Illinois University; Donald McLean, Oakland Community College; Joe Morris, Northwestern State University; James E. Newman, Rio Hondo Community College–Police Academy (California); James T. Nichols, Tompkins Cortland Community College; Tom O'Connor, North Carolina Wesleyan University; Jerald L. Plant, Milwaukee Area Technical College; Carroll S. Price, Penn Valley Community College; Chester L. Quarles, University of Mississippi; James Sewell, Florida Department of Law Enforcement; Sandra M. Hall Smith, Indiana University Northwest; B. Grant Stitt, University of Nevada at Reno; and Gary W. Tucker, Sinclair Community College. Any errors in the text are, however, the sole responsibility of the coauthors.

Finally, thanks to our photo consultant, Bobbi Peacock; our photo researcher, Terri Wright; our editors at Delmar Cengage Learning, Product Manager Anne Orgren and Senior Acquisitions Editor Shelley Esposito, for their outstanding advice, support and encouragement; our copyeditor, Robin Gold; and our production editor at Buuji, Sara Dovre Wudali.

ABOUT THE AUTHORS

ABOUT THE AUTHORS

Kären Matison Hess, Ph.D., has written extensively in the field of law enforcement and conducts seminars on communication in law enforcement. She was a member of the English department at Normandale Community College and president of the Institute for Professional Development. Dr. Hess is a graduate of the University of Minnesota, where she concentrated on educational psychology and instructional design.

Other Cengage texts Dr. Hess has coauthored are *Community Policing: Partnerships for Problem Solving*, Fifth Edition; *Criminal Investigation*, Ninth Edition; *Criminal Procedure; Introduction to Law Enforcement and Criminal Justice*, Ninth Edition; *Juvenile Justice*, Fifth Edition; *Management and Supervision in Law Enforcement*, Fourth Edition; *Private Security*, Fifth Edition; and *Careers in Criminal Justice and Related Fields: From Internship to Promotion*, Sixth Edition.

Dr. Hess is a member of the Academy of Criminal Justice Sciences, the American Association of University Women, the American Correctional Association, the American Society for Industrial Security, the American Society of Criminologists, the International Association of Chiefs of Police, the Minnesota Association of Chiefs of Police, the Police Executive Research Forum and the Text and Academic Authors Association, which has named her to their Council of Fellows. She is also a member of the TAA Foundation board of directors.

Christine Hess Orthmann, M.S., has been writing and researching in various aspects of criminal justice for over 20 years. She is a coauthor of *Corrections for the Twenty-First Century* and *Criminal Investigation*, Ninth Edition, as well as a major contributor to *Introduction to Law Enforcement and Criminal Justice*, Ninth Edition; *Constitutional Law*, Fifth Edition; *Community Policing: Partnerships for Problem Solving*, Fifth Edition; and *Juvenile Justice*, Fifth Edition. Orthmann is a member of the Text and Academic Authors Association (TAA) and the Academy of Criminal Justice Sciences (ACJS), as well as a reserve officer with the Rosemount (Minnesota) Police Department.

ABOUT THE CONTRIBUTOR

Henry Lim Cho holds an M.A. in Human Services with an emphasis on Criminal Justice Leadership from Concordia University–St. Paul, Minnesota. He has worked in the field of criminal justice for more than 10 years, having held positions in private security and as a community service officer, police officer and detective. He currently holds the rank of Sergeant with the Rosemount (Minnesota) Police Department. Sgt. Cho has experience as a use-of-force instructor and a crime scene investigator. His professional memberships include the Minnesota Police and Peace Officer's Association, International Association of Identification–Minnesota Chapter, Minnesota Sex Crimes Investigator Association, High Technology Crime Investigation Association, National White Collar Crime Center, and Fraternal Order of Police. Sgt. Cho has been published in the *Minnesota Police Journal* and has appeared as a featured profile contributor in *Introduction to Law Enforcement and Criminal Justice*, Ninth Edition, by Kären M. Hess.

SECTION I

The Basics behind Effective Police Operations

Police operations deal with what officers do in the field as they "serve and protect." To fulfill their responsibilities, law enforcement officers have been given great power, power entrusted to them by the people they serve and defined by the laws of the land, state and municipality. This section presents an overview of police operations starting with the context in which those services are provided.

The society served, the laws it has enacted, the individuals entering law enforcement and the police organization itself have undergone great changes in the past decade—today's law enforcement uses mission statements, value statements, goals, objectives, policies, procedures and regulations to provide a basic structure within which officers normally function. Because law enforcement deals with such diverse problems, officers also must expect to use discretion while safeguarding citizens' constitutional rights (Chapter 1).

Law enforcement demands that its officers be multi-faceted and well rounded. Officers must understand the

complex communication process and the barriers that often exist within that process and within our diverse society. Officers also must be skilled in making field inquiries, interviewing and interrogating, and they must know how to do so while protecting the constitutional rights of victims, suspects and witnesses. Further, officers must record the information they have obtained in effective, reader-friendly reports, and they must know how to use the various records available (Chapter 2). In addition, officers need several profession-specific skills. They must understand and become skilled at conducting stops and frisks, making arrests, conducting searches and participating in undercover operations, all without violating anyone's constitutional rights (Chapter 3).

CHAPTER 1

Police Operations in Context

DO YOU KNOW . . .

- What police operations are and what they include?
- What changes have affected police operations?
- How our society has changed?
- How our law enforcement officers have changed?
- How the police organization may change?
- What the Commission on Accreditation of Law Enforcement Agencies (CALEA) is and how it affects police operations?
- How advances in technology are affecting police operations?
- What community policing is?
- What a mission and a mission statement are?
- What the relationship between goals and objectives is?
- What police discretion is and what positive contributions it makes?
- What problems are associated with discretion?
- What balance presents a major challenge for law enforcement?

CAN YOU DEFINE?

bifurcated society
broken windows metaphor
community policing
discretion
dog shift
goals
mission
mission statement
objectives
participatory leadership
police operations
policy
procedures
racial profiling
regulations
selective enforcement

INTRODUCTION

Just what do police officers do? What skills must they possess, and in what ways does the community rely on their services? Historically, police officers have been viewed as law *enforcement* officers, concerned with keeping the law from being broken and apprehending those who break it. This function, however, has broadened considerably, as evidenced in the label *peace officer* replacing *police officer* in many departments. Although *peace officer* is a general term that covers all licensed law enforcement officers, including state troopers, sheriff's deputies, conservation officers, and the like, it also speaks to the expanded responsibilities of police officers to act proactively to serve the community and problem-solve in an effort to keep the peace as well as to handle crime and disorder as it occurs. No matter what priorities a law enforcement agency may have, certain basic police operations will be found.

police operations Those activities conducted in the field by law enforcement officers as they "serve and protect." They usually include patrol, traffic, investigation and general calls for service.

Police operations refers to activities conducted in the field by law enforcement officers as they "serve and protect," including patrol, traffic, investigation and general calls for service.

Before looking at specific police operations and the skills required to perform them effectively and efficiently, it is important to understand the *context* in which these operations occur. Although police operations have changed little over the last hundred years, the public served and the laws enacted by that public, the officers providing the services, the police bureaucracy itself and the community's involvement have changed and will continue to change.

This chapter begins by examining the various changes affecting police operations. This is followed by another important context affecting police operations: the department's mission and values, reflected in goals, objectives and tasks to be accomplished. Next the policies, procedures and regulations to fulfill the department's mission are discussed. The chapter concludes with yet another area greatly influencing operations—discretion; the discussion includes ethical decision making, the negative and positive sides of discretion and the interaction of discretion and critical thinking skills.

A VIEW OF CONTEMPORARY AMERICAN LAW ENFORCEMENT

In 2008, *Police* magazine ran a 12-part series of articles painting a portrait of American law enforcement operations. Following are some of their conclusions (Griffith, 2008, p.10):

- There are not enough cops. Hardly anyone wants to pay for more. And nobody is quite sure how to add more men and women to the "Thin Blue Line."
- The demographics of who serves in law enforcement are changing in terms of race, ethnicity, gender, and even age.
- Training methods are rooted more in tradition and convention than in the realities of what you face on the street. Updating these methods elicits howls from some trainers.
- The public doesn't really hate you. Some of it doesn't love you that much either.
- You will likely gravitate toward a specialty such as K-9, SWAT, or investigations at some point in your career. This trend will be even more prevalent as we move deeper into this century.

- Women will play a greater role in law enforcement in this century. They won't find it easy to balance career and family. Neither will their male counterparts.
- Patrol is still one of the most critical operations in law enforcement. It is both the "protect" and "serve" part of the job.
- SWAT's focus on physical strength and endurance is being challenged by politicians more interested in diversity than tactical performance.
- Since 9/11, you've actually done a [expletive deleted] fine job [of] improving your ability to prevent and respond to terrorist attacks. . . . Unfortunately, you still can't relax your guard.
- Policymakers make rules of engagement for the least common denominator of officers. This is true, even though the experience level and education level of the vast majority of American law enforcement officers far exceeds that common denominator.
- Regardless of where you work, no matter how affluent or remote, violent criminal gangs are going to be a big problem for you in the coming years. Gang investigators we have talked to say you can thank Hollywood and the music industry for making gang culture so attractive to kids.
- Using less-lethal force can be controversial. Not using less-lethal force can be even more controversial. Weapons technology will likely outpace policy and the political will of your local government.[1]

All of these observations are discussed in this text. Griffith concludes, "The truth is that the state of American law enforcement is a very fluid thing," noting that while the *Police* staff was working on addressing issues their audience wanted addressed, the world economy "went down a rabbit hole and we are all now living in Recessionland" (2008, p.10). The "economic meltdown" is greatly affecting American law enforcement.

CHANGES AFFECTING POLICE OPERATIONS

Law enforcement is affected by a changing public and society, changing law enforcement officers, a changing police bureaucracy, standards set forth by the Commission on Accreditation for Law Enforcement Agencies (CALEA), advances in technology and a change in community involvement.

A Changing Public and Society

The U.S. population is changing, and these trends will undoubtedly affect police operations:

- An aging U.S. population—Experts at the Population Division of the U.S. Census Bureau project by 2020, nearly 61 million Americans will be over age 65, and by 2040 that number will climb to 92 million. The increase is the result of the aging of the baby boomers as well as of the increased life

[1]Police Magazine, Bobit Business Media

expectancy. When our country was founded, the average life expectancy was 35. In 2005 it was 77.8 years. Law enforcement is now seeing more elderly victims of crime, who are considered "vulnerable adults." Such victimization most commonly occurs through abuse or fraud. Several factors contribute to this increased victimization rate, including a larger number of elderly citizens in the population and a greater willingness of such victims to report "private" family matters than was seen in previous generations.

- An increasingly racially diverse population—In 1950 the U.S. population was 87 percent White; that percentage is projected to drop to 51 percent by 2050. Population statistics projections expect immigration to propel the U.S. population total to 438 million by 2050, from 303 million in 2008. The racial and ethnic profile of Americans will continue to shift, with non-Hispanic Whites assuming a minority status (Haub, 2008).
- A growing number of single-parent households—One-parent families numbered 12 million in 2000 (32% of all family groups); single-mother families increased from 3 million (12%) in 1970 to 10 million (26%) in 2000, and single-father families grew from 393,000 (1%) in 1970 to 2 million (5%) in 2000 (Fields and Casper, 2001, p.7). (The official U.S. Census is done only every 10 years, so 2000 is the most recently available data.)
- A widening gap between the wealthy and the poor—A report from the Congressional Budget Office indicates incomes for the wealthiest Americans are rising twice as fast as those of the middle class. This economic disparity has led to a **bifurcated society**—the "haves" and the "have nots."

bifurcated society

Divided into two distinct socioeconomic groups, upper and lower.

Our society is becoming older and has more minorities, more immigrants and more single-parent households, while the gap between the rich and poor continues to expand.

These trends underscore the need for those in the criminal justice field to be culturally sensitive to the public they serve, especially those who work as directly with that public as police officers do. Many theories have addressed how our existing system of laws and law enforcement affects and is affected by our evolving society.

Another major change affecting police operations is the type of officer performing them.

A Changing Law Enforcement Officer

Historically, law enforcement has attracted young White men out of the military. These men frequently had a high school education or less and were used to following orders without questioning authority. This is no longer true. Many people entering the field have no military experience. Furthermore, the ranks of today's police departments are less exclusively White men because more women and minorities are being actively recruited and promoted, a change that has led to greater racial and gender heterogeneity among those in leadership positions within law enforcement organizations.

Police departments are achieving greater diversity, recruiting more women and minorities to better reflect the demographics of the populations they serve.
© AP Images

Today's police recruits include fewer people with military backgrounds and more women and minorities. New recruits have more education and value on-job satisfaction more than material rewards. They also are expected to perform more diverse operations.

More Women and Minorities As noted by Harrington (2001, p.21), "In 1968 the Indianapolis Police Department made history by assigning the first two female officers to patrol on an equal basis with their male colleagues." Since that time, women have entered the field of law enforcement in increasing numbers and played a critical role in the development of modern policing." Yet, overall, the number of women in law enforcement has remained small and the pace of increase slow. Some data seem to indicate the representation of women has actually declined in recent years (Dodge, 2007, p.82). The most recent research shows that only 14.3 percent of sworn personnel are female, with an annual increase of only 0.5 percent over the last several years. At this rate, women will not achieve parity within the police profession for at least another 70 years, and many have cautioned that time alone is insufficient to substantially increase their numbers. Furthermore, it is estimated that only 1 percent of police chiefs are women.

Data on the number of minority sworn law enforcement officers is limited and outdated. The U.S. Department of Justice reports that in large city police departments, the percentage of minority full-time sworn personnel was 29.8 percent in 1990 and rose to 38.1 percent in 2000 (*Police Departments in Large Cities,* 2002, p.3). Of these, 20.1 percent were Black, non-Hispanic; 14.1 percent were Hispanic (any race); 2.8 percent were Asian/Pacific Islander; and 0.4 percent were American Indians. Doubtless, these percentages have grown since 2000.

Despite gains made during the past several decades, women and minorities continue to be underrepresented among the ranks of the police. In addition to recruiting more women and other minority officers, departments are also progressively raising the educational standards for officer candidates.

Better Educated Traditionally, emphasis was placed on potential officers' physical strength, height, weight and such abilities as firearms skills. This focus began to change slightly during the 1920s and 1930s, when August Vollmer, considered by many as the father of professional policing, began advocating higher education for those entering law enforcement. In addition, the Wickersham Commission (1937) and the President's Commission on Law Enforcement and the Administration of Justice (1967) both recommended post-secondary education for law enforcement officers.

Research examining the effects of higher education on police officers' performance has produced varied and sometimes seemingly contradictory results. Some studies have found officers with more education perform more effectively and have a better capacity to handle the variety of tasks involved in modern policing, but other studies have concluded that higher-educated officers burn out more quickly and experience greater job dissatisfaction.

Information from the U.S. Census Bureau reinforces the value of a college education. For example, workers (in general, not strictly in law enforcement) 18 and over with a bachelor's degree earn an average of $51,206 a year, while those with a high school diploma earn $27,915. Workers with an advanced degree make an average of $74,602 a year, and those without a high school diploma average $18,734 annually.

Today college is what high school was a generation ago. An increasing number of agencies require either a college degree or some college credits. Legal barriers no longer stand in the way of police departments requiring college education. In *Davis v. Dallas* (1986), a U.S. court of appeals upheld a requirement by the City of Dallas that entry-level police recruits have completed 45 college credits with a C average.

McFall (2006, p.45) cites the experience and observations of Major Stelmack of the Baltimore County Police Department: "When I started [as a police officer], they taught me how to fill out a report, do mouth-to-mouth resuscitation and drive a police car in an emergency. Now we need to be hiring people who have the temperament to deal with society. They have to be open-minded. They have to deal with people from different classes, different backgrounds and different ethnic groups. They have to have excellent oral communication skills and be able to write. They have to come on board with some understanding of technology. They have to be able to mediate. And they have to be problem solvers." Such skills and understanding are greatly enhanced through education. Another change occurring in law enforcement throughout the country is the existence of three or four distinct generations within a single department. (NOTE: This is not to be confused with legacy hiring, which is the practice of hiring successive generations within the same family.)

Different Generational Values It has been noted that today's younger police officers come from distinctly different backgrounds than previous groups. Although different sources vary somewhat in the year they attribute to a given generation and some call a specific generation by different names, the most common breakdown is

1922–1945	Veterans, Silents or Traditionalists
1946–1964	Baby Boomers
1965–1980	Generation X
1981–2000	Generation Y, Millennials, Echo Boomers

Each generation has distinct attitudes, behaviors, expectations, habits and motivations (Hammill, 2005). Tables 1.1 and 1.2 compare the personal and lifestyle characteristics of the four generations and their workplace characteristics.

Slahor (2007, p.66) notes, "The Generation Xers and the Millennials multitask. Their work stations and home have music, computer screen images and the TV news, all while they're talking on their cell phones [or texting]!" Harrison (2007, p.150) calls the individuals between ages 18 and 25 Gamers or Generation Next, saying that 90 percent of the latest generations use the Internet daily, about half send text messages daily, and more than half have gotten a tattoo, had a body piercing or have dyed their hair a nontraditional color. He stresses, "With the advent of interactive technologies and online social networking as well as a growing chasm between the wired and unwired worlds, never has the gap between the generation 'in charge' and those that follow it been as wide."

In addition to having different backgrounds and values from the "traditional" police recruit, police officers now are often called on to perform operations well beyond what traditionally has been provided. Given the changing needs of the public, the new type of person entering law enforcement and the growth of new services, it is logical that the bureaucracy directing police operations must also change.

Table 1.1 Personal and Lifestyle Characteristics by Generation

	Veterans (1922–1945)	Baby Boomers (1946–1964)	Generation X (1965–1980)	Generation Y (1981–2000)
Core Values	Respect for authority Conformers Discipline	Optimism Involvement	Skepticism Fun Informality	Realism Confidence Extreme fun Social
Family	Traditional nuclear	Disintegrating	Latch-key kids	Merged families
Education	A dream	A birthright	A way to get there	An incredible expense
Communication Media	Rotary phones One-on-one Write a memo	Touch-tone phones Call me anytime	Cell phones Call me only at work	Internet Picture phones E-mail
Dealing with Money	Put it away Pay cash	Buy now, pay later	Cautious Conservative Save, save, save	Earn to spend

Source: Greg Hammill. "Mixing and Managing Four Generations of Employees." *FDU Magazine*, Winter/Spring 2005. Fairleigh Dickinson University, 1000 River Road, Teaneck, NJ 07666.

Table 1.2 Workplace Characteristics by Generation

	Veterans (1922–1945)	Baby Boomers (1946–1964)	Generation X (1965–1980)	Generation Y (1981–2000)
Work Ethic and Values	Hard work Respect authority Sacrifice Duty before fun Adhere to rules	Workaholics Work efficiently Crusading causes Personal fulfillment Desire quality Question authority	Eliminate the task Self-reliance Want structure and direction Skeptical	What's next Multitasking Tenacity Entrepreneurial Tolerant Goal oriented
Work is . . .	An obligation	An exciting adventure	A difficult challenge A contract	A means to an end Fulfillment
Leadership Style	Directive Command-and-control	Consensual Collegial	Everyone is the same Challenge others Ask why	*TBD
Interactive Style	Individual	Team player Loves to have meetings	Entrepreneur	Participative
Communications	Formal Memo	In person	Direct Immediate	E-mail Voicemail
Feedback and Rewards	No news is good news Satisfaction is a job well done	Don't appreciate it Money Title recognition	Sorry to interrupt, but how am I doing? Freedom is the best reward	Whenever I want it, at the push of a button Meaningful work
Messages That Motivate	Your experience is respected	You are valued You are needed	Do it your way Forget the rules	You will work with other bright, creative people
Work and Family Life	Ne'er the twain shall meet	No balance Work to live	Balance	Balance

*As this group has not spent much time in the workforce, this characteristic has yet to be determined.
Source: Greg Hammill. "Mixing and Managing Four Generations of Employees." *FDU Magazine*, Winter/Spring 2005. Fairleigh Dickinson University, 1000 River Road, Teaneck, NJ 07666.

A Changing Police Bureaucracy

A basic principle held by Sir Robert Peel, often called the father of modern policing, was that the police must be organized militarily. The military model of the Metropolitan Police of London (established in 1829) was adopted in the United States and has been the model for our police departments since that time. Figure 1.1 illustrates this traditional pyramid of authority and organizational hierarchy.

This model, however, is now being questioned by many, partially because of the changes in police recruits and the trend toward community policing. Some police departments are moving away from the paramilitary model and adopting a business or corporate model that flattens the organization and reduces the number of management and supervisory positions while increasing the number of officers. These officers are becoming better trained to act independently while providing more field services—that is, police operations.

It is important at this point in the discussion to recognize the differences between appearance and image (external) and philosophy and approach (internal). Some departments have attempted to shift their appearance to match

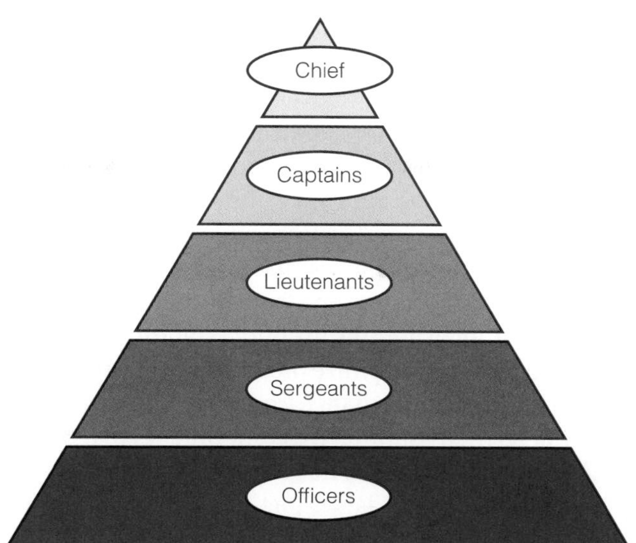

FIGURE 1.1
Traditional Pyramid of Authority and Organization Hierarchy.

the less militaristic approach, for example, by adopting a more "friendly" look in having officers wear business casual suits, but these departments have frequently encountered a plethora of negative issues involving police officer identity, safety, effectiveness and public perception. Beyond being impractical, such attire often makes it more difficult for officers to gain compliance from "bad guys" or be taken seriously by the public. There is much to say about a "uniform" and officer presence and how our society expects a police officer to *look*. Thus, although it is entirely possible for agencies to modify the behavioral approach and response of officers to be less militaristic, the ability to alter the external image and appearance of law enforcement has met with less success. The net result has been that police still look like they always have, but they are now expected to act quite differently.

The police bureaucracy may become less militaristic and may move toward a team approach to providing services. This includes decentralization and a shift from management to leadership.

Many people, particularly Gen-Xers, no longer depend on the authority of somebody "above" them to dictate their opinions or control their actions. They are more independent, preferring to make up their own minds and accepting responsibility for their own actions. They still, however, need the support and guidance of a leader. Many police organizations are undergoing a change from an authoritarian management style to a leadership style that focuses on teamwork. This style, called **participatory leadership**, allows officers to influence decisions affecting them and seeks to form a cohesive team.

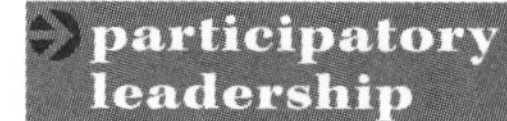

Allows officers to influence decisions affecting them and seeks to form a cohesive team.

Participatory leadership is usually highly motivating to all members of the team. In progressive police departments, the role of rank-and-file officers is elevated significantly, with their input being critical in decision making. It is further expected that rank-and-file officers will be in close contact with the citizens they serve and, therefore, can reflect citizen concerns as decisions are made and can provide leadership.

A type of leadership closely related to the participatory style is transformational leadership, which combines the principles of shared leadership, shared vision, and the continuing improvement of the individual: "Transformational leadership uses the concepts of individualized consideration, idealized influence, inspirational motivation, and intellectual stimulation, which are referred to as the 'four I's of leadership'" (Bynum, 2008, p.72).

Another trend stemming from participatory leadership is customized leadership, which incorporates an understanding of generational differences. In this style, supervisors customize their leadership styles toward individual subordinates to gain optimal performance from each employee. For example, a supervisor need not offer as many supportive compliments to a Baby Boomer as to a Millennial.

Many of the changes in the police bureaucracy result from a desire to comply with the standards set forth by the Commission on Accreditation of Law Enforcement Agencies.

Standards Set Forth by the Commission on Accreditation of Law Enforcement Agencies (CALEA)

CALEA is an independent, nonprofit corporation with a professional staff governed by a 21-member commission board. Eleven members must be from law enforcement; the remaining members represent businesses, academia, the judiciary and state/provincial and local government. Members are appointed by the four founding law enforcement organizations and serve without compensation.

> The Commission on Accreditation for Law Enforcement Agencies, Inc. (CALEA), was created in 1979 as a credentialing authority through the joint efforts of law enforcement's major executive associations:
>
> - International Association of Chiefs of Police (IACP)
> - National Organization of Black Law Enforcement Executives (NOBLE)
> - National Sheriffs' Association (NSA)
> - Police Executive Research Forum (PERF)
>
> The purpose of CALEA's Accreditation Programs is to improve the delivery of public safety services, primarily by: maintaining a body of standards, developed by public safety practitioners, covering a wide range of up-to-date public safety initiatives; establishing and administering an accreditation process; and recognizing professional excellence.
>
> Specifically, CALEA's goals are to:
>
> - Strengthen crime prevention and control capabilities;
> - Formalize essential management procedures;
> - Establish fair and nondiscriminatory personnel practices;
> - Improve service delivery;
> - Solidify interagency cooperation and coordination; and
> - Increase community and staff confidence in the agency.

> The CALEA Accreditation Process is a proven modern management model; once implemented, it presents the Chief Executive Officer (CEO), on a continuing basis, with a blueprint that promotes the efficient use of resources and improves service delivery—regardless of the size, geographic location, or functional responsibilities of the agency. ("About CALEA", 2007)

The Commission on Accreditation of Law Enforcement Agencies (CALEA) certifies law enforcement agencies that meet the standards set by the commission.

Counterpoint

ARGUMENTS AGAINST ACCREDITATION

Although few dispute the need for law enforcement agencies and officers to hold themselves to high professional standards, some criticism has befallen the accreditation process because it can potentially impede an agency's discretion, whether in the form of overly restrictive policies, limitations on hiring practices, or some other impact on police operations. Consider, for example, the experience of one suburban police agency in Minnesota that attempted to move toward accreditation during the early 1990s. During this process, the department realized a surge in policy requirements so great that officers were overwhelmed, which led to a disruption in proactive policing out of fear of violating one of the new, relatively unknown and unfamiliar policies. Furthermore, accreditation mandated new officer candidates hold a 4-year college degree, which significantly limited the pool of qualified individuals the agency could hire. In the end, the agency chose practicality over the "gold label" of accreditation.

The CALEA *Standards for Law Enforcement Agencies,* Fifth Edition (2008) are used by agencies throughout the country and will be referred as they relate to specific police operations.

Consider next how technology has changed law enforcement.

Advances in Technology

Law enforcement has come a long way since 1931 when Dick Tracy, the hard-hitting, extremely intelligent comic strip detective chased bad guys using his two-way wrist radio that few readers believed could actually exist. Finn (2007, p.96) observes, "The information- and intelligence-led policing models of today place an emphasis on delivering timely, organized, and relevant information to front-line officers that provides them with the means for carrying out more thorough investigations without having to leave their patrol zones." The accelerated advances in communication such as cell phones, Blackberries, PDAs, MDTs, video streams and other devices, products and applications have created what Marshall (2008) refers to as "the equivalent of a technology tsunami."

Advances in technology are affecting every aspect of law enforcement.

Although the introduction of technology has allowed law enforcement the ability to work more efficiently and effectively, it has also provided several challenges. One of the most obvious challenges involves those officers who are not as technologically savvy, often the older and more experienced generations of police officers, being placed at an operational disadvantage compared with younger, less experienced yet more technologically adept officers. The flip side to this challenge, however, occurs when younger generations become overly dependent on technology and lack the ability to respond appropriately to calls in the absence of all of their technical "tools" (e.g., not being able to run an individual's criminal history before making contact).

A specific example of applied advances in technology is the Los Angeles Police Department's Smart Car, which is equipped with state-of-the-art technology to connect officers to vital information systems, effectively making the car a mobile office. A computer in the trunk processes the infrared scans of license plates, identifying stolen cars and outstanding warrants. The Smart Cars also have facial and fingerprint recognition technology, and the COPLINK technology is an analysis-and-decision support tool for rapidly identifying criminal suspects, relationships and patterns (Davis, 2007, pp.28–35).

Technology has in fact, changed the very nature of police work. Chuck Wexler (2008, pp.2, 7), Executive Director of the Police Executive Research Forum (PERF), provides a perspective on police technology:

> Technological advances in policing are almost entirely a development of the last 30 years or so. In 1967, President Lyndon Johnson's Commission on Law Enforcement and the Administration of Justice found that police agencies were suffering from an almost total lack of contact with the scientific and technological communities. In the 1960s, there hadn't been any major advances in police technology since the development of two-radios in patrol cars in the 1920 and 1930s the commission found. We didn't even have a 911 system to handle emergency calls.
>
> Compare that to the situation today, beginning with the hundreds of ways that computers help police to measure and analyze crime patterns; maintain sophisticated databases at the local, state, and federal levels regarding crimes, criminals, firearms, DNA, fingerprints, and other information; monitor officers' performances; bring information about local crime conditions to community residents; and so on. There have also been tremendous technological advances in police communications gear; less-lethal weapons; and cameras at crime hot spots and in patrol cars, to name a few areas.
>
> Technology clearly is a force-multiplier that enables officers to be more productive . . .
>
> There is no doubt in my mind that today's law enforcement agencies are much more effective than those of a generation ago in actually preventing crime and bringing down crime rates. And no one would question that technology has played an enormous role in that fundamental change in the quality of policing.

Scheider (2008) notes, "Technology can be leveraged in specific ways to enhance the implementation of the community policing philosophy. Technology can increase the effectiveness of problem-solving and partnership initiatives and assist in the implementation of organizational changes designed to institutionalize these processes." Problem solving and partnerships are the cornerstones of community policing.

A Change in Community Involvement: Community Policing

When Peel established the London Metropolitan Police, he set forth a number of principles, one of which foreshadowed community policing: "The police are the public and the public are the police." The Upper Midwest Community Policing Institute (n.d.) defines **community policing** as "an organization-wide philosophy and management approach that promotes community, government and police partnerships; proactive problem solving; and community engagement to address the causes of crime, fear of crime and other community issues."

community policing
Involves empowering citizens to help local law enforcement provide safer neighborhoods; usually includes an emphasis on foot patrol, partnerships and problem solving.

Miller et al. (2010, p.xix) suggest that community policing offers one avenue for increasing neighborhood safety: "Community policing is not a program or a series of programs. It is a philosophy, a belief that working together, the police and the community can accomplish what neither can accomplish alone. The *synergy* that results from community policing can be powerful. It is like the power of a finely tuned athletic team, with each member contributing to the total effort. Occasionally heroes may emerge, but victory depends on a team effort."

Community policing differs from earlier efforts such as team policing, community relations, crime prevention programs or neighborhood watch programs. Community policing involves a rethinking of the role of the police and a restructuring of the police organization.

Trends in Police Operations

GEO-POLICING

A new trend in policing is called "Geo-policing," which is essentially a hybrid between community policing and foot patrolling beats.

Community policing usually assigns specific officers to specific neighborhoods and actively involves them in helping the neighborhood solve its problems. Table 1.3 presents basic differences between traditional policing and community policing.

Community policing is proactive, empowering citizens to help local law enforcement provide safer neighborhoods. It usually includes an emphasis on foot and bicycle patrol.

Community policing goes much further than traditional community relations programs or neighborhood watch programs, although it often includes these components. Community policing means that officers get to know the citizens in their assigned areas—those who are law-abiding and those who are

Table 1.3 Traditional versus Community Policing: Questions and Answers

Question	Traditional Policing	Community Policing
Who are the police?	A government agency principally responsible for law enforcement.	Police are the public and the public are the police: the police officers are those who are paid to give full-time attention to the duties of every citizen.
What is the relationship of the police force to other public service departments?	Priorities often conflict.	The police are one department among many responsible for improving the quality of life.
What is the role of the police?	Focusing on solving crimes.	A broader problem-solving approach.
How is police efficiency measured?	By detection and arrest rates.	By the absence of crime and disorder.
What are the highest priorities?	Crimes that are high value (e.g., bank robberies) and those involving violence.	Whatever problems disturb the community most.
What, specifically, do police deal with?	Incidents.	Citizens' problems and concerns.
What determines the effectiveness of police?	Response times.	Public cooperation.
What view do police take of service calls?	Deal with them only if there is no real police work to do.	Vital function and great opportunity.
What is police professionalism?	Swift effective response to serious crime.	Keeping close to the community.
What kind of intelligence is most important?	Crime intelligence (study of particular crimes or series of crimes).	Criminal intelligence (information about the activities of individuals or groups).
What is the essential nature of police accountability?	Highly centralized; governed by rules, regulations and policy directives; accountable to the law.	Emphasis on local accountability to community needs.
What is the role of headquarters?	To provide the necessary rules and policy directives.	To organizational values.
What is the role of the press liaison department?	To keep the "heat" off operational officers so they can get on with the job.	To coordinate an essential channel of communication with the community.
How do the police regard prosecutions?	As an important goal.	As one tool among many.

Source: Malcolm K. Sparrow. *Implementing Community Policing: Perspectives on Policing*. Washington, DC: National Institute of Justice, November 1988, pp.8–9.

not. It means they listen to the citizens and treat them as a business treats its customers. Community policing also capitalizes on people's natural tendency to subscribe to the Not In My Back Yard (NIMBY) philosophy. The closer to home police can get their message, the more likely they are to enlist community support.

A general philosophy behind community policing is explained by Wilson and Kelling (1982), who suggest that crime and social disorder are "inextricably linked" (p.31). They use a **broken windows metaphor** to describe the deterioration of neighborhoods. Broken windows that go unrepaired make a statement that no one cares enough about the quality of life in the neighborhood to bother fixing things that need repair. In a later article, Wilson and Kelling (1989, p.49) contend, "Community-oriented policing means changing the daily work of the police to include investigating problems as well as incidents. It means defining as a problem whatever a significant body of public opinion regards as a threat to community order. It means working with the good guys, and not just against the bad guys."

broken windows metaphor

Broken windows in a neighborhood make a statement that no one cares enough about the quality of life in the neighborhood to bother fixing little things that need repair.

The devastated economy of 2008 and 2009 and the collapse of risky mortgages provide a present-day example of this theory in the challenge of potentially

This poverty-stricken, run down, high crime, inner-city urban neighborhood in the South Bronx section of New York illustrates the disrepair and disorder described in Wilson and Kelling's broken window theory.

dangerous empty vacant homes: "Communities across the nation are seeing deserted houses in greater numbers than ever in neighborhoods of all socio-economic levels. Left empty, these homes deteriorate. The grass grows out of control, windows get shattered, swimming pools turn slimy and green, walls get spray painted with graffiti. Worse yet, these vacant houses become magnets for squatters, thieves and teens looking for a place to party" (Partington, 2008, p.83).

Scheider (2009) points out that the broken windows metaphor "stresses the importance of including communities in the change process, with the primary goal being the development of informal social control mechanisms within the communities in question and not merely increased enforcement of minor offenses." The philosophy of community policing and its effect on police operations will be found throughout this text as it is actually implemented in the field.

This text provides a chance to engage in some thought-provoking, critical thinking about important issues in police operations. To do so effectively requires an understanding of the basis for police operations. The functions undertaken by law enforcement officers should be viewed not as isolated activities, but rather as part of a master plan to accomplish the mission of the law enforcement agency.

MISSION AND VALUES

"Organizational mission statements represent the core purpose of the organization and should represent the organization's reason for existence. . . . The value and purpose of mission statements are that they serve as a steadfast guide for the activities of organizational members" (DeLone, 2007, pp.219, 220).

An agency's **mission** is its reason for existence, its purpose. This is often embodied in a **mission statement**.

mission
An organization's reason for existence, its purpose.

mission statement
Written statement of an organization's reasons for existence or purpose.

Mission statements should be short, believable, easy to understand, easy to remember and widely known. They should make work meaningful. Officers who see themselves as serving an important function will be more productive and more satisfied in their profession than will those who feel no sense of mission.

Consider the following example:

> The Charlotte-Mecklenburg Police Department will build problem-solving partnerships with our citizens to prevent the next crime and enhance the quality of life throughout our community, always treating people with fairness and respect.

Mission statements often are accompanied by the set of values on which they are based. These values must be shared by department members and the public served, or they will be meaningless. Ideally, these values also are consistent with the overall cultural values of the state and the nation. The values underlying the Charlotte-Mecklenberg Police Department mission statement are as follows:

We value:

- Our Employees
- People
- Partnerships
- Open Communications
- Problem Solving
- Integrity

Many police departments emphasize the goals of forming partnerships with the community and serving as positive role models for young citizens.
© AP Images/Tim Shaffer

- Courtesy
- The Constitution of North Carolina
- The Constitution of the United States[2]

Many departments are now encouraging supervisors to have their own type of mission statement in the form of a personal leadership philosophy (PLP). It is the same concept as an agency's mission statement, yet it provides individual supervisors their own goals and expectations. It is the mission statement on a more cellular level.

Mission and value statements are important to law enforcement agencies and should be the driving force behind police operations. They are, however, only the starting point. The next steps are to develop goals and objectives that will accomplish the mission and then to decide what specific tasks must be undertaken to accomplish the goals and objectives.

GOALS, OBJECTIVES AND TASKS

Goals may vary from one police department to another, but they usually focus on the following:

- To preserve the peace.
- To protect civil rights and civil liberties.
- To prevent crime.
- To enforce the law.
- To provide services.
- To improve the quality of life in the community.
- To participate in partnerships to solve problems related to crime and disorder.

Although the words *goals* and *objectives* often are used interchangeably, most authorities agree that a goal is a more general term, referring to a broad, nonspecific desired outcome such as those previously listed. Goals are usually long range. Objectives, in contrast, are more specific outcomes, usually with a listing of specific tasks and a timetable attached.

Goals are broad, general intentions. **Objectives** are specific activities to accomplish goals.

goals
Broad, general purposes.

objectives
Specific activities to accomplish a goal.

The distinction between goals and objectives is clarified in the California Council on Criminal Justice's *A Guide for Criminal Justice Planning:*

> Goal—A statement of broad direction, a general purpose of intent. A goal is general and timeless and is not concerned with a particular achievement within a specified time period.
>
> Objective—A desired accomplishment that can be measured within a given time and under specifiable conditions. The attainment of the objective advances the system toward a corresponding goal.

[2]Charlotte-Mecklenburg Police Department, Charlotte, NC

Goals give purpose to what may appear to be relatively unimportant tasks. An inscription carved in 1730 in a church in Sussex, England, proclaims, "A vision without a task is but a dream, a task without a vision is drudgery, a vision and a task is the hope of the world."

Consider, for example, the differences in perspective of the following three bricklayers. In response to the question, What are you doing? the first bricklayer replies, "I'm making $15 an hour laying these stupid bricks." The second replies, "I'm building a wall." And the third says, "I'm part of a team that's building a cathedral so people can worship."

dog shift
Typically the shift from 11 P.M. to 7 A.M.

Or consider the difference in attitude between those police officers on the **dog shift** (typically, 11:00 P.M. to 7:00 A.M.) who see the drug pusher just arrested as nothing more than an annoyance and those officers who believe they have helped make the neighborhood safer, perhaps even saving a life.

Specific objectives or individual tasks in isolation may seem to accomplish little, but in combination they provide the direction needed to achieve the broad goals sought by the department. Common goals *are* important to team building.

How are objectives accomplished? Usually police departments establish policies that cover specific tasks that must be undertaken in basic police operations. They then create procedures to accomplish these tasks.

Policies

policy
A guiding principle or course of action.

Goals and objectives are more easily achieved with written policies guiding the police department's activities. A **policy** is a statement of principles that guide decisions: "By definition, policy is a course of action, a guiding principle or procedure considered expedient, prudent, or advantageous" (Scoville, 2008, p.56). Policies provide guidance and help maintain organizational control and ensure accountability within an organization. In addition, they provide a basis for fair discipline. Written policies should be generated for those areas in which directions are needed, including public and press relations; personal conduct; personnel procedures and relations; and specific law enforcement operations with emphasis on such sensitive areas as the use of force, the use of lethal weapons, search and seizure, arrests and custody. However, officers must use common sense in differentiating between the "letter of the policy" and the "spirit of the policy," the difference being in doing things right versus doing the right thing (Burch, 2008, p.69). This is especially true when an officer must use discretion, as discussed shortly.

Procedures

procedures
Step-by-step instructions for carrying out department policies.

After policies are developed and put in writing, the next step is to identify procedures to carry out the policies, that is, guidelines for action or established methods. **Procedures** are step-by-step instructions for carrying out departmental policies. Written procedures promote a uniformity of action that is especially important for ongoing calls for service or when a large number of officers perform the same services. Written procedures also may reduce civil liability. Figure 1.2 illustrates a directive containing a goal, a policy and the procedures for implementing the policy.

Mytown Police Department

Date issued: 01-01-20xx
Page 1 of 1

Procedure directive no. xx-xxxx

Effective date: 01-01-20xx
Subject: Community service officer in service operations

Goal:

To provide community service officers with uniform procedures for in-service operations. The procedures will document community service officer (CSO) activities and provide reference material for a CSO training manual. The CSO in-service operation is new. As the CSO's tasks expand, additional procedures will be added to this directive.

Policy:

Community service officers will respond to calls only when directed by the dispatcher or supervisor or by the patrol officer's request. Community service officers will notify dispatch immediately when observing any criminal or suspicious activity. Community service officers will not respond to any call, emergency or not, as an emergency vehicle.

Procedure:

I. Responding to Calls

A. When a CSO is responding to a call at the same time as a patrol officer, the CSO will stop or slow down to allow the patrol officer to arrive on the scene first. This will prevent a CSO from entering into a situation that is or could become dangerous.

B. When a CSO is directed to a call where a patrol officer is not assigned or that a patrol officer has requested a CSO to handle, the CSO will call for assistance in any of the following circumstances:

1. Any situation that the CSO determines on arrival as being dangerous or that could escalate into a dangerous situation.

2. Any situation where a criminal violation has taken place and a suspect is still on the scene, leaving the scene or likely to return to the scene.

3. Any situation in which the CSO has not had training or experience or that the CSO feels unable or not equipped to handle.

II. Reports

A. The CSO will turn in all reports, including daily logs, to the report basket in the squad room unless otherwise specified.

B. A supervisor will review and approve all reports and handle accordingly.

C. A supervisor will place the CSO's daily report in the administrative in-basket.

John J. Doe
Chief of Police

FIGURE 1.2
Sample Goal, Policy and Procedure Directive

Policies and Procedures Manuals

If a policies and procedures manual is to be credible, it must be easy to understand as well as concise. Manuals that are hundreds of pages long will gather dust on a shelf.

Regulations

regulations
Rules governing the actions of employees of the city, including police department personnel.

Regulations and procedures are similar and have the same intent: to guide conduct. **Regulations** are rules put out by a lower level of government, for example, a municipality, governing the actions of employees of the municipality, including police department personnel. These orders have the force of law for those people under their jurisdiction. Regulations are to a certain extent restrictive in that they force officers to adhere to certain codes of conduct. Like procedures, regulations should be in writing. Regulations help officers in decision making by eliminating discretionary action in certain areas.

A Final Note and Caution

Police chiefs and supervisors cannot establish goals, objectives and policies in a vacuum. *All* officers, particularly those in the field, can contribute to understanding problems and can assist in developing policies and procedures. Officers in face-to-face contact with community members usually are the best informed about problems in the field and potential solutions. These officers, in turn, will better identify and understand problems through direct contact and discussion with representative community members.

Goals, policies, procedures and regulations help make police departments efficient and effective. They are extremely important and deserve care in development and periodic evaluation. It must always be remembered, however, that not everything can be anticipated. Further, for every rule an exception usually can be found. Too many rules can be detrimental, limiting a department and its officers' flexibility. Flexibility is vital to law enforcement and includes the necessity for officers to use discretion.

DISCRETION

discretion
The freedom to act or decide a matter on one's own.

Discretion is the ability to act or decide a matter on one's own. Police use discretion because no set of policies and procedures can prescribe what to do in every circumstance. The International Association of Chiefs of Police (IACP) "Police Code of Conduct" states, "A police officer will use responsibly the discretion vested in his position and exercise it within the law. The principle of reasonableness will guide the officer's determinations, and the officer will consider all surrounding circumstances in determining whether any legal action will be taken."

Discretion *must* be allowed for several reasons. One reason is that the law *overreaches,* seldom addressing exceptions that might arise. For example, although a highway may have a posted speed limit of 55 miles per hour (mph), a driver exceeding this limit may have very good reasons for doing so. Such a driver might be a volunteer firefighter on the way to a fire, an undercover police officer tailing a car, a parent taking a seriously injured child to the hospital or a man taking his wife who is in labor to the hospital. Technically, these people are speeding—but should they be given tickets? The law overreaches in each of these instances.

Another reason discretion is allowed is because human behavior is too varied and complex to be accommodated by inflexible legal rules, and in some cases, the law may be better served by not being enforced. Consider the following explanations from motorists clocked at 50 mph in a 35 mph zone: "I've just come from my mother's funeral, and I'm very upset;" or "I just got fired;" or "I haven't ever received a speeding ticket in my life. I teach driver education at the high school."

Discretion makes enforcement of our laws *equitable,* that is, humanistic, considering the spirit rather than the letter of the law or, often, of a policy. Discretion also gives officers a sense of control over their jobs, which are, in many cases, primarily reactive.

Discretion allows for equitable enforcement of our laws and for police officers to grow morally and professionally.

Most officers appreciate the chance to work through a citizen's problem from beginning to end. They also appreciate the acknowledgment that they have something to contribute in the form of expertise, imagination and creativity, as well as problem-solving ability.

The ability to decide when to impose legal sanctions on those who violate the law, whether issuing traffic tickets or arresting someone, is known as **selective enforcement**. This type of discretion has only recently been recognized by police administrators and the general public as a proper aspect of officers' authority. Although such discretion is acknowledged as a necessity for effective policing, it does have some drawbacks.

selective enforcement
The ability to decide when to impose legal sanctions on those who violate the law, whether issuing traffic tickets or arresting someone.

Problems with Officer Discretion

Problems associated with officer discretion include
- Lack of accountability.
- Unpredictability.
- Inconsistency and allegations of racial profiling.

Discretionary actions may also confuse citizens because they are not sure how they will be treated from one situation to the next. Discretion can be unpredictable from one officer to the next. For example, one traffic officer may allow up to 5 mph over the speed limit before stopping a motorist. Another may allow 10 mph over. The driver who gets a ticket for exceeding the limit by 5 mph when the driver who is going 10 mph over the limit does not get a ticket will see the situation as unfair.

Most importantly, discretion is often applied inconsistently. Equality under the law has always implied that people should receive similar treatment when they perform relatively the same acts. However, discretion lets officers treat different people differently. This may be seen as discrimination and, in fact, sometimes is. Some officers are harder on minorities, men or juveniles. This may be conscious or unconscious discrimination, but it does make for inconsistent enforcement of the laws. An example of such inconsistent, biased enforcement of laws is seen in **racial profiling**, when an officer uses a person's race to assess the likelihood of criminal conduct or other wrongdoing. Racial profiling is discussed in depth in Chapter 5. Officer discretion, while necessary, must also be limited.

racial profiling
Inconsistent, discriminatory enforcement of the law; an officer uses a person's race to assess the likelihood of criminal conduct or wrongdoing.

Limits on Discretion

A major challenge facing law enforcement is finding the balance between a department's clear-cut goals, policies and procedures and its officers' discretionary actions.

Two factors must be kept in mind: (1) the primary goals of the department and (2) maintaining a balance between a need for clear policies and procedures and the accompanying need for discretion when exceptions arise. In addition, officers will be called on to use critical-thinking skills in performing police operations.

Discretion and Critical-Thinking Skills

To use discretion wisely, police officers need to develop their critical-thinking skills. Critical thinking includes a broad range of skills, such as problem solving, identifying perceptions, generating concepts from observations, applying concepts to police problems, designing systematic plans of action and approaching social problems from several different perspectives. As a result of learning to think critically, students and future police officers will

- Learn to use their diverse backgrounds and those of others to resolve social problems in a more effective, acceptable manner.
- Learn specific ways to move from lower-order to higher-order thinking skills.
- Be better prepared to enter the world of police work and further their existing or future careers.

SUMMARY

Police operations are activities conducted in the field by law enforcement officers as they "serve and protect," including patrol, traffic, investigation and general calls for service. Those engaged in police operations must consider the important changes affecting them, including changes in the public and society served, changing law enforcement officers, a changing police bureaucracy, standards set forth by the Commission on Accreditation for Law Enforcement Agencies (CALEA), advances in technology and a change in community involvement.

Our society is becoming older and has more minorities, more immigrants and more single-parent households, and the gap between rich and poor continues to expand. Our law enforcement officers also have changed. Today's police recruits include fewer people with military backgrounds and more women and minorities. New recruits have more education and value job satisfaction more than material rewards. They also are expected to perform more diverse operations.

Another change is anticipated in the police bureaucracy itself. The police bureaucracy may become less militaristic and may move toward a team approach to providing services. This includes decentralization and a shift from management to leadership. Yet another influence on law enforcement is the CALEA, which certifies law enforcement agencies that meet the standards set by the commission. Advances in technology are also affecting every aspect of police operations.

A further change is the trend toward community policing, which is proactive and empowers citizens to help local law enforcement provide safer neighborhoods. Community policing usually includes an emphasis on foot and bicycle patrol.

Those in law enforcement should understand the context in which police operations are performed and the changes that have occurred, and they should understand the foundation for these operations. Most law enforcement agencies are guided by missions. An agency's mission is its reason for existence, its purpose. Often, this is embodied in a mission statement. This mission is accomplished most effectively by clearly stated goals and objectives. Goals are broad, general intentions. Objectives are specific activities to accomplish goals. The ways these objectives are to be carried out are frequently described in policies and procedures.

Officers need to follow policies, procedures and regulations, but they also need to use discretion. Discretion allows for equitable enforcement of our laws and for police officers to grow morally and professionally. Discretion is not without its problems, including a lack of accountability, unpredictability and the potential for inconsistency and allegations of racial profiling. A major challenge facing law enforcement is finding the balance between a department's clear-cut goals, policies and procedures and its officers' discretionary actions.

APPLICATION

General Directions

When you complete each chapter, you will be asked to apply the information to develop suggested policies and procedures appropriate for your area. The appendix at the end of the book contains a form to use for this purpose. As with any other type of administrative writing, policies and procedures should be clearly written. Consider the following guidelines:

- Use short, simple words, avoiding police jargon.
- Use short, simple sentences: 10 to 15 words.
- Use short paragraphs: 2 to 3 sentences.
- Use lists when possible.
- Use active verbs: Write *Clean the gun daily* rather than *The gun should be cleaned daily.*
- Use illustrations and diagrams for clarification.
- Have three or four individuals read and evaluate the policy and procedure.

Most important, keep things simple. Avoid the tendency to impress rather than to express.

Instructions

Write a policy for writing policies, that is, outline what policies should be written for. Then write at least five procedures to be used when writing policies.

AN EXERCISE IN CRITICAL THINKING

At the end of each chapter, you will be presented with exercises in critical thinking. These exercises were written by Waldo Asp, Normandale Community College, and are based on actual decisions of state appeals courts or state supreme courts throughout the country. Read each situation carefully. Then consider the alternative responses given and select the *most logical* statement based on what you have read in the chapter.

On September 4, State Trooper Berg was on routine patrol when he stopped a car driven by Carl Lundberg for a traffic violation. Trooper Berg arrested Lundberg for breach of the peace and placed him in the squad car's back seat. Carl's brother, Allen Lundberg, went to the scene of the arrest and, without identifying himself, got into his brother's car with the apparent intention of driving it away.

Trooper Berg got out of his vehicle, approached the as-yet-unidentified individual, and asked him to get out of the car and leave. Only after A. Lundberg got out of the car did he identify himself as the suspect's brother. Trooper Berg again asked A. Lundberg to leave the scene, but A. Lundberg persisted in questioning Trooper Berg as to why he could not take the car to avoid having it towed. Trooper Berg continued to insist that A. Lundberg leave the scene.

> The verbal sparring continued to escalate to such a point that it drew the attention of several individuals in the parking lot of a shopping mall across the street. Various witnesses testified that A. Lundberg yelled obscenities at Trooper Berg, "leaned over and pointed to his buttocks," and gave Trooper Berg "the finger." Witnesses also testified that Trooper Berg physically turned A. Lundberg around and "gave him a shove toward the parking lot," at which point A. Lundberg "kind of turned around and came close to hitting Trooper Berg's arm." That is when Trooper Berg told him he was under arrest.

Meanwhile, as Trooper Berg was dealing with A. Lundberg, C. Lundberg (who was in the back of the squad car) managed to cause $500 damage to the squad's interior by kicking the door.

1. Considering the way this incident unfolded, which statement best represents how Trooper Berg should have handled this event?
   a. This demonstrates that sometimes sticking to policies and procedures is not worth the trouble that is caused, for the general public will not accept impersonal execution of procedures.
   b. Officers need to understand the reasoning behind operations and be able to explain them to citizens, thereby possibly avoiding violent actions and breaches of the peace.
   c. In this case, there was insufficient evidence to support a criminal conviction for obstructing legal process.
   d. Mere words (regardless of tone, loudness, agitation and word choice) cannot be used as a basis for a disturbing the peace charge.
   e. Only Carl Lundberg's actions should be prosecuted. Allen Lundberg should be released.
2. Officer involvement with the community would have helped Trooper Berg in what way?
   a. Witnesses might corroborate the yelled obscenities and other actions by Allen Lundberg, as well as Trooper Berg's responses.
   b. Some community members could talk the Lundbergs into cooling off and could assist Trooper Berg in physically escorting Allen away from the scene to prevent the escalation of anger.
   c. Many would enjoy the power and authority of becoming "assistant officers" with the rights of enforcing the law, as well as the status of being considered "officers and gentlemen."
   d. Fair, compassionate and excellent police service is possible only when responsibilities are not piled on one individual.
   e. With expanded opportunities for misconduct, more eyes are needed to keep watch for undesirable activity.

DISCUSSION QUESTIONS

1. What purposes do goals serve in a police department?
2. What do you consider the most important goal for a police department?
3. What are the advantages of having written policies?
4. Are value statements necessary? How can officers best be involved in developing a department's values?
5. Who should be involved in policy development?
6. Is discretion more of an advantage or a disadvantage for police officers?
7. Have you observed police discretion in operation?

GALE EMERGENCY SERVICES DATABASE ASSIGNMENTS

- Use the Gale Emergency Services database to answer the discussion questions as appropriate.
- Use the Gale Emergency Services database to research articles and materials on *participatory leadership and management.* Be prepared

to discuss the advantages and disadvantages of participatory leadership and/or management with the class.

- Use the Gale Emergency Services database to research articles and materials on *law enforcement accreditation*. Be prepared to discuss your findings with the class.
- Read and outline "Law and the Parameters of Acceptable Deviance" by Mark A. Edwards.
- Read and outline "Community Policing: Exploring the Philosophy" by David M. Allender.

REFERENCES

"About CALEA" September 19, 2007. CALEA Online, http://www.calea.org/Online/AboutCALEA/Commission.htm

Burch, Jay. "The Loss of Common Sense in Policing." *Law and Order*, November 2008, pp.69–74.

Bynum, Ray. "Transformational Leadership and Staff Training in the Law Enforcement Professions." *The Police Chief*, February 2008, pp.72–81.

Commission on Accreditation of Law Enforcement Agencies. *Standards for Law Enforcement Agencies,* 5th ed. Fairfax, VA: CALEA, 2006, updated 2008.

Davis, Paul. "Technology Serves as a Force Multiplier." *Law Enforcement Technology,* June 2007, pp.28–35.

DeLone, Gregory J. "Law Enforcement Mission Statements Post-September ll." *Police Quarterly,* June 2007, pp.218–235.

Dodge, Mary. "Women in Policing: Time to Forget the Differences and Focus on the Future." *Criminal Justice Research Reports,* July/August 2007, pp.82–84.

Fields, Jason and Casper, Lynne M. *America's Families and Living Arrangements: Population Characteristics 2000.* U.S. Census Bureau, Current Population Reports (CPR), June 2001. (P20-537)

Finn, Richard. "The IMPACT of Implementing Technological Change." *The Police Chief,* October 2007, pp.96–105.

Griffith, David. "The State of American Law Enforcement." *Police,* December 2008, p.10.

Hammill, Greg. "Mixing and Managing Four Generations of Employees." *FDU Magazine Online,* Winter/Spring 2005. http://www.fdu.edu/newspubs/magazine/05ws/generations.htm

Harrington, Penny E. *Recruiting & Retaining Women: A Self-Assessment Guide for Law Enforcement.* Los Angeles, CA: National Center for Women & Policing, 2001. (NCJ 185235)

Harrison, Bob. "Gamers, Millennials, and Generation NEXT: Implications for Policing." *The Police Chief,* October 2007, pp.150–160.

Haub, Carl. "U.S. Population Could Reach 438 Million by 2050, and Immigration Is Key." Washington, DC: Population Reference Bureau, 2008.

Marshall, Mark A. "The Cutting Edge of Law Enforcement Technology." *PoliceOne.com News,* January 2, 2008. http://www.policeone.com/pc_print.asp?vid=1645861

McFall, Ellen. "Changing Profession Requires New Level of Education." *The Police Chief,* August 2006, pp.45–47.

Miller, Linda S.; Hess, Kären Matison; and Orthmann, Christine Hess. *Community Policing: Partnerships for Problem Solving,* 5th ed. Clifton Park, NY: Delmar Publishing Company, 2010.

Partington, Karie. "Abandoned Homes and 'Broken Windows.'" *Law and Order,* October 2008, pp.83–85.

Police Departments in Large Cities, 1990–2000. Washington, DC: U.S. Department of Justice, Bureau of Justice Statistics, Special Report, May 2002. (NCJ 175703)

Scheider, Matthew C. "The Role of Technology in Community Policing." *Community Policing Dispatch,* November 2008.

Scheider, Matthew C. "Broken Windows and Community Policing." *Community Policing Dispatch,* January 2009.

Scoville, Dean. "Rules of Engagement." *Police,* October 2008, pp.56–63.

Slahor, Stephenie. "Four Generations on the Job." *Law and Order,* December 2007, pp.63–67.

U.S. Census Bureau, Washington, DC, February 25, 2009.

Upper Midwest Community Policing Institute, brochure, no date.

Wexler, Chuck. "Policing and Technology: Tapping the Potential to Protect Communities." *Subject to Debate,* June 2008, pp.2, 7.

Wilson, James Q., and Kelling, George. "The Police and Neighborhood Safety: Broken Windows." *Atlantic Monthly,* March 1982, pp.29–38.

Wilson, James Q., and Kelling, George. "Making Neighborhood Safe." *Atlantic Monthly,* February 1989, pp.46–52.

CASE CITED

Davis v. Dallas, 777 F.2d 205 (5th Cir. 1985), cert. denied, 476 U.S. 1116 (1986)

CHAPTER 2

Communication

The Foundation of Police Operations

DO YOU KNOW . . .

- What positive outcomes effective communication can produce?
- In what directions communication might flow?
- What databases can be of value to law enforcement?
- What special communication problems law enforcement officers may encounter?
- What some criminal justice entities believe law enforcement 10-codes should be replaced with?
- What special populations may pose especially challenging communication issues?
- When slurred speech may not be the result of intoxication?
- When police officers can stop a person to ask questions?
- What rights *Miranda v. Arizona* grants to suspects?
- What would make a confession inadmissible in court?
- What purposes written police reports serve?
- Who the likely audiences of police reports are?
- What the characteristics of effective police reports are?
- What two amendments police must balance when dealing with the media?

CAN YOU DEFINE?

absolute privilege
admission
beachheading
closed question
cognitive interview
conditional privilege
confession
felony syndrome
field inquiry
grapevine
informant
interoperability
interrogation
interview
leading question
Miranda warning
open question
primary victim
privileged information
rapport
reader-friendly writing
secondary victim
statement
totality of circumstances

INTRODUCTION

Communication at any level is an inexact art. But misunderstood communication can have grave consequences in police work. Communication skills are critical to every aspect of effective police operations.

Communication is all around us. We are continually bombarded by spoken and written messages, yet most people give little thought to its importance, nor are they trained in communicating effectively.

Effective communication can produce several positive outcomes and can be used to inform, persuade, diffuse, guide, motivate, reassure and negotiate.

In contrast, ineffective communication can result in confusion, false expectations, wrong conclusions, negative stereotypes, frustration, anger, hostility, aggression and even physical confrontations.

Police officers routinely communicate in every facet of their jobs, not only when they interview and interrogate individuals, but also during their interactions with the public, with coworkers in their departments and with professionals in other fields. Officers also may testify in court and fulfill public speaking assignments, especially those for school-age children and youths.

This chapter begins with a discussion of the lines of internal communication—horizontal and vertical as well as technological advances in communication and problems associated with using radios and cell phones to communicate. This is followed by a look at special populations that may pose especially challenging communication problems. A brief discussion of using language as a tool or a weapon follows. The chapter then turns to communicating to obtain information: the field inquiry and the interview including interviewing and interrogating techniques. This is followed by a discussion of the role of informants and anonymous tips and the interrogation, including the use of the *Miranda* warning. Next, report writing is discussed, including the importance of field notes as the basis of operational reports and how such notes might be supplemented by videotaping. This is followed by a discussion of written reports, including their purposes, audiences, ways to make them reader friendly and the content and characteristics of effective reports. Next is a brief look at computer-assisted report entry and records. The chapter concludes with a discussion on communicating with the media.

LINES OF COMMUNICATION WITHIN AN AGENCY

Communication within an agency may flow in different directions. It may flow vertically downward from the chief or upward from line officers. It may also flow outward or horizontally among those on the same "level" within the organization.

Internal communication may be vertical (downward or upward) or horizontal (lateral).

In addition to the more formal lines of internal communication, informal channels also exist, called the **grapevine** or the "rumor mill." This powerful line of communication can help or hurt an agency. The grapevine can be used

grapevine
A network of informal, internal channels of communication. Also called the *rumor mill.*

A Saginaw Township, Michigan, police officer uses his cell phone and a map to check a location. Using the cell phone avoids interrupting dispatch calls.
© Ray Malace

positively to disseminate information quickly and as a barometer of what the workforce is thinking. However, negative information, allowed to grow unchecked, can undermine an agency's mission. Departments typically devise policies, under the area of police officer conduct, that cover the rumor mill phenomenon, yet there may be times when such rumors are allowed to persist and go unaddressed. Some of this "allowance" is attributed to the police culture because bringing an issue such as rumors to the administration may be viewed as complaining, which is not respected among law enforcement.

Communication between officers in the field, officers and headquarters, and officers and local, state and national data sources as well as information sharing among agencies has been enhanced greatly through advancing technology.

TECHNOLOGICAL ADVANCES IN COMMUNICATION

Law enforcement communications began with whistles and rattles and has advanced to handheld radios, laptop computers in patrol cars, photo cell phones and Enhanced 9-1-1, whose geolocation feature allows law enforcement to quickly trace where a wireless call is coming from. Many wireless devices can now display and send images of a crime scene or a suspect to hundreds of officers, using only a phone and a digital camera. Furthermore, many departments have outfitted their squad cars with cameras and recording systems that are able to download to a central, fixed station server via Wi-Fi, as well as having an onboard global positioning system (GPS) that allows dispatch to monitor the real-time location of squads.

An intranet—a Web site inside a department firewall that serves the mission of the department and is not available to the public—can streamline communications and manage information cost-effectively. For example, many agencies have access to secured Web sites that police officers can use to retrieve and complete all of the necessary reports and forms associated with various calls and activities. All of these documents are shared on a secure network with other facets of the criminal justice system and can be uploaded directly to the courts and jails as soon as officers submit them. Brown (2008, p.37–38) shares what his agency learned when it developed its intranet:

- Get buy-in from advocates early on in the process, preferably from chain-of-command going vertical.
- To create the buy-in, show how the intranet will benefit the department.
- Consolidate forms and manuals by locating people in the departments who know their whereabouts and get the most current versions for posting.
- Consider creating all forms with Acrobat PDF. The reader version is free. The user can open the form, fill in the blanks, print it and sign and date it, ready to turn in for approval.
- Find someone internally who is technology-savvy. Credibility and department knowledge go a long way.
- Design the main menu with your organizational chart in mind. Consider starting at the top and working down.
- Make the intranet project a real project with a task list and a timeline to stay on track.
- Spell check, times three.
- Prepare the unveiling in advance.

Regional or countywide intranets are becoming increasingly popular. In addition to making operations more efficient for patrol, these Web sites also assist law enforcement and criminal justice administration. For example, in Dakota County, Minnesota, city police departments can log onto a secured Web site known as CJIIN, the Criminal Justice Information Integration Network, from which administration can quickly tabulate statistics for various crimes, calls for service, and so on because the network compiles all of the information for them.

Communications systems are the one tool that law enforcement officers use every day. A newly created program of the U.S. Department of Justice, Office of Justice Programs, National Institute of Justice (NIJ) is the National Law Enforcement and Corrections Technology Center (NLECTC) Communications Technologies Center of Excellence (COE). The center is designed to engage the law enforcement community in improving communications and developing the tools law enforcement needs. The COE works with law enforcement to identify technology requirements and encourages input from law enforcement practitioners. The COE tracks the research and development of communications technologies and products in both the academic community and the private sector, as well as research and development efforts funded by the NIJ (Mulvihill, 2008, p.60).

The trend toward community policing is bringing more officers out of the squad car to patrol on foot, bikes, motorcycles and horses. Although this move puts officers closer to the citizens in the community, it also pulls them away from their vital link to real-time data—the vehicle-mounted laptop. Again, technology is available to assist such officers with their mobile police operations.

The BlackBerry smartphone, for example, has e-mail, voice telephone and wireless Web access, making it a powerful communications tool (Careless, 2008, p.12). The device can be loaded with specialized law enforcement programs such as BIO-key PocketCop or Info-Cop, transforming the BlackBerry into a highly capable handheld data terminal. Bio-key PocketCop lets BlackBerry users query the FBI's National Crime Information Center (NCIC) database as well as other state and motor vehicle databases. Info-Cop also does this and lets officers download photos and look up license plates. The Tequesta (Florida) Police Department (TPD) uses BlackBerries on the beat. The TPD chief says they choose the BlackBerry for its "one-unit fits all potential. By using all the services available from BlackBerry, the officers stay in constant communication with the station, citizens and are able to leave information with their contacts. The officers are truly self-contained in the field. They have cell phone, direct connect, e-mail and calendar. In addition, they can run warrant and information checks on people, run drivers' license checks, and print citations from the machine. If we are running a campaign against running red lights, the brochure is downloaded to the BlackBerry and the officer can print it out for violators or persons he meets on the street" (Careless, p.15).

Even with this capability on hand, whether in the form of a BlackBerry or as a squad car laptop, police officers still rely heavily on the radio and dispatcher to retrieve critical information when their hands are full in dealing with incidents. There are many situations that either do not allow or make it unsafe for an officer to check such information by himself or herself. Departments must also be cognizant of the need to train officers in how to operate in the absence of technology, such as when equipment fails or services go down or are otherwise inaccessible. An overreliance on technology can actually impede officer effectiveness and safety in certain situations.

Geoghegan (2009, p.40) reports, "Today's law enforcement officer functions more efficiently thanks to the numerous remote database tools now available. Through the use of compact PDAs, wireless phones and laptops, police officers can gain instant access to criminal records from a host of databases." She suggests that rather than setting up its own infrastructure, agencies may want to use wireless technology solutions available from A&T, Sprint/Nextel or Verizon Wireless, all of which provide integrated communications strategies tailored to suit the needs of individual police departments.

AVAILABLE DATABASES

As law enforcement officers increasingly rely on access to information while in the field, emerging technology will ensure they are automatically receiving the most current data. Dorsey and Smith (2008, p.44) stress, "In today's digital environment, information is more important than ever for the patrol officers, investigators and crime analysis supporting our communities."

Among the valuable databases are the Law Enforcement Information Exchange (LInX), CrimeCog, the National Crime Information Center (NCIC), the Law Enforcement National Data Exchange (N-DEx), the Law Enforcement Online service (LEO) and the OneDOJ Initiative.

The Law Enforcement Information Exchange (LInX)

The LInX, a regional information-sharing system developed, coordinated, and largely funded by the U.S. Naval Criminal Investigative Service (NCIS), has begun to "revolutionize law enforcement in the 21st century" (Dorsey and Smith, 2008, p.44). This state-of-the-art collaborative information-sharing program is officer-friendly, making access and retrieval of data easy; enhances officer safety by providing current information to officers in the field; and improves law enforcement efficiency and effectiveness by allowing more rapid identification and processing of offenders following the reporting of a crime. LInX is currently operating in seven regions around the country: Washington/Oregon; Hawaii; New Mexico; Gulf Coast, Texas; Florida/Georgia; Hampton Roads and Richmond, Virginia; and the Washington, DC region. Nearly 500 law enforcement agencies are using LInX daily, and more than 20,000 law enforcement professionals have been trained in and are using LInX to achieve investigative and operational successes (Dorsey and Smith, p.44).

CrimeCog

CrimeCog, an Internet-based information-sharing and records-management source reserved exclusively for use by law enforcement and justice systems, is powered by E*Justice™ and is already used by large cities and counties across the country (Siuru, 2007, p.79). CrimeCog Technologies Inc. has exclusive U.S. rights to develop and sell access to the E*Justice software via Internet connections, allowing even the smallest law enforcement agency to use the powerful capabilities of E*Justice for a low monthly fee.

Siuru (2007, p.81) observes, "Today, law enforcement requires effective collaboration between agencies and jurisdictions, especially with respect to homeland security. CrimeCog connects each subscribing agency to other local, state and federal agencies, sharing criminal justice information required to locate, arrest and adjudicate suspects. The service allows searching warrants, jail bookings, master names, arrests/incidents/field interviews, court cases/convictions and receiving caution alerts."

The National Crime Information Center (NCIC)

The FBI's NCIC is an online real-time transaction-processing database that maintains information on millions of records. Established in 1967, this database is the forerunner of newer information-sharing systems in the country. Connecting to this system, patrol officers can run local, state and federal database checks ranging from driver's license and vehicle registration, to arrest reports, stolen/recovered property and even emergency phone numbers of business owners. The system handles nearly 4.5 million transactions daily and offers fingerprint matching capability, digital image data storage and a mobile imaging unit to electronically capture fingerprint and camera images and incorporate them into an NCIC database query.

The National Data Exchange (N-DEx)

Another initiative of the FBI is the N-DEx, an Internet-based information system aimed at eventually linking the more than 18,000 law enforcement agencies in the nation electronically to share information beyond state boundaries. According to the FBI ("N-DEx: Welcome to the Future," 2008), once fully operational and fully deployed in 2010, N-DEx will include a full range of capabilities:

- Nationwide searches from a single access point.
- Searches by "modus operandi" and for clothing, tattoos, associates, cars, etc.—linking individuals, places and things.
- Notifications of similar investigations and suspects.
- Identification of criminal activity hotspots and crime trends.
- Threat level assessments of individuals and addresses.
- Visualization and mapping features.

All of these capabilities include safeguards to protect privacy and civil rights. According to Bush (2008, p.12), "The vision of the N-DEx is clear: to share complete, accurate, timely and useful information across jurisdictional boundaries and to provide new investigative tools that will enhance the ability of the United States to fight crime and terrorism."

The Law Enforcement Online Service (LEO)

LEO was launched in July 1995 by FBI staff who foresaw what the information-sharing powerhouse called "the Internet" was to become. According to its Web site ("Law Enforcement Online"),

> LEO supports the FBI's ten priorities by providing cost-effective, time-critical national alerts and information sharing to public safety, law enforcement, anti-terrorism and intelligence agencies in support of the Global War on Terrorism. LEO is provided to members of the law enforcement communities at no cost to their respective agencies. It is the mission of LEO to catalyze and enhance collaboration and information exchange across the FBI and mission partners with state-of-the-art commercial off-the-shelf communications services and tools, providing a user-friendly portal and software for communications and information exchange.
>
> LEO is a 7 days a week, 24 hours a day online (real-time), controlled-access communications and information sharing data repository. . . . LEO also supports antiterrorism, intelligence, law enforcement, criminal justice, and public safety communities worldwide.

Lindsey (2008, p.82) points out, "The high degree of LEO's integrity and accessibility is complemented by its versatility to its users. Once online, members have access to the entire suite of services provided. These include information-sharing services such as chat, e-mail that is secure between LEO members, access to relevant special interest groups (SIGs), use of Virtual Command Centers, e-learning modules, and an e-library. SIGs can be formed for a variety of reasons, including an entity's mission and location, a group's specialized skill or a particular event."

OneDOJ Initiative

The OneDOJ Initiative is a one-stop storefront for federal law enforcement information designed to allow state, local, and tribal law enforcement partners to get information from all of the Department of Justice's investigative components: the Bureau of Alcohol, Tobacco, Firearms and Explosives (ATF); the Drug Enforcement Administration (DEA); the Federal Bureau of Investigation (FBI); the U.S. Marshals Service (USMS); and the Bureau of Prisons (BOP)—with a single query (Hitch, 2007, p.26).

PROBLEMS IN USING RADIOS AND CELL PHONES TO COMMUNICATE

Special problems in communicating via radios and cell phones include keeping police communications secure, interference on the line and dropped calls, lack of interoperability and lack of a common language.

Communication Security

Many citizens have police scanners that allow them access to dispatcher-to-officer and officer-to-officer communications. Some criminals also use scanners, so security precautions must be taken. Listening in on cell phone transmissions is prohibited under the Electronic Communications Privacy Act of 1986, but enforcing the law is impractical. Therefore, conversations are not safe on mobile phones. As with cell phone conversations, wireless data transmissions are susceptible to interception.

Although digital technology adds a level of security greater than the analog transmissions made over police radio frequencies, it is not totally secure. Consequently, data encryption, which "scrambles" transmitted data, is considered the best way to keep outsiders from accessing inside information. As this technology becomes more accessible and affordable, more departments across the country will move toward digital radio with encryption capabilities.

Also, as increasing numbers of agencies go online, using the Internet to access and share data, keeping information secure in this medium has also become a challenge.

Interference on the Line and Dropped Calls

As more people use wireless channels to communicate, the interference encountered has also increased. Interference occurs when radio channels assigned to public safety are intermingled among and adjacent to commercial channels such as cell phones.

Another problem occurs when technology to enhance communication experiences a glitch or "goes down." Earlier, communication systems were relatively uncomplicated, consisting of a microphone and a speaker, with users simply talking over them. Today's communication systems have controllers, microprocessors and software, all of which can experience problems.

In July 2004, the Federal Communication Commission (FCC) unanimously approved the Consensus Plan to eliminate 800-megahertz interference by realigning the current licensing of 800-megahertz systems into two distinct blocks: one for public safety and private wireless systems and one for wireless carriers such as cellular service providers.

Wireless coverage gaps (that is, dropped calls) and interruptions are other problems officers may encounter. As investigators and officers travel, they may pass in and out of wireless coverage areas, such as when driving through a tunnel, into a parking garage or simply traveling in an area with limited cellular coverage. These dead zones may cause officers to lose their connections, locking up their applications and requiring them to restart their applications, which takes time and usually requires re-logging onto a network (Lee, 2008, pp.42–43). Such interruptions can lead to a loss of unsaved work and to officer frustration in having to retype any work in progress. Unexpected automatic software updates sent directly to devices can also interrupt an officer's work and lead to time and data loss.

Recall the mass chaos that occurred in September 2005 after Hurricane Katrina knocked out communications throughout the New Orleans area. This event highlighted the particular vulnerability of cell towers and land lines, one response to which was that wireless carriers now have dedicated units to provide law enforcement agencies with products and services to ensure they can communicate in dead zones and even during the worst disasters: "Mobile cell towers, handsets on standby and companies' dedicated disaster response teams can help your agency stay connected" (Basich, 2009, p.40).

Lack of Interoperability

"The need to provide first responders with an improved system for interoperable communications remains an urgent national priority, despite the painful lessons of 9/11 and Hurricane Katrina. Even with the attention being paid to interoperability, emergency officials around the country cannot be confident they'll be able to communicate with each other when they need to most" (Kane, 2009, p.52).

interoperability

The ability of public safety officials to communicate with each other seamlessly in real time over their wireless communications network either by voice or through data transmissions.

Interoperability refers to the ability of public safety officials to communicate with each other seamlessly in real time over their wireless communications network. Gavigan (2008, p.58) defines interoperability as "the ability of emergency response agencies to talk to one another via radio communication systems, to exchange voice and/or data with one another on demand, in real time, when needed and when authorized." She notes the absence of emergency response interoperability across the country is "a long-standing, complex and costly problem."

A successful seven-year interoperability project in Washington, DC, is the Capital Wireless Information Net (CapWIN): "Primary and secondary responders have always had an awareness of the need to communicate across jurisdictions and disciplines, but it has been only in the new millennium that these capabilities were effectively extended to in-the-field use" (Mulholland, 2008, p.88). Mulholland notes that as with other reports regarding interoperable initiatives and reviews of federal information-sharing programs, the CapWIN project demonstrated that the primary challenge was not technological, but political.

To overcome political issues, early in the project, law enforcement agencies, fire departments, emergency medical services and transportation stakeholders from the District of Columbia, Maryland, Virginia, and the federal government met and agreed to share information: "As a result, CapWIN, a system designed by practitioners for practitioners, so successfully met the needs of the 'boots in the field' that a recent review by the IACP [International Association of Chiefs of Police] for compliance with National Incident Management System standards found CapWIN to be fully compliant, with only minor recommendations for enhancement" (Mulholland, 2008, p.88).

A national approach to working toward interoperability is SAFECOM, a communications program in the Office for Interoperability and Compatibility run by the Department of Homeland Security to provide research, development, testing and evaluation, guidance, tools, and templates on communications-related issues (Gavigan, 2008, p.58). Its mission is to improve emergency response through more effective, efficient interoperable wireless communications. The SAFECOM Interoperability Continuum includes governance, standard operating procedures, technology, training and exercises and usage, as shown in Figure 2.1.

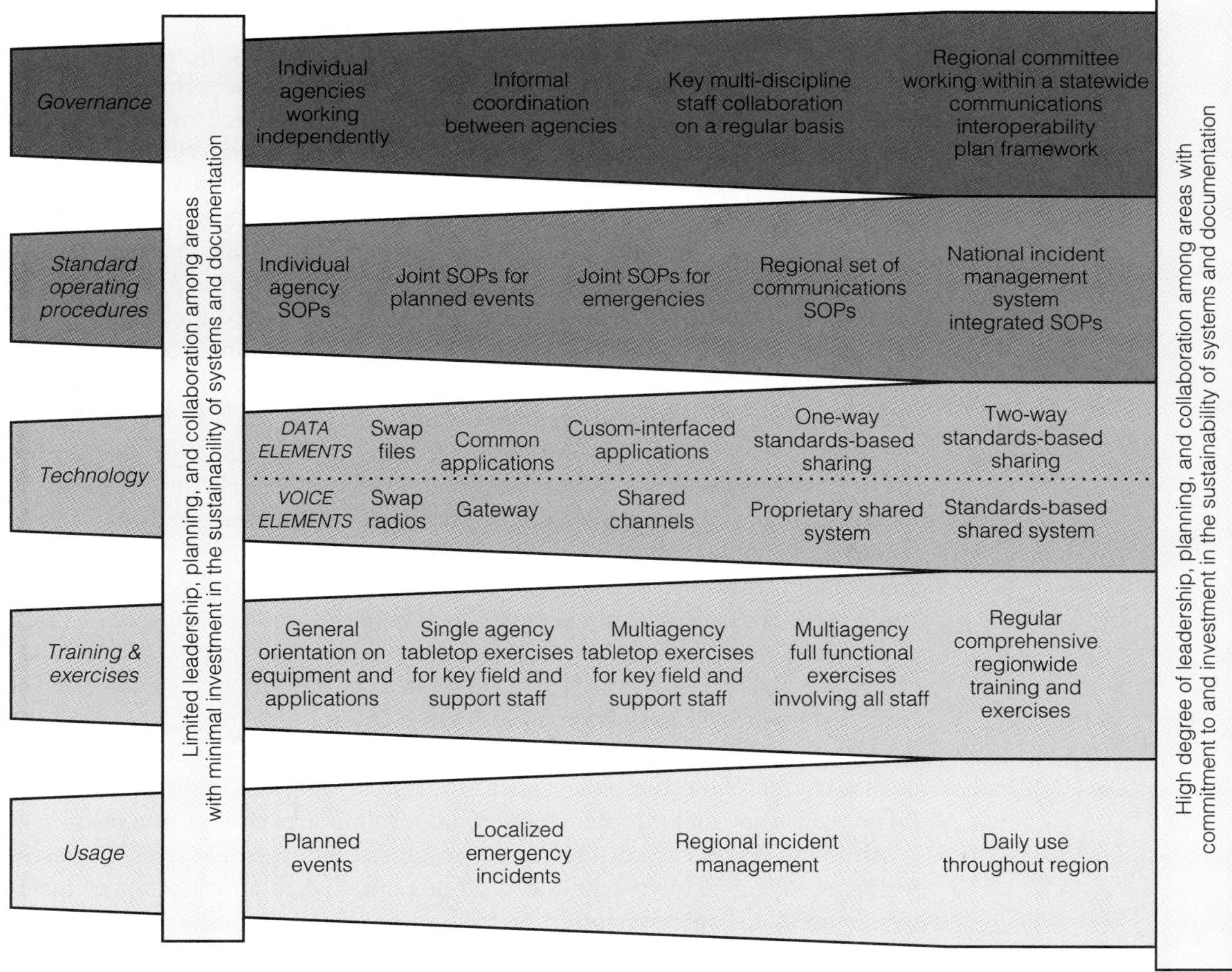

FIGURE 2.1 SAFECOM Interoperability Continuum
Source: "Interoperability Continuum." 2004. Washington, DC: Department of Homeland Security. Retrieved from http://safecomprogram.gov/NR/rdonlyres/54FϕC2DE-FA7ϕ-48DD-A56E-3A72A8F35066/ϕ/Interoperability_Continuum_Brochure_2.pdf on December 10, 2009.

Wright (2008, p.44) stresses that public safety officers need comprehensive communications interoperability: "The end goal is for first responders and other government personnel to be able to communicate using any communications device (new or legacy radio, smart-phone, traditional phone, IP phone, or softphone) with any media (voice, video, text messages, and data). This more comprehensive kind of interoperability enhances public safety by providing greater situational awareness and enabling a unified chain of command."

Galvin (2009, p.60) asserts, "Creating an interoperable public safety network is a financial investment that, cities will find, pays big dividends." Interoperability is a priority for law enforcement and is critical in large-scale emergencies. However, much of the time law enforcement officers spend communicating is with individuals one-on-one, not only in trying to determine what problems exist in a community, but in investigating and solving crimes. At times, this results from lack of a common language.

Lack of a Common Language

O'Toole and Reyes (2008, p.72) point out, "In addition to relying solely on police radios, many officers today communicate from their cruisers through mobile data computer transmissions, cellular telephone calls, text messaging, and e-mail. Communications between and among law enforcement officers and agencies have improved significantly in the past few years, and police first responders and administrators alike have acquired and embraced numerous technological innovations. Unfortunately, however, these officers are not always speaking the same language; thus, *the largest obstacle remaining in the way of interoperability is in the human ability to communicate effectively*" [emphasis added].

O'Toole and Reyes (2008, p.72) recall the memorable line from the classic *Cool Hand Luke*: "What we've got here is . . . failure to communicate." They give as an example in policing a routine radio transmission between a Maryland State Police (MSP) trooper and a Montgomery County, Maryland, police dispatcher. The trooper was monitoring the county police radio channel in his cruiser when he came upon a minor vehicle collision. Forgetting that he was tuned to the county police radio channel, he interrupted a routine dispatch on the county channel and transmitted, "I have a 10-50 southbound 270, prior to 495." To the trooper a 10-50 was an accident, and he was simply informing his dispatcher that he was assisting in a minor collision. However, to the Montgomery County Police a 10-50 was the code for "officer in trouble." Because the trooper was assisting at the collision, he was away from his radio and did not respond to calls from the Montgomery County Police, who then sent officers from two police districts to assist a trooper who they believed was in trouble. This lack of communication did not cause any major problem, but it did result in wasted time and resources.

Although there is no national uniform standard in 10-codes, typically neighboring agencies do have a standard. In any case, when considering an interagency incident, officers should be trained and have common knowledge to use plain English over radio traffic instead of 10-codes.

The Department of Homeland Security recommends that first responders replace their 10-codes with "plain English" communications.

O'Toole and Reyes (2008, p.72) quote Chief Scoff of the Arlington County, Virginia, Police Department: "It is our responsibility, as police leaders, to remove any remaining impediments to effective communications between law enforcement officers and agencies. In today's working environment, it makes no sense that an officer in one jurisdiction might fail to understand a critical piece of information overheard on the police radio because we failed to provide for a common speaking platform."

It is, however, critical to recognize the difference between interagency communication challenges, where the possibility of misunderstanding is high, and routine communication practices in the field among officers in the same department. In the latter case, 10-codes are still extremely common and have high pertinence to officer safety. As any first-line officer will attest, having codes when dealing with active incidents give the officers a distinct safety advantage. Consider the example of one officer telling his partner to "go 10-15" with a suspect. The suspect does not have any idea that the 10-code means "arrest him or her," which gives the arresting officer an edge for safety and leaves less time for suspects to think about what they might do if they had had that knowledge before being in handcuffs.

Another effort to enhance communication is seen in efforts to develop a more advanced system to access emergency care.

THE NEXT GENERATION 9-1-1

The 9-1-1 system began in the United States in 1967 when President Lyndon Johnson's Commission on Law Enforcement and Administration of Justice recommended that police departments choose a single number to call nationwide. The first Enhanced 9-1-1 system is reported to have gone online in Chicago in 1976 (Larson, 2008, p.4). "While the existing E9-1-1 system has been a success story for more than 30 years, technological advances have stretched it to its limit. New wireless and IP-based devices that are capable of delivering messages via text and video are being developed and utilized at a steadily increasing rate" (Hixson et al., 2007, p.18). Thus, a critical need exists for an Internet Protocol (IP)–enabled Next Generation 9-1-1 (NG9-1-1) system able to adapt rapidly to new technology and support new devices. Slahor (2008, p.18) reports, "Additions such as IP (Internet Protocol)–based communications, shared infrastructure, increased flexibility/redundancy, and seamless voice, data, and video communications are on the horizon, ready to lead the way to better planning and development of the 'Next Generation of 9-1-1'."

Before looking at specific ways in which officers communicate with citizens and suspects, consider some of the problems officers might have in communicating with and understanding certain individuals.

PROBLEMS IN COMMUNICATING WITH A DIVERSE PUBLIC

Officers might have difficulty understanding the elderly, individuals who speak little or no English or who have different cultural backgrounds and those with disabilities or diseases that may impair their ability to communicate.

Communicating with the Elderly

Serving and protecting the aging U.S. population is a special challenge for law enforcement. The U.S. Census Bureau predicts that by 2030, the population over age 65 will nearly triple to more than 70 million people, and older people will make up more than 20 percent of the population.

Problems in communicating with the elderly can arise from the age differences between, and corresponding generational concerns of, senior citizens and law enforcement officers. However, perhaps the greatest challenge will be for officers to recognize when they are interacting with an elderly person who has Alzheimer's disease who is either lost, shoplifting or driving erratically. Such persons may forget where they live, where they left their cars or even their names.

An individual with Alzheimer's disease may have slurred, incoherent speech resembling intoxication.

If Alzheimer's disease is suspected, officers should look for an identification (ID) bracelet or other identification. Officers should identify themselves and explain what they will be doing, even if obvious. Officers should also maintain eye contact when speaking and try to keep a calm atmosphere. Physical restraints should be avoided if possible because they are almost certain to cause the person to lash out, verbally and physically.

Communicating with Non-English-Speaking Immigrants

"More than 47 million people in the United States speak a language other than English. Of those, about 19 million are classified as having limited English proficiency. Overall, nearly 2.6 million adults in the country speak no English at all. For law enforcement, the reality in the field speaks even more loudly than the statistics" (Holt, 2008, p.54). Holt notes that law enforcement officers face daily situations where they must communicate with individuals who have limited English skills, often a dangerous situation for all involved: "Miscommunication between an officer and a victim or suspect can spark further conflict, delay needed help and escalate already tense situations." Concurring, Moore (2008b, p.106) states, "Dealing with individuals who do not speak English in the course of an emergency call can turn out to be a nightmare if a miscommunication takes place."

Language and cultural barriers can also severely hinder an investigation. It can be extremely difficult to interrogate these types of people, and if an officer does not speak the suspect's language, everything is then translated through an interpreter (who typically has no law enforcement background). Many of the tactics and nonverbal communication involved in interrogation can be lost in this translation, which is frustrating to the investigator, the victim and sometimes the suspect.

One way to enhance communication with non-English-speaking people is to recruit bilingual officers. Another approach is for English-speaking officers to learn the language most commonly used by the immigrant population in their jurisdiction. Traditional language classes are not necessarily effective because they include writing and "polite" conversation, not what police officers need. They need to master a small number of phrases with specific applications to street situations to maintain control until someone fluent in the target language arrives.

Another way to overcome language barriers is to compile a list of bilingual citizens in the community. This is easiest in large cities and those that have colleges and universities. Legal problems may arise, however, if confidential information is involved. When interviewing a suspect in custody, credentials count, and a court will only recognize certified translators. Often, incidents involving language barriers occur at times when it is difficult to find a certified translator, making it difficult to properly investigate or resolve an incident.

Another approach to the language barrier is to subscribe to the *language line*, a translation service offered by AT&T that provides direct interpretation for police and other emergency service units responding to calls in more than 140 languages. This service, however, is not without potential drawbacks.

AN OFFICER'S PERSPECTIVE
The Downside of Translators

I once had a domestic abuse incident involving a Somali family and decided to use a language line Somali interpreter. This interpreter could barely speak English, and I later discovered he had asked the female victim why she had called the police over the incident. Apparently it is not acceptable for a woman in that culture to report an abusive husband. This had nothing to do with what I wanted translated. When using a translator who has no law enforcement background, it is important to keep in mind that, if it involves their primary culture, you may find barriers with them as well. You are dependent on them as your communication, and they have the power to place bias in the translation without either party's knowledge.

—*Sgt. Henry Lim Cho*

Technology is also available to help officers communicate with diverse populations, such as point talk translators. Electronic voice translators that convey basic instructions in the subject's own language are also available.

Communicating with Those from a Different Culture

Even when language is not a barrier, communication problems may result from customs and cultural differences in gestures, body language, body space expectations and the like. For example, the Asian custom of coin rubbing to cure children of diseases leaves marks on the skin that may be misinterpreted by teachers or police officers as signs of child abuse. It is also reported that officer gender can come into play, with some individuals from non-Western cultures refusing to listen to female officers.

Another example: Unlike most Americans who know they should remain seated in their car if stopped by police, a Nigerian will usually get out of his car to show respect and may ignore a request to step back because it makes no sense

This officer's knowledge of sign language helps him communicate more clearly with a hearing-impaired person.
© Ray Malace

to him. Furthermore, in Nigeria, the distance for conversation is much closer, sometimes even less than 15 inches, and direct eye contact signifies deception, rudeness or defiance. These cultural differences could easily cause communication problems and conflict between an officer and an immigrant citizen.

Other cultural issues related to immigration may make communication even more difficult. *The Police Chief's Guide to Immigration Issues* (2007, p.7) states, "Immigration is not a new issue; in fact, it has been an essential part of the fabric of American society since the nation's inception. The distinction of 'legal' and 'illegal' immigration has existed since 1882, when Congress passed the Chinese Exclusion Act—one of the nation's first immigration laws established to keep immigrant populations out of the United States, Additionally, police response to the immigrant community is not new either. For centuries, police agencies have sought to understand the cultures and perspectives of the growing international communities within their jurisdictions."

Figures from the U.S. Census Bureau indicate that of the 34.2 million persons in the 2005 U.S. Census survey, 12 percent were foreign born, bringing to local communities multiple cultures, languages and "often unique perspectives on, or fears of, the police."

The *Guide to Immigration Issues* (2007, p.10) notes the challenges facing law enforcement:

- One major city agency launched a new outreach initiative to work closely with its immigrant communities on the same day the local sheriffs department cross-deputized each deputy as a U.S. Immigration and Customs Enforcement (ICE) agent to pursue and arrest illegal immigrants.
- Some cities have been faced with divided community opinion on "flashpoint" issues such as day laborer hiring sites—some calling for the police to support such locations, while others contend that most laborers at these sites are illegal and should be arrested.

- Community groups are seeking to support immigrants while other groups are focusing on undocumented immigrants and enforcement actions.
- Governing body leaders are seeking to protect undocumented immigrants and other leaders are seeking to deport them.

The estimated number of illegal immigrants is growing at a rate of 100,000 to 300,000 a year. These non-English-speaking immigrants often cluster together in relatively poor neighborhoods where crime rates are high, leading non-immigrants to equate these newly arrived individuals with crime and disorder.

In addition, many new immigrants come from countries where the police are feared rather than respected. The police in those countries keep secret files and have broad arrest powers. They may brutalize citizens, force confessions from them or simply imprison them without any "due process." In fact, due process may be a concept unknown to immigrants. Many immigrants also distrust government and public institutions, especially banks, and keep their money and valuables at home or at their businesses, making them vulnerable to crime. Again, their fear of the police will work against them because they are unlikely to report the crimes or to assist the police in investigating them.

The Police Executive Research Forum (PERF) report, *Police Chiefs and Sheriffs Speak Out on Local Immigration Enforcement*, states, "Increased enforcement of immigration law will have a significant chilling effect on crime reporting in immigrant communities. Fear of arrest and deportation will give illegal immigrants an even greater incentive to stay 'under the radar' and avoid drawing attention to themselves" (2008, p.15). This problem is compounded when the immigrant (legal or illegal) does not understand or speak English.

Communicating with Individuals with Disabilities or Conditions Affecting Speech

When people think of "cultural diversity," they typically think of racial, ethnic or even religious groups existing within mainstream America. Yet, in fact, the largest minority group in the United States, an estimated 49 million, consists of individuals with disabilities. The U.S. Department of Justice (DOJ) estimates that about 20 percent of Americans have disabilities, a figure likely to rise as the population ages and baby boomers grow older (Kanable, 2008, p.68).

To ensure that people with disabilities are treated fairly, the Americans with Disabilities Act (ADA) was enacted in 1990. The DOJ explains, "Under the Americans with Disabilities Act, people who have disabilities are entitled to the same services law enforcement provides to anyone else. They may not be excluded or segregated from services, be denied services, or otherwise treated differently than other people." The ADA defines a person who has a disability as one who has a physical or mental impairment that substantially limits one or more major life activity, has a record of such an impairment, or is regarded as having such an impairment.

The Americans with Disabilities Amendments Act went into effect January 1, 2009, establishing new definitions of key terms, particularly the legal definition of a disability, and expanding on the definition of "substantially limits" by stating that the question of whether a major life activity is "substantially limited" should not be interpreted strictly. The act also broadens the group of individuals eligible for protection under the "regarded as" portion of the ADA: "The Amendments Act adds clarification providing that an individual who is "regarded as" having a disability is one who has been subjected to discrimination based on an actual or perceived physical or mental impairment—whether or not the impairment limits or is perceived to limit a major life activity" (Collins, 2009, p.12). Collins notes that it is too soon to tell what effect the Amendments Act will have on police departments or municipalities, but most experts expect an increase in the number of ADA-related lawsuits.

Knowing who is disabled and, therefore, protected by ADA, is sometimes difficult. Some disabilities are obvious: paralysis and blindness, for example. Other disabilities, however, are not immediately apparent. Likewise, many conditions or diseases that impair speech are not immediately apparent and may be mistaken for intoxication or being under the influence of drugs. Nonetheless, officers must adhere to and abide by ADA requirements that prohibit discrimination against qualified individuals with disabilities in the delivery of government services, programs or activities.

Blindness and deafness are two of the most common disabilities officers may encounter. The *visually impaired* comprise more than 11.5 million individuals, according to the National Society to Prevent Blindness. When interacting with people who are blind, police officers should not only identify themselves, but offer to let the people feel their badges as well. The *hearing impaired* are among those with "invisible" handicaps. Police officers will interact more effectively with citizens who are hearing impaired if they understand that most deaf people are not good lip-readers. In addition, the speech of individuals who have been deaf since birth may sound garbled and even unintelligible.

The speech of a person who has been deaf since birth may be mistaken for that of one who is intoxicated or using drugs.

How deaf people communicate depends on several factors, including the type of deafness, the age at which the person became deaf, the individual's personality and intelligence, speech and speech-reading abilities, general language skills and educational background. To communicate with an individual who is hearing impaired, officers should get the person's attention by gently tapping a shoulder or waving and speak slowly and clearly using short sentences. It is helpful to learn sign language. The services of a certified interpreter should be used whenever possible. In fact, several court cases have addressed when such services are required by law.

People with epilepsy also may present communication problems. Epilepsy is a disorder of the central nervous system in which a person tends to have recurrent seizures. It may alter behavior, movement, perception and sensation. Some seizures impair consciousness and may last from a few seconds to several minutes.

An epileptic seizure can look like intoxication or the influence of street drugs, as all may involve impaired consciousness, incoherent speech, glassy-eyed staring and aimless wandering.

The person may be confused or need to rest after a seizure. A person having a seizure will generally regain his or her faculties within several minutes, whereas a drunk or high person will not.

Communicating with Individuals Who Are Mentally Ill

Historically, mentally ill individuals were locked away from society in insane asylums. Long-term institutionalization or hospitalization was the norm. Likewise, mentally retarded individuals were placed into special schools, usually hidden away from society. In the mid-1960s, however, this changed, and a massive deinstitutionalization movement occurred, placing mentally disabled individuals into the community, but without the support they formerly had. The continuing trend of deinstitutionalization has directly affected police, requiring them to acquire a new set of communication skills.

The National Institute for Mental Health (NIMH) estimates that almost 58 million Americans, nearly 20 percent of the population, suffer from a diagnosable mental disorder in a given year. Law enforcement officers need to know about mental illness because of the high likelihood they will come into contact with mentally ill people as officers work their beats, contacts that can be dangerous to the officer as well as to anyone involved in the contact. The recommended way to contact a person with mental illness is to have two officers present, one to make the contact and the other one to provide cover for that officer (Siegfried and Arlotti, 2008, p.48).

Many departments participate in crisis intervention teams (CITs), sometimes referred to as the Memphis Model because the first CIT was organized in Memphis, Tennessee. A CIT is more than a law enforcement initiative; many other players are involved: "Crucial to CIT's model are family members, the consumers, the mental health community, and, finally, law enforcement, all working on the same page. . . . CIT succeeds because it respects the dignity of the mentally ill. It works to divert these individuals from the criminal justice system and into more appropriate surroundings whenever possible. And it takes a reasonable caring approach" (Moore, 2008a, p.61).

Mentally ill people may find it difficult to get to a clinic to receive follow-up service or ongoing outpatient care. They may even forget appointments or go off their treatment plans. As a result, they often stop refilling or taking needed medication, which eventually leads to behavior that brings them into contact with the law. Although many proclaim the inappropriateness of using the criminal justice system to handle situations involving mentally disordered individuals, few have focused attention on the appropriateness of using informal dispositions, including no police action, mediation, separation, lecturing and transports to homes or homeless shelters

Making Referrals Officers should know how to determine when someone needs referral to mental health professionals or a mental health court, how to access those resources and the procedures for formal commitment of individuals who pose a threat to themselves or others.

Communicating with Individuals Who Are Mentally Retarded or Autistic

The ADA ensures that people with developmental disabilities, such as mental retardation or autism, remain a part of our nation's increasingly diverse workforce. To avoid future potential litigation, officers need to be able to communicate effectively with those who are developmentally disabled.

Interacting with Individuals Who Are Mentally Retarded Recognizing mental retardation is the first step in dealing with it effectively. Often those who are retarded are adept at camouflaging their disability. When interacting with mentally retarded individuals, officers should try to find a quiet, private setting, be patient and speak slowly, using simple language and, if possible, visual aids, pictures or diagrams. Officers should be aware that people who are mentally retarded often try to please others and may, therefore, make untruthful statements thinking it is what the officer, or someone else, wants to hear.

Interacting with Individuals Who Are Autistic Autism is a developmental disability that typically becomes apparent before a child reaches age three.

Some indicators that an individual may be autistic include the individual avoiding eye contact, lack of verbal response (many autistic people do not speak), speaking in monotone, repeating exactly what an officer says, engaging in repetitive physical actions, not responding to verbal commands or sounds, not understanding body language or recognizing a police uniform, dressing inappropriately for the weather and not asking for help.

When responding to situations involving autistic individuals, officers should approach the person in a quiet, nonthreatening manner and talk in a moderate, calm voice. Instructions should be simple and direct, such as "stand up" or "go to the car now." They should understand that touching the autistic person may cause a protective "fight or flight."

If a crime has been committed and an officer must take an autistic individual into custody, the suspect should be segregated until a mental health professional can evaluate him or her. Also, use caution when considering an autistic suspect's statements because they may confess to crimes they did not commit because of their desire to please and willingness to accept an authority figure's version of events.

Communicating with the Homeless

The homeless, some 3.5 million people (National Law Center on Homelessness and Poverty, 2008, p.5) who are sleeping on the streets, constitute an ever-increasing social problem in the 21st century. They also pose a dual problem for police: Some break the law, and some become victims. The homeless are frequently *victims* of crime and violence, and law enforcement is responsible for protecting the homeless from those who would take advantage of them. Another problem is that those who advocate for the homeless sometimes break the law—for example, taking over unoccupied private homes as well as unoccupied public buildings and demanding that these buildings be made into homeless shelters. On the other hand, countless citizens do not want people sleeping in their parks. They cite problems such as littering, stealing, panhandling, drinking, doing drugs and public urinating and defecating. Many homeless people also suffer from mental illness and, if unable to pay for medication, can present erratic behavior that can bring them into contact with law enforcement.

In general, communities simply do not want the homeless around. Citizens clamor for their city councils to pass laws against sleeping in the street. And when city councils oblige, the social problem becomes a law enforcement problem.

The change in public attitudes toward the homeless is illustrated in cities that have toughened regulations on panhandling, sleeping in public places and other behavior associated with the homeless. Police may be asked to enforce regulations that prohibit lying down on benches in parks, panhandling, fighting, or disrobing and urinating or defecating outside toilet facilities. Because they have no home, most homeless people have lost the privilege of voting. Because they have no home, most cannot simply pick up the phone to call for help when needed.

The Albuquerque (New Mexico) Police Department has developed teams to address the gap between crisis intervention and long-term services, especially for those who are chronically homeless but nonviolent and who often fall through the cracks. According to Kyrik (2008, p.58), their Homeless Strategic Outreach Team includes Albuquerque Police Department officers, health care outreach workers, job counselors from Goodwill industries and a contract psychiatrist. Kyrik says that these innovative teams "take the burden off of beat cops."

Police must first see the homeless as individuals and as possible victims and then do all they can to protect them from victimization. Police must also consider the reality that, many times, the homeless are offenders and need appropriate diversion and treatment alternatives to prevent further criminal behavior. Police should also be aware of what kinds of assistance are available for the homeless and make this information known, including helping them obtain services.

COMMUNICATION AS A TOOL OR A WEAPON

Effective communication can be a powerful public relations tool and a means to implement community policing. A positive, service-type attitude begins with communication skills. Officers who use harsh, commanding words put people on the defensive. Many people, if pushed, will push back. Recognizing this tendency, officers must resist the temptation to engage in verbal confrontations and, instead, remain calm, using logic and reason in speaking with others. For example, compare the command "Come here!" with the request "Excuse me, but I need to talk with you for a minute."

In any use-of-force transaction, officers must use professional language so their communication becomes a tool for controlling the situation instead of a weapon used against the officer should the incident be reviewed. Training in verbal skills teaches officers to be assertive, not aggressive. Using Verbal Judo is discussed in Chapter 3.

An officer's ability to effectively communicate directly affects his or her ability to perform a vital function of policing—obtaining information.

COMMUNICATING TO OBTAIN INFORMATION

A tremendous amount of time is spent communicating during police operations. Although much information officers receive may seem irrelevant to the law enforcement mission, it is important to the person conveying the information and should be treated accordingly. Officers who listen empathetically to citizens' concerns will promote public relations, enhance the department's image and foster community policing. If they are truly "to serve and protect," officers must listen to their "clients."

The majority of officers' communicating time should be spent listening rather than speaking. Skillfully phrased questions can elicit a wealth of information. Active listening can greatly enhance the quality of the information obtained whether the communication involves a brief stop, a formal interview or an interrogation.

THE FIELD INQUIRY

field inquiry
The unplanned questioning of a person who has aroused a police officer's suspicions.

A **field inquiry** is the unplanned questioning of a person who has aroused a police officer's suspicions. It is not an arrest but could lead to one. Field inquiries are also referred to as "reasonable suspicion" investigatory stops or *field contacts*, and a card on which the information is recorded is called the *field contact card.*

The Authority to Stop

Law enforcement officers are expected to stop and question people acting suspiciously. If an officer stops someone for questioning (a reasonable suspicion investigatory stop or field inquiry) and the officer believes the person may be armed, the officer can also pat down the person's outer clothing for weapons.

The right to stop and question suspicious people was established in the landmark case of *Terry v. Ohio* (1968).

Briefly, this case involved Detective McFadden, an officer with 30 years of investigative experience, who observed three men who "just didn't look right" standing outside a jewelry store. After watching the men repeat a routine nearly a dozen times, McFadden suspected they were casing the store for a "stickup" and might be armed. Deciding to investigate their activity further, McFadden approached the men, identified himself as a police officer, asked for their names and then decided to act.

He turned one man, John Terry, around, and made a quick "pat down" of Terry's outer clothing and felt a pistol in one pocket. Keeping Terry between himself and the others, McFadden ordered all three men to enter the store, where he asked the store owner to call for police while he patted the outer clothing of the others. McFadden removed the revolver from Terry's pocket and another gun from the coat of a man named Chilton. Terry and Chilton were formally charged with carrying concealed weapons. When Terry and Chilton were brought to court, their lawyers moved that the guns could not be used as evidence, claiming they were illegally seized.

The trial judge disagreed, ruling that on the basis of McFadden's experience, he had reasonable cause to believe the defendants were conducting themselves suspiciously and some interrogation was warranted. For his own protection, the detective had the right to frisk the men whom he believed to be armed. The men were convicted, and both appealed their conviction to the U.S. Supreme Court. Before the Court's decision was handed down, Chilton died. Therefore, the Court's review applied only to Terry.

The Court recognized Detective McFadden as a man of experience, training and knowledge, and certainly "a man of reasonable caution." And as a man of "*ordinary care* and prudence," he waited until he had strengthened his suspicions, making his move just before what he believed would be an armed robbery. Given these facts, the Court upheld the trial court verdict, adding that McFadden had to make a quick decision when he saw the three men gathered at the store, and his actions were correct.

A *stop* must be based on a reasonable suspicion that the person stopped is about to be or is actually engaged in criminal activity. For example, the person fits a description of a suspect, doesn't "fit" the time or place, is acting strangely, is known to associate with criminals, is loitering, runs away, is present at a crime scene and the area is a high-crime area. The stop may be all that occurs, it may lead to a patdown, or it may progress to an arrest, depending on the information received.

Rutledge (2008b, p.68) points out, "The U.S. Supreme Court has said that not every interaction between police and citizens amounts to a search or seizure requiring some kind of suspicion. If you simply walk up to an individual on the street and start talking, without blocking the way or ordering the person to stay and talk to you, the person has not been detained and you have nothing to justify." This was the ruling in *United States v. Mendenhall* (1980) when the Court held, "There is nothing in the Constitution which prevents a policeman from addressing questions to anyone on the streets."

More recently, the Supreme Court, in *Hiibel v. Sixth Judicial District Court of Nevada* (2004), has upheld a Nevada law that makes it a crime for a person stopped for questioning, a *Terry* stop, to refuse to tell the police his name. In *Hiibel*, the Court said that asking questions is an important part of any police investigation and does not violate the Fourth Amendment. Citing a series of Supreme Court decisions, the Court stated that it is "clear that questions concerning a suspect's identify are a routine and accepted part of many *Terry* stops." Detaining a person for questioning is an important police function that easily generates hostility because people resent restriction of their freedom. Officers must be flexible. Some inquiries will be brief and simple; others extremely complex.

THE INTERVIEW

The interview is an important type of routine communication used by police officers. It differs from the impromptu field inquiry in that an **interview** is the planned questioning of a witness, victim, informant or other person with information related to an incident or case. An interview is a "broad-based

interview
The planned questioning of a witness, victim, informant or other person with information related to an incident or a case.

inquiry using open-ended questions to obtain facts, sequence of events or alibis, which may or may not be true" (Sturman, 2008, p.44). To be effective, interviews should be based on specific goals and objectives.

A quality interview is often the deciding factor in solving a crime and having a successful prosecution. A successful investigator presents prosecutors with well-documented, detailed interviews of the victim, suspect, and all witnesses.

A quality interview promotes the victims' and public's confidence in law enforcement and increases the likelihood of guilty pleas. It reduces the hours often spent re-interviewing witnesses; directs investigators to additional suspects, evidence, and victims; and helps in recovering property. It may also reduce the false arrests and improve department morale.

The Importance of Rapport

rapport
A relationship of mutual trust, conformity, accord and respect; a sense between two people that they can communicate comfortably and openly.

Building rapport is essential in successful interviewing. **Rapport** basically means a relationship of mutual trust, conformity, accord and respect. It is a sense between two people that they can communicate comfortably and openly. This can be difficult to achieve between someone in a position of authority, such as a police officer, and someone under scrutiny, such as a suspect, or someone under emotional distress, such as a victim of a violent crime. Police rapport building is not always a quick and effortless endeavor, and different approaches work better with different suspects, as well with different police officer types. However, several basic suggestions may help facilitate the development of rapport between an officer and an individual they are interviewing.

Sturman (2008, p.46) states, "A professional, yet friendly, approach to the person being interviewed is the most effective way to establish rapport. A quick way to do this is by finding some common ground or interest . . . . By reading the suspect's personality, you can establish rapport by changing topics to discuss points of interest common to both of you. Try to connect with the suspect on one of the many similarities most people have. For example, common ground might be found in weather, family, work frustrations, bills, children, etc."

Rapport may also be fostered when an officer tries to fill a simple want or need the interviewee may have before getting into any details, particularly in the case of interrogations. For example, asking the person if he or she would like to use the rest room or have something to drink can help dissipate tension and get the interview off to a better start. Finally, when addressing the interviewee (whether victim, witness or suspect) and throughout the duration of the contact, it is crucial to speak to interviewees with respect, regardless of what they are accused of having done.

Setting the Stage

The ideal setting for an interview can involve many factors, but the main thing is to keep the room simple and free of distractions, such as phones, clocks and magazines (Sturman, 2008, p.44). The space should be relatively small (10 feet by 10 feet) and void of excess furniture. Barriers such as a desk or table between the interviewer and interviewee should be eliminated. The number of people in the room should also be limited. If there is a window in the room, the interviewee should be seated facing away from it.

Recording Interviews

Phillips (2008, p.162) notes, "Law enforcement professionals conduct interviews with hundreds or perhaps even thousands of individuals every year, and each interview is as different as the background and personality of the interviewee. So, what happens when an interview turns into a case of 'he said, she said'?" One way to avoid this situation and to protect officers against false allegations is to record the interview. Anand (2008, p.60) suggests, "Tired of the debate over who said what, many agencies use new digital technology to record all interviews." Some states, such as Minnesota, have mandated a policy of recording suspect interviews when feasible (Scales Law), and others strongly encourage departments to conduct such recordings.

Types of Questions

Sumpter (2008b, p24) observes, "Asking questions is truly an art form, one that must be mastered to properly elicit needed information." Officers should distinguish between three types of questions: closed, leading and open.

A **closed question**, *limits* the amount or scope of information that the witness can provide, for example, "How many shots did you hear?" or "Did you see the suspect shove the victim?" Such questions may require a yes or no answer and should be avoided when seeking to obtain information. A **leading question** *suggests* an answer, for example "You wanted your boss dead, isn't that correct?" Sumpter (2008, p.23) stresses, "It is important the officer maintains a neutral position, encouraging the interviewee to express the information developed in his head and not something created by the officer." An **open question** allows for an *unlimited* response from the witness in his or her own words. Usually open-ended questions are most effective in interviewing. For example: "Tell me what happened." Sumpter explains, "Open questions create a two-way conversation, allowing the interviewee to answer on his terms and take the answers into the conversational direction he prefers. Open questioning is the best indicator of the interviewee's cooperation. . . . Sometimes the answers to these questions are lengthy, but the interviewee must be allowed to answer without interruption."

closed question
Limits the amount or scope of information that a person can provide, for example, "What color was the car?" (the opposite of an open-ended question).

leading question
One that suggests an answer, for example, "You wanted your boss dead, isn't that correct?"

open question
One that allows for an unlimited response from the witness in his/her own words, for example, "What can you tell me about the car?" (the opposite of a closed-ended question).

Whether officers are seeking to comfort the victim of a crime while obtaining information or seeking to obtain information from a witness, certain techniques can make interviews more effective.

INTERVIEWING TECHNIQUES

Interviews should be structured around the investigatory elements of the incident or crime. The need for careful planning and advance preparation cannot be overstated. In a preliminary interview at a crime scene, officers have extremely limited time for such planning. Consequently, they need to know their priorities in advance. They should obtain as much information as possible, identify and locate the offender(s), and broadcast the information or alert other officers and departments about the offense and identity of the offender(s).

Officers should not use police terminology when interviewing people because it will increase the incriminating atmosphere of the questioning. For example, use *take property* rather than *rob, have sex with* rather than *rape*, or *private use* rather than *embezzle*.

Phrasing Questions

Evidence shows that the phrasing of questions can definitely influence answers. In one study, for example, observers who were asked, "How tall was the basketball player?" estimated his height to be, on average, about 79 inches. Those asked, "How short was the basketball player?" responded with an estimated average of about 69 inches.

To minimize the inadvertent biasing of memory, witnesses should give an uninterrupted narration before being asked specific questions. Interrogation should also take place as soon as possible so that misleading information from various sources does not become part of the remembered event.

Follow-up questions can reduce or eliminate confusion and clarify statements that seem to contradict previously stated facts. Contradictory statements by an individual may be innocent, due simply to an error in memory, or may indicate deception. Skilled questioning can uncover lies told as part of a witness's or suspect's statement.

Avoiding Contaminating an Interview

Interviewing a person on a noisy, busy street with many onlookers may cause problems. Table 2.1 presents tips for avoiding interview contamination.

Table 2.1 Tips for Avoiding Interview Contamination

Focus on Interview Environment	
Questions to Consider	**Strategies to Use**
Where should the interview take place?	A location free of distractions.
How should the room be configured?	Without barriers (e.g., desk or plants) between interviewer and subject.
Who should conduct the interview?	One interviewer builds rapport and engenders trust more easily. Two interviewers should use team approach; one asks questions and the other takes notes.
Focus on Interviewer's Behavior	
Questions to Consider	**Strategies to Use**
How can interviewers encourage subjects to talk?	Use an open and relaxed posture, facing the subject; lean forward, make eye contact, nod, and occasionally say "uh huh" and "ok."
How can interviewers encourage subjects to listen?	Speak slowly, softly, and deliberately; avoid stressing or emphasizing one word over another.
Focus on Interviewer's Questions	
Questions to Consider	**Strategies to Use**
What is a model for posing questions?	A funnel, with open-ended followed by closed-ended questions.
What are the benefits of open-ended questions?	Gather complete information, minimize the risk of imposing views on subject, and help assess subject's normal behavior.
What are the benefits of closed-ended questions?	Elicit specific details, ensure accuracy, and help detect deviations or changes in subject.
How can interviewers ensure thoroughness?	Address the basics of who, what, when, where, how, and why.
What are other cautions during questioning?	Never ask questions that disclose investigative information and lead the subject toward a desired response.

Source: Vincent A. Sandoval. "Strategies to Avoid Interview Contamination." *FBI Law Enforcement Bulletin*, October 2003, p.8.

Interviewing Witnesses and Victims: The Lifeblood of Criminal Cases

A witness is a person other than a suspect who is asked to give information about an incident or another person. A witness may be a victim, a complainant, an observer of an event, a scientific specialist who has examined physical evidence or a custodian of official documents.

Officers must take accurate notes on what witnesses see, smell or hear. Officers also must evaluate the witnesses' credibility on a number of intangible factors, such as their ability to articulate, their intelligence, their opportunity to observe, their sobriety and their stress level at the time of observation.

Officers must realize that a crime of violence can put witnesses in shock. A **primary victim** is one actually harmed. A **secondary victim** is not actually harmed but suffers along with the victim—a spouse or parent, for example. Therefore, witnesses to a criminal event may also be considered victims of the crime.

primary victim
One who actually is harmed.

secondary victim
One who is not actually harmed but who suffers along with the victim—a spouse or parent, for example.

Oetinger (2007, p.40) notes, "Even though crimes involving violence or the loss of property affect over 30 million people in the United States every year, just a small percentage of these individuals and family members obtain the services they need to manage the stress that develops upon falling victim to crime." Jordan et al. (2007, p.44) likewise note that victims of crime are often neglected in the criminal justice system, even though state laws define victim rights such as "the right to be treated with fairness, dignity, and respect; to be informed and present throughout the entire criminal justice process; to be reasonably protected from the accused; and to be entitled to seek restitution."

Effective interviewing helps officers obtain needed information and helps victims' and witnesses' future mental and emotional well-being. Officers should begin interviewing and questioning victims and witnesses only after establishing psychological and physical equilibrium. Insensitive questioning can compound the trauma.

Standard 55 "Victim/Witness" states, "In its own best interests, law enforcement has a role to play in victim/witness assistance, a role that no other component of the criminal justice system can effectively duplicate" (CALEA, 2006).

Standard 55.2.2. specifically addresses the issue of victim and witness intimidation, requiring that agency provides "appropriate assistance to victims/witnesses who have been threatened or who, in the judgment of the agency, express specific, credible reasons for fearing intimidation or further victimization." According to Spadanuta (2008, p.51), such assistance is vital: "Winning the fight against witness intimidation is the first step toward the successful prosecution of gang-related crimes." Bune (2008, p.78) stresses, "Criminal victimization has a widespread impact, requiring extra attention and effective response strategies by agencies." Bune emphasizes, "Law enforcement professionals and victim services personnel must be proactive in utilizing practical strategies and effective response mechanisms to ensure that crime victims are treated with the sensitivity, dignity and the respect they deserve." As Jordan et al. (2007, p.50) point out, "When crime victims perceive that they have been treated with compassion, fairness, and respect, they are more likely to cooperate in the investigation of the crime committed against them, making an agency's job easier at first response and as cases progress through the justice system."

privileged information
Data that does not need to be divulged to the police or the courts because of the existence of a special relationship, such as that between spouses or between lawyers and their clients.

absolute privilege
Information or testimony that cannot be received; there are no exceptions (see *privileged information*).

conditional privilege
The official information privilege; that is, the information can be received but the source of the information can be protected.

cognitive interview
Interviewing method that puts witnesses mentally back at the scene of an incident and encourages them to tell the whole story without interruption.

Police officers should assure themselves that the witnesses they interview can and will testify. However, some information may be "off limits." **Privileged information** is information that need not be divulged to the police or the courts. Two kinds of privileges exempt witnesses from testifying: absolute and conditional. An **absolute privilege** permits no exceptions. For example, conversations about social, business and personal affairs are often private and privileged. Such conversations include communications between physicians and patients, lawyers and clients, husbands and wives or others under a special obligation of fidelity and secrecy. A **conditional privilege** usually takes the form of the "official information privilege." An example is asking the court to not disclose an informant's identity.

Although witnesses may often be the only source of information available for solving a case, they are also fallible. One way to help witnesses recall events more accurately is the cognitive interview.

The Cognitive Interview

The **cognitive interview** puts witnesses mentally back at the scene of an incident and encourages them to tell the whole story without interruption. Most such interviews have five phases: (1) introduction to establish rapport, (2) open-ended questioning asking for a narrative of the event, (3) probing memory codes by asking the interviewee to close his or her eyes and concentrate on a specific portion of the narrative, again using open questioning, (4) review the information obtained to be sure it is accurate and perhaps jog the interviewee's memory more, and (5) close, getting information about the witness—the background information usually collected first.

Interviewing Children

Officers may be particularly challenged when interviewing a child witness. Depending on the child's age, the witness may have a limited comprehension of what took place or may lack the vocabulary to adequately relate what was seen. Also, depending on the type of incident and type of interview taking place, officers may benefit from using trained professionals such as social service agents or staff from private companies who are experienced in interviewing children.

Interviewers of children should avoid leading questions, repeated interviews and linguistically confusing questions. It is important the interview be conducted in a safe, child-friendly environment, preferably a room with child-sized furniture. Before the interview begins, however, the child and the adult who brought the child should be introduced to the interviewer and any others who will be present. Then, the child should be taken on a brief tour of the building, pointing out where the restrooms are and where the accompanying adult will be waiting for the child, as well as explaining what will happen during the interview.

Interviewers should not wear a uniform or gun. The child should be praised indicating approval, for example, "You're doing a good job of telling me what happened." As with adult witnesses, officers should ask open-ended questions and avoid criticism.

Statements

If an interview yields important information, often a statement is taken. Hess and Orthmann (2010, p.183) explain, "A **statement** is a legal narrative description of events related to a crime. It is a formal, detailed account. It begins with an introduction that gives the place, time, date and names of the people conducting and present at an interview. The name, address and age of the person questioned are stated before the main body of the statement." The body of the statement is the person's account of the incident. A clause at the end states that the information was given voluntarily. The person making the statement reads each page, makes any needed corrections, initials each correction and then signs the statement.

statement
A legal narrative description of events related to a crime.

The Certified Forensic Interviewer Program

The Center for Interviewer Standards and Assessment (CISA) has developed the Certified Forensic Interviewer (CFI) program. Benefits of obtaining a CFI certificate include the following (2003, p.44):

- Reduces exposure to liability.
- Helps establish credibility as an expert witness.
- Promotes officers with proven knowledge and training.
- Stands out when the next promotion comes around.
- Raises professional standards and accountability.
- Increases confession and conviction rates.
- Ensures consistent, predictable techniques.

INFORMATION FROM INFORMANTS

An **informant** is a person who provides information in a criminal action and whose identity must be protected. Because of an informant's residence, occupation, associates or lifestyle, that person may be in a better position than a police officer to obtain information about a particular crime. Law enforcement commonly categorizes informants based on how reliable an informant has proven to be. Those who have previously worked successfully with law enforcement may be known as "credible informants" or CIs.

informant
A human source of information in a criminal action whose identity must be protected.

Often an informant's tip, along with some corroboration, can establish probable cause to arrest. The amount of corroboration needed to establish probable cause depends on the informant's credibility and source of information. And although officers often know informants' identities, having worked with them regularly, many times police receive information about crime from individuals who refuse to identify themselves, calling into question the reliability of the tip.

ANONYMOUS TIPS

Citizens are constitutionally protected through Fourth Amendment provisions from being forcibly detained by the government based solely on the false accusations of pranksters and those harboring grudges. In *Alabama v. White* (1990), the Supreme Court held that an anonymous tip can provide the foundation for reasonable suspicion if the tip predicts future activities the officer can corroborate.

Officers must use sound judgment in how they respond to an anonymous tip, using court rulings as guidelines for what is legally allowed.

In *Florida v. J. L.* (2000), the Supreme Court held that an anonymous tip that a person is carrying a gun is not, without more, sufficient to justify a stop and frisk of that person. An officer must have a reasonable suspicion that a suspect is engaged in criminal activity and may be armed.

THE INTERROGATION

The terms *inquiry, interview* and *interrogation* are often confused. In police terminology, *inquiry* usually refers to conversations held with citizens during routine patrol. *Interviews*, as just discussed, are planned questionings of people having information about incidents. In contrast, an **interrogation** is the questioning of a hostile witness or suspect from whom officers try to obtain facts related to a crime as well as an admission or confession. An **admission** contains some information about the elements of the crime but falls short of a confession. A **confession** is information supporting the elements of a crime given by a person involved in committing that crime.

interrogation
The questioning of suspects from whom officers try to obtain facts related to a crime as well as admissions or confessions related to the crime.

admission
Statement containing some information concerning the elements of a crime, but falling short of a full confession.

confession
Information supporting the elements of a crime that is provided and attested to by any person involved in committing the crime; can be oral or written.

Interrogations carry an implied suspicion of criminal knowledge or involvement and must be handled differently from interviews. PERF has published *Model Procedures for Police Interrogation* (Caplan, n.d.), which states, "[An] interrogation occurs whenever an officer engages in conduct which he should know is likely to elicit an incriminating response from the suspect" (p.1).

Sumpter (2008a, p.14) suggests that investigators make an interrogation appear to be a simple conversation that builds rapport and gains information and weakens the suspect's stance: "If the officer gives the suspect the floor, he can subtly and subconsciously work the suspect to his favor by utilizing some basic tools." Sumpter explains how mirroring, pacing, and leading can help achieve these goals (p.14):

> *Mirroring*
>
> Mirroring is the process of consciously modeling the suspect's behaviors, such as speech pattern, posture, and other personal gestures. We swear if he swears, use our hands if he uses his, and raise our voice if he does. . . .
>
> *Pacing*
>
> While mirroring the verbal interaction, we subtly begin pacing nonverbal behavior. As the suspect changes posture, we subtly do the same. When the suspect leans back or forward in his chair, we will do the same. . . . Both mirroring and pacing send a subconscious message that brings us closer to passing the compatibility test.
>
> *Leading*
>
> Once we have mirrored and paced the interview to the point where there is verbal and nonverbal agreement, we will turn the table and lead the suspect in our direction. Leading is a process where we gauge the listener's cooperation from our nonverbal behaviors. When the time is right, change your posture for 30 seconds to see if there is a similar change in the suspect. If there is a similar

change, then rapport is strong, but if not, go back and try again. It is time for questioning when true rapport is gained.

Although interrogation is a vital law enforcement tool, it is susceptible to abuse and, consequently, is closely regulated by law. The landmark Supreme Court decision regulating police interrogation is *Miranda v. Arizona* (1966).

The *Miranda* Decision

In *Miranda v. Arizona*, 23-year-old Ernesto Miranda was arrested and interrogated about a rape and kidnapping. He confessed to the crimes but had not been told of his rights because police, aware Miranda had been arrested before, assumed he already knew his rights. The Supreme Court ruled (in a 5–4 decision) that the officers erred in not informing Miranda of those rights again: "The Fifth Amendment privilege is so fundamental to our system of constitutional rule and the expedient of being given an adequate warning as to the availability of the privilege so simple, we will not pause to inquire in individual cases whether the defendant was aware of his rights without a warning being given. Assessments of the knowledge the defendant possessed, based on information as to his age, education, intelligence, or prior contact with authorities, can never be more than speculation; a warning is a clear-cut fact (*Miranda v. Arizona*)."

In *Miranda v. Arizona*, the Court established the following rights applied to custodial interrogations:

- The suspect has the right to remain silent.
- If the suspect gives up the right to remain silent, anything that the suspect says can be used in a court of law against him or her.
- The suspect has a right to speak to an attorney and to have an attorney present when being questioned by the police.
- If the suspect cannot afford one, an attorney will be appointed to represent the suspect *before* questioning begins.

In *Miranda*, the Supreme Court held that these warnings are required before custodial interrogation. "Custodial" was defined as referring to the situation of a person who is "in custody" (under arrest) or *otherwise deprived of freedom of action in any significant way*. The test to determine if *Miranda* safeguards are triggered is whether a reasonable person in the suspect's position would conclude that he is not free to go (Caplan, n.d., p.2).

Many officers carry a card with the ***Miranda* warning** printed on it, clearly spelling out the suspect's rights, and read it verbatim to suspects. Of importance is whether the suspects understand each right. If, for example, a suspect speaks only Spanish, the warning might be read from a card bearing the warning in Spanish.

Miranda warning
A statement of a suspect's rights when that suspect is being questioned: the rights to remain silent, to talk to an attorney and to have an attorney present during questioning, the attorney to be provided free if a suspect cannot afford one.

Another important facet of the *Miranda* decision is whether suspects are willing to give up these rights and talk to the police. If they do so, a signed waiver should be obtained. When reading *Miranda* rights to juveniles, special care should be taken to ensure the suspect understands the warnings. Furthermore, "Officers should honor a juvenile suspect's request to speak to a parent or guardian before waiving his rights" (Caplan, n.d., p.9). As a further precaution for police, Caplan (p.12) recommends, "In major felony cases, the notification of rights, the waiver and the subsequent questioning should be videotaped."

If at any time during an interrogation the suspect decides he or she wants a lawyer, either by direct request or through a comment such as, "Maybe I ought to have a lawyer," all questioning must end until legal counsel has been secured. The court has even held that a suspect's question, "Do you think I ought to have an attorney?" was an assertion of rights requiring an immediate cessation of the interrogation. It should be noted that the police should *never* give legal advice, as this could be used against them later if the case goes to trial.

It is not necessary to give a suspect the *Miranda* warnings if the officer does not intend to question the suspect, taking what is known as the *silent approach*. Other situations not involving "custodial interrogation" and, therefore, not invoking *Miranda* include brief on-the-scene questioning or investigatory questioning during a temporary detention, such as a *Terry* stop; roadside questioning following a routine traffic stop or other minor violation for which custody is not ordinarily imposed; routine booking questions attendant to arrest; nontestimonial identification procedures, such as fingerprinting, conducting a lineup, or taking voice, blood or handwriting samples; conducting a sobriety test; volunteered, spontaneous statements by a suspect, even if in custody; and questioning by a private citizen (Caplan, n.d., pp.2–7).

Two key elements when deciding if *Miranda* applies are (1) the *custodial* nature of the questioning (i.e., Would a reasonable person in the suspect's position conclude that he or she is not free to go?) and (2) the *authority* of the person asking the questions (e.g., A private citizen or an agent of the law?). *Miranda* applies only to custodial interrogation by police. However, when police engage the help of a private citizen to get around *Miranda* requirements, that citizen has effectively become an agent of the police. The situation of an undercover agent questioning a suspect illustrates how both elements are needed for *Miranda* to apply:

> The rule prohibiting the use of private individuals to circumvent *Miranda* also precludes interrogation by a "jail plant" or undercover agent while the suspect is in custody. *Miranda* prevents interrogation of custodial suspects by a "jail plant" in the absence of warnings and waiver, but it does not bar statements made by suspects while in custody that are overheard by undercover agents. Moreover, no rule prohibits an undercover agent from questioning to the fullest extent possible a suspect who is not in custody and who has not been charged. An encounter between an undercover agent and a suspect on the street is not custodial because the suspect does not know that he is dealing with a police officer and believes that he is free to leave. (Caplan, p.7)

totality of circumstances

All relevant variables in an arrest, including an individual's age, mentality, education, nationality and criminal experience, as well as the reason for the arrest and how it was explained to the individual being arrested. During an interrogation, it also includes whether basic necessities were provided and the methods used during the interrogation.

The Supreme Court ruled in *Yarborough v. Alvarado* (2004) that the *Miranda* custody standard is the same for juveniles as it is for adults. Officers must distinguish between a *Terry* "detention" and a *Miranda* "custody." Although no bright-line rule exists for determining whether a particular police-suspect encounter is a *Terry* stop or an arrest, courts currently use the **totality of circumstances** test, that is, considering all relevant variables in a situation, including an individual's age, mentality, education, nationality and criminal experience. During an interrogation, it also includes whether the *Miranda* warning was given, if basic necessities were provided, the length of the questioning and the methods used during the interrogation.

Which Comes First: *Miranda* Warning or Questioning?

Officers must be cognizant of the legal pitfalls surrounding questioning before *Mirandizing*. In *Missouri v. Seibert* (2004), Patrice Seibert was afraid she would be charged with neglect when her son, who had cerebral palsy, died in his sleep. Two of her other sons and their friends burned the mobile home to hide the circumstances of the son's death and left an unrelated mentally ill 18-year-old male to die in the fire so it would appear that the son was not left alone. Five days later, the police arrested her but did not read her rights.

At the police station, an officer questioned Seibert for 30 to 40 minutes until she eventually confessed to the fatal arson. The officer then gave her a 20-minute break from questioning. When he returned, he read her the *Miranda* rights and obtained a signed waiver to continue the questioning. The officer resumed questioning and was successful in getting Seibert to repeat her confession. At trial, the officer testified that he had purposely decided to question the suspect first to the point of obtaining a confession, then give the *Miranda* warning and repeat the questioning until he elicited from her the same information she had provided before being *Mirandized*. Seibert was convicted of second-degree murder. The case found its way to Missouri Supreme Court, which overturned the conviction saying that because the interrogation was nearly continuous, the second statement was clearly the product of the invalid first statement. The U.S. Supreme Court upheld this finding, suggesting that such tactics constituted a deliberate end run around the spirit and intent behind *Miranda*. Such deliberate questioning first and then *Mirandizing* and requestioning, sometimes referred to as **beachheading**, is unconstitutional.

beachheading
Deliberate questioning first and then *Mirandizing* and requestioning, an unconstitutional interrogation strategy.

Waiving the *Miranda* Rights

If an individual waives his or her *Miranda* rights, special care must be taken with individuals who do not speak English well, who are under the influence of drugs or alcohol, who appear to be mentally retarded or who appear to be hampered mentally in any way. It is preferable to get the waiver in writing. Caplan (n.d., pp.9, 12, 14) suggests these interrogation guidelines for suspects who waive their *Miranda* rights:

- Officers should honor a juvenile suspect's request to speak to a parent or guardian before waiving his rights.
- In major felony cases, the notification of rights, the waiver and the subsequent questioning should be videotaped.
- Any direct request for counsel requires all questioning to end. A request to speak to someone other than an attorney, such as a parent, friend or even a probation officer, is not an assertion of the right to counsel.
- When a suspect attempts to reach an attorney but is not successful, most courts hold that he has asserted his right and cannot be questioned.

Interrogating without *Mirandizing*

Giving suspects the *Miranda* warning may inhibit suspects from talking by causing them to "lawyer up." FBI statistics show that the national clearance rate for violent crimes plunged 28 percent after the *Miranda* decision and has never recovered: "Officers are not well-advised to give unnecessary *Miranda* warnings, risking the needless loss of a potential confession" (Rutledge, 2009, p.62). One way to avoid giving the *Miranda* warning is to ask a suspect to come to the station to be interviewed, voluntarily, without arrest. The admonitions might be worded, "You're not under arrest. You're free to leave anytime you want, OK?" Such a statement is known as a "Beheler admonition," based on the Supreme Court ruling in *California v. Beheler* (1983). In this case, the Court ruled that no reasonable person in Beheler's position would have felt himself to be under arrest when he had been expressly advised that he was not, and when he came and went voluntarily without police restraints on his freedom (Rutledge, p.64). Several factors that also indicate a lack of arrest or restraint in addition to giving a "Beheler admonition" are

- The suspect agrees to talk and brings himself in.
- No restraints or threats of detention or arrest are used.
- The suspect is questioned for an hour or two, with breaks allowed.
- The suspect is allowed to leave and is arrested sometime later (Rutledge, 2009, p.65).

The more of these factors that are present, the more likely the lack of a *Miranda* warning will be acceptable to the courts.

As a general rule, *Miranda* warnings are also not required when officers question someone during a routine traffic stop or a *Terry* stop (Scarry, 2008, p.22).

Providing Consular Rights Warnings to Foreign Nationals

Law enforcement officers must provide consular rights warnings to arrested or detained foreign nationals, that is anyone who is not a U.S. citizen. The U.S. State Department recommends the following notice be read to detained foreign nationals:

> As a non-U.S. citizen who is being arrested or detained, you are entitled to have us notify your country's consular representative here in the United States. A consular official from your country may be able to help you obtain legal counsel and may contact your family and may visit you in detention among other things. If you want us to notify your country's consular officials, you can request this notification now, or at any time in the future. After your country's consular officials are notified, they may call or visit you. Do you want us to notify your country's consular officials?

Under appropriate circumstances, law enforcement must also notify the foreign nationals' consular officials.

Ethical Considerations in Interrogation

The use of deception during interrogations is highly controversial. Many interrogators feel it is a vital tool to elicit information, while others hold deception to be highly unethical. Many types of deception have been used during interrogations:

- Misrepresenting the nature or seriousness of the offense—for example, telling a suspect that the murder victim was still alive.
- Role-playing manipulative appeals to conscience—for example, projecting sympathy, understanding and compassion; using the good cop/bad cop routine.
- Misrepresenting the moral seriousness of the offense—for example, offering the suspect excuses, such as that a rape victim "asked for it."
- Using promises—for example, suggesting that a suspect's conscience will be eased.
- Misrepresenting identity—for example, pretending to be a reporter or a cellmate.
- Fabricating evidence.

Considering the use of fabricated documents during interrogation, the Supreme Court has recognized that the duties of law enforcement may require limited officially sanctioned deception in the course of a criminal investigation (Mount, 2007, p.10). For example, in *United States v. Russell* (1973) the Court said, "Criminal activity is such that stealth and strategy are necessary weapons in the arsenal of the police officer."

Playing arrestees against each other can also help investigators elicit a confession. With this strategy, interrogators typically start with the suspect most likely to waive his or her rights and confess: "This will often be the youngest, or the one with the cleanest record, or the one who looks most scared, or the person you believe has the least amount of involvement in the crime. . . . Even if the first suspect doesn't admit anything, you can return him to the cell with a big 'Thanks for everything, Danny,' right in front of his cellmate" (Rutledge, 2008a, p.61).

Culhane et al. (2008) studied how current law enforcement, future law enforcement and laypeople saw interrogation techniques and found that current law enforcement officers favored the use of "passive" interrogation techniques more than the student and layperson groups and that all three groups minimally endorsed aggressive interrogation techniques such as the good cop/bad cop (p.366). Culhane et al. (p.380) conclude, "The limited endorsement of aggressive techniques by all three groups suggests that there may be a concern for the well-being of suspects as well as a growing understanding of admissibility issues related to coerced confessions by those currently in law enforcement."

Use of Force or Coercion during Interrogation

In addition to giving the *Miranda* warning, officers must avoid any force or coercion during interrogation because any incriminating statements, admissions or confessions that result from such tactics are likely to be of little use in building a case against the suspect. In 1944, the Supreme Court ruled to exclude from evidence confessions obtained by beating, threats and promises, as well as those obtained under conditions that were "inherently coercive."

Confessions obtained by force or under "inherently coercive" conditions are inadmissible in court.

The Court measured what is or is not inherently coercive by reviewing the totality of circumstances in each case where the admissibility of the confession was at issue.

Detecting Deception

Lies are generally told for one of the following reasons:

- Prosocial: to protect someone, to benefit or help others.
- Self-enhancement: to save face, avoid embarrassment, disapproval or punishment.
- Selfish: to protect self or to conceal a misdeed
- Antisocial: to hurt someone intentionally or gain something.

Officers can detect subtle signs that a suspect is lying by watching the face and neck, particularly the eyes. An increase in the blinking rate or changes in pupil dilation are part of the fight-or-flight reaction and cannot be easily controlled. If this reaction is noticed, the officer should immediately begin an aggressive line of questioning (Sumpter, 2009, p.20). An increase in breathing rate and sweating may also indicate deception, as may the appearance of red blotches rising from the collar line to the ears (Sumpter).

Many believe the ability to detect deception is greatly enhanced through use of technological instruments such as the polygraph and the voice stress analyzer (VSA).

Truth Detection Technology

A polygraph, which literally means "many writings," scientifically measures and records a subject's physiological reactions to specific questions in an effort to detect deception. As a polygraph operator asks a series of predetermined questions, changes in the subject's respiration, depth of breathing, blood pressure, pulse and electrical resistance of the skin are measured and graphed for analysis.

A polygraph might be used to clear suspects; confirm victim, witness and informant statements; or locate evidence. Polygraphs are sometimes used as part of an exploratory exam to further investigate the criminal involvement of someone already in custody for a different offense. Although the polygraph gives investigators another tool to use in their quest for information, the results are rarely admissible in court. Polygraph results can only be allowed into evidence if both prosecution and defense agree to its admissibility, which is unlikely as the results are likely to support one side or the other. Naturally, it is not because either side is sure to have an issue if the other side desires the results to be admitted. The polygraph is not regarded as a valid scientific instrument as the Supreme Court ruled in *Frye v. United States* (1923) and *Daubert v. Merrell Dow Pharmaceuticals, Inc.* (1993).

Some contend polygraph results violate hearsay rules because it is impossible to cross-examine a machine. However, even though polygraph results are not presently admissible in court, any confession obtained as a result of a polygraph test is admissible (Hess and Orthmann, 2010, p.197).

Another type of truth detection instrument is VSA, which is gaining popularity among law enforcement agencies, with departments across the country spending millions of dollars on VSA software programs in recent years (Damphousse, 2008, p.8). Unlike the polygraph, the VSA does not limit the subject to only "yes" or "no" responses; it can analyze any spoken word. However, according to a study by the NIJ, two of the most popular VSA programs being used by police departments were found to be no better than flipping a coin in detecting deception. On a positive note, the study also found that the mere presence of a VSA program during an interrogation may deter false answers (Damphousse).

Before the terrorist attacks of September 11, 2001 (9/11), research into deception and credibility assessment was minimal. Now, however, 50 such laboratories in the United States alone are undertaking such research: "Several universities and private companies are trying to develop the next generation of lie detection technologies by using functional magnetic resonance imaging, electroencephalography, near-infrared light, and other strategies to directly access brain function" (Gordon, 2008, p.73). However, most of this experimental research will not necessarily translate to an investigative role, and many such technologies will never be practical for police use (Gordon, p.74). Noting that the polygraph remains the standard truth test for most law enforcement and government agencies, Gordon reports that the American Polygraph Association (APA) has a compendium of 80 research projects involving 6,380 examination as well as 12 studies of the validity of field examination, providing an average accuracy of 98 percent.

No matter what type of technology is used, the results must always be used as an investigative aid, a supplement to a thorough investigation—never as a substitute for it.

Documenting Confessions

A confession can be given orally or in writing, but it must always be voluntary to be admissible. Documenting confessions is vital because a properly documented confession increases the likelihood of swift, successful prosecutions. Videotaped interrogations and confessions are becoming increasingly popular in law enforcement agencies nationwide to quell accusations of police brutality and reduce doubts concerning the voluntariness of confessions. Hess and Orthmann (2010, p.193) caution, "Even though a confession is highly desirable, it may not be true, it may later be denied, or there may be claims that it was involuntary. A confession is only one part of the investigation. Corroborate it by independent evidence." Usually the corroboration of independent evidence is contained in an officer's written report.

REPORT WRITING

Writing good reports is one of the most important skills law enforcement officers can possess. An estimated 20 percent of frontline officers' time is spent writing reports (Brewer, 2007, p.36). As O. W. Wilson and Roy C. McLaren wrote three decades ago, "Almost everything that a police officer does must be reduced to writing. What is written is often the determining factor in whether a suspect is arrested in the first place, and if he is arrested, whether he is convicted and sentenced. The contents of written reports, in fact, often have a great bearing in life-and-death situations. To say that officers need to be proficient in report writing is an understatement."

Although investigative skills are important, they mean little if the report that synthesizes the investigation's findings crumbles under courtroom scrutiny: "Your investigative report may be the one pivotal piece of documentation that makes a difference in the prosecution of a murderer or a serial rapist. You certainly don't want it to be the weakest link in the investigation and provide a gap for an offender to get away with their crimes" (Swobodzinski, 2007, p.47).

Cases can be made or lost on an officer's report alone. It has often been said that a good report is more important than a good arrest. Well-constructed police reports help expedite case processing and can alleviate the overall burden on the criminal courts because solid, effective reports are more likely to encourage plea bargaining. Indeed, plea bargaining is often considered a trial by police report.

In addition, officers often are judged by their reports. A shoddy report makes the reader question the officer's intelligence, education, competence or integrity—or perhaps all of these. Keep in mind, "Your reputation and that of your department often rest on your written words" (Arp, 2007, p.100).

In today's litigious society, where anyone can sue anyone else for practically anything, law enforcement agencies and officers are not immune to becoming the target of a lawsuit. For this reason, well-written reports can reduce legal liability for both the officer and the department by clearly documenting the actions taken throughout the investigation. Jetmore (2008, p.29) points out,

> Writing a good investigative report proves difficult without significant knowledge of the legal concepts inherent to the profession. The tools of our trade include exceptional knowledge of basic principles relative to local, state, and federal law. These include knowledge of what constitutes a crime; probable cause; arrest, search and seizure; the exclusionary rule; the various U.S. Supreme Court decisions we deal with on a daily basis (e.g., *Miranda v. Arizona*); and departmental policy and procedure.
>
> Opinions differ on how much information we should include in the police report narrative. Many believe reports should be short, concise and provide only the details necessary to relay the basic information required. Others (myself included) believe officers should record all facts that may be relevant to a case.

Figure 2.2 shows the typical path of an investigative report. The number of times the report loops between the supervisor and the officer, or between the prosecutor and the officer, depends on how carefully (or carelessly) the officer constructs the report to begin with.

The Importance of Field Notes

Effective field notes are the basis for all types of reports and for further investigation of cases and incidents. Notes should be taken as soon after an incident as possible and should be kept in a notebook. Most officers prefer loose-leaf

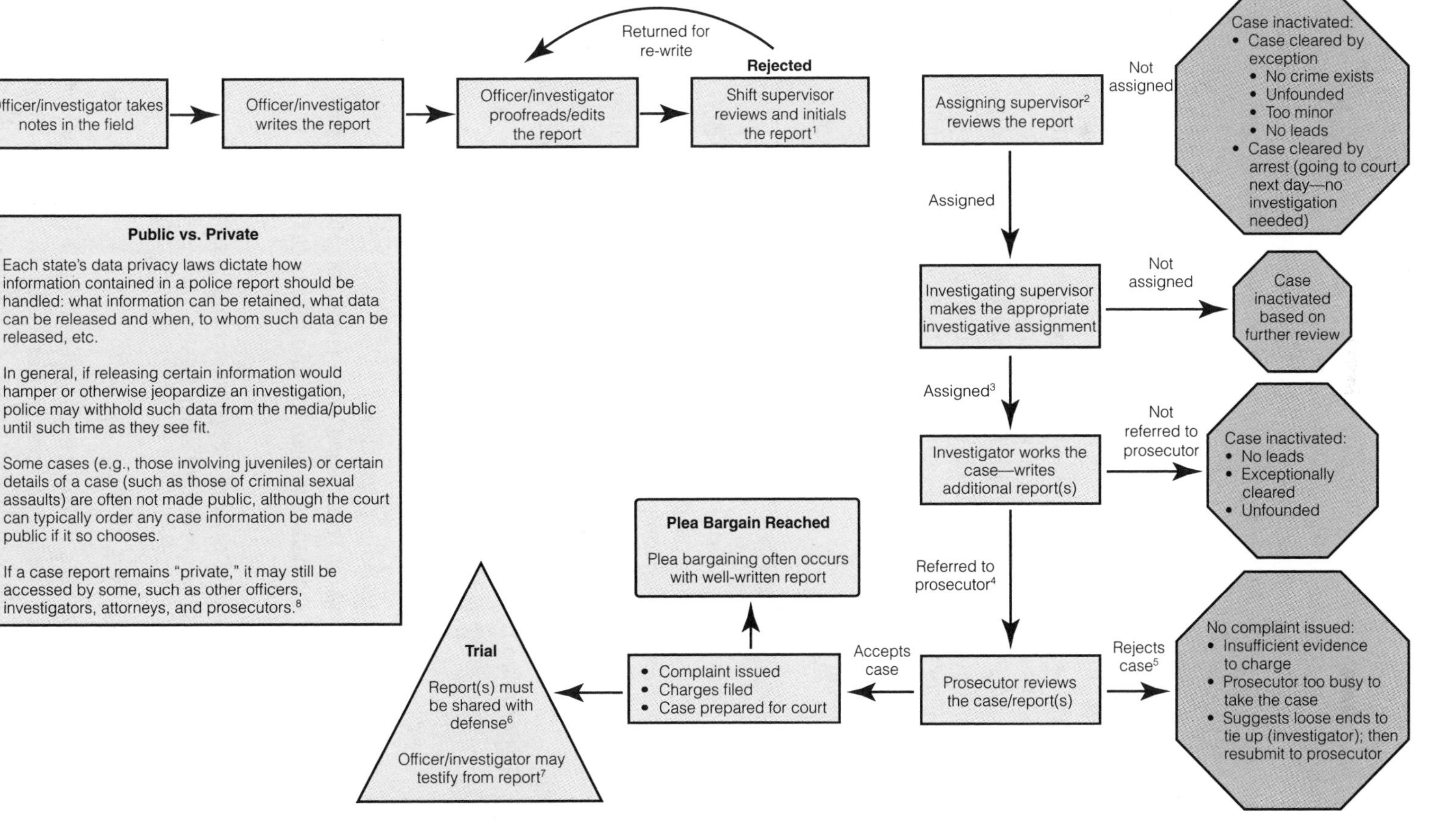

1 Often the report is simply handwritten by the officer, given to the shift supervisor for a cursory review/initialing, and then sent off for transcription before going to an assigning supervisor.
2 Assigning supervisor is typically of higher rank (lieutenant, captain, etc.).
3 In smaller departments, the case may go to a generalized investigator. In larger departments, several investigative units may exist (homicide, arson, motor vehicle theft, etc.).
4 Case can proceed to prosecutor with or without an arrest having been made.
5 A rejection does not necessarily mean case is not prosecutable at a later date. It means only that a complaint is not issued at that time.
6 Who has access to the report(s) at trial varies by state. For example, in Minnesota, the judge and jury do not automatically receive the report(s).
7 The report itself is not evidence, but any testimony the officer/investigator provides based on the content of a report becomes part of the trial record (testimonial evidence).
8 Check with your state's data privacy law. Laws vary from state to state regarding what can be retained, what must be released, and when information must be released. Consideration must also be given to whether or not release of information would hamper any ongoing investigations.

FIGURE 2.2 Typical Path of an Investigative Report.
Note: Because this process varies from department to department, this flowchart illustrates a generalized oversimplification of one way an investigative report might travel from origination to final disposition.
Source: From HESS/ORTHMANN. *Criminal Investigation*, 9E © Delmar Learning, a part of Cengage Learning, Inc. Reproduced by permission. www.Cengage.com/permissions, p.73.

notebooks because they are easily organized, and notes can be removed and used as needed for writing reports or for testifying in court.

The ABCs of effective field notes are accuracy, brevity, clarity and completeness. Accuracy is ensured by repeating information, spelling names and verifying numbers. Brevity is accomplished by omitting the articles *a*, *an* and *the*; by omitting all other unnecessary words; and by using common abbreviations. However, even common abbreviations can be misunderstood. For example, many people hear *P.C.* and think *personal computer* or *politically correct*. Police officers, however, are likely to think *probable cause* or *penal code*. Context often helps make the meaning obvious.

Clarity includes legibility. Notes that cannot be deciphered a few weeks later because of sloppy handwriting are worthless. A clear picture of what happened during an incident or at a crime scene depends on careful, complete notes that contain answers to six basic questions: who, what, where, when, why and how. This is as true of misdemeanors as of felonies. Prosecutors contend that many police officers suffer from the **felony syndrome**; that is, they obtain complete information only on felony cases, deeming these to be "real" cases, with misdemeanors given much less time and attention. To the people involved, however, every incident or crime is important. Further, many more civil suits against police officers and departments arise from misdemeanor cases than from felony cases.

felony syndrome
Obtaining complete information on only felony cases, deeming them to be the only "real" police work.

Purposes of Reports

Police officers write many kinds of reports, including incident reports, continuation or supplemental reports, arrest reports, property and inventory reports, vehicle reports, missing-person reports, bias-motivated crime reports, domestic violence reports, police pursuit reports and crash reports. These reports serve many important purposes.

Reports are used to

- Permanently record facts.
- Provide details of a criminal incident to be used in a follow-up investigation.
- Provide a basis for prosecution.
- Provide data for federal and state crime reporting systems.
- Document the past and plan for future services.

Operations budgets and overall department budgets depend a great deal on accurate documentation of patrol activities.

The Audience

A basic premise of effective writing is that it is reader based. All too often, writers try to *impress* their readers rather than to *express* their ideas clearly. They equate big words and long sentences with big brains and extensive education. WRONG. Reader-based writing avoids the tendency to impress.

The audience for police reports includes other officers, supervisors, other professionals within the criminal justice system and laypeople such as insurance investigators, social workers and reporters.

Hess and Orthmann (2008, p.7) stress, "**Reader-friendly writing** avoids police jargon and abbreviations and communicates in plain, simple language. It is written as it would be spoken, and it considers its audience."

reader-friendly writing
Avoids police jargon and communicates in plain, simple language; it is written as it would be spoken, and it considers who the audience is.

Common Problems with Reports

The most common problems in police reports include misspelled words; unfamiliar abbreviations; confusing or unclear sentences; missing information, such as elements of the crime; missing work addresses and phone numbers; extreme wordiness and overuse of police jargon; missing or incomplete witnesses' names and addresses; and use of assumptions.

The Effective Report

The basic content of a police report includes an introduction, the body and a conclusion. The information answers the same questions answered in field notes: who, what, where, when, why and how. Good reports have the same characteristics as good field notes as well as several additional characteristics.

Effective reports are accurate, brief, clear, complete, legible, objective, grammatically correct and correctly spelled. Effective reports are also written in the past tense and in chronological order. They use verbs rather than nouns when possible, avoid sexist language and can "stand alone."

Some police departments have their officers tape or dictate their reports. Increasing numbers of agencies throughout the country are moving toward digital dictation of reports, where an officer records his or her report verbally and this dictation is later transcribed by clerical staff. The officer then signs off on the final report once it is drafted and appears accurate.

Computer-Assisted Report Entry

Many police departments use word-processing packages for report writing, and others go even further and use computer-assisted police report entry systems. Mobile technology is enabling officers to construct reports in the field, as information is obtained.

Online Citizen Reporting

Increasing numbers of departments, including the San Francisco Police Department, allow citizens to file online police reports for lost property, theft, vandalism and graffiti, vehicle tampering, vehicle burglary, and harassing phone calls (Gitmed, 2007, p.127).

In accessing the local department's Web site and pulling up the page with the crime report form, citizens are able to complete an online report with such required fields as name, address, type of incident, and loss experienced. Before the citizen can submit the report, a warning appears stating the penalties for filing a false report. Gitmed (2007, p.124) notes, "Trying to obtain police reports from tourists, who would rather get back to their vacations than deal with filing a report, and trying to obtain a copy of these reports for insurance purposes can be a logistical nightmare." Gitmed (pp.124–125) suggests the following benefits of citizen online reporting:

> The benefits of online reporting can be seen from the perspective of both the law enforcement agency providing the service and from citizens using the service. Agencies have the ability to serve citizens as they normally would while keeping officers on the street. This prevents busy or understaffed departments from having to create "no-response" policies for low- priority calls. Staff resources can also be better allocated as online reports gradually replace telephone reports and the workload for desk officers becomes manageable compared with a never-ending stream of citizens visiting police station lobbies to report crimes. The monetary savings are quite substantial when considering the volume of reports that are taken online as opposed to having officers take reports and write them. Depending on the vendor an agency chooses, online reporting systems can also facilitate crime tips, special form submissions, and volunteer applications and can even serve as a 3-1-1 system, so that citizens can conveniently report abandoned vehicles, barking dogs, or even streetlight outage.

Before leaving the discussion of communication, one other important kind of communication should be considered—that between law enforcement and the media.

INTERACTION AND COOPERATION WITH THE MEDIA

Law enforcement needs the media, and the media needs law enforcement. Keys to success in dealing with the media include

- Having a clear policy on what information is to be released to the press and what is not.
- Treating all reporters fairly.
- Being as sensitive to the need for the privacy of victims and witnesses as to the need of the public to know what is going on.

When Captain Sullenberger put US Airways Flight 1549 down in the Hudson River, US Airways CEO Parker provided an excellent example of dealing with the media by speaking with them right away, within two hours of the incident. He was empathetic, expressing concern about the victims and the community, and he dealt with facts and information, not with what he thought (Rosenthal, 2009, p.6).

Garner (2009, p.54) offers the following guidelines for dealing with the media during a crisis:

- Tell the truth.
- Never say "No Comment."
- Keep consistent media rules during an incident.
- Do not hide; remain highly visible.
- Convey a sense of normalcy.
- Do no harm.
- Stay calm and in control.

The police and the media have a symbiotic relationship, with each benefiting from the actions and efforts of the other. Here North Miami Beach, Florida, Police Chief Rafael Hernandez talks to the media about the search for the killer of Miami police officer James Walker during a news conference. Hernandez is flanked by Miami Police Chief John Timoney, right, and members of several police agencies to his rear.
© AP Images/J. Pat Carter

Knowing what to do and not to do, officers must also be aware of the public's "right to know" and the privacy rights of victims and witnesses.

Police departments must balance the public's "right to know" and reporters' First Amendment rights to publish what they know with the police's need to withhold certain information and to protect the privacy of victims and witnesses—Sixth Amendment rights.

Some larger departments have a public information officer (PIO) who is the only one authorized to release information to the media. Other departments allow those officers involved in specific cases to be interviewed by reporters interested in the cases. Media organizations should be told who their contacts will be. Whether a department has a PIO or permits individual officers to talk with the media, the department should always remember that most of what the public knows about law enforcement comes from the media. Their support for an agency is often directly related to the time and resources an agency spends on managing its message.

Moore (2007, p.106) suggests, "Over the past few years the growing antipathy between law enforcement and the media has turned into the 800-pound gorilla in the room. . . . Reporters bring their biases and political agendas to their jobs, just like everyone else. And many media outlets are dominated by factions that look upon police and the military with suspicion and, sometimes, outright hostility."

Donlon-Cotton (2008, p.14) says, "All too often law enforcement is forced to be on the defensive with the media. The media sniff out some sort of sensational story and then law enforcement is forced to be defensive and reactive, automatically losing some advantage." Unfortunately, the old adage appears to hold true: "If it bleeds, it leads."

54

CALEA STANDARD 54 on public information states, "Agencies have an obligation to inform the public and news media of events that affect the lives of citizens in the community with openness and candor. Policies should be developed that govern what information should be released, when it should be released and by whom." (*Standards for Law Enforcement Agencies*, 2006)

Standards can ensure that the media is a friend rather than a foe of a police department. As with other areas of law enforcement, effective communication is the key.

SUMMARY

Effective communication can produce several positive outcomes. It can be used to inform, persuade, diffuse, guide, motivate, reassure and negotiate. Communication can be vertical (downward or upward) or horizontal (lateral). Among the valuable databases available to law enforcement are the Law Enforcement Information Exchange (LInX), CrimeCog, the National Crime Information Center (NCIC), the Law Enforcement National Data Exchange (N-DEx), the Law Enforcement Online service (LEO) and the OneDOJ Initiative.

Special problems in communicating include keeping police communications secure, interference on the line and dropped calls, lack of interoperability and lack of a common language. The Department of Homeland Security recommends that first responders replace their 10-codes with "plain English" communications.

Special populations that may pose especially challenging communication issues include the elderly, individuals who speak little or no English or have different cultural backgrounds and those with disabilities or diseases that may impair their ability to communicate, including blindness, deafness, epilepsy, Alzheimer's disease, mental illness, mental retardation or autism. The speech of a person who has been deaf since birth or who has epilepsy or Alzheimer's disease may be mistaken for intoxication.

Effective communication in the field is critical to successful police operations and includes field inquiries, interviews and interrogations. The right to stop and question suspicious people (field inquiries) was established in the landmark case of *Terry v. Ohio*. In *Miranda v. Arizona*, the Supreme Court established the following rights applied to custodial interrogations:

- The suspect has the right to remain silent.
- If the suspect gives up the right to remain silent, anything that the suspect says can be used in a court of law against him or her.
- The suspect has a right to speak to an attorney and to have an attorney present when being questioned by the police.
- If the suspect cannot afford one, an attorney will be appointed to represent the suspect before questioning begins.

Confessions obtained by force or under "inherently coercive" conditions are inadmissible in court.

In addition to verbal communication skills, police officers also need effective writing skills for both field notes and reports. Reports are used to permanently record facts, to provide details of a criminal incident to be used in a follow-up investigation, to provide a basis for prosecution, to provide data for federal and state crime reporting systems and to document the past and plan for future services. The audience for police reports includes other officers, supervisors, other professionals within the criminal justice system and laypeople such as insurance investigators, social workers and reporters.

Effective reports are accurate, brief, clear, complete, legible, objective, grammatically correct and correctly spelled. Effective reports are also written in the past tense and in chronological order. They use verbs, avoid sexist language and can "stand alone."

Police departments must balance the public's "right to know" and reporters' First Amendment rights to publish what they know with the police's need to withhold certain information and to protect the privacy of victims and witnesses—Sixth Amendment rights.

APPLICATION

As head of the public relations department, you have noticed an increase in complaints against officers who have mistaken a disability or physical problem as intoxication. Officers have no guidelines on how to determine whether what appears to be alcohol- or drug-induced intoxication is indeed alcohol- or drug-induced intoxication.

INSTRUCTIONS

Use the form in the Appendix to write a policy regarding communicating with individuals who *appear* to be under the influence of alcohol or drugs. Then write the procedures needed to carry out the policy.

AN EXERCISE IN CRITICAL THINKING

On April 13, Joel Powell's car was stopped, and he and a companion were arrested a few miles away from, and a few minutes after, the burglary of a supper club. The burglary had been reported by an eyewitness whose descriptions of the event and the car involved were transmitted by radio to area police officers. Powell's car matched the description of the car in which the burglars left the scene. It was also traveling in the same direction on the same road. After Powell and his passenger had been taken into custody, the car was sealed, towed and searched. It contained two bank bags with about $500 in currency and coin, later identified as club property, and various tools, including pry bars, mauls, tire irons and a hacksaw.

1. Must the factual basis for stopping a vehicle arise from the officer's personal observation?
   a. When stopping a vehicle, officers must have a warrant when they do not personally observe a felony being committed.
   b. Arresting officers may rely on any communicated information when a possible felony is to be investigated.
   c. The basis for stopping a vehicle may be supplied by information acquired from another person as well as other law enforcement officials.
   d. Arresting officers must have personal knowledge of the facts constituting probable cause.
   e. Six factors must be considered:
      1. The particular description of the offender or the vehicle in which the offender fled.
      2. The size of the area in which the offender might be found.
      3. The number of people in that area.
      4. The known or probable direction of the offender's flight.
      5. Observed activity by the particular offender.
      6. Knowledge or suspicion that the offender has been involved in other criminality of the type presently under investigation.

      Not all of these factors were clearly or completely communicated, so the stop is not supported.

DISCUSSION QUESTIONS

1. When you communicate with another person, are you aware of whether that person is really listening? How can you tell?
2. Do you feel the average citizen with whom you communicate is going to understand any legal language you may use to describe an offense?

3. What language barriers or other cultural barriers would you be likely to encounter in your community?
4. At night, you confront a suspicious man walking in an elite neighborhood. You stop to question the man, but he refuses even to give his name. What are you going to do? Elaborate and justify your decision.
5. How would you warn a suspect of his rights if, while you were interviewing this person, he suddenly said, "I committed the crime"?
6. What are some positive outcomes of good incident reports?
7. How do the media affect police operations?

GALE EMERGENCY SERVICES DATABASE

- Use the Gale Emergency Services database to answer the Discussion Questions as appropriate.
- Use the Gale Emergency Services database to research articles on *deception*. List the difficulties in detecting deception. State and support your opinion on whether deception is a viable tool in interrogation.
- Use the Gale Emergency Services database to research articles on *interoperability*. Outline the benefits realized and challenges faced to date and be prepared to share your findings with the class.
- Use the Gale Emergency Services database to find and outline one of the following articles:
  - "Subtle Skills for Building Rapport: Using Neuro-Linguistic Programming in the Interview Room" by Vincent A. Sandoval and Susan H. Adams
  - "When an Informant's Tip Gives Officers Probable Cause to Arrest Drug Traffickers" by Edward M. Hendrie
  - "The Montgomery County CIT Model: Interacting with People with Mental Illness" by Rodney Hill, Guthrie Quill and Kathryn Ellis
  - "Law Enforcement and the Elderly: A Concern for the 21st Century" by Lamar Jordan
  - "Strategies to Avoid Interview Contamination" by Vincent A. Sandoval
  - "Criminal Confessions: Overcoming the Challenges" by Michael R. Napier and Susan H. Adams
  - "Documenting and Reporting a Confession with a Signed Statement: A Guide for Law Enforcement" by Timothy T. Burke
  - "The Americans with Disabilities Act: A Practical Guide for Police Departments" by Thomas D. Colbridge
  - "Contact with Individuals with Autism: Effective Resolutions" by Dennis Debbaudt and Darla Rothman
  - "Working with Informants: Operational Recommendations" by James E. Hight
  - "The Psychological Influence of the Police Uniform" by Richard R. Johnson
  - "Detecting Deception" by Joe Navarro and John R. Schafer
  - "Offenders' Perceptual Shorthand: What Messages Are Law Enforcement Officers Sending to Offenders?" by Anthony J. Pinizzotto and Edward E. Davis
  - "The Public Safety Wireless Network (PSWN) Program: A Brief Introduction" by Derek Siegle and Rick Murphy

REFERENCES

Anand, Radhika. "Trends in Recording Police Interviews." *Law Enforcement Technology*, February 2008, pp.60–65.

Arp, Don Jr. "Effective Written Reports." *Law and Order*, April 2007, pp.100–102.

Basich, Melanie. "Wireless When You Need It." *Police*, January 2009, pp.40–44.

Brewer, Brad. "ABCs of Mobile Reporting." *Law and Order*, November 2007, pp.36–44.

Brown, Ralph. "Inside a Law Enforcement Intranet." *Law Enforcement Technology*, April 2008, pp.32–38.

Bune, Karen. "Focusing on What's Vital for Victims." *Law Enforcement Technology*, June 2008, pp.78–85.

Bush, Thomas E., III. "N-DEx: A National System for Local Information Sharing." *The Police Chief*, February 2008, p.12.

Caplan, Gerald M. Model Procedures for Police Interrogation. Washington, DC: Police Executive Research Forum, no date.

Careless, James. "The BlackBerry: A Surprisingly Powerful Crime-Fighting Tool." *Law and Order*, January 2008, pp.12–16.

"Certified Forensic Interviewer Program." *Law and Order*, May 2003, pp.42–45.

Collins, John M. "Americans with Disabilities Amendment Act: What It Means for Law Enforcement Agencies." *The Police Chief*, January 2009, pp.12–13.

Commission on Accreditation of Law Enforcement Agencies. *Standards for Law Enforcement Agencies*, 5th ed. Fairfax, VA: CALEA, 2006, updated 2008.

Culhane, Scott E.; Hosch, Harmon M.; and Heck, Cary. "Interrogation Technique Endorsement by Current Law Enforcement, Future Law Enforcement, and Laypersons." *Police Quarterly*, September 2008, pp.366–386.

Damphousse, Kelly R. "Voice Stress Analysis: Only 15 Percent of Lies about Drug Use Detected in Field Test." *NIJ Journal*, March 2008, pp.8–13. (NCJ 221500).

Donlon-Cotton, Cara. "Proactive Media Relations." *Law and Order*, March 2008, pp.14–17.

Dorsey, Michael, and Smith, Douglas. "Law Enforcement Information Exchange (LInX). *Law and Order*, July 2008, pp.44–48.

Galvin, Robert. "Getting with the Times." *Law Enforcement Technology*, February 2009, pp.60–67.

Garner, Gerald W. "Surviving the Circus: How Effective Leaders Work Well with the Media." *The Police Chief*, March 2009, pp.52–57.

Gavigan, Jennifer. "SAFECOM Offers Real Communications Help." *Law and Order*, July 2008, p.58.

Geoghegan, Susan. "Telecommunications Technology in Policing." *Law and Order*, January 2009, pp.40–43.

Gitmed, William. "Citizens Reporting Crimes Online: *The Police Chief*, August 2007, pp.124–131.

Gordon, Nathan J. "Today's Instruments for Truth Testing." *The Police Chief*, September 2008, pp.70–78.

Hess, Kären M., and Orthmann, Christine Hess. *For the Record: Report Writing in Law Enforcement*, 6th ed. Rosemount, MN: Innovative Systems-Publishers, Inc., 2008.

Hess, Kären M., and Orthmann, Christine Hess. *Criminal Investigation*, 9th ed. Clifton Park, NY: Delmar Publishing Company, 2010.

Hitch, Vance. "OneDOJ." *The Police Chief*, April 2007, pp.26–31.

Hixson, Roger; Cobb, Bob; and Halley, Patrick. "9-1-1: The Next Generation." *9-1-1 Magazine*, January/February 2007, pp.18–24.

Holt, Greg. "Mobile Language Interpretation Program." *Law and Order*, July 2008, pp.54–56.

Jetmore, Larry F. "Investigative Report Writing." *Law Officer Magazine*, February 2008, pp.26–30.

Jordan, Suzanne; Romashkan, Irina; and Werner, Serema. "Launching a National Strategy for Enhancing Response to Victims: A Logical Next Step in Community Policing." *The Police Chief*, October 2007, pp.44–50.

Kanable, Rebecca. "ADA Compliance." *Law Enforcement Technology*, January 2008, pp.68–75.

Kane, Kevin. "Radio Communications Bandwidth Melting Pot." *Law Enforcement Technology*, February 2009, pp.52–56.

Kyrik, Kelly. "Albuquerque Police Department Homeless Strategy." *Police*, June 2008, pp.58–61.

Larson, Randall D. "I Don't Think We're in Hayleyville Anymore." *9-1-1 Magazine*, January/February 2008, p.4.

Law Enforcement Online. http://www.leo.gov/

Lee, Ed. "Best Practices in Mobile Data Communications." *Law Enforcement Technology*, March 2008, pp.40–45.

Lindsey, Jeffrey C. "Law Enforcement Online: A Powerful Partner for Information Sharing." *The Police Chief*, May 2008, p.82.

Moore, Carole. "Making Friends with the Media." *Law Enforcement Technology*, January 2007, p.106.

Moore, Carole. "Diffusing Crisis." *Law Enforcement Technology*, June 2008a, pp.56–63.

Moore, Carole. "Lost without Translation." *Law Enforcement Technology*, October 2008b, pp.100–107.

Mount, David C. "Strategic Deception Revisited: The Use of Fabricated Documents during Interrogation—Permissible Ploy or Prohibited Practice?" *The Police Chief*, June 2007, pp.10–11.

Mulholland, David J. "Challenges and Successes of the CapWIN Project: Lessons Learned from the Inside." *The Police Chief*, June 2008, p.88.

Mulvihill, Rick. "NLECTC—Communications Technologies Center of Excellence: Serving Law Enforcement Today, Planning for Tomorrow." *The Police Chief*, October 2008, pp.60–67.

National Law Center on Homelessness and Poverty. *2008 Annual Report*. Washington, DC: The National Law Center on Homelessness and Poverty, 2009.

"N-DEx: Welcome to the Future." Washington, DC: Federal Bureau of Investigation, April 21, 2008.

Oetinger, Thomas. "Providing Better Service to Victims of Crime." *The Police Chief*, October 2007, pp.40–43.

O'Toole, William C., and Reyes, Eddie. "Making a Successful Transition to Common Radio Language." *The Police Chief*, May 2008, pp.72–75.

Phillips, Amanda. "Bearing True Witness on Thy Neighbor." *Law Enforcement Technology*, October 2008, pp.162–165.

Police Chief's Guide to Immigration Issues. Arlington, VA: International Association of Chiefs of Police, July 2007.

Police Chiefs and Sheriffs Speak Out on Local Immigration Enforcement. Washington, DC: Police Executive Research Forum, April 2008.

Rosenthal, Rick. "Training the Media." *ILEETA Digest*, January/February/March 2009, p.6.

Rutledge, Devallis. "The *Bruton* Rule." *Police*, March 2008a, pp.61–63.

Rutledge, Devallis. "No Explanation Required." *Police*, September 2008b, pp.68–70.

Rutledge, Devallis. "Non-Custodial Stationhouse Interrogations." *Police*, January 2009, pp.62–65.

Scarry, Laura L. "When Are *Miranda* Warnings Required During Traffic Stops?" *Law Officer Magazine*, August 2008, pp.22–24.

Siegfried, Mike, and Arlotti, Kevin. "Contacting Mentally Ill Subjects." *Police*, December 2008, pp.48–51.

Siuru, Bill. "CrimeCog Information System Technology." *Law and Order*, April 2007, pp.79–81.

Slahor, Stephenie. "Next Generation 9-1-1." *Law and Order*, March 2008, pp.18–21.

Spadanuta, Laura. "Can I Get a Witness?" *Security Management*, November 2008, pp.51–58.

Sturman, Shane G. "Every Law Enforcement Officer Needs to Know How to Conduct a Criminal Interview and Interrogation." *Police*, October 2008, pp.44–50.

Sumpter, J. L. "The Art of a Conversation." *Law and Order*, July 2008a, pp.14–15.

Sumpter, J. L. "Open and Closed Questioning." *Law and Order*, October 2008b, pp.23–24.

Sumpter, J. L. "Subtle Signs of Deception." *Law and Order*, January 2009, p.20.

Swobodzinski, Kimberle. "The Crime Scene Report." *Law Officer Magazine*, February 2007, pp.47–49.

Wilson, O. W., and McLaren, Roy C. *Police Administration*. New York: McGraw-Hill, 1977.

Wright, Morgan. "Crisis Collaboration." *9-1-1 Magazine*, July 2008, pp.44–46.

CASES CITED

Alabama v. White, 496 U.S. 325 (1990)

California v. Beheler, 463 U.S. 1121 (1983)

Daubert v. Merrell Dow Pharmaceuticals, Inc., 509 U.S. 579 (1993)

Florida v. J. L., 529 U.S. 266 (2000)

Frye v. United States, 54 App. D.C. 46, 293 F. 1013 (1923)

Hiibel v. Sixth Judicial District Court of Nevada, Humboldt County, 542 U.S. 177 (2004)

Miranda v. Arizona, 384 U.S. 436 (1966)

Missouri v. Seibert, 542 U.S. 600 (2004)

Terry v. Ohio, 392 U.S. 1 (1968)

United States v. Mendenhall, 446 U.S. 544 (1980)

United States v. Russell, 411, U.S. 423 (1973)

Yarborough v. Alvarado, 541 U.S. 652 (2004)

CHAPTER 3

Operational Skills

Performing within the Law

DO YOU KNOW . . .

- What balance between freedom and order police officers must maintain?
- What two amendments restrict arrests and searches?
- What a stop and frisk involves?
- What constitutes an arrest?
- When officers may arrest someone?
- Why understanding and skill in making legal arrests are critical?
- How substantive and procedural criminal law differ?
- What the Exclusionary Rule is and its relevance to police operations?
- How officers arrest someone?
- How much force can be used in making an arrest?
- What three use-of-force tests are established in *Graham v. Connor?*
- When handcuffs should be used in conjunction with an arrest?
- What less-lethal weapons police officers have available?
- What police activity can be an obstacle to community policing?
- When a search can be conducted?
- How a search conducted with a warrant is limited?
- When a search warrant is *not* needed?
- How officers search a person and a building?

CAN YOU DEFINE?

arrest
compliance
continuum of contacts
curtilage
de facto arrest
due process of law
Exclusionary Rule
exigent circumstance
frisk
functional equivalent
good faith
"in the presence"
mere handcuff rule
patdown
plain view
positional asphyxia
probable cause
procedural law
stop
stop-and-frisk situation
substantive law

INTRODUCTION

The basic skills discussed in this chapter—stopping and frisking, arresting and searching—may be needed in a variety of situations. These skills are used often, and they are strictly governed by law and usually by department policies and procedures as well.

Police officers are expected to be familiar with the basic rules of criminal procedure. It is not the intent of this text to go into the details of any of these basic rules but rather to remind the reader of their critical importance in police operations. Chapter 2 discussed the importance of obtaining information legally. This chapter focuses on making legal arrests and searches.

Law enforcement officers must maintain a balance between "freedom to" and "freedom from."

In a democracy such as ours, law enforcement has the awesome responsibility of ensuring that citizens have freedom *to* live, remain free, pursue happiness and have due process of the law. Law enforcement has also been charged with protecting society—that is, giving citizens freedom *from* crime and violence as well as *from* unreasonable search and seizure by the government. The conflict between these two competing responsibilities is sometimes referred to as due process versus crime control. Police officers must strike a balance between the rights of individuals and those of our country and between the rights of law-abiding citizens and those of criminals. Officers must *act* to fulfill their responsibilities but always within the constraints of the law.

Guarantees against unlawful arrests and searches are found in the Fourth and Fifth Amendments to the U.S. Constitution.

The Fourth Amendment states, "The right of the people to be secure in their persons, houses, papers and effects, against unreasonable searches and seizures, shall not be violated, and no warrants shall issue but upon probable cause, supported by oath or affirmation, and particularly describing the place to be searched, and the persons or things to be seized." The Fourth Amendment protects the fundamental right to privacy that lies at its core. Its guarantees extend to arrest warrants as well as to search warrants. It does *not,* however, prohibit arrests or searches without a warrant.

The Fifth Amendment provides that no person shall be "deprived of life, liberty, or property without due process of law and protect those suspected of crime against self-incrimination" (*Miranda*). Both the Fourth and the Fifth Amendments should be kept in mind throughout this text and, indeed, throughout an officer's career.

This chapter begins with an explanation of the common procedure of stopping and frisking someone acting suspiciously. Next, legal arrests are described, including when they can be made and the importance of ensuring that they are legal. This is followed by a discussion of procedures for making legal arrests and the issues of handcuffing, excessive and deadly force, and the implications of the use of force. The chapter concludes with a discussion of legal searches, including procedures for searching both people and places. This chapter contains more court cases than other chapters simply because of the topic: acting within the law while making arrests and conducting searches. The principles (and cases) discussed in this chapter will have relevance throughout the remaining sections of this text.

STOP AND FRISK

Law enforcement officers are expected to stop and question people acting suspiciously, as discussed in the preceding chapter. If an officer stops someone for questioning (an investigatory stop or field inquiry) and the officer believes the subject may be armed, the officer can also pat down the subject's outer clothing for weapons. This action *is* considered a search, albeit a very limited one.

A **stop-and-frisk situation** is one in which law enforcement officers

- Briefly detain (*stop*) a suspicious person for questioning (this is *not* an arrest).
- And *if* they reasonably suspect the person to be armed, they are allowed to pat down (*frisk*) the person's outer clothing (this *is* a limited search for weapons).

stop-and-frisk situation
One in which law enforcement officers briefly detain a suspicious person for questioning and pat the person's outer clothing to assure that they are not armed.

The right to stop and frisk suspicious people was established in the landmark case of *Terry v. Ohio* (1968), as presented in detail in Chapter 2. Recall that is how Detective McFadden, based on 30 years' experience as an investigator, stopped and frisked three men loitering outside a jewelry store because he suspected they were planning an armed robbery of the store. The frisk did, in fact, reveal two revolvers concealed in the men's coats, and when the case ultimately came before the Supreme Court, the detective's actions were upheld as legal. The stop, frisk and subsequent seizure of the weapons as evidence did not violate the suspects' constitutional rights.

The justification behind Detective McFadden's response in the *Terry* situation can be explained by considering the **continuum of contacts**, the almost limitless variation of contacts between the public and the police. Figure 3.1 illustrates how police action must correlate to an individual's actions to be constitutionally justified—police action becomes increasingly intrusive on individual freedom as the reasons for thinking criminal activity is afoot build. Harr and Hess (2008, p.187) state, "While the intent of the Constitution is to prevent the government from intruding on people's lives when they have done nothing wrong, this freedom, as with all constitutional rights, is not absolute. When police have lawful reason to act, it is expected they will, and they have the right to do so. The U.S. Supreme Court has clearly stated that police have a responsibility, in fact a duty, to act to prevent crimes and apprehend criminals and has shown continued support for law enforcement."

continuum of contacts
Almost limitless variations of contacts between the public and the police, ranging from no contact to incarceration or even the death penalty.

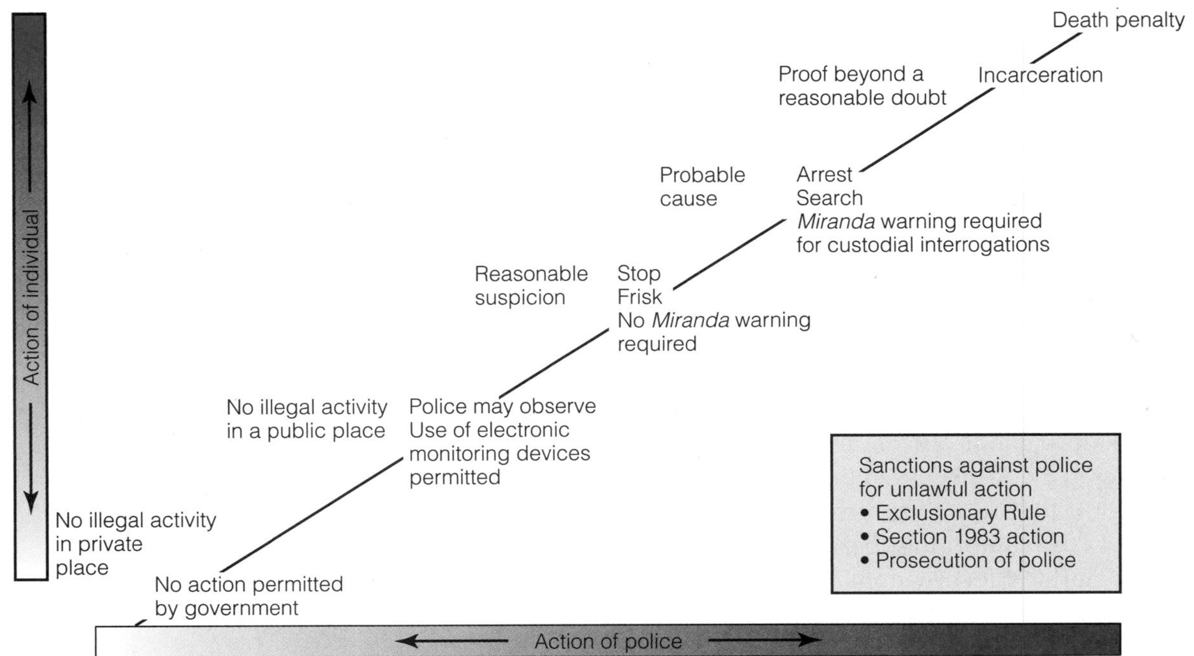

FIGURE 3.1 The Continuum of Contacts between Individuals and the Police
Source: From HARR/HESS. *Constitutional Law and the Criminal Justice System*, 3E. © 2005 Wadsworth, a part of Cengage Learning, Inc. Reproduced by permission. www.cengage.com/permissions

The Stop

stop
Brief detention of a suspicious person by law enforcement officers for questioning.

The stop is the first point on the continuum of contacts where police have the constitutional authority to interfere with a person's freedom. The **stop** in a stop and frisk must be based on a reasonable suspicion that the person detained is about to be or is actually engaged in criminal activity. The most common reasons for a stop were discussed in Chapter 2.

Several Supreme Court cases have set guidelines for law enforcement in determining when a stop is constitutional. In *United States v. Sokolow* (1989), the Court ruled, "In evaluating the validity of a stop such as this, we must consider the 'totality of the circumstances—the whole picture'." In *Alabama v. White* (1990), the Supreme Court held that reasonable suspicion is a less demanding standard than probable cause. Because the police made the stop on reasonable suspicion, it was legal.

In *Florida v. Bostick* (1991), the Supreme Court ruled that the location of a police-citizen encounter is only one factor to be considered in determining whether a seizure occurred: "In order to determine whether a particular encounter constitutes a seizure, a court must consider all the circumstances surrounding the encounter to determine whether the police conduct would have communicated to a reasonable person that the person was not free to decline the officers' requests or otherwise terminate the encounter."

The Supreme Court ruled in *Illinois v. Wardlow* (2000) that unexplained flight from the police is pertinent in developing reasonable suspicion necessary for a stop and frisk. In this case, officers patrolling an area of Chicago known for heavy narcotics trafficking observed Wardlow standing on the sidewalk holding an opaque bag. Wardlow looked in the direction of the officers and immediately fled, causing the officers to give chase. When they caught him, one officer conducted a patdown for weapons based on his experience that guns were commonly present during drug deals. A hard object in the shape of a gun was felt in the opaque bag. When the officer opened the bag, he found a loaded handgun. Wardlow was arrested for a weapons violation.

The trial court held that the officer's actions were a lawful stop and frisk. Two appellate courts, however, reversed, and the case eventually came before the Supreme Court. Noting that the officers were bound by the *Terry* standard of reasonable suspicion, the Court ruled that although Wardlow's presence in a high-crime area was insufficient, in and of itself, to justify reasonable suspicion of criminal activity, it was a relevant fact the officers could consider. Wardlow's unexplained flight was another pertinent factor, as Justice Rehnquist rationalized, "Headlong flight—whenever it occurs—is the consummate act of evasion: it is not necessarily indicative of wrongdoing, but it is certainly suggestive of such." This consideration of multiple relevant factors continued the long-standing totality of circumstances test for officers in justifying reasonable suspicion.

A stop-and-frisk situation is one in which officers briefly detain a suspicious person for questioning, and if they reasonably suspect the person to be armed, they may pat down the person's outer clothing. © AP Images/Branimir Kvartuc

In *Hiibel v. Sixth Judicial District Court of Nevada* (2004), the Supreme Court ruled that police may properly request a person's name in a *Terry*-type stop. In this case, a Nevada rancher was stopped and asked for identification 11 times. He refused 11 times and was arrested and charged with the misdemeanor of refusing to identify himself. He was convicted and fined $250. Both the Nevada Supreme Court and the U.S. Supreme Court upheld his conviction. Jurisdictions differ on how they classify the crime of refusing to identify oneself or providing a false identity. In general, however, using someone else's real identity is more severe than making one up.

The stop may be all that occurs, it may lead to a patdown, or it may progress to an arrest, depending on the information received.

The Frisk

frisk
A brief patdown following a stop to determine if a person is armed.

patdown
A brief feeling of a person's outer clothing to determine if a weapon is present. Also called a *frisk*.

The **frisk** or **patdown** in a stop and frisk is conducted for the officers' safety and must be based on a reasonable suspicion that the person is armed. *Minnesota v. Dickerson* (1993) established that a frisk that goes beyond that authorized in *Terry* is invalid. The frisk cannot extend to a search for evidence. However, if during the frisk an officer feels what would reasonably be evidence, such as a packet of marijuana, the officer can retrieve the evidence under the "plain feel" doctrine discussed later in the chapter. If the stop turns into an arrest, a more thorough search can be conducted, also discussed later in the chapter.

Although a stop and frisk falls far short of an actual arrest and a full-blown search, it is *not* to be taken lightly, as the Court made clear in the *Terry* decision: "It is simply fantastic to urge that such a procedure [stop and frisk], performed in public by a police officer, while the citizen stands helpless, perhaps facing a wall with his hands raised, is a 'petty indignity.'" And, as noted, the stop might escalate into an arrest, depending on the specific circumstances.

LEGAL ARRESTS

Making an arrest is one of the most important and extreme steps law enforcement officers take in their daily duties. The frequency of its occurrence, the nonserious nature of many offenses for which arrests are made, the poor character of many people subjected to it and their lower socioeconomic status must never lull officers into forgetting the lofty place arrest holds in our law. The police responsibility in arrests is clearly defined.

Arrest Defined

The common meaning of *arrest* is simply "to stop." In a cardiac arrest, for example, the heart stops beating. Its meaning in the context of law enforcement is also generally known, that is, to seize and hold in jail or prison. The legal definition of *arrest* is somewhat narrower.

arrest
The official taking of a person into custody to answer criminal charges. Arrest involves at least temporarily depriving the person of liberty and may involve the use of force.

An **arrest** is the official taking of a person to answer criminal charges. This involves at least temporarily depriving the person of liberty and may involve the use of force.

When Arrests Can Be Made

The Fourth Amendment stresses the importance of having an arrest warrant when making an arrest (or conducting a search). The courts have, nonetheless, recognized other circumstances in which an arrest can legally be made.

The law's ideal is for arrests to be made under an arrest warrant where a neutral judge stands between the person to be arrested and the arresting officer and calmly determines that probable cause exists for the arrest. But the law also recognizes that the practical necessities of keeping the public peace often demand that police officers make arrests without a warrant.

An arrest can legally be made

- With an arrest warrant.
- Without an arrest warrant
    - When any offense (felony or misdemeanor) is committed in an officer's presence.
    - When officers have probable cause to believe a person has committed a felony and no time is available to obtain a warrant.
    - For specifically enumerated misdemeanors, such as shoplifting in some jurisdictions.

In the Presence **"In the presence"** does not refer to proximity, but rather to the officer's senses—that is, what the person making the arrest perceives through his or her senses. *Atwater v. Lago Vista* (2001) gave police the authority to arrest the driver of a vehicle for violations punishable only by a monetary fine, widening police authority in traffic-related stops. In this case, a police officer saw Atwater and her small children unrestrained in the front seat of her truck. The officer stopped the truck, confirmed that Atwater was violating the seat belt statute, handcuffed her and drove her to the police station. There she had to surrender her personal property, was photographed and placed in a jail cell for about an hour. Atwater sued the officer, the police chief and the city, claiming her Fourth Amendment right to be free from unreasonable seizures had been violated. In deciding the case, Justice Souter stated, "If an officer has probable cause to believe that an individual has committed even a very minor criminal offense in his presence, he may, without violating the Fourth Amendment, arrest the offender."

"in the presence"
Perceived by an officer through the senses (does not refer to proximity).

Probable Cause Basic to lawful arrests is the concept of *probable cause.* **Probable cause** means it is more likely than not that a crime has been committed by the person whom a law enforcement officer seeks to arrest. An officer's *probable cause* to conduct an arrest depends on what the officer knew *before* taking action. An often-quoted definition of probable cause is from *Brinegar v. United States* (1949): "Probable cause exists where the facts and circumstances within the officers' knowledge, and of which they had reasonably trustworthy information, are sufficient in themselves to warrant a man of reasonable caution in the belief that an offense has been or is being committed."

probable cause
The fact that it is more likely than not that a crime has been committed by the person whom a law enforcement officer seeks to arrest. An officer's probable cause to conduct an arrest depends on what the officer knew *before* taking action.

In *Illinois v. Gates* (1983), the Supreme Court ruled that probable cause is a practical, nontechnical concept that should not be weighted in terms of "library analysis by scholars using tests." Rather, the test for probable cause under the Fourth Amendment should be a "totality of the circumstances test."

Two recent cases further clarify when a person can be arrested (seized) during a traffic stop. In *Brendlin v. California* (2007), police stopped a car to check its registration without reason to believe it was being operated unlawfully. One officer recognized Brendlin, a passenger in the car, as a parole violator and arrested him. A search of the car found, among other things, methamphetamine paraphernalia. Brendlin appealed his conviction of violating parole, and the California Court of Appeals reversed the decision, saying suppression of the evidence was unwarranted because a passenger is not seized as a constitutional matter absent additional circumstances that would indicate to a reasonable person that he was the subject of the officer's investigation or show of authority. The Supreme Court disagreed, stating, "When police make a traffic stop, a passenger in the car, like the driver, is seized for Fourth Amendment purposes, and so may challenge the stop's constitutionality." Collins (2007, p.10) notes that the decision broke no new ground in the law of motor vehicle stops and passenger searches. Collins also points out that passengers may successfully have any evidence so obtained suppressed and may sue police for violating their constitutional rights while illegally stopping the driver.

In a second case, *Virginia v. Moore* (2008), two police officers received a radio report alerting them that Moore was driving on a suspended license. They arrested him, and a search of his car turned up crack cocaine. Moore appealed his conviction to the Virginia Supreme Court, which reversed the decision, saying the officers should have simply issued a citation as state law required. The Supreme Court, however, disagreed, saying, "The police did not violate the Fourth Amendment when they made an arrest that was based on probable cause, but prohibited by state law, or when they performed a search subsequent to the arrest." Spector (2008, p.12) contends, "It seems that in *Virginia v. Moore*, the U.S. Supreme Court has done a great favor to law enforcement officers and administrators in eliminating many of the concerns about violations of state statute arrest procedural rules." It is not a Fourth Amendment violation even if an arrest violates state laws (Scarry, 2008b, p.22), as Rutledge (2008, p.66) explains, "For federal civil liability purposes and to determine admissibility of evidence, the Supreme Court has ruled that state restrictions do *not* prevail over constitutional standards."

No precise formula for determining probable cause exists that can be applied to every case, just as no precise formula for determining reasonable suspicion for a stop exists. Both must be determined from the individual facts and circumstances of each case. Table 3.1 summarizes the basic differences between a stop and an arrest.

Probable cause can be either observational (what the officer sees) or informational (what the officer is told). *Observational probable cause* includes suspicious conduct, being high on drugs, associating with known criminals, the existence of a criminal record, running away, presence in an unusual place or at an unusual time, presence in a high-crime area, presence at a crime scene, failure to answer questions, failure to provide identification, providing false information and physical evidence. The more factors that are present, the greater the probable cause is. *Informational probable cause* consists of communications

Table 3.1 Stop versus Arrest

	Stop	Arrest
Justification	Reasonable suspicion	Probable cause
Warrant	None	Maybe
Officer's intent	To investigate suspicious activity	To make a formal charge
Search	Patdown for weapons	Full search for weapons and evidence
Scope	Outer clothing	Area within suspect's immediate control
Record	Minimal—field notes	Fingerprints, photographs and booking

Source: J. Scott Harr and Kären M. Hess. *Constitutional Law and the Criminal Justice System*, 4th ed. Belmont, CA: Wadsworth Cengage Learning, 2008, p.214. Reprinted by permission.

from official sources, such as wanted posters, statements from victims and information from informants.

The Importance of Lawful Arrests

"Almost every state limits police authority to arrest, especially without warrants—even when the officers have probable cause. Some of these statutory limitations are complicated, allowing arrest at certain time, with various jurisdictional limitations, and for particular crimes, and many of the statutes are peppered with a number of exceptions" (Spector, 2008, p.12). Although it is preferable to have an arrest warrant, it is not required to arrest a suspect on probable cause while in a public place. "However, an arrest warrant is necessary, with few exceptions, if the suspect is in their own home" (Scarry, 2008a, p.22). An exception to this requirement is when officers are in "hot pursuit" of an offender, with probable cause to arrest, and that individual flees into their own residence; in this situation, officers may lawfully enter that residence without a warrant to affect the arrest. Two other exceptions to this warrant requirement are consent and emergency situations.

Because arrests deprive individuals of their freedom, it is crucial that law enforcement officers are skilled at making *lawful* arrests.

Skill in making arrests is critical because

- Fundamental rights to personal liberty and privacy are involved.
- The law of arrest is strict and technical.
- Arrest is often the first step in criminal proceedings.
- Illegal arrests may taint crucial evidence of guilt.
- Police performance quality is judged by arrests.
- Arrests may lead to civil suits and criminal prosecution of officers.
- Arrests may endanger officers' lives.

Arrests Involve the Fundamental Rights to Personal Liberty and Privacy In every arrest, the right to personal liberty is involved. This is the fundamental right to come and go or stay when or where one may choose—the so-called right to freedom of locomotion. This right is embodied in the common law of England and is protected by our state constitutions and the U.S. Constitution.

Although the essential nature of the right to personal liberty cannot be denied, it is, nevertheless, not absolute. It is limited by the fact that people do not live in a vacuum, isolated from others. Their survival demands that they live and work in a society whose well-being is also vital. Therefore, when people commit offenses against society's law, their right to personal liberty can be restrained for the common good. In other words, they can be arrested, and their arrest is justified if made according to **due process of law**, that is, the fundamental principles of justice embodied in the Fifth and Fourteenth Amendments. The power of arrest is inherent in the right of society to defend itself. It has long been recognized that offenders may be arrested on criminal charges and be detained for trial even though they may ultimately be proved innocent of wrongdoing.

due process of law

The fundamental principle of American justice. It requires notice of a hearing or trial that is timely and that adequately informs the accused persons of the charges; it also gives the defendant an opportunity to present evidence in self-defense before an impartial judge or jury and to be presumed innocent until proven guilty by legally obtained evidence.

The Law of Arrest Is Strict and Technical It severely limits the power of apprehension. It was formulated in England during the 17th and 18th centuries, when conditions as well as standards were far different from those of today. The professional police officer was unknown, and the fate of those arrested for crimes was fraught with danger.

In that era, people arrested on serious charges were rarely granted bail. Prisoners awaited court action in jails overrun with disease and corruption and where the dreaded jail fever was common. They were kept in irons for the jailers' safety. If they escaped from the easily breached lockups, their wardens were held personally responsible. Because the jails were run for profit and fees were charged for almost every aspect of prison life, a poor person was in desperate straits.

This state of affairs led to the development of arrest laws greatly restricting the right to arrest. The courts, wanting a neutral judicial official to stand between the people being arrested and those doing the arresting, made it clear that an arrest was to be made only on the basis of a warrant issued by a judge. The courts also recognized the need to arrest without a warrant, but they spelled out the conditions under which such arrests could be made.

For example, the courts clearly distinguished between arresting without a warrant for a serious felony and arresting without a warrant for a minor misdemeanor. A warrantless arrest for a misdemeanor was limited to offenses committed in the arresting person's presence, whereas arrest for a felony without a warrant was not so limited. There was less justification for arresting people without a court order for minor offenses and subjecting them to the attendant dangers than for doing so for serious offenses that affected the whole community.

The ironclad law of arrest has survived the conditions that brought it about. Modern statutes and court decisions have remedied some technicalities of former times, but the old common law still controls many aspects of arrest, despite the arrival of professional police officers and vastly improved detention facilities and procedures. Legislatures and judges have hesitated to change concepts and procedures where the rights to personal liberty and privacy loom so large.

Arrest Is Often the First Step in Criminal Proceedings In the community's timeless attempt to keep the public peace through its criminal law, arrest by police officers is often the first step in criminal proceedings against wrongdoers. Despite the law's ideal that a court-issued warrant precedes an arrest, there is often no time in actual practice to apply for a warrant. The arrest must be made "now or never." Because police officers' duties often demand that they arrest people without the protection of a warrant, officers must know both the substantive and the procedural criminal law of their jurisdiction.

Substantive law deals with content, or what behaviors are considered crimes. **Procedural law** deals with process, or how the law is applied.

substantive law

Deals with the content of what behaviors are considered crimes; defines the elements of crimes and the punishments for them.

procedural law

Deals with process, or how the law is applied.

Substantive law defines the elements of crimes and the punishments for each crime. For example, premeditation is an element in first-degree murder, and the punishment upon conviction might be life imprisonment or even death. Crimes and their punishments are decided by elected bodies such as Congress and state legislatures.

Procedural law governs how the law is enforced and is perhaps of greater importance to law enforcement officers than substantive law. Procedural law tends to be more controversial than substantive law. Although some laws are controversial (for example, those governing "victimless crimes" such as prostitution, gambling and use of marijuana), other laws, such as those allowing criminals to "get off" because of a technicality, are even more controversial. It seems to many people that the criminals have all the rights and that victims' rights are ignored. This is largely because the framers of our Constitution had, themselves, experienced life under rule of a tyrannical government and believed it was better to risk letting the guilty go free than to risk recreating a society where the innocent suffered injustice at the hand of an arbitrary government.

Laws concerning crimes and arrest are complicated, and officers are allowed no margin of error in deciding whether the conduct, when not committed in the officers' presence, constitutes a felony and thus justifies arrest without a warrant. At one time, determining whether an offense was a felony or a misdemeanor was not difficult. The inherent seriousness or nonseriousness of the offense served as the guide. But this is no longer true. Legislatures have created felonies that are not inherently serious and misdemeanors that are. Officers must know the law.

The law will justify officers' actions if they proceed on the basis of probable cause or reasonable grounds. Yet, when they arrest without a warrant, they are responsible for exercising good judgment in hectic, fluid situations where mistakes are bound to occur.

Illegal Arrests May Taint Crucial Evidence of Guilt

Although illegal arrests will not immunize defendants against criminal prosecution, they may lead to the inadmissibility of crucial evidence of guilt. Unfortunately, "Virtually every law enforcement officer will sometime in the course of his or her career encounter the bitter taste of having important evidence excluded from a criminal trial due to a Fourth Amendment violation" (Ivy and Orput, 2007, p.8). Physical evidence obtained by search and seizure incident to an illegal arrest, such as recovered stolen property or burglary tools, will be considered tainted and therefore suppressed under the Exclusionary Rule.

Exclusionary Rule

Courts cannot accept evidence obtained in illegal searches and seizures, regardless of how relevant the evidence is to the case (*Weeks v. United States*, 1914).

The **Exclusionary Rule** established that the courts cannot accept evidence obtained in illegal searches and seizures, regardless of how relevant the evidence is to the case (*Weeks v. United States*, 1914).

This principle is also referred to as "The Fruit of the Poisonous Tree" doctrine, meaning if the initial search is tainted because it is unconstitutional (the "poisonous tree"), anything that the search produces as evidence (the "fruit") will also be tainted and will be inadmissible in court.

Weeks v. United States applied only to federal cases. Nearly a half century later, *Mapp v. Ohio* (1961) established that the Exclusionary Rule applies to all state criminal proceedings under the due process clause of the Fourteenth Amendment. Verbal evidence, such as incriminating statements obtained in the immediate aftermath of an illegal arrest, may also be barred from the jury's consideration. However, any evidence discovered during a search incident to a lawful arrest (i.e., one supported by probable cause) is presumed legally obtained and, thus, is not suppressible in most state courts (Rutledge, 2008, p.70).

good faith

Belief that one's actions are just and legal.

If officers are not aware that they are violating someone's constitutional rights, they are said to be acting in **good faith**, and the Exclusionary Rule may not apply: "The good faith exception often comes into play when the government is executing arrest or search warrants. If such warrants are later found to be invalid, . . . the evidence obtained while executing the warrants is still admissible because the officers were acting in 'good faith'" (Harr and Hess, 2008, p.197). Objectively reasonable good faith circumstances that may prevent suppression and liability often occur in the following instances: search warrants, arrest warrants, misidentification, consent and invalid statutes (Rutledge, 2007a, p.71).

Massachusetts v. Sheppard (1984) established that if police were relying on a search warrant that had been approved by a magistrate but was later declared invalid, any evidence seized during that search would be admissible at trial. In a similar case, *United States v. Leon* (1984), the Court held, "Once the warrant issues, there is literally nothing more the policeman can do in seeking to comply with the law. Penalizing the officer for the magistrate's error, rather than his own, cannot logically contribute to the deterrence of Fourth Amendment violations."

In *Arizona v. Evans* (1995), the Supreme Court extended this logic to include information coming through "official channels," ruling that if officers reasonably rely on such information, and if the information turns out to be erroneous, any evidence developed from this information need not be suppressed because the officers themselves were not intentionally engaged in misconduct (Rutledge, 2009, p.78).

Murray v. United States (1988) established that evidence initially seen by police during an illegal search could be admissible if later recovered under a valid warrant. Another relevant ruling occurred in *Arizona v. Evans* (1995), where the Supreme Court held that the Exclusionary Rule does not require suppression of evidence gained during arrests made on the basis of computer errors by clerical court employees.

The Quality of Police Performance Is Judged by Arrests The community's judgment of the quality of its police department frequently turns on the actions of officers in the more visible, dramatic areas of responsibility, such as apprehending felons. The public pays much less attention to officers' performance in the less colorful aspects of police work, even though extensive time and effort are necessarily required, for example, directing traffic.

Arrests May Result in Civil Suits or Criminal Prosecutions Scarry (2007a, p.138) notes, "Arrestees sometimes threaten officers with the fateful words, 'I'm gonna sue you!' Some follow through, others do not, but regardless, officers involved in a serious incident resulting in injuries for the arrestee know such a threat may become a reality. And most also know such a lawsuit may be subject to a statute of limitations." If a lawsuit is not filed within the time specified by state statute, the claim can no longer be filed. The hazard of lawsuits against police officers is discussed in detail in Chapter 14.

Arrest Is Extremely Dangerous and Sometimes Life Threatening for Police Officers Arrests put police officers in jeopardy every time they take this drastic step. The peril exists not only with hardened criminals where possible violence is an obvious, ever-present concern, but also with people who do not have criminal records. Ordinary people often lose all sense of emotional and mental balance when arrested. They can react to their loss of freedom and the danger to their reputation in unexpected ways and may resist fiercely rather than submit to the command of the apprehending officers.

Arrests can also lead to dangers for the community at large. For example, an arrest that may seem particularly brutal and inhumane can bring about immediate and violent community reaction, as in the 1965 Watts riot.

PROCEDURES FOR MAKING LEGAL ARRESTS

The actual arrest is usually made by an officer stating to a person, "You are under arrest for . . ." The person being arrested should be told clearly—not in police jargon or legalese—the reason for the arrest. Officers should always be on guard when making arrests because people can react violently to being arrested, even those who appear meek and incapable of violence.

Depending on the circumstances, the person may first be handcuffed for the officer's safety. The arrested person should be searched for weapons and destructible evidence, as discussed later in this chapter. If the arrested person is to be questioned, the *Miranda* warning must be given before any questions are asked. However, "excited utterances," or things that suspects in custody spontaneously say in those initial moments surrounding an arrest, can still be used against them in a court of law under "hearsay" statutes, regardless of whether the arrestee has been *Mirandized* or not.

In a typical arrest situation officers should

- Announce the arrest and the reason for it.
- Handcuff the person if warranted.
- Search the arrested person for weapons and evidence.
- Give the *Miranda* warning if questions are to be asked.

De Facto Arrests

de facto arrest
A detention without probable cause that is factually indistinguishable from an arrest.

A **de facto arrest** is a detention without probable cause that is factually indistinguishable from an arrest. In *Kaupp v. Texas* (2003), the Supreme Court held that without probable cause for arrest, it is unlawful for law enforcement to transport a suspect against his or her will to the station for questioning.

THE USE OF FORCE IN MAKING AN ARREST

"The management and applications of police use of force are, perhaps the most important, complex, and pressing issues in modern law enforcement. The use of force—including deadly force—is at once necessary to achieve law enforcement tools and contrary to the core mission, to protect life" (Ederheimer and Johnson, 2007, p.1).

1 CALEA STANDARD 1 "Law Enforcement Role and Authority" states, "Few issues outweigh the concern raised in a community when it is perceived that members of a law enforcement agency use inappropriate levels of force. A community rightfully expects that its law enforcement agency will issue weapons only to those agency members legally authorized to carry same as a condition of their duties, and that weapons and tactics are only utilized in conformance with sound policies, procedures, and training." (*Standards for Law Enforcement Agencies*, 5th edition, 2006)

Durose et al. (2007, p.1) report, "Of the 43.5 million persons who had contact with police in 2006, an estimated 1.6 percent had force used or threatened against them during their most recent contact, a rate relatively unchanged from 2002 (1.5 percent)." Durose et al. (p.7) also report that of stopped drivers, an estimated 0.8 percent of the 17.8 million persons indicated police used or threatened to use force against them. In cases where force was used, the most common actions were pushing or grabbing (43.4 percent) or pointing a gun (15.2 percent) (p.10).

Moore (2008, p.82) notes, "Arrests caught on tape often reflect what—to the average citizen—appears to be an overreaction or too much force." She recommends that the best defense is a good offense, consisting of creating legally "bulletproof" policies regarding use of force when making arrests.

Guidelines for use of force when making an arrest:

- No resistance—use no force.[1]
- Resistance—use only as much force as necessary to gain control.
- Threat or perceived threat to officer's life or the life of another—use deadly force.

[1]Technically, mere "officer presence" is considered to be a use of force, albeit the extreme minimum level.

Force has been defined as the amount of effort required to gain compliance from an uncooperative subject. **Compliance** is a complete lack of physical resistance. A suspect willingly, although perhaps not enthusiastically, obeys the conditions and lawful orders of police. Many use-of-force incidents occur when the subject is intoxicated or under the influence of drugs.

compliance
A complete lack of physical resistance.

In *Graham v. Connor* (1989), the landmark case concerning police use of force, the Supreme Court acknowledged, "The reasonableness of a particular use of force must be judged from the perspective of a reasonable officer on the scene, rather than with the 20/20 vision of hindsight. The calculus of reasonableness must embody allowance for the fact that police officers are often forced to make split-second judgments—in circumstances that are tense, uncertain, and rapidly evolving—about the amount of force that is necessary in a particular situation."

Graham v. Connor established a three-prong test for use of force: (1) the severity of the crime, (2) whether the suspect poses an immediate threat to the safety of law enforcement officers or others and (3) whether the suspect is actively resisting arrest or attempting to evade arrest by flight.

Gender Differences in Use of Force

Several studies have examined whether a gender difference exists in police use of force, with the general consensus being that female officers tend to emphasize communication and de-escalation of potentially violent situations. Basich (2008, p.46) reports, "Female officers often bristle at the idea of their tactics being different from those of men, but they agree that for most women, communication is their first line of defense. Women are sometimes criticized for talking too much, . . . but a tendency to rely on communication skills without resorting to violence when possible can be a very good trait." Many law enforcement professionals advocate learning what "Doc" Thompson, founder and president of the Verbal Judo Institute, teaches.

Verbal Judo

Miller (2008, p.62) offers the following scenarios:

Scenario A.

Officer: Give me your driver's license and registration.
Subject: Why?
Officer: You were speeding, sir.
Subject: No, I wasn't.
Officer: Yes, you were. My radar put you at 59 miles per hour, and this is a 45-mile-per-hour zone.
Subject: Radar can be wrong. Anyway, I just came off a 55-mile-per-hour road . . .

Scenario B.

Officer: Good afternoon, sir. I'm Officer Jones of the Metropolitan Police Department. The reason I stopped you is that I clocked you driving

73 miles per hour in a 45-mile-per-hour zone. Is there a reason you were driving that fast?

Subject: No, no reason.

Officer: May I see your driver's license?"

In the first scenario, the subject goes on the defensive, becomes argumentative and wrests control of the situation, whereas in the second scenario the officer maintains control by using Verbal Judo techniques. Effective communication skills are critical to gaining compliance from subjects and managing the "intercalated" situations involving arrest, search and seizure and use of force. Verbal Judo, or as some call it, tactical communication, is a skill that, like any other, can be learned. In contrast to deliberate tactical communication, "natural communication" is what we say without really thinking. Officers spend a great deal of time learning to fall and punch without hurting themselves but little time learning to communicate to enhance compliance rather than backing a suspect into a corner where they are likely to become defensive and resistant to commands (Miller, 2008, p.66). What Verbal Judo teaches is this: "Aim for peace, but be prepared for war." Using the image of a "Peace Warrior" who holds olive branches in one hand and arrows in the other, Thompson advises, "Always extend the olive branches of peace to all, but hold the arrows of war ready. Always treat people with respect, but have a plan to kill them."

Thompson explains how the peace warrior approaches a subject, considering how we are all alike with respect to basic needs (Miller, 2008, p.69):

- To be respected, not disrespected.
- To be asked, not told, what to do.
- To be told why.
- To be given options, not threats.
- To be given a second chance.

AN OFFICER'S PERSPECTIVE

Natural versus Tactical Communication

The noble goal of Verbal Judo is to maintain control. However, there is a persuasive argument against using this form of communication in that agencies that institute this style of communication as policy risk restricting or impairing an officer's natural communications skills, which may be, in many cases, a more effective form of communication. Although Verbal Judo can be valuable and highly successful at times, there are other times when it can make you sound "textbook" and unnatural, and lead to a failure to properly empathize with those you come into contact with. Much like discretion in law enforcement, it is important to allow officers flexibility in communication styles and to give them a variety of tools to use when dealing with the many dynamic situations they will encounter. It is also important to allow officers to choose which tools to use in specific circumstances because the job has too many variables to be defined in black-and-white terms.

—Sgt. Henry Lim Cho

Usually communication is placed at the low level in use of force models.

Use of Force Models

Use of force applications must be broad enough to allow officers reasonable options in the field, yet specific enough to provide guidance. The Federal Law Enforcement Training Center (FLETC) "Use of Force Model" provides officers with various options categorizing the reasonable officer's perception to how a subject will or will not submit to arrest in one of five levels:

- Compliant Level—subject is cooperative and complies with the officer's commands.
- Resistive (Passive) Level—subject directs no physical energy to the arrest, yet does not follow the officer's commands. An example is a protestor who sits on the ground and ignores an officer.
- Resistive (Active) Level—subject directs energy and physical strength to resisting arrest but not directly at the officer. For example, grabbing a fence and refusing to let go. Verbal subject resistance can be included in this level. Compliance techniques include joint manipulation or restraints, leverage techniques, pressure points or even pepper spray. Officers may warn the subject before using any of these techniques.
- Assaultive (Bodily Harm) Level—a direct, physical attack on the officer. Use-of-force options include striking with hands, fists, elbows and knees; kicking; baton strikes; and forcefully directing the subject to the ground.
- Assaultive (Serious Bodily Harm or Death) Level—an attack where officers reasonably believe that they or others would be subject to serious bodily injury or death. The appropriate officer response is deadly force.

Use-of-Force Continuums

Means and Seidel (2009b, p.31) explain, "Use-of-force models and continuums were developed over time to help officers manage the increased number of force options available. Use of force continuums go from no force to deadly force with numerous alternatives between these two extremes. In some instances, the mere presence of an officer is enough to keep the peace or to stop a crime from happening. If visible presence is not enough to stop a negative situation from escalating, verbal commands may succeed, for example 'Please stop that' or 'Listen to me.'" Figure 3.2 presents one use-of-force continuum that depicts the escalation from no force to extraordinary force.

Such force continuums are not without their critics, who point out that policing is not linear and that such continuums do not reflect the real world of confusion, fear and sometimes an overwhelming sense of urgency that officers may face in violent confrontation with offenders. Force continuums may also cause hesitation and intensify officers' natural reluctance to use significant force even facing a serious threat. Every use-of-force situation is unique.

Means and Seidel (2009b, p.31) point out, "The difficulty in constructing useful models is the long list of important variables or 'force factors' an officer must weigh during a use-of-force event. No simple model can take into account the number or the relative importance of each force factor present during an incident." Among such variables are the suspect's known or apparent gender,

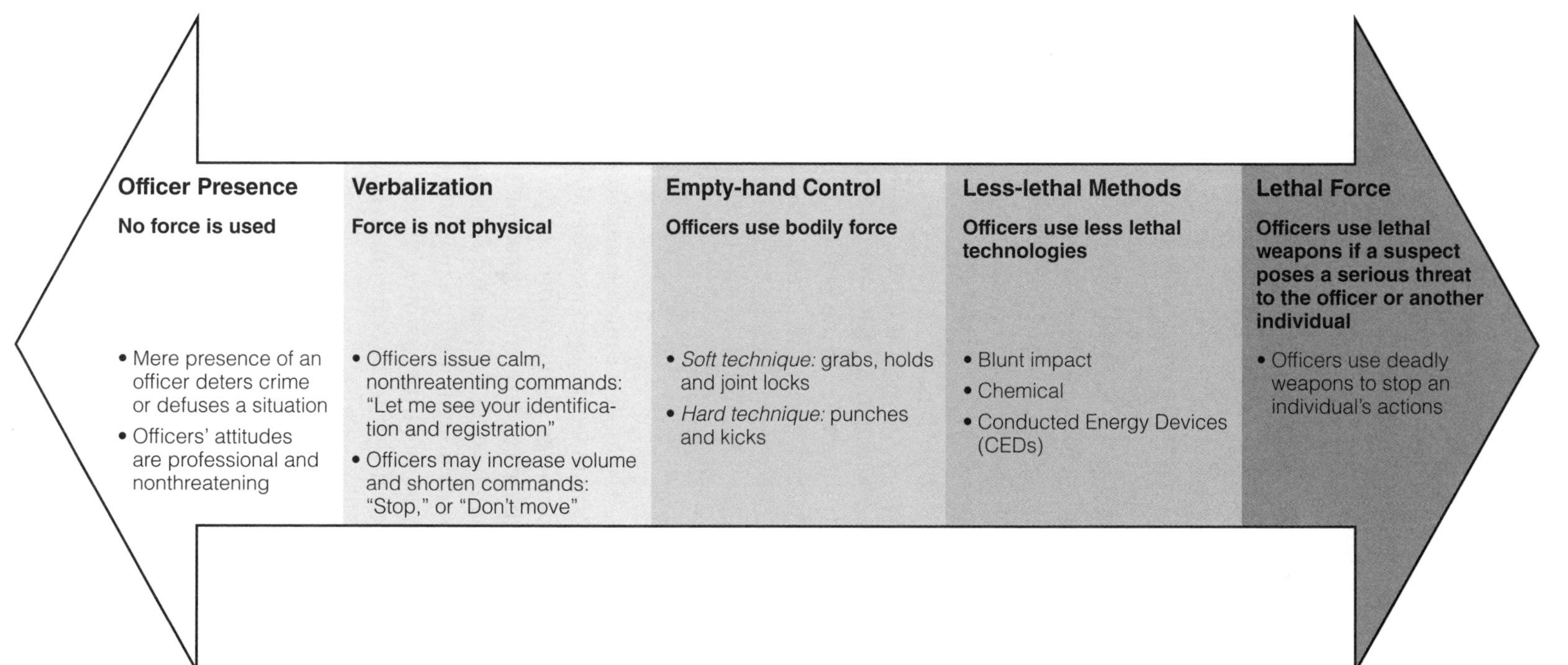

FIGURE 3.2 A Continuum in the Use of Force
Data source: National Institute of Justice, http://www.ojp.usdoj.gov/nij/topics/law-enforcement/use-of-force/continuum.htm

age, size, strength, condition and personal weapon proficiency as well as the weapons available to the suspect and the suspect's known or apparent motivation to harm or escape, propensity for violence, and current state of mind.

Using Forcible Entry to Arrest (or Search)

The right of law enforcement officers to use force to enter a building to make an arrest is almost 400 years old: "In all cases where the King is a party, the Sheriff, if the doors be not open, may break the party's house, either to arrest him, or do other execution of the King's process, if otherwise he cannot enter. But before he breaks it, he ought to signify the cause of his coming and to make request to open the doors" (*Semayne's Case*, 5 Coke, 918 [1603]).

The use of forcible entry to arrest was firmly established early on in common law, even though a fundamental liberty of people includes protecting their homes. The home as a sanctuary and place of refuge is embodied in the Fourth Amendment to the Constitution and in state constitutions and protects homes against unjustified invasion. Even under common law, officers' authority to break the doors of a house to arrest was eventually drastically limited. It had to be shown that officers had reasonable cause to break and enter to arrest. They had to justify such extreme and drastic actions.

The Knock and Announce Rule As a general rule, before crossing the threshold of a house in such emergency cases, officers must identify themselves, make known their purpose, demand admittance and be refused. This requirement frequently is embodied in statutes. The rule was established to protect the right to privacy of citizens, to reduce the risk of possible violence to both police and occupants, and to prevent unnecessary destruction of private property. The rule applies equally to whether police are executing an arrest or a search warrant. Most of the cases discussed in this section happen to apply to search warrants, but the basic rule applies to either. Geoghegan (2007, p.99) explains, "Most officers find it judicious to know and announce their presence and intentions. 'Surprise' entries can lead to misunderstanding on the suspect's part, creating situations that can escalate into unnecessary violence."

The knock-and-announce notice is consistent with the presumption of innocence and lessens the danger arising from ambiguous conduct, bad information, mistaken identity and other practical hazards of everyday police work. It makes clear to those within a dwelling what the object of the breaking is and prevents them from justifiably considering it an aggression to be resisted.

Guidance on how long officers must wait after the announcement and using force to enter is provided in *United States v. Banks* (2003), where the Court ruled that 15 to 20 seconds between an officer's knock and announcement of a search warrant and actual forced entry was "reasonable," overturning a lower court ruling: "The issue comes down to whether it was reasonable to suspect imminent loss of evidence after the 15 to 20 seconds the officers waited prior to forcing their way. . . . We think that after 15 or 20 seconds without a response, police could fairly suspect that cocaine would be gone if they were reticent any longer." In its unanimous ruling, the Court announced it would continue to take a case-by-case "totality of the circumstances" approach to deciding the constitutionality of police searches.

Three years later, in what Devanney (2007, p.28) called "arguably the most important decision from the United States Supreme Court in decades on the laws of search and seizure," the Court ruled 5–4 in *Hudson v. Michigan* (2006) that peace officers with search warrants may enter homes *without* knocking and *without* the risk of having any seized evidence thrown out at trial. In this case, Detroit officers approached Hudson's home, announced "Police, search warrant," but did not knock. Three to 5 seconds later, they opened the door and entered. The Supreme Court upheld the legality of the entry, even though it was made with only a 3- to 5-second delay. Judge Scalia noted that the negative social costs of allowing the exclusionary rule to be used in knock-and-announce violations would be considerable and would flood the courts with alleged claims and would, in many cases amount to a "get-out-of-jail-free card" for criminals. Hilton (2007, p.38) cautions, "Some police departments have interpreted the Supreme Court's recent *Hudson v. Michigan* (2006) ruling as a license to execute warrants without knocking, announcing, and waiting a reasonable amount of time for a resident to answer the door before entering. That interpretation is both wrong and dangerous. Failure to adhere to the requirements of the knock-and-announce rule can result in terrible tragedy and extremely expensive litigation."

One way to avoid claims of improper or illegal procedure is to conduct an audio/video recording of knock-notice announcements and entry, providing evidence of officers' compliance with knock notice and the time waited before forcing entry. Another way to avoid problems is to obtain a no-knock or quick-knock warrant, which provides a tactical advantage for law enforcement, especially in drug-related and other high-risk cases. Such warrants allow officers to enter without the requisite knock-announce-and-wait, instead allowing officers to announce who they are as they cross the threshold of the building, maximizing the element of surprise (Heinecke, 2007, p.30).

Level of Destruction If forcible entry is justified, the breaking must be done with the least amount of destruction. Only the slightest force is necessary to constitute a breaking. For example, pushing open an unlocked yet closed door constitutes forcible entry. In *United States v. Ramirez* (1998), the Supreme Court held, "Excessive or unnecessary destruction of property in the course of a search will violate the Fourth Amendment, even though the entry itself is lawful and the fruits of the search are not subject to suppression."

The Use of Handcuffs in Making an Arrest

Handcuffs have been used for more than 200 years to allow officers to restrict prisoners' mobility, thus offering some degree of safety. Agencies need a handcuffing policy that addresses handcuffing for all arrestees, with adaptations for special circumstances, such as people with physical injuries or disabilities.

Nance and Hallford (2008, p.55) note, "Tragically, the lives of many officers have been lost at the hands of suspects who attacked without warning as the officer attempted to apply handcuffs. The handcuffing process is perhaps the most opportune time for a suspect to attack an officer because of the officer's close proximity to the suspect and the fact that the officer's attention is divided between controlling the suspect and applying handcuffs." Nance and Hallford recommend that before asking a suspect to put his arms behind his back, the officer grasp the suspect's upper arm allowing him to more safely

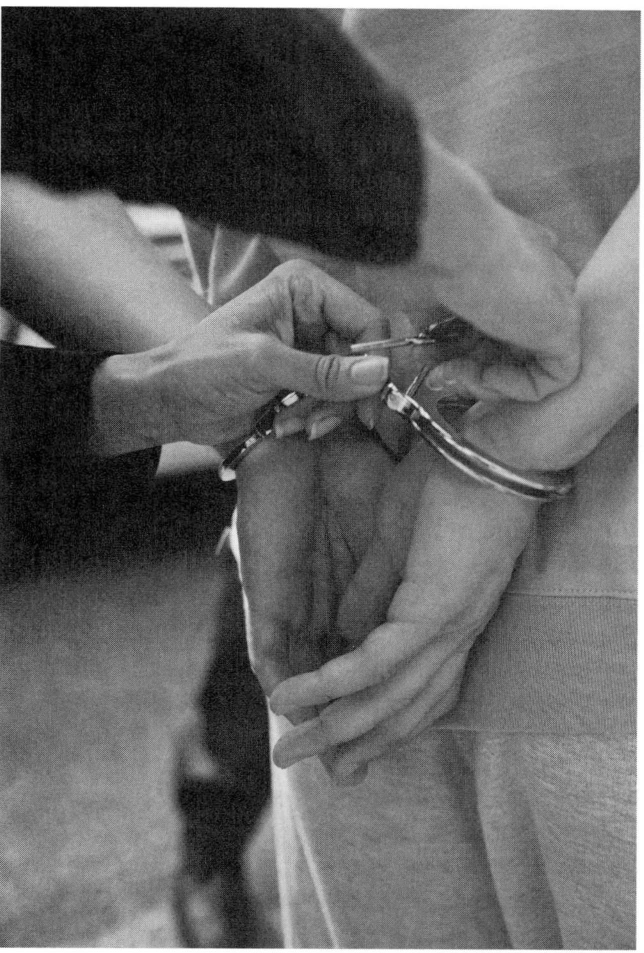

Although handcuffing in some instances is vital to protecting an officer's life, to automatically handcuff every suspect arrested may leave the officer and the department open to a charge of objectively unreasonable handcuffing and a lawsuit.
© Radius Images RF/Alamy

gauge a suspect's intent: "The *Lateral Arm Transitional Control Hold* (L.A.T.C.H.) places you in a position of relative safety while enabling you to anticipate suspect's resistance. In addition, it enables you to smoothly transition to familiar techniques to handcuff, create distance, or take the suspect to the ground." Many law enforcement agencies have a policy stating, "In the interest of officer safety, all persons arrested and transported shall be handcuffed." This policy has been called the **mere handcuff rule**. But such a rule, making mandatory the application of a form of force in all arrests, conflicts with the Fourth Amendment's "objective reasonableness" standard for use of force.

mere handcuff rule
A policy stating that in the interest of officer safety, all persons arrested and transported shall be handcuffed. It disregards the fact that handcuffing is a form of force and should be used only if the situation warrants.

Whether an arrested person should automatically be handcuffed while being transported is controversial. Officer discretion may be advisable.

It is a common saying among law enforcement officers that "hands kill." This puts the emphasis on always watching a suspect's hands when dealing with suspects and is one of the primary justifications for using handcuffs. Although handcuffing in some instances is vital to protecting an officer's life, to automatically handcuff every suspect arrested may leave the officer and department open to a lawsuit charging objectively unreasonable handcuffing. Discretion might be used with the very young, the very old and the physically disabled, always remembering, however, that these individuals can still pose a threat to officers' safety. In some scenarios, officers must use "creative handcuffing" to address an individual's specific physical needs and limitations while protecting themselves, as officer safety is primary.

Use of tight handcuffs has been seen by some courts as a violation of the Fourth Amendment: "Several courts have addressed the issue of whether tight handcuffs can constitute excessive force under the Fourth Amendment, but no general rule says handcuffs must be loose or at what level the handcuffs become too tight" (Scarry, 2007b, p.50). Using the *Graham v. Connor* standard on use of force, the reasonableness of the application and tightness of handcuffs should depend on the totality of circumstances of each case. Scarry (p.51) cites several instances where courts have ruled against police officers where evidence showed that the officers had notice of the handcuffs' tightness but did not respond reasonably to the subject's pleas.

Because tightness can be subjective, many academies and departments train officers to use a technique such as the two-finger rule, which is similar to the guideline used when placing a collar around a dog's neck. If an officer can comfortably fit the tips of the fore finger and middle finger between the cuff rim and the suspect's wrist, the handcuffs are generally deemed to be appropriately tight. The cuffs can then be double-locked to prevent further tightening. There are, of course, variations to this rule, and no absolute standard exists.

In some instances, officers go beyond handcuffs and use leg restraints or may even "hog-tie" extremely violent, unmanageable suspects. Be aware, however, this can pose an extreme hazard to the bound subject. **Positional asphyxia** may result if a person's body position interferes with breathing, as when a subject is in maximum restraints and placed prone on the ground or the back seat of a patrol car. Especially at risk of positional asphyxia are obese people whose weight can be displaced to the diaphragm, cutting off breathing; suspects who are acutely intoxicated from alcohol or drugs and, because of their state, may not realize they are suffocating; and suspects who have struggled violently before being restrained, making them susceptible to respiratory muscle fatigue.

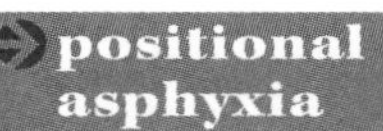

A type of strangulation that results if a person's body position interferes with breathing.

Because of the dangers and liability associated with hogtying challenging subjects, many police departments are moving away from this method and replacing it with the use of hobble restraints, which are leg, ankle, knee and elbow restraints designed for transporting prisoners in a upright sitting position.

Excessive Force

As officers carry out their daily duties, moving up and down the continuum of contacts and making countless, on-the-spot decisions regarding how much force to use, one hazard is ever-present—the possibility of going a fraction beyond the amount of force necessary to achieve a legitimate police objective. Stepping over that invisible line puts officers knee-deep into the area known as *excessive force*, that is, using an amount or frequency of force greater than that required to compel compliance.

Of the hundreds of thousands of police-citizen contacts that occur every day, the only ones that seem to receive media attention are those involving charges of excessive force, estimated to be less than 0.5 percent of all calls for service. Despite their relative infrequency, police misconduct, brutality and excessive use of force do exist and are real problems for law enforcement.

In 1997 in a single police brutality claim in New York, the city and the police union paid $9 million to a Haitian immigrant, Abner Louima, who was tortured in a stationhouse bathroom. One officer, believing Louima had punched him during the arrest, sought revenge by sodomizing Louima with a broomstick. This was a clear case of police brutality (excessive force).

In *Scott v. Harris* (2007), Deputy Scott attempted to pull Harris over for speeding. When Harris fled, Scott pursued and attempted to stop him by ramming Harris' vehicle with his police cruiser. Harris crashed and was rendered a quadriplegic. Harris sued Scott claiming he had used excessive force. The Supreme Court, however, held, "Because the car chase respondent initiated posed a substantial and immediate risk of serious physical injury to others, Scott's attempt to terminate the chase by forcing respondent off the road was reasonable. . . .Viewing the facts in the light depicted by the videotape, it is clear that Deputy Scott did not violate the Fourth Amendment."

Plitt (2008) presents a 10-item quiz to test an officer's knowledge of excessive force. As you read, answer each question true or false.

1. There are constitutional limits on the types of weapons and tactics you can use on the street.
2. Your intent and your state of mind at the time you use force can be important factors in determining if your use of force was legal.
3. You must always retreat if possible before using deadly force.
4. You must first see a suspect's weapon before you can use force.
5. You must always use the least amount of force possible to gain control.
6. You cannot lawfully shoot a fleeing felon.
7. You may not use force to temporarily detain someone for purposes of a *Terry* stop.
8. Information you discover after force was used can be a factor in determining if the force you used was legally justified.
9. Courts and juries are permitted to evaluate your use of force by considering what you could have done differently.
10. Your uses of force in prior incidents can be considered in court in evaluating whether your use of force in the current situation was legally proper.

All of the preceding *except* question 6 are false. Although *Tennessee v. Garner* (1985) held that officers could not shoot a fleeing felon who was simply fleeing to escape, if the suspect posed a danger to the officer or others, such a shooting may be justified.

The Use of Nonlethal or Less-Lethal Weapons in Making Arrests

Less-lethal weapons for use with violent, combative suspects include tear gas and other chemical irritant sprays, impact weapons, conducted energy devices (CEDs) such as the TASER, foams, nets and K-9s.

Some of the most common nonlethal weapons are chemical irritant sprays, such as tear gas, chemical mace, and oleoresin capsicum (OC), more commonly called pepper spray. OC can be delivered in a cone-shaped spray, a fog, a directed stream, a splatter stream or a foam.

Chemical irritants, in addition to being used in aerosol spray form, can be placed inside pellets and fired from a rifle, similar to paintballs. The PepperBall System, used by many police departments across the country, combines kinetic impact technology with OC pepper powder irritant. These devices are effective to about 30 feet but can also be deployed at point-blank range without causing great bodily harm.

As with all other impact or extended impact systems, certain target areas are off limits. For example, officers are not allowed to hit in the neck or head with a PR-24, or straight stick, and the same applies for the PepperBalls. However, most department policies also recognize that a suspect contact can escalate into a deadly force matter, at which time all restrictions on less-lethal targeting are off and deadly force with less-lethal weapons directed at typically restricted areas may be allowed.

Most conventional chemical agents work as either lachrymators, causing intense eye irritation and tearing, or as respiratory irritants, which make it difficult to breathe. Other less-lethal devices that use directed kinetic energy in projectile form are impact weapons such as bean-bag rounds and rubber bullets.

Although death and serious injury rarely result from use of these less-lethal impact projectiles, death has occurred, often caused by improper shot placement. Certain areas of the body are very vulnerable to impact injury, whereas others are relatively resistant.

Less-lethal devices that remove the need for accurate shot placement on a limited target area are CEDs, with the best known being the TASER™. An acronym for Thomas A. Swift Electric Rifle, the TASER is a conducted energy weapon that fires a cartridge with two small probes that stay connected to the weapon by high-voltage, insulated wire. Although prior generations of TASER stun technology have had limited success in stopping extremely motivated subjects or those under the influence of drugs or alcohol, the advanced TASER is able to incapacitate even the most focused combatants.

The TASER is not without critics. Several studies have linked TASER use with deaths; however, the *Study of Deaths Following Electro Muscular Disruption* (2008) by the National Institute of Justice reports, "Although exposure to CED is not risk free, there is no conclusive medical evidence within the state current research that indicates a high risk of serious injury or death from the direct effects of CED. Therefore, law enforcement need not refrain from deploying CEDs provided the devices are used in accordance with accepted national guidelines. (For example, *Electronic Control Weapons*, a model policy of the International Association of Chiefs of Police.)"

Other less-lethal alternatives include a "sticky foam" that hardens like taffy and can effectively immobilize a person. Another alternative is an aqueous (water-based) foam similar to that used by firefighters that incapacitates suspects by filling the space so the person cannot see or hear, although they can still breathe. Air bags in the rear seat of squad cars offer a third option to immobilize combative suspects.

A "tool" long used by law enforcement that is now gaining acceptance as an alternative means of force is the K-9. Police service dogs can enhance the safety of officers, bystanders and suspects and help officers avoid resorting to deadly force. A source of K-9–related case law can be found on the Web site of Terry Fleck, an expert in the field of canine legalities.

Emphasis on CEDs and other less-lethal options may make handheld impact weapons obsolete because historically such handheld devices have filled a use-of-force gap between fisticuffs and firearms (Scoville, 2009, p.50). Scoville suggests that if you ask the average citizen what constitutes "police brutality," most would think of a cop with a baton or some other "club" beating on a suspect. Nonetheless, says Scoville (p.51), "Batons are probably one of the most valuable tools a police officer can have on his belt. They don't malfunction. They provide you with greater distance from the threat in lieu of having to use deadlier force. You will never hit a person harder with your hand than you will with your baton. The baton is the best equalizer, the best low technology weapon on a law enforcement officer's belt." The newer, telescoping batons can be an even more powerful persuader for compliance.

Voodoo Science and Less-Lethal Weapons The general public is often confused about the risks of less-lethal weapons, with civil libertarians saying one thing and law enforcement agencies saying something else. Heal et al. (2009) call most of the so-called research of libertarians "Voodoo Science," which they characterize as a " catchall" term for any junk science that misleads or mischaracterizes the evidence (pp.26–27): "Simply put, much of the 'science' cited by detractors of non-lethal options is either fundamentally flawed, misunderstood, mischaracterizes the evidence or ignores influences beyond the control of the user. It is an exceedingly rare occurrence when any of this so-called 'science' is subject to peer review by objective researchers, cited in reports by other researchers or scientists, used in supporting references, or corroborated with other research by bona fide scientific or academic institutions."

Laser light technologies, acoustic devices and malodorants are all under development as less-lethal alternatives (Ijames and Ederheimer, 2007, pp.86–87).

The Use of Deadly Force in Making Arrests

Using deadly force is perhaps the hardest decision a law enforcement officer faces. The use of such force is prescribed by state and federal statutes and basically requires that deadly force be used only in self-defense or in defense of another. Until 1985, it was legal in many states for officers to use deadly force to prevent a felon from escaping. This practice, however, terminated following *Tennessee v. Garner* (1985), when, as noted, the Supreme Court ruled that law enforcement officers cannot shoot "fleeing felons" unless they present an "imminent danger to life": "The use of deadly force to prevent the escape of all felony suspects, whatever the circumstances, is constitutionally unreasonable. It is not better that all felony suspects die than that they escape. Where the suspect poses no immediate threat to others, the harm resulting from failing to apprehend him does not justify the use of deadly force to do so."

Up Close

THE SCIENCE OF FORCE

A nonprofit Force Science™ Research Center at Minnesota State University in Mankato opened in 2004 to study human dynamics so officers can be better trained, make better decisions and keep themselves and their communities safe. Research conducted at the center seeks to define the limits of human performance and the parameters of danger and has provided the following insights into "extreme encounters":

> [Research at the center showed that] males, especially, tended to use their hands and arms to assist them in turning. This often brought their gun up and forward, and could create the allusion that they were consciously pointing the gun at the officer. Actually this wasn't true because the suspect would continue rotating away from the officer to flee. But based on the split-second perception of threat, the officer could decide to shoot in self-defence . . . and by the time the bullet arrived, the suspect would be further turned and end up shot in the side or back. To someone who didn't understand the dynamics involved, it would look like the deliberate, illegal "execution" of a fleeing, nonthreatening subject. This would be disastrous for the officer. The bottom line: If an officer dealing with a determined, armed suspect waits to shoot until he sees a gun pointed at him, it's too late. (p.11)
>
> In addition to keeping officers safer, a number of officers who have been charged criminally or sued civilly have been exonerated because of what we could reconstruct based on force science. (p.12)
>
> We've been able to document that when the average officer is shooting rapidly (as he would be in the adrenalized stress of defending his life), it takes him an average of two additional seconds to process the information and stop pulling the trigger once he perceives the threat has ended. . . . (p.13)
>
> Don't dismiss safety fundamentals. For instance, if you can't see a suspect's hands on a vehicle stop, you're casting your fate to the wind if you approach. Our studies have proved that wherever a suspect may have his hands hidden from sight in a car, he can reach a gun and shoot at you faster than you can react—even with your gun on target and your finger on the trigger. (p.13)

Source: Charles Remsberg. "New Force Science™ Center Unravels Vital Mysteries of Extreme Encounters." *The Law Enforcement Trainer*, Third Quarter, 2004, pp.8–13.

The Duty to Warn

If a felon is fleeing and an officer believes that the felon is a significant threat to the officer or others, the officer should shout a loud warning, "Stop or I'll shoot!" before firing. The warning should be loud enough that in addition to the fleeing felon, *everyone* who might be a witness to both the fleeing and the use of deadly force will hear the warning. Table 3.2 summarizes when a warning is preferred or required in using specific types of force.

Written Reports on Use of Force

Means and Seidel (2009a, p.29) stress, "A well-written, detailed use-of-force report is the department and officer's best friend in post-incident reviews, whether in court or in internal administrative matter. An old law enforcement proverb says, 'If it's not in the report, it didn't happen.'" Some officers believe that the more detail they include, the more a defense attorney can pick the incident apart. In actuality, most defense attorneys now do not ask for an internal affairs investigation, but rather conduct a thorough investigation on their own (Means and Seidel). What commonly happens is several years after an incident, an officer is sued for excessive force. The plaintiff's case has been fully documented with evidence and statements gathered at the time of the incident. However, the defense side has no detailed use-of-force report, or possibly no

Table 3.2 Type of Force and Whether a Warning Is Required or Preferred

Type of Force	Is a Warning Required?	Is a Warning Preferred?
Use of deadly force	Yes, if feasible, in all states.	A warning is required.
Use of less lethal shotguns and similar less-lethal device	A warning should be provided, if feasible, by officers in Alaska, Arizona, California, Guam, Hawaii, Idaho, Montana, Nevada, Oregon, Washington and the Northern Mariana Islands.	Yes, if feasible, in all states. Note that many manufacturers of less-lethal equipment now "require" that a warning be given before using their equipment against a suspect.
Batons	Probably not, unless the baton is being used in such a way as to be considered deadly force (such as with a blow to the head).	Yes, if feasible, in all states.
Canine deployment	Probably yes, at least in Alaska, Arizona, California, Guam, Hawaii, Idaho, Montana, Nevada, Oregon, Washington and the Northern Mariana Islands.	Yes, if feasible, in all states.
Oleoresin Capsicum	Probably not.	Yes, especially in those situations where the substance is used against a number of individuals such as during unlawful "protests."

Source: David N. Lesh. "The Duty to Warn." *The Law Enforcement Trainer*, March/April 2003, p.18. Reprinted by permission.

report at all, and no internal investigation. The officer may not even remember the incident and is in about as bad a position as possible.

The accuracy and completeness of force reports are extremely important. Officers need to be fluent in the language of force. Some practitioners suggest that agencies change the name *Use of Force Report* to *Subject Resistance Report*, focusing on the subject's actions (resistance) that led the officer to use force.

Use of Force and Community Policing

An integral part of the community policing philosophy is that the police must become a part of the community rather than stand apart from it. This places police in a somewhat difficult position as they try to become a part of the very entity over which they must exercise power and authority. Facing the potential dilemma of having to use force against the very citizens with whom they are seeking to form partnerships, this arrangement also presents a paradox—the ability of police to use force to secure a peaceful community.

Use of force can be a serious obstacle to the community policing philosophy.

Adding to this challenge is the seemingly disproportionate use of force against minorities and those of lower socioeconomic status. Miller and Hess (2010, p.49) observe

> Because police-enforcement efforts focus on common criminals, who are frequently poor, the most use of force by the police will be directed against this part of the population. Citizens in White suburban areas. . . may never see a police officer use force. The most negative experience they are likely to have with a police officer is receiving a traffic ticket.

> When people from these widely separated communities talk about the police, it seems as though they are speaking of entirely different entities. On the one hand, police may be referred to as brutal, racist aggressors whereas others describe them as professional, helpful, efficient protectors.

The public must be educated about the legitimate use of force required to maintain peaceful neighborhoods. They might also have input into policies on the use of force as well as incidents involving alleged excessive use of force.

LEGAL SEARCHES

The Fourth and Fifth Amendments also restrict police officers in when they can search and for what. As with an arrest, a search usually should be conducted with a *warrant*. Procedures for obtaining and executing search warrants vary by locality, but generally search warrants may be issued if

- The property was stolen or embezzled.
- Possession of the property is a crime.
- The property is in the possession of someone who intends to use it to commit a crime.
- The property was used in committing a crime.
- The items tend to show that a crime was committed or that a specific person committed the crime.

Three principal justifications have been established by the courts for the right to search.

A search may be legally conducted if

- A search warrant has been issued.
- Consent is given.
- It is incidental to a lawful arrest.

Search Warrants

Ideally, all searches would be conducted with a search warrant. Typically, an officer or prosecutor drafts a search warrant explaining what is being searched for and where they expect to find such evidence, based on probable cause, and brings it before a judge. The judge reviews the warrant and either signs it to be active (if they believe probable cause exists) or denies it.

Wilson v. Arkansas (1995) held that the "knock and announce" requirements are part of the reasonableness inquiry and that officers must knock and announce *before* they enter. As with an arrest warrant, officers seeking to search premises under the authority of a search warrant can break down a door to gain admittance if they are denied entrance. Even with a search warrant, however, the search must be limited.

A search conducted under the authority of a search warrant must be limited to the area specified in the warrant and for the items described in the warrant.

Exceptions to the Search Warrant Requirement

Ten exceptions to the search warrant requirement are (1) execution of an arrest warrant, (2) frisks, (3) incident to arrest, (4) automobiles, (5) consent, (6) plain view/feel, (7) abandoned property, (8) open fields, (9) inventory and (10) exigent circumstances.

Arrest Warrant Execution Officers can search for a suspect in the suspect's home to execute an arrest warrant if they have probable cause to believe the suspect is there. This exception applies *only* to the suspect's home. They cannot conduct a search of any other location even though they have the arrest warrant. For other locations, a search warrant is generally required, although exceptions have been allowed by the courts. Scarry (2009, p.20) notes that officers *may* enter a third party's home to serve an arrest warrant without a search warrant under three circumstances: reason to believe the suspect lives at the third party's residence, consent and exigency. *Maryland v. Buie* (1990) established that officers may make a limited protective sweep of a home during an arrest if the circumstances warrant.

Frisks As previously discussed, *Terry v. Ohio* established that officers can conduct a patdown of an individual they have stopped if they believe the person is armed and dangerous. This is a protective search for weapons only. The Supreme Court has identified additional factors that could contribute to a reasonable suspicion that a suspect might be armed and dangerous and, thus, could justify a frisk for the officer's safety, including (Rutledge, 2007b, p.38)

- Violent nature of the suspected crime
- Visible bulges, holster, ammo, and so forth
- Menacing gesturers or verbal threats
- Citizen tips of weapons or violence
- Information from bulletins or broadcasts
- Prior experience with the suspect
- Number of suspect and officers
- Size of suspects and officers
- Remote location of the encounter
- Obscure location lacking public visibility
- Late night or early morning hour
- Evasive conduct by the suspect
- Metallic clicking sounds
- Suspect's attempt to hide something
- Resistant or obstructive behavior
- Unprovoked flight on approach of police
- High-crime nature of the area
- Refusal to ID
- Suspicious clothing (such as a long coat on a warm day)
- The officer's training and experience

Such factors should be clearly stated in any report of the incident. These factors can also play a role in the other exceptions to the search warrant requirement, such as search incident to arrest.

Search Incident to Arrest *Chimel v. California* (1969) established that officers can search a person they have arrested for weapons and for evidence, but the search must be limited to the area within the arrested person's immediate control, sometimes referred to as the person's "wing span." It is entirely reasonable for the arresting officer to search for and seize any evidence on the arrestee's person to prevent its concealment or destruction and the area from within which the arrestee might gain possession of a weapon or destructible evidence.

The area within a person's control includes women's purses, chairs suspects are sitting on at the time of arrest and the entire interior of an automobile if the person is in a car at the time of the arrest. (The trunk is not included in this exception.) *New York v. Belton* (1981) decided that an automobile's interior could be searched after a passenger was arrested.

Automobile Exception *Carroll v. United States* (1925) established that because automobiles are mobile, officers may search them without a warrant if they have probable cause to believe the car contains evidence of a crime. This is the only exception allowing officers to search without a warrant even if they have time to get one. Probable cause alone supports the warrantless search. This exception includes the car's trunk, as well as suitcases within the trunk if the officers have probable cause to believe they contain evidence. Further, this exception applies to all kinds of motorized vehicles. *California v. Carney* (1985) declared that this exception applied to mobile campers.

Maryland State Police make a random vehicle check at the entrance ramp to the Baltimore Washington International Airport. Earlier in the day, police were stopping all vehicles entering the terminal area as part of a security check.
© Joe Giza/Reuters/CORBIS

Consent The consent must be voluntary, and it must be given by a person who has the authority to do so. No threats can be used. The officers do not need to identify themselves as law enforcement officers. The consent can be withdrawn at any time during the search. Property owners cannot give consent to allow their tenants' apartments to be searched.

If two occupants of a residence or apartment are present and one person consents but the other does not, no consent search can be conducted, as established by the Supreme Court's ruling in *Georgia v. Randolph* (2006): "A physically present co-occupant's stated refusal to permit entry renders warrantless entry and search unreasonable and invalid."

Plain View If officers are performing their duties and come across evidence or contraband that is easily seen—that is, it is in **plain view**—they may seize it. As the Supreme Court explained in *Katz v. United States* (1967), "The Fourth Amendment protects people, not places. What a person knowingly exposes to the public, even in his own home or office, is not a subject of Fourth Amendment protection." Officers can use a flashlight, provided they have a right to be at the location in the first place. The question of whether officers using binoculars or telescopic devices can seize evidence they discover under the plain view exception is controversial. Some courts have allowed it; others have not.

plain view
Term describing evidence that is not concealed, that is easily seen by officers while performing their legal duties.

Similar to not requiring an arrest warrant to allow officers to arrest someone they see committing a crime, a search warrant is not required for officers to seize contraband or other evidence that is in plain sight. Officers may not, however, act merely on reasonable suspicion and manipulate suspected evidence to determine its illegality. The evidence must be immediately recognizable as such.

In *Arizona v. Hicks* (1987), while conducting a lawful yet warrantless search of an apartment for a gunman immediately following a shooting, an officer noticed several pieces of expensive-looking stereo equipment that seemed out of place in the otherwise poorly furnished room. Suspecting the items were stolen, the officer recorded the equipments' serial numbers, moving some of the pieces in the process. A later check on the serial numbers revealed the items were indeed stolen. A search warrant was obtained, and the equipment was seized.

Suspect Hicks was charged with and convicted of robbery. Upon appeal, however, the Supreme Court reversed, ruling, "Moving the equipment . . . did constitute a 'search' separate and apart from the search for the shooter, victims, and weapons that was the lawful objective of [the officer's] entry into the apartment." The Court held that probable cause, not merely reasonable suspicion, to believe that items seen are contraband or evidence of criminal activity is required for the items to be seized under the "plain view" exception to the warrant requirement.

Plain Feel The *Minnesota v. Dickerson* case (1993) mentioned in the discussion of stop and frisk established the legitimacy of "plain feel" if probable cause is established. In this case, the Supreme Court ruled unanimously that a police officer may seize contraband discovered during a patdown search for weapons if it is immediately apparent to the officer that the object is an illegal substance. The officer may not, however, "manipulate" the object to determine whether it is actually contraband: "To this Court, there is no distinction as to which sensory perception the officer uses to conclude the material is contraband. An experienced officer may rely upon his sense of smell in DUI stops or in recognizing the smell of burning marijuana in an automobile. The sound of a shotgun being racked would clearly support certain reactions by an officer. The sense of touch, grounded in experience and training, is as reliable as perceptions drawn from other senses. 'Plain feel' therefore, is no different than plain view."

Despite this holding, the evidence against Dickerson was ruled inadmissible at trial because the police officer testified he had determined the lump contained cocaine only after squeezing, sliding and manipulating it. The Court said such manipulation was a search, not a limited patdown for protection.

Luggage Searches The Court's reasoning in *Dickerson* has been applied to searches of luggage. In *Bond v. United States* (2000), the Court extended its "look, but don't touch" policy when it ruled police officers can visually inspect travelers' luggage but not squeeze or physically manipulate a bag to determine whether it contains drugs or other contraband. To do so would constitute a warrantless search, thus requiring probable cause.

Thermal Imaging The use of technology that enables officers to see or hear into a subject's home has been heavily restricted by the law. Although wiretapping, electronic surveillance and other sound-monitoring devices have been addressed by the court many times during the last few decades, a relatively recent issue involves the use of thermal imaging devices. In *Kyllo v. United States* (2001), the Supreme Court ruled the use of technology-enhanced surveillance equipment is a "search" within the meaning of the Fourth Amendment if it reveals any information about the inside of a subject's home that police could otherwise know only by entering.

In this case, police were suspicious Kyllo was growing marijuana in his home, which was part of a triplex. Aware that indoor marijuana cultivation typically requires use of high-intensity lamps, agents used thermal imaging to monitor the amount of heat emanating from Kyllo's unit. The scan showed Kyllo's garage roof and a side wall were relatively hot compared with the rest of the home and noticeably warmer than the neighboring units. This evidence, combined with an offer made by Kyllo to a police informant to supply marijuana, was used to obtain a search warrant. The search netted 100 marijuana plants, weapons and drug paraphernalia, and Kyllo was indicted on federal drug charges.

The lower court reasoned the thermal imaging technology did not reveal any intimate details about the activities inside the home, merely amorphous hot spots, and compared the level of intrusion to that involved in warrantless aerial surveillance. However, the majority of the Supreme Court disagreed, recalling the decision in *Katz v. United States* (1967) that individuals always retain the expectation of privacy in their homes: "To withdraw protection of this minimum expectation would be to permit police technology to erode the privacy guaranteed by the Fourth Amendment." Thus, police use of sense-enhancing technology constitutes a search that is presumptively unreasonable without a warrant ("Thermal Imaging of a . . .," 2001, p.13).

Abandoned Property *Abandoned property* refers to anything an individual throws away, including bags or purses discarded while being chased by the police. In *California v. Greenwood* (1988), the Court upheld the right of officers to search through an individual's garbage that had been placed on the curb. Some states, however, are more restrictive. New Jersey and Hawaii, for example, prohibit police from going through garbage without a warrant.

Open Fields The house and the area immediately surrounding it, called the **curtilage**, cannot be searched without a warrant. The curtilage is basically a person's yard and is protected by the Constitution. Open fields, however, are not. *Oliver v. United States* (1984) held that open fields are not protected by the Constitution and that, even if they are posted with "No Trespassing" signs, police can search them without a warrant. In this case, police were headed for a marijuana patch.

curtilage
A house and the area immediately surrounding it.

Border Searches In *United States v. Flores-Montano* (2004), Chief Justice Rehnquist stated, "Time and again, we have stated that searches made at the border, pursuant to the long-standing right of the sovereign to protect itself by stopping and examining persons and property crossing into this country, are reasonable simply by virtue of the fact that they occur at the border."

Routine searches are also allowed at places other than actual borders, under the **functional equivalent** doctrine. The functional equivalent doctrine refers to places other than actual borders where travelers frequently enter or exit the country, such as international airports.

functional equivalent
Refers to places other than actual borders where travelers frequently enter or exit the country, such as international airports.

Inventory Most police departments will automatically conduct an inventory of impounded vehicles. An inventory search protects the owner's property, it protects the law enforcement agency against claims that property in its possession has been lost or stolen, and it uncovers any danger that may exist to police because of property in their possession, such as a bomb. Inventorying must be a standard department procedure for this exception to be used.

Exigent Circumstances An **exigent circumstance** occurs when an emergency exists and there is no time for the officers to obtain a search warrant. That is, the evidence could be destroyed or gone by the time they obtained the warrant. This is a frequently used exception and also the most difficult to justify. Once the right to search is established, officers should make certain they conduct the searches legally.

exigent circumstances
Conditions surrounding an emergency situation in which no time is available to secure an arrest or search warrant.

PROCEDURES FOR LEGALLY SEARCHING PEOPLE

The least intrusive search is a patdown or frisk of a person's outer clothing as a protective search for weapons. In the case of arrest, the search is more thorough and also includes a search for weapons. In a search incident to arrest, certain basic guidelines should be followed.

When searching a person, officers should

- Handcuff the subject if warranted.
- Be on guard, keeping themselves at arm's length from the person being searched.
- Keep the subject facing away from the searching officer.
- Be aware of where the service weapon is and keep it as far from the subject as possible.
- Be systematic and thorough.
- Keep the person under control, preferably off balance.
- Use the back of the hand when patting down or searching the "private" areas of someone of the opposite sex (crotch area of both males and females; breast area of females).

The FBI and most police departments have a policy that individuals to be searched are handcuffed first for officer safety. If more than one suspect is to be searched, all except those currently being searched should be ordered to lie on the ground, facing away from the person being searched. If two officers are at the search scene, one conducts the search while the other officer stands guard.

PROCEDURES FOR LEGALLY SEARCHING BUILDINGS

Officers often must search buildings in response to either alarms or calls from citizens. Such searches are fraught with danger and require extreme caution.

Chimel v. California (1969) established that officers entering a structure to make a lawful arrest could look into areas within the arrestee's immediate control to deter the arrestee from obtaining a weapon or destroying evidence. In *Maryland v. Buie* (1990), the Supreme Court allowed the arresting officers to make a protective sweep of the immediately adjoining spaces where a potential assailant might be concealed. Such a *Buie* sweep does not require any suspicion that an assailant is present, but must be limited to immediately adjoining spaces, not through the entire premises.

Officers arriving at a building to search it should arrive as quietly as possible to preserve the element of surprise. To make certain no one escapes from within the building, observation posts should be set up and maintained while the search is being conducted. A thorough search depends on having enough officers to visually contain the building as well as to thoroughly and systematically search the inside.

The building search itself must be carefully planned. If time permits, the building's owner should be contacted to learn as much as possible about its layout and possible hiding places. The number of floors, including basements and attics, should be determined. Usually one door is selected as the entry/exit door for the search team. In some instances, however, officers enter the front and back of the building simultaneously.

Once inside the building, all officers must know what each is doing. Each should have a clear assignment to carry out. A system of communication should be established to maintain contact. Should a suspect be located, assistance should be called for immediately. The search should continue, however, as more than one suspect might be in the building.

As officers search the building, they should use proven techniques. For example, when entering a room or a building, they should look into the structure from both sides of the doorway without exposing any more of the body than necessary. They should always keep low and move rapidly. If the building is dark, they should use a flashlight without becoming a target.

One of the most dangerous moments in searching a building occurs when officers come to a *corner*. An armed suspect could be around that corner. In such instances, mirrors and periscopes can be invaluable.

When searching a building officers should

- Get as much information as possible before starting the search.
- Plan carefully. Set up an entry/exit point, learn the interior layout, assign personnel to cover each area.
- Arrive quickly and quietly.
- Set up containment positions around the building.
- Make sure enough personnel are available.
- Make use of solid cover during the search.
- Use proper search techniques.

Officers also should take safety precautions when searching to avoid coming into contact with material that is contaminated and could result in acquiring hepatitis B or HIV. The risk factor in this area is ever increasing. Protecting against such hazards is discussed in-depth in Chapter 14.

An aerial view of four customs officers and a K-9 checking cargo for bombs and other threats. A dog frequently lessens the dangers associated with such searches.
© Dennis Mac Donald/ PhotoEdit

USING K-9s IN SEARCHES

Dogs (K-9s) can be invaluable in conducting searches for suspects, evidence, drugs and bombs. Numerous cases have addressed whether the use of detector dogs constitutes a search, with the court generally ruling that dog sniffs of inanimate items or in public locations are *not* searches. For example, in *United States v. Place* (1983), the Supreme Court held that a dog sniff of lawfully detained luggage in a public place does not constitute a search. In *City of Indianapolis v. Edmond* (2000), the Court extended this principle to the dog sniff of the exterior of a vehicle to which police have legitimate access. A dog sniff of the exterior of a warehouse or garage from a public location is not usually considered a search. The Supreme Court has never directly addressed the issue, but lower court cases generally consider a dog sniff of a person to be a search. Because state courts may find dog sniffs are searches under their own constitutions, officers should consult their laws related to using a dog to sniff items, locations or people for the presence of contraband.

Despite the many benefits gained by using K-9s, officers must also be aware of some of the drawbacks and limitations. Some days a dog may not perform well, missing drugs or contraband.

SUMMARY

While conducting police operations involving arrests and searches, law enforcement officers must maintain a balance between "freedom to" and "freedom from." Guarantees against unlawful arrests and searches are found in the Fourth and Fifth Amendments to the U.S. Constitution.

A stop-and-frisk situation is one in which law enforcement officers briefly detain (stop) a suspicious person for questioning (this is *not* an arrest) and, *if* the officers suspect the person is armed, they are allowed to pat (frisk) the person's outer clothing (this *is* a limited search for weapons).

An arrest is the official taking of a person to answer criminal charges. This involves at least temporarily depriving the person of liberty and may involve the use of force. An arrest can legally be made with an arrest warrant or without an arrest warrant (1) for any offense (felony or misdemeanor) committed in an officer's presence, (2) when officers have probable cause to believe a person has committed a felony and no time is available to obtain a warrant, or (3) for specifically enumerated misdemeanors, such as shoplifting in some jurisdictions. Probable cause refers to a situation where it is more likely than not that a crime has been committed by the person whom a law enforcement officer seeks to arrest. An officer's probable cause to conduct an arrest depends on what the officer knew *before* taking action.

Skill in making arrests is critical because arrest involves fundamental rights to personal liberty and privacy, the law of arrest is strict and technical, arrest is often the first step in criminal proceedings, illegal arrests may taint crucial evidence of guilt, the quality of police performance is judged by arrests, arrests may lead to civil suits or criminal prosecution of officers, and arrests may endanger officers' lives.

To make lawful arrests, officers must know both substantive and procedural law. Substantive law deals with content, or what behaviors are considered crimes. Procedural law deals with process, or how the law is applied. An illegal arrest may result in evidence being excluded under the Exclusionary Rule, which established that the courts cannot accept evidence obtained in illegal searches and seizures, regardless of how relevant the evidence is to the case (*Weeks v. United States,* 1914).

In a typical arrest situation, officers should announce the arrest and the reason for it, handcuff the person if warranted and then search the person arrested for weapons and evidence. The person should be given the *Miranda* warning if any questions are to be asked. Use of force when making an arrest is always an issue. If there is no resistance, no force should be used. If resistance occurs, only as much force as necessary to overcome the resistance should be used. If a threat to an officer's life exists, the use of deadly force is authorized in most departments. *Graham v. Connor* established a three-prong test for use of force: (1) the severity of the crime, (2) whether the suspect poses an immediate threat to the safety of law enforcement officers or others and (3) whether the suspect is actively resisting arrest or attempting to evade arrest by flight. Handcuffing may be considered a use of force. Whether an arrested person should automatically be handcuffed while being transported is controversial. Officer discretion may be advisable.

Less-lethal weapons available for use with violent, combative suspects include tear gas and other chemical irritant sprays, impact weapons, CEDs, foams, nets and K-9s. Use of force can be a serious obstacle to the community policing philosophy.

A search may be legally conducted if a search warrant has been issued, consent is given or it is incidental to a lawful arrest. A search conducted under the authority of a search warrant must be limited to the area specified in the warrant and for the items described in the warrant. Ten exceptions to the search warrant requirement are (1) execution of an arrest warrant, (2) frisks, (3) incident to arrest, (4) automobiles, (5) consent, (6) plain view/feel, (7) abandoned property, (8) open fields, (9) inventory and (10) exigent circumstances.

When searching a person, officers should handcuff the subject if warranted; be on guard, keeping themselves at arm's length from the person being searched; keep the subject facing away from the searching officer; be aware of where the service weapon is and keep it as far from the subject as possible; be systematic and thorough; keep the person under control, preferably off balance; and use the back of the hand when patting down or searching the private areas of individuals of the opposite sex.

When searching a building, officers should get as much information as possible before starting the search, plan carefully, arrive quickly and quietly, set up containment positions around the building and make sure enough personnel are available. They should set up an entry/exit point, learn the interior layout and assign personnel to cover each area. They should also use available cover and proper search techniques.

APPLICATION

You are a Bigtown patrol officer. You notice that transporting and booking a person arrested as a misdemeanant takes from one to three hours. This seems counterproductive because you are out of service during that time, not available for other calls, and the arrested person will usually be released from jail in a short time, often even before you finish the reports. You feel that issuing a citation to the person without formal procedures of arrest and booking would more than serve the purpose and would release you for more important duties. You approach your sergeant and pose your recommendations to her. She asks you to "put it in writing."

INSTRUCTIONS

Use the form in the appendix at the end of this book to make your policy and procedure. The policy will include the following:

> The policy of the Bigtown Police Department for releasing people from custody who have been arrested for a misdemeanor will change effective (date). Any person cited for a misdemeanor whom the officer feels will appear in court as promised may be given a written citation by the officer.
>
> *When a Citation May Be Issued.* Give several circumstances or conditions that may exist whereby officers could issue a citation to such a person who also has no previous criminal record.

Justifications for Not Issuing a Citation. In completing this policy, you should insert what form is to be used when issuing a citation, what reports are necessary and also that issuing a citation means suspects should be entered in the arrest log and assigned a log number and a case number. You should indicate what needs to appear in the citation notification form.

AN EXERCISE IN CRITICAL THINKING

At 7:40 A.M. on June 27, Officer Steve Sjerven was in the crossover preparing to turn south on Highway 65 to help the driver of an apparently disabled car. As he waited to turn, he saw a red pickup truck heading south on Highway 65 and made eye contact with the driver and sole occupant of the truck. The driver abruptly turned the truck right onto Tower Systems Road and appeared to immediately disappear. Not seeing the pickup truck or any dust that might be expected from a truck traveling down a gravel road, the officer concluded that the truck must have immediately pulled into a driveway. As the officer pulled up to assist the disabled car, he saw the pickup emerge and turn south onto Highway 65—a very short time after having turned onto Tower Systems Road. Inferring that the driver had turned off Highway 65 to avoid him, the officer motioned the driver of the pickup to stop. The driver did so, identified himself as Mark Johnson and admitted that his license had been revoked.

1. As the U.S. Supreme Court's decisions require only that an officer have a "particular and objective basis for suspecting the particular person stopped of criminal activity," what is your judgment of Officer Sjerven's approach?
   a. Because Johnson's action can be explained as consistent with lawful activities, Officer Sjerven should not stop him.
   b. The officer's suspicion, though nothing more than a hunch, was later verified by the stop.
   c. Sjerven stopped Johnson on mere whim, caprice or idle curiosity, and so should be disciplined for poor judgment in operational skills.
   d. Inferences and deductions might well elude an untrained person, but a trained police officer is entitled to draw inferences on the basis of "all of the circumstances."
   e. If the observed facts are consistent with innocent activity, then the stop is invalid.

DISCUSSION QUESTIONS

1. The Fifth Amendment provides that no person shall be "deprived of life, liberty or property without due process of law." What does this really mean? Explain your answer as if you were giving a lecture to a high school class.
2. Substantive law is concerned with the content of the law. Criminal law defines what behaviors are illegal and imposes punishments for engaging in them. Name five types of behavior the law does not tolerate.
3. When officers make an arrest without a warrant, they act at their own peril and are allowed no margin of error. Why is this statement written so stringently?
4. Describe a good example of "reasonable grounds of suspicion."
5. What search situations are officers likely to find themselves in? How can they best prepare themselves?
6. Discuss how you felt when you read about the Abner Louima case. Do you think this incident could have been prevented?
7. Do you feel that given the awesome power police hold, they can ever be true partners with citizens in community policing?

GALE EMERGENCY SERVICES DATABASE ASSIGNMENTS

- Use the Gale Emergency Services database to answer the Discussion Questions as appropriate.
- Use the Gale Emergency Services database to research recent incidents where *excessive force* was alleged against the police. Outline the characteristics that bring on alleged excessive

force situations. Be prepared to share your outline with the class.

- Use the Gale Emergency Services database to find and outline one of the following articles:
  - "Flight as Justification for Seizure: Supreme Court Ruling" by Michael E. Brooks
  - "Reviewing Use of Force: A Systematic Approach" by Sam W. Lathrop
  - "Using Drug Detection Dogs: An Update" by Jayme S. Walker
  - "Deadly Force: A 20-Year Study of Fatal Encounters" by Larry C. Brubaker
  - "U.S. Land Border Search Authority" by M. Wesley Clark
  - "Inferring Probable Cause: Obtaining a Search Warrant for a Suspect's Home without Direct Information that Evidence Is Inside" by Edward Hendrie
  - "Consent Searches: Factors Courts Consider in Determining Voluntariness" by Jayme Walker Holcomb
  - "Obtaining Written Consent to Search" by Jayme Walker Holcomb
  - "Consent Searches Scope" by Jayme Walker Holcomb
  - "Use-of-Force Policies and Training: A Reasoned Approach" by Thomas D. Petrowski
  - "Use-of-Force Policies and Training: A Reasoned Approach (Part Two)" by Thomas D. Petrowski
  - "Force Continuums: A Liability to Law Enforcement?" by George T. Williams

REFERENCES

Basich, Melanie. "Women Warriors." *Police*, June 2008, pp.44–49.

Collins, John M. "Recent Decision in *Brendlin v. California* Provides Good 'Law Review' on Seizures of Persons." *The Police Chief*, September 2007, pp.10–11.

Commission on Accreditation of Law Enforcement Agencies. *Standards for Law Enforcement Agencies*, 5th ed. Fairfax, VA: CALEA, 2006, updated 2008.

Devanney, Joe. "Supreme Court Ruling: Knock-and-Announce." *Law and Order*, April 2007, pp.28–31.

Durose, Matthew R.; Smith, Erica L.; and Langan, Patrick A. *Contacts between Police and the Public, 2005.* Washington, DC: Bureau of Justice Statistics Special Report, April 2007. (NCJ 215243)

Ederheimer, Joshua, and Johnson, Will. "Introduction." *Strategies for Resolving Conflict and Minimizing Use of Force*, edited by Joshua A. Ederheimer. Washington, DC: Police Executive Research Forum, April 2007, pp.1–11.

Geoghegan, Susan. "*Hudson v. Michigan* and Forced Entry." *Tactical Response*, March/April 2007, pp.96–99.

Harr, J. Scott, and Hess, Kären M. *Constitutional Law and the Criminal Justice System*, 4th ed. Belmont, CA: Wadsworth Cengage Learning, 2008.

Heal, Sid; Bovbjerg, Viktor; and Kenny, John. "Voodoo Science and Non-Lethal Weapons." *Tactical Response*, January/February 2009, pp.24–28.

Heinecke, Jeannine. "'Knock, Knock.' 'Who's There?'" *Law Enforcement Technology*, February 2007, pp.30–37.

Hilton, Alicia M. "Clearing Up Knock-and-Announce Confusion." *Police*, August 2007, pp.38–43.

Ijames, Steve, and Ederheimer, Joshua. "Less-Lethal Weaponry and Less-Lethal Force Decision-Making." In *Strategies for Resolving Conflict and Minimizing Use of Force*, edited by Joshua A. Ederheimer. Washington, DC: Police Executive Research Forum, April 2007, pp.71–89.

Ivy, Peter and Orput, Peter "Defendants Must Demonstrate Standing before the Exclusionary Rule Applies." *Minnesota Police Chief*, Spring, 2007, pp.8–11.

Means, Randy, and Seidel, Greg. "Keys to Winning with the Use of Force: Avoiding Peripheral Poisonings." *Law and Order*, March 2009a, pp.28–30.

Means, Randy, and Seidel, Greg. "Maintaining Proportionality and Managing Force Escalations." *Law and Order*, February 2009b, pp.31–32.

Miller, Christa. "The Art of Verbal Judo." *Law Enforcement Technology*, August 2008, pp.62–72.

Miller, Linda S., and Hess, Kären M. *Community Policing: Partnerships for Problem Solving*, 6th ed. Clifton Park, NY: Delmar Cengage Publishing, 2010.

Moore, Carole. "On Cameras." *Law Enforcement Technology*, November 2008, p.82.

Nance, Richard, and Hallford, David. "Cuffing with Useful Force." *Police*, May 2008, pp.55–57.

Plitt, Emory A. "Test Your 'Excessive Force' I.Q." *PoliceOne News*, February 28, 2008.

Remsberg, Charles. "New Force Science™ Center Unravels Vital Mysteries of Extreme Encounters." *The Law Enforcement Trainer*, Third Quarter, 2004, pp.8–13.

Rutledge, Devallis. "The 'Good Faith' Doctrine." *Police*, June 2007a, pp.70–71.

Rutledge, Devallis. "How to Justify Officer Safety Searches." *Police*, October 2007b, pp.36–40.

Rutledge, Devallis. "Fourth Amendment Supremacy." *Police*, June 2008, pp.66–70.

Rutledge, Devallis. "Official Misinformation." *Police*, March 2009, pp.78–81.

Scarry, Laura L. "False Arrest Claims." *Law Officer Magazine*, May 2007a, pp.138–139.

Scarry, Laura L. "Tight Handcuffs: A Fourth Amendment Violation?" *Law Officer Magazine*, December 2007b, pp.50–53.

Scarry, Laura L. "Arrest Warrants: The Standard to Enter a Suspect's Home." *Law Officer Magazine*, November 2008a, pp.22–25.

Scarry, Laura L. "Is It a 4th Amendment Violation When an Arrest Violates State Law?" *Law Officer Magazine*, June 2008b, pp. 22–24.

Scarry, Laura L. "Someone Else's Home: When an Arrest Warrant Isn't Enough." *Law Officer Magazine*, March 2009, pp.20–24.

Scoville, Dean. "Do We Still Need Batons?" *Police*, March 2009, pp.50–54.

Spector, Elliot B. "U.S. Supreme Court Diminishes Effect of Arrests That Violate State Procedural Rules." *The Police Chief*, November 2008, pp.12–13.

Study of Deaths Following Electro Muscular Disruption: Interim Report. Washington, DC: National Institute of Justice, June 2008.

"Thermal Imaging of a Residence Constitutes a Search." *NCJA Justice Bulletin*, June 2001, p.13.

Thompson, George. "Verbal Judo Tactics & Techniques." *PoliceOne.com News*, April 4, 2008.

CASES CITED

Alabama v. White, 496 U.S. 325 (1990)
Arizona v. Evans, 514 U.S. 1 (1995)
Arizona v. Hicks, 480 U.S. 321 (1987)
Atwater v. Lago Vista, 532 U.S. 318 (2001)
Bond v. United States, 529 U.S. 334 (2000)
Brendlin v. California, 551 U.S. 249 (2007)
Brinegar v. United States, 338 U.S. 160 (1949)
California v. Carney, 471 U.S. 386 (1985)
California v. Greenwood, 486 U.S. 35 (1988)
Carroll v. United States, 267 U.S. 132 (1925)
Chimel v. California, 395 U.S. 752 (1969)
City of Indianapolis v. Edmond, 531 U.S. 32 (2000)
Florida v. Bostick, 501 U.S. 429 (1991)
Georgia v. Randolph, 547 U.S. 103 (2006)
Graham v. Connor, 490 U.S. 386 (1989)
Hiibel v. Sixth Judicial District Court of Nevada, Humboldt County, 542 U.S. 177 (2004)
Hudson v. Michigan, 547 U.S. 586 (2006)
Illinois v. Gates, 462 U.S. 213 (1983)
Illinois v. Wardlow, 528 U.S. 119 (2000)
Katz v. United States, 389 U.S. 347 (1967)
Kaupp v. Texas, 538 U.S. 626 (2003)
Kyllo v. United States, 553 U.S. 27 (2001)
Mapp v. Ohio, 367 U.S. 643 (1961)
Maryland v. Buie, 494 U.S. 325 (1990)
Massachusetts v. Sheppard, 468 U.S. 981 (1984)
Minnesota v. Dickerson, 508 U.S. 336 (1993)
Murray v. United States, 487 U.S. 533 (1988)
New York v. Belton, 453 U.S. 454 (1981)
Oliver v. United States, 466 U.S. 170 (1984)
Scott v. Harris, 550 U.S. 372 (2007)
Semayne's Case, 5 Coke, 918 (1603)
Tennessee v. Garner, 471 U.S. 1 (1985)
Terry v. Ohio, 392 U.S. 1 (1968)
United States v. Banks, 540 U.S. 31 (2003)
United States v. Flores-Montano, 541 U.S. 149 (2004)
United States v. Leon, 468 U.S. 897 (1984)
United States v. Place, 462 U.S. 696 (1983)
United States v. Ramirez, 523 U.S. 65 (1998)
United States v. Sokolow, 490 U.S. 1 (1989)
Virginia v. Moore, 553 U.S. _____ (2008)
Weeks v. United States, 232 U.S. 383 (1914)
Wilson v. Arkansas, 514 U.S. 927 (1995)

SECTION II

Getting the Job Done: Basic Police Operations

Most police operations books begin and end in this section. But a law enforcement officer must never forget that the actual operations themselves are only half the job.

To perform police operations professionally, officers must always keep in mind the content of the first section. They must consider the context in which they operate—the citizens they serve as well as the colleagues with whom they work. Law enforcement officers are an integral part of this context, not a separate entity. They do not operate in a vacuum. Officers must use effective communications skills, and they must do so while staying within the law.

With this solid foundation, now focus on the actual operations law enforcement officers perform. At the heart of police operations is patrol, often called the backbone of the police organization (Chapter 4). Activities conducted

during patrol often include other functions performed by officers, such as traffic enforcement (Chapter 5); responding to crime, disorder and quality-of-life issues (Chapter 6); deterring violence (Chapter 7); dealing with emergencies (Chapter 8) and securing our homeland (Chapter 9). The next section will focus on specialized police operations.

CHAPTER 4

Patrol

The Backbone of Police Operations

DO YOU KNOW . . .

- How patrol is typically described?
- What functions patrol typically performs?
- How the majority of patrol time is spent?
- How crowds can be classified?
- What methods of patrol have been used and the advantages and disadvantages of each?
- What type of patrol has the most mobility and flexibility and is usually the most cost effective?
- What the Kansas City Preventive Patrol Experiment found?
- What most affects the possibility of on-scene arrests?
- What two basic causes account for delays in calling for service?
- What basic change in perspective problem-oriented policing requires?
- What the SARA problem-solving process consists of?

CAN YOU DEFINE?

differential police response strategies
directed patrol
discovery crimes
impact evaluation
involvement crimes
problem-oriented policing (POP)
process evaluation
proportionate assignment
proximate
response time

INTRODUCTION

Usually the most complex, burdensome and dangerous aspects of police service are performed by uniformed patrol officers. The work may be carried out in an atmosphere emotionally charged with hostility—an environment that breeds distrust and danger—and in situations that require officers to be clergy, psychologists, therapists or many other types of professionals who deal with human problems.

Patrol service has been described as the backbone of the police department.

Theoretically, patrol officers are the most valuable people in the organization. To a certain extent, all activity radiates from them. But such a concept is not totally supported by such measures as salary, working conditions and authority.

This chapter begins with a brief overview of the importance of patrol and its historical organizational contradiction. This is followed by a look at the typical functions performed by patrol and the various methods of patrol, including foot, automobile, motorcycle, bicycle, Segway, mounted, air, personal vertical takeoff and landing aircraft, water, special-terrain, K-9–assisted and combined patrol. Next, patrol techniques and strategies are examined, including results of the classic Kansas City Preventive Patrol Experiment, area and shift assignment modification, response time, differential police response strategies and use of directed patrol. Then attention shifts to the critical role problem solving plays in patrol effectiveness. The chapter concludes with a discussion of patrol and community policing.

THE IMPORTANCE AND "PLACE" OF PATROL

Historically, the identity and importance of patrol has suffered from an organizational contradiction: "If patrol personnel are skeptical of their place in the law enforcement hierarchy, it is understandable. For while many a department still pays lip service to patrol constituting the backbone of law enforcement, empirical observations may lead one to conclude otherwise. For larger agencies, it is commonly accepted that the road to promotion is not via patrol, but through coveted positions along the administrative or investigative path" (Scoville, 2008, p.42).

The fact is, the most crucial people on the law enforcement team are lowest on the totem pole. A police department's ability to carry out its mission of providing public service and controlling crime depends greatly on the uniformed patrol officers' capabilities. Oldham (2007, p.33) notes, "For the average citizen, the most powerful person in his life is the beat patrol officer. After all, this officer can immediately deprive someone of his freedom. If the situation warrants, the officer can also immediately take his life." Griffith (2008, p.10) likewise asserts, "There is no resource more valuable to an agency than its patrol officers, yet many treat these cops as disposable. Civilians and even some law enforcement brass have a tendency to judge the value of an officer by his or her rank."

Most of the country's police agencies are small, employing fewer than 20 officers. These departments assign almost all the officers to patrol, delegating additional special duties as needed. In a police agency with only one officer, that officer performs all roles from chief to records clerk, with the majority of the time spent serving a patrol function.

PATROL FUNCTIONS

41.1 CALEA STANDARD 41.1 "Patrol" states, "Patrol is considered to be a primary law enforcement function and embraces much more than the act of patrolling. It is defined as a generalized function in which officers may be engaged in a variety of activities which can range from traditional response to requests for service to alternate strategies for the delivery of police services." (*Standards for Law Enforcement Agencies*, 5th edition, 2006)

Lansdowne (2007, p.1), in noting that the core of a police department is patrol, explains, "The most difficult, dangerous, complex job in the police department is the patrol officer that answers calls every day. Everybody else is support to that patrol person." In addition, patrol officers are frequently first responders, courageous and dedicated to duty (Griffith, 2007, p.10).

Every patrol division performs different tasks, although some are common to all. Patrol duties are not usually described in great detail, except when officers answer specific calls for service. "Routine" patrol means different things to individual officers, supervisors and departments. For example, one officer on routine patrol may feel that if nothing is "happening," time can best be spent talking to citizens and getting to know the patrol areas. Another officer might feel the time should be spent looking into suspected gang activity. A third officer might feel this is the time to catch up on current events by reading the newspaper.

The police presence is intended to deter crime and give citizens a feeling of being protected. Officers help reduce racial tensions in large-city ghettos, and often conduct educational programs and provide help to drunks, the mentally ill, street people or patrons of prostitution who may be at risk of robbery.

Among the important patrol functions are

- Responding to crime calls for service.
- Responding to noncrime calls for service.
- Controlling traffic.
- Assisting at the scene of a crime.
- Conducting preliminary investigations.
- Gathering intelligence.
- Making arrests.
- Patrolling public gatherings and special events.
- Assisting at the scene of a fire and other medical calls.
- Providing community service and general peacekeeping activities.
- Partnering with others to solve problems related to crime and disorder.

The patrol response to crime calls for service is the focus of Chapter 6. The following section of this chapter, however, will discuss the remaining basic functions of patrol, aside from the vital task of responding to criminal actions.

Noncrime Calls for Service

Responding to calls for service is an important function of patrol officers. Many calls involve missing persons, damage to property, lost and found property, missing and stray animals, escort services, people locked out, licensing, inspections and city ordinance violations (e.g., open burning of leaves, noise complaints, etc.).

Television programs have made the *missing persons* function of the police department seem routine. In actuality, however, unless foul play is suspected or the person missing is a juvenile, mentally handicapped or in need of medication, the police often do not become involved in missing person cases. If no crime has been committed and the missing person's safety is not in jeopardy, the police department performs an administrative function, recording the information to be used in helping to identify individuals who are unconscious, who are found wandering (senility) or who are found dead and have no identification on them. The policy in some agencies may involve having an officer write a short report and submit a statewide alert, through dispatch, to check the welfare of the missing person if a police contact is made. Some agencies will only assist after a certain amount of time has passed and if there are certain suspicious variables involved, such as the person was intoxicated at the time they went missing. Also, if the missing person is a juvenile, a thorough report is done and a possible search-and-rescue plan enacted, along with the likely execution of an Amber Alert (discussed in greater detail in Chapter 11). The National Crime Information Center (NCIC) includes a missing person file with four specific categories and criteria for entry: (1) disabled, (2) endangered, (3) involuntary (abducted, kidnapped) and (4) juvenile.

Citizens who experience *property damage* are likely to call the police. If the incident poses danger, the first priority of responding officers is to make sure the scene is safe to themselves and others, before proceeding to dealing with danger. If danger does exist, officers must act to remove the danger. For example, if a tree has fallen on power lines and hot wires are on the ground, police should rope off the area and call the power company. If no danger is inherent in the situation, officers should determine if the damage is the result of criminal or noncriminal actions. If it is criminal property damage, for example, the work of vandals, officers should conduct a thorough investigation. If it is a noncriminal (and nondangerous) situation, for example, a tree fallen on a home, police officers should advise the complainant of alternatives in taking care of the damage. The complainant usually should also be advised to notify his or her insurance agent.

The police department may also serve a *lost and found* function. People who find valuable property are likely to turn it in to the police department. Conversely, people who have lost items of value are likely to request assistance from the police department. In this situation, again, the police department plays primarily an administrative function, maintaining accurate records of lost or found property.

Some police departments also have the responsibility for *missing and stray animals,* especially unlicensed dogs. And they may be called on to deal with dangerous animals, such as bears, or with trapped animals, such as a raccoon up a chimney of a home.

Police may be called on to provide *escort service* to celebrities and other public figures who are either extremely popular or unpopular. Police may also provide escort services for dangerous cargoes, such as those containing highly flammable materials, hazardous wastes and the like, or for oversized cargoes. In addition, police may be asked to provide escort services for funeral processions or for very valuable cargoes, such as large sums of cash. Little agreement exists on when escort services are appropriate or on how they should be provided; that is, should they include red flashing lights and sirens, or proceed as though on general patrol?

The police may also be called to assist *people locked out* of their cars or homes. In such instances, it is usually preferable to have the civilian call a locksmith. If this is not possible, officers should check the identity of the person requesting assistance. Imagine the predicament of a police officer who assists a burglar in breaking and entering.

The police department is sometimes involved in *licensing* handguns. It is to the department's advantage to know who owns what kind of weapons in its jurisdiction. In addition, the police are in a position to investigate applicants for a license and to determine if such a license should be granted. They also may do background investigations on applicants for liquor licenses, taxi licenses and tow truck licenses. The police department is also involved in other types of licensing, such as issuing animal licenses, licenses for holding parades or for blocking off streets for community functions.

In addition, because officers routinely patrol the entire area over which the department has jurisdiction, many decision makers believe officers should be responsible for *inspections* to ensure adherence to fire codes, health codes and building codes. This is another area of controversy because such activities are extremely time consuming. They do present the advantage of familiarizing officers with the people and buildings on their beats. However, such activities take officers off the street and into buildings where they are no longer on preventive patrol but rather are serving functions that could easily be carried out by inspectors specifically hired for the jobs, usually at less cost.

In many areas, police are also responsible for checking the weight of trucks. Police are used in this capacity because they must be on the scene anyway to issue tickets to overweight trucks or to stop trucks that bypass the scales completely. Some contend, however, that the patrol officers in the vicinity could be called in for either of the preceding situations and that it might be more practical not to use patrol officers in this capacity.

Between 80 and 90 percent of all calls for police service are of a non-criminal nature.

Whether police officers should spend time in all these activities is somewhat controversial. Yet, proposals to eliminate such social service functions fail to recognize the relationship between social-service-type calls and more serious crime. For example, a domestic disturbance can end in a serious assault or even homicide.

In addition, police are the only agencies available 24/7 for immediate help, which is one reason they are so often called to intervene in *domestic disputes.* Such disputes usually occur at night and commonly involve people who have been drinking. Police officers often are expected to defuse such situations without making an arrest. And they frequently are called to the same scene time and again. Such calls may lull officers into complacency, making them vulnerable should a normally routine call turn out to involve crazed, weapon-wielding individuals. Dealing with domestic disputes is discussed in detail in Chapter 7.

Controlling Traffic

Patrol officers also serve a *traffic* function by directing traffic, responding to traffic crash calls, issuing tickets for traffic violations and the like, as discussed in detail in Chapter 5.

Assisting at the Scene of a Crime

Responding to calls about *crimes in progress* or recently committed and conducting the *preliminary investigations* are other important functions of patrol officers. Because they are on patrol and readily available to respond, they are usually first on the scene. This is the type of call most officers consider to be "real" police work. On such calls, patrol officers are responsible for aiding injured victims, securing the scene, interviewing victims and witnesses and arresting any suspects present at the scene. In smaller departments, patrol officers may also continue the investigation and *gather intelligence.* In larger departments, the investigation may be turned over to the detective division. The investigative function is discussed in Chapter 10.

Making Arrests

Making arrests is one of patrol officers' most serious and important responsibilities, as discussed in Chapter 3. Officers are commonly granted much discretion in this area, allowed to decide whether to arrest or not, and make decisions that can drastically change the futures of those engaged in unlawful activity. Frequently, a simple warning is the best alternative. However, in some situations, such as certain domestic violence incidents, officers are legally mandated to arrest, with statutory provision restricting their discretionary powers. Patrol officers deal with a wide variety of criminal and noncriminal situations; they also commonly deal with several such situations within a brief time, often without much background information.

Special Events

Many functions performed by patrol officers can also be required in handling *special events.* Patrol officers are often an essential part of large public gatherings, including sporting events, rock concerts, parades, celebrations and political rallies. The presence of uniformed patrol officers helps ensure peaceful assembly and prevents unlawful actions. Patrol officers also help expedite the traffic flow of both vehicles and pedestrians.

Crowds may be classified as self-controlled, active or explosive.

Handling explosive crowds is discussed in Chapter 6.

One trend is to hire off-duty patrol officers to perform the crowd-control function, particularly if the event is sponsored by private business or industry. Other alternatives include using volunteers or reserves to handle crowd-control problems.

Assisting at the Scene of a Fire

The first action of police officers who come upon an *uncontrolled fire* is to call the fire department. Only then should any attempts be made to control or suppress the fire. Other functions the police may serve include traffic control, ensuring that firefighting equipment can arrive quickly at the scene and helping search for and rescue people trapped by the fire. If children are trapped in a burning home, rescuers should check under beds and in closets because children frequently try to hide from the smoke and flames. Police officers can also provide crowd control, assist with first aid, transport injured people to the nearest medical facility and guard any personal property removed from the burning structure. Assisting with other emergency situations is the focus of Chapter 8.

The Community Service and Peacekeeping Function

In addition to their enforcement function, patrol officers also serve an important *peacekeeping function*. Although this function occupies the majority of the officers' time, it is largely unrecorded and unaccounted for. The public often misunderstands this function. When they see officers driving around simply observing the area, citizens often criticize the police for not chasing criminals or for not finding the "jerks" who "ripped off" their apartment when they were gone. Further, the peacekeeping function is seldom included in police training. The tendency is to think that all officers need is a little common sense. Consequently, texts, manuals and training sessions seldom include this important patrol function, leaving officers to "play it by ear." Patrol functions are summarized in Table 4.1.

To serve these various functions, officers have a variety of patrol methods from which to choose.

PATROL METHODS

The methods of patrol departments use vary, depending on local needs. Most jurisdictions use some form of foot patrol in combination with automobile patrol.

Patrol methods include foot, automobile, motorcycle, bicycle, Segway, mounted, air, water, special-terrain vehicle and K-9 assisted.

Table 4.1 Patrol Officer Functions

Function	Situations
Noncrime calls for service (80–90 percent of calls for service)	Noise and party calls Domestic disturbances Property owner/tenant disputes Nuisance complaints
Traffic control	Traffic delays Pedestrian problems Crashes Traffic violations Drunken drivers
Preliminary investigations	Scene security Emergency first aid Evidence procurement Victim/witness statements
Arrests	Warrants Suspect transport Court testimony
Public gatherings	Sporting events Political rallies Rock concerts Parades Special events
Community service	Speeches and presentations Auto and home lockouts Babies delivered Blood transported Home/business security checks

Foot Patrol

Foot patrol is the oldest form of patrol. Its use declined with the introduction of the police cruiser, but it has again gained prominence, largely because of the move toward community policing. Its primary advantage is close citizen contact. Other advantages include the enhanced rapport between officers and the citizens and its proactive, rather than reactive, nature, seeking to address neighborhood problems before they become crimes. Experiments with foot patrol conducted in Newark, New Jersey; Flint, Michigan; Oakland, California; Houston, Texas; and Boston, Massachusetts have yielded similar results—foot patrol programs improve public relations between the police and the community but do not affect crime rates. Miller (2008) says,

> While the actual effect of foot patrol officers on crime statistics is still being debated, surveys clearly show that citizens feel safer and more confident in their local police department when the officers are a living, breathing presence in their daily lives. Ironically, however, it is the foot patrols that are often the first to undergo budget cuts in favor of more flashy special tactics and investigative units.
>
> For patrol cops to do their jobs effectively, they must adopt a constructive territoriality about their patrol areas, sometimes known as owning the beat. By

> becoming increasingly familiar with the geography, economy, personality, and sociology of their beats, patrol cops come to know intuitively where's normal or what's out of place for their respective neighborhoods.
>
> Additionally, by adopting the optimal blend of professional detachment and emotional involvement in their neighborhoods, patrol officers develop what the business world calls buy-in, a personal stake in the welfare of their patrol community, a situation in which it is important to them to keep the peace and provide the highest quality of service: "This is my territory, and I'm going to do everything I can to make sure that it stays safe."

Craven (2009) acknowledges past results indicating that foot patrol had little effect on crime. However, he also reports, "Significant changes have been recorded . . . [D]epartments that take the positive elements of foot patrols and combine their efforts with data analysis that focuses on the time, location, and type of crime, may use the finding to develop strategies to decrease crime and enhance the quality of life in their communities," the focus of Chapter 6. The following key initiatives are suggested to help departments make foot patrol succeed (Craven):

- Determine the date, time and location of service calls by types, and create representative maps to aid in efficient and effective deployment.
- Complement statistical analysis with a community survey to obtain the opinions of residents and business owners regarding priority issues.
- Invite the community to participate in planning sessions.
- Recruit a range of individuals (both officers and civilians) to use various models of patrol, demonstrating that both police and civilians can address public expectations through a variety of approaches such as volunteer efforts with neighborhood watch programs and crime-prevention programming.

Craven stresses (2009), "Foot patrols should be developed as part of a proactive, integrated problem-solving strategy, and not as a reactive response to an incident, by taking five steps to develop and deploy successful foot patrols: (1) establish a structure for long-term implementation and evaluation, (2) establish criteria for locating foot patrols in the community, (3) establish overarching program goals and objective for implementing each foot patrol/beat location, (4) establish baseline information on the foot patrol area to assist with developing strategies, and (5) establish focused areas for implementing foot patrols."

One technique used during foot patrol is the *knock and talk*, where an officer knocks on a resident's door and asks if they can talk. It can be used to discover perceived problems or in investigations.

Foot patrol is not without its disadvantages, however. It is relatively expensive, it may interfere with the officer's ability to communicate with dispatch or obtain information available from them, and limits officers' ability to pursue suspects in vehicles as well as their ability to respond rapidly to calls for service in another area. However, technology has improved to the extent that officers are no longer tied to a patrol car for radio access and can request backup from a patrol car if needed. In addition, the geography of some jurisdictions, such as rural areas, makes the use of foot patrol highly impractical.

Automobile Patrol

Automobile patrol reverses the advantages and disadvantages of foot patrol. Unlike officers on foot, officers in squad cars can pursue suspects in vehicles and can respond rapidly to service calls in other areas. They also can transport equipment needed to process crime scenes as well as suspects they have arrested, and can have ready access to a variety of tools, such as their laptop computers, paperwork, additional weapons, emergency medical equipment and kits and other valuable supplies. Officers in squad cars can patrol a larger area in less time, or the same area as an officer on foot can, but more frequently.

Communication with the citizenry, however, is greatly reduced. In addition, the physical act of driving requires much of the officers' attention, diverting it from attention to subtle signs that criminal activity may be taking place. A further disadvantage is that automobiles are restricted in the areas they can access. Despite these disadvantages, automobile patrol continues to be a mainstay of the patrol division.

Automobile patrol has the greatest mobility and flexibility and is usually the most cost-effective patrol method.

To offset costs, many departments are buying refurbished highway patrol cars or using (and marking) vehicles seized from narcotics deals. Research on the effectiveness of the automobile patrol in preventing crime suggests that crimes prevented by a passing squad car are usually committed as soon as the police have gone.

41.3.1 CALEA STANDARD 41.3.1 states, "Conspicuously marked patrol cars are readily identified as law enforcement agency vehicles from every view and from a long distance, even at night. Conspicuous marking increases safety, serves as a warning to potential violators, and provides citizens with a feeling of security. Markings, if used, should include exterior mounted emergency lights, the agency's name, the emergency telephone number, and reflective materials placed on the sides and rear of the vehicle, such as reflective striping, lettering, or decals." (*Standards for Law Enforcement Agencies*, 5th edition, 2006)

Although most departments use vehicle patrol, departments vary in whether the vehicles are assigned to an officer or taken home when off duty, the number of officers assigned to each car, and the technology available in the vehicle.

Assigned Vehicle Programs Whether officers should be assigned their own patrol car and whether they should be able to take them home are disputed, often argued, emotionally charged issues. Many departments see such programs as a valuable recruiting tool. Numerous studies have been conducted on assigned/take-home police vehicles and car pool vehicles. Almost all support the use of take-home programs. The City of Oxford, Ohio, "Take Home Police Vehicle Program," implemented in 1997, found the program to be fiscally sound in its management and implementation by extending the life of the car, reducing major mechanical maintenance and encouraging "ownership" and "pride" in the vehicle by the officer assigned.

Data from a Florida jurisdiction, in which costs were compared between assigned and pool vehicles, found that the vehicle life of an assigned car was 5 years, whereas the average life cycle of a pooled car was 1.8 years. In addition, the total cost per assigned vehicle was $50,754, with an average cost per mile of $0.56, compared with a total cost of $65,309 for a pooled car and an average of $0.73 per mile. This analysis found that the most notable cost savings was in deputy's lost time at the beginning and end of each shift for equipment change-out, vehicle inspections, and equipment checks. The average amount of time loss was approximately 40 minutes per shift or approximately 11 days a year (Salisbury, 2007).

Research conducted on the Tacoma (Washington) Police Department's Assigned Vehicle Program (AVP), adopted in 1999 found that the benefits of assigning vehicles and allowing them to be taken home far outweigh costs and that police productivity was significantly enhanced through such a program (Lauria, 2007, p.192). Numerous other evaluations of take-home vehicle programs by departments across the country have reached similar conclusions.

Such programs are not without their drawbacks, however. Departments with take-home vehicles usually require more police cars than do those that share vehicles; if only select officers are assigned cars, other officers may feel they are not being treated equitably; take-home cars make it obvious where officers live and are more easily stolen or vandalized than are those parked in a secured police lot; assigned vehicles might be used for personal gain; and it is arguable who should pay the commuting costs.

One-Officer versus Two-Officer Patrol Units Whether automobile patrol should have one or two officers per vehicle is controversial. Arguments can be made for either. One-officer units are more cost effective from a personnel point of view, allowing for twice the coverage and twice the power of observation. In addition, officers riding alone may be more careful and more attentive to what is happening around them because they have no one to distract them with conversation.

Two-officer units are more cost effective in the number of patrol vehicles required and may increase officer safety. Some unionized departments' contracts stipulate that two officers be assigned to each patrol car. Some departments use two-officer units only in high-crime areas or only at night.

Many studies have concluded that one-officer cars are more cost-effective, but that such economic savings may come at the expense of officer safety: "Number crunching does not in and of itself resolve the matter. In examining the thousands of law enforcement officers assaulted during 2006, the U.S. Department of Labor found that an overwhelming number were assigned to single-officer vehicle patrols" (Scoville, 2008, p.40).

Efficient communication among one-officer units on patrol and a clear policy on when to call for backup is one way to increase the safety of single officers on patrol. Other ways include K-9–assisted patrol and vehicle-mounted video.

In-Car Video (ICV) Increasingly popular are compact, high-resolution video cameras mounted by the squad car's rearview mirror. Although initially many officers were uneasy about having a camera record their actions, in a recent *Police* survey, a "resounding 93 percent of respondents whose agencies have in-car videos now approve of the practice" (Basich, 2009, p.18). The survey found that 59.6 percent of agencies currently use in-car videos, with 36.3 percent of those agencies equipping all their cars with the videos. Respondents reported evidence and liability protection as the top benefits to law enforcement.

ICV cameras can record whatever happens in front of the car through a wide-angle lens. The camera is turned on and off by the officer and is supplemented by a lightweight, wireless microphone worn by the officer. The actual recording unit and tape are stored in a fireproof, bullet-resistant vault in the squad's trunk, inaccessible to suspects and officers alike. Therefore, any charges of tampering are avoided.

The cameras are used to document exactly what is said and done during a police stop, be it a traffic violation or a driving while intoxicated (DWI) stop. Such recorded documentation helps officers write their incident reports, assist in internal affairs investigations and help settle court cases. One such camera captured the murder of a Texas police officer and was key in gaining a conviction. Often people who are stopped and are acting belligerently will change their attitude completely when they learn they are being videotaped. In addition, the tapes serve a valuable training purpose.

41.3.8

CALEA STANDARD 41.3.8 states, "If in-car audio or video recording systems are used, a written directive establishes guidelines for situations for use; data security and access; and data storage and retention schedule." (*Standards for Law Enforcement Agencies*, 5th edition, 2006)

If officers need to leave their vehicles, they can still record what they encounter using VIDMIC, a shoulder microphone equipped with a video and audio recorder and a still camera (Garrett, 2008, p.122). Data shows that when such video evidence is collected and a suspect alleges officer misconduct, the officer is exonerated 96.2 percent of the time (Garrett, p.127).

Global Positioning and Information Systems (GPS/GIS) "Global positioning satellite (GPS) tracking is a powerful law enforcement tool for monitoring vehicles, packages, contraband and people with satellite photos, near real-time location updates and detailed reporting features" (Orput and Ivy, 2008, p.8). This technology is vital for both global positioning systems (GPS) and geographic information systems (GIS).

GPS is a satellite-based navigation system consisting of a network of 31 actively broadcasting satellites placed into orbit by the U. S. Department of Defense. The satellites circle the earth twice a day in precise orbits and transmit signal information to GPS receivers on the ground, which use triangulation to calculate the user's exact location.

Many GPS systems have added automatic vehicle location (AVL) software: "AVL/GPS is there to ensure officer safety. If an officer does not respond to the radio, then the dispatcher should immediately 'ping' that officer's location and advise a field supervisor. The time lost looking for an officer without an AVL/GPS start point can be the difference between life and death" (Brewer, 2007, p.53). More progressive departments are using live GPS that allows dispatch and supervisors to monitor, via a secured server, real-time locations of all squads without pinging.

Brewer notes, "AVL is a major benefit to patrol supervisors when deploying resources at an in-progress dynamic incident. Being able to actually see the scene on a map or better with an orthographic overlay is another way to help reduce the demands on the supervisor. When responding units are in quadrants, the supervisor has a visual picture of the best way to redeploy those units." Many departments use GPS-enabled AVL systems to keep track of resources and better manage their patrol districts. Hubbard (2008, p.A01) notes,

> Across the country, police are using GPS devices to snare thieves, drug dealers, sexual predators and killers, often without a warrant or court order. Privacy advocates say tracking suspects electronically constitutes illegal search and seizure, violating Fourth Amendment rights of protection against unreasonable searches and seizures, and is another step toward George Orwell's Big Brother Society. Law enforcement officials, when they discuss the issue at all, said GPS is essentially the same as having an officer trail someone, just cheaper and more accurate. . . . Most of the time judges have sided with police.

GIS are also vital to police: "Every incident called in to a 911 center is associated with a real-world location where people need help. Immediate location awareness for dispatch and first responders during an incident can often mean the difference between life and death. Today the majority of law enforcement agencies use some degree of geographic information systems (GIS) mapping technology to locate callers and provide first responders with critical information before arriving on scene" (Wandrei, 2007, p.56).

Voice-Activated Patrol Car Equipment—Project 54 Patrol vehicles have a broad array of high-tech radios, computers, GPS, video cameras, radars, lights, sirens and databases available to field officers. In many police vehicles, these can all be activated by voice commands, for example engaging emergency lights and siren, accessing NCIC, activating radar, and the like. According to Molnar (2007, p.20), "Voice recognition makes patrol work safer and easier." He describes Project 54, which takes its name from the classic TV show *Car 54, Where Are You?*, as a platform designed to integrate real-time information processing for patrol vehicles and the control of in-car equipment through speech command.

Motorcycle Patrol

Motorcycle patrol was first used more than 100 years ago by officers in Pittsburgh, Pennsylvania, to patrol the streets and enforce traffic regulations. Most police departments have their motorcycles marked with the same insignia as their patrol cars. Motorcycle patrol has many of the same advantages as automobile patrol, especially speed and maneuverability. Motorcycles have greater access than automobiles to some areas and are better suited to heavy traffic, narrow alleys and rugged terrain.

Some departments, in their quest to improve their patrol division's efficiency and effectiveness, have begun exploring alternative vehicles for patrol. Here, a New York Police Department detective demonstrates the Vectrix eco-friendly electric motor scooter, which the department's motorcycle division will be trained to use.
© AP Images/Kathy Willens

Disadvantages include motorcycles' relatively high cost to operate; their limited use in bad weather; their inability to carry large amounts of equipment, evidence or prisoners; and the danger involved in riding them. Proper protective clothing and helmets are a must. A motorcycle also offers officers much less protection than a squad car should a person in a vehicle being pursued decide to start shooting.

Bicycle Patrol

Bicycle patrol is not new. In the 1880s, police in many large cities patrolled on bicycles. But automobile patrol displaced bicycle patrol for nearly 100 years until 1988 when bicycle patrol was reintroduced in Seattle, Washington. Bicycle patrol is growing in popularity. According to Wes Branham, president of the Law Enforcement Bicycle Association (LEBA), there is now a bicycle unit in nearly every major police department: "It's been really successful. The big trend is in community policing and this is community policing at its very best" (Moore 2007, p.58).

A study by the Cincinnati, Ohio, Police Department compared activity of patrol officers on bikes with those in cars and found that bike patrol officers reported significantly more activity in many categories, including arrests, crimes discovered, warrants served and motorist assists. Bicycle officers are also an important public relations tool, helpful in bringing citizens closer to the police. Another study that examined bike patrol versus motor patrol in several cities found a higher amount of contact with the public by police officers patrolling on bicycles (Menton, 2007, p.78).

Another benefit to bicycle patrol is its cost effectiveness. For the cost of one police cruiser, several bicycle patrol officers can be outfitted. Bicycles are

Bicycle patrols are becoming increasingly popular because of their ease in operation, their relatively low operational costs and their acceptance by the public.
© AP Images/Alan Diaz

also very maneuverable and good for enforcing bicycle, motorized scooter, rollerblading and skateboarding ordinances. On the Las Vegas strip, where most of the elite casinos are located, all patrol is on bicycle: on the streets, in the parking areas and inside the casinos when officers respond to calls. Motor patrols go on the strip only when called for emergencies.

Additional advantages of bicycles include their stealth factor, allowing officers to sneak up on situations such as drug buys, and their green factor, referring to their environmentally friendly power source. Furthermore, bicycle patrol provides a good source of exercise and promotes the physical fitness of officers. Bicycles often are used in parks and on beaches and have many of the same advantages and disadvantages as motorcycles. Like motorcycles, bicycles leave the patrol officer extremely vulnerable. Officers should have the proper safety equipment and follow all basic safety practices while on bicycle patrol.

Segways

A newer method of patrol is the Segway Personal Transporter, commonly known as the "Segway PT" or simply a "Segway." Introduced in 2001, they are now being used by police departments throughout the country and for tasks ranging from patrol to hazardous material (hazmat) response. With only two wheels and a gyroscope balance system, the Segway was initially a hard sell as a viable patrol vehicle, but it has since caught on and now provides many law enforcement agencies with an enhanced way to patrol: "Because riders stand an additional eight inches off of the ground, they have an improved perspective on sidewalks and streets and inside buildings, and are also more visible and approachable in community policing situations" (Basich, 2008, p.22).

A Metropolitan Transportation Authority officer uses a Segway to patrol the Union Station in Los Angeles, California. Here he is giving directions to a family on vacation.
© AP Images/Damian Dovarganes

Bradley (2008, p.48) observes, "Whether they're used as a platform for engaging area youths in conversation or as a new avenue for patrol and quick response, Segway Personal Transporters (PTs) offer police agencies many possibilities. In the sweltering heat of Albuquerque, New Mexico, police officers have found that Segway PTs do more than prevent crime and catch crooks; they draw crowds." According to one Segway officer, "Before we got Segways, we would walk miles and miles. Now, we're able to respond to calls more quickly and not be as tired" (Bradley, p.48). The Segway moves by syncing its gyros and electronics with the officer's body. When the officer leans forward, the Segway goes. The further the officer leans, the faster the device goes, up to 12.5 miles per hour (mph).

Mounted Patrol

The greatest advantage of mounted patrol is that officers on horseback are usually more acceptable than K-9s as crowd-control instruments and are much more effective at controlling a disorderly crowd than officers on foot or in any kind of vehicle (other than a tank). One horse and rider is equal to 10 foot patrol officers in a crowd-control situation.

Mounted officers can often handle 911 calls and other emergencies with more speed and visibility than foot patrols. In addition, mounted patrol members can help search for evidence at crime scenes, round up stray animals after a truck has tipped over and search for lost children or bodies in tall corn or fields.

Mounted patrol is decreasing in the United States but is still used in some large cities for crowd and traffic control and in some rural jurisdictions. Expense is one of the main disadvantages of mounted patrol.

Air Patrol

"The value of airborne law enforcement has been demonstrated since 1929, when the New York City Police Department started a fixed-wing (airplane) aviation unit to combat a growing menace of barnstormers" (Solosky, 2009, p.38). Air

Mounted patrol serves important symbolic and practical functions. They are especially good for crowd control; 1 horse and rider is equal to 10 foot patrol officers in a crowd-control situation.

patrol is highly effective when large areas are involved. For example, searching for a suspect, an escaped convict, a lost child or a downed aircraft can all be accomplished most efficiently by air. Using technology such as infrared or other heat sensory detectors can also help aerial surveillance be more effective in locating hidden or elusive suspects. Small airplanes and helicopters are used as eyes in the sky to report traffic tie-ups and to work along with police cars to conduct criminal surveillance or to detect, clock and stop speeding vehicles and can reduce the hazards and costs associated with high-speed pursuits.

Helicopters are valuable in rescue efforts during disasters such as fires in tall buildings, floods and earthquakes. Police aircraft and helicopters are also a cost-effective way to transport prisoners long distances. Air patrol, however, is quite expensive to operate and maintain. Other disadvantages include citizen complaints about the noise and about being spied on.

Nonetheless, "In the past 10 years, thanks in large part to the military surplus program, more law enforcement agencies are starting their own aviation units to take advantage of this strong and powerful asset. Today, there are approximately 800 U.S. law enforcement agencies flying aircraft" (Solosky, 2009, p.38).

Personal Vertical Takeoff and Landing Aircraft

A promising new method of patrol is the personal vertical takeoff and landing (VTOL) aircraft. Cowper (2004, p.36) says, "The VTOL aircraft bring with them capabilities that will allow the creation of new and innovative tactics vitally necessary for police to be successful in the future." Cowper asks, "What if the majority of pursuits could be conducted by aircraft capable of following, monitoring and containing a suspect without disrupting traffic or further endangering innocent bystanders, helping to coordinate the deployment of ground units from a distance until the suspect could be safely cornered and captured?" At present, the helicopter is the only practical VTOL available to law enforcement, but a search of VTOL online provides interesting reading of what might be in store in the near future.

Water Patrol

Water patrol units are extremely specialized and not in great use except in areas with extensive coasts or a great deal of lake or river traffic. Like aircraft, boats are expensive to buy, operate and maintain. Further, those who operate them must have special training. Nonetheless, boats are the best means to effectively control violators of water safety regulations as well as to apprehend drug and gun smugglers. They are also valuable in rescue operations during times of flooding as well as in dragging operations for drowning cases.

A trend in water patrol is the use of personal watercraft (PWC) or Jet Ski, which has a very shallow draft, high maneuverability and stability. They are also easy to operate. The front compartment allows for storage of a ticket book, high-powered binoculars and a portable breath test. Many are equipped with public-address systems, sirens and lights.

In Miami Beach, Florida, for example, officers on personal watercraft find they can approach areas not accessible to conventional patrol boats because of shallow water, low bridges or other impediments. The watercraft have been used in search and recovery, in recovering drowning victims, in deterring boating law violations (including reckless operation and DUI violations), in checking fishing licenses and catch limits and in improved public relations.

Special-Terrain Vehicles

Police departments responsible for areas with extensive coastlines may also rely on jeeps or amphibious vehicles to patrol the beaches. Those who must patrol where snow is common frequently rely on snowmobiles. Departments whose jurisdiction includes remote parts of the country, including hundreds of acres of desert, may also use jeeps or all-terrain vehicles (ATVs). An additional advantage of ATVs is that they can carry a substantial amount of support equipment. Special-terrain vehicles are useful for rescue missions as well as for routine patrol.

K-9–Assisted Patrol

The K-9–assisted patrol is becoming more popular, with even smaller departments beginning to establish K-9 units. The K-9 unit can be used to control crowds, break up fights, recover lost articles or find evidence. In addition, dogs can provide protection for a one-officer patrol.

Detector dogs are specially trained to sniff out narcotics, explosives or bodies (live and cadaver). Drug- and bomb-sniffing dogs are used extensively in international airports and border checkpoints. Tracker dogs can follow the scent of a fleeing suspect or a missing person. Search and rescue K-9s were used after the Oklahoma City bombing and the September 11, 2001, terrorist attack on the World Trade Center to locate trapped or deceased victims. Besides detection, canines can be trained and used for apprehension, chasing down and "holding" fleeing suspects until officers can gain physical control of such individuals. Dogs may be cross-trained in both detection and apprehension.

K-9 units are also an asset to public relations efforts. They can be used for demonstrations at state fairs or in local schools, showing how well trained and under control the animals are. According to a *Police* magazine survey ("Almost 50% of Agencies Routinely Use K-9s," 2008, p.14), the majority of agencies (74 percent) use the "iconic American police dog," the German shepherd. The second most popular breed used is the Belgian Malinois (44 percent). Like other forms of specialized patrol, K-9–assisted patrol has disadvantages. One drawback occurs when a police dog is trained to work with only one handler. Should that handler become ill or disabled or be killed, the dog must be retrained. Further, if a K-9 handler is wounded, the dog may not allow emergency personnel near the officer to help. To counter such problems, many departments are cross-training their dogs to work with two handlers. Another difficulty is that a K-9, like most dogs, is territorial, and its handler and its K-9 cruiser are part of its territory. It may become aggressive without being told to do so if its handler or cruiser is approached by strangers.

Because many dogs are donated, training generally constitutes the greatest expense of K-9 units. The training usually takes 10 to 12 weeks and can cost one to two thousand dollars per team, in addition to the officer's salary during this time. The other major expense is modifying the patrol car, removing the back seat and replacing it with a platform. Some units are equipped with a radio-controlled door or window opener that allows officers to release their K-9s from a distance. An alternative is for officers to leave a back window rolled down so the dog can get out of the car if called. Other costs of maintaining a canine unit include annual, routine veterinary care and food.

Another factor to consider when implementing a K-9 program is the potential increase in vulnerability to lawsuits, particularly in cases involving searches and use-of-force issues. Because law enforcement officers use K-9s to find people, clear buildings, sniff out bombs and locate evidence or contraband, their use implicates the Fourth Amendment. In *United States v. Place* (1983), the Supreme Court held that the exposure of luggage to a canine sniff in a public place did not constitute a search. However, courts are divided over when a dog sniff constitutes a search, and state courts may find dog sniffs are searches under their own state constitutions. Courts have also ruled police use of K-9s as a use of force, some going so far as to deem it lethal force. However, as one officer stated in defending the "lethality" of his K-9, "I can recall the dog. I can't recall a bullet." As noted in Chapter 3, one source of K-9 related case law is the Web site of Terry Fleck, an expert in canine legalities.

Combination Patrol

No single patrol method or combination of methods is best. Usually, the greater the variety of methods available, the more effective a department will be. Which methods of patrol to use will vary depending on the department's physical jurisdiction, the types of crimes occurring, the size of the department, the training of its officers and its budget. Once a department knows which methods it has available, it can determine effective patrol techniques.

PATROL TECHNIQUES AND STRATEGIES

Patrol is, indeed, an essential function of law enforcement, yet it is not always as effective as it could or should be: "One of the things we learned from Sept. 11 was that attacks on America will come from within, and that means that good cops doing routine police work will come across these people if we actively do police work and take our responsibilities seriously" (Stockton, 2008, p.8).

To improve effectiveness, numerous patrol techniques and strategies have been tried and evaluated throughout the years, including routine patrol, rotating or fixed area and shift assignments, rapid response, differential police response and directed patrol. Perhaps the most classic study of patrol as it is traditionally performed is the Kansas City Preventive Patrol Experiment.

The Kansas City Preventive Patrol Experiment

Although this study was conducted in 1972, it is still the most comprehensive study of the effects of routine patrol. In this experiment, 15 beats in Kansas City were divided into three groups, each with five beats:

Group 1—Reactive Beats: No routine patrol, responding only to calls for service.

Group 2—Control Beats: Maintained their normal level of routine preventive patrol.

Group 3—Proactive Beats: Doubled or tripled the level of routine preventive patrol.

The Kansas City Preventive Patrol Experiment found that increasing or decreasing routine preventive patrol had no measurable effect on

- Crime.
- Citizens' fear of crime.
- Community attitudes toward the police on delivery of police services.
- Police response time.
- Traffic accidents.

Says Klockars (1983, p.130), commenting on the findings of the Kansas City experiment, "It makes about as much sense to have police patrol routinely in cars to fight crime as it does to have fire fighters patrol routinely in fire trucks to fight fire." Although the Kansas City experiment demonstrated the limited effect that increasing or decreasing the number of officers engaged in unstructured random patrol appears to have, other studies have found changing area and shift assignments can have a significant effect.

Area and Shift Assignments

Patrol shifts typically divide the 24-hour period into three 8-hour shifts. One common division is 7:00 A.M. to 3:00 P.M., 3:00 P.M. to 11:00 P.M. and 11:00 P.M. to 7:00 A.M. (the dog shift). Sundermeier (2008, p.60) describes the 12-hour shift used by the Lincoln (Nebraska) Police Department, providing "excellent coverage during peak times—typically late afternoon and evening and on into the early morning hours on weekends." A day shift and night shift provide 24-hour coverage with another shift scheduled from early afternoon to early morning. Staggering start times provides constant coverage at the beginning and end of shifts. The 10-hour schedule provides a day off for every day worked plus four hours of flextime during each two-week pay period. The department also continues the traditional 8-hour shift schedule for those officers who preferred to work that way.

Whatever time periods are used, scheduling shifts can be made much easier by software: "While it may not be possible to manage all the functions that scheduling software programs can perform with just one click of a mouse—although it's close—the time savings offered by these new products are significant" (Mills-Senn, 2008, p.62).

Software can also make the assignment of beats easier and more effective. The municipality served by the department typically is divided into geographic areas—beats—on the basis of personnel available for patrol. Many departments rotate shifts or areas or both. Other departments assign permanent shifts, areas or both, feeling this allows officers to become more familiar with their assignments and, consequently, more effective in patrolling. Regardless of whether an agency uses rotating or permanent beat assignments, having officers allocated to various beats tends to reduce disparities in how officers take calls, for example, having only one or a few officers who actively respond to calls throughout the jurisdiction while others are able to avoid responding at all. A U.S. Bureau of Justice Statistics study (*Community Policing in Local Police Departments*, n.d.) found that 90 percent of all local law enforcement agencies serving populations of 50,000 or more helped facilitate community policing goals by giving patrol officers responsibility for specific geographic beats.

The shifts and areas new officers are assigned to depend on the supervisor's philosophy. Some departments assign rookies to high-crime areas and "fast" shifts to help them learn their new job more rapidly and to assess their performance. Other departments assign rookies to the slowest shifts and the lowest crime areas to allow them to ease into their new job. Two basic forms of shift scheduling are used. The first assigns equal numbers of patrol officers to each of the three shifts. The second assigns officers based on anticipated need.

As departments become more proactive, many are using *proportionate assignment*, which considers not only the number of calls but many other factors as well. In **proportionate assignment**, area assignments are based on the data available from requests for service, taking into account the amount and severity of crime occurring in various areas, population density, routes to the areas and any special problems that might be involved, such as large groups of non-English-speaking citizens. Boundaries of the patrol beat are determined by considering how rapidly a responding car can cover the area, and assignments are made so that in normal circumstances police can respond within three minutes.

proportionate assignment
Determination of area assignments by requests for service based on available data. No area is larger than the time it takes a car to respond in three minutes or less.

Response Time

Patrol effectiveness is frequently measured in **response time**, the time elapsed between when the call is received and when the police arrive on the scene. One reason for rapid response is the opportunity to apprehend a

response time
The time elapsed from when the need for police arises and when they arrive on the scene.

person engaged in criminal activity. However, as Klockars (1983, p.130) stresses, "Police currently make on-scene arrests in about 3 percent of the serious crimes reported to them. If they traveled faster than a speeding bullet to all reports of serious crimes, this on-scene arrest rate would rise to no higher than 5 percent."

Spelman and Brown (1991) replicated the citizen reporting component of the Kansas City Experiment response time analysis and found, "In the cities we studied, . . . *arrests that could be attributed to fast police response were made in only 2.9 percent of reported serious crimes*" (p.164). Spelman and Brown attribute this low response-related arrest rate largely to the fact that 75 percent of all serious crimes are **discovery crimes**; that is, they are completed before they are discovered and reported. This is in direct contrast to **involvement crimes**, in which the victim and suspect confront each other.

discovery crimes
Offenses that have been completed and whose scenes have been abandoned before the crimes are noticed. In contrast to *involvement crimes*.

involvement crimes
Offenses in which the victim and the suspect confront each other. In contrast to *discovery crimes*.

Citizen reporting time affects the possibility of on-scene arrests more than does police response time. Citizens delay calling the police because of decision-making problems or problems in communicating with the police.

After citizens decide to call the police, they may encounter other problems: no phone available, not knowing what number to call or not being able to communicate clearly with the person receiving the call. Response time is also increased when the department does not have enough patrol officers available for such duty at any particular time. Nonetheless, citizens *expect* a rapid response when they call. This expectation could be modified, however. The response may not need to be immediate, and it may not have to be made by a sworn officer. Many police departments are implementing differential police response strategies.

Differential Police Response

differential police response strategies
Practice of varying the rapidity of response as well as the responder, based on the type of incident and the time of occurrence.

proximate
Closely related in space, time or order; very near.

Differential police response strategies vary the rapidity of response as well as the responder based on the type of incident and the time of occurrence. Differential police response strategies replace the traditional "first-come, first-served" and as-fast-as-possible response, depending on the type of incident and whether it is in progress, proximate or cold. Usually, if a crime is in progress, the response will be immediate and made by a sworn officer. If it is **proximate**, that is, recently committed, response to the call may be put ahead of other, less urgent calls. If the incident is "cold," that is, it happened several hours before, the response may be "as time permits" or even by appointment.

The most common alternatives used in differential response strategies include response by sworn or nonsworn personnel and whether it is immediate, expedited, routine or by appointment. Other alternatives for minor crimes include contact by telephone, mail, referral or no response. For example, a major personal injury would require an immediate response by sworn personnel, whereas a minor noncrime call might be handled by a referral. As long as callers are told what to expect and the reasoning behind the type of response selected, they usually are satisfied with the response, even if it is delayed up to several hours or scheduled as an appointment for the following day.

Directed Patrol

If a department's goals are clear, and if the department has kept accurate records on calls for service and on crimes committed in the community, then based on this data, patrol time should be effectively structured to provide the best service and protection possible. It is usually much more productive to have officers' discretionary time directed toward accomplishing specific department objectives than to expect each officer simply to do his or her "thing." **Directed patrol** uses officers' discretionary patrol time to focus on specific department goals. These goals are often identified through problem-oriented policing.

directed patrol
Use of officers' discretionary patrol time to focus on specific department goals.

PATROL AND PROBLEM-ORIENTED POLICING

Problem-oriented policing (POP)—that is, grouping calls for service to identify specific problems—was first formally introduced by Herman Goldstein in 1979. Based on 20 years of research, this approach suggests a fundamental shift in perspective.

problem-oriented policing (POP)
A proactive approach to patrol and policing that focuses on problems to be solved rather than incidents to be responded to.

Problem-oriented policing requires a shift in perspective from incident driven to problem driven; from reactive to proactive.

In this approach, police are trained to think not in terms of incidents but in terms of problems. According to Goldstein (1990, p.33), "In handling incidents, police officers usually deal with the most obvious, superficial manifestations of a deeper problem—not the problem itself." He contends that "incidents are usually handled as isolated, self-contained events. Connections are not systematically made among them, except when they suggest a common crime pattern leading to identifying the offender." What is needed, suggests Goldstein (p.33), is a different approach—problem-oriented policing: "The first step in problem-oriented policing is to move beyond just handling incidents. It calls for recognizing that incidents are often merely overt symptoms of problems. This pushes the police in two directions: (1) It requires that they recognize the relationships between incidents (similarities of behavior, location, persons involved, etc.); and (2) it requires that they take a more in-depth interest in incidents by acquainting themselves with some of the conditions and factors that give rise to them."

Problem-oriented policing has been used to address many community problems, such as burglaries, graffiti, sex offenses and trespassing. The SARA problem-solving technique has contributed greatly to its effectiveness.

The SARA Problem-Solving Process

The problem-solving process called SARA consists of four stages:

- Scanning—identifying the problem
- Analysis—learning the problem's causes, scope and effects
- Response—acting to alleviate the problem
- Assessment—determining whether the response worked

Excellence in Problem-Oriented Policing (2002, pp.2–3) describes each of these four stages:

Scanning:

- Identify recurring problems of concern to the public and the police.
- Prioritize problems.
- Develop broad goals.
- Confirm that the problems exist.
- Select one problem for examination.

Analysis:

- Try to identify and understand the events and conditions that precede and accompany the problem.
- Identify the consequences of the problem for the community.
- Determine how frequently the problem occurs and how long it has been taking place.
- Identify the conditions that give rise to the problem.
- Narrow the scope of the problem as specifically as possible.
- Identify a variety of resources that may be of assistance in developing a deeper understanding of the problem.

Response:

- Search for what communities with similar problems have done.
- Brainstorm interventions.
- Choose among the alternative solutions.
- Outline a response plan and identify responsible parties.
- State the specific goals for the response plan.
- Identify relevant data to be collected.
- Carry out the planned activities.

Assessment:

- Determine whether the plan was implemented.
- Determine whether the goals were attained and collect pre- and postresponse qualitative and quantitative data.
- Identify any new strategies needed to augment the original plan.
- Conduct ongoing assessment to ensure continued effectiveness.

Assessment that determines if a response was implemented as planned.

Assessment that determines if a problem declined.

Assessing Responses to Problems According to Eck (2002, p.6), "You begin planning for an evaluation when you take on a problem. The evaluation builds throughout the SARA process, culminates during the assessment and provides findings that help you determine if you should revisit earlier stages to improve the response." Figure 4.1 illustrates the problem-solving process and evaluation.

Eck (2002, p.10) describes two types of evaluations to conduct: **process evaluation** that determines if the response was implemented as planned and **impact evaluation** that determines if the problem declined. Table 4.2 provides

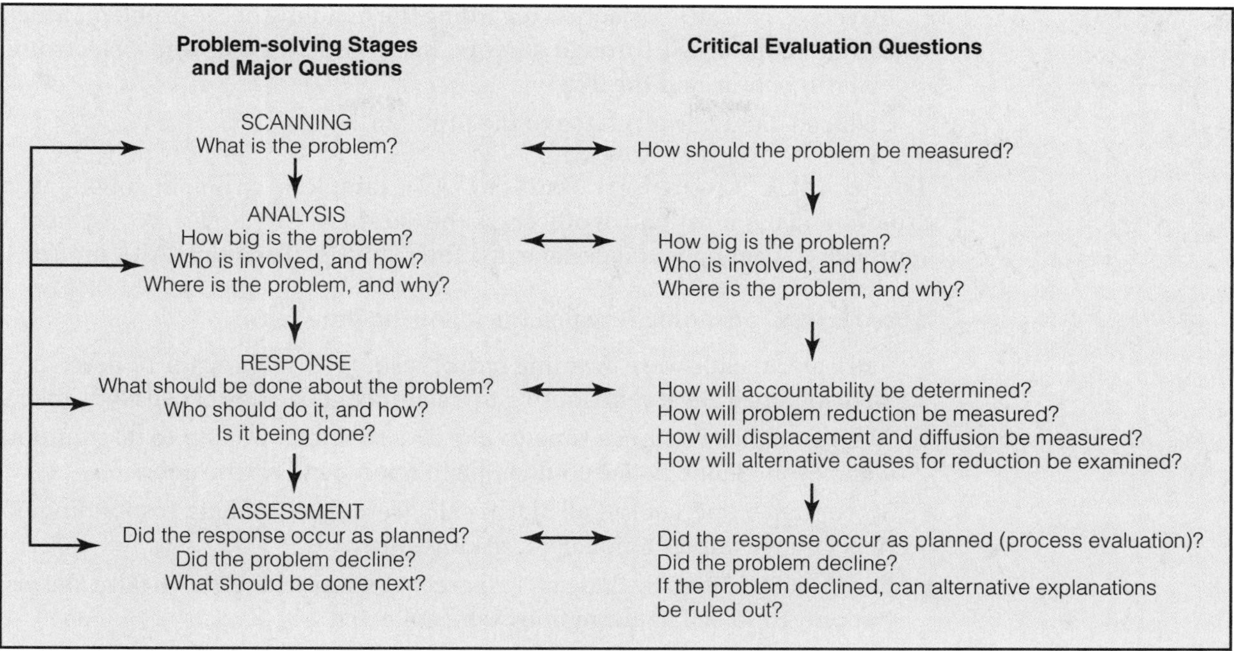

FIGURE 4.1 The Problem-Solving Process and Evaluation
Source: John E. Eck. *Assessing Responses to Problems: An Introductory Guide for Police Problem-Solvers*. Washington, DC: Office of Community Oriented Policing Services. 2002, p.6.

guidance in interpreting the results of process and impact evaluation. Several nontraditional measures will indicate if a problem has been affected by the interventions (Eck, p.27):

- Reduced instances of repeat victimization
- Decreases in related crimes or incidents
- Neighborhood indicators: increased profits for legitimate businesses in target area; increased use of area/increased (or reduced) foot and vehicular traffic; increased property values; improved neighborhood appearance; increased occupancy in problem buildings; less loitering; fewer abandoned cars; less truancy

Table 4.2 Interpreting Results of Process and Impact Evaluations

		Process Evaluation Results	
		Response implemented as planned, or nearly so	**Response not implemented, or implemented in a radically different manner than planned**
Impact Evaluation Results	Problem declined	A. Evidence that the response caused the decline	C. Suggests that other factors may have caused the decline, or that the response was accidentally effective
	Problem did not decline	B. Evidence that the response was ineffective, and that a different response should be tried	D. Little is learned; perhaps if the response had been implemented as planned, the problem would have declined, but this is speculative

Source: John E. Eck. *Assessing Responses to Problems: An Introductory Guide for Police Problem-Solvers*. Washington, DC: Office of Community Oriented Policing Services, 2002, p.10.

- Increased citizen satisfaction regarding the handling of the problem, which can be determined through surveys, interviews, focus groups, electronic bulletin boards and the like
- Reduced citizen fear related to the problem

The SARA Model in Action An example of problem solving in a situation facing most patrol officers is the Salt Lake City Police Department's approach to dealing with false alarms. Their solution used the SARA model.

Scanning Scanning revealed the following problems:

- False alarm calls were draining patrol resources, making up 12 percent of all dispatched calls, contributing to a significant backlog of calls for service.
- Average police response time to alarm activations was up to 40 minutes, well beyond when police could hope to apprehend an intruder.
- More than 99 percent of all alarm calls were false, making responding officers increasingly complacent, risking injury.
- Nearly $500,000 of the budget (1.2 percent) was attributable to false alarms, but only $150,000 in alarm fines were collected.
- False alarms had three main causes: user errors resulting from insufficient training; inadequate verification by alarm company monitoring stations; and improper installation, inferior equipment and application at the alarm site.

Analysis Analysis revealed that past efforts to reduce the volume of false alarms through permits, warnings, fines and suspensions had only a modest effect. Examining other approaches tried elsewhere, from cost recovery to alarm industry regulation to outsourcing alarm administration, similarly proved only moderate effectiveness. Police response to alarms was most effective and efficient if the police had verification that an alarm activation indicated suspicious activity. Private security guards were ideally suited to make the initial verification. A legal opinion established that police were under no legal obligation to respond to all alarm activations.

Response The police department proposed to the city council that a verified alarm response ordinance be required in all alarm activations and that eyewitness verification of suspicious activity be identified by alarm company personnel or a private guard before notifying the police department. A campaign was then conducted to inform the public, elected officials and the alarm industry about the purposes and advantages of verified response, and the police department conducted training for private security officers.

Assessment The police department experienced a 90 percent decrease in alarm-related calls for service during the first nine months, representing 6,338 fewer calls for service or the equivalent of five full-time patrol officers (valued at about $400,000). There were fewer backlogs of calls for service, and responses to high-priority calls for service dropped from five to three minutes.

Alarm owners benefit by achieving a 6- to 15-minute alarm activation response compared to the 40-minute average the police provided. The alarm industry benefited by now providing customers with a valued quick response.

By using problem-oriented policing and no longer attempting to manage a private sector problem, the Salt Lake City's verified response alarm ordinance provides a long-term solution to a problem the department had struggled with for 20 years.

PATROL AND COMMUNITY POLICING

Patrol officers can be catalysts for joint police and community problem-solving endeavors. Part of the evolution to community policing involves a shift in the patrol methods used, such as greater use of foot, bicycle, mounted and K-9–assisted patrol. Community policing also involves the redeployment of patrol officers from vehicles into small, decentralized police posts. Some of the most effective community policing strategies used by patrol officers are quite simple and cost nothing. For example, the Burger King in Charles County, Maryland, was the first business in the country to set aside space as a "writing station" for officers. According to the owner, the main reason for setting up the writing stations was to help employees feel safer and to take an active part in community-police relations.

Another example is New York City's Cab Watch. The New York Police Department helped train Cab Watch taxi drivers to report incidents and provided the drivers with donated 911-direct wireless phones. In its first two years, Cab Watch expanded from the 50-driver pilot program to more than 1,700 who have alerted police to hundreds of incidents, as well as helping save lives in car crashes and building fires.

Other strategies are more complex and involve numerous partnerships with patrol officers. One such strategy is the Model Neighborhood Program, used in West Valley City, modeled after the Los Angeles Police Department (LAPD) Model Neighborhood Program. The program is a partnership of city, county and federal agencies; the community; and the local police department. The local officer assigned to the area gets the names and addresses of property owners and then coordinates with. U.S. Department of Housing and Urban Development (HUD) personnel and task force members of the police department to plan and conduct an area sweep serving arrest warrants, evicting problem tenants and identifying specific "hot spots" needing extra attention. Coordination with local government agencies responsible for graffiti removal, impounding abandoned cars and trash pickup is also undertaken. At the same time, the local city attorney or ordinance enforcement officer works with the police to contact owners of neglected property and invites them to participate in the program by evicting problem tenants, renovating their properties and implementing screening procedures for new tenants. If owners are unwilling to improve their property, abatement procedures are initiated to confiscate and raze the property.

SUMMARY

Patrol service has been described as the backbone of the police department. Officers on patrol serve many functions. Among the important patrol functions are responding to noncrime calls for service, controlling traffic, assisting at the scene of a crime, conducting preliminary investigations, gathering intelligence, making arrests, patrolling public gatherings and special events, assisting at the scene of a fire, providing community service and general peacekeeping activities and partnering with others to solve problems related to crime and disorder. Between 80 and 90 percent of all calls for police service are of a noncriminal nature. Patrol officers are often responsible for maintaining order with large groups of people. Crowds may be classified as self-controlled, active or explosive.

Methods of patrol include foot, automobile, motorcycle, bicycle, Segway, mounted, air, water, special-terrain vehicles and K-9 assisted. Automobile patrol has the greatest mobility and flexibility and is usually the most cost-effective method of patrol.

Different patrol techniques have met with varying degrees of success. The Kansas City Preventive Patrol Experiment found that increasing or decreasing routine preventive patrol had no measurable effect on crime, citizens' fear of crime, community attitudes toward the police on delivery of police services, police response time or traffic accidents. Regardless of the patrol strategy used, police effectiveness is greatly influenced by citizen involvement. Citizen reporting time affects the possibility of on-scene arrests more than does police response time. Response time is often lengthened because citizens delay calling the police because of decision-making problems or problems communicating with the police.

Problem-oriented policing requires a shift in perspective from incident driven to problem driven; from reactive to proactive. It often depends on the SARA technique. The SARA problem-solving technique has contributed greatly to policing effectiveness and consists of four stages:

- Scanning—identifying the problem
- Analysis—learning the problem's causes, scope and effects
- Response—acting to alleviate the problem
- Assessment—determining whether the response worked

APPLICATION

The local chamber of commerce has asked that you assign an officer to foot patrol in the business district because of numerous problems, such as vandalism, shoplifting, boisterous conduct by young people and general disruption of business because of gang activity.

You realize foot patrol is proactive, designed to prevent crime and deal with social problems before they become overtly criminal. The city council wants you to proceed; it will add an officer to your department to provide this service.

Instructions

Write a policy and procedure that would offer guidelines to an officer and satisfy the business community's request. Keep in mind that foot patrol is an important assignment with many advantages over automobile patrol: more person-to-person contact, high visibility, enhanced public relations, the potential to be proactive and solve problems and increased community support.

Begin the policy with a statement of need. Consider that the officer, being highly visible, may need more supervision. Who will supervise the officer, and what will the officer's duties be? Some type of communication with the officer while on duty must be established, and a system of assignment decided on. Decide what parameters would be useful to officers on foot patrol when they employ the directed-patrol approach and problem-oriented policing. List expectations for the officer's conduct and responsibilities while serving this important function.

AN EXERCISE IN CRITICAL THINKING

At 2:04 A.M. on a Friday, a burglar alarm went off at Prior Lake Marine, a business located on the outskirts of Prior Lake. Officer Ferderer of the Prior Lake Police Department, responding to the dispatcher's request at 2:07 A.M. for assistance in investigating a burglary in progress, drove toward the burglary scene. The only car he saw was a red 2000 Honda Accord with three men in it proceeding on a residential street just two blocks from Prior Lake Marine and headed away from that area. Ferderer turned and stopped the car about a mile from the scene at approximately 2:15 A.M.

Ferderer waited until Officer Gliniany of the Savage Police Department arrived to assist, then approached the car on foot. Another officer arrived a short time later. The three men in the car were all in short-sleeved shirts and jeans and were sweating heavily (their bodies were literally "soaked with sweat"). Although it was a warm night, the heavy sweating was obviously inconsistent with the men having just been driving around. Ferderer could see that the driver and the rear-seat passenger were wearing tennis shoes and that the front-seat passenger was barefooted. In fact, as Gliniany testified, the front-seat passenger's feet were muddy.

After telling the men in the front seat to put their hands on the dashboard, Ferderer asked the driver, Terry Theis, what he was doing in the area. He said he had stopped to "take a leak" and that he, Rolland Moffatt and Gerald Moffatt were on their way to New Prague to visit a friend. Ferderer asked who the friend was, but apparently no name was given. Ferderer told the men there had just been a burglary in the area and he was checking it out. He did not tell the men they were suspects.

A decision was made to separate the men from one another by placing them in separate squad cars. Ferderer did this by removing each man, one at a time, frisking him for weapons and then placing him in a squad car.

After the three men were placed in separate squad cars, Officer Gliniany contacted Officer Brandt, who was with officers at the burglary scene, and asked Brandt if there were footprints at the scene. Brandt reported there were.

Under instructions radioed by a police sergeant at the burglary scene, the officers told each of the two men with shoes to take off one tennis shoe. At this point, Theis said he asked one officer if he was under arrest, and the officer said, "No, you're being detained." One officer got the third tennis shoe, that of the barefoot front-seat passenger, by reaching in and removing it from the floor of the front-seat passenger side, where it was in open view. It was then about 2:45 A.M. Officer Klegin of the Savage Police Department, who had been dispatched at 2:20 A.M., drove to the scene of the stop, arriving about 15 minutes after the shoes had been seized, picked up the three shoes and drove them to the burglary scene. There he compared the distinctive treads of the tennis shoes, each a different brand, with the two different fresh tennis shoe footprints he found. He concluded that the pattern and size of each print had been made by two of the men.

Ten to 15 minutes after Officer Klegin picked up the shoes, Sergeant McColl contacted the officers, then handcuffed the three men, told them that they were being taken into custody, gave them *Miranda* warnings and impounded the stopped car. This occurred at 3:16 A.M., 61 minutes after the car was stopped.

A search warrant was obtained, and the car was searched. Three pairs of gloves, a box of tools, a crowbar and other items were found in the trunk.

1. Did the police violate the Fourth Amendment rights of Rolland and Gerald Moffatt and Terry Theis in stopping their car a short distance from the burglary scene?
   a. Yes; before receiving a search warrant, neither the stop, the limited investigation nor the seizing of shoes would be considered justified or proper.
   b. Yes; police obtained probable cause to arrest shortly before 2:45 A.M., but before that time a stop would not be lawful.
   c. No; observing the only car in the area moments after the report of burglary justifies stopping the vehicle.
   d. Yes; the observation that the three men were soaked with sweat and gave a lame reason for being in the area justified the stop.

e. Yes; the police have a right to stop any vehicle at any time as long as an officer has a hunch there is possible suspicious activity, so this stop was lawful.

2. Was the conduct of the police diligent and reasonable?
   a. No; there are no good reasons for placing each man in a separate squad car, and no such action should occur before they are given a *Miranda* warning and told they are under arrest.
   b. Yes; while conducting a limited investigation, officers must get all available information within half an hour, including any search. Further, confiscating the shoes so they could be taken to the burglary scene for comparison with footprints requires a warrant.
   c. No; once the officers frisked for weapons and put the three men in the squad cars, they converted what might have been a detention into an arrest for which there was no probable cause—no weapons were found.
   d. Yes; this was diligent and reasonable police action because of the small police department and the facts that it was a burglary investigation (not just a petty offense) and there were three men involved; it was not in the interest of the police or public to release them quickly and allow them to get away with evidence of their guilt.
   e. No; the 20-minute "bright line" rule by the American Law Institute, for the length of an investigative detention, makes this hour-long detention illegal.

DISCUSSION QUESTIONS

1. Which of the following is the most complex objective of patrol: crime prevention, crime repression, apprehending offenders or recovering stolen property? Why?
2. What factors should be considered when using K-9–assisted patrol? What restrictions should be placed on such patrol?
3. Which is the most effective method of patrol: foot patrol, bicycle patrol, one-officer patrol vehicle, two-officer patrol vehicle or some other method?
4. What factors should be considered in determining the most suitable patrol methods to use in a police agency? How do these factors affect the choice of patrol methods?
5. What are the relative strengths and weaknesses of foot patrol and automobile patrol? How can these two patrol methods be combined to enhance the effectiveness of patrol efforts?
6. Why do the patrol officers' behaviors vary so widely from community to community?
7. How might the organizational contradiction embodied in the patrol function be reduced?

GALE EMERGENCY SERVICES DATABASE ASSIGNMENTS

- Use the Gale Emergency Services database to answer the Discussion Questions as appropriate.
- Use the Gale Emergency Services database to research the *various incidents that occur on patrol* and *the various types of patrol* that agencies use. Can you determine a pattern or correlation in how the types of incidents handled influence the method of patrol used?
- Use the Gale Emergency Services database to find and outline one of the following articles:
  - "Looking Inward with Problem-Oriented Policing" by Terry Eisenberg and Bruce Glasscock
  - "Police on Horseback: A New Concept for an Old Idea" by John C. Fine
  - "Using Drug Detection Dogs: An Update" by Jayme S. Walker

REFERENCES

"Almost 50% of Agencies Routinely Use K-9s." *Police*, March 2008, p.14.

Basich, Melanie. "Rapid Transit." *Police*, May 2008, p.22.

Basich, Melanie. "Officers Overwhelmingly Approve of In-Car Video." *Police*, February 2009, p.18.

Bradley, Jennifer. "Mission Creep: Agencies are Deploying Segways in a Variety of Ways." *Law Officer Magazine*, April 2008, pp.48–52.

Brewer, Brad. "AVL/GPS for Front Line Policing." *Law and Order*, November 2007, pp.46–54.

Commission on Accreditation of Law Enforcement Agencies. *Standards for Law Enforcement Agencies*, 5th ed. Fairfax, VA: CALEA, 2006, updated 2008.

Community Policing in Local Police Departments, 1997 and 1999. Washington, DC: Bureau of Justice Statistics, no date. (NCJ 184794) www.ojp.usdoj.gov/bjs/

Cowper, Tom. "Vertical Takeoff and Landing Aircraft for 21st Century Policing." *Law and Order*, September 2004, pp.36–41.

Craven, Kym. "Foot Patrols: Crime Analysis and Community Engagement to Further the Commitment to Community Policing." *Community Policing Dispatch*, February 2009.

Eck, John E. *Assessing Responses to Problems: An Introductory Guide for Police Problem-Solvers.* Washington, DC: Office of Community Oriented Policing Services, 2002.

Excellence in Problem-Oriented Policing: The 2002 Herman Goldstein Award Winners. Washington, DC: National Institute of Justice, COPS and Police Executive Research Forum, 2002.

Garrett, Ronnie. "Smile, You're on VIDMIC." *Law Enforcement Technology*, June 2008, pp.122–127.

Goldstein, Herman. *Problem-Oriented Policing.* New York: McGraw-Hill, 1990.

Griffith, David. "Brothers in Arms." *Police*, July 2007, p.10.

Griffith, David. "In Praise of the Patrol Officer." *Police*, January 2008, p.10.

Hubbard, Ben. "Police Turn to Secret Weapon: GPS Device." *Washington Post*, August 13, 2008, p.A01.

Klockars, Carl B. *Thinking about Policing: Contemporary Readings.* New York: McGraw-Hill, 1983.

Lansdowne, William M. "'The Core of the Department Is Patrol': An Interview with San Diego Police Chief William M. Lansdowne." *Subject to Debate.* August 2007, pp.1, 6.

Lauria, Donald T. "Cost-Benefit Analysis of Tacoma's Assigned Vehicle Program." *Police Quarterly*, June 2007, pp.192–217.

Menton, Chris. "Bicycle Patrols versus Car Patrols." *Law and Order*, June 2007, pp.78–81.

Miller, Laurence. "Practical Police Psychology." *PoliceOne.com News*, April 18, 2008.

Mills-Senn, Pamela. "Right on Schedule." *Law Enforcement Technology*, March 2008, pp.62–67.

Molnar, J. P. "Smart Talk." *Law Officer Magazine*, November 2007, pp.20–23.

Moore, Carole. "Hit the Pavement." *Law Enforcement Technology*, April 2007, pp.56–65.

Oldham, Scott. "Protect and Serve?" *Law and Order*, September 2007, p.33.

Orput, Peter and Ivy, Pete. "Mobile Tracking Devices." *Minnesota Police Chief*, Summer 2008, pp.8–9.

Salisbury, Tom. "Manatee County Sheriff's Office Memorandum." Accessed November 30, 2007. http://www.manateesheriff.com/pdf/budget/AssignedVsPooledVehicles.pdf

Scoville, Dean. "Working on the Front Lines." *Police*, July 2008, pp.38–48.

Solosky, Kenneth J. "Your Eye in the Sky." *Law Officer Magazine*, February 2009, pp.38–43.

Spelman, William G. and Brown, Dale K. "Response Time." In *Thinking about Police: Contemporary Readings*, 2nd ed., edited by Carl B. Klockars and Stephen D. Mastrofski. New York: McGraw-Hill, 1991, pp.163–167.

Stockton, Dale. "Intervene and Prevent." *Law Officer Magazine*, February 2008, p.8.

Sundermeier, Jon. "A Look at the 12-Hour Shift: The Lincoln Police Department Study." *The Police Chief*, March 2008, pp.60–63.

"Take Home Police Vehicle Program." City of Oxford, Ohio, Web site. http://www.cityofoxford.org/Page.asp?NavID=984

Wandrei, Greg. "Instant Access to Vital Information: The Role of GIS." *Law Enforcement Technology*, November 2007, pp.56–61.

CASE CITED

United States v. Place, 462 U.S. 696 (1983)

CHAPTER 5

Traffic

Policing in a Country on the Move

DO YOU KNOW . . .

- What three functional areas police traffic services include?
- What the basic purposes of traffic enforcement are?
- What syndromes are common in the driving public?
- Who is responsible for traffic enforcement?
- How the problem of speeding in residential areas can be addressed?
- What the difference between aggressive driving and road rage is?
- What the number one problem of traffic enforcement is?
- What strategies are being used to deter DUI?
- What balance must be maintained in an effective pursuit policy?
- What issues should be addressed in a pursuit policy?
- What a hazardous materials enforcement program should include?
- What the responsibilities of officers responding to a crash scene are?

CAN YOU DEFINE?

blood-alcohol concentration (BAC)
cruising
drug recognition expert (DRE)
drug recognition technician (DRT)
dual motive stop
enforcement index
implied consent law
nystagmus
pretext stop
pursuit
racial profiling
road rage
scofflaws
selective enforcement
traffic calming

INTRODUCTION

The United States is truly a nation on the move. Citizens feel it is their *right* to drive vehicles, even though it really is a privilege, and they resent any limitations imposed on this "right." At the same time, they also expect city and state governments to keep the roadways in good condition and the police to keep traffic moving. Besides simply keeping traffic flowing, officers involved in this important aspect of police work are also charged with helping at and investigating crashes involving vehicles. Police also must deal with criminals who use vehicles in committing their crimes. This often involves high-speed chases. At the opposite end of the spectrum is law enforcement's responsibility to educate the driving public about their responsibilities and the rules and regulations they must obey.

More officer time is spent on traffic patrol than on any other police activity. Unfortunately, like patrol in general, traffic services are often perceived as unglamorous and rank low on the department's and community's priority list: "Addressing traffic-related concerns is increasingly challenging because of dwindling municipal budgets, competing resources, and rising crime rates. [Yet] [t]he ease with which motorists can move about in a safe manner is an important attribute of a prosperous and livable community" (Maggard and Jung, 2009, p.46).

61.1

CALEA STANDARD 61.1 focuses on traffic, stating, "Activities undertaken by the agency that directly affect the movement and control of vehicles and pedestrians include point traffic control, traffic engineering, school crossing supervision, and other activities related to the design and implementation of plans and programs that expedite the movement of vehicles and pedestrians. . . . The agency may perform a variety of diverse, traffic-related services including providing general assistance, emergency assistance, public information, and directions; identifying and reporting roadway and roadside hazards; checking abandoned vehicles; and locating and recovering stolen vehicles." (*Standards for Law Enforcement Agencies*, 5th edition, 2006)

Police traffic services (PTS) are divided into three major areas:

- Traffic direction and control.
- Traffic enforcement.
- Crash investigation.

This chapter begins with a discussion of traffic direction and control. This is followed by a discussion of traffic enforcement and specific traffic violations, including failure to obey seat belt laws; speeding; red-light running and failing to obey a stop sign; aggressive, reckless or careless driving and road rage; and driving under the influence. Next the traffic stop is examined, including the use of automated citations and the issues surrounding pretext stops and biased profiling. This is followed by an in-depth look at recognizing and stopping drivers under the influence of alcohol and drugs. High-speed pursuits and hazardous materials enforcement are presented next. Then crash management and investigation are discussed. The chapter concludes with a look at the relationship between traffic, community policing and problem solving.

Directing traffic is a hazardous duty. Each year many officers are injured or killed by careless drivers.
© AP Images/Gregory Bull

TRAFFIC DIRECTION AND CONTROL

Traffic direction and control (TD&C) is a planned assignment and may take place regularly at such places as schools before and after closing, rush hour, major sporting events, parades, funerals and the like. It may also take place during unexpected or emergency events, such as civil disturbances or natural disasters, or when a high-profile political figure or celebrity is in town. In addition, TD&C is part of an officer's responsibility at crash scenes.

TD&C requires great skill in nonverbal communication. The tools officers normally use are their hands, eyes and a whistle. At night or in poor weather conditions, a vital tool is a flashlight or lighted cone. Seldom can verbal commands be issued. Officers get attention by short blasts on their whistles, use of their flashlights and by making eye contact with drivers. Officers provide direction with their hands, motioning drivers to stop, turn or go straight.

Officers engaged in traffic direction and control should plan carefully how best to position themselves, considering both their visibility to oncoming traffic and their personal safety. Safety precautions include wearing reflective Day-Glo vests and, at night, using flashlights with cones attached. Officers must also consider in the overall plan how best to keep the traffic moving, including pedestrian traffic.

Whistles are "great attention getters" for traffic officers, especially those who are smaller in stature (Grossi, 2008b, p.34). One long whistle blast means stop all traffic, and two short blasts get the drivers started again. Officers should always be alert for "unconscious" drivers: "Traffic officers must assume that the motoring public, including older drivers, are operating on a system that devotes 90 percent of their in-car driving time to their CD player, GPS, cell phone, coffee or newspaper; and that the appearance of either emergency lights, a traffic cop, highway flares or bright orange cones will only serve to short-circuit their brains" (Grossi).

High Visibility

The Manual on Uniform Traffic Control Devices (2007) has mandated that highway workers wear high-visibility safety garments and apparel while working on or near the roadway, and this includes law enforcement. The Occupational Safety and Health Administration (OSHA) and many states are also mandating and enforcing the use of "hi-viz" garments by all roadway workers, including law enforcement (Beck, 2008). Officers who are working special traffic enforcement details, such as Safe & Sober, Night Cap and the like are required to wear high visibility traffic vests for the duration of their participation in such grant-funded events.

The Cruising Problem

Since the 1950s, cruising has been a favorite pastime of teenagers and young adults. **Cruising**—driving around and around a predetermined, popular route, usually through the heart of a town or city—gives teenagers a chance to see who is going out together and what kinds of cars other teenagers are driving, to pick up dates and to spend their socializing hours in a relatively inexpensive way. When teenagers got out of hand in the 1950s and 1960s, police used existing curfew or loitering laws to send them home, a task easy to do in a small town.

cruising
Driving around and around a predetermined, popular route, usually through the heart of a town or city; a social activity of teenagers.

By the 1970s, however, cruising had become a problem in major urban areas. Some cities passed cruising ordinances that prohibited a car from passing a specific point more than a certain number of times within a specific period. In addition, cruising is often associated with johns seeking prostitutes, drug addicts seeking drug buys, or potential robbers or burglars staking out possible targets. Further, it has become associated with drive-by shootings, certainly of grave concern to any community and its police.

TRAFFIC ENFORCEMENT

A primary responsibility of traffic services is enforcing a municipality's and state's traffic rules and regulations, which are enacted for the safety of all citizens: "There's nothing a law enforcement agency can do that has as much potential to save lives and prevent injury [as does traffic enforcement]" (Bolton, 2009, p.90).

The two basic purposes of traffic enforcement are to control congestion and to reduce crashes. Enforcement can also detect criminal activity.

Enforcement action taken against traffic violators serves a dual purpose. First, it allows the court to evaluate the propriety of a motorist's conduct and administer appropriate punitive sanctions directly against that driver. Second, enforcement acts as a deterrent to other drivers in preventing future violations because citizens who know that traffic laws are enforced are more likely to comply with the rules of the road. Nonetheless, many drivers routinely break traffic laws, believing their minor infractions will not be noticed or result in tickets. Particularly troublesome are offenders who have had their driver's license permanently revoked because of continued traffic infractions and because their mentality is commonly one of "I can't lose something I've already lost."

The I-won't-get-a-ticket syndrome is common among the driving public.

Although most people respect the aims and efforts of police officers in traffic enforcement as applied to *other* drivers, many motorists turn critical of the same enforcement actions when they become the subject of a traffic stop. A common complaint of those ticketed for traffic violations is that the police should be focusing on catching real criminals instead of pulling people over for driving a little faster than the speed limit.

Even some police officers do not regard traffic enforcement as "real" police work, contending that writing traffic citations could be done by nonsworn personnel. Indeed, nonsworn personnel are helpful in many areas, such as parking violations. However, stopping vehicles can be just as dangerous, if not more so, as responding to calls. In addition, a crucial, frequently unrecognized aspect of traffic enforcement is the potential apprehension of wanted suspects.

Someone willing to commit a serious criminal act usually has little reservation about breaking traffic laws. People who commit crimes are also the ones driving with revoked licenses, expired tags, or burned-out taillights or headlights. Thus, the potential for exposure of other crimes during a traffic stop makes traffic enforcement a duty of all officers, not just those assigned to highway patrol or other specific traffic units.

Even if a traffic enforcement unit exists, traffic enforcement is the responsibility of all officers.

Bolton (2008a, p.66) contends, "Ideally, traffic enforcement is integrated into the daily work goals of routine patrol operations. When all officers—rather than simply a specialized division or overtime detail—are responsible for enforcement activity, the result is likely to be more consistent action addressing crash and traffic problems in their areas. It has also been proven that aggressive traffic law enforcement positively affects crime detection and deterrence."

A good example of the potential for traffic enforcement to lead to a criminal apprehension occurred when state trooper Charles Hanger stopped Timothy McVeigh's car because it lacked license plates. Trooper Hanger, unaware of the driver's involvement in the day's earlier terrorist bombing of the Alfred P. Murrah Building, cited McVeigh for, among other things, the absence of license tags and carrying a concealed gun. While McVeigh sat in a jail cell being processed into the system for his offenses, investigators handling the bombing's aftermath were searching for suspects, including McVeigh. Their database search turned up a "hit," and the trooper was credited with apprehending the terrorist, McVeigh, who was later convicted and executed for his role in the bombing.

Traffic enforcement is a large part of proactive policing. Sanow (2009, p.6) contends, "Traffic enforcement equals crime prevention," noting, "Aggressive traffic enforcement is a win-win. It reduces crime and increases safety. As a result of a focused traffic enforcement effort, Oklahoma County, Oklahoma, has already documented a 90 percent reduction in crashes and a 90 percent reduction in criminal activity."

The International Association of Chiefs of Police (IACP) Highway Safety Committee and the 3M Traffic Safety Systems Division have partnered for more than a decade in recognizing police officers who use license plates to solve serious, nontraffic crimes. The "Looking Beyond the License Plate Award" substantiates and documents the importance of license plates as a critical law enforcement tool to track and identify offenders because it is generally accepted that most serious crime involves a motor vehicle (Ashton, 2008, p.28).

The Illinois Association of Chiefs of Police program, "Looking Beyond the Safety Belt," recognizes that law enforcement officers who initiate a traffic stop based solely on a safety-belt violation often discover other crimes or situations leading to an arrest. Casstevens (2008, p.44) describes two safety-belt stops that resulted in arrests. In the first, a driver was stopped for a seat-belt violation, and the officer found proceeds from residential burglaries. After being arrested, the driver confessed to 11 burglaries in that area and several others in surrounding areas. In a second situation, a state trooper stopped a driver for not wearing a seat belt. The driver fled on foot; one passenger was wanted on an active warrant. After investigation, the identity of the driver was determined and officers also determined that the vehicle was wanted in connection with several burglaries and home invasions, as well as a sexual assault: "Study after study shows that more arrests are made as a result of traffic stops than any undercover operation" (Casstevens, p.45). Technology such as automated license plate recognition (ALPR) programs assists in efforts to check for suspicious vehicles, stolen vehicles or license plates, outstanding unpaid parking citations and wanted felons.

Automated License Plate Recognition

ALPR or simply license plate recognition (LPR) systems were introduced in the United States in 2004 and have become a valuable tool for law enforcement. ALPR technology uses special cameras to photograph vehicle license plates and then uses optical character recognition (OCR) software to read the plate number and compare it with wanted vehicle databases that are updated every few minutes. This technology can read and compare more than 4,000 license plates an hour in real time (Beery, 2008, p.77). Haug (2009, p.64) says, "Through the use of ALPR systems, investigators are able to solve numerous crimes that go well beyond simple auto theft." ALPR can provide data officers can use for ongoing investigation in areas such as violent crimes, burglaries or any other targeted criminal activities and can also increase revenue related to traffic and parking citations and vehicle impounds (Beery, p.76). Stockton (2009, p.8), a strong advocate for this technology, states, "I'm absolutely convinced that LPR has the potential to be even more important to public safety and policing than DNA."

Being cited for a traffic violation is one of the most common ways citizens come in contact with the police. Here a trooper issues a traffic ticket for speeding. The State Highway Patrol in Ohio is trying to lower traffic deaths by concentrating troopers at perilous intersections and dangerous stretches of road instead of giving out tickets at random sites or speed traps.
© AP Images/EricAlbrecht

Traffic Violators and Violations

Most drivers stopped for traffic violations are not terrorist bombers or other wanted criminals—they will be average everyday people, most of whom are not necessarily actively refusing to conform to society's laws. They simply are not paying attention. Judging by the millions of traffic citations and parking tickets issued every year, operating a motor vehicle in compliance with all the laws is mastered by only a few motorists. Despite their good intentions and interest in community safety, hundreds of thousands of people—young and old, male and female, of all races, national origins, occupations and religions—violate traffic laws.

Violations range from failing to wear a seat belt or put children in the proper child safety seats, to changing lanes or turning without signaling, to ignoring "no parking" or "no turn on red" signs, to speeding or running red lights. The most serious traffic violations involve aggressive driving that may turn to road rage, or driving under the influence of alcohol or drugs. The reasons given for violations range from being late for an appointment; to "just keeping up with traffic"; to "getting away with something"; to being distracted by cell phones, radios, a steaming cup of coffee, screaming children or conversation with other passengers; to being daydreamers whose thoughts are far away from the responsibilities of driving a vehicle.

Using a cell phone while driving has been determined so serious a distraction that it has become the subject of legislation. California, New York,

New Jersey, Connecticut, Washington state and the District of Columbia already have hands-free cell phone laws in place, and more states are considering such legislation (Garrett, 2008a, p.6). Minnesota prohibits the operation of a motor vehicle while using a wireless communication device to compose, read or send an electronic message when the vehicle is in motion or in traffic—this is the "no texting while driving" law, which an increasing number of states are also considering enacting.

Critics argue that if cell phones are banned because they distract drivers, perhaps all vehicle radios should be removed, passengers should not be allowed to talk, and drivers should be prohibited from eating or drinking while behind the wheel. The focus should be on a driver's ability, or inability, to obey traffic laws, regardless of whatever else is occurring in the vehicle. Some drivers can observe the law while talking on the phone, especially when using hands-free equipment, whereas other drivers simply ignore the laws.

Seat Belt Laws

One of the most prevalent motor vehicle violations is the failure to buckle up. In 1994, because safety belt use stood at only 12 percent, the New York legislature approved a bill creating the nation's first mandatory seat belt law. By 2008, seat belt use had climbed to 83 percent, with a statistically significant increase to 90 percent for seat belt use among occupants on expressways ("Seat Belt Use in 2008," p.1). According to the survey, seat belt use continued to be higher in states in which vehicle occupants can be pulled over solely for not using seat belt ("primary law" states). In 2007, seat belt use in rear seats was 76 percent, 11 percent higher than in 2006, and was higher among states with laws requiring belt use in all seating positions (Ye and Pickrell, 2008, p.1). An estimated 15,147 lives were saved in 2007 through use of seat belts in motor vehicles, and an estimated 76,936 lives were saved from 2003 through 2007 through such use ("Lives Saved in 2007," 2008, p.1). An additional 2,788 lives were saved by front-end air bags.

The leading cause of death for children age 2 to 14 in the United States is motor vehicle crashes, with an average daily fatality rate of 5 children age 14 and younger; another 568 children are injured (on average) in motor vehicle crashes each day ("Children," 2006, p.1). According to "Child Passenger Safety" (n.d.), these deaths and injuries were largely caused by the nonuse or improper use of child seats and seat belts. Motor vehicle crashes are also the leading cause of death for 15- to 20-year olds ("Young Drivers," 2007, p.1). In fact, one in four crash fatalities involve someone 16 to 24 years of age (Garrett, 2008b, p.8). Forty-seven states have addressed younger driver skills by requiring some form of three-stage graduated licensing (supervised learner, intermediate, and full). Graduated licensing, increased seat belt use and reduced access to alcohol are considered the three core components in an effective plan to save the lives of novice drivers (Bolton, 2008b, p.106).

Paralleling the institution of seat belt laws in 1994 was North Carolina's *Click It or Ticket Program* to increase use of seat belts, which has since become a national effort. The National Highway Traffic Safety Administration (NHTSA) Click It or Ticket (CIOT) Web site calls the program "the most successful seat belt enforcement campaign ever." The program uses heavy publicity and a solid public information and education campaign from mid-May to the beginning of June (Memorial Day). The primary audience continues to be men ages 18 to 34, whom research shows are less likely to wear seat belts.

Speeding

One of the most basic risk factors in traffic safety is speed: "Higher driving speeds lead to higher collision speeds and thus to severer injuries. Higher driving speeds also provide less time to process information and to act on it, and the braking distance is longer" ("The Relation between Speed and Crashes," 2009, p.1). According to the NHTSA, "Speeding is one of the most prevalent factors contributing to traffic crashes. The economic cost to society of speeding-related crashes is estimated at $40.4 billion per year. In 2007, speeding was a contributing factor in 31 percent of all fatal crashes, and 13,040 lives were lost in speeding-related crashes ("Speeding," 2007, p.1).

Many drivers, particularly younger, less experienced ones, fail to anticipate hazards in the road and overestimate their ability to control their vehicle when the unexpected happens—another driver cuts in front of them, a dog runs across the street, a tire blows or they hit an icy patch in the road. Some drivers subscribe to the philosophy that it is safer to "go with the flow" of traffic, even if it is 10 miles an hour over the posted speed limit, than to obey the traffic law and make other drivers maneuver their speeding vehicles through numerous lane changes to get around slower traffic. Still others, lost in thought or conversation, are completely unaware of the speed at which they are traveling. Sometimes, compliance with the speed limit can be obtained simply by reminding drivers to check their speedometers. Other times, aggressive ticketing campaigns are needed to get drivers to slow down.

The Problem of Speeding in Residential Areas Numerous studies have shown that traffic-related issues continue to be citizens' number one complaint to police (Casstevens, 2008, p.45). Speeding in residential areas makes citizens fear for children's safety; makes pedestrians and bicyclists fear for their safety; and increases the risk of vehicle crashes as well as the seriousness of injuries to other drivers, passengers, pedestrians and bicyclists struck by a vehicle.

Speeding can be addressed through engineering, education and enforcement responses.

traffic calming
Describes a wide range of road and environment design changes that either make it more difficult for a vehicle to speed or make drivers believe they should slow down for safety.

Engineering responses are preventative in nature and include posting warning signs and signals; installing stop signs, speed limit signs and computerized speed display boards; painting crosswalks; using turn prohibitions; designating streets as one-way; and using traffic calming alternatives. **Traffic calming** involves modifying road design and environmental conditions to make it more difficult for a vehicle to speed. Some traffic calming measures are speed bumps and humps, rumble strips, cul-de-sacs, narrowing the road, putting bends and curves in the road, permitting parking on both sides of residential streets and timing traffic signals for vehicles traveling the desired speed. "Without traffic calming to intervene and prevent accidents, the number of traffic crashes and fatalities would rapidly escalate" ("A World without Traffic Calming," 2009).

Installing a radar speed display in a problem area is another engineering effort to reduce speeding. Such displays show the speed limit and the approaching motorist's speed, and are often set to flash when drivers exceed the posted speed limit. Some departments mount a speed display on the back of a patrol car that they park alongside a problem area. Dixon (2008, p.42) notes, "Radar speed signs are quickly becoming the traffic calming solution of choice around school zones, neighborhood streets, parks and other locations where pedestrian safety is of particular concern."

Education responses include conducting anti-speeding public awareness campaigns, informing complainants about actual speeds, instituting neighborhood speed watch programs, and providing realistic driver training.

Enforcement responses include using photo radar, using speed display boards, ticketing speeders, arresting the worst offenders and training citizen volunteers to monitor speeding.

Measures to reduce speeding in residential areas that seem to have *limited effectiveness* include reducing speed limits, increasing fines and penalties, erecting stop signs, installing speed bumps and rumble strips, and reengineering vehicles. However, these measures used in conjunction with education and other engineering responses may prove to be effective.

Curbing Illegal Street Racing Informally organized street races cause the deaths of numerous drivers and spectators every year. "Illegal races can result in mass casualties and a growing outlaw culture in your community" (Petrocelli, 2007, p.20). In California alone, illegal street racing claims the lives of nearly 100 people each year (Bernstein et al., 2007). Petrocelli suggests, "Today, street racing is a problem in almost every American community, as technology such as the Internet and text messaging have made it easy to stage underground races for substantial audiences" (p.20).

Strategies that may reduce street racing include using undercover officers and vehicles, videotaping or photographing the racing activities, developing interagency enforcement teams, working with the media to publicize the problem, developing an alternative site for racing, and making Internet contact through street racing groups' Web sites and the department's own Web site. If these don't work, law enforcement should adopt a zero tolerance policy: "Written enforcement action can be taken for careless driving, reckless driving, and racing on public streets. Non-participants (starters, timers, those who block street) can be charged with trespassing or obstructing public passage. Applicable curfew laws can be enforced to winnow crowds. And you can deprive the racers of their tracks by getting the local government to install speed bumps on particularly troublesome streets" (Petrocelli, 2007, p.21).

Officers are reporting seeing an increase in a particularly dangerous form of racing called "cutting the gap," which involves "impromptu speed contests in which racers weave in and out of traffic" (Bernstein et al., 2007). One detective describes this kind of racing as "a game of chicken—like a real-life video game. They are driving souped-up vehicles where their skills don't match the cars" (Bernstein et al.) Griffith (2007, p.12) contends, "Cutting the gap is nothing short of attempted murder. It should be treated that way."

Using Decoy Patrols Some jurisdictions are using decoy or dummy patrol vehicles to reduce speeding and traffic violations. These unmanned vehicles provide high visibility parked along side the road in areas experiencing traffic problems. However, such squads may fall victim to vandalization, as happened in Durham, North Carolina, when a decoy highway patrol car left parked along Interstate 85 had its windows smashed and tires slashed. The deterrent effect of such decoys is also often only temporary, until the driving public recognizes that no officer is actually on-scene to issue citations. Nonetheless, decoy patrol vehicles have proven effective in many jurisdictions.

Speed Enforcement Technology The conventional radar unit is the oldest electronic speed enforcement technology in use and is still the "tool of choice" for most traffic officers. A controversial new speed enforcement device is photo radar. Photo speed enforcement is also being used. These units are typically mounted in the rear of a sport-utility vehicle parked at roadside and aimed at a 22-degree angle at oncoming traffic. The radar detects a speeding car, records its speed, license number and the driver's face. It then generates a ticket that is mailed to the driver.

Another type of speed enforcement is drone radar, which capitalizes on the fact that many motorists have radar detection units in their vehicles. (Radar detector use in cars is legal in most states, but its use in commercial vehicles was banned in all states by a directive of the U.S. Department of Transportation [USDOT] in 1995.) Drone radar has the sole purpose of triggering these radar detection units, thereby slowing their drivers in most instances. The units can be connected with speed display signs that announce, "You are going X miles" to alert drivers they are speeding. However, once drivers discover that a drone radar unit is operating and that no tickets are forthcoming, the effectiveness of the unit is lost, and the unit should be moved.

Red-Light Runners

When people are in a hurry and are speeding or are distracted, they are also more likely to run red lights and stop signs. Public awareness of the problems associated with red light running might be raised through press conferences, billboards, and posters. Suggested engineering improvements include warning signs, pavement markings, skid resistance, bigger or brighter signs and signals, and timing of traffic signal phases. Another approach is to install automated red light cameras.

For some people looking for faster ways to get from point A to point B, the stop sign or red stoplight has become a personal nemesis, seen not as a device to enhance traffic flow and safety but as an enemy to be beaten. Getting "caught" at the light is more than an inconvenience; it's a mild form of defeat. Some license plate sprays may foil traffic cameras by bouncing back the flash of the camera to overexpose the license plate, but these sprays do not work if flashless digital cameras are used.

Another potential concern is the availability of signal-changing devices. A mechanism called a mobile infrared transmitter, or MIRT, is the trigger device in traffic preemptions systems. Although no cities have reported this as a problem, several cities are urging their legislators to pass legislation specifically banning the use of MIRTs by unauthorized individuals.

Tailgating

Tailgating is a factor in many crashes. However, "Driving too closely behind another car, or tailgating, has been one of those traffic infractions on U.S. roadways that has defied law enforcement officers for years" (Galvin, 2008, p.40). It is difficult for law enforcement to enforce the highway safety industry's 3-second rule—the guideline stating that the distance traveled in 3 seconds is the *minimum* distance a driver should be from the vehicle in front of him or her—because it is considered by many to be a subjective judgment (Galvin, 2009, p.70).

Aggressive Driving and Road Rage

Aggressive driving has become one of the leading safety hazards on our highways and, according to several studies, is considered to be more dangerous than drunk driving or driving without seat belts. The NHTSA defines *aggressive* driving as occurring when "an individual commits a combination of moving traffic offenses so as to endanger other persons or property." The NHTSA distinguishes aggressive driving from road rage, saying that behaviors of aggressive drivers include tailgating, making erratic or unsafe lane changes, exceeding speed limits or driving too fast for conditions, weaving in and out of traffic, and ignoring traffic control devices such as stop lights and yield signs. Aggressive driving often precipitates road rage. The NHTSA defines **road rage** as "an assault with a motor vehicle or other dangerous weapon by the operator or passenger(s) of one motor vehicle on the operator or passenger(s) of another motor vehicle and is caused by an incident that occurred on the roadway."

road rage
An assault with a motor vehicle or other dangerous weapon by the operator or passenger(s) of one motor vehicle on the operator or passenger(s) of another motor vehicle and is caused by an incident that occurred on the roadway.

Aggressive driving is a traffic violation; road rage is a criminal offense.

Recognizing the danger posed by aggressive drivers, jurisdictions throughout the country are implementing special teams to tackle this growing threat. For example, the Washington State Patrol has dedicated 10 new police vehicles to its Aggressive Driver Apprehension Team to target dangerous speed and aggressive drivers (Ursino, 2007, p.36).

Driving under the Influence

Another serious traffic violation that may earn a driver some jail time is driving under the influence of alcohol or drugs. Whether called *driving while intoxicated* (DWI), *driving under the influence* (DUI), *driving under the influence of liquor* (DUIL) or some other designation, those who do so are a critical problem for the community. Every 33 minutes, someone in this country dies in an alcohol-related crash. Law enforcement agencies take nearly 1.5 million drunk and drug intoxicated drivers off the road each year because of tougher laws, sobriety checkpoints and saturation patrols. And yet, an estimated 2,000 alcohol-impaired driving trips occur for every arrest. A Mothers Against Drunk Driving (MADD) brochure states, "Those injured and killed in drunk driving collisions are not 'accident' victims. The crash caused by an impaired driver is a violent crime."

Nationwide, DUI is the number one traffic law enforcement problem.

Yet police officers frequently simply issue a ticket and perhaps write a brief report, making prosecution extremely difficult. In some states, such as Minnesota, the first DWI offense, barring any aggravating factors, is only a misdemeanor crime and is citable. However, for every DWI offense after that, or if there are aggravating factors in the initial offense (e.g., excessive recklessness or speed, children in the vehicle, etc.), the offender is jailed. It is important to understand the various differences between state laws concerning DWI.

One reason officers may be detoured from enforcing DWIs is the weak punishments DWI offenders receive. Officers are commonly frustrated by how prosecutors treat DWI cases, often as just another traffic ticket. Offenders usually are able to bargain a weak punishment, frustrating officers because of all of the work and time it takes to process a DWI. A typical DWI from traffic stop to disposition lasts 2 hours, with many taking much longer, depending on the variables involved. Recognizing and stopping impaired drivers will be discussed in greater detail shortly.

Selective Traffic Enforcement and the Enforcement Index

selective enforcement
The ability to decide when to impose legal sanctions on those who violate the law, whether issuing traffic tickets or arresting someone.

Officers cannot possibly stop and ticket every traffic violator. Consequently, most police departments rely on **selective enforcement**, the ability to decide when to impose legal sanctions on those who violate the law. Selective traffic enforcement plans allocation of police personnel and equipment by studying the violators and road conditions that contribute to collisions.

61.1.1

ACCORDING TO CALEA STANDARD 61.1.1 ("Traffic,"), "The ultimate goal of selective traffic law enforcement is to reduce traffic collision. This may be achieved through the application of such techniques as geographic/temporal assignment of personnel and equipment and the establishment of preventive patrols to deal with specific categories of unlawful driving behavior. The techniques used should be based on collision data, enforcement activity records, traffic volume, and traffic conditions. The objective is to direct appropriate enforcement efforts toward violations, not only in proportion to the frequency of their occurrence in collision situations but also in terms of traffic-related needs identified in the agency's service community. (*Standards for Law Enforcement Agencies*, 5th edition, 2006)

enforcement index
Standard suggesting that for each fatal and personal injury crash, between 20 and 25 convictions for hazardous moving violations indicates effective traffic enforcement.

Many police departments also use the **enforcement index**, a figure based on the ratio of tickets issued for hazardous driving violations to the number of fatal and personal injury crashes. The IACP and the National Safety Council suggest that an index of between 1:20 and 1:25 is realistic for most cities, that is, for each fatal and personal injury crash, between 20 and 25 convictions for hazardous moving violations indicate effective traffic enforcement. For some cities, the ratio may be higher; for others, lower. The index provides only a starting point for setting traffic enforcement goals and evaluating results.

Given the wide array of traffic violations and violators, it is critical that traffic enforcement be conducted fairly and uniformly. Departments must have clear policies on when motorists should be stopped and on the appropriate action to take.

THE TRAFFIC STOP

Police encounters with citizens involving traffic infractions will almost always be emotional, and drivers' reactions will vary greatly, from anxiety to remorse, fear, surprise, anger or even hate. The first words officers say to violators set the tone for the rest of the contact. If officers are belligerent, the violators may be belligerent. If officers are pleasant, chances are the violators will be pleasant—but not always. Officers dealing with traffic violators should *never argue*. Motorists who want to debate their driving actions will never be convinced that they are wrong and the officer is right. Further, officers should not try to justify the enforcement action, as this only adds to the drivers' preconceived idea that the officer is wrong, prejudiced or "picking on them."

Instead, officers should try to make the traffic contact an educational encounter for the driver, not a belittling or degrading experience. Motorists can be given information so they will be less likely to violate the law again. Studies have shown that many traffic stops by courteous, respectful officers have a positive effect on the citizens' perceptions of the police, even though a citation may be issued.

The stop should be made in a safe place, if possible, not necessarily the first available place. Dispatch should be notified of the stop and of the car's description and license number. After parking safely (many departments instruct officers to park behind the stopped vehicle and slightly to the left, leaving an alley of safety to protect the officer from passing traffic) and leaving the light bar flashing, the officer should approach the car cautiously and stand clear of the driver's door, which could be swung open unexpectedly.

Pennsylvania v. Mimms (1977) established that police officers may order the driver of a vehicle to exit the vehicle during a stop for a traffic violation. In some states, officers may also use a handheld fingerprint scanner, known as Identix Integrated Biometric Identification System (Identix IBIS), to identify wanted and missing people who are stopped. Officers can call into the National Crime Information Center (NCIC) database and remotely compare a suspect's fingerprints to that database.

Officers have great discretion in traffic enforcement. After making a stop, they usually do one of three things: (1) simply talk to the motorist and explain how the motorist has violated the law, perhaps warning the driver verbally, (2) issue a warning ticket or (3) issue a citation. The third action causes motorists to become irate, often acting illogically. Motorists have been known to make ridiculous and profane statements, to tear up tickets and to curse at officers.

Sometimes such behavior stems from the fear of being discovered as "wanted" by the police and of being arrested on the spot.

Automated Citations

Automated citations have simplified the traffic stop process. With handheld computers, which prompt officers for the information to be entered, citations can be issued on the spot and are legible and complete. Some handheld computers read the magnetic stripe on the driver's license in the same way magnetic tapes are read on credit cards. The information is saved and downloaded into the main processing unit at the end of the shift, or, in some jurisdictions, it can be uploaded into a server that includes all participating agencies.

Automated citations, electronic citations or e-tickets usually allow the officer to choose from pull-down menus to input appropriate code violations and other information. Multiple violations are easy to add, and the entire record can be saved with a paper copy printed for the driver. The entire process can be completed within 3 to 4 minutes, a great reduction from the standard 10 to 20 minutes needed to write out a citation (Griffin, 2009, p.30). Although this process is extremely convenient and efficient, like most computerized systems, it can experience technical problems. Thus, it is a good idea to keep a paper citation book handy for such instances.

Benefits of e-tickets include (Griffin, 2009)

- Eliminating handwritten tickets and the need to enter the same information into a separate database(s)
- Getting officers and drivers off the roadside more quickly
- Eliminating errors and duplicate entries by law enforcement, courts, clerks and other staff
- Increasing the accuracy of information
- Giving officers more time to patrol by reducing paperwork
- Saving clerical time for clerks, courts and agencies because data is transferred electronically
- Improving timeliness by making data available electronically

Hillard (2008, p.58) summarizes the key benefit: "With a mobile computer equipped with electronic traffic citation software, officers can clear a traffic stop three to five times faster, thereby reducing the risk on the roadside."

scofflaws
Persistent lawbreakers.

Handheld computers can also be used to deal with **scofflaws**—persistent lawbreakers. For example, when officers issue a parking ticket, they can run a check on the license and determine if other parking tickets are outstanding. If there are outstanding tickets, officers can have a boot put on one of the vehicle's tires so the vehicle cannot be moved before it can be towed to the impound garage. Handheld computers can also store and produce on command lists of stolen vehicles and revoked driver's licenses and can produce the daily logs that formerly required quantities of time and were tedious to complete.

As a final note, an officer who issues a traffic citation accepts the obligation to pursue that action through the courts by preparing evidence, obtaining witnesses, testifying and performing the necessary functions to ensure a conviction.

Pretext Stops

A **pretext stop**, also called a **dual motive stop**, is one in which an officer stops a vehicle not only for a traffic violation but also because the driver looks suspicious. For example, an officer sees a suspicious-looking driver and follows the vehicle, hoping a violation occurs to justify a stop. The officer may then use the stop as a pretext to investigate the driver as well as the violation. Is such a stop legal? The states disagree. At the heart of the issue is the intent of the stop.

pretext stop
A stop in which the officer is stopping a vehicle to investigate not only a traffic violation but also the fact that the driver looks suspicious. Also called a *dual motive stop*.

dual motive stop
A stop in which the officer is stopping a vehicle to investigate a traffic violation and because the driver looks suspicious. Also called a *pretext stop*.

The question of pretext stops was clarified in *Whren v. United States* (1996). In this case, plainclothes officers patrolling a high-drug area in an unmarked vehicle saw a truck waiting at a stop sign for an unusually long time. The truck then turned suddenly without signaling and sped off at an "unreasonable" speed. The officers stopped the vehicle supposedly to warn the driver about the illegal turn and speed (traffic violations). When they approached the vehicle, they saw plastic bags of crack cocaine in the truck and arrested the driver.

The motion to suppress the evidence (cocaine) was denied, with the Supreme Court ruling, "The temporary detention of a motorist upon probable cause to believe he has violated the traffic laws does not violate the Fourth Amendment's prohibition against unreasonable seizures, even if a reasonable officer would not have stopped the motorist absent some additional law enforcement objective." In other words, the validity and constitutionality of a stop does not depend on whether police officers "would have" made the stop but rather whether the officers "could have" made the stop. The real purpose of a stop, even if ulterior, does not render the stop and subsequent search invalid if there was, in fact, a valid reason for the stop, such as in this case traffic violations.

Racial Profiling

Closely linked to the question of pretext stops is the issue of racial profiling. **Racial profiling**, or biased-based profiling, is the selection of individuals based solely on a common trait of a group, including, but not limited to race, ethnic background, gender, sexual orientation, religion, economic status, age, cultural group, or any other identifiable group (CALEA, 2006, p.1–6). It is most often encountered when officers use discretionary authority in encounters with minority motorists, typically in the context of a traffic stop,

racial profiling
Inconsistent, discriminatory enforcement of the law; an officer uses a person's race to assess the likelihood of criminal conduct or wrongdoing.

In October 2001, the Supreme Court refused to hear the only remaining case docketed for the year concerning an equal protection claim in a case where police officers stop people based primarily on racial or ethnic descriptions, in effect, upholding the ruling of the U.S. Court of Appeals for the Second Circuit in *Brown v. City of Oneonta*. In this case, the court held that when law enforcement officers have a description of a suspect that consists of the suspect's race and gender, and have no evidence of discrimination, they can act on the description without violating the Equal Protection Clause of the Fourteenth Amendment.

The court noted that subjecting officers to an equal protection strict-scrutiny analysis in making investigative detentions or arrests could hinder police work. Officers fearful of personal liability might fail to act when they are expected to. The court held, "Police work, as we know it, would be impaired and the safety of all citizens compromised. . . . The most vulnerable and isolated would be harmed the most. And, if police effectiveness is hobbled by special racial rules, residents of inner cities would be harmed most of all."

The Commission on Accreditation for Law Enforcement Agencies (CALEA) has added a prohibition against racial profiling Although conceding that profiling can be a useful tool in law enforcement, bias-based profiling is prohibited (Standard 1.2.9).

In 1999, Connecticut became the first state to pass racial profiling legislation, requiring every municipal police agency and the state police to collect race data for every police-initiated traffic stop. Since that time, measures dealing with racial profiling have been introduced in many states. Data collection is a large issue in many departments.

The Police Executive Research Foundation (PERF) has published *By the Numbers: A Guide for Analyzing Race Data from Vehicle Stops* (Fridell, 2004). The purposes of this Community Oriented Policing Services–supported document are "(1) to describe the social science challenges associated with data collection initiatives so that agencies and other stakeholders can be made fully aware of both the potential and limitations of police-citizen contact data collection, and (2) to provide clear guidelines for analyzing and interpreting the data so that the jurisdictions collecting them can conduct the most valid and responsible analyses possible with the resources they have" (Fridell, p.2).

The Racial Profiling Data Collection Center at Northeastern University, funded by a grant from the Bureau of Justice Statistics, features a Web site that explains the purpose of data collection as well as its benefits and limitations:

Focus on Data Collection?

In the late 1990s, in response to allegations of racial profiling, jurisdictions around the country began to track information about those who are stopped, searched, ticketed, and/or arrested by police officers. These data collection efforts are an attempt to provide the tangible numbers that will enable police and community leaders to better understand their policing activities. With this understanding, departments will be able to examine and revamp policing strategies based on effectiveness, reconfigure deployment of police resources, or take other measures.

Data collection includes both the collection of the numbers and objective analysis of the data, which is often done through a scholarly partnership between the police department and outside experts. Data analysis allows law enforcement collaboration with community stakeholders to discuss the results and the ways police resources can be used most effectively. Though many departments have begun to collect some data on traffic stops, the resources discussed on this Web site offer additional ways to use such data both to improve police/community dialogue and increase officer accountability.

BENEFITS OF DATA COLLECTION

The implementation of data collection systems has led to countless benefits for police departments and communities around the country. Data collection processes can:

- Send a strong message to the community that the department is against racial profiling and that racial profiling is inconsistent with effective policing and equal protection
- Build trust and respect for the police in the communities they serve
- Provide departments with information about the types of stops being made by officers, the proportion of police time spent on high-discretion stops, and the results of such stops
- Help shape and develop training programs to educate officers about racial profiling and interactions with the community
- Enable the development of police and community dialogue to assess the quality and quantity of police-citizen encounters

- Allay community concerns about the activities of police
- Identify potential police misconduct and deter it, when implemented as part of a comprehensive early warning system
- Retain autonomous officer discretion and allow for flexible responses in different situations

LIMITATIONS OF DATA COLLECTION

While jurisdictions can derive many benefits from implementing data collection systems, they also face several potential challenges. Such challenges may include the following:

- Concerns about extra-budgetary expenditures associated with collecting data
- Developing a benchmark against which the data can be compared
- The potential burden an improved data collection procedure will have on individual officers in the course of a normal shift
- The potential for police disengagement from their duties, which may lead to officers scaling back on the number of legitimate stops
- The challenge of ensuring that officers will fully comply with a directive to collect stop data
- Ensuring that data is recorded on all stops made, and that the data collected is correct
- The difficulty of determining the race or ethnicity of the persons stopped
- Once data is collected and analyzed, the difficulty of making a definite conclusion about whether racial profiling exists or not, as this question requires more than a "yes" or "no" answer

These challenges may seem daunting, and there are no easy answers to any of them. If a law enforcement agency is aware of these challenges from the outset, however, it will be better able to address them when they arise. Hundreds of jurisdictions are successfully collecting data despite these challenges.

Source: Institute on Race & Justice, Northeastern University.

Another area of traffic enforcement often associated with enhanced liability is officers' "public duty" to get drunken or drugged drivers off the road.

RECOGNIZING AND STOPPING DRIVERS "UNDER THE INFLUENCE"

"Every 30 minutes someone dies in an alcohol-related crash. Alcohol is a factor in 6 percent of all traffic crashes and over 40 percent of all fatal crashes" ("Drunk Driving," n.d.). In 2007, an estimated 12,998 people were killed in alcohol-impaired driving crashes—a decline of 3.76 percent from 2006 ("2007 Traffic Safety Annual Assessment," 2008).

Most police officers are familiar with the common physical symptoms of the person under the influence of alcohol or drugs: slurred speech, bloodshot or watery eyes, delayed reactions, lack of coordination, staggering, smell of alcoholic beverage on breath or clothing, confusion, dizziness, nausea, exaggerated actions. Officers must be cautious, however, because many of these symptoms can be produced by medical conditions such as diabetes, epilepsy, heart attack or concussion. Driving actions that tend to indicate a DUI suspect include

- Unusually slow or excessive speeds for driving conditions or posted limits.
- Erratic starts and stops.
- Weaving or drifting between the center line and fog line in a lane, or straddling the center line.
- Failing to signal turns and lane changes.
- Problems making turns (either too wide or cutting across the curb).
- Driving the wrong direction on a roadway.
- Repeated use of horn in traffic.

Any one of these actions by itself may indicate only carelessness or haste, but a combination of such actions provides probable cause for an officer to stop the car. The officer must then determine if the driver is "under the influence."

Field and Chemical Tests for DUI

nystagmus
The involuntary bouncing or jerking of the eye, a possible cause of which is intoxification.

blood-alcohol concentration (BAC)
The weight of alcohol in grams per milliliter of blood.

Common standardized field sobriety tests (SFSTs) include the heel-to-toe straight line walk, the finger-to-the-nose test, a balance test, a one-leg stand, counting backwards, and reciting the alphabet from a certain letter to another letter. One test used by most officers is the horizontal gaze nystagmus (HGN) test. **Nystagmus** is the involuntary jerking or bouncing of the eye, a possible cause of which is intoxication. In performing an HGN test, a thoroughly trained officer moves a pencil or fingertip in front of a driver's face and watches the driver's eyes for several things: equal tracking (making sure both eyes track the same) of the moving object, lack of smooth pursuit, distinct nystagmus ("bouncing" of the eye) at maximum deviation, and onset of nystagmus before 45 degrees. The officer may also check for vertical nystagmus. The way a driver performs on these various HGN tests can indicate to a trained officer the motorist's level of intoxication. According to Rao (2003, p.233), "The three recommended tests—walk and turn, one-leg stand and horizontal gaze nystagmus . . . have been shown to be almost 90 percent accurate in identifying persons with a BAC above 0.10 percent."

Chemical tests are also used. Because alcohol is absorbed directly into the bloodstream, its level of concentration can be tested. The **blood-alcohol concentration (BAC)** test represents the weight of alcohol in grams per milliliter of blood. A BAC of .08 represents 80 milligrams of alcohol per 100 milliliters of blood. (Some states use the term *blood-alcohol level [BAL].*) States set specific blood-alcohol levels considered to indicate legal intoxication, with all 50 states setting the limit at .08.

A driver's blood-alcohol concentration can also be documented through a breath test, called a breath alcohol equivalent (BAQ) test. The same percentage should be obtained from both the breath and the blood test. Many squads carry a small, portable preliminary alcohol screening (PAS) device, also known as a preliminary breath test or PBT, that can display a BAC level after a person suspected of drunken driving blows into it.

A note about breath tests: If a PBT in the field indicates a driver is over the legal BAC limit, a more conclusive and accurate test is required. Currently, however, the use of the Intoxilyzer machine, a nonportable device used by police departments nationwide, is being challenged by defense attorneys from several states because of a technical issue with the machine. In Minnesota, for example, the pending status of this case has prevented police officers from giving offenders the option of a breath test, thus restricting officer's choices to either a blood or urine sample only. If an offender requests a blood sample, he or she cannot be jailed because the results of the blood test are not immediate. In addition, it is costly, timely and often dangerous to take blood from offenders. The status of this legal challenge is being monitored.

Recognizing the Driver under the Influence of Drugs

Often the symptoms of an individual impaired by drugs are very similar to those exhibited by an intoxicated person. This has given rise to a new specialty, the **drug recognition expert (DRE)** or **drug recognition technician (DRT)**. These experts are police officers with more than 80 hours of classroom training and 100 hours of field certification training, in addition to passing rigorous written and practical tests. Such specialists perform in the field, train other officers within the department and can serve as expert witnesses in court cases requiring such testimony.

drug recognition expert (DRE)
Specially trained individual who can determine if someone is under the influence of drugs. Also called *drug recognition technician*.

drug recognition technician (DRT)
See *drug recognition expert*.

Using speed or meth often results in changes in physical condition and appearance, conditions that commonly allow officers to identify such "speed freaks" and "meth heads" (Grossi, 2009, p.24). The first is *body odor*: "To put it plainly: speed freaks stink. Chronic meth use causes tweakers to sweat constantly. In addition to the odor of methamphetamine oozing from their pores, their hair and skin are usually greasy."

The second characteristic is *twitches*: "Speed freaks constantly move their heads and look around, left, right and behind. Their hands will be constantly busy too; they constantly touch themselves and their hair, and adjust their clothing. They'll also be continually shifting their weight from foot to foot."

The third characteristic Grossi (2009, p.26) describes is a *rapid pulse*, noting that all people being stopped by the police may have rapid pulses because they are nervous. But speed freaks may have pulse rates in the mid to high 100s: "Sometimes the veins in their neck will be pulsing visibly." Other characteristics include dilated pupils and rapid, paranoid, disconnected speech.

People suspected of being under the influence of drugs or alcohol may be asked to take a blood, urine or breath test. If they refuse, the consequences can be extremely negative because of the concept of implied consent.

Implied Consent

The **implied consent law** states that those who request and receive driver's licenses must agree to take tests to determine their ability to drive. Refusal will result in license revocation. The implied consent law is based on the precept that driving an automobile is not a personal right but a privilege. Permission to drive a motor vehicle is given under whatever conditions and terms are considered reasonable and just by the granting state. Courts have uniformly upheld this principle.

implied consent law
A law stating that those who request and receive driver's licenses agree to take tests to determine their ability to drive; refusal will result in revocation of the license.

In theory, no one is deprived of his or her constitutional rights by the implied consent law, nor is anything demanded of the driver that was not required before the law was enacted. The implied consent law gives drivers a choice: "If you wish to drive an automobile on the public highways of this state, you shall be deemed to have consented to submit to certain prescribed circumstances and conditions (such as breath tests). If you fail to submit to such tests, your privilege to drive on the state's highways will be revoked."

Videotaping Drivers

Many police departments have made it standard practice to videotape individuals stopped for DWI. This does not violate the person's constitutional rights. *Pennsylvania v. Muniz* (1990) is the leading case on Fifth and Sixth Amendment issues in videotaping drivers under the influence. The question before the Supreme Court was whether the police must give motorists suspected of DWI the *Miranda* warning before asking routine questions and videotaping them. The Court said, "No. The privilege against self-incrimination protects an accused from being compelled to testify against himself or otherwise provide the state with evidence of a testimonial or communicative nature, but not from being compelled by the state to produce real or physical evidence."

However, even though it is not a violation of a person's constitutional rights, videotaping a DWI stop may not be in the best interests of the prosecution. Unless the suspect is "falling down drunk," the videotape may actually work in the suspect's favor. Too often an officer's word appears to contradict what a jury sees on videotape. This is not because the officer has embellished the facts. It is because the jury is untrained at detecting intoxication at levels as low as .08 BAC in a defendant viewed on a video monitor.

Strategies to Deter DUI

Traffic officers cannot do the job alone. Effective strategies to address the problem of impaired driving must include tougher laws, tougher judges and frequent and ongoing awareness campaigns to keep impaired drivers out of the driver's seat.

Strategies to deter DUI include educating drivers through awareness campaigns and establishing sobriety checkpoints and saturation patrols. Additional efforts aimed at repeat offenders include using ignition interlocks and enacting vehicle forfeiture programs.

Education and Awareness Campaigns Young people must be educated about the dangers of driving drunk and about the hazards of driving while high on pot, speed, cocaine, crack or various other drugs used today for recreation, escape and thrills. Two active national organizations committed to reducing drunk driving by raising awareness of the dangers it poses are Mothers Against Drunk Driving (MADD) and Students Against Drunk Driving (SADD).

Founded in 1980, MADD's purpose, according to its brochure, is "to stop drunk driving and to support victims of this violent crime" ("Help Keep Families Together," n.d.). SADD programs have been organized in many high schools throughout the country to help new teenage drivers acknowledge the serious responsibilities that accompany a license to drive. Common SADD activities include designated driver programs for "special" events where underage drinking is likely, such as homecoming and prom, and staging mock crashes and funerals for students to "witness" the deadly consequences of irresponsible driving.

Sobriety Checkpoints and Saturation Patrols Many states are using sobriety checkpoints to deter and detect drunk drivers. In *Michigan Department of State Police v. Sitz* (1990), the Supreme Court ruled, "Sobriety checkpoints are constitutional" because the states have a "substantial interest" in keeping intoxicated drivers off the streets and that the "measure of intrusion on motorists stopped at sobriety checkpoints is slight." The Court also cautioned against random stops, authorizing only well-conceived, carefully structured programs.

Drug Checkpoints In *City of Indianapolis v. Edmond* (2000), the Supreme Court ruled that police may not set up drug interdiction roadblocks because the Fourth Amendment requires that even a brief seizure of a motorist by the roadside requires a suspicion that the motorist committed a crime. As Justice O'Connor wrote, "We cannot sanction stops justified only by the generalized and ever-present possibility that interrogation and inspection may reveal that any given motorist has committed some crime."

61.1.10 CALEA STANDARD 61.1.10 suggests several countermeasures in various combinations in selective alcohol enforcement programs: "Selective assignment of personnel at the time when, and to the locations where analyses have shown that a significant number of violations and/or collisions involving incidence of drinking-driving collisions to ascertain the characteristic violation profile of the problem drinker who drives; selected alcohol related collision investigations and analyses of findings; selective roadway checks for deterrence purposes; and selective enforcement of drinking driving laws through concentration on existing laws and the expeditious processing of violators." (*Standards for Law Enforcement Agencies*, 5th edition, 2006)

Dealing with Repeat Drunk Drivers No matter how severe the consequences of drunk driving are, it seems some drivers are always willing to push their luck by continuing to get behind the wheel while intoxicated. The NHTSA's research shows that DWI offenders have usually committed between 200 and 2,000 unapprehended drunk driving violations before their first arrest, and that an estimated 60 to 80 percent of people with suspended licenses continue to drive.

Ignition interlocks are one solution aimed at the major problem of recidivism in DWI. An ignition interlock monitors how much a person has had to drink, and if the person has had too much, the vehicle will not start. To prevent someone other than the convicted DWI offender from using the system, a breath code is established.

Several states have *vehicle forfeiture* legislation permitting the permanent confiscation of vehicles of repeat DUI/DWI offenders—drive drunk; lose your car.

Legal Liability

The decision to arrest a drunk driver is not discretionary if the state has a law against drunk driving (which all states do). Arresting impaired drivers is an officer's *public duty*, a principle established in *Carleton v. Town of Framingham* (1993). In this case, an officer had spoken with an intoxicated driver inside a store but had put off taking him into custody, deciding instead to wait outside the store until the driver got into his car. When the officer then attempted a traffic stop for DUI, the intoxicated driver refused and continued driving, which resulted in a head-on collision and a lawsuit against the police.

ENFORCEMENT AND PURSUIT

Pursuit is usually thought of as an officer in a police car pursuing a suspect in a vehicle; however, foot pursuits are also common and hazardous.

Foot Pursuit

Grossi (2008a, p.28) notes, "Foot chases remain some of the most emotionally charged and dangerous contacts officers make." Foot pursuits get the adrenalin flowing: "Like most high-risk contacts, when adrenaline starts flowing, officer safety tactics can go right out the window" (Grossi). It is recommended that officers consider a number of factors before chasing a suspect on foot, including the environmental factors involved, the time of day, what communications are available for backup and what physical condition the officer is in: "Even if you do catch the perp, if you've burned up all your energy during the rundown, will you have enough left to cuff and stuff your prize catch?" (Grossi).

Vehicle Pursuit

pursuit
An active attempt by a law enforcement officer on duty in a patrol car to apprehend one or more occupants of a moving motor vehicle, providing the driver is aware of the attempt and is resisting apprehension by maintaining or increasing his speed or by ignoring the law enforcement officer's attempt to stop him. Can also refer to a foot chase.

As with foot pursuit, vehicle pursuits can be extremely hazardous. A vehicle **pursuit** is "an active attempt by a law enforcement officer on duty in a patrol car to apprehend one or more occupants of a moving motor vehicle, providing the driver of such vehicle is aware of the attempt and is resisting apprehension by maintaining or increasing his speed or by ignoring the law enforcement officer's attempt to stop him" (Nugent et al., n.d., p.1). This definition establishes four key points: (1) that the law enforcement officer is in a patrol car and, therefore, should be recognizable as a law enforcement officer; (2) that the driver is aware that the law enforcement officer is trying to stop him or her and resists the attempt; (3) that the reason for the pursuit may embrace traffic offenses, including speeding itself, and felonies; and (4) that the vehicle speed may vary (Nugent et al.). Yates (2009) explains the importance of pursuits:

> Vehicle pursuits are no doubt one of the most dangerous activities that occur in law enforcement. Pursuits are particularly unique in that their dangers are often aimed directly at innocent victims; studies suggest that more than 300 civilians are killed each year in police vehicle pursuits. Despite the dangers, all but just a few agencies across the country have continued the practice of vehicle pursuits. Obviously the function of crime control and apprehending criminals is the reason why vehicle pursuits continue, but agencies must balance the need to apprehend criminals versus the danger that is placed on society. Several court cases through the years combined with an increased awareness of the dangers of vehicle pursuits have caused more police agencies to restrict their police pursuits. While these restrictions range greatly from a "violent felony only" policy to specific categories of evaluation before a pursuit can continue, these restrictions have no doubt minimized the dangers to our officers and the communities they serve.

An effective pursuit policy must balance crime control efforts against the threat a pursuit poses to public safety and officer and department liability.

The nature of this balance is seen in the evolution of the legal decisions regarding police pursuit, as well as in police pursuit policies (Alpert, 2008). Lum and Fachner (2008, p.8) stress, "The balance between crime control and safety/liability is a central framework in the discourse on police pursuits and is reflected in police policies, research and practice. However, in addition to these on-going concerns, two equally important and contemporary contexts should also motivate pursuit policy reform and data collection. These contexts include the advent of a new era of policing that emphasizes proactivity, prevention, and problem-solving, accompanied by an increasing use and demand for information and analysis to support those innovations and hold officers and agencies accountable for the resulting outcomes."

Pursuit Policies and Data

In 2002, the IACP developed the National Police Pursuit Database, a user-friendly Web-based database for storing pursuit information enabling law enforcement leaders to set pursuit guidelines, make informed policy and training decisions and generate statistical reports to assist in analysis and comparison with other jurisdictions. Analysis of the 7,737 policies currently in the database indicates that 94.8 percent of the policies allowed pursuit (Lum and Fachner, 2008). This database can help departments develop their pursuit policies to balance deterrence and safety, and allow departments to meet the demands of proactive police innovations including directed (hot spots) patrol, problem-oriented policing, CompStat, crime analysis, information-driven management, zero tolerance, community policing and evidence-based policing: "These innovations change the use and symbolic meaning of police vehicles, in turn significantly altering the nature, frequency, risk, and consequences of high-speed pursuits" (Lum and Fachner).

Some departments have a "chase-them-all" policy. Others chase only those vehicles involved in felonies. And a few departments have a "no-chase" policy. Among the reasons given for initiating a pursuit, traffic violations were the most common (42.3 percent), followed by a belief that the vehicle was stolen (18.2 percent) and the belief that the driver was intoxicated (14.9 percent). Felonies initiated pursuits more often than misdemeanors (Lum and Fachner, 2008, p.56).

Issues that should be addressed in a pursuit policy include (Lum and Fachner, 2008, p.40):

- **Supervision, monitoring, and accountability.**
- **Safety.**
- **Driving conditions.**
- **Vehicles involved.**
- **Situational context.**
- **Devices and tactics used.**

Pursuits were recorded by 89.0 percent of the departments; 84.9 percent kept in communication. Public safety was specifically mentioned in 95.9 percent of the policies; officer safety in 84.9 percent; suspect safety in 34.2 percent.

Driving conditions such as weather, visibility and traffic variables are commonly included in pursuit policies—91.8 percent of the policies said both weather considerations and traffic considerations were discretionary; 57.5 percent said visibility considerations were discretionary. Relatively few policies allow pursuing officers to drive the wrong way during pursuit (19.2 percent) or go off road in their pursuit (5.5 percent). And only 4.1 percent placed limits on officer speed.

Regarding the number of vehicles involved, 84.9 percent of the policies allowed more than one vehicle to pursue; 54.8 percent allowed unmarked cars to pursue until a marked car was available; 53.4 percent allowed motorcycles to be used until a marked car was available; 28.8 percent mentioned air support; 15.1 percent said unmarked cars could not be used; and 11.0 percent said motorcycles could not be used.

Situational context includes the type of offense involved and whether the suspect is known. The type of offense limited pursuits in 47.9 percent of the policies—pursuit allowed for any offense (52.1 percent), misdemeanors or worse (21.9 percent), felonies only (12.3 percent);, and no mention (8.2 percent). That suspect identification must end the pursuit was required in only 4.1 percent of the policies.

Various devices and tactics may be used during pursuit. Roadblocks and tire deflation could be used according to 61.6 percent of the policies; intentional collisions could be used in 57.5 percent; any contact was considered "deadly force" in 60.3 percent; and paralleling could be used in 32.9 percent.

Only 6 percent of the pursuits studied actually employed some form of termination method. Most pursuits ended when the suspect stopped (35.7 percent), the suspect crashed (18.4 percent) or the suspect eluded the police (17.9 percent). In only 0.8 percent was the officer involved in a crash (Lum and Fachner, 2008, p.66). When a termination method was used, the most common method was tire deflator (3.4 percent). Other methods used, which were identified in fewer than 1 percent of the policies, were roadblocks, rolling roadblocks and the Pursuit Intervention Technique (PIT) maneuver, in which the violator is spun to a stop.

Pursuit policies can take several forms. One type of pursuit management can be viewed as a continuum, ranging from low-risk interdiction actions such as trailing of low-level offenders (those presenting a low-to-moderate public threat such as persons engaged in traffic offenses and less serious crimes), to high-risk interdiction involving vehicle contact maneuvers and possible discharge of firearms for offenders engaged in life-threatening felonies that justify the use of deadly force (Ashley, 2004). Disengagement from the pursuit is always an option.

Whenever pursuit does occur, if damage results, officers and their departments may face lawsuits.

Liability Issues

At issue usually is whether police officers violate the Fourteenth Amendment's guarantee of substantive due process by causing death through deliberate or reckless indifference to life in a high-speed automobile chase to apprehend a suspected offender. The Supreme Court, in *County of Sacramento v. Lewis* (1998), held, "In high-speed vehicle pursuit cases, liability in Section 1983 cases ensues only if the conduct of the officer 'shocks the conscience.' The lower standard of 'deliberate indifference' does not apply." Justice Souter noted that an officer's decision to pursue a fleeing suspect often is made in a "split-second . . . in circumstances that are tense, uncertain and rapidly evolving." Officers are forced to "balance on the one hand the need to stop a suspect and show that flight from the law is no way to freedom, and, on the other, the high-speed threat to everyone within stopping range, be they suspects, their passengers, other drivers or bystanders."

More recently, in *Scott v. Harris* (2007), the Supreme Court backed the police in the pursuit case (Scarry, 2007, p.58). Harris sued Officer Scott for pursuing his vehicle and ramming it, resulting in injuries to Harris that left him a quadriplegic: "The issue in the case was 'Whether a law enforcement official can, consistent with the Fourth Amendment, attempt to stop a fleeing motorist from continuing his public-endangering flight by ramming the motorist's car from behind. Put another way: Can an officer take actions that place a fleeing motorist at risk of serious injury or death in order to stop the motorist's flight from endangering the lives of innocent bystanders?' The Court's answer: Yes" (Means, 2007, p.43). The Court held, "A police officer's attempt to terminate a dangerous high-speed car chase that threatens the lives of innocent bystanders does not violate the Fourth Amendment, even when it places the fleeing motorist at risk of serious injury or death."

An advance in technology that may help officers engaged in pursuits is the DriveCam. This is a black box recorder that automatically records everything a driver sees, hears and feels for the 10 seconds before and after a crash, missed accident, abusive driving or other event of interest.

ENFORCEMENT AND TRANSPORTATION OF HAZARDOUS MATERIALS

In many states, traffic enforcement also includes enforcing truck weight limits, enforcing bicycle and pedestrian regulations and regulating transportation of hazardous materials. More than 13,000 transportation-related hazardous materials (HM or hazmat) accidents occurred in 2006, with 85 percent occurring on the nation's highways or railways (Hanson, 2007, p.80). Yet traffic enforcement of transporting hazardous materials is often overlooked. Most traffic codes do not include dealing with the transportation of hazmat.

A hazardous materials enforcement program should consist of

- Terminal audits.
- Shipper and other audits.
- Road enforcement.
- Technical assistance and enforcement training.
- Emergency response.

The police should conduct periodic audits at transporters' hazardous materials terminals to ensure compliance with regulations, and they should conduct periodic audits of those who pack the materials to be transported. Police should conduct periodic inspections on the highway as well.

The Electronic Emergency Response Management System (E2RMS) was developed to enhance the response to a terrorist attack or major hazmat spill by improving communications and access to timely and actionable information: "E2RMS uses an automated, software-based rule engine . . . to analyze transportation and critical infrastructure data to predict and automatically send alerts when a material in transportation poses a threat" (Moses, 2007, pp.52–53). With this system, authorized transporters and shippers can call a toll-free number to determine whether a specific vehicle is where it is supposed to be at any given time.

In addition, training should be made available to carriers and shippers, as well as to other law enforcement agencies in the state. Finally, law enforcement should have clearly established emergency response plans in case an accident or terrorist incident involving hazardous materials should occur: "Protecting officers and the community at large, in a hazmat situation, begins with surveying businesses and other vulnerable areas before an incident occurs" (Hanson, 2007, p.82). The emergency hazmat response is discussed in Chapter 8.

CRASH MANAGEMENT AND INVESTIGATION

Motor vehicle traffic crashes were the leading cause of death in the United States in 2005 ("Motor Vehicle Traffic Crashes," 2008, p.1). According to the NHTSA, in 2007, "There were an estimated 7,024,000 police-reported traffic crashes, in which 41,059 people were killed and 2,491,000 people were injured; 4,275,000 crashes involved property damage only" ("Overview," 2007).

The a-crash-won't-happen-to-me syndrome is common among the American driving public.

When a crash does happen, people are frequently in shock or disbelief. They may be dazed or seriously injured. They may be hysterical. They may be belligerent.

At a crash scene, officers are responsible for

- Managing the scene, including protecting it, attending to injuries, keeping traffic moving and restoring normal traffic flow.
- Investigating and reporting the cause(s) of the crash, including the possibility of a crime (e.g., criminal vehicular operation, etc.).

Formerly vehicle collisions were called *accidents*; however, this term implied a rather random, causeless chain of events that resulted in the crash of one or more vehicles. Recognizing that many, if not most, such incidents happen because of some identifiable factor(s) or reason(s), not by chance or coincidence, these collisions are now referred to as *crashes*. A spokesperson for the USDOT estimates it costs $200 billion for motorists to wait during traffic slowdowns and stoppages caused by crashes and that such crashes cause secondary incidents and increased air pollution (Galvin, 2007, p.34).

Officers called to major crashes often have multiple responsibilities, such as administering first aid to injured drivers, passengers and possibly pedestrians, while keeping the traffic situation from causing further damage and injury. After the victims have been tended to and removed from the scene, investigation of the crash can commence.
© AP Images/Chuck Liddy

Responding to a Crash Call

Officers called to the scene of a crash usually must proceed as rapidly as possible, treating it as an emergency because injuries are often involved. However, be aware that in responding to a crash, your mindset can drastically change: "And like a pursuit, heart rate and blood pressure rise, tunnel vision develops, and adrenaline flows. *Bottom line*: You can't do any good unless you get there. Take the necessary time appropriate for the situation and get there safely" (Molnar, 2008, p.20).

Once there, officers should park to protect the scene, but not to endanger other motorists coming on the scene. Once the scene is protected, the first responsibility is to attend to the victims. If injuries are serious, an ambulance or rescue squad should be called immediately. During this time, one officer should be keeping the traffic moving.

Crash scene management is critical because the more severe results of a crash can occur after the initial collision. This can include the injured not being properly or promptly cared for, other vehicles becoming involved in the crash, fires starting, hazardous materials leaking or other matters that increase the probability of injury or property loss and increase congestion.

The National Incident Management System (NIMS) developed by the U.S. Department of Homeland Security has a traffic incident management system (TIMS) that adapts well to the control of traffic incidents. When an incident occurs, the incident commander is expected to

- Take immediate steps to stabilize the incident, provide for life safety and establish traffic control. A perimeter for the scene needs to be established and evacuate persons as required.
- Evaluate the situation and call for needed assistance.
- Triage the injured and provide appropriate field treatment and emergency care transportation.

- Extend the area of operation to ensure safe and orderly traffic flow through and around the incident scene.
- Provide for the safety, accountability and welfare of personnel, a responsibility that will be ongoing throughout the incident.
- Restore the roadway to normal operations after an incident has been cleared.

Sometimes problems arise at a crash scene when police, firefighters and emergency medical services (EMS) personnel converge on the scene. For example, firefighters often arrive on the scene with a fire truck and police officers feel it is simply in the way. The police may demand it be moved because it is obstructing traffic. What they should realize, however, is that fire trucks are brought to crash scenes for two very specific purposes: (1) the equipment officers may need is already on the truck, and (2) the truck provides good traffic control, protecting the crash scene and those responding to it.

Crash Investigation and Reconstruction

After victims have been tended to, officers should turn their attention to the crash investigation phase. In minor crashes, the so-called fender benders, a thorough investigation is seldom required. Officers should make certain the drivers involved exchange insurance information and complete the required forms. Many major crashes, including those involving disabling injuries and fatalities, are investigated by officers with specialized training. Such serious collisions often require a reconstruction of the crash, and the services of a crash reconstruction specialist may be required.

Crash investigation usually begins with taking statements from those involved and from any witnesses. It has been suggested that officers not ask bystanders if they are witnesses to the crash, because they might not want to get involved. A better question is, What did you see happen? After statements are taken, a physical examination of the vehicles involved and the scene is conducted. Officers should measure the location of skid marks, the final position of vehicle(s), roadway widths, distances to bridge abutments, utility poles and the like. Molnar (2008, p.21) advises police to listen to the voice of the roadway: "The roadway shows you the vehicle(s)' path prior to collision, the roadway surface factors affecting that path, the area where the actual crash occurred and the paths each vehicle took after impact."

Photographs and careful notes are also critical in most serious crash investigations. A crash investigator should have a camera and be skilled in its use. Investigators should photograph debris showing approximate point of impact—for example, broken glass, dirt from the underside of the vehicles and tire imprints or skid marks in soft material such as mud, snow and sand. Also, photographs should be taken of more permanent evidence: roadside objects, view obstructions, traffic signs, vehicular damage, road and tire marks and the roadway environment.

Many law enforcement agencies are now using surveying techniques to map crash scenes: "Law enforcement professionals trained in forensic mapping are using total stations to map fog lines, street width, center lane dividers, utility poles, skid marks and any other details that might help explain the circumstances of a crash" (Pope, 2007b, p.57). With this information, officers can usually determine the speed of each vehicle at impact within 2 miles per hour and use such information in court (Pope). Such precise measurements are typically used in prosecutable fatalities, so it is important to have as much evidence as possible.

The availability of this technique to crash investigations means law enforcement no longer needs to shut down roadways to take all the needed measurements, saving the driving public much frustration, especially when crashes occurred during rush hour: "As the use of technology that is traditionally reserved for construction planning, building maps and determining ownership boundaries continues to grow among law enforcement teams, even more police officers across the country will be able to work more accurately, efficiently, and, most importantly, safely in order to protect the public" (Pope, 2007a, p.37).

Brown (2008, p.44) observes, "Collision investigators no longer respond merely to gather information for insurance companies. These days, people are being tried for offenses ranging all the way up to murder for killing someone while behind the wheel. Furthermore, defense lawyers now hire highly educated engineering firms for their defense, and going up against an engineer can intimidate some officers. Having the training and technology to back up your investigations is imperative because no matter how many collisions your agency investigates each year, it's just a matter of time until you're hit with a potentially criminal fatal collision."

Of assistance in accident reconstruction might be the "black box. These "black boxes" or Event Data Recorders (EDR) were designed to tell a car when to deploy its airbag, but the data contained has also been instrumental in determining the cause of a crash.

Crashes Involving Pedestrians In 2007, 4,654 pedestrians died in traffic crashes—a 13 percent decreased from 1997. On average, a pedestrian is killed in a traffic crash every 113 minutes and injured in a traffic crash every 8 minutes ("Pedestrians," 2007, p.1). A disproportionate number of pedestrian victims are children. Nearly 33 percent of pedestrians killed or injured in traffic crashes are under the age of 15, yet this group represents only about 15 percent of the total U.S. population (*Pedestrian Safety*, n.d.).

Pedestrian Safety: Report to Congress (2008, p.1) notes that many technologies are being developed to help ensure pedestrians the right-of-way, but they need further research and are not yet market ready. In the meantime, the Pedestrian Safety Campaign offers one effective approach. "The Pedestrian Safety Campaign" (n.d.), developed by the U.S. Department of Transportation's Federal Highway Administration, consists of ready-made outreach materials that states and communities can customize and use locally. These materials are currently being used in over 400 communities nationwide.

Crashes involving pedestrians are very different from those involving only vehicles and, thus, require different investigative techniques. However, like vehicle crash investigations, photographs should be taken at all pedestrian-involved crash scenes, including photographs of the victim, the vehicle involved and the roadway.

Fake "Accidents"

Staged auto crashes are always a possibility. Ambulance-chasing personal injury mills include a "capper" or "runner" who spreads the word that anyone involved in an auto collision can come to their agency for help. Some crashes are arranged for insurance fraud purposes.

Crash Reduction Strategies

One strategy to reduce crashes is use of decoy patrols as described earlier in the chapter. Another way to reduce crashes is through educational programs for beginning drivers.

Crash Reports

Complete and accurate crash reports are critical to selective enforcement and other traffic safety measures. Some agencies are one to two months behind in manually entering data from traffic incidents, making the data no longer "real time." To combat this problem, many agencies are turning to electronic report forms.

Legal Liability

Crashes frequently result in lawsuits, so careful documentation of all facts is important. In addition, crash-scene management and investigation may also be the target of lawsuits, with the officers involved, their department and their city being named as defendants. Accurate, complete documentation helps should a lawsuit be initiated and helps identify areas to be targeted for selective enforcement.

Legal liability in crash cases generally involves three areas of public duty: (1) to warn and protect other motorists, (2) to render assistance and (3) to secure the scene. Not all traffic services involve enforcement or crashes. Much of it deals simply with keeping the traffic flowing smoothly.

TRAFFIC AND COMMUNITY POLICING

In many communities, traffic is considered a serious problem, one that plagues quiet residential communities and crime-ridden inner cities alike. Citizens want to see police on the street, and citizens don't want to see police ignoring traffic violations.

An approach to safety on our roadways emphasizing partnerships and citizen involvement is the Safe Communities program, sponsored by the USDOT. Increasing from a few sites in 1996 when the program began to 755 Safe Community Programs by December 1999, the program was operating in every state, the Pacific Territories and Puerto Rico. The program is based on the philosophy that communities are in the best position to affect improvements in motor vehicle and other transportation-related safety problems. According to its Web site ("Safe Communities," n.d.),

> The Safe Communities approach represents a new way community programs are established and managed. All partners participate as equals in developing solutions, sharing successes, assuming risks, and building a community

structure and process to continue improvement of community life through the reduction of injuries and costs.

A Safe Community expands resources and partnerships, increases program visibility, and establishes community ownership and support for transportation injury prevention programs. As the Safe Community concept addresses all injuries, transportation and traffic safety becomes positioned within the context of the entire injury problem. . . .

Four main characteristics define Safe Communities:

1. Injury data analysis and (where possible) data linkage
2. Expanded partnerships, especially with health care providers and businesses
3. Citizen involvement and input
4. An integrated and comprehensive injury control system.

. . . The objective of Safe Communities is to promote community-based solutions to address transportation safety and other injury problems.

The Safe Communities Service Center helps further this objective by monitoring and tracking activities conducted by the USDOT and NHTSA, as well as other federal, state and local partners. The center also catalogs information, resources and materials so it can link community coalitions directly to providers who can service their specific needs. The center is continually identifying a national network of Safe Community practitioners, marketing best practices, facilitating new partnerships, promoting citizen involvement, evaluating campaign progress, and initiating a number of other ways to build Safe Communities. The center is located at the NHTSA regional office in Fort Worth, Texas. In addition to services provided within its interactive Web site, it provides one-stop shopping for a community's needs for information and resources related to constructing Safe Communities.

TRAFFIC AND PROBLEM-ORIENTED POLICING

The 2001 Winner of the Herman Goldstein *Excellence in Problem-Oriented Policing* was awarded to the California Highway Patrol (CHP) for its Corridor Safety Program: A Collaborative Approach to Traffic Safety (Helmick et al., 2001, pp.32–35). The program used the SARA model to address a high rate of fatal crashes on an infamous stretch of rural highway in California, the roadway where actor James Dean was killed in the late 1950s, dubbed "Blood Alley."

Scanning

Scanning was rigorous, with 550 qualifying roadway segments examined. The selection process incorporated a variety of quantitative measures of the safety challenges on roadways throughout the state, along with more subjective information from traffic safety officials. Three years of collision and victim data were reviewed to minimize any statistical anomalies. Segments less than eight miles in length and those with an average daily traffic count of 1,000 vehicles or fewer were eliminated. Also, to be included in the selection pool, potential corridors had to pass through or be adjacent to an urban area and fall under the jurisdiction of the CHP. Segments with fewer than five deaths in three years were also eliminated. Based on statistical rankings and input from local experts, recommendations for corridor selection were presented to CHP's executive management, which selected State Routes 41/46.

Analysis

The CHP formed a multidisciplinary task force consisting of 31 members representing the CHP, Caltrans [California Department of Transportation], local governments, fire departments, city police departments, state legislators, local public works departments and federal transportation officials. This task force studied the physical characteristics that might adversely affect safety: the adequacy of regulatory and advisory signage; the number of traffic or passing lanes; the presence of roadway shoulders and medians, and their size; the presence or absence of guardrails and other safety aids; the condition of the pavement; and the presence or lack of landscaping. The task force found that much of the corridor was quite remote, largely without cellular phone service and having too few call boxes. Call response times for emergency services depended on the EMS unit with jurisdiction over the area, sometimes not the closest unit. The roadway lacked adequate shoulders and medians, and existing signage was confusing and inadequate, as were existing passing and merging lanes. Being an east-west route, glare was a problem during sunrise and sunset. Various roadway curves also contributed to poor visibility.

The task force also looked at collision and traffic data and found that the primary collision factors spoke to the presence of aggressive driving and of impatient drivers who made unwise passing decisions when stuck behind large, slow-moving vehicles. The top five collision factors were unsafe turning, driving on the wrong side of the road, improper passing, driving under the influence and unsafe speed. The task force also found that collisions occurred most frequently on Friday, Saturday and Sunday between 1:00 and 6:00 P.M. Collision times and days reflected the presence of "weekend-warriors" who traveled to the coast on the weekends to escape the valley heat. It also suggested that many involved in collisions were local farm workers with limited English skills who were unfamiliar with California rules-of-the-road.

Response

Proposed solutions fell into four categories: enforcement, emergency services, engineering and education.

Enforcement Special enforcement operations were implemented and funded through federal traffic safety grants. Ultimately, officers worked 2,922 overtime hours, offered assistance and services to motorists 2,837 times and issued 14,606 citations.

Emergency Services Additional emergency roadside call boxes were installed. A CHP helicopter was permanently assigned to the roadway, and agreements were reached with emergency service providers that the closest units should respond to collision scenes, without regard to jurisdictional boundaries.

Engineering Several physical changes were made in the roadway. Raised-profile thermoplastic striping was installed where passing was allowed in one direction. In no-passing zones, a widened center median with rumble strips and thermoplastic striping was installed. Outside shoulders were treated with rumble strips. Several signing, striping and maintenance projects were completed. "Stop Ahead" warning signs were posted at key intersections, and chevron signs were installed to warn of impending curves.

Education A variety of educational programs and materials involved the local media, businesses, government and residents in reminding motorists to drive safely. Two million color flyers emphasizing safe driving habits were printed and distributed through educational institutions, newspapers, local businesses, restaurants, recreational facilities and government agency offices. Large and small posters were posted in restaurants and in local businesses. In addition, three kick-off news conferences were held just before the Memorial Day weekend in three separate locations along the corridor.

Assessment

The efforts were quite successful with fatal collisions reduced by 10 percent and injury collisions reduced by 32 percent. Over the five years of available data, it is estimated that the safety initiatives have saved 21 lives and prevented 55 injuries. As Helmick et al. (2001, p.33) suggest, "Extraordinary traffic safety benefits can result from systematically identifying corridors, analyzing the causes of dangerous conditions, forming specific recommendations for action, and evaluating the resulting collision trends."

AN AREA TRAFFIC OFFICER (ATO) PROGRAM

An innovative program that combines community policing and a focus on problem solving was recently instituted in Irvine, California. The Irvine Area Traffic Officer (ATO) Program is aimed at implementing problem-solving strategies with an emphasis on long-lasting solutions using community input and is intended to

- Identify and resolve traffic problems through a single point of contact.
- Increase monitoring of area of concern.
- Build close-knit relationships with community residents, business owners, and school administrators.
- Establish proactive, long-term solutions that consider input from other city departments and key personnel.
- Explore innovative methods of moving vehicles more effectively through the city in a safe and efficient manner.
- Affirm a commitment to increasing reliable two-way communication, which the community expects from its local government (Maggard and Jung, 2009, p.46).

The program has divided Irvine into three areas, each assigned an ATO responsible for investigating and resolving complex traffic-related issues in his or her respective geographic area: "The ATOs work hand-in-hand with area motor officers, patrol officers, traffic engineers, land use planners, and key personnel from Irvine Public Works Department to address traffic issues in a comprehensive and collaborative manner" (Maggard and Jung, 2009, p.46).

The ATOs have achieved significant results. They have improved school safety by making improvements to school parking/loading areas to enhance overall safety and maximize traffic flow, determined the need for additional crosswalks, revised access plans and determined the need for additional speed limit and cautionary signs. ATOs have also addressed the issue of abandoned vehicles, which can become unsightly and be targets for vandalism and other criminal activity. In addition, the ATOs have worked closely with major retail shopping centers and business owners to improve circulation and safety issues by enhancing directional signage and increased parking enforcement.

Another area of concern that has been addressed is construction traffic. ATOs work well ahead of development projects in collaboration with construction superintendents to address such issues as the delivery of building supplies, truck routes, roadway closures, detour barriers, roadway excavation and appropriate construction signage. Residential traffic has also been a focus, especially speed enforcement. ATOs frequently deploy radar speed boards throughout the city that post the legal speed limit and inform drivers of their speed.

Maggard and Jung (2009, p.50) conclude, "The benefits of establishing an ATO program far outweigh those of the traditional approach of addressing traffic management issues." Such a program can stretch existing law enforcement resources, giving the example of the Irvine Police Department's three area commanders previously assigned to resolve chronic circulations issues now having time to address their primary responsibilities while ATOs focus exclusively on traffic-related inquiries. Maggard and Jung also note that since the inception of the ATO program, traffic accidents have decreased by 6 percent. "A program that improves safety and communication while reducing the strain on law enforcement resources should be viewed as a success by any measure" (p.50).

SUMMARY

Police traffic services (PTS) are divided into three functional areas: traffic direction and control, traffic enforcement, and crash investigation. The two basic purposes of traffic enforcement are to control congestion and to reduce crashes. Enforcement can also detect criminal activity. Despite officers' efforts to maintain a high-profile, aggressive traffic presence, the I-won't-get-a-ticket syndrome is common among the driving public. Even if a traffic enforcement unit exists, traffic enforcement is the responsibility of *all* officers. Speeding can be addressed through engineering, education and enforcement responses.

Some of the more challenging and hazardous motorist behaviors involve aggressive driving, road rage and driving under the influence. Aggressive driving is a traffic violation; road rage is a criminal offense. Nationwide, DUI is the number one traffic law enforcement problem. Strategies to deter DUI include educating drivers through awareness campaigns and establishing sobriety checkpoints and saturation patrols. Additional efforts aimed at repeat offenders include using ignition interlocks and enacting vehicle forfeiture programs.

Another problem area for traffic officers is pursuit. An effective pursuit policy must balance crime control efforts against the threat a pursuit poses to public safety and officer and department liability. Pursuit policies should address such issues as supervision, monitoring, and accountability; safety; driving conditions; vehicles involved; situational context; and devices and tactics. A frequently overlooked area in traffic enforcement involves transportation of hazardous materials. A hazardous materials enforcement program should consist of terminal audits, shipper and other audits, road enforcement, technical assistance and enforcement training and emergency response.

Dealing with motor vehicle crashes is another function of traffic services. Such crashes are the leading cause of death for people ages 1 to 33, yet the a-crash-won't-happen-to-me syndrome is common among the American driving public. At a crash scene, officers are responsible for managing the scene, including protecting it, attending to injuries, keeping traffic moving and restoring normal traffic flow. Officers are also responsible for investigating the cause(s) of the crash, including the possibility of a crime.

APPLICATION

The chief of police in your agency approaches you over concern with the inconsistency of written crash reports in your department. Officers have been writing accident reports for incidents that have occurred on both public and private properties. Although no law prohibits writing state accident reports on private property, your chief is concerned that having no consistent policy may expose your agency to liability. Currently, officers are allowed discretion regarding whether to write the accident reports on private property. Your chief has asked you as a supervisor to create a policy for writing accident reports that meet local, state and national criteria along with remaining consistent for the public you serve.

INSTRUCTIONS

With current local, state and national criteria in mind, draft a policy for your agency outlining what criteria needs to be met to write a state accident report. In addition, make the policy consistent, stating whether all accidents are required to be written as long as it meets the criteria, or if only certain accidents are required to be written. Also, in the event that an accident does *not* need to be reported, what is required of the officer responding to that call? Officers should also consider legal liability and refer to other local agencies' policies regarding this matter.

EXERCISES IN CRITICAL THINKING

On July 15 at 2:14 A.M., Officer Geasone was working patrol and pulled into a gas station in his marked squad car. As he pulled in he observed a lone driver, who was already parked in the lot, get out of his vehicle from the driver side and enter the gas station. Officer Geasone entered the gas station and made small-talk with the driver while waiting in line with him to buy refreshments. In speaking with the driver, Officer Geasone noticed the odor of an alcoholic beverage on the driver's breath. He further observed the driver to have bloodshot, watery eyes and slurred speech. Officer Geasone did not actually observe the driver driving the vehicle, nor did he conduct a traffic stop on him. When he engaged the driver in conversation, his intent was not to inquire if the driver was intoxicated.

1. Does Officer Geasone have probable cause to pursue a DWI investigation?
   a. No, because Officer Geasone did not at anytime observe the driver driving, and therefore did not observe any driving conduct. Because there was no development of probable cause from driving conduct, Officer Geasone cannot pursue a DWI investigation at this point.
   b. Yes, because Officer Geasone observed the driver get out of the driver seat of the vehicle as he arrived at the gas station. He further observed that the driver was alone

at the time. Although he did not conduct a traffic stop, based on that information Officer Geasone has probable cause to continue this investigation.

c. No, because Officer Geasone cannot use general conversation with the driver while in the gas station as usable probable cause that the driver was driving under the influence of the vehicle. Officer Geasone further cannot go back for an initial stop since he did not have any reason to suspect that the driver was drinking until he spoke to him in the gas station.

d. Yes, because Officer Geasone does not need driving conduct alone to continue with a DWI investigation. The time of day and all the other factors that Officer Geasone became aware of while making contact with the driver, along with Officer Geasone observing the driver in control of the vehicle in the parked position is probable cause enough to continue an investigation.

e. No, because Officer Geasone's contact with the driver in the gas station was not directly related to looking to develop further probable cause if the driver was intoxicated. The conversation was general, and therefore has no correlation to probable cause.

On March 10 at 9:00 P.M., Officer Wagon received road and driving complaints from multiple complainants regarding one driver who was "all over the road." Dispatch was able to get a license plate that listed the registered owner's address near the area of the complaints. The vehicle was also described as a unique classic collector corvette. The record on the registered owner of the vehicle came back with several previous DWI convictions on record. Officer Wagon was not able to respond to the area quickly enough to observe the vehicle driving but did, however, arrive at the registered owner's address shortly after the call. Officer Wagon did not observe the driver driving at anytime. Upon arrival, Officer Wagon observed, by peering through a garage window, that the suspected vehicle was parked inside the residential garage. Officer Wagon knocked on the door of the residence and made contact with the registered owner of the vehicle.

Officer Wagon could clearly observe that the registered owner was intoxicated. Officer Wagon observed the odor of an alcoholic beverage emitting from the man's breath, bloodshot watery eyes, slurred speech and inability to stand up. The registered owner would not exit his residence, did not admit to driving and insisted he had been home for a long time. The registered owner continued speaking with Officer Wagon through his open front door but would not cooperate in answering questions related to the complaints. Officer Wagon was not able to get a hold of any of the complainants. The registered owner stated that he was not the only one home at the residence, but Officer Wagon did not observe anyone else. The registered owner eventually grew tired of speaking with the officer and closed his door.

1. Could Officer Wagon take the registered owner from his residence since he was actively speaking with him with an open door to his residence? Could Officer Wagon then continue with a DWI investigation and conduct field sobriety tests based on multiple complainant reports and a previous history?
   a. Yes. Officer Wagon was not able to make contact with any of the complainants and was not able to get a description of the actual driver of the vehicle but does not need it when responding to a road and driving complaint. The complaint alone is enough probable cause to continue with a DWI investigation in this situation.
   b. Yes. Officer Wagon did not observe the registered owner drive or in control of the vehicle at any time and only made contact with the registered owner when he was already in his residence. However, once Officer Wagon made contact with the registered owner, the officer developed more probable cause.
   c. No, because there is no probable cause to indicate that the registered owner of the vehicle was driving at the time of the reports. Officer Wagon did not have probable cause to pursue a DWI investigation. Furthermore, Officer Wagon did not

observe the driver of the vehicle between the time he had parked and went inside his residence, which left a time where he plausibly could have consumed alcohol, even though it was a matter of minutes between the call and the response to the residence. There was also no hot pursuit in this incident.

d. No, because it does not matter who the registered owner of the vehicle was or if he were home alone, even if Officer Wagon had that information. The registered owner was inside his residence the entire time he was speaking with the officer. He did not invite the officer into his residence and would not cooperate in answering questions about driving recently. There is nothing the police could do about it either way.

DISCUSSION QUESTIONS

1. What should be the top priority in a traffic program? Justify your selection.
2. Your municipality has an ordinance stating that it is against the law to drink and drive. Obtain a copy of that ordinance and bring it to class. What is the legal limit for intoxication? Do you feel the legal limit justifies the penalty if one is convicted? Would you suggest some modifications in the law as you see it enforced?
3. Three tests are usually given to determine if a person is under the influence of alcohol while driving: a breath test, a urine test and a blood test. From evidence that might be presented in court, which test would you favor if you were a police officer? What are the advantages and disadvantages in administering each test?
4. Is a pursuit policy justified in a police department, or should officers be allowed to make a discretionary decision to chase without the benefit of a specific policy?
5. Should officers expose those they are pursuing to hazardous roadblock conditions or be given permission to ram cars? If so, what restrictions should apply, if any?
6. Radar detectors used by motorists are a source of irritation to most traffic officers. Do you feel they should be declared illegal to possess and use, as they have been in some states?
7. Most warning tickets issued by officers are never formally recorded on a driver's record. Are such tickets an effective tool in obtaining compliance to traffic laws?

GALE EMERGENCY SERVICES DATABASE ASSIGNMENTS

- Use the Gale Emergency Services database to help answer the Discussion Questions as appropriate.
- Use the Gale Emergency Services database to research *road rage*. Write a brief (two- to three-page) report on the characteristics of this type of driver and the effects of aggressive driving.
- Use the Gale Emergency Services database to read and outline one of the following articles to share with the class:
    - "The Role of Race in Law Enforcement: Racial Profiling or Legitimate Use?" by Richard G. Schott
    - "Collecting Statistics in Response to Racial Profiling Allegations" by Karen J. Kruger
    - "High-Speed Police Pursuits: Dangers, Dynamics and Risk Reduction" by John Hill
    - "Alexandria CARES and BABY-1: Protecting the Future" by Dianne Gittins
    - "Battling DUI: A Comparative Analysis of Checkpoints and Saturation Patrols" by Jeffrey W. Greene

REFERENCES

Alpert, G. P. "Police Pursuits after *Scott v. Harris*. Far from Ideal?" Washington, DC: *Police Foundation*, Ideas in American Policing Series, Lecture given on February 18, 2008.

Ashley, Steve. "Reducing the Risks of Police Pursuit." Spofford, NH: The Police Policy Studies Council, 2004. http://www.theppsc.org/Staff_Views/Ashley/reducing_the_risks_of_police_pursuit.htm

Ashton, Richard J. "Looking beyond the License Plate." *The Police Chief*, January 2008, pp.28–31.

Beck, Kirby. "Tomorrow's Uniforms Today: Visibility." *Law and Order*, September 2008, pp.34–39.

Beery, Craig. "Busted . . . At the Speed of Light." *Law Officer Magazine*, January 2008, pp.76–79.

Bernstein, Sharon; Abdollah, Tami; and Blankstein, Andrew. "Street Racing Takes on a Deadly New Form." *Los Angeles Times*, October 11, 2007.

Bolton, Joel. "IACP Law Enforcement Challenge—Part VI: Traffic Enforcement Tactics." *The Police Chief*, January 2008a, p.66.

Bolton, Joel. "Traffic Safety 2008." *The Police Chief*, December 2008b, p.106.

Bolton, Joel. "Why Are Traffic Laws Enforced?" *The Police Chief*, February 2009, p.90.

Brown, Weston. "Collision Investigation: Know and Use the Tech behind Vehicle Crashes." *Law Officer Magazine*, February 2008, pp.44–47.

Casstevens, Steven. "Traffic Enforcement Is Real Police Work." *Law and Order*, August 2008, pp.44–46.

"Child Passenger Safety." NHTSA Web site, no date. Accessed: http://www.nhtsa.gov

"Children." Washington, DC: NHTSA Traffic Safety Facts, 2006. (DOT HS 810 803)

"Click It or Ticket." NHTSA Web site, no date. Accessed: http://www.nhtsa.gov

Commission on Accreditation of Law Enforcement Agencies. *Standards for Law Enforcement Agencies*, 5th ed. Fairfax, VA: CALEA, 2006, updated 2008.

Dixon, John. "Radar Speed Signs." *Law Officer Magazine*, December 2008, pp.42–50.

"Drunk Driving." Itasca IL: National Safety Council, no date.

Excellence in Problem-Oriented Policing: The 2001 Herman Goldstein Award Winners. Washington, DC: National Institute of Justice, COPS and the Police Executive Research Forum, 2001.

Fridell, Lorie A. *By the Numbers: A Guide for Analyzing Race Data from Vehicle Stops*. Washington, DC: Police Executive Research Forum, 2004.

Galvin, Bob. "Mapping Choices Abound as Crashes and Traffic Mount." *Law Enforcement Technology*, August 2007, pp.34–45.

Galvin, Bob. "New Tech Targets Tailgaters: Using LIDAR to Slow Down Life in the Fast Lane." *Law Officer Magazine*, April 2008, pp.40–43.

Galvin, Bob. "Laser Device Takes on Tailgating." *Law Enforcement Technology*, January 2009, pp.70–73.

Garrett, Ronnie. "Hang Up and Drive." *Law Enforcement Technology*, July 2008a, p.6.

Garrett, Ronnie. "A New Sheriff in Town." *Law Enforcement Technology*, February 2008b, p.8.

Griffin, Michelle. "Going Mobile: Building a Case for e-Ticketing." *Law Officer Magazine*, February 2009, pp.30–33.

Griffith, David. "Death Race." *Police*, November 2007, p.12.

Grossi, Dave. "Foot Pursuit Tactics: Plan Your Moves and Know the Suspect's." *Law Officer Magazine*, April 2008a, pp.28–29.

Grossi, Dave. "Tactics for Traffic Management: Be Prepared, Day and Night." *Law Officer Magazine*, December 2008b, pp.32–35.

Grossi, Dave. "Night Crawlers: How to Spot Speed Freaks and Meth Heads." *Law Officer Magazine*, February 2009, pp.24–28.

Hanson, Doug. "Hazardous Duty." *Law Enforcement Technology*, April 2007, pp.80–85.

Haug, Scot. "Kootenai County Goes High Tech: A Case Study in License Plate Recognition." *Law Officer Magazine*, January 2009, pp.64–68.

Helmick, D.O.; Keller, John; Nannini, Robert; and Huffaker, Alice. "Corridor Safety Program: A Collaborative Approach to Traffic Safety." *The Police Chief*, July 2001, pp.32–35.

"Help Keep Families Together." Irving, TX: Mothers Against Drunk Driving (MADD) (undated brochure).

Hillard, Terry. "Deploying an eTicketing Solution." *Law and Order*, January 2008, pp.58–61.

"Lives Saved in 2007 by Restraint Use and Minimum Drinking Age Laws." Washington, DC: NHTSA Traffic Safety Facts, November, 2008. (DOT HS 811 049)

Lum, Cynthia, and Fachner, George. *Police Pursuits in an Age of Innovation and Reform. The IACP Police Pursuit Database*. Arlington, VA: International Association of Chiefs of Police, September 2008.

Maggard, David L., and Jung, Daniel. "Irvine's Area Traffic Officer Program." *The Police Chief*, March 2009, pp.46–50.

The Manual on Uniform Traffic Control Devices, 2003 Edition. Washington, DC: U.S. Department of Transportation, Federal Highway Administration, December 2007.

Means, Randy. "Vehicle Ramming and *Scott v. Harris*." *Law and Order*, September 2007, pp.43–45.

Molnar, J.P. "Crash Investigation." *Law Officer Magazine*, November 2008, pp.20–21.

Moses, Tom. "Smarter Technology for Hazmat Response." *9-1-1 Magazine*, July 2007, pp.52–54.

"Motor Vehicle Traffic Crashes as a Leading Cause of Death in the United States, 2005." Washington, DC: NHTSA Traffic Safety Facts, April 2008. (DOT HS 810 936)

Nugent, Hugh; Connors, Edward F.; McEwen, J. Thomas; and Mayo, Lou. Restrictive High-Speed Police Pursuits. Washington, DC: U.S. Department of Justice, no date. (NCJ 122025)

"Overview." Washington, DC: NHTSA Traffic Safety Facts, 2007. (DOT HS 810 993)

Pedestrian Safety. Itasca, IL: National Safety Council, no date.

"The Pedestrian Safety Campaign." Washington, DC: U.S. Department of Transportation Federal Highway Administration, no date.

Pedestrian Safety: Report to Congress. Washington, DC: U.S. Department of Transportation, Federal Highway Administration, Office of Safety, August 2008.

"Pedestrians." Washington, DC: NHTSA Traffic Safety Facts, 2007. (DOT HS 810 994)

Petrocelli, Joseph. "Street Racing." *Police*, April 2007, pp.20–21.

Pope, Cori Keeton. "Rebuilding a Wreck." *9-1-1 Magazine*, April 2007a, pp.36–37.

Pope, Cori Keeton. "Survey Technology for Crash Reconstruction." *Law and Order*, April 2007b, pp.56–63.

Rao, Angelo. "Transportation Services." In *Local Government Police Management*, 4th ed. edited by William A. Geller and Darrel W. Stephens. Washington, DC: International City/County Management Association, 2003, pp.207–238.

"The Relation between Speed and Crashes." Leidschendam, the Netherlands: Institute for Road Safety Research, April 2009.

"Safe Communities." Washington, DC: NHTSA, no date. Accessed: http://www.nhtsa.gov/portal/site/nhtsa/menuitem.fdfb2e086bb579e4fb8e5f8dcba046a0/

Sanow, Ed. "Traffic Enforcement Equals Crime Reduction." *Law and Order,* March 2009, p.6.

Scarry, Laura L. "*Scott v. Harris*: U.S. Supreme Court Backs Police in Pursuit Case." *Law Officer Magazine*, July 2007, pp.58–61.

"Seat Belt Use in 2008—Overall Results." Washington, DC: NHTSA Traffic Safety Facts. September 2008. (DOT HS 811 036)

"Speeding." Washington, DC: NHTSA Traffic Safety Facts, 2007. (DOT HS 810 998)

Stockton, Dale. "New Year, New Challenges: Synergy, Technology & Video." *Law Officer Magazine*, January 2009, p.8.

"2007 Traffic Safety Annual Assessment—Alcohol-Impaired Driving Fatalities." Washington, DC: NHTSA Traffic Safety Facts, August 2008. (DOT HS 811 016)

Ursino, Brian. "Washington State Patrol's Target Zero." *Law and Order*, September 2007, pp.36–38.

"A World without Traffic Calming." *The Traffic Calmer Newsletter*, January 2009.

Yates. Travis. "Analysis of the IACP Report: 'Police Pursuits in an Age of Innovation and Reform.'" *PoliceOne.com News*, March 23, 2009.

Ye, Tony Jianqiang, and Pickrell, Timothy M. "Seat Belt Use in Rear Seats in 2007." Washington, DC: NHTSA Traffic Safety Facts, April 2008. (DOT HS 810 933)

"Young Drivers." Washington, DC: NHTSA Traffic Safety Facts, 2007. (DOT HS 811 001)

CASES CITED

Brown v. City of Oneonta, 221 F.3d 329 (2nd Cir.2000), cert. denied, 122 S.Ct. 44 (2001)

Carleton v. Town of Framingham, 418 Mass. 623, 627 (1994)

City of Indianapolis v. Edmond, 531 U.S. 32 (2000)

County of Sacramento v. Lewis, 523 U.S. 833 (1998)

Michigan Department of State Police v. Sitz, 496 U.S. 444 (1990)

Pennsylvania v. Mimms, 434 U.S. 106 (1977)

Pennsylvania v. Muniz, 496 U.S. 582 (1990)

Scott v. Harris, 550 U.S. 372 (2007)

Whren v. United States, 517 U.S. 806 (1996)

CHAPTER 6

Crime, Disorder and Quality-of-Life Issues

Responding to the Call

DO YOU KNOW . . .

- What the official sources of information about crime are?
- What index offenses the FBI compiles statistics on?
- What technologies assist law enforcement in addressing crime and disorder issues?
- What the responsibilities of officers responding to a criminal action call are?
- What the preliminary investigation of a crime consists of?
- What issues may lead to civil disobedience in the 21st century?
- How police departments should be prepared to deal with demonstrations and violence?
- What crisis situations police officers may face?
- What the number one rule is when dealing with hostage situations, barricaded subjects or attempted suicides?

CAN YOU DEFINE?

chain of custody
chain of possession
civil disobedience
collective efficacy
Crime Index
flashbangs
geographic information systems (GIS)
hot spots
incivilities
preliminary investigation
property crimes
Stockholm syndrome
Uniform Crime Reports (UCRs)
violent crimes

INTRODUCTION

Responding to calls about crime is a basic function of law enforcement and has been a defining priority throughout the history of policing. Many believe this is the only true function of the police and that in a perfect world, one free of all crime, police would be unnecessary. Of course, police operations involve more than just handling crime. By the same token, the response to crime is not new, nor has it always been solely the responsibility of law enforcement.

"The reason people commit crime has been debated since crime was first defined. Some blame crime on the failings of the criminal justice system—understaffed police forces, lenient judges, overcrowded jails and prisons and overworked, burned-out probation and parole officers. Others blame society and the overwhelming absence of personal and community responsibility and accountability—abusive parents, permissive parents, inadequate schools and incompetent teachers, the decline of religion, media violence, drugs and high rates of unemployment" (Hess, 2009, p.92). It is apparent that many of the suggested causes of crime are well beyond the control of law enforcement. It takes a total community effort in most cases.

The English, beginning with the reign of Alfred the Great (871–899), were expected to catch criminals under the Frankpledge system. If a crime was committed, everyone in the community was to raise a "hue and cry." Failing to catch an offender meant paying a fine, which forced the entire realm to engage in law enforcement. Modern policing has returned to the idea of engaging the community to help combat crime because crime is not just a law enforcement problem. It is everyone's problem.

Preliminary data from the Federal Bureau of Investigation (FBI) Uniform Crime Report (UCR) show that both violent and property crime decreased in the United States during 2008 when compared with crime data for 2007, with a decrease of 2.5 percent in reported violent crime and a drop of 1.6 percent in reported property crime (*Crime in the United States*, 2008). Figures released by the Bureau of Justice Statistics (BJS) from its National Crime Victimization Survey showed that the percentage of households experiencing crime remained stable between 2005 and 2006 (Rand and Catalano, 2007, p.1).

Many contend the added "eyes and ears" of the citizenry has contributed to the stable or declining crime rate. Paradoxically, some citizens have grown increasingly fearful of crime and victimization. Some studies have found those who watched the most local television news reported the highest levels of fear of crime. Media accounts of crime usually focus on the most serious, sensational cases. The sensationalized media accounts may explain why the levels of citizens' fear of crime appear to be unrelated to the actual levels of crime in their neighborhoods. Study after study shows that the media focuses on crime and violence to the neglect of other aspects of law enforcement.

Some surveys indicate the country as a whole appears to feel safer in its neighborhoods and homes today than citizens did several decades ago. A 1975 poll that asked, "Is there any area near where you live—that is, within a mile—where you would be afraid to walk alone at night?," found 45 percent of respondents replied yes, they were fearful of walking alone after dark. In answer to that same question in 2008, only 37 percent responded that they were fearful to walk alone at night (*Sourcebook . . .*, n.d., Table 2.37). Those reporting the most fear were minority females, 18 to 20 years old, with a high school education who earned under $20,000 in a clerical type job and lived in the West (Table 2.38).

This chapter begins with a look at how crimes are classified and measured, including a discussion of the Uniform Crime Reports, the National Incident-Based Reporting System and the National Crime Victimization Survey. Next, crime mapping is presented, followed by a look at how police respond to calls about crimes. The chapter then examines the police response to disorder and civil disobedience; and crisis situations involving hostages, barricaded individuals and suicide attempts. The chapter concludes with a look at how crime and disorder are related to both community policing and problem-oriented policing.

CLASSIFYING AND MEASURING CRIME

The U.S. Department of Justice administers several statistical programs to measure the magnitude, nature and impact of crime in America. The FBI collects and disseminates crime statistics through its UCR Program and the National Incident-Based Reporting System (NIBRS). The BJS collects detailed crime information via its National Crime Victimization Survey (NCVS).

The official sources of information about crime are the Uniform Crime Reports (UCR), the National Incident-Based Reporting System (NIBRS) and the National Crime Victimization Survey (NCVS).

Uniform Crime Reports (UCRs)
The FBI's national crime reporting system, published annually as *Crime in the United States*.

Crime Index
Term identifying the FBI's Uniform Crime Report program (UCR); includes the violent crimes and the property crimes.

violent crimes
Offenses in which physical contact with the victim occurs, including assault, murder, rape and robbery; sometimes called *crimes against persons*.

property crimes
Offenses in which no physical contact with the victim occurs, including arson, auto theft, burglary and larceny/theft.

Although the UCR and NCVS programs each have unique strengths, they are conducted for different purposes and use different methods. Therefore, caution is needed in comparing crime trends presented by the UCR and NCVS because, as each examines the nation's crime problem from a unique perspective, their results are not comparable. Nonetheless, the information they produce together provides a more comprehensive view of crime in the United States than either could produce alone.

Uniform Crime Reports

The FBI gathers statistics on reported crimes from local, county and state law enforcement agencies throughout the country and reports the findings annually in their **Uniform Crime Reports (UCRs)**, called *Crime in the United States*. According to the FBI (*Crime in the United States*), the law enforcement agencies active in the UCR Program during 2006 represented 17,000 law enforcement agencies serving 94.1 percent of U.S. citizens.

When the UCR program was launched in 1929, seven offenses were chosen to serve as an index for gauging fluctuations in the overall volume and rate of crime reported to law enforcement: "Known collectively as the **Crime Index**, these offenses included the **violent crimes** of murder and nonnegligent manslaughter, forcible rape, robbery and aggravated assault and the **property crimes** of burglary, larceny-theft and motor vehicle theft. By congressional mandate, arson [a property crime] was added as the eighth Index offense in 1979" (*Crime in the United States,* p.1) [boldface added].

The FBI's Uniform Crime Reports contain statistics on violent crimes (murder, aggravated assault causing serious bodily harm, forcible rape, robbery) and property crimes (burglary, larceny/theft, motor vehicle theft and arson).

2008 Crime Clock

One violent crime	**Every 22.8 seconds**
One murder	Every 32.3 minutes
One forcible rape	Every 5.9 minutes
One robbery	Every 1.2 minutes
One aggravated assault	Every 37.8 seconds
One property crime	**Every 3.2 seconds**
One burglary	Every 14.2 seconds
One larceny-theft	Every 4.8 seconds
One motor vehicle theft	Every 33.0 seconds

FIGURE 6.1
2008 Crime Clock
Source: *Crime in the United States, 2008.* Washington, DC: Federal Bureau of Investigation, September 2009.

A summary of the figures for the Index crimes committed in 2007 is presented in Figure 6.1. This graphic does not imply regularity in the commission of the Index offenses. Rather, it shows the annual ratio of crime to fixed time intervals. Figure 6.2 shows the distribution of the offenses.

The UCR program is undergoing major revision, moving from its current system of summary counts to a more comprehensive, detailed reporting system, the NIBRS. This system is intended to replace the traditional eight offenses of the FBI Crime Index with detailed incident information on 46 offenses representing 22 categories of crimes.

National Incident-Based Reporting System

Although the UCR counts incidents and arrests for the eight Crime Index Offenses and arrests only for other offenses, NIBRS provides detailed incident information on 48 Group A offenses representing 22 categories of crimes. NIBRS also distinguishes between attempted and completed crimes:

> NIBRS data can be directly traced back to original information collected by the local agency to allow for data quality checks that were impossible under the Summary Program. Now, with the advances in technology and computing resources, leveraged by incident-based crime reporting, the information relayed to law enforcement can be monitored from the initial response until its final report to the FBI. These capabilities in combination with a state program designed to foster quality control can substantially increase the chance of identifying effort in the data and improving the quality of those data. (Barnett-Ryan and Swanson, 2008, p. 19).

Table 6.1 shows the NIBRS Group A offenses, comparable to the UCR Index offenses. Table 6.2 shows the Group B offenses—the "other" offenses, or Part II offenses. Table 6.3 shows the data to be obtained for each offense.

FIGURE 6.2
Percent Distribution of Part I Offenses
Data source: http://www.fbi.gov/ucr/cius2008/offenses/index.html

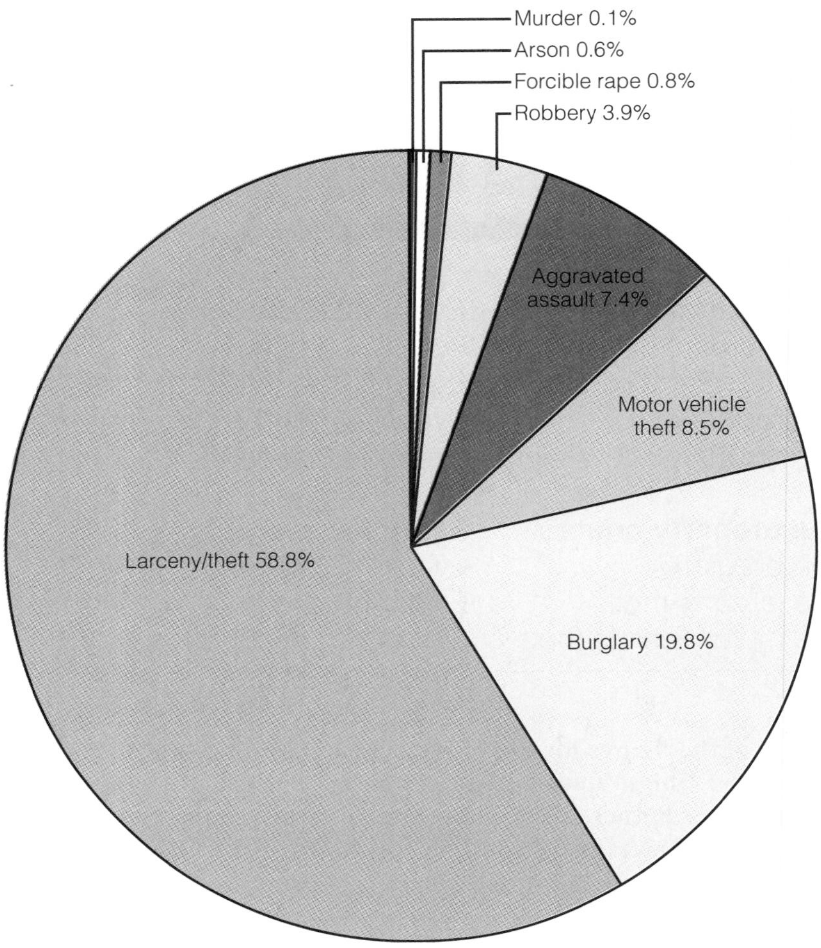

National Crime Victimization Survey

Conducted by U.S. Bureau of the Census personnel and reported through the BJS, the NCVS is an ongoing survey of a nationally representative sample of approximately 49,000 households to collect information on crimes suffered by individuals and households, whether or not those crimes were reported to law enforcement. All household members age 12 and older (about 101,000 people) are interviewed every six months for three years. New households are continuously rotated into the sample.

Since its inception in 1973, the NCVS has been the primary source of information on the characteristics of criminal victimization and on the number and types of crimes *not* reported to law enforcement authorities. Following are highlights from the 2006 NCVS:

- Males experienced higher rates of victimization than females: 28 violent victimizations per 1,000 males age 12 or older and 23 violent victimizations per 1,000 females age 12 or older.
- An estimated 25 percent of all violent crime incidents were committed by an armed offender. A firearm was involved in 9 percent of these incidents.
- Violent and property crime rates in urban and suburban areas were stable between 2005 and 2006.

Table 6.1 The NIBRS Group A Offenses

Arson	Kidnapping/abduction
Assault offenses	Larceny/theft offenses
Aggravated assault	Pocket picking
Simple assault	Purse snatching
Intimidation	Shoplifting
Bribery	Theft from building
Burglary/breaking and entering	Theft from coin-operated machines
Counterfeiting/forgery	Theft from motor vehicle
Destruction/damage/vandalism of property	Theft of motor vehicle parts/accessories
Drug/narcotic offenses	All other larceny
Drug/narcotic violations	Motor vehicle theft
Drug equipment violations	Pornography/obscene material
Embezzlement	Prostitution offenses
Extortion/blackmail	Prostitution
Fraud offenses	Assisting or promoting prostitution
False pretenses/swindle/confidence game	Robbery
Credit card/ATM fraud	Sex offenses, forcible
Impersonation	Forcible rape
Welfare fraud	Forcible sodomy
Wire fraud	Sexual assault with an object
Gambling offenses	Forcible fondling
Betting/wagering	Sex offenses, nonforcible
Operating/promoting/assisting gambling	Stolen property offenses
Gambling equipment violations	Weapon law violations
Sports tampering	
Homicide offenses	
Murder/nonnegligent manslaughter	
Negligent manslaughter	
Justifiable homicide	

Source: Brian A. Reaves. *National Incident-Based Reporting System: Using NIBRS Data to Analyze Violent Crime*. Washington, DC: Bureau of Justice Statistics Technical Report, October 1993, p.1.

Table 6.2 The NIBRS Group B Offenses

Bad checks	Nonviolent family offenses
Curfew/loitering/vagrancy	Peeping Tom
Disorderly conduct	Runaway
Driving under the influence	Trespassing
Drunkenness	All other offenses
Liquor law violations	

Source: Brian A. Reaves. *National Incident-Based Reporting System: Using NIBRS Data to Analyze Violent Crime*. Washington, DC: Bureau of Justice Statistics Technical Report, October 1993, p.2.

From Measuring Crime to Predicting Crime—Becoming Proactive

These various data collection programs have created a documented history of crime problems throughout our country and have helped the national law enforcement community gain better insight into trends in criminal activity and victimization in the United States. As beneficial as these programs have been and continue to be, increasingly sophisticated computerized mapping tools now enable police at the local level to track and analyze crime directly affecting their community. In addition to real-time capabilities, this technology also has forward-looking capabilities, meaning it affords agencies a degree of predictability in forecasting future crime in their community, allowing the department to become proactive.

Table 6.3 NIBRS Data Elements

Administrative Segment:
1. ORI [Originating Agency Identification] number
2. Incident number
3. Incident date/hour
4. Exceptional clearance indicator
5. Exceptional clearance date

Offense Segment:
6. UCR offense code
7. Attempted/completed code
8. Alcohol/drug use by offender
9. Type of location
10. Number of premises entered
11. Method of entry
12. Type of criminal activity
13. Type of weapon/force used
14. Bias crime code

Property Segment:
15. Type of property loss
16. Property description
17. Property value
18. Recovery data
19. Number of stolen motor vehicles
20. Number of recovered motor vehicles
21. Suspected drug type
22. Estimated drug quantity
23. Drug measurement unit

Victim Segment:
24. Victim number
25. Victim UCR offense code
26. Type of victim
27. Age of victim
28. Sex of victim
29. Race of victim
30. Ethnicity of victim
31. Resident status of victim
32. Homicide/assault circumstances
33. Justifiable homicide circumstances
34. Type of injury
35. Related offender number
36. Relationship of victim to offender

Offender Segment:
37. Offender number
38. Age of offender
39. Sex of offender
40. Race of offender

Arrestee Segment:
41. Arrestee number
42. Transaction number
43. Arrest date
44. Type of arrest
45. Multiple clearance indicator
46. UCR arrest offense code
47. Arrestee armed indicator
48. Age of arrestee
49. Sex of arrestee
50. Race of arrestee
51. Ethnicity of arrestee
52. Resident status of arrestee
53. Disposition of arrestee under 18

Source: Brian A. Reaves. *National Incident-Based Reporting System: Using NIBRS Data to Analyze Violent Crime*. Washington, DC: Bureau of Justice Statistics Technical Report, October 1993, p.2.

TECHNOLOGICAL ADVANCES IN ANALYZING, RESPONDING TO AND PREVENTING CRIME AND DISORDER

Law enforcement's ability to understand the extent of crime and patterns to its occurrence is continuously evolving, and with it has come an enhanced capacity for police to tailor their response to suit a community's specific crime and disorder problems.

15 CALEA STANDARD 15 states, "Crime analysis represents a system utilizing regularly collected information on reported crimes and criminals to prevent and suppress crime and to apprehend criminal offenders. Crime analysis is a scientific process in the sense that it involves the collection of valid and reliable data, employs systematic techniques of analysis, and seeks to determine, for predictive purposes, the frequency with which events occur and the extent to which they are associated with other events. The collection, analysis and distribution of readily available crime data information to affected personnel will enhance agency effectiveness." (*Standards for Law Enforcement Agencies*, 5th edition, 2006)

Crime analysts have several tools available. Tactically, the fundamental function of crime analysis is to provide law enforcement and its support staff with crime series, patterns, and trends and to help develop information to improve chances of apprehending criminals and preventing crimes (Paletta and Belledin, 2008, p.37). Peed et al. (2008, p.20) stress, "By taking full advantage of crime analysis, law enforcement agencies can combine geographic data with a wealth of local crime and administrative data to paint a more comprehensive picture of *why* crime happens where it does (or does not), rather than simply noting where it does and does not happen."

Technologies that greatly assist law enforcement in analyzing and responding to crime and disorder issues include mapping, geographic information systems, geographic systems and CompStat.

MAPPING CRIME

Mapping crime has evolved from using color-coded push pins to user-friendly mapping software, designed for examining and predicting crime and criminal behavior: "From Alaska to the East Coast, law enforcement agencies are using crime mapping to communicate with their communities and focus their resources and investigations. The benefits of this technological tool are countless, and the options for implementation are growing" (Bradley, 2008, p.64).

According to the National Institute of Justice (NIJ), "The ability to visualize how crime is distributed across the landscape (i.e., crime mapping) gives analysts and policy makers a graphic representation of crime and its related issues. Simple maps help law enforcement leaders direct patrols to areas where they are most needed. Complex maps help policymakers and investigators observe trends and respond more intelligently to changing issues. For example, detectives may use maps to understand the hunting patterns of serial criminals, determine where these offenders might live, and identify their next likely target" ("NIJ Crime Mapping Resources," 2007). Crime mapping may also be used to track registered sex offenders in communities.

When the Police Executive Research Forum (PERF) surveyed police agencies in 2005 and 2006 to identify the most widely used antiviolence strategy, the highest-ranking program cited by 63 percent of the respondents was hot spot enforcement (*Violent Crime in America*, 2008, p.3). **Hot spots** are locations of persistent calls regarding crime and disorder, and the 2008 PERF survey focused on "hot spots" enforcement:

hot spots
Clusters of crime in certain geographic areas.

> In general, hot spot enforcement refers to police efforts to identify the location—a residence, a store, a nightclub or other particular address; a street corner; a city block; a neighborhood—that generates the most calls to 911 or other indicators of criminal activity. Then, police analyze the types of crimes being committed at each hot spot and devise ways of reducing the crime. Because hot spots are often plotted as dots on a map, and the police response often involves sending more officers to the location, hot spots enforcement is sometimes called "putting cops on the dots." . . . [N]early 9 out of 10 agencies use hot spots enforcement efforts directed either at larger hot spot areas like neighborhoods, smaller hot spot places like intersections, or both. . . . (p.3)

> Strategies used to deal with *homicide/shooting* hot spots included problem analysis and problem solving (77 percent), community policing/partnerships (73 percent), enhanced traffic stops and field interviews (69 percent), targeting known offenders (69 percent and most frequently mentioned as the most effective strategy), directed patrol (64 percent), intervening at problem locations (64 percent), mobile suppression or saturation unit (63 percent), warrant service (62 percent), checks on probationers and parolees (62 percent), and use of overtime for saturation patrol (61 percent).... (p.4)
>
> Strategies used to deal with *robbery* hot spots included problem analysis and problem solving (93 percent), directed patrol (91 percent and most often identified as the most effective strategy), community policing/partnerships (89 percent), surveillance operations (86 percent), enhanced traffic stops and field interviews (80 percent), and targeting known offenders (80 percent).... (p.5)
>
> Strategies to deal with *aggravated assault* hot spots included problem analysis (82 percent), community policing/partnerships (76 percent), intervening at problem locations (74 percent), targeting known offenders (63 percent), and directed patrol (61 percent and most often identified as the most effective strategy).... (p.6)
>
> Strategies to deal with *gang violence* hot spots included targeting known offenders (89 percent, and most often identified as the most effective strategy), directed patrol (86 percent), problem analysis and problem solving (85 percent), and enhanced traffic stops and field interviews (84 percent). (p.7)

Given that prevention is one of the primary goals of proactive policing, hot spots enforcement may provide police with a new way to break the vicious cycle of crime: "Hot spots policing may be to the new millennium what problem-oriented policing was to the 1990s" (Wexler, 2008, p.29).

In addition to mapping hot spots, mapping can be used to map key buildings. Several floor planning software programs are available to law enforcement, including the CAD Zone, which was originally developed to draw crime scenes but is also ideal for creating floor plans and site plans for tactical planning purposes (Mills-Senn, 2008). Another program called FloorView captures as much detail as desired for both the interior and exterior of any facility as well as mapping information about the areas surrounding the building and aerial photographs.

Information from mapping is often enhanced by geographic information systems (GIS).

Geographic Information Systems (GIS)

geographic information systems (GIS)
Creating, updating and analyzing computerized maps.

Geographic information systems (GIS) enhance traditional mapping by adding information from various other databases. For example, modern GIS software can generate maps that correlate crime with vacant housing units, schools, or parks; income level of a census tract; patterns of car thefts; and locations of chop shops. Much like with any form of technology in law enforcement, agencies can choose from many different types of GIS software, which allows departments to select programs better tailored to their specific needs. Cook and Burton (2008, p.126) explain, "In a GIS-focused law enforcement agency, databases, in-vehicle computers, mobile devices and GPS tracking equipment enable cost-effective data input and output systems and empower data analysis and dissemination to all who need it—officers, investigators, crime analysts, street supervisors and upper-level managers." Peed et al. (2008, p.24) state,

> Because police solutions to crime are necessarily about where crime takes place, the ability to visualize and analyze geographic patterns becomes paramount. Advancements in crime mapping, geographic information systems (GIS) software, and other spatial analysis software have greatly enhanced the field of crime analysis. GIS approaches are gaining acceptance and prominence by effectively combining criminological theory and geographic analysis principles to address practical law enforcement problems. Continuing improvements in GIS software have made it possible to better assemble, integrate, and create new ways of analyzing data. Not only can analysis, with the help of GIS software, assemble multiple and disparate sets of demographic, economic, and social data; they can also create new units of analysis that more accurately model human behavior. . . .
>
> There are some significant benefits to adopting an integrated analysis model:
>
> - Understanding the big picture. Combining both intelligence analysis and crime analysis can help executives see all pieces of the puzzle.
> - Enhanced enforcement tactics. To implement a broader range of tactics for responding to crime patterns and to respond with efficiency and effectiveness, police officers need to understand both the what *and* the why of criminal behavior.
> - Real-world analytic approaches. Combining intelligence analysis and crime analysis avoids overly simplistic solutions. It allows for a more realistic and integrated analytical model, without unnecessary duplication of efforts.

Global Positioning Systems (GPS)

GIS can be combined with global positioning systems (GPS) and photomapping technology to help investigators spatially piece together clues that are spread out over large areas such as high speed chase scenes (Corbley, 2008, p.101). Any crime that spans a large area may leave a trail of evidence such as weapons, blood or bullet casings that can be mapped and analyzed using GPS: "There can be no doubt that the proliferation of GPS functionality in policing technologies dramatically improves capabilities across a wide spectrum of law enforcement operations" (Smith, 2009, p.144). GPS is at the core of emerging law enforcement technologies such as automatic vehicle location (AVL) systems and offender-tracking systems. Some departments use crime mapping technology for long-term strategic planning and to enhance their real-time response to crime. In addition, many departments have enhanced their crime analysis by using CompStat.

CompStat

CompStat, short for "computer statistics" or "comparison statistics," began in 1994 in New York City. Since that time, "CompStat has become synonymous with progressive police management, and police departments large and small are adopting the principles of CompStat in order to identify crime problems,

Table 6.4 Has Your Department Implemented a CompStat-Like Program?

Department Size	Percent Yes	Percent No, But Planning	Percent No
Small (50–99 Sworn)	11.0	29.3	59.8
Large (100+ Sworn)	32.6	25.6	41.8

Due to rounding, rows may not add to 100.
Source: David Weisburd, Stephen D. Mastrofski, Rosann Greenspan and James J. Willis. "The Growth of CompStat in American Policing." *Police Foundation Reports*, April 2004, p.6. Washington, DC: Police Foundation. Reprinted by permission.

select tactics for dealing with specific crime situations, and conduct relentless follow-up and assessment to learn about what works best" (Bond, 2007, p.6). The CompStat process is "a goal-oriented, information-driven management process that stresses both operational strategy and managerial accountability. Its goal is to reduce crime and enhance the community's quality of life. The CompStat process consists of four components: (1) collection and analysis of crime data, (2) development of strategy to address problems, (3) rapid deployment of resources, and (4) follow-up and accountability" (Geoghegan, 2006, pp.42–43).

Nationwide, about one-third of large departments (those with 100+ sworn officers) have implemented a CompStat-like program and another 26 percent are planning such a program, as shown in Table 6.4.

According to Lt. Cahhal of the Los Angeles County Sheriff's Department, "With the automation of the CompStat module, shift managers and even deputies can view crime statistics and do their own analyses within seconds" (Miller, 2008, p.141).

Beyond Crime Analysis

Many law enforcement agencies are not using crime analysis technology to its full potential, to intervene in crime patterns and move beyond merely responding to crime after the fact (Casady, 2008, p.40). Effective crime analysis can use several processes, including the traditional crime analysis process, the SARA model, the intelligence cycle model and others, but the most difficult aspect of preventing crime and arresting criminals is the transition between analysis and response: "It is here that the analyst loses direct control over the process and must pass the baton to the operational units" (Bruce and Ouellette, 2008, p.30). Building on routine activity theory, which suggests that crime occurs when a motivated offender and a suitable target occur in the same time and space in the absence of a committed guardian, Bruce and Ouellette point out that although directed patrol is a "default response" to a crime pattern, hot spot or problem, it can be effective for some issues and can result in both suppression and apprehension. Agencies have many more potential responses beyond directed patrol at their disposal: apprehending offenders, hardening potential targets, and suppressing underlying opportunities for crime.

Issues Related to Disseminating Crime Information to the Public

As beneficial as this technology is for police operations, it has raised some legitimate concerns. For example, given communities' growing desire for access to timely information about crime and disorder in their neighborhoods, how much of this crime data should be made so readily available? Although technically such data is public information, and citizens do have a right to know about crime in their communities, how do law enforcement agencies address victims' right to privacy?

The National Center for Victims of Crime has published *Beyond the Beat: Ethical Considerations for Community Policing in the Digital Age* (2008). The publication describes how recent advances in one-way communications such as online crime statistics, crime maps, and sex offender registries can help combat crime but may also present ethical challenges. Other concerns involve the possible revitalization of informal redlining methods used by some insurance and banking companies. Although a neighborhood identified as a high-crime area could benefit from positive local interventions, it could also be flagged (i.e., redlined) as undesirable, resulting in residential flight and causing more damage to an already disadvantaged area. Real estate agents and homeowners may become concerned about decreasing property values if crime maps lead to the perception their neighborhoods are unsafe.

Despite great advances in detecting crime and apprehending criminals, crimes will continue to be committed, and when crime and disorder problems surface, law enforcement must respond.

RESPONDING TO CALLS ABOUT CRIME AND DISORDER

How police officers respond to calls about committed crimes depends on several important variables:

- What specific crime is involved?
- Is the crime still in progress?
- How many suspects are involved?
- Do we know their identity?
- Are weapons involved?
- Are there other aggravating circumstances regarding the suspect(s), for example, are they intoxicated, mentally imbalanced, and so forth?
- Are there victims involved or injured?
- Is there a danger to the public?
- Could a hostage situation develop?
- What weather and environmental factors can affect a response?
- How many officers are needed to respond?
- How many officers are available?
- Where are they?

Sometimes answers to all these questions are available. More often, however, responding officers lack much of this information.

Responsibilities of officers responding to a call regarding a criminal act include

- Arriving as rapidly, yet as safely, as possible.
- Caring for any injured people at the scene.
- Apprehending any suspects at the scene.
- Securing the scene.
- Conducting a preliminary investigation.

Arriving at the Scene

Whether the police arrive with red lights and sirens will depend on the nature of the information to which police are responding. The element of surprise may be important if the crime is believed to be still in progress. At other times, such as in assault cases, the siren may be desirable because it may frighten off the attacker. Each specific call must be assessed for whether the added speed of response available through the use of red lights and siren is an advantage. Recall the Kansas City Preventive Patrol Experiment, which showed that rapid response time did not greatly improve chances of making an arrest at the scene. In addition, the more rapid the response, the greater the likelihood of a crash en route involving the responding squad or citizens who happen to be in the way.

The NIJ has produced a guide for law enforcement officers (*Crime Scene Investigation* . . . , 2000, p.11), which states the following policy regarding initial response when arriving at a crime scene: "The initial responding officer(s) shall promptly, yet cautiously, approach and enter crime scenes, remaining observant of any persons, vehicles, events, potential evidence, and environmental conditions." Procedures listed in the guide for initial responders include noting or logging dispatch information (e.g., address/location, time, date, type of call, parties involved) and remaining alert and attentive.

The actual arrival may be fraught with danger; consequently, officers should make use of cover if it is thought the suspect might still be at the scene. If the element of surprise is important, officers should have a system of hand signals to coordinate their arrival and approach to the scene. Communication with other officers is critical and is typically done via radio, although alternatives to using the main channel include switching over to a tactical talk-around channel on the radio or using push-to-talk cell phones.

Grossi (2007b, pp.24–25) offers three objectives for a safe, efficient response to "in-progress" calls. First, anticipate the unexpected and assume the worst; consider shutting down your lights and siren, close your vehicle doors quietly, lower your radio and silence your equipment. Second, if possible, isolate innocent bystanders. Third, control and take into custody the suspect: "Remember the contact and cover principles: firm, clear and concise verbal commands given by only one officer; watch the suspect's hands; hands kill; and 'no' people belong on the ground." A "no" person is considered one who resists an officer's commands, in contrast to "yes" people who comply, surrender and are able to be taken into custody while remaining standing. Defiance and failure to comply is a danger to officers; thus "no" people must be immobilized by commanding them to get down on the ground before an officer can safety approach, cuff and search the individual.

The next two responsibilities, attending to injured people and apprehending suspects at the scene, may occur in reverse order, depending on the situation.

Attending to Injuries and Apprehending Suspects

Usually injuries and suspects at the scene are considered emergency matters to be attended to immediately upon arrival. If the injuries are not life threatening and the suspect is considered dangerous, apprehending that suspect will take precedence over attending to the injuries. The NIJ general policy states, "The initial responding officer(s) arriving at the scene shall identify and control any dangerous situations or persons" (*Crime Scene . . .*, 2000, p.12). Control of physical threats ensures the safety of officers and others at the scene.

Once dangerous situations or people have been brought under control, "the initial responding officer(s') next responsibility is to ensure that medical attention is provided to injured persons while minimizing contamination of the scene" (*Crime Scene . . .*, 2000, p.13). The guide (p.14) also suggests, "Assisting, guiding, and instructing medical personnel during the care and removal of injured persons will diminish the risk of contamination and loss of evidence." As soon as emergency matters are tended to, the primary responsibility of the police is to secure the crime scene.

Securing the Crime Scene

The first officer to arrive on the crime scene automatically incurs the critical responsibility of securing the crime scene from unauthorized intrusion or other contamination: "Controlling, identifying and removing persons at the crime scene and limiting the number of persons who enter the crime scene and the movement of such persons is an important function of the initial responding officer(s) in protecting the crime scene" (*Crime Scene . . .*, 2000, p.14). If more than one officer responds to the call, the scene can be secured immediately by one officer while the other officer handles any emergency situation.

Officers should consider any crime scene as highly dynamic and make the preliminary survey of the layout carefully while preserving crime scene integrity. Sometimes securing the scene is as simple as closing a door, but other times it is more complex. In a bank robbery, for example, the entire lobby is usually secured and closed for business until the preliminary investigation is completed. Outdoor crime scenes are generally roped off or barricaded. Only those individuals with official business should be allowed into the crime scene. In many cases, authorized personnel such as other police officers who are curious, or administrators who arrive on scene to "check things out," are responsible for compromising or contaminating a crime scene. As a general rule, no one should be allowed on the scene other than those who are actually investigating or processing it (after the incident has been secured). A way to deter curiosity seekers is to require all personnel who enter the scene, from the chief of police down through patrol officers, to write a detailed report stating their reason for being there and what they did on the scene. This requirement serves as a reminder that anyone entering a crime scene can be called into court to testify about what they saw and did—a clear deterrent to those who were present for no good reason—and makes personnel think twice before entering a scene where their actions may compromise any evidence.

The NIJ (*Crime Scene . . .*, 2000, p.15) suggests setting well-defined, liberal and controllable boundaries is a critical aspect in preserving the integrity of evidentiary material: "Defining and controlling boundaries provides a means for protecting and securing the crime scene(s). The number of crime scenes and their boundaries are determined by their location(s) and the type of crime. Boundaries shall be established beyond the initial scope of the crime scene(s) with the understanding that the boundaries can be reduced in size if necessary but cannot be as easily expanded." In many cases, crime scene investigators will set up two boundaries, one that expands well beyond the scene and another that is just at the border of the scene. This dual barrier creates a buffer zone that gives authorized personnel a work space just outside and around the actual crime scene, thereby improving scene integrity. It also acts as an added buffer for the media and public onlookers by keeping such individuals beyond the outermost boundary.

In some departments, this is where the responsibilities of the responding officers end. They keep the scene secure until investigators or detectives arrive to conduct the investigation, especially in crimes such as murder, as discussed in Chapter 10. The NIJ policy regarding this "changing of the guard" states, "The initial responding officer(s) at the scene shall provide a detailed crime scene briefing to the investigator(s) in charge of the scene" and "Turn over responsibility for the documentation of entry/exit" (*Crime Scene* . . . , p.17). The *Crime Scene* guide (p.17) also notes, "All activities conducted and observations made at the crime scene must be documented as soon as possible after the event to preserve information. Documentation must be maintained as a permanent record." In other departments, particularly smaller agencies that lack the resources for a designated crime scene unit, the responding officers may conduct the preliminary investigation and, perhaps, the entire investigation. If the crime itself is complicated and severe, even larger local departments may enlist assistance or additional support from state-level law enforcement agencies.

The Preliminary Investigation

The more information and evidence that can be obtained immediately after a crime has been committed, the better the chances of identifying the person responsible and of successfully prosecuting the case. The officers responding to the call are usually in the best position to obtain this information and evidence.

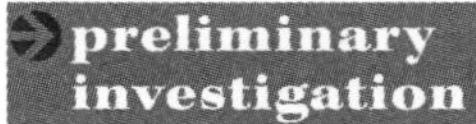

The on-the-scene interviews of victims and witnesses, interrogations of suspects and search of the crime scene itself.

The **preliminary investigation** of a crime involves on-the-scene interviews of victims and witnesses, interrogation of suspects and a search of the scene itself.

The preliminary investigation is not so much an "investigation" in the traditional sense, where days, weeks, months, even years of tracking leads, developing suspects and refining theories go into the eventual solving of a crime. (The complete investigation itself is discussed in Chapter 10.) Compared with this level of examination, the preliminary investigation is a rather superficial on-site assessment and collection of evidentiary details observed by the initial responding officer(s) and relayed by witnesses.

In larger departments, if a suspect is apprehended at the scene, interrogation is usually done at the police department by experienced, trained investigators. Interviewing and interrogating were discussed in Chapter 2. Witnesses should be separated and their statements recorded.

Officers arriving at the scene are often responsible for recognizing and gathering evidence as part of the preliminary investigation. Therefore, officers must know the elements of each crime and what evidence will prove them.

Curiosity seekers can destroy valuable evidence and contaminate a crime scene, so it is necessary to cordon off the area. © AP Images/Danny Johnston

Recognizing and Collecting Physical Evidence The crime-scene search is, for certain offenses, the most important part of the investigation. A large part of the preliminary investigation centers around whether officers can obtain evidence that a crime has been committed and been committed by a particular person. Evidence may be the turning point determining whether a case can be made and a criminal convicted.

Although some crimes, such as forgery, embezzlement, identity theft and credit-card fraud, have no crime scenes and yield little to no physical evidence, many crimes do have crime scenes and provide physical evidence. The value of any physical evidence used in court to verify that a crime has been committed, to identify the person(s) who did it and to obtain a conviction often depends on the officers who arrive first at a crime scene. In most cases, the officers who protect and search a crime scene play a critical role in determining whether a case can be made.

Experienced officers anticipate finding certain types of evidence in specific crimes. In many offenses, criminals contact the physical surroundings and leave evidence linking themselves to victims and crime scenes. Violent crimes, for example, often involve a struggle and frequently yield evidence such as blood, skin, saliva, semen or other DNA evidence; hairs; fibers; fingerprints; and weapons. Property crimes, in contrast, commonly yield evidence such as tool marks on doors, windows, safes, money chests, cash registers and desk drawers, as well as fingerprints. Recognizing and collecting evidence are examined in greater depth in Chapter 10.

All preliminary investigations must be systematic and thorough. The finding of some answers does not mean that all answers have been uncovered. Likewise, the finding of some evidence does not mean that more may not exist. One is mindful of the question once considered the epitome of the obvious, Who's buried in Grant's tomb? Those who answer "General Ulysses S. Grant" are only half right. His wife, Julia, is buried with him. Professional police officers must get *all* the facts and information, not just the obvious.

When evidence is found, it must be carefully marked (often with the officer's badge number), placed in a secure container, sealed, tagged, recorded in the officer's notebook and, as soon as practical, placed in the property or evidence room. It must be kept secure until it is needed for trial. The **chain of possession**, or **chain of custody**, documents who has had control of the evidence from the time it is discovered until it is presented in court. Any time evidence is taken from the property room, it must be signed for. When it is returned, it is examined to be sure that it has not been altered in any way.

chain of possession

See *chain of custody*.

chain of custody

Documented account of who has had control of evidence from the time it is discovered until it is presented in court. Also called *chain of possession*.

Crime-Scene Units

Because most local police departments have fewer than 20 sworn officers, they seldom have special teams of criminal investigators. In such cases, a crime-scene team consisting of patrol officers assigned crime-scene duty as a collateral duty is often of value.

The crime-scene unit, after conducting a preliminary survey of the crime scene, determines the actual crime-scene perimeter and search area. They set the search objectives as well as the equipment and personnel needed and also develop a theory of the crime. In addition, they identify and protect transient evidence and prepare a narrative description of the scene.

In some departments, after these functions are performed, the work of the crime-scene unit is complete, and the case is turned over to an investigative or detective division. In smaller departments, however, the crime-scene unit may conduct the entire investigation.

Examples of Specific Crime-Related Call Responses

Law enforcement has traditionally been expected to deal with criminal activity and to be proactive in preventing such activity when possible.

Theft Auto theft is one of the most common calls police respond to, as introduced in the last chapter. Automated license plate recognition (ALPR) programs help officers identify thousands of stolen vehicles every year. Another technique used to apprehend car thieves in action is a "bait" car, equipped with hardware and software that allows police to track the vehicle by GPS, and to shut down the vehicle's engine and lock the doors remotely.

One form of theft officers will need to respond to is fraudulent credit card purchases because this type of crime is becoming increasingly prevalent. Criminals use fraudulent credit cards to steal billions of dollars in merchandise every year, costing U.S. businesses $3.2 billion in losses in 2007 (Petrocelli, 2008b, p.16). As with many crimes, the victims often do not report the theft to police, feeling the credit card issuer is responsible. However, police can do little about this problem without the help of credit card companies, retail stores and credit card users. Investigating credit card fraud is difficult, expensive and time consuming, and conviction rates are fairly low for this offense. One reason this crime is so challenging for law enforcement is that it often crosses jurisdictional, even international, borders. It is also relatively easy to commit, and, considering the low likelihood of arrest, prosecution and conviction for this crime, the benefits to credit card thieves far outweigh the risks.

Identity theft is another challenge that law enforcement can do little about. According to the NIJ, "Identity theft has become perhaps the defining crime of the information age, with an estimated 9 million or more incidents each year" ("Introduction," 2007). Approximately one out of every four people in the United States will become a victim of identity theft, the fastest-growing crime in the United States (Barton (2008, p.14).

The NIJ notes that no accepted definition of identity theft existed until Congress passed the federal Theft and Assumption Deterrence Act of 1998: "This statute defines identity theft very broadly, making it easier for prosecutors to conduct their cases, but does little to help researchers because identity theft is composed of numerous crimes committed in widely varying venues and circumstances" ("Defining Identity Theft," 2007).

Law enforcement can help combat identity theft by taking a complete police report, providing victim assistance, advising victims to contact all of their financial institutions, and instructing them to contact the fraud units of the three principal credit card reporting agencies: Equifax, Experian (formerly TRW) and TransUnion (Barton, 2008).

Patrolling Motels Law enforcement can prevent crime and improve the chances of apprehending criminals by keeping a watch on motels, which have historically presented problem for police: "Transitory populations and apathetic management make motels havens for prostitution, truancy, and human smuggling. In recent years, even the war on drugs has had an impact" (Scoville, 2008, p.27). Keeping a watch on hotels and motels usually helps identify problem establishments. Key indicators of criminal activity on such properties include the number of calls for service they generate, the types of vehicles in the parking lot, and the amount of traffic occurring there: "When law enforcement officers take initiative and target motel undesirables, they can dramatically impact problems generated both at the motels and elsewhere" (Scoville).

Responding to Drive-By Shootings Research suggests that drive-by shootings can be triggered by road rage or by personal disputes, but are most often associated with street gangs and street drug dealers. Gang members and drug dealers are not likely to take their grievances to the police but are much more apt to retaliate with their own drive-by shooting, resulting in a cycle of attack, counterattack, reprisal and retribution and may lead to a claim of self defense (Petrocelli, 2007a, p.20). Officers responding to a drive-by shooting must determine whether it was a planned assault or a random attack and should canvass the neighborhood. In extreme cases, road blocks might be set up. Other actions officers can take are presented in Chapter 12, which deals with the gang and drug problems.

Immigration and Crime Before leaving the discussion of responding to a call for crime-related service, consider the issues facing law enforcement and the immigration problem and crime: "Across the country, in communities large and small, residents and policy makers are grappling with the issues raised by a population of immigrants who have entered the United States illegally. For state and local police and sheriff's departments, the main issues are the extent to which they should be involved in inquiring about immigration status during encounters on the street, reporting non-criminal illegal immigrants to federal authorities, and otherwise helping to enforce federal immigration laws" (*Police Chiefs and Sheriffs Speak Out on Local Immigration Enforcement*, 2008, p.1). Each agency must decide for itself whether being in the country illegally is a crime in itself, calling for deportation.

Petrocelli (2008a, p.22) contends, "Young illegal aliens loitering in front of businesses waiting for work can be a catalyst for crime." These day laborers are mainly young males lacking education and skills and do not speak English. Large numbers of such day laborers can create traffic problems, litter, loiter, interrupt businesses and intimidate citizens passing by. From a law enforcement perspective, the main problem caused by day laborer sites is the deterioration of a neighborhood, and arresting day laborers can be frustrating, time-consuming and fruitless for officers. Often, the best officers can do is contain the problem by organizing and maintaining day labor sites where day laborers can assemble without directly affecting the rest of the community (Petrocelli).

A study of the "particularly tricky problem" of preventing crime and disorder at day laborer sites found the politically charged nature at such sites to be a serious obstacle; most day laborers are illegal immigrants, and many people have strong opinions about immigration, some viewing them as valuable resources providing cheap labor for jobs others will not do, but others seeing them as criminals who take jobs, commit other crimes, and cause community disorder (Guerette, 2007). The first step for an agency in approaching the problem is to analyze the community's attitudes toward these sites, focusing on any disorder and crime associated with the sites, rather than on trying to shut them down.

RESPONDING TO CALLS REGARDING DISORDER AND QUALITY-OF-LIFE ISSUES

Closely associated with the problem of crime is the problem of disorder and quality-of-life issues. When disorder occurs, police are expected to deal with it. In 1982, Wilson and Kelling (p.31) set forth their classic broken windows theory, writing,

> At the community level, disorder and crime are usually inextricably linked, in a kind of developmental sequence. Social psychologists and police officers tend to agree that if a window in a building is broken *and is left unrepaired*, all the rest of the windows will soon be broken. This is as true in nice neighborhoods as in run-down ones. Window-breaking does not necessarily occur on a large scale because some areas are inhabited by determined window-breakers whereas others are populated by window-lovers; rather, one unrepaired broken window is a signal that no one cares, and so breaking more windows costs nothing. (It has always been fun.) . . .
>
> The citizen who fears the ill-smelling drunk, the rowdy teenager or the importuning beggar is not merely expressing his distaste for unseemly behavior; he is also giving voice to a bit of folk wisdom that happens to be a correct generalization—namely, that serious street crime flourishes in areas in which disorderly

> behavior goes unchecked. The unchecked panhandler is, in effect, the first broken window. (p.34)

The link between disorder and crime and whether social and physical disorder lead directly to more serious offenses has been debated. However, collective efficacy may help explain this link. **Collective efficacy** refers to cohesion among neighborhood residents along with expectations of informal social control in public places that inhibits both crime and disorder.

collective efficacy
Cohesion among neighborhood residents combined with shared expectations for informal social control of public space that inhibits both crime and disorder.

According to Miller, Hess and Orthmann (2010, pp.64–65), "Broken windows and smashed cars are visible signs of people not caring about their community. Other less subtle signs include unmowed lawns, piles of accumulated trash and graffiti, often referred to as **incivilities**. Incivilities include rowdiness, drunkenness, fighting, prostitution and abandoned buildings." The community can be enlisted to deal with the physical incivilities.

incivilities
Subtle signs of a community not caring about disorder, including rowdiness, drunkenness, fighting, prostitution and abandoned buildings.

Jones (2009, p.20) describes a dramatic increase (14 percent) in calls for service in Suwanee, Georgia, that was forcing the department to operate strictly reactively, no longer able to maintain its traditional open communication and positive relationship with the community. Analysis of the department's calls-for-service data revealed that the vast majority of calls were from neighborhoods, not businesses or public areas. Residents in one neighborhood called the department every day to complain about speeders, potholes and many other quality-of-life issues. The department decided to use community outreach through the homeowners associations already in place in the community.

In 2002, the department established the Police and Citizens Together (PACT) program to encourage community residents to work together to maintain the quality of life in their own neighborhoods. The first year focused on the neighborhood that had been calling every day. Through PACT, each homeowners association has its own police officer with whom they can become familiar and build a relationship. The officers hold meetings at least three times a year.

PACT achieved its major goal of halting the spiraling increase calls for service, actually reducing such calls even though the community was growing rapidly. Officers were given time to work proactively, problem solving with residents to address issues of concern: "Officers are empowered to assist directly and residents do not feel the need to make repeated calls for service" (Jones, 2009, p.26). A further goal was also reached—keeping Suwanee's crime rate low, with the crime rate not keeping pace with the population growth.

Responding to Disorderly or Troublesome People

Disorderly or troublesome people may include panhandlers, prostitutes, inebriates, and individuals who are mentally ill or homeless.

Panhandlers The public has two vastly different views on panhandling: Some, including many civil libertarians and homeless advocates, sympathize, believing that panhandling is essential to destitute people's survival and should not be prohibited by the government. Some even see panhandling as an expression of the plight of the needy, and an opportunity for those more fortunate to help. Others, however, see panhandling as a blight that contributes to community disorder and crime, as well as to panhandlers' shame as their basic problems go unaddressed. Those with the latter view believe panhandling should be regulated by the government.

Two types of panhandling are passive and aggressive: "Passive panhandling is a silent solicitation; the panhandler generally lets his appearance speak for itself. Aggressive panhandling involves some type of verbal interaction usually accompanied by a physical action. . . . Passive panhandling plays on a citizen's sense of generosity; whereas aggressive panhandling plays more on a citizen's sense of fear" (Petrocelli, 2007c, p.20). Police are more apt to take action against aggressive panhandlers, but according to one study, police made arrests for panhandling in about 1 percent of all encounters (Petrocelli).

Unfortunately, laws prohibiting panhandling seldom control the problem, nor does "shooing" them away. Petrocelli (2007, p.21) suggests officers build a strong file on a chronic offender, so that if an arrest is made, the case is strong. Video surveillance, officer decoys and citizen complaints also help build a case. Restraining orders might forbid a panhandler to frequent certain areas or establishments. Some departments use a voucher system by which concerned citizens buy vouchers from area merchants good only for basic necessities, not for liquor or cigarettes. This system allows sympathetic citizens to donate, knowing their contribution will be used as intended. Petrocelli (p.21) concludes, "Chronic panhandlers are a thorn in the side of police because they commit a very obvious crime but are rarely arrested. To properly handle the problem, clearly define who you are dealing with, gather public support, and develop a response that will eliminate the problem."

Prostitutes Petrocelli (2009, p.20) asserts, "For as long as there have been men and women, there has been the exchange of valuables for sexual favors, though there rarely have been societies that allowed prostitution. Sanctions have varied from fines to death, yet prostitution has flourished in every stratum of society in every part of the world. Prostitution takes many different forms from high-priced call girls who meet clients in hotel rooms to street prostitutes who ply their trade in public." A closely related crime, and much more serious, is human trafficking. Of all alleged human trafficking incidents reported by task forces for 2007–2008, nearly 83 percent involved allegations of sex trafficking (Kyckelhahn et al., 2009, p.1). These individuals are forced into prostitution.

Street-level prostitution can directly affect a neighborhood's quality of life, attracting strangers to an area and providing opportunities for other street level crimes. Jetmore (2008, p.96) notes, "As police officers, we recognize that arresting streetwalkers and their customers is like squeezing a balloon. When the heat (the squeeze) is on, prostitutes and their customers just move to another area."

Street sweeps are largely ineffective. Law enforcement in many jurisdictions has shifted from attacking the supply to targeting the demands, but this strategy alone does not reduce the problem: "Any effective policy is going to incorporate a balanced attack against the suppliers and those who demand it" (Petrocelli, 2009, p.20). Although street prostitution accounts for only 10 to 20 percent of the prostitution problem, it has the greatest negative impact on the community (Petrocelli). It also has a negative impact on the prostitutes themselves.

Many prostitutes are homeless, and most have limited education and few ties with the community. Most did not choose prostitution as a career but sell themselves to survive, often as a result of addiction to drugs or alcohol and a lack of skills or resources. Departments might consider setting up program presenting opportunities for offenders to get out of the business, serve restraining orders to prohibit them from returning to certain high-risk areas or place curfews to ensure they do not work during peak hours. Proposed solutions include having all "johns" make the court appearance on the same date, allowing the judge and public to see the magnitude of the problem, shaming offenders by publishing their names, sending them warning letters, or sending them to "john schools" where they learn about the legal and health consequences of their behavior (Petrocelli, 2009). Other strategies involve distributing pamphlets to the public outlining the dangers of paying for sex, especially in cities that host conventions. Reporting abandoned buildings and working to restrict or eliminate motel rooms available by the hour can also help reducing opportunities for prostitution.

Often prostitutes find their "johns" in bars. Bars can present yet another challenge for law enforcement.

Problems around Bars It is common knowledge that alcohol lowers inhibitions. Alcohol makes many people feel powerful and unconcerned about the consequences of their actions. Individuals who drink too much often get into fights and may end up assaulting someone or being assaulted themselves. Generally speaking, certain "problem" bars account for the majority of violent incidents, including bars that tolerate disorderly conduct, yelling and profanity and whose clientele includes drug users, drug sellers and prostitutes (Petrocelli, 2008c, p.16). Other characteristics of bars where violence is likely to occur are those that do not sell food, are overcrowded and are poorly ventilated.

Law enforcement should work with the bar owners association in the community, attend their meetings and have a police representative at any alcohol licensing procedures. Drink servers should be trained to identify those who have had too much to drink and who are acting aggressively. Because much of the violence in and around bars occurs at closing, departments might consider adding supplemental patrols to trouble spots during this relatively brief time. Some bars serve non-alcoholic drinks and food for an hour after normal closing time, allowing an hour "cooling off" period as well as staggering the exodus from the bar.

The New York Police Department, in an effort to address the crime and disorder often associated with bars and nightclubs, partnered with the New York Nightlife Association to jointly consider how to address the problem (Kelly, 2008, pp.52–53). The working group came up with a series of 60 best practices, 47 of which applied to security, employees, age verification, club policies, and police-community relations. The remaining 13 related to reporting crimes, including physical and sexual assaults.

Individuals Who Are Mentally Ill "If you work the street, you're going to deal with crazy people" (Petrocelli, 2007b, p.22). The most common call, where mentally ill persons are involved, is disturbing the peace. It is recommended that agencies maintain a database of incidents involving mentally ill citizens as well as a list of mental health services available 24 hours per day (Petrocelli).

Many agencies now provide crisis incident team (CIT) training to help officers identify individuals who need mental health treatment, thereby preventing such individuals from ending up in jail for "disturbing the peace"—or dead. Some departments have specially designated CIT officers to respond to mental illness calls on a specific beat or area of responsibility. These officers often operate as part of a network to handle the community's mentally ill population.

Some community-based programs partner mental health practitioners from local government and private practice with local law enforcement to conduct officer safety and de-escalation training. In most departments, however, calls involving mentally ill subjects fall to all patrol officers, not just to a specialized unit of CIT officers.

In some cases, unfortunately, use of force is necessary. The courts have held that in certain situations police use of force against a mentally ill person is justifiable and necessary for the protection and safety of the officer and public. The operational triangle, shown in Figure 6.3, has safety as its foundation. Only after safety is established should officers attempt to achieve a relationship with a mentally ill subject. Communicating with individuals who are mentally ill was discussed in Chapter 2.

Many of those who are mentally ill are also homeless as a result of the deinstitutionalization that occurred in the 1960s and 1970s.

The Homeless Although it is not against the law to be homeless, many people living on the streets, by virtue of their lack of residence, do engage in illegal activity or otherwise contribute to a community's level of disorder. With no place to sleep, use the bathroom, keep their belongings, dump their trash, get drunk or take care of other private matters, the homeless have to conduct such "business" in public.

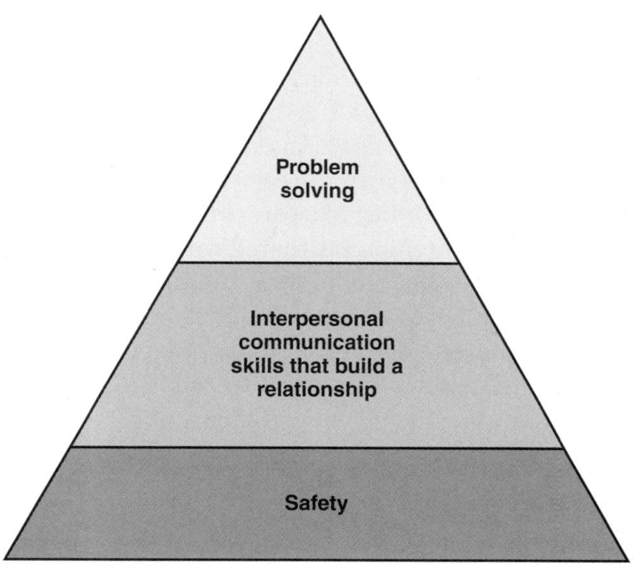

FIGURE 6.3
Operational Triangle for Responding to Individuals Who Are Mentally Ill
Source: Douglas Gentz and William S. Goree, "Moving Past What to How—The Next Step in Responding to Individuals with Mental Illness." *FBI Law Enforcement Bulletin*, November 2003, p.15.

A large percentage of homeless adults are unemployed and, without income, many resort to panhandling or stealing just to be able to eat. National data indicate 20 percent of homeless people eat one meal a day or less. Addicts often turn to crime to support their habits or engage in crime while under the influence of alcohol and other drugs. Nearly half of all homeless people suffer from chronic health problems such as high blood pressure, arthritis, diabetes or cancer, and more than half lack medical insurance. Such health factors undoubtedly add to the stress of homelessness and may contribute to either the increased perpetration of crime by or vulnerability to crime of those afflicted. Victimization among the homeless is relatively common, with many reporting having had money or possessions stolen directly from them and having had money or possessions stolen while unattended.

Thus, although homelessness may begin as a social service issue, with entire families living on the streets or in cars, when it becomes combined with the economic factor of unemployment, the medical factors of mental illness or substance abuse, and the increased risk of victimization, it can quickly become a criminal justice issue.

Some departments are providing sensitivity training to educate officers about the specific needs and concerns of homeless people. Other agencies have formed alliances between officers, city officials, local businesses, homeless shelters and human services outreach workers to provide a coordinated response to the multiple issues surrounding homelessness.

One of the most important challenges is reducing violent attacks against homeless people. Attacks increased 65 percent from 2005 to 2006 and more than 170 percent since 2001. The 2006 attacks included beatings, stabbings, burnings, and rapes and fatalities ("Violent Crimes against Homeless," 2007, p.4). Jurisdictions across the country have begun modifying their statutes to designate crimes against the homeless as hate crimes.

The operational triangle in Figure 6.3 could also be applied when responding to homeless people. Safety first, followed by communication to build rapport (as discussed in Chapter 2), concluding with problem solving.

The challenges to law enforcement when responding to troublesome people can be much greater when the situation is not one-on-one but instead involves a crowd bent on civil disobedience.

CIVIL DISOBEDIENCE

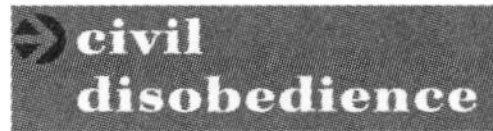

Intentional breaking of a law to prove a point or to protest something.

Civil disobedience consists of breaking a law to prove a point or to protest something. Civil disobedience occurs daily around the world, from the fight against apartheid in South Africa, to the quest for autonomy of ethnic groups in Europe, to demonstrations in Washington, DC, against racism or for a more responsive government. The antiwar protests across America following the U.S.–led invasions in Iraq and other Middle East countries are recent and ongoing examples of these events. Our society, like many others around the globe, is filled with dissension. And law enforcement officers are called on to control or suppress these demonstrations.

The purpose in most cases of civil disobedience is to protest some governmental or institutional policy. Although most protests start out lawfully and are relatively peaceful demonstrations, emotions may become inflamed, legal

During this anti-war protest in San Francisco, the presence of police officers helped ensure that the demonstration remained orderly and nonviolent.
© AP Images/Danny Johnston

barriers are crossed, and a classic civil disobedience situation develops. A civilly disobedient person breaks the law to prove a point. The act is done openly. A law is violated because people feel the law violates their sense of what is right, and they are willing to accept punishment for their actions supporting their beliefs. The United States was born through the efforts of dissenters, and some of our greatest Americans, now regarded as heroes, were lawbreakers in their time. George Washington, Benjamin Franklin, John Adams and Alexander Hamilton were all civilly disobedient and considered traitors until success crowned their efforts.

Nonviolent lawbreaking begins when participants are willing to be punished by the courts for their lawbreaking. From there, demonstrators may become violent lawbreakers, frequently disregarding the rights of others. The extreme result of this type of action is anarchy, chaos, revolution and bloodshed. The police generally agree that nonviolent protest is one thing to contend with, but violent protest—which can result in property damage, looting, personal injuries and, in some cases, death—infringes on the rights of police officers as well as of other citizens.

Whether demonstrations are violent or nonviolent, police have been designated by our society as the correct vehicle for coping with the various kinds of demonstrations occurring in the 21st century.

Issues Leading to Civil Disobedience

Issues leading to civil disobedience include

- Overt racism and bias.
- Human rights concerns.
- Environmental concerns.
- Animal rights concerns.
- Pro-life and pro-choice conflicts.

Racism and Other Biases Historically, the Ku Klux Klan has been the epitome of violent racism. However, other groups are now contending for this dubious title. A group known as the skinheads poses a threat to minorities of several types, including homosexuals, Jews and "people of color," whom they call "mud people."

Skinheads get their name from their practice of shaving their heads, although some have let their hair grow out so they are not as easily recognized by police. Acting in groups, they attack ruthlessly, often beating or stomping their lone victims. They often display patches bearing American flags, German swastikas and such slogans as "White Supremacy" and "WAR," an acronym for White Aryan Resistance.

Most states have enacted some type of hate crime penalty-enhancement statute that allows courts to issue more severe sentences for people convicted of criminal actions motivated by bigoted, prejudiced and hateful beliefs. Hate crimes are discussed in depth in Chapter 10.

Human Rights Concerns Violent civil rights protests swept the country in the 1950s and 1960s and are being seen again. Gay rights issues, the rights of individuals with communicable diseases such as AIDS and the right to die are among the most hotly debated controversies.

Environmental Concerns Environmental protest issues include nuclear waste disposal and logging versus forest preservation. Activist groups such as Earth First have forced municipal police and rural police into thinking about dealing with protests and the unique circumstances they present. One key problem with the rural protests and demonstrations is that most of the law enforcement officers who have to deal with them know the protesters.

Animal Rights Concerns Campaigns to protect certain species of animals have been around for decades and usually are confined to fund-raising efforts and massive informational mailings. However, one group, the Animal Liberation Front (ALF), has been described as a terrorist group because of the extreme measures its members undertake for their "cause." For example, the ALF has been associated with more than 80 break-ins since 1977, including one that caused $3.8 million in damages to a University of California (Davis) animal research facility.

Pro-Life and Pro-Choice Conflicts Conflicts between pro-life and pro-choice groups are common and often make headlines as groups of pro-lifers seek to shut down abortion centers and pro-choicers seek to stop them. What may begin as a relatively peaceful march around an abortion center or clinic may escalate rapidly into a violent, destructive confrontation resulting in property damage and personal injuries. Political careers have been made and destroyed on this single issue. The courts also have become involved in the controversy. And police officers are likely to have their own views on this highly personal issue.

Pro-life demonstrators and others involved in the harassment of doctors and patients feel it is their moral obligation to protest the taking of unborn human lives. They assert their First Amendment rights in such protests. However, the

U.S. Supreme Court ruled in *Madsen et al. v. Women's Health Center Inc., et al.* (1994) that a Florida statute establishing a 300-foot zone around clinics to protect them from abortion protesters was constitutional. In addition, it was constitutional to restrict excessive noisemaking within the earshot of, and the use of images observable by, patients inside the clinic, and to create a 300-foot buffer zone around the residences of clinic staff.

Responding to Demonstrations and Civil Disturbances

"Perhaps there is no greater challenge for police officers in a democracy than that of managing mass demonstrations. It is here, after all, where the competing goals of maintaining order and protecting the freedom of speech assembly meet" (Wexler, 2006, p.i). A key to responding to demonstrations is advance planning and preparation. Although officers may not know exactly when they may need to intervene, they can anticipate what types of intervention might be necessary depending on their locality. A police department responsible for a jurisdiction in which animal research is being conducted or in which an abortion clinic is located should be prepared for demonstrations that might turn violent.

To deal with demonstrations and possible violence, police departments should

- Assess their risks.
- Develop contingency plans.
- Have a call-out system for off-duty officers.

Another key to effectively handling civil disorder incidents is a coordinated response among agencies, including police, fire and corrections personnel. Police departments should know what additional emergency medical personnel might be available and how to contact them. Police departments might also coordinate with corrections personnel regarding the handling and transportation of arrestees.

Some departments use a cross-arm carry to remove arrestees; others use stretchers. Whatever the method, departments must have a sound policy on use of force during demonstrations, and officers should use only as much force as is necessary to control the crowd. Because many, if not most, demonstrations involve citizens' exercising their freedoms of speech and expression, any police action taken to reduce or stop that activity necessarily falls under court scrutiny. The Supreme Court has stated, "Freedom of individuals to oppose or challenge police action without risk of arrest is one of the principal characteristics by which we distinguish a free nation from a police state."

Videotaping a demonstration and the police response can counter any claims of police brutality. If a demonstration gets big enough and violent enough, a jurisdiction may call on the National Guard for help. This request usually has to be made by the sheriff to the governor.

Vernon (2008, pp.64–65) describes an annual ritual at a university when, on the first hot day of spring, the fraternity students engage in a massive water fight. A large bucket of water was thrown into an open window of a vehicle, distracting the driver who bumped into the curb, shaking up his pregnant wife who seemed to be going into labor. Vernon was called to the scene and summoned the three available units. When the biggest officer and Vernon approached the crowd, they were met with whistles and cat calls and saw one frat boy mixing mud with the water in his bucket. Vernon held his hand up, palm forward and shouted with a smile, "I come in peace. Before I am executed, take me to your leader." They presented a "massive, Viking-like fraternity member" and identified him as their leader. Vernon asked to speak before getting doused. He shouted "You know this is your street. We in the police department know this is your street." Then I told them how they may have unknowingly put a life in danger. Visibly shocked by this news they agreed to return to their rooms and send a delegation with him to the dean's office. Vernon points out, "All situations have their own unique factors, so there no cookie-cutter strategy. Dealing with crowds can be very volatile and dangerous. There are, however a few basic principles to consider:

1. Assess the crowd's motives.
2. Select the appropriate posture or emotion—ranging from a strong command presence to a show of force.
3. Consider crowd psychology, including allowing them to save face.
4. Target leadership.
5. Make a swift decision."

He cautions that just as a small fire can turn into a firestorm in minutes, an unruly crowd can turn into a full-blown riot very quickly. Officers have a window of opportunity of just a few minutes to prevent this.

Police Management of Mass Demonstrations: Identifying Issues and Successful Approaches (Narr et al., 2006) provides detailed information on planning and preparation, training, intelligence and information management, roles and responsibilities, crowd control and use of force, and media relations. This report (pp.73–74) concludes,

> Over the past fifteen years, mass demonstrations have created significant challenges for law enforcement agencies. From spontaneous disorder after athletic events to highly organized protests against international monetary policies, local law enforcement agencies have encountered demonstrations that require seemingly every available resource to contain. In addition, police actions seem to be the subject of increased monitoring by third parties, including news agencies, amateur reporters and civil rights organizations, all of whom are armed with video cameras. . . .
>
> Agencies must balance a number of conflicting demands when managing demonstrations. These include allowing legitimate groups to express their First Amendment rights; protecting innocent bystanders; safeguarding municipal and private property; ensuring unimpeded commerce and traffic; containing unruly protestors with the appropriate type and amount of force; preventing injuries to officers; and, all the while, projecting professionalism and proficiency.

In addition to the challenge of demonstrations and civil disobedience, police sometimes face the challenge of large celebratory crowds. The death of a 21-year-old college student outside Fenway Park in 2004 on the night the Red Sox beat the Yankees for the American League pennant is a reminder that crowd control is a tough challenge for the police.

CRISIS SITUATIONS

Another form of disorder law enforcement officers must be prepared to deal with is that accompanying crisis situations. Frequently, negotiation techniques are called upon to prevent such crises from escalating to violence. In some critical incidents, such as hostage taking, barricaded suspects, snipers, terrorist acts and other high-risk incidents, special weapons and tactics (SWAT) teams may be used.

Police officers may face crises that include hostage situations, barricaded individuals and suicide attempts.

Hostage Situations

When police respond to a call about a crime in progress or a terrorist group in action, they may encounter a hostage situation. The FBI and most police departments divide hostage takers into four distinct categories: (1) the criminal trapped at the crime scene or escaping from the crime scene who uses bystanders as shields or bargaining tools, (2) terrorists, (3) prisoners and (4) mentally unstable individuals. Category 1 is considered the "traditional" hostage situation. Grossi (2007a, p.30) offers a somewhat different classification, suggesting that hostage takers usually fall into three categories: revenge seekers, power seekers and attention seekers. The most dangerous hostage situation is usually one involving terrorists; terrorists are usually willing to die for their cause and have little problem killing others. The most prevalent and usually least dangerous hostage situation involves the mentally disturbed. Whatever the motivation, it is important to recognize which type of hostage situation is involved because the negotiation process is directly affected.

The first two hours of a hostage situation are usually the most dangerous. Stress and anxiety are high in the hostage taker, hostage and rescue personnel. As time passes, the hostage and captor may emotionally bond in a phenomenon called the **Stockholm syndrome** whereby, through the process of transference, hostages begin to feel positively toward their captors and negatively toward the police, and the captors return these positive feelings. This syndrome makes it less likely that the hostage taker will harm the hostages: "The Stockholm syndrome is understandable as a predictable and normal response to abnormal circumstances. The development of an emotional bond between persons who share a life-threatening experience, a bond that can unite them against outsiders, can be seen as an adaptive human response to the violent scenarios played out with them as hapless, reluctant, and helpless players" (Slatkin, 2008, p.77).

Stockholm syndrome

In a hostage situation, the process of transference, with the hostages feeling positive toward their captors (and negative toward the police) and the captors returning these positive feelings.

Because the first few hours of a hostage incident are so volatile, it is important for those responding to the high-anxiety situation to *slow everything down* in an effort to avoid "tunnel vision." Beyond allowing time for captors and hostages to calm down, other benefits to stalling include having enough time to adequately contain and isolate the scene, being able to call in the appropriate personnel for the response, and allowing enough time to devise a plan.

The number one rule in hostage situations is to slow things down.

If a strategy that involves negotiation of some type is selected, it is critical that someone skilled in hostage negotiations should be available to talk with the hostage holder. The FBI hostage negotiator course emphasizes "negotiators don't command; commanders don't negotiate." To have the person in command of the containment of the situation also conduct the negotiations is usually not the best approach. The commander at the scene should devote full attention to the entire situation. In addition, if the hostage taker knows the negotiator is also the person in command, the hostage taker also knows that individual has the authority to grant requests. With the commander as negotiator, the advantage of stalling while waiting for authorization is lost.

Because the majority of hostage situations involve mentally unstable captors, many hostage negotiation teams include mental health professionals. In addition to mentally disturbed hostage takers, police may need to deal with those under the influence of alcohol.

SWAT members may attempt to facilitate the victim's rescue and the perpetrator's apprehension by distracting the hostage holder so a tactical plan can be implemented. In hostage situations and in some high-risk entries, some police departments have used **flashbangs**, devices that explode with a loud bang and emit a brilliant, temporarily blinding light. Flashbangs should not, however, be used when the elderly or small children are a part of the situation because they may panic. Flashbangs also may create a lot of smoke, reducing visibility, and they may set off smoke alarms.

flashbangs
Devices that explode with a loud bang and emit brilliant light; used by police as a diversion.

The Officer as Hostage An officer being held hostage should first calm himself down and then use verbal defusing skills, as would be used with an emotionally disturbed person, to calm the hostage taker and to find out who and what the officer is dealing with (Grossi, 2007a, p.31). As in other hostage situations, it is important to slow things down and try to get the hostage taker to see the officer as a human, rather than as a law officer.

Officers should practice escape techniques such as having a cutting tool within reach in the event of being duct-taped, hiding a handcuff key on your body and being able to retrieve and use it and if, policy allows, carrying a backup gun (Grossi, 2007). The three best times to attempt an escape are (1) during the early stages of the incident when the scene is still disorganized, (2) when the suspect relaxes a bit thinking you aren't going to fight back and (3) any time the captor is distracted or you can create a distraction (Grossi, p.33). Perhaps most important is to have a plan for such a situation beforehand and train for it: "With the right training, the right mind-set and a mastery of all your tactics

Armed police officers wearing bulletproof vests take up position behind a car outside a small branch of the Bankers Trust office, which was being held up by a lone gunman. The gunman, who was holding six hostages, demanded 10 million dollars in gold and the release of several Symbionese Liberation Army members.
© UPI/Bettmann/Corbis

(physical, firearms, emotional), you can survive and win a hostage-cop situation" (Grossi, p.33).

Many techniques used in hostage situations are also appropriate when responding to a situation in which an individual is barricaded or threatening suicide.

Barricaded Individuals and Suicide Attempts

"Crisis negotiation is a complex discipline. Negotiating with an armed barricaded person holding hostages can be a prolonged and stressful event. When a uniformed officer responds to an event that becomes a barricade incident, he may not have the luxury of patiently waiting the 45 to 60 minutes for the tactical team and crisis negotiators to arrive. Negotiations by one of the first responders may not be just an option, it may be an absolute necessity" (Massock, 2008, p.39).

In these scenarios, officers must first ensure their own safety and obtain as much information about the subject and incident as possible. Massock (2008, p.40) recommends against using a bullhorn or loudspeaker to make contact, and suggests either telephone or voice-to-voice as better alternatives. The first responder should introduce himself as an officer and ask the subject for his name, the conditions of the others with him (do not refer to them as hostages), and his own condition. The subject should be allowed to talk uninterrupted, even if yelling and screaming. Being a good listener is critical for successful negotiations. It is recommended that officers not respond to demands or a timeline and that honesty is the best approach. The first responder is key to gathering intelligence about the situation, information that will be used to brief the negotiator when he or she arrives and thus holds immense value for resolving the incident (Massock, p.42).

Police departments need clear guidelines about how to handle life-threatening situations such as those involving barricaded individuals and those who are threatening suicide. Of prime importance are the lives of those involved. If no danger exists for the police or the public, it is often best to talk the situation out or simply wait it out.

The number one rule in barricaded-individual or suicide-attempt situations is to slow things down.

In some instances, negotiations fail and the barricaded subject takes his or her own life. Or there may be no hostage or barricaded situation; the person simply commits suicide. Although some suicidal individuals come to police attention through an acute episode of crisis behavior, others are suffering from the more chronic condition of mental illness.

If officers respond to a successful suicide, they must secure the scene and conduct a thorough investigation, keeping in mind that, to many people, suicide is a stigma. Family members may hide or destroy evidence of a suicide, including a note that may have been left. This may be done so that insurance can be collected. Sometimes those intent on dying set up a situation in which they get the police to pull the trigger, a phenomenon known as victim-precipitated homicide or, more commonly, suicide by cop.

Suicide by Cop (SBC) Suicide by cop (SBC) is a well-recognized phenomenon and a troubling trend (Porter and Parra, 2008). As with other crisis incidents, officers should attempt to slow down the situation when possible. However, the pacing of the event ultimately rests in the hands of the subject. Consider the following comments from mental health experts and an officer involved in such incidents (Porter and Parra):

- This type of suicide is essentially the same mechanism that would cause people to commit suicide for any reason: that they are desperate and depressed and they don't see any way out (neuropsychiatrist).
- Sometimes it would occur to somebody it may be better to have it occur by somebody else because then they feel that somehow that's not technically suicide (neuropsychiatrist).
- In many cases, officers show tremendous restraint when confronted by people with weapons. But in others, police have to do what they are taught to do. Officers have to protect themselves and other people. When someone pulls out a weapon, officers are well within the continuum of what they are trained to do (police captain).

A final step for officers involved in an SBC incident that ends in the subject's death is for the officer to recognize the range of emotions that may follow the shooting and to receive timely critical incident stress debriefing. Officers involved in SBC shootings have reported feeling angry at and used by the perpetrator, guilty for shooting someone who was not necessarily dangerous but in dire psychological pain, and a sense of failure for not recognizing the "set up." When officers do not work through these emotions, their ability to respond effectively to future incidents is severely compromised, making the officer vulnerable to potentially fatal errors in judgment and leaving the department susceptible to lawsuits. The mere instant it takes an officer to second-guess a course of action is all the time a subject needs to pull the trigger. Furthermore, officers unable to resolve the incident in their own minds may succumb to overwhelming feelings of guilt and failure and become, themselves, suicidal.

Officer Suicide According to Perin (2007, p.14), "If an officer does not deal with stress in a healthy manner, depression, burn-out and suicide could be the result." Sanow (2008, p.6) says of police officers, "We kill ourselves by a 3 to 1 ratio more than we are killed by others. The ratio may actually be much higher because many police suicides are purposefully misclassified on death certificates as accidents or undetermined deaths. The rate of police suicide is also more than three times that of the general population. And those rates are increasing compared with a decade ago."

One precipitant appears to be retirement, with retired law enforcement personnel being 10 times more likely to commit suicide than are age-matched peers (Honig and White, 2009). Officers who retired because of a disability had a suicide rate of 2,616 per 100,000 compared with age-matched peers having a rate of 34 per 100,000.

About 97 percent of officer suicides involve a duty weapon according to Perin (2007, p.14), who notes that officers have a special relationship with their guns: "It is a source of control, of confidence and of comfort." Many officer suicides are made to look accidental or duty-related because of the stigma attached to the act; an officer killed in the line of duty receives a hero's funeral and has his or her name memorialized on a wall at the National Law Enforcement Officers Memorial Fund in Washington, whereas officers who commit suicide get no such honor (Cowen, 2008). Additional factors are emotional and financial implications associated with the different causes of death, with survivors of officers killed "in the line of duty" being better emotionally supported, better able to accept the death, and typically eligible for financial compensation from the federal government as well as college scholarships for their children.

Negotiating with another officer is extremely difficult and presents both advantages and disadvantages for the negotiation (Christol, 2009, p.35). The advantages include that rapport is often already built because they may know one another, there is a common bond as police officers, it is easier to empathize because the negotiator knows what the officer may be going through, and background information is usually easier to obtain. The disadvantages are that the negotiator represents an agency that may be the cause of the situation, the suicidal officer knows police tactics and skills, and he may blame other officers for not recognizing his situation. Christol (p.37) recommends not conducting negotiations alone and using extreme caution, as anyone willing to kill himself or herself may be willing to also kill you.

CRIME, DISORDER AND COMMUNITY POLICING

An effective police response to crime and disorder requires community mobilization and active citizen involvement because, in the long run, vibrant neighborhoods are the best defense against crime. The law enforcement community has recognized this principle in embracing community policing and seeking to address and solve local problems through partnership with residents.

As discussed, since the advent of community policing, many departments across the country have focused on the aggressive enforcement of disorder offenses. These aggressive strategies are popularly known as "zero-tolerance," "order-maintenance" and "quality-of-life" policing. Following their seminal article, "Broken Windows," Wilson and Kelling (1989, p.49) contend, "Like it or not, the police are about the only city agency that makes house calls around the clock. And like it or not, the public defines broadly what it thinks of as public order, and holds the police responsible for maintaining order. Community-oriented policing means changing the daily work of the police to include investigating problems as well as incidents. It means defining as a problem whatever a significant body of public opinion regards as a threat to community order. It means working with the good guys, and not just against the bad guys."

Some agencies, such as the San Diego (California) Police Department, have taken community policing "up a notch," to a strategy called *neighborhood policing*. Numerous examples of communities coming together to deal with problems of crime and disorder using problem-oriented policing are available.

CRIME, DISORDER AND PROBLEM-ORIENTED POLICING

"Designing Out Crime: The Chula Vista Residential Burglary Reduction Project"[1] is one of the Herman Goldstein Award winners for excellence in problem-oriented policing.

Although residential burglary rates had declined in Chula Vista in the mid-1990s, the number of burglaries was still unacceptably high in 1996, when more than 900 of 52,000 households were victimized. The program used the SARA model to address the problem.

Scanning

A resident survey reinforced the need to focus on residential burglary: 82 percent of respondents indicated that they were concerned about burglary, making it the second-highest ranked crime or disorder problem in the city after the problem of speeding vehicles. It was imperative that potential buyers and builders saw Chula Vista neighborhoods as safe places to live because 30,000 new housing units were scheduled for construction during the next 20 years.

Analysis

To better understand the dynamics of the burglary problem, project staff carefully examined all sides of the crime triangle—victim, offender and location. The police department undertook an extensive study of the factors that attracted burglars to specific homes, as well as those protective devices that were most effective at preventing burglaries. Researchers and sworn police staff interviewed more than 250 victims and 50 burglars, conducted more than 100 street-view environmental assessments, and reviewed more than 1,000 incident reports

[1]Source: Adapted from "Designing Out Crime: The Chula Vista Residential Burglary Reduction Project." In *Excellence in Problem-Oriented Policing: The 2001 Herman Goldstein Award Winners.* Washington, DC: National Institute of Justice, Community Oriented Policing Services and the Police Executive Research Forum, 2001, pp.27–37.

of burglaries committed against single-family homes. Key findings from the analysis phase included

- Doors without deadbolt locks were targeted.
- Windows with single-paned glass were targeted.
- Windows with simple stock latches were easily defeated.
- Sliding glass doors without specialized pin locks were easily rocked off their tracks.
- Homes that appeared unoccupied were targeted.
- A relatively frequent and highly preventable type of burglary, particularly in newer neighborhoods, was the open garage door burglary.
- In 94 percent of the burglaries, points of entry other than the front door were hidden from the street, either by high shrubbery or solid wood fencing.

An additional review of police department data revealed during the previous 18 months, 569 single-detached homes had reported a burglary or attempted burglary. Analysis indicated 70 percent of the residential burglaries had occurred during daylight hours, but only 58 percent had occurred during weekdays. (If burglaries were occurring randomly, 71 percent should have occurred on weekdays.)

Response

Chula Vista police developed an array of solid, practical responses based heavily on crime prevention through environmental design (CPTED) principles and, to a lesser extent, public education efforts. Environmental protections were thought to be especially appropriate for Chula Vista, which lacked the around-the-clock surveillance provided by a strong Neighborhood Watch program—particularly in newer residential areas.

Police also focused on changing construction standards for new homes, realizing if they could negotiate built-in burglary prevention features, it would achieve target hardening and make such homes less attractive to would-be burglars. They developed a mutually beneficial, collaborative relationship with the new housing development and building industry. Such "burglar-resistant" features would lower the incidence of burglary and provide an attractive selling point to home buyers.

Project staff approached home development executives about partnering in the effort to prevent burglaries. Developers agreed to several design modifications of new homes, including installing deadbolt door locks on vulnerable garage service doors, using only windows that met strict forced-entry resistance standards and installing pin locks on all sliding glass doors. Developers agreed to distribute a safety and security brochure spelling out ways to prevent burglary and a brochure on antiburglary landscape ideas. Developers also required that garage doors be kept shut, in accordance with homeowners' association rules. Finally, developers agreed to task each newly created homeowner's association with setting up and maintaining a permanent Neighborhood Watch program.

Assessment

Although the long-term impact of the antiburglary project will not be felt for some time, the initial results are very promising. Residential burglary rates in Chula Vista dropped 29 percent in 1999. Burglaries declined 13 percent in

National City, which borders Chula Vista to the North, and 16 percent in the City of San Diego, which borders Chula Vista to the South.

In assessing the effectiveness of antiburglary home design modifications, police found that a home in a new-construction neighborhood where the developer had agreed to install burglary prevention features was 37 percent less likely to be burglarized than was a home in the adjacent mixed-age neighborhoods.

The department was able to conclude that the use of their collaborative problem-solving model led to a win-win situation that will continue to provide a payoff for all members of the Chula Vista community well into the 21st century.

SUMMARY

The official sources of information about crime are the Uniform Crime Reports (UCR), the National Incident-Based Reporting System (NIBRS) and the National Crime Victimization Survey (NCVS). The FBI's Uniform Crime Reports contain statistics on violent crimes (murder, aggravated assault causing serious bodily harm, forcible rape, robbery) and property crimes (burglary, larceny/theft, motor vehicle theft and arson). Technologies that greatly assist law enforcement in analyzing and responding to crime and disorder issues include mapping, geographic information systems, geographic profiling systems and CompStat.

One major function of law enforcement is to respond when a crime has been committed. Responsibilities of officers responding to a call regarding a criminal act include arriving as rapidly, yet as safely, as possible; caring for any injured people at the scene; apprehending any suspects at the scene; securing the scene; and conducting a preliminary investigation. The preliminary investigation involves on-the-scene interviews of victims and witnesses, interrogation of suspects and a search of the scene itself.

In addition to dealing with crime, police officers are also often called upon to deal with situations involving disorder and civil disobedience. Civil disobedience consists of breaking a law to prove a point or to protest something. Issues leading to civil disobedience include overt racism and bias, human rights concerns, environmental concerns, animal rights concerns and pro-life and pro-choice conflicts. To deal with demonstrations and possible violence, police departments should assess their risks, develop contingency plans and have a call-out system for off-duty officers.

Police officers may face crises that include hostage situations, barricaded individuals and suicide attempts. Sometimes when police respond to a call regarding a crime, a hostage situation develops. The number one rule in hostage situations, as well as in crisis situations involving barricaded individuals or those threatening to commit suicide, is to slow things down.

APPLICATION

The chief of police of the Bigtown Police Department notices there is no policy or written procedure to guide patrol officers when they receive a call to a crime scene. Past analysis of reports indicates that many officers have made their own policies about what their responsibilities are. No uniformity exists. The chief calls you in as the head of the patrol division and instructs you to formulate a policy and procedure for all officers when responding to a crime.

INSTRUCTIONS

Use the form in the appendix at the end of this book to make the policy and procedure. The overall policy of how such calls are to be regarded and the specific procedures to be followed, including priorities, should be addressed.

AN EXERCISE IN CRITICAL THINKING

On June 13 at 10:00 P.M., Officer Cha and Officer Ericsen responded to a report of a suicidal male who was believed to be intoxicated. The call came out with details of unknown weapons. Officers Cha and Ericsen had previous dealings with this suspect, having responded to the residence several times before, and were aware that he had fought and resisted arrest with the police in the past. The officers were also aware that the suspect was an alcoholic. The officers responded to the residence and made contact with the suspect, who was intoxicated. The suspect had admitted to drinking and stated he was feeling "down" but stated that he did not want to kill himself. The suspect cooperated with the officers and spoke with a mental health representative, who believed that the suspect was okay to be released. A neighbor friend agreed to watch him for the night as he was still extremely intoxicated. The officers cleared the residence.

Shortly afterward, the officers received another call back to the residence. Dispatch again stated the suspect threatened suicide. The officers arrived on scene and saw the suspect in his backyard; he requested that the officers come meet him there. As Officers Cha and Ericsen approached him in the low light, they observed the suspect reaching into his jacket with his right hand in a motion suggesting that he was pulling out a gun. The suspect also yelled, "Kill me!" several times, and refused to show his hands after several loud verbal commands by both officers.

1. If you were responding as a back up officer, how would you assist your partners in this situation?
   a. Set up a perimeter around the incident to prevent innocent bystanders from accidently or intentionally entering a dangerous zone.
   b. Back up the officers until the situation was under control.
   c. Wait for more officers, or officers with special training such as SWAT, to respond.
   d. Attempt to apprehend the suspect alone.
   e. Start interviewing neighbors and possible witnesses.
2. After several loud verbal commands, the suspect eventually complied and pulled his hands out (empty) very quickly. The officers did not observe any weapons and placed the suspect in custody while holding adequate cover.
   a. Was deadly force justified in this situation? Why, and what are the guidelines?
   b. What other types of force would be justified in this situation?
   c. After taking the suspect into custody, what would be your procedure? Would you just jail him?

DISCUSSION QUESTIONS

1. What forces spark crime and disorder in our streets?
2. Select a recent popular movie you have seen that contains scenes of crime, disorder or quality-of-life issues. Compare your reactions with those of other students. Discuss its effects on the general population who may see it.
3. Does your community have more or less crime and disorder than average? On what do you base your opinion?
4. Have you ever participated in a demonstration? If so, what was the cause? How did you feel about participating? Was it peaceful?
5. Is homelessness a problem in your community? If so, how does your police department deal with it?
6. Have there been any instances of the police having to interact with the mentally ill in your community? Were they handled well by the police?
7. Have there been instances of suicide by cop in your community? If so, what were the circumstances and were the police justified in using deadly force?

GALE EMERGENCY SERVICES DATABASE ASSIGNMENTS

- Use the Gale Emergency Services database to help answer the Discussion Questions as appropriate.
- Use the Gale Emergency Services database to find and outline one of the following articles:

- "The Montgomery County CIT Model: Interacting with People with Mental Illness" by Rodney Hill, Guthrie Quill and Kathryn Ellis
- "CompStat Design" by Jon M. Shane
- "CompStat Implementation" by Jon M. Shane
- "Hostage/Barricade Management: A Hidden Conflict within Law Enforcement" by Gregory M. Vecchi

REFERENCES

Barnett-Ryan, Cynthia, and Swanson, Gregory. "The Role of State Programs in NIBRS Data Quality." *Journal of Contemporary Criminal Justice*, February 2008, pp.18–31.

Barton, Liz. "Tips to Help Prevent Identity Theft during Tax Season." *The Police Chief*, March 2008, pp.14–15.

Beyond the Beat: Ethical Considerations for Community Policing in the Digital Age. Washington, DC: National Center for Victims of Crime, 2008.

Bond, Brenda J. "CompStat: Let's Focus on Communication and Coordination." *Subject to Debate*, September 2007, pp.6–7.

Bradley, Jennifer. "Crime Mapping." *Law Officer Magazine*, February 2008, pp.64–67.

Bruce, Christopher W., and Ouellette, Neil F. "Closing the Gap between Analysis and Response." *The Police Chief*, September 2008, pp.30–34.

Casady, Tom. "Beyond Arrest: Using Crime Data to Prevent Crime." *The Police Chief*, September 2008, pp.40–42.

Christol, Tim. "Negotiating with a Fellow Officer." *Tactical Response*, January–February, 2009, pp.34–38.

Commission on Accreditation of Law Enforcement Agencies. *Standards for Law Enforcement Agencies*, 5th ed. Fairfax, VA: CALEA, 2006, updated 2008.

Cook, Dave, and Burton, Scott L. "GIS Enterprise Technology Investment Yields Proactive, Intelligence-Led Policing." *The Police Chief*, August 2008, pp.126–127.

Corbley, Kevin. "GPS Photo-Mapping in Law Enforcement." *Law Enforcement Technology*, January 2008, pp.96–101.

Cowen, Alison Leigh. "Suicide Bigger Threat for Police than Criminals." *The New York Times*, April 8, 2008.

Crime in the United States: Preliminary Annual Uniform Crime Report—January to December 2008. Washington, DC: Department of Justice, Federal Bureau of Investigation. Accessed June 1, 2009. http://www.fbi.gov/ucr/08aprelim/index.html

Crime Scene Investigation: A Guide for Law Enforcement. Washington, DC: Department of Justice, National Institute of Justice, January 2000. (NCJ 178280)

"Defining Identity Theft." *Identity Theft—A Research Review.* Washington, DC: National Institute of Justice, July 2007.

"Designing Out Crime: The Chula Vista Residential Burglary Reduction Project." In *Excellence in Problem-Oriented Policing: The 2001 Herman Goldstein Award Winners.* Washington, DC: National Institute of Justice, Community Oriented Policing Services and the Police Executive Research Forum, 2001, pp.27–37.

Geoghegan, Susan. "CompStat Revolutionizes Contemporary Policing." *Law and Order*, April 2006, pp.42–46.

Grossi, Dave. "Officer-as-Hostage: Survival Tips." *Law Officer Magazine*, February 2007a, pp.30–33.

Grossi, Dave. "Responding to In-Progress Crimes." *Law Officer Magazine*, December 2007b, pp.24–25.

Guerette, Rob T. *Disorder at Day Laborer Sites.* Washington, DC: Community Oriented Policing Services Guide No. 44, 2007.

Hess, Kären M. *Introduction to Law Enforcement and Criminal Justice*, 9th ed. Belmont, CA: Wadsworth, Cengage Learning, 2009

Honig, Audrey L., and White, Elizabeth K. "By Their Own Hand: Suicide among Law Enforcement Personnel." *Community Policing Dispatch*, April 2009.

"Introduction." *Identity Theft—A Research Review.* Washington, DC: National Institute of Justice, July 2007.

Jetmore, Larry F. "The Oldest Profession: Investigating Street-Level Prostitution." *Law Officer Magazine*, October 2008, pp.92–96.

Jones, Michael. "Police and Citizens Together: The Suwanee PACT Program." *The Police Chief*, April 2009, pp.20–26.

Kelly, Raymond W. "Formulating Best Practices for Nighttime Establishments." *The Police Chief*, May 2008, pp.52–58.

Kyckelhahn, Tracey; Beck, Allen J.; and Cohen, Thomas H. *Characteristics of Suspected Human Trafficking Incidents, 2007–2008.* Washington, DC: Bureau of Justice Statistics Special Report, January 2009. (NCJ 224526)

Massock, Bill. "Negotiations for First Responders." *Law and Order*, December 2008, pp.39–42.

Miller, Christa. "CompLink CompStat Analyzer Automates Crime Data Analysis." *Law Enforcement Technology*, October 2008, pp.136–142.

Miller, Linda J.; Hess, Kären Matison; and Orthmann, Christine Hess. *Community Policing: Partnerships for Problem Solving*, 6th ed. Clifton Park, NY: Delmar Publishing Company, 2010.

Mills-Senn, Pamela. "Tactical Mapping Aids." *Law Enforcement Technology*, February 2008, pp.18–24.

Narr, Tony; Toliver, Jessica; Murphy, Jerry; McFarland, Malcolm; and Ederheimer, Joshua. *Police Management of Mass Demonstrations: Identifying Issues and Successful Approaches.* Washington, DC: Police Executive Research Foundation, 2006.

"NIJ Crime Mapping Resources." *Justice Resource Update*, Vol. 1, Issue 1, 2007. Accessed: http://www.ncjrs.gov/justice-resupd.html

Paletta, Kevin, and Belledin, Stacy. "Finding Out What You Don't Know: Tips on Using Crime Analysts." *The Police Chief*, September 2008, pp.36–39.

Peed, Carl; Wilson, Ronald E.; and Scalisi, Nicole J. "Making Smarter Decisions: Connecting Crime Analysis with City Officials." *The Police Chief*, September 2008, pp.20–28.

Perin, Michelle. "Police Suicide." *Law Enforcement Technology*, September 2007, pp.8–16.

Petrocelli, Joseph. "Patrol Response to Drive-By Shootings." *Police*, 2007a, pp.20–21.

Petrocelli, Joseph. "Patrol Response to Mentally Ill Subjects." *Police*, 2007b, pp.22–23.

Petrocelli, Joseph. "Patrol Response to Panhandling." *Police*, 2007c, pp.20–21.

Petrocelli, Joseph. "Patrol Response to Day Laborer Sites." *Police*, 2008a, pp.22–23.

Petrocelli, Joseph. "Patrol Response to Fraudulent Credit Card Purchases." *Police*, 2008b, pp.16–19.

Petrocelli, Joseph. "Patrol Response to Violence around Bars." *Police*, 2008c, pp.16–18.

Petrocelli, Joseph. "Patrol Response to Street Prostitution." *Police*, 2009, pp.20–22.

Police Chiefs and Sheriffs Speak Out on Local Immigration Enforcement. Washington, DC: Police Executive Research Forum, April 2008.

Porter, Ira, and Parra, Esteban. "Provoking Police to Shoot to Kill: A Troubling Trend." Delewareonline, July 7, 2008. Accessed http://pqasb.pqarchiver.com/delawareonline/access/1742773091.html?FMT=ABS&date=Jul+07,+2008

Rand, Michael, and Catalano, Shannan. *Criminal Victimization, 2006.* Washington, DC: Bureau of Justice Statistics Bulletin, December 2007. (NCJ219413)

Sanow, Ed. "Use CIT Two Ways." *Law and Order*, May 2008, p.6.

Scoville, Dean. "Room Service." *Police*, June 2008, pp.27–30.

Slatkin, Arthur. "The Stockholm Syndrome Revisited." *The Police Chief*, December 2008, pp.76–86.

Smith, Kurt. "GPS Technology in Policing: Ride the Wave to Make Better Decisions." *The Police Chief*, April 2009, pp.144–145.

Sourcebook of Criminal Justice Statistics Online. Washington, DC: Bureau of Justice Statistics, no date.

Vernon, Bob. "Unruly Crowd or Riot?" *Law Officer Magazine*, January 2008, pp.64–65.

Violent Crime in America: What We Know about Hot Spots Enforcement. Washington, DC: Police Executive Research Forum, May 2008.

"Violent Crimes against Homeless Are Rising, Organization Reports." *Criminal Justice Newsletter*, March 1, 2007, pp.4–5.

Wexler, Chuck. "Foreword." In Narr, Tony; Toliver, Jessica; Murphy, Jerry; McFarland, Malcolm; and Ederheimer, Joshua. *Police Management of Mass Demonstrations: Identifying Issues and Successful Approaches*, Washington, DC: Police Executive Research Foundation, 2006, pp.i–ii.

Wexler, Chuck. "Conclusion." In *Violent Crime in America: What We Know about Hot Spots Enforcement.* Washington, DC: Police Executive Research Forum, May 2008, pp.29–30.

Wilson, James Q., and Kelling, George L. "The Police and Neighborhood Safety: Broken Windows." *The Atlantic Monthly*, March 1982, pp.29–38.

Wilson, James Q., and Kelling, George L. "Making Neighborhoods Safe." *The Atlantic Monthly*, February 1989, pp.46–52.

CASE CITED

Madsen v. Women's Health Center, Inc., 512 U.S. 753 (1994)

CHAPTER 7

Violence

At Home, in the Classroom, on the Job

DO YOU KNOW . . .

- Who is at risk of being a victim of domestic violence?
- What law enforcement's responsibility is when domestic violence occurs?
- How dangerous police response to a domestic violence call is?
- What the Minneapolis experiment established?
- What *Thurman v. City of Torrington* (1984) established?
- Whether incidents of school violence can be anticipated or are always a surprise?
- What three-pronged approach is an effective response to the issue of school violence?
- What controversial measures have been taken to make schools safer?
- What similarities exist between school and workplace violence?
- If warning signs typically precede incidents of workplace violence?

CAN YOU DEFINE?

battered woman syndrome
battering
bullying
elder abuse
expressive violence
instrumental violence
lockdown
stake-in-conformity variables
zero-tolerance policies

INTRODUCTION

Violence has accompanied every stage of our country's existence from its birth to the present and is often involved in ensuring law and order. Indeed, one of the great ironies of police authority is the ability to use force to achieve a peaceable society. Violence is connected with some of the most positive events of U.S. history: independence from England through the Revolutionary War, the emancipation of slaves and preservation of the Union following the Civil War, and the expansion and stabilization of frontier society via vigilante violence. Some of the nation's most violent criminal figures, such as Al Capone, John Dillinger, Jessie James and Bonnie and Clyde, were popular folk heroes.

Even today, our nation is drawn into a violent fight for the preservation of its values, including the freedom to live in peace. A statement made by Martin Luther King, Jr., nearly 40 years ago seems eerily prophetic in light of recent events: "The choice today is no longer between violence and nonviolence. It's between nonviolence and nonexistence."

Many fear violence is becoming a way of life in the United States, and there exists among the public a common perception that violent crime is spinning out of control. True, violence occurs throughout the United States and directly touches the lives of millions of people. However, the reality is that violent crime is down, as discussed in Chapter 6.

The dominant expression of violent behavior in the United States involves acts of *interpersonal* violence that occur nearly everywhere, every day. Domestic violence is a major challenge for law enforcement. In addition, bar fights, street fights, beatings, slashings, stabbings and shootings are the types of violent transactions most likely to require a police response. These "garden-variety" acts of violence require police officers to possess excellent communication skills. Police may also have to resort to violence themselves.

Children are also demonstrating an increased capacity for violence, which has crept into our schools and made students fearful of victimization by their classmates. Metal detectors, surveillance cameras and drug- and weapons-detector dogs are a growing presence on school campuses nationwide. When the final bell rings and the class day is over, the violence is carried over onto the extracurricular activities fields, where kids are taught to compete and win at all costs. Aggression is rewarded and even modeled by the parents who, in front of their own children, shamelessly hurl more than words at coaches, umpires and parents of the opposing team.

Workplace violence also captures headlines, as the media report more murder-suicide stories involving disgruntled employees who return to the office seeking vengeance against the "higher ups" or workplace bullies who wronged them. Stress at home, in the classroom and on the job moves with people as they go from point A to point B, sometimes manifesting as road rage. Drivers run each other off the road, assault each other during postcrash confrontations and shoot each other for taking the parking spot they had been waiting for.

While reading this chapter, keep in mind that because the police have a monopoly on the *legitimate* use of force, they have the authority to impose themselves on conflicts as third-party agents of social control. Therefore, police-citizen encounters are *always* potentially coercive relationships. This is a particularly important factor when considering the role of the police in controlling "typical" violent encounters. The dangers implicit in these encounters, for both the police and the citizens involved, are thoroughly documented in research on violence.

This chapter begins with an overview of domestic and family violence and the various forms of partner abuse, including battered women, battered men and gay domestic violence. Next is a look at the police response to calls of domestic violence and the challenges presented by incidents of stalking. Then child abuse and neglect often referred to as maltreatment, is looked at very briefly—it is discussed in detail in Chapter 11. The section on domestic and family violence concludes with abuse of the elderly and community policing and domestic violence. Next the chapter examines the increasingly publicized issue of school violence and how police are expected to respond in efforts to keep our nation's students and teachers safe. The final domain of violence presented in this chapter concerns that found in the American workplace. The chapter concludes with problem-oriented policing and violence.

VIOLENCE: AN OVERVIEW

Newscasts and headlines in 2006 and 2007 consistently reported increases in violent crime in the United States:

- "Startling New Stats Show Cross-Country Crime Spike," *ABC News*, October 2006
- "Report Outlines Rising Crime Wave," *CBS News*, October 2006
- "FBI Stats Show Spike in Violent Crime," *ABC News*, December 2006
- "Violent Crime Is Up for 2nd Straight Year," *Washington Post*, December 2006
- "Spike in Violent Crime Creates Fears for the Future," *CBS News*, January 2007
- "PERF Releases Violent Crime Report Showing 24 Months of Alarming Trends,' *Subject to Debate*, March 2007
- "FBI: Violent Crime Still Increasing," May 2007

In 2007, however, violent crime began to decrease. According to *Crime in the United States 2007*, the estimated volume of violent crime declined 0.7 percent when compared with 2006 data. Preliminary figures for 2008 show a similar decline. Nonetheless, according to the FBI's 2007 Crime Clock, one violent crime occurred every 22.4 seconds. Particularly troubling is when violent crimes are perpetrated not by strangers but by people who know one another, whether they are family, school friends or coworkers.

DOMESTIC AND FAMILY VIOLENCE

It seems contradictory that the social unit people depend on for love and support can also foster violence. But this is true in thousands of homes. Although people who live together usually form close relationships, they may also take their hurts and frustrations out on others within the family. The psychology around this is that those we love the most can also hurt us the most. An intergenerational cycle of violence is taught by parents who use physical force to discipline their children. Some parents even say, while administering a spanking or beating, "This hurts me more than it hurts you," truly believing it is their responsibility to physically punish children who misbehave. Many parents also teach their children to defend themselves and to "fight their own battles." Children come to learn that "might makes right."

Risk Factors for Domestic Violence Victimization

Domestic violence knows no bounds. It occurs in families of all races, ethnicities and religions and across all socioeconomic and educational levels, although it is more likely to involve law enforcement at the lower economic levels. Sampson (2007, pp.10–14) describes the most common risk factors and says in summary, "Being young, Black, low-income, divorced or separated, a resident of rental housing, and a resident of an urban area have all been associated with higher rates of domestic violence victimization among women. For male victims the patterns were nearly identical: being young, Black, divorced or separated, or a resident of rental housing" (p.13).

A comprehensive review of current research on domestic violence reveals a high correlation between alcohol and substance abuse and domestic violence by abusers and an increased likelihood of domestic abusers being involved in other criminal activity, findings that have direct implications for law enforcement: "Law enforcement should carefully check domestic violence suspects' status in regard to outstanding warrants, pending cases, probationary or parole status and other concurrent criminal justice involvement" (Klein, 2008, p.22).

The tensions of our complex society, the prevalence of drug and alcohol abuse, and the fact that people are living longer, often creating an emotional and economic strain, all contribute to the problem of domestic violence. Such violence may be threatened or actual; it may be physical, sexual or psychological/emotional.

Wives, husbands, significant others, children, elders—in fact, anyone within a family unit—may be at risk of becoming victims of domestic violence.

The Extent of the Problem

Research shows that domestic violence-related police calls constitute the single largest category of calls received by police, accounting for between 15 and more than 50 percent of all calls. Such data emphasize the need for law enforcement agencies to commit as much time, resources and attention to the problem of domestic violence as they do to other major types of crime (Klein, 2008, p.6).

Many criminal justice scholars speculate "family" violence is the most widespread form of violence in the country (Sherman, n.d., p.1). However, domestic violence is often viewed by others, including those in law enforcement, as a family matter. Even victims may hold this perception, agonizing over the decision to report abuse to authorities. The victim wrestles with feelings of fear, loyalty, love, guilt and shame; often there is a sense of responsibility for other victims in the household. The victim also knows that reporting is a risk. All too often police or prosecutors minimize or ignore the problem, and the victim is left alone to face an attacker who will respond with anger at being reported or incarcerated.

Victims often do not want to press charges and do not want the victimizers to be put in jail. A victim may fear retaliation, and not want to give up the

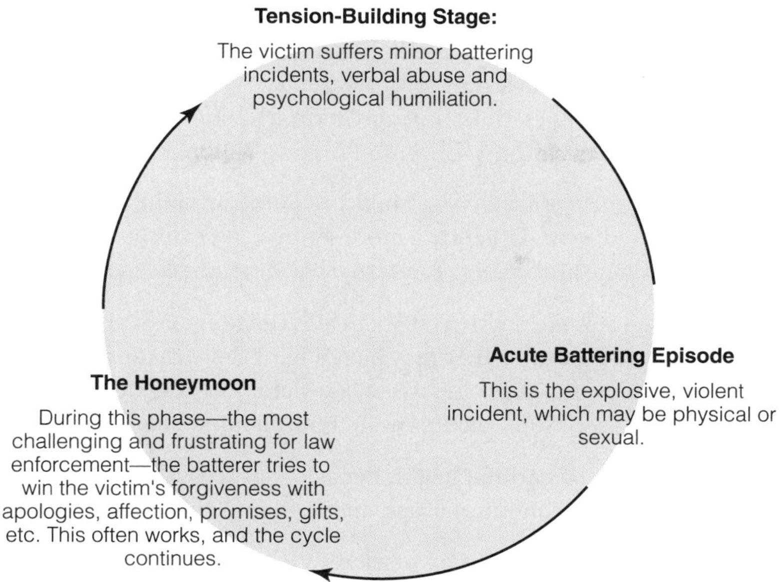

FIGURE 7.1
Three-Stage Cycle of Abuse

abuser's income or companionship. All victims want is for the violence to stop. It seldom does, however, and instead continues in an increasingly frequent and severe three-stage cycle of abuse shown in Figure 7.1.

The cycle theory of violence was developed by Dr. Lenore Walkers, whose research in the 1970s established the concept of the "battered woman syndrome." According to this theory, domestic violence continues to cycle because of the delay commonly experienced in bringing domestic violence cases to court. Police are generally called during the acute battering phase, and by the time the case is processed for prosecution, the honeymoon phase has set in and the victim is ready to forgive the batterer (Hill, 2008, p.3). The Stockholm syndrome is another explanation for victims recanting their statements: "When victims are isolated, mistreated, placed in fear for their lives, and made dependent on their captors to supply everything they need to survive, they begin to develop positive feelings for the people who victimize them" (Hill, p.3).

Not only does such violence tend to be self-perpetuating; it can also be passed from one generation to the next. The National Coalition Against Domestic Violence (NCADV) cautions that 60 percent of boys who witness domestic violence will grow up to batter, and 50 percent of the girls who witness such abuse will grow up to be battered women.

INTIMATE PARTNER VIOLENCE

According to the Centers for Disease Control and Prevention (CDC), "Intimate partner violence (IPV) is a serious, preventable public health problem that affects millions of Americans. The term 'intimate partner violence' describes physical, sexual, or psychological harm by a current or former partner or spouse. This type of violence can occur among heterosexual or same-sex couples and does not require sexual intimacy. IPV can vary in frequency and severity. It occurs on a continuum, ranging from one hit that may or may not impact the victim to chronic, severe battering" ("Intimate Partner Violence: Definitions," 2008).

The CDC estimated the cost of IPV in 1995 at $5.8 billion, which, when updated to 2003 dollars, exceeded $8.3 billion. The cost includes medical care, mental health services and lost productivity. IPV can affect health in many ways, and the longer the abuse goes on, the more serious the effects on the victims ("Understanding Intimate Partner Violence," 2006):

> Many victims suffer physical injuries. Some are minor like cuts, scratches, bruises, and welts. Others are more serious and can cause lasting disabilities. These include broken bones, internal bleeding, and head trauma.
>
> Not all injuries are physical. IPV can also cause emotional harm. Victims often have low self-esteem. They may have a hard time trusting others and being in relationships. The anger and stress that victims feel may lead to eating disorders and depression. Some victims even think about or commit suicide.
>
> IPV is linked to harmful health behaviors as well. Victims are more likely to smoke, abuse alcohol, use drugs, and engage in risky sexual activity.

The National Institute of Justice (NIJ) stresses, "Violence by an intimate partner is linked to both immediate and long-term health, social and economic consequences. Factors at all levels—individual, relationship, community, and societal—contribute to intimate partner violence. Preventing intimate partner violence requires reaching a clear understanding of those factors, coordinating resources, and fostering and initiating change in individuals, families, and society" ("Intimate Partner Violence," 2007).

Battered Women

Under English common law, a woman was her husband's property, and he could beat her with a stick as long as the stick was no larger in diameter than his thumb—hence, the well-known phrase "rule of thumb." Unfortunately, many modern-day relationships suffer under this archaic concept, but today it is called **battering**—the use of physical, emotional, economic or sexual force to control another person. Whether the batterer is consciously applying his "rule of thumb" to keep "the little woman" in line, or whether he is merely continuing a cycle of abuse witnessed as a child that later came to define how relationships "worked," the behavior of battering is about power and control. It is violence, and it can take many forms. It happens among married and unmarried couples. It may surface after a once-happy relationship takes a wrong turn, or battering may have actually been an element of a relationship as it was forming. And, as Turner and Rizzo (2009, p.5) contend, "Crimes of violence against women are prominent in all communities, whether small or larger."

battering
The use of physical, emotional, economic or sexual force to control another person.

Batterers are not only violent; most are also extremely jealous, suspicious, possessive, and extremely insecure. They generally have very traditional ideas about the relationship between men and women and often try to isolate their wives or girlfriends from family and friends. Battering tends to worsen over time, sometimes ending in death.

Leaving an abusive marriage does not guarantee the battering will end. Women separated from their husbands experience intimate partner violence at rates significantly higher than married, divorced, widowed or never married women, and divorced women are victimized by an intimate partner at the second highest rate among the marital categories.

Violence against Women: Identifying Risk Factors (2004, p.ii) reports on two research studies whose findings were remarkably similar: "Being sexually or physically abused both as a child and as an adolescent is a good predictor of future victimization. Child sexual abuse on its own, however, did not predict adult victimization. Women who were victims of both sexual and physical abuse before adulthood were more likely to become adult victims of physical or sexual abuse than women who had experienced only one form of abuse or women who had not been early victims of abuse."

In addition to the risk factors already discussed, several types of "special needs" victims of domestic violence have been identified. An estimated 17 percent of *pregnant women* are battered, with the abuse either beginning or intensifying during pregnancy. Battered *immigrant women* face the triple threat of being held in isolation by their batterers, being isolated by language barriers and often being fearful and distrusting of the police and government in general. As society becomes more culturally and ethnically diverse, law enforcement must be aware that woman are still viewed as property in many different cultures, where it is acceptable within the family to treat woman this way. Battered woman of these cultures also face the additional threat of being ostracized by their own family and community and, thus, are extremely unlikely to cooperate with our criminal justice system's efforts to bring their batterers to justice.

Women with disabilities are also more vulnerable to physical, emotional and sexual abuse. Physical disabilities resulting from injury (e.g., paralysis, amputation), disease (e.g., multiple sclerosis) or a congenital condition (e.g., cerebral palsy) can prevent victims from escaping violent situations. Abusers may also withhold mobility-assisting apparatuses, such as prosthetic devices or wheelchairs. Sensory disabilities, such as vision and hearing impairments, may severely hinder abused women's ability to seek help because, although they may be able to physically escape the violent environment itself, they often face communication and mobility challenges once outside. Mental impairments, including mental retardation, mental illness and cognitive disabilities caused by head trauma, also increase a woman's risk of abuse because they may limit victims' ability to physically defend themselves and diminish their problem-solving capacity such that they do not know how to seek or where to go for help.

Finally, *women married to police officers* face the difficulty of seeking help from their abuser's colleagues, some of whom may even be the batterer's close friends. According to Gallo (2004, p.132), "Research suggests violence may occur more frequently in police families than among the general public." It is sometimes a "don't ask, don't tell" situation, ignored, hidden or denied, protected by the "blue wall of silence."

Despite officers' sworn duty to uphold the law, they are susceptible to the same stresses that spark abuse in others' relationships, perhaps even to a greater degree. The abused intimate may also struggle with the added consequence of a complaint leading to the officer's loss of employment. If the officer is the sole bread-winner in the family and the only source of health insurance and other benefits, a loss of employment could financially devastate a family with young children or those with chronic medical conditions. A 1997 federal law known as the Lautenberg Amendment to the Gun Control Act prohibits any person with a misdemeanor domestic violence conviction from possessing or purchasing a firearm. Unable to carry a weapon, officers are not likely to keep their jobs. Thus, a victimized police spouse wishing only to have the violence stop, not to get the batterer fired, may choose not to report the abuse, or may recant a previous statement of abuse due to financial considerations.

The International Association of Chiefs of Police (IACP) has issued a policy statement, *Domestic Violence by Police Officers* (effective in 2003), which begins, "This policy recognizes that the profession of law enforcement is not immune from members committing domestic violence against their intimate partners.... This policy offers a comprehensive, proactive approach to domestic violence by police department employees with an emphasis on victim safety. It delineates a position of zero tolerance by the department. The policy includes in the section on patrol response: The responding officers shall make an arrest if probable cause exists."

Theories about Why Men Batter Four theories generally explain why some men batter in intimate relationships (Sampson, 2007, pp.7–8):

> *Psychological theory*: Battering is the result of childhood abuse, a personality trait (such as the need to control), a personality disturbance (such as borderline personality), a psychological disorder or problem (such as posttraumatic stress, poor impulse control, low self-esteem, or substance abuse).
>
> *Sociological theory*: Sociological theories vary but usually contain some suggestion that intimate violence is the result of learned behavior. One sociological theory suggests that violence is learned with a family, and a partner-victim stays caught up in a cycle of violence and forgiveness. If the victim does not leave, the batterer views the violence as a way to produce positive results. Children of these family members may learn the behavior from their parents (boys may develop into batterers and girls may become battering victims). A different sociological theory suggest that lower income subcultures will show higher rates of intimate abuse, as violence may be a more acceptable form of settling disputes in such subcultures. A variant on this theory is that violence is inherent in all social systems and people with resources (financial, social contacts, prestige) use these to control family members, while those without resort to violence and threats to accomplish this goal.
>
> *Feminist or societal-structural theory*: According to this theory, male intimates who use violence do so to control and limit the independence of women partners. Societal traditions of male dominance support and sustain inequities in relationships.
>
> *Violent individuals theory*: Although the full extent of violence batterers perpetuate is unknown, there is evidence that many batterers are violent beyond domestic violence, and many have prior criminal records for violent and nonviolent behavior. This suggests that domestic violence batterers are less unique and are more accurately viewed as violent criminals, not solely as domestic batterers.

Battered Men

Men are not the only intimate partners who batter. The reverse is sometimes true. Although not as prevalent as wife battering, husband or boyfriend battering does exist. Some women are much larger and stronger than their husbands or boyfriends and may beat them at will. Others are physically inferior to the men in their lives, but the men, when hit, will not hit back. Further, women tend to use weapons as equalizers; therefore, the physical harm may be greater. Husbands and boyfriends can also be emotionally abused through belittling, name-calling, ridiculing in public and the like. In extreme cases, some battered women use their abuse as justification to kill their batterers, a phenomenon known as **battered woman syndrome**, now recognized as a legal defense by the courts. Movies such as *The Burning Bed* have helped publicize the predicament of women beaten by their husbands and the lengths to which they may go to end the abuse.

battered woman syndrome
Defense used by women who have been beaten by their husbands and who then kill those husbands, apparently while completely sane and in control.

Some studies suggest a trend in young women becoming more aggressive in domestic relationships. For example, a longitudinal study involving 360 couples found

> Many young women believe they can hit male partners with impunity; significantly more young women than young men believed that their hitting would not injure their partner, that the police would not intervene, and that their partner would not hit back. However, these beliefs are misguided, as women's abuse does have consequences. . . . Women inflict a substantial minority of domestic injuries and deaths, . . . women make up as many as one-quarter of police arrests for abuse in some jurisdictions, . . . and men do abuse women who abuse them. (Moffitt et al., 2001, p.23)

Regarding the limited research thus far on the subject, Sampson (2007, p.8) states, "Less is known about women who use violence in relationships, particularly the extent to which it may be in self-defense, to fight back, or to ward off anticipated violence." She also notes, however, "Clearly there are women who use violence in relationships provocatively outside the context of fighting back or self-defense" (2007, p.9).

Men are less likely to report acts of violence against them by their intimate partner, fearing negative reactions of others. Men who endure abuse often let it go unreported because such victimization is not socially or culturally acceptable, nor is it often believed by the general public. This is true for men who are sexually assaulted by woman as well. And although there are many resources now for battered and abused woman and children, similar resources for battered men are exceedingly rare because they are still an extreme minority.

Gay Domestic Violence

Although calls involving battered men are generally not considered the "traditional" type of domestic call, police responding to calls of domestic violence between gay or lesbian partners may find themselves in even more unfamiliar territory. Nonetheless, partner abuse among the gay community does exist and is increasingly being brought to the attention of law enforcement. A survey by Burke et al. (2001, p.5) of 73 self-identified gay adults found

- 28 percent of respondents report having been threatened with physical harm by a partner.
- 31 percent of respondents report actually being physically harmed by a partner.

- 22 percent of respondents report experiencing vandalism or property destruction at the hands of a partner.
- 19 percent of respondents report being pressured into sexual activities by a partner.

The survey also indicated many of those who had been victimized did not report their victimization to the police out of fear of retaliation, fear of loss of emotional support, a desire to avoid embarrassment or shame, fear of being "outted," a distrust of law enforcement and lack of confidence in the courts.

Teen Dating Violence

The CDC classifies dating violence as a type of intimate partner violence because it occurs between two people in a close relationship, despite the participants' youthful age ("Understanding Teen Dating Violence," 2008). Three common types of teen dating violence are physical, emotional and sexual. Such dating violence can negatively affect health throughout life, such as engaging in drug and alcohol use, having eating disorders and being depressed, and even attempting suicide. Research shows that people who harm their dating partners are more depressed, have lower self-esteem and are more aggressive than their peers. Additional warning signs for dating violence include the use of threats or violence to solve problems, alcohol or drug use, inability to manage anger or frustration, poor social skills, association with violent friends, problems at school, lack of parental supervision or support, and witnessing abuse at home ("Understanding Teen Dating Violence").

RESPONDING TO DOMESTIC VIOLENCE CALLS

Legislative bodies have placed the burden of settling domestic disputes largely on the shoulders of the police. The police response to calls of domestic violence must be unbiased and executed without regard to the victim's gender or the gender of their abuser. An effective response to domestic disputes requires special skills, especially communications and negotiating skills, by law enforcement. Family violence has a strong tendency to repeat itself, and officers often are called back several times—sometimes in the same evening. It also tends to escalate. Effective handling of the first few calls can greatly decrease the number of further calls.

In most crimes, the responsibilities of the responding officers are clear-cut: gather evidence supporting the elements of the crime, determine who is responsible and make an arrest. Responsibilities in domestic violence calls are much less clear-cut. Often, it is not at all obvious who is responsible. Frequently both parties are at fault, but the violence must still be ended. Even if one party is clearly to blame, it is usually a mistake for officers to take sides in a domestic dispute. They must maintain their objectivity.

Police responding to a domestic violence call involving a fellow officer may find it particularly challenging to remain objective, yet they must adhere to department policy regarding the handling of such calls because of ethical and professional obligations and because the integrity of the policing profession and the community's trust are at stake.

Police responding to a call in which the man claims to be the victim often have difficulty believing a woman can physically abuse a man. Officers may downplay the seriousness of the call and may actually blame the man for being weak or cowardly. As with any other assault, one involving a woman battering a man must be investigated thoroughly. If probable cause exists to believe an assault has occurred and the woman did it, she should be arrested. It may also be difficult to sort out who the primary aggressor is when police respond to a domestic call and find both partners disheveled, bruised and hostile.

Responsibilities at the scene of domestic violence include

- Stop the violence.
- Separate those in conflict.
- Administer medical assistance if required.
- Determine if assault has occurred.
- If no probable cause for an arrest exists, mediate the situation. Get them to talk it out, to stop shouting and fighting and to start talking and thinking about their situation.
- If mediation is not possible, order the abusive spouse out of the house.
- Suggest possible solutions and sources of assistance to the abused person.
- If probable cause supporting the crime of assault does exist, make an arrest.

Police officers responding to a domestic violence call are responsible for investigating it thoroughly as an assault and for making an arrest if probable cause exists.

A comprehensive, collaborative response strategy is one that considers the response to a domestic violence incident and includes action before and after an incident as illustrated in Table 7.1.

Additional strategies for responding to domestic violence include educating potential victims and offenders, encouraging domestic violence victims and witnesses to call the police, encouraging other professionals to screen for domestic violence victimization and make appropriate referrals, providing victims with emergency protection and services after an assault, assessing the threat of repeat victimization, arresting offenders, issuing and enforcing restraining orders, aggressively pursuing criminal prosecution of severe domestic violence cases and publicizing convictions, establishing special domestic violence courts, and providing treatment for batterers (Sampson , 2007, pp. 28–41).

Arresting both parties in a domestic violence incident (dual arrest) usually has limited effectiveness because there is almost always one primary aggressor (Sampson, 2007, p.41). The victim may feel safe expressing anger against the batterer when the police are there, making it appear as though it is a "mutual combat" situation. Consequently, more than 20 states have enacted primary aggressor or "predominant aggressor" laws.

The importance of an effective law enforcement response to a domestic violence call is clear: "Research indicates that the actions of law enforcement, such as follow-up home visits after incidents, can encourage victim reports of domestic violence" (Klein, 2008, p.12). In contrast, research also shows that

Table 7.1 Matrix of Responses to Domestic Violence

Strategic Focus	Strategic Times for Responses	Goal	Police Role	Other Agencies, Organizations, Group
At-risk population	Before incidents	Prevention; persuade those at risk that, if abused, call the police	Alert and educate at-risk victim population; educate/warn at-risk offending population	Public health organizations, domestic violence coalitions, schools and educators, medical professionals
Peers and neighbors of at-risk individuals	Ongoing	Getting peers and neighbors to call the police if they learn of domestic abuse	Educate these groups about the importance of calling the police to reduce the violence	Public health organizations, domestic violence coalitions, educators
Injured women and men	During medical care	Screen the injured for domestic violence; raise awareness of available services; provide medical care	Engage the medical profession and link medical professionals with appropriate referral organizations	Medical professionals
Individual incident	During	Violence cessation	Stop the violence; identify primary aggressor; accurately identify abuse history	Medical and public health professionals
Immediately after incident	After, ongoing	Prevent revictimization	Assist with victim safety; develop tailored strategies for victim and offender based on risk/physical violence history; increase focus on high-risk offenders; ensure victim is linked with needed resources; increase focus on high-risk victims; ongoing monitoring	Domestic violence victim advocates, victims' friends and family, shelters, victim services, criminal justice system, treatment services

Source: Rana Sampson. *Domestic Violence*. Washington, DC: Office of Community Oriented Policing Services, Problem-Oriented Guides for Police, Problem-Specific Guides Series, Guide No. 45, 2007, p. 25.

victims who thought the criminal justice response was insufficient were less likely to report future incidents (Klein). Studies have found that victim dissatisfaction generally includes four basic "themes": (1) an adverse personal outcome (victim arrested, child protection called), (2) the police made assumptions or did not listen, (3) the police took sides, and (4) nothing happened (absence of a strong court sanction) (Klein, p.43). In summary, the research concludes, "The single, most appreciated service officers can deliver to the greatest number of victims is arresting their abusers" (Klein).

The Danger of Domestic Calls

It is commonly thought that a domestic call can be one of the most dangerous calls police officers receive. Indeed, some calls are extremely dangerous, even fatal, for the responding officer(s).

Responding to a domestic violence call is hazardous, but not as hazardous as is often thought.

A hearse carrying the body of fallen Capitol Police Officer John Gibson turns off Memorial Drive and into Arlington Cemetery in Arlington, Virginia, during his funeral procession. Officers who are called upon to deal with violence can become victims of that violence themselves.

Because researchers originally did not separate domestic disputes from other types of "disturbance" calls, using data from *all* disturbance calls "stretched the findings beyond what they reasonably meant" (Sampson, 2007, p. 1). Furthermore, the frequency of domestic disturbance calls likely adds to the "overblown" claims of dangerousness regarding such calls in terms of injury to officers (Sampson, 2007).

Documenting Evidence of Domestic Violence

After the abuser has been arrested and removed from the scene, a thorough investigation is needed, including comprehensive interviews with the victim and any witnesses. Information should be obtained about the frequency and intensity of the domestic violence as well as any previous police contacts.

Photographs should be taken of injuries and of indications of the level of violence, such as tipped-over or broken furniture, smashed objects and the like. Any evidence of the violence should be properly collected. Keep in mind bruises often do not show up until several hours after a battering, perhaps even a day or two later. Furthermore, many victims change their minds within 24 hours of filing a complaint of abuse and try to drop charges against their batterer.

As with videotaping statements, photographing evidence may be necessary insurance in cases where victims are uncooperative in seeing the case through to prosecution and can also help remind victims why they must stand firm in pressing charges.

Arresting Batterers

Traditionally, the police response to a domestic call regarding wife battering has been to try to mediate the situation or to simply get the batterer out of the house for the night. Unless the police were threatened or actually assaulted, arrests seldom were made. Today, arrests are not made because often the police do not have the legal authority to do so unless they actually witness the assault or unless the victim presses charges. Sometimes, making an arrest only adds to the violence as the batterer seeks to avoid being arrested. Other times, the victim changes her mind and refuses to cooperate with the police. In addition, such cases are often not prosecuted vigorously.

For several decades, researchers have sought to assess the effects of arrest on intimate partner violence and how such a response compares with more informal, therapeutic intervention methods such as on-scene counseling and temporary separation. Although many studies throughout the years have produced inconsistent findings, researchers have now come to a general consensus about the benefit of arrest.

The Minneapolis Domestic Violence Experiment In 1981, the NIJ and the Minneapolis Police Department conducted what many now consider one of the most influential social science studies ever completed. The study, led by Lawrence W. Sherman (Sherman and Berk, 1984), examined three police responses to domestic violence calls and their effects on reducing future abuse:

- Arrest the suspect.
- Give only advice to the suspect.
- Order the suspect to leave the premises.

Instances of repeat violence were examined through a review of police records and interviews with the victims. Although the effectiveness of advising compared with separating is inconclusive from this study, the effectiveness of arrest is clear.

In the Minneapolis experiment, arrest was clearly more effective in reducing future violence than was advice or sending the suspect away.

The finding—that police should arrest suspects in domestic violence cases, rather than giving them on-the-spot counseling or other types of more lenient treatment, because arrests reduce recidivism—affected police policies nationwide and led Congress to fund grant programs encouraging law enforcement agencies to establish "pro-arrest."

Follow-up studies replicating the Minneapolis experiment, however, yielded less conclusive results. In some cases, offenders who were arrested had higher levels of recidivism than did those who were not arrested. Such findings led some, including Sherman, to call for the repeal of mandatory arrest laws. After further research examining the dynamics between socioeconomic status, domestic violence and the likelihood of repeated abuse, Sherman developed a community-specific law enforcement policy advocating mandatory arrest of batterers in neighborhoods with low unemployment and discretionary arrest in those with high unemployment. His reasoning was based on findings that arrest increased recidivism among unemployed suspects by 52 percent but reduced subsequent violence by 37 percent among batterers who were employed. Sherman's conclusion: Officers should be allowed discretion in deciding whether to make an arrest.

More recently, as Klein (2008, p.16) reports, "A major reexamination of a series of fairly rigorous experiments in multiple jurisdictions finds that arrest deters repeat abuse." A further finding was that no site showed evidence that arrest was associated with increased re-abuse. A major study reported by the National Crime Victim Survey (NCVS) based on 2,564 partner assaults reported between 1992 and 2002 found that police involvement, whether arrest occurred or not, had a strong deterrent effect: "The positive effects of police involvement and arrest are not dependent upon whether or not the victim or a third party reported the incident to law enforcement. Nor are they dependent upon the seriousness of the incident assault, whether a misdemeanor or felony" (Klein, p. 16). Thus, based on multiple studies in diverse jurisdictions, "Arrest should be the default position for law enforcement in all domestic violence incidents" (Klein, p.17).

States laws fall into one of three policy categories regarding arrests in domestic violence cases (Hirschel et al., 2007, p18):

- Arrest is mandatory (22 states and the District of Columbia).
- Arrest is preferred (6 states).
- Arrest is at the officer's discretion (22 states).

These laws also delineate the circumstances in which officers can make an arrest. For instance, the law might state an officer can make an arrest *only*

- In cases of felonies.
- Within a certain number of hours of the incident.
- If the couple is married, blood related, living together or has a child together.

The policies of a jurisdiction govern whether officers can decide to arrest or whether they are required to do so. In addition, the policy in a jurisdiction may require more of the police than state law. For example, a state law may say that an arrest is preferred in domestic violence cases, but a jurisdiction may choose to make an arrest mandatory (Hirschel et al., 2007).

In formulating a response, police might consider the difference between **instrumental violence** (that used to control) and **expressive violence** (that resulting from hurt feelings, anger or rage). Arrest may work best for batterers who use instrumental violence, but other methods, such as learning to mediate differences, may work better with batterers who use expressive violence. Again, however, this difference may not matter depending on state law and jurisdictional policies, where officers have no choice but to arrest.

instrumental violence
That used to exert control.

expressive violence
That resulting from hurt feelings, anger or rage.

"Failure to Protect" Lawsuits In many states, officers who have evidence that an assault has occurred have no choice but to make an arrest. The case largely responsible for this change in approach is *Thurman v. City of Torrington* (1984), in which Tracey Thurman, over a period of eight months, contacted Torrington police on at least 11 separate occasions to report threats upon her life and the life of her child made by her estranged husband, Charles Thurman.

Between October 1982 and June 1983, Charles's threatening behavior became more violent, and after he smashed Tracey's windshield while she was inside the vehicle, he was placed on probation and ordered to stay away from her. However, Charles, ignoring the conditions set for his probation, continued to threaten Tracey, and the police continued to respond to her calls with an "oh, no, not again" attitude. On May 6, 1983, she obtained a court-issued restraining order forbidding Charles from assaulting, threatening and harassing her. And on June 10, 1983, when Charles went to her house demanding to see her, Tracey called the police asking he be picked up for violating his probation. About 15 minutes later, expecting police to arrive shortly, Tracey went outside to talk to Charles, who then stabbed her 13 times in the chest, neck and throat. Ten minutes later (25 minutes after her call), a single officer arrived on the scene to witness Charles drop a bloody knife and kick Tracey in the head as she lay on the ground. Tracey Thurman sued the police department for "failure to protect."

At the trial, the department defended its "hands off" response as a means of promoting domestic harmony by refraining from interference in marital disputes. The jury, however, decided the police response had been less than adequate, evidencing a pattern of deliberate indifference by the police department to the complaints of the plaintiff Tracey Thurman and to its duty to protect her. The court added an officer may not "automatically decline to make an arrest simply because the assaulter and his victim are married to each other."

Tracey was awarded $2.6 million dollars. The case resulted in the passage of the Family Violence Protection and Response Act in Connecticut and has resulted in more than 60,000 arrests. The message in the law is clear: Domestic violence is a crime.

Thurman v. City of Torrington (1984) established that domestic violence is an assault rather than simply a family affair. Officers and departments can be sued for "failure to protect."

Police departments that develop and implement pro-arrest policies in domestic assaults can substantially reduce the risk of being sued for federal civil rights violations alleging discrimination. Another way to reduce liability and exposure to lawsuits is to require officers responding to domestic assault calls to document when and why no arrest was made—for example, there was a lack of probable cause because no injuries were visible on the victim, no signs of a struggle, and the like.

Batterer Intervention Programs (BIPs)

Batterer intervention programs (BIPs) are also known as spouse abuse abatement programs or SAAPs." Several studies have found little or limited support for court-ordered treatment for batterers. Some studies have found the batterer's "stake-in-conformity" as the most significant factor in rehabilitation. **Stake-in-conformity variables** include marital status, employment, residential stability and age—all variables offenders might lose if convicted for a repeat offense.

stake-in-conformity variables

Include marital status, employment, residential stability and age—all variables offenders might lose if convicted for a repeat offense.

The NIJ report *Batterers' Intervention Programs: Where Do We Go from Here?* notes that most BIP programs are based on the Duluth Model. The report concludes that the programs in Broward County, Florida, and Brooklyn, New York, show little or no effect on re-offense rates, and no impact on batterers' attitudes about domestic violence (Jackson et al., 2003).

The Controversial Duluth Model The Duluth Model, designed in 1981, is a coordinated community response of law enforcement, the criminal and civil courts and human service providers to hold offenders accountable for their behaviors. The program helps offenders understand how their beliefs about women, men and marriage contribute to their abusive behavior and that intentional violence is a choice used to control an intimate partner.

Labriola et al. (2008, p.252) studied randomly assigned misdemeanor domestic violence offenders in the Bronx, New York, to either a batterer program or not and to either monthly or graduated judicial monitoring, with the latter involving reduced court appearances for compliance and increased appearances for noncompliance. The researchers found that neither approach reduced the re-arrest rates for any offense, for domestic violence, or for domestic violence with the same victim. The researchers found similar results after one year, with victim interviews showing that neither program assignment nor monitoring schedule significantly affected re-abuse.

Schwartz and DeKeseredy (2008, p.178) suggest, "Attempting to solve the problem of interpersonal violence by dealing with the private problems of individuals is a strategy doomed to failure." They contend that male peer support gives permission to men to assault women or to ignore those who do so.

Helping Victims Deal with the Assault

Besides arresting the abuser, officers responding to calls of domestic assault can help battering victims by making them aware of the many resources available to them. Support groups, counseling programs and shelters have been established throughout the country to help victims of domestic violence. Other strategies that also may effectively address the problem include establishing programs to rehabilitate those who commit domestic violence, and using protective and restraining orders and ensuring that such orders are adhered to.

Restraining Orders A civil restraining order (RO), also called a temporary restraining order (TRO) or order for protection (OFP), is a legally enforceable document that limits physical contact between abuser and abusee. Furthermore, a TRO is valid anywhere a victim might go within the country.

Article IV, Section 1 of the U.S. Constitution contains the phrase, "Full faith and credit shall be given in each state to the public acts, records, and judicial proceedings of every other state." This provision allows such things as marriage licenses and driver's licenses to have nationwide validity, regardless of which state issued them.

Federal law requires officers to honor out-of-state protection orders, and given the technology and information-sharing databases now prevalent in law enforcement, agencies and their officers are no longer excused for remaining ignorant of such orders. In fact, officers may be held liable for not checking for any existing protection orders when encountering these situations; failure to check may be considered a dereliction of duty.

Using GPS to Track Abusers Thirteen states have passed legislation expanding the use of global positioning devices to include domestic abusers and stalkers who have violated orders for protection. Currently about 5,000 domestic abusers are being tracked nationwide, but it is still challenging to protect families who live in rural areas or where there are not enough police officers to respond quickly (Green, 2009).

In cases of extreme violence, judges have been known to order global positioning system (GPS) use before trial, as a condition of bail or as a sentence, but this measure often leads to complaints by the American Civil Liberties Union and others critics that it allows too much leeway for judges. With the economic downturn, states have cut funding previously allocated for training police and judges in GPS use.

STALKING

Another type of domestic violence requiring an enhanced awareness by and response of law enforcement is stalking. If the goal of domestic abuse is to exert power and control over a victim, often through fear, stalking certainly qualifies as such abuse. The Office for Victims of Crime (OVC) defines stalking as "the willful or intentional commission of a series of acts that would cause a reasonable person to fear death or serious bodily injury and that, in fact, does place the victim in fear of death or serious bodily injury." California passed the first stalking law in 1990, and now stalking is a crime in every state (Petrocelli, 2007b, p.22).

Current data indicate an estimated 3.4 million persons age 18 or older are victims of stalking each year (Baum et al., 2009, p.1). The most common types of stalking behavior reported are receiving unwanted phone calls (66 percent), receiving unsolicited letters or email (31 percent) or having rumors spread about oneself (36 percent). About half (46 percent) of stalking victims experienced at least one unwanted contact per week, and 11 percent had been stalked for 5 years or more (Baum et al.). The risk of stalking victimization is highest for individuals who are divorced or separated—34 per 1,000 individuals. Women are at greater risk than men, but women and men are equally likely to report their victimization to police. About 1 in 4 stalking victims reports some form of cyberstalking such as e-mail (83 percent) or instant messaging (35 percent). The NIJ stresses that although cyberstalking does not involve physical contact with a victim, it is still a serious crime ("Stalking," 2007).

Nearly three in four stalking victims know their offender in some capacity. Most stalking cases involve a male offender and a female victim who had a prior intimate relationship with each other. In addition to this primary category of intimate or former intimate stalking, two other categories exist: acquaintance stalking, where the stalker and victim may know each other casually and may even have dated once or twice but were never intimate; and stranger stalking, commonly found in cases involving celebrities and other public figures, where no prior relationship between the stalker and victim exists.

The Police Response

Velazquez et al. (2009, p.30) emphasize, "Since the first laws against stalking were passed in the 1990s, police departments have worked to understand this crime and enforce the laws against it. To respond effectively to cases of stalking, officers must understand the nature of the crime, its legal definition, its many forms, its associations with other crimes, and its impact on victims."

Law enforcement officers should instruct victims to record specific incidents and their initial, visceral reactions either in a notebook or audio taped in a stalking log: "A well-kept stalking log, supported by physical evidence (phone recordings, e-mails, etc), will not only be strong evidence at a trial, but will empower the victim" (Petrocelli, 2007b, p.23).

Officers should also obtain as much information about the stalker as possible and then make an effort to talk with the suspect, recording the conversation if possible. It should be made clear that stalking is a crime and must stop or an arrest will be made. An official report of the conversation and the suspect's reactions should be filed (Petrocelli, 2007b).

CHILD ABUSE AND MALTREATMENT

Because child abuse and maltreatment commonly occur within a family setting, it can be considered a special subtype of domestic violence. But such abuse can also be perpetrated by people outside the family, and now, with the Internet reaching into homes across the country, strangers many miles away are able to victimize children online, creating new challenges for law enforcement and the criminal justice system as a whole. Because of the unique dynamics involved in interacting with child victims and the technical issues surrounding such incidents as Internet crimes against children, we will save the bulk of this discussion for Chapter 11, the chapter devoted to issues concerning youths and juvenile justice.

For now, however, it is enough to acknowledge that, in families where spousal abuse is occurring, it should also be considered a possibility that child abuse is occurring, or may occur in the future. At the very least, child endangerment exists. Millions of children witness violence in their homes; even when they are not themselves the direct targets of abuse, children may be victimized through continued exposure to abusive relationships. Officers responding to a domestic call involving adults must remain aware of the "invisible victimization" suffered by children who witness violence in the home and tend to these young victims as well. Often, when adults are arrested for domestic violence, additional charges of *endangering children* should be made if children were present during the abuse, and those children should also be taken into protective custody.

Children themselves may become perpetrators of family violence, when they are grown and turn abusive to their elderly parents. Thus, the elderly may be as vulnerable to violence as children are.

ELDER ABUSE

In 1900, the average life expectancy of U.S. residents was only 47 years. A century later, that figure has nearly doubled, and the elderly—those age 65 and up—will soon outnumber children for the first time in our country's history. The U.S. Bureau of the Census projects that by 2030, the U.S. population over age 65 will number about 70 million, more than double the number of seniors in 1998. Census data also reveals the fastest-growing segment of the elderly population is occurring among Americans age 85 and older. According to the NIJ, "This aging population will require more care and protection than is currently available" ("Elder Abuse," 2007).

With the increasing number of elderly comes an increasing number of elder abuse cases. **Elder abuse** includes the physical and emotional trauma, financial exploitation and general neglect of a person aged 65 or older. In the 1990s, elder abuse was criminalized including the creation of mandatory-reporting legislation and increased penalties for elder abusers. According to the National Center on Elder Abuse ("Elder Abuse: Frequently Asked Questions," 2007),

elder abuse
The physical and emotional trauma, financial exploitation and/or general neglect of individuals over 65 years of age.

> Elder abuse is a term referring to any knowing, intentional, or negligent act by a caregiver or any other person that causes harm or a serious risk of harm to a vulnerable adult. The specificity of laws varies from state to state, but broadly defined, abuse may be
>
> - *Physical Abuse*—Inflicting, or threatening to inflict, physical pain or injury on a vulnerable elder, or depriving them of a basic need.
> - *Emotional Abuse*—Inflicting mental pain, anguish, or distress on an elder person through verbal or nonverbal acts.
> - *Sexual Abuse*— Nonconsensual sexual contact of any kind.
> - *Exploitation*—Illegal taking, misuse, or concealment of funds, property, or assets of a vulnerable elder.
> - *Neglect*—Refusal or failure by those responsible to provide food, shelter, health care or protection for a vulnerable elder.
> - *Abandonment*—The desertion of a vulnerable elder by anyone who has assumed the responsibility for care or custody of that person.

Elder abuse affects people of all races and ethnicities, religions, socioeconomic groups and educational levels. Findings from the oft-cited *National Elder Abuse Incidence Study* (1998) suggest that more than 500,000 Americans aged 60 and older were victims of domestic abuse in 1996. This study also found that only 16 percent of the abusive situations are referred for help—84 percent remain hidden. Although a couple of studies estimate that between 3 percent and 5 percent of the elderly population have been abused, the Senate Special Committee on Aging estimates that there may be as many as 5 million victims every year.

The 2004 Survey of State Adult Protective Services (APS), the "most rigorous national study of state-level APS data conducted to date," showed a 19.7 percent increase in the combined total of reports of elder and vulnerable adult abuse and neglect and a 15.6 percent increase in substantiated cases in the four years since the last survey was conducted in 2000. In the overwhelming majority of cases (89.3 percent), the alleged abuse was reported to have occurred in a domestic setting. Types of maltreatment substantiated included self-neglect (37.2 percent), caregiver neglect (20.4 percent), financial exploitation (14.7 percent), emotional/psychological/verbal abuse (14.8 percent), physical abuse (10.7 percent), sexual abuse (1 percent) and other (1.2 percent) (*The 2004 Survey of State Adult Protective Services*, 2006, p.1).

Just as it is difficult to understand how parents could abuse their children, it is difficult to understand how adult children could abuse their elderly parents. Literature suggests multiple causes of abuse and that most instances are not intentional and preconceived but are the result of the accumulation of stress and limited knowledge and resources for the person providing care. Elderly victims, however, often allow the abuse to continue, being either unwilling or unable to report it. For example, an elderly parent being "cared for" at home by a grown child may fear that reporting the abuse will lead to the caretaker's arrest and incarceration, thus forcing the elderly victim into a nursing home. On the other hand, if the elder reports the abuse and the caretaker is not arrested, the elder may end up in an even more violent situation with an abusive caretaker seeking retaliation for being "told on."

Elderly parents may choose not to report abuse because they feel guilty, ashamed and embarrassed that their own children are mistreating them. It is very common for individuals of this older generation to consider it inappropriate to discuss these matters with anyone outside of the family, and many do not view such treatment as a police issue. Sometimes elderly parents either do not know who to report abuse to or are physically unable to report it, perhaps because they are bedridden with no access to a telephone or they have no visitors. Other times, the abused elders are so disoriented, confused or otherwise impaired they do not recognize their mistreatment as abusive.

Elderly residents in nursing homes also have been abused, physically and sexually, by caregivers and sometimes even by other residents. As with the elderly parents living with their children, nursing home residents may have no way to contact help and may fear retribution if they claim they are being abused.

Many other elderly people are not physically abused; they are simply neglected, deprived of all but the most basic necessities. Still others are financially exploited, targeted by unscrupulous scam artists and bilked out of their life savings, or defrauded by caregivers or relatives.

Warning Signs of Elder Abuse

The National Center on Elder Abuse ("Elder Abuse: Frequently Asked Questions," 2007) lists warning signs that there could be an elder abuse problem:

- Bruises, pressure marks, broken bones, abrasions, and burns may be an indication of physical abuse, neglect, or mistreatment.
- Unexplained withdrawal from normal activities, a sudden change in alertness, and unusual depression may be indicators of emotional abuse.
- Bruises around the breasts or genital area can occur from sexual abuse.

- Sudden changes in financial situations may be the result of exploitation.
- Bedsores, unattended medical needs, poor hygiene, and unusual weight loss are indicators of possible neglect.
- Behavior such as belittling, threats, and other uses of power and control by spouses are indicators of verbal or emotional abuse.
- Strained or tense relationships, frequent arguments between the caregiver and elderly person are also signs.

Research on Elder Abuse

Research on elder abuse and neglect is 30 to 40 years behind that associated with other issues such as child abuse and domestic violence, which places an increasingly large population of elders at risk and poses a huge hurdle for prosecutors in bringing elder abuse cases (McNamee and Murphy, 2006). One NIJ study that followed a group of elderly individuals for 16 months to document the difference between accidental and intentional bruising found that accidental bruising occurred in predictable locations in the geriatric population, with 90 percent of all bruises occurring on the extremities. No accidental bruises were seen on the ears, neck, genitals, buttocks, or soles of the feet.

McNamee and Murphy also describe NIJ-funded researchers who have studied elder deaths and have identified four categories of potential markers of abuse:

1. *Physical condition/quality of care.* Specific markers include documented but untreated injuries; undocumented injuries and fractures; multiple, untreated, and/or undocumented pressure sores; medical orders not followed; poor oral care, poor hygiene, and lack of cleanliness of residents; malnourished residents who have no documentation for low weight; bruising on nonambulatory residents; bruising in unusual locations; statements from family concerning adequacy of care; and observations about the level of care for residents with nonattentive family members.
2. *Facility characteristics.* Specific markers include unchanged linens; strong odors (urine, feces); trash cans that have not been emptied; food issues (unclean cafeteria); and documented problems in the past.
3. *Inconsistencies.* Specific markers include inconsistencies between the medical records, statements made by staff members and/or observations of investigators; inconsistencies in statements among groups interviewed; and inconsistencies between the reported time of death and the condition of the body.
4. *Staff behaviors.* Specific markers include staff members who follow an investigator too closely; lack of knowledge and/or concern about a resident; unintended or purposeful verbal or nonverbal evasiveness; and a facility's unwillingness to release medical records.

Risk Factors for Elder Abuse

The National Center on Elder Abuse ("Risk Factors for Elder Abuse," 2007) explains the risk factors associated with elder abuse:

> Although the factors listed below cannot explain all types of elder maltreatment, because it is likely that different types (as well as each single incident) involve

different casual factors, they are some of the risk factors researchers say seem to be related to elder abuse.

Domestic Violence Grown Old

It is important to acknowledge that spouses make up a large percentage of elder abusers, and that a substantial proportion of these cases are domestic violence grown old: partnerships in which one member of a couple has traditionally tried to exert power and control over the other through emotional abuse, physical violence and threats, isolation, and other tactics.

Personal Problems of Abusers

Particularly in the case of adult children, abusers often are dependent on their victims for financial assistance, housing, and other forms of support. Oftentimes they need this support because of personal problems, such as mental illness, alcohol or drug abuse, or other dysfunctional personality characteristics. The risk of elder abuse seems to be particularly high when these adult children live with the elder.

Living with Others and Isolation

Both living with someone else and being socially isolated have been associated with higher elder abuse rates. These seemingly contradictory findings may turn out to be related in that abusers who live with the elder have more opportunity to abuse and yet may be isolated from the larger community themselves or may seek to isolate the elders from others so that the abuse is not discovered. Further research needs to be done to explore the relationship between these factors.

Other Theories

Many other theories about elder abuse have been developed. Few, unfortunately, have been tested adequately enough to definitively say whether they raise the risk of elder abuse or not. It is possible each of the following theories will ultimately be shown to account for a small percentage of elder abuse cases.

- **Caregiver stress.** This commonly stated theory holds that well-intentioned caregivers are so overwhelmed by the burden of caring for dependent elders that they end up losing it and striking out, neglecting, or otherwise harming the elder. Much of the small amount of research that has been done has shown that few cases fit this model.
- **Personal characteristics of the elder.** Theories that fall under this umbrella hold that dementia, disruptive behaviors, problematic personality traits, and significant needs for assistance may all raise an elder's risk of being abused. Research on these possibilities has produced contradictory or unclear conclusions.
- **Cycle of violence.** Some theorists hold that domestic violence is a learned problem-solving behavior transmitted from one generation to the next. This theory seems well established in cases of domestic violence and child abuse, but no research to date has shown that it is a cause of elder abuse.

The Police Response

Albrecht (2008, p.44) contends, "It's in your best interest (and your duty as a mandated reporter in nearly all states) to respond, ask questions, investigate all potential crimes and check on the health and viability of any elderly person under the care or control of someone." Most elder abuse does not happen in retirement or nursing homes; it occurs in the home of the senior citizen, with the most common perpetrator being the spouse (Petrocelli, 2007a, p.16). Responding officers must proceed with respect and caution and must also be aware of the laws governing elder abuse in their state. The skills used in dealing with domestic violence and abused children apply to investigating elder abuse (Petrocelli).

Elder abuse should be defined and documented as a crime separate from assault, battery, burglary, murder or some other category. This would accomplish two purposes: raise awareness of the problem and help outline a proper police response to the problem. Law enforcement should first try to prevent such abuse by empowering the elderly with information about how to protect themselves. Police should identify the at-risk population such as those elderly dependent on others for some or all of their basic daily needs. Officers should also recognize and understand why the elderly are abused and develop a strategy to meet their needs.

Petrocelli (2007a) recommends that officers investigating a report of elder abuse in a residence observe the general condition of the residence. Has the garbage been taken our? Has the mail been brought in? Are there dirty dishes in the sink? How does the house smell?

After determining the living conditions, officers should interview the alleged victim, paying attention to nonverbal cues: "Is a suspected perpetrator hovering in the area, refusing to leave the senior alone to answer questions? Is the potential victim answering the questions by looking the officer in the eye and giving direct responses or is he or she averting eye contact and giving ambiguous answers?" Petrocelli (2007a) also suggests assessing the potential victim's mental state: "What is the day/month? Who is the president? What is 6 plus 8?"

Because physical evidence of assault or neglect is vital to establishing a charge of elder abuse, officers responding to a call where physical abuse is suspected should examine the elderly victim for indicators such as fractures, bruises, burns, lacerations and punctures. Officers should look for the presence of old and new wounds and be alert to difficulties the elderly victim has with walking or sitting, recognizing that mobility impairment is also a normal part of aging.

Evidence of psychological abuse is more difficult to detect but may manifest as depression, a change in personality, a loss of interest in themselves and their surroundings, anger or agitation.

Law enforcement must also respond to financial abuse of the elderly including stealing, embezzling or misusing money or possessions, savings or stocks; misusing the person's property or other resources; and denying the elderly a home. Sometimes the grown children are responsible for financially exploiting their elderly parents, a relatively easy crime to commit if the adult child is the victim's guardian, has power of attorney for the elderly parent, or has been given other rights over the victim's estate and person.

Elder abuse also includes neglect that may take the form of abandonment or denial of food, shelter, clothing, basic hygiene practices and medical attention. Often abusers rely on overmedicating their victims to control them.

Although interviewing abused elders directly is a preferred police response, often the victim is confused or unable to grasp what has happened. Elderly victims may have impaired mental abilities or memories. In such instances, information provided by other people becomes extremely important. If elderly victims live at home, all those who have contact with the victims should be interviewed. If elderly victims live with one of their children, all family members should be interviewed. If elderly victims live in a nursing home, other residents of the home as well as the care providers should be interviewed. The past record of the institution should be looked into, including any violations of licensing standards reported to the state department of human services or whatever agency issues licenses to nursing homes.

Cooperative Efforts

As with other areas of domestic violence, cooperative efforts in responding to elder abuse are critical and can include social workers, mental health workers, elder protective services, hospital workers, shelters for the elderly and transportation services. As stressed throughout this text, multiagency partnerships and a focus on community policing have been shown to increase the effectiveness of police response to crime. The application of such collaborative efforts to the issue of domestic violence is as promising as it is to any other police operation, yet it faces the same challenges found with other areas involving partnerships. These same collaborative efforts might be used to address school violence.

SCHOOL AND COLLEGE VIOLENCE

The CARD Report (Crime Analysis, Research & Development)—*Crime in Schools and Colleges* states, "Schools and colleges are valued institutions that help build upon the nation's foundations and serve as an arena where the growth and stability of future generations begin. Crime in schools and colleges is therefore one of the most troublesome social problems in the nation" (Noonan and Vavra, 2007). As noted earlier, educators are commonly the ones who detect and report to authorities incidents of suspected child abuse or family violence. Educators may also, however, be first-hand witnesses to and, on occasion, victims of violence, as the aggression experienced at home by some children finds its way onto school grounds. A variety of elements may lead police in a certain jurisdiction to have to respond to incidents of school violence.

Although incidents of school and college violence are to be taken seriously and have received much media attention in recent years, such publicity has also generated a widespread, baseless fear that today's schools are teeming with youths more valueless and violent than ever before. Current research suggests differently. Analysis of data submitted to the FBI's National Incident-Based Reporting System from 2000 to 2005 indicates that, of the more than 17 million incidents reported during this period, only 3.3 percent occurred at schools and colleges (Noonan and Vavra, 2007). In these incidents of school violence, most (38.0 percent) of the offenders were 13- to 15-year-olds, followed by those age 19 or older (18.2 percent). The majority (76.7 percent) of offenders were males and

White (71.1 percent). The relationship between offender and victim most often reported was "acquaintance," which, when combined with "otherwise known" were 3.3 times more likely to occur than were other relationships. Personal weapons (hands, fists, feet) were 3.4 times more likely to have been reported than was any other weapon type. Knives and other cutting instruments were used as weapons more often than were guns, by a ratio of 3.2 to 1.

Statistics from *Indicators of School Crime and Safety: 2008* (Dinkes et al., 2009) acknowledge that our nation's schools are relatively safe but that crime and violence still occur. Using the enrollment figure of an estimated 55.5 million students in prekindergarten through grade 12 during the 2006–2007 school year, Dinkes et al. report (pp.v–vii),

- There were 27 homicides and 8 suicides of school-age youth (ages 5–18) at school or about 1 homicide or suicide of a school-age youth at school per 1.6 million students.
- Students ages 12 to 18 were victims of about 1.7 million nonfatal crimes, including thefts and violent crimes.
- Four percent of students ages 12 to 18 reported being victimized at school during the previous six months. Less than half of a percent reported serious violent victimization.
- Ten percent of male students in grades 9 to 12 reported being threatened or injured with a weapon on school property compared with 5 percent of female students.
- A greater percentage of teachers in city schools reported being threatened with injury or physically attacked than did teachers in suburban, town, or rural schools.
- Eighty-six percent of public schools reported that one or more serious violent incidents, thefts, or other crimes had occurred.
- Twenty-four percent of public schools reported that student bullying was a daily or weekly problem.
- Twenty-three percent of students ages 12 to 18 reported there were gangs at their schools.
- Thirty-two percent (ages 12–18) reported having been bullied at school.
- Twelve percent (grades 9–12) said they had been in a fight on school property.
- Six percent (grades 9–12) reported they had carried a weapon on school property during the previous 30 days.
- About 5 percent of students (ages 12–18) reported being afraid of attack or harm at school.
- Seven percent (ages 12–18) reported avoiding a school activity or one or more places in school in the previous 6 months because of fear of attack or harm.
- The majority of students (ages 12–18) reported that their school had a student code of conduct (96 percent) and a requirement that visitors sign in (94 percent). Ten percent reported the use of metal detectors at their schools.

Data from the National Center for Education Statistics covering the 2007–2008 school year indicate that 48 percent of schools reported at least one student threat of physical attack, but only 9 percent reported such a threat with a weapon (Neiman and DeVoe, 2009). About 13 percent of city schools reported at least one gang crime, a higher percentage than that reported by suburban (5 percent), town (5 percent) or rural schools (3 percent).

LAW ENFORCEMENT IN SCHOOLS AND COLLEGES

Law enforcement has become increasingly involved in maintaining safe environments for learning at all levels of education. At the K–12 level, the most common form of law enforcement involvement is the school resource officer or SRO. At the college/university level, the most common form of law enforcement is a campus-based police department.

The School Resource Officer (SRO)

A police-school liaison program was developed in 1958 in Flint, Michigan, with the cooperation of school authorities, parents, social agencies, juvenile court officials, businesses and the police department. The foundation for the police-school liaison program established a workable relationship with the police department and the public school system. This program gradually evolved into what is today the SRO program.

Part Q of Title I of the Omnibus Crime Control and Safe Streets Act of 1968 defines the SRO as "a career law enforcement officer, with sworn authority, deployed in community-oriented policing, and assigned by the employing police department or agency to work in collaboration with school and community-based organizations." According to the National Association of School Resource Officers, school-based policing is the fastest growing area of law enforcement.

Although SROs have traditionally educated students about topics such as pedestrian safety and the dangers of substance abuse through programs such as Drug Abuse Resistance Education (D.A.R.E.), their role has greatly expanded. SROs do not enforce school regulations, which are the responsibility of the school superintendent and staff. Instead, officers typically enforce all violations of law that occur on school property or have school staff involved. This includes all crimes, including status violations such as tobacco use, involving students who attend school. This also includes crimes such as fraud or assault that may be committed by school staff. SROs also work with students, parents and school authorities to apply preventive techniques to problems created by antisocial youths including counseling children and their parents, referring them to social agencies to treat the root problems, referring them to drug and alcohol abuse agencies and being in daily contact in the school to check their progress.

SROs may patrol elementary school areas until school starts in the morning, during the noon hour and after school, watching for suspicious people or automobiles and for infractions of safety rules. SROs also check the middle school areas for anyone loitering around the building or grounds trying to pick up students in the area. These officers are an invaluable resource to the police department because they usually have an opportunity to build rapport with the youth in the community because the SRO position is usually a long-term one, if not indefinite. SROs are often aware of rumors of crimes that will happen or have happened involving students. They know the kids in the community and who they are all connected to. If the youths are considered "problem kids," the officer may already have established a relationship with the child and his or her parents.

Another important area SROs are involved in is *liaison work with other interested agencies,* including juvenile courts, social agencies, mental health agencies, other schools and private organizations. Officers often coordinate their efforts with these other agencies to better treat children. Finally, *recreational participation* is a type of interaction with youths that breaks down many walls of resentment. Officers who participate in organized athletics with youngsters build a rapport that is carried over into their other contacts with those youths.

Campus Law Enforcement

The first official campus police force was formed at Yale University in 1894. In 1968, a New York study of campus police found that most chiefs and officers had not completed high school and had little or no training or background in law enforcement; most departments worked out of the boiler room, reporting to the maintenance department; and more than one third of all the officers were more than 60 years old (Peak et al., 2008, p.258). In reviewing the evolution of campus policing in America during the past 20 years, the following summary can be made:

> What is most evident is that these contemporary organizations have generally experienced a marked increase in the use of the title "Police Department" (with a concomitant decline in the designation of "Security Department"), the nature of reporting lines (they now typically report to the central administration as opposed to a head of campus buildings and grounds), and greater diversity among administrative-level personnel. There also have been slight increases in the number of administrators having graduate degrees. Furthermore, today more campus police agencies have full police powers, statewide jurisdiction, and greater numbers of full-time sworn personnel, agency ranks, and activities/responsibilities. They also report more positive relations with local area police agencies, a more detailed hiring process, and higher levels of mandatory annual in-service training; and they are generally very much engaged in disaster planning and terrorism readiness. (Peak et al., 2008, p. 258)

During the 2004–2005 school year, 74 percent of the 750 law enforcement agencies serving four-year universities and colleges with 2,500 or more students employed sworn law enforcement officers having full arrest powers. The other campuses hired nonsworn security officers. Two-thirds (67 percent) of campus law enforcement agencies used armed patrol officers (Reaves, 2008, p.1).

One of campus law enforcement's major responsibilities is adhering to the crime reporting requirements of the Clery Act, named in memory of 19-year-old university freshman Jeanne Ann Clery who was raped and murdered while asleep in her residence hall room on April 5, 1986. The Jeanne Clery Disclosure of Campus Security Policy and Campus Crime Statistics Act, signed into law in 1990, is the landmark federal law, originally known as the Campus Security Act, that requires colleges and universities to disclose information about crime on and around their campuses. Because the law is tied to federal student financial aid programs, it applies to most institutions of higher education, both public and private. It is enforced by the U.S. Department of Education.

The law was first amended in 1992 to add a requirement that schools afford the victims of campus sexual assault certain basic rights, and was amended again in 1998 to expand the reporting requirements. Subsequent amendments in 2000 and 2008 added provisions dealing with registered sex offender notification and campus emergency response, respectively. The 2008 amendments also added a provision to protect crime victims, "whistleblowers" and others from retaliation. Violators can be fined as much as $27,500 per nonreported incident.

Responsibilities of law enforcement officers in schools and on college campuses can be quite varied. Consider, as an example, the responsibilities of officers at the Fort Hays State University (Kansas) Police Department, which employs nine full-time, armed, state certified police officers: "The officers are responsible for a full range of public safety services, including criminal investigations, enforcement of criminal statutes and city ordinances, collection of data for the required statistical crime reports, motor vehicle accident investigations, civil commitments for persons in need of care, traffic and parking enforcement, emergency management, enforcement of FHSU rules and regulations, and the security of the university's physical assets" (Howell et al., 2008, p.20).

Bullying

Research suggests that many of the roots of crime and violence may stem from what is often ignored throughout the educational system—incidents of bullying and harassment. According to Olweus' (1992) groundbreaking study, former school bullies in Norway had a fourfold increase in the level of relatively serious, recidivist criminality as young adults.

Although some parents, other adults and even students tend to dismiss schoolyard bullying as a "rite of passage," a simple cycle of the big kids "picking on" the little kids, who in turn grow up to be the big kids who pick on the little kids, and so on, the U.S. Department of Education asserts **bullying** is more than just big versus small: "Bullying involves intentional, repeated hurtful acts, words or other behavior. There is a real or perceived power imbalance between bully and victim" (Peterson, 2001, p.18). Thus, the two key components of bullying are *repeated harmful* acts and an *imbalance of power*. Sampson (2008, p.1) states, "Perhaps more than any other school safety problem, bullying affects students' sense of security. . . . Bullying is widespread and perhaps the most underreported safety problem on American school campuses." Bullying may be

bullying
Intentional, repeated hurtful acts, words or behavior.

- Physical—hitting, kicking, spitting, pushing, punching, poking, hair-pulling, biting
- Verbal—name-calling, taunting, gossip, malicious teasing, making threats
- Psychological/Emotional—rejection, humiliation, ostracism, intimidation, extortion, spreading rumors, manipulating social relationships, berating personal characteristics such as perceived sexual orientation
- Sexual—harassment and actual abuse

Bullying is a serious concern in the issue of school violence because of its far-reaching and long-lasting impacts beyond a specific "episode" between bully and victim. Bullying can also lead to criminal behavior later in life.

Most students do not report bullying to adults (teachers or parents), fearing retaliation, that they would not be believed or that their teacher would tell the bully who told on him; feeling shame at not standing up for themselves; or thinking it was worse to be thought of as a snitch (Sampson, 2009, p.5). Because of this reluctance to tell, teachers and school resource officers may not think they have a problem. *Indicators of School Crime and Safety: 2008* reported that a fourth of schools thought bullying occurred daily or weekly, but a third of students reported being bullied. Sampson (pp.19–23) suggests the following approaches to address bullying:

- Enlist the school principal's commitment and involvement. . . .
- Use a multifaceted, comprehensive approach including establishing a schoolwide policy addressing bullying and providing guidelines for teachers, other staff and students on actions to take if bullying occurs, educating and involving parents, adopting strategies to deal with bullies and victims, encouraging students to report bullying and to be helpful to classmates. . . .
- Increase student reporting of bullying by setting up a bully hot line or having a "bully box" where students can drop a note about bullying. . . .
- Develop activities in less-supervised areas such as schoolyards, lunchrooms, lavatories. . . .
- Reduce the time students can spend with less supervision such as recess, lunch breaks and class changes. . . .
- Stagger recess, lunch and/or class-release times. . . .
- Monitor areas where bullying can be expected. . . .
- Assign bullies to a particular location or to particular tasks during release time. . . .
- Post classroom signs prohibiting bullying and listing the consequences for it.

Approaches that do *not* appear to be effective including training students in conflict resolution and peer mediation, adopting a "zero tolerance" policy, providing group therapy for bullies, and encouraging victims to simply "stand up" to bullies (Sampson, 2009, pp.23–24).

Attention must also be paid to victims of bullying. Some victims of bullying suffer such humiliation and loss of self-esteem they become violent toward themselves. The effects of bullying can also lead its victims to turn their anger and frustration outward.

School Shootings

"Statistically, shootings and other homicides are a rare event in U.S. schools. . . . [However] school shootings can be a very real and very frightening part of school violence in this country. Each attack has a terrible and lasting effect on the students, school and surrounding community—and on the nation as a whole. Even one school shooting is too many" (Schuster, 2009).

Consider the following excerpt from a 15-year-old boy's journal: "I hate being laughed at. But they won't laugh after they're scraping parts of their parents, sisters, brothers and friends from the wall of my hate." These words were written by Kip Kinkel, who later killed both of his parents and then went on a shooting spree at his high school in Springfield, Oregon, killing two students and wounding two dozen more. A year later came the tragedy at Columbine

On March 22, 2005, police forensic vans sit outside Red Lake Senior High School in Red Lake, a northern Minnesota Indian reservation. The day before a student shot and killed nine people and then turned the gun on himself.
© John Gress/Reuters/CORBIS

High School in Littleton, Colorado, where two shooters killed a dozen students and a teacher and wounded 23 others before turning their guns on themselves. Further investigation revealed the shooters had been plotting for a year to kill at least 500 and blow up their school.

School shootings have occurred throughout the United States, from Alaska to Florida, from Pennsylvania to California. Despite the geographic spread, a common thread seems to pull a majority of these events together: "Many of the recent shooters have felt put upon at school. Even the Secret Service worries about bullying. A study run by its National Threat Assessment Center found that in about two-thirds of 37 school shootings over the last 25 years, the attackers felt 'persecuted, bullied, threatened, attacked or injured'" (Peterson, 2001, p.17). Although some school shooters were described as socially isolated, others have been quite popular. Some were bullied, some were not. They came from both intact and broken families, and academic performance ranged from excellent to failing (Peterson, 2001, p.19). It is important to avoid overgeneralizing or making faulty assumptions based on backward logic. Although the majority of school shooters may have experienced bullying, it cannot be said that the majority of kids who are bullied will become violent or go on shooting rampages.

Following traditional law enforcement protocol, many have tried profiling the shooters and victims involved in school violence, searching for a pattern that may help predict or prevent similar events in the future. Teachers and others should avoid relying on profiles or checklists of danger signs to identify the next youth likely to bring lethal violence to a school.

School violence almost never occurs without warning.

Early Warning Signs Although use of profiles and checklists is strongly discouraged, early warning signs of violent behavior have been recognized that, when presented in combination, might aid in identifying and referring children who may need help. Such early warning signs include social withdrawal, excessive feelings of isolation or rejection, being a victim of violence, feelings of being picked on, low school interest and poor performance, expression of violence in writings and drawings, uncontrolled anger, patterns of impulsive and chronic bullying, discipline problems, past history of violent and aggressive behavior, drug and alcohol use, affiliation with gangs, possession of firearms, and threats of violence. None of these signs alone is sufficient for predicting aggression and violence.

The Police Response

As the nature of school and campus violence has changed over the years, so too has law enforcement's response to such incidents. The tragic events at Columbine fundamentally changed how police react to school shootings. During the Columbine rampage in 1999, the police did what they were trained to do—contain the situation and wait for a SWAT team. However, it took the SWAT team 45 minutes to assemble and get there; during that time Eric Harris and Dylan Klebold shot 10 of the 13 people who were killed that day. One victim bled to death. Since then, police across the country have established "active-shooter" protocol: "It [active-shooter training] calls for responding officers to rush toward gunfire and step over bodies and bleeding victims, if necessary, to stop the gunman—the active shooter—first" (Banda, 2009). This response is considerably different from that expected of police in other highly volatile or dangerous situations, where they are trained to take cover and wait for backup. A basic premise of the active-shooter response is that there is not enough time to wait for backup because it is assumed that the shooters will continue killing and have already committed themselves to dying in the altercation rather than surrendering by way of negotiation or communication.

This active-shooter response was used by the Virginia Tech police, fire and EMS responders during the deadliest school shooting in U.S. history, when Seung-Hui Cho "methodically murdered" 32 students and faculty and wounded 23 more. Larson (2008, pp.40–42) describes the police response:

> At 9:41, the first 9-1-1 call of the shooting went to the Blacksburg (Virginia) police department, which when it learned the shooting was on the Virginia Tech campus, immediately transferred the call to the VTPD. Within a minute, VTPD dispatched all available officers to an active shooting at Norris Hall and requested all county EMS units to respond. Police arrived at 9:45 and heard shots. They hesitated briefly to make sure they were not being fired upon and then rushed to the entrances, which Cho had chained shut. At 9:50 officers used a shotgun to shoot open the lock of an entrance Cho had not chained and followed the sounds to the second floor. At 9:51 Cho shot himself in the head just as police reached the second floor. The second floor was secured by 9:52 and medics entered to begin triage. In those 11 minutes Cho had fired 174 rounds, and as noted, had plenty of additional ammunition to continue his deadly shooting spree had the approach of the police not caused him to shoot himself.

Another trend, particularly among smaller departments, is toward more cross-training and pooling of resources. A comprehensive, step-by-step discussion of police response to school violence is beyond the scope of this text; however, several publications focus in their entirety on this subject. A particularly useful document published by the IACP, based on the input of more than 500 experts and 15 focus groups with a diverse range of disciplines addressing school violence, is the *Guide for Preventing and Responding to School Violence*.

IN SEARCH OF SAFER SCHOOLS

Beres (2008) suggests, "A combination of community policing, school resource officers and physical security can go a long way toward guaranteeing a safe school environment. This combination should have as its basis a well-thought-out and practiced plan for any crisis, natural or manmade."

An effective three-pronged approach to school security encompasses crisis planning, security technology and school/law enforcement/community partnerships.

Crisis Planning

Every agency and institution affected or involved during an episode of school violence must decide in advance how they plan to respond, knowing that no two situations will be exactly the same and that even the best-laid plans will require on-the-spot, last-minute adjustments. For police, the first step is generally to obtain blueprints or floor plans and to conduct walk-throughs of local schools. The next step is to actually train the response and to make such training exercises routine. Some departments stage mock disasters to test their emergency preparedness for acts of school violence and to identify areas that need improving. Such drills often highlight the importance of collaboration and communication with other agencies to an effective response.

46.1.5 CALEA STANDARD 46.1.5 states, "The planning function is vital to the success of the critical incident plan. Preparation of a documented incident action plan is one of the first responsibilities of the planning function. This function is also responsible for collecting and evaluating information about the incident, the status of resources, and anticipated equipment and manpower needs.

The planning function is typically tasked with assembling information on current and alternative strategies, identifying needs for special resources,, providing predictions on incident potential, and preparing recommendations for release of resources." (*Standards for Law Enforcement Agencies*, 5th edition, 2006)

In addition to having a plan, many schools are using security technology to enhance school safety.

Security Technology

A second prong in the effort to achieve safer schools involves security technology, such as weapons screening programs, entry control systems and surveillance cameras.

Recognizing that a significant proportion of school violence is perpetrated by those who neither attend nor work at the school, many districts are implementing entry control systems, such as mandatory sign-in for all visitors and photo ID cards, to make it easier to spot outsiders. Video cameras are also being installed as a way to curb school violence. Most cameras are not actively monitored but, rather, tape on a continuous loop and are reviewed only when an incident is reported.

Surveillance cameras are also of great value on college campuses, which are spread out geographically. As an example, Franklin & Marshall College in Lancaster, Pennsylvania, installed 21 closed-circuit television (CCTV) cameras outlining the campus perimeter, on campus parking lots and specific locations in the local neighborhood where a large number of students reside. The CCTV system "has proven itself a sound deterrent to criminal activity in the campus area and has paid for itself by assisting in numerous incidents that were deterred by their presence" (Morin, 2008, p.22). A second major technological enhancement was installing a campus-wide emergency siren and notification system.

Southern Illinois University has implemented a text "e-alert" system whereby students can be texted a message about any campus emergency. This system is controversial, however, because most professors maintain a policy of not allowing cell phones to be on in the classroom because they are distracting and make it easier for students to cheat, either by texting a friend for an answer or taking pictures of the test questions (Donald, 2008).

Although many other schools have found positive benefits in using video cameras and other security devices, technology cannot replace the human factor.

Lessons Learned from Campus Shootings

Since the widely publicized and tragic shooting incidents at Virginia Tech in April 2007 and Northern Illinois University in February 2008, several organizations and task forces have recommended that campuses create behavioral threat assessment/behavioral intervention teams as a key measure for preventing violence before it can occur (Margolis and Healy, 2009). The *Virginia Tech Special Task Force Report* calls for implementation of systems that link "troubled students to appropriate medical and counseling services either on or off campus, and to balance the individual's right with the rights of all others for safety." The report also recommends, "Incidents of aberrant, dangerous, or threatening behavior must be documented and reported immediately to a college's threat assessment group, and must be acted upon in a prompt and effective manner to protect the safety of the campus community" (Margolis and Healy). The Florida Gubernatorial Task Force for Campus Safety recommends, "That each college and university develop a multidisciplinary crisis management team, integrating and ensuring communication between the university law enforcement or campus security agency, student affairs, residential housing, counseling center, health center, legal counsel, and any other appropriate campus entities to review individuals and incidents which indicate 'at-risk' behavior. The team should facilitate the sharing of information, timely and effective intervention, and a coordinated response when required" (Margolis and Healy, 2009). Such threat assessment task forces are one example of how partnerships can enhance school and campus security.

Partnerships

In cannot be emphasized enough that, as with so many other areas of police operations, partnerships are a vital component in an effective response to school violence. Partnerships to address the issue of school violence can take many forms and involve numerous entities.

The Safe Schools Pyramid developed by the Center for the Prevention of School Violence (illustrated in Figure 7.2) reflects the importance of the community policing concept in school safety. The community sits at the pyramid's base because the school environment often mirrors what's happening in the community. Community problems can disrupt the school environment and impede learning. The SRO is the first level of the pyramid itself, depicting the SRO's function as an integral connection between the school and the community.

Operation CleanSWEEP San Bernardino County, California, has developed its own three-pronged approach to school safety through Operation CleanSWEEP (Success With Education/Enforcement Partnership), a triple partnership between the office of the superintendent of schools, the sheriff's department and the court system. Using juvenile citations, security assessment and special projects, this triumvirate tackled the problem of school crime and violence perpetrated by youths who previously had received neither genuine punishment nor rehabilitative guidance. Results of the program have been resoundingly positive, with participating school campuses reporting a decline in numbers of fights and acts of disruption and an increased feeling of safety among students and faculty (Penrod, 2001).

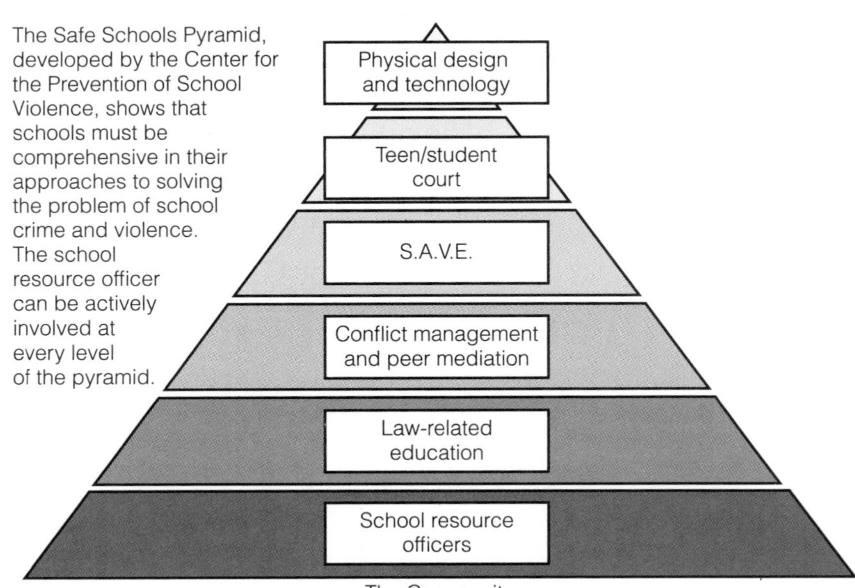

FIGURE 7.2
The Safe School Pyramid
Source: http://www.ncdjjdp.org/cpsv/safe_schools_pyramid.html. Copyright © Center for the Prevention of School Violence. Center for the Prevention of School Violence allows republishing for educational purposes.

OTHER EFFORTS TO PREVENT SCHOOL VIOLENCE

Some schools have supplemented their violence prevention efforts with programs, policies and procedures aimed at problematic student behavior. Intervention and behavior modification programs have proven successful in some jurisdictions. Another approach to preventing school violence is for those involved with students, particularly law enforcement officers, to have the skills to de-escalate juvenile aggression. For youths who pose no immediate danger but whose aggression appears to be manifestly deliberate, de-escalation tactics include reminding, warning or confronting the student; verbally removing the student (telling the student to leave); and physically removing or restraining the youth. In cases where no immediate danger is perceived and the youth's aggression might stem from an underlying emotional status, de-escalation strategies include giving the student space and time, listening reflectively to what is on the student's mind, and counseling positively (Golden, 2004, p.34).

Some schools have adopted controversial measures to prevent school violence, including zero-tolerance policies or school security procedures known as lockdowns.

Most such policies and procedures focus on the possession of weapons and other contraband on school property. And although it seems to make good sense that schools, in fulfilling their duty to maintain a safe learning environment, should restrict what students are allowed to carry on campus, policies and procedures aimed at achieving the goal of safety are not without controversy.

Zero-Tolerance Policies

zero-tolerance policies
School policies that mandate predetermined consequences or punishments for specific offenses, for example, suspension or expulsion for possession of drugs or a weapon.

Zero-tolerance policies mandate predetermined consequences for specific offenses. Such policies must be used with common sense. Consider, for example a case from Fort Myers, Florida, where school officials saw a knife on the floor of the passenger's side of an honor student's car while she was in the school. The knife, which had a 5-inch blade, had been left in the car after she moved some possessions over the weekend. The girl, 18, spent Monday in jail on a felony charge of possession of a weapon on school property. Further, the girl was not allowed to participate in her graduation ceremony because the principal insisted, "A weapon is a weapon." In thinking about these words, recall the data presented earlier in the chapter indicating that "personal" weapons, such as hands, fists and feet, were used more than three times as often in incidents of school violence than were any other type of weapon. Students cannot be expected to check their hands, fists and feet at the door, so common sense must prevail when implementing and interpreting school policies.

lockdowns
Periods when students are detained in classrooms while police and dogs scour the building searching for contraband or any danger to a safe educational environment.

Proactive Lockdowns

Another controversial effort aimed at preventing school violence is the planned but unannounced lockdown. Some schools are taking a **lockdown** approach not as a reactive response to a crisis, but rather as a proactive step to avoid a crisis.

Many legal issues must be considered when planning such a lockdown, so collaboration with the district attorney's office is usually required. An "amnesty time" is announced during which students can turn over any illegal substances or weapons without penalty and can list such items in their lockers. While part of the lockdown team searches the campus for contraband, another part meets with students to discuss what is occurring.

Although some criticize such lockdowns as being frightening or intimidating to students, and some students complain they feel threatened when their day is interrupted by the police, this approach has, thus far, not been challenged in court or before a school board. In addition to curbing the possession of drugs and weapons in the public schools, these lockdowns demonstrate the cooperation between law enforcement and the school system.

Proactive lockdowns may be effective in locating and securing weapons that might be used in incidents of school violence, but they are used very infrequently in very few schools. Zero-tolerance policies fall dangerously short in their effectiveness if students believe any prohibited items they bring to school will go unnoticed. In fact, many weapons are discovered only after they have been used in a violent episode. Metal detectors, again, are used rather infrequently, especially in smaller schools and in smaller communities, despite statistics showing these jurisdictions are also vulnerable to fatal school violence.

So although these efforts are seen as luxuries for those schools able to afford them, they cannot be relied on alone and are no substitute for the power of partnerships between students, teachers, officers, parents and other community members.

WORKPLACE VIOLENCE

The third major setting for violence for which law enforcement must prepare a response is the workplace. A Security Director News Poll found that workplace violence topped security directors' concerns for 2009 (Stelter, 2009b, p.2). In response to the question, "What do you consider the biggest security risk in 2009?," 49 percent responded workplace violence, followed by intellectual property theft (27 percent) and terrorism (24 percent). "Violence in the workplace is a serious safety and health issue. Its most extreme form, homicide, is the fourth-leading cause of fatal occupational injury in the United States. According to the Bureau of Labor Statistics Census of Fatal Occupational Injuries (CFOI), there were 564 workplace homicides in 2005 in the United States out of a total of 5,702 fatal work injuries" ("Workplace Violence," 2007).

The Occupational Safety and Health Administration (OSHA) reports that some 2 million American workers are victims of workplace violence each year and that it can strike anyone, anywhere, although some workers are at increased risk, including those who exchange money with the public; deliver passengers, goods, or services; or work alone or in small groups, during late night or early morning hours, in high-crime areas, or in community settings and homes where they have extensive contact with the public. Included in the latter group are health care and social service workers such as visiting nurses, psychiatric evaluators, and probation officers; community workers such as gas and water utility employees, phone and cable TV installers, and letter carriers; retail workers; and taxi drivers ("Workplace Violence," 2002). Hospital emergency room employees seem particularly vulnerable to workplace violence, with 86 percent of emergency room nurses reporting being victims of workplace violence in the past three years and 20 percent reporting that they experienced workplace violence "frequently" (Entwistle, 2008, p.17).

Standards for Responding to Workplace Violence

Although there are currently no specific OSHA standards for workplace violence, the following sections of the Federal Register are relevant: Section 5(a)(1) of the OSH Act, often referred to as the General Duty Clause, requires employers to "furnish to each of his employees employment and a place of employment which are free from recognized hazards that are causing or are likely to cause death or serious physical harm to his employees." Section 5(a)(2) requires employees to "comply with occupational safety and health standards promulgated under this Act" ("OSHA Standards," 2007).

The Society for Human Resource Management (SHRM) is collaborating with the American Society for Industrial Security (ASIS) International to develop an American National Standards Institute (ANSI)–accredited standard addressing workplace violence (Stelter, 2009a, p.2). The *Workplace Violence Prevention and Intervention American National Standard* will be based on the existing ASIS workplace violence prevention and response guideline, published in 2005. The new standard is expected to be completed in 2010.

ANSI has administered and coordinated the U.S. private sector voluntary standardization system for more than 90 years. Founded in 1918 by five engineering societies and three government agencies, the institute is a private, nonprofit membership organization supported by a diverse constituency of private and public sector organizations. Although such a document is intended primarily for security and human resources personnel, it can also help law enforcement in formulating a policy on the police response to workplace violence.

Types of Workplace Violence

Workplace violence is not new. Accounts of workplace violence can be found in the early 1980s, usually involving shootings at post offices. The most publicized of post office shooting was August 20, 1986, when a letter carrier, Patrick Sherrill, facing possible dismissal, walked into the Edmond, Oklahoma, post office where he worked and shot 14 people to death before killing himself. Workplace shootings have continued into the 21st century. In December 2007, a man walked into the Westroads Mall in Omaha, Nebraska, and shot nine people to death (Daniels, 2008, pp.1).

Rugala and Isaacs (2004, p.12) point out, "Contrary to popular opinion, sensational multiple homicides represent a very *small* number of workplace violence incidents. The majority of incidents that employees/managers have to deal with on a daily basis are lesser cases of assaults, domestic violence, stalking, threats, harassment (to include sexual harassment), and physical and/or emotional abuse that make no headlines." Law enforcement is seldom involved unless the behaviors cause actual physical harm or death.

Specialists agree that workplace violence falls into four broad categories (Rugala and Isaacs, 2004, p.13):

Type 1: Violent acts by criminals who have no other connection with the workplace but enter to commit robbery or another crime.

Type 2: Violence directed at employees by customers, clients, patients, students, inmates, or any others for whom an organization provides services.

Type 3: Violence against coworkers, supervisors, or managers by a present or former employee.

Type 4: Violence committed in the workplace by someone who doesn't work there but has a personal relationship with an employee—an abusive spouse or domestic partner.

Type 1 violence accounts for the "vast majority"—nearly 80 percent—of workplace homicides (Rugala and Isaacs, 2004).

Similarities between School and Workplace Violence

Researchers have noted some striking similarities between school and workplace violence.

Similarities between school and workplace violence include the perpetrators' profiles, the targets, the means and the motivation.

The perpetrators are frequently loners with poor social skills, often obsessed with violence and weapons. The targets include authority figures and peers who are in conflict with the perpetrators. The perpetrators often bring an arsenal of weapons and kill all who get in their way. The common motive is revenge, believing they have been treated unjustly. Most are suicidal and feel they have nothing left to lose. School and workplace violence also tend to provide early warning signs before acts of violence.

The caution issued previously regarding the hazards of profiling perpetrators of school violence also applies to attempts at identifying those at risk of committing workplace violence. Workplace violence experts cite three key factors in such incidents: (1) the personality of the perpetrator, (2) the particular stress and (3) the specific setting. Precipitating events for workplace violence might include problems at home, use of drugs or alcohol, missed promotions and terminations.

Early Warning Signs

Harne (2008, p.102) stresses, "It is rare for an employee to just snap. There are, in fact, frequent warning signs that a person is troubled and might become violent prior to any incident. Red flags include displays of harassing or threatening behavior during the course of employment and some aspect of the employee's personal life in turmoil."

Behaviors that could indicate potential for violence include outbursts of anger or rage without provocation, an increase in unsolicited comments about firearms or other dangerous weapons and violent crimes, talk of previous incidents of violence, an escalation of domestic problems into the workplace and paranoid behavior (Gane, 2007, p.140). Additional warning signs include increasing belligerence, hypersensitivity to criticism, apparent obsession with a supervisor or coworker or employee grievance, extreme disorganization, noticeable changes in behavior, and homicidal/suicidal comments or threats (Rugala and Isaacs, 2004, pp.21–22).

As with school violence, workplace violence rarely occurs without warning.

Though companies must be vigilant to the early warning signs of potential violence, they also must be aware of a legal limitation imposed by the Americans with Disabilities Act (ADA). The act severely restricts "profiling" of employees through observation of traits presumed to be potentially violent.

Workplace violence may be the result of the presence of gang members in the workforce or a spillover of domestic violence. Although the problem of domestic violence creeping into the workplace is to be taken seriously, workplace violence victims are more likely to be victimized by a stranger than by someone they know.

Policies on Workplace Violence

The ASIS *Workplace Violence Prevention and Response Guidelines* (2005, p.19) say a written workplace violence policy should include a "No Threats, No Violence" policy that is clearly communicated to all employees: "The policy will state the employer's commitment to provide a safe workplace, free from violence or the threat of violence. It will also set forth a code of employee conduct that clearly defines unacceptable behavior and prohibits all violence and threats on-site and during work-related off-site activities."

The policy should also include the role of law enforcement and when police should be called: "While not every workplace incident will reach the level of criminal conduct, cases that involve physical assault or significant destruction of property or serious threats, especially with a weapon, will as a general rule require intervention by law enforcement and possibly other public safety agencies as well" (*Workplace Violence Prevention*, 2005, p.38). Any business owner or manager knows that if life or personal safety is in danger, a call to 9-1-1 will bring a rapid response from law enforcement.

The Police Response

Most law enforcement agencies have established procedures for responding to crisis situations. Once police arrive, their immediate responsibility is to control the situation and eliminate the threat. In severe cases, they also gather evidence and interview witnesses for criminal prosecution. However, emergency response is not the only law enforcement role in workplace violence. The ASIS *Guidelines* state, "Employers should be aware that establishing contact and exchanging information with local police or sheriff's departments before a violent act occurs can be very helpful in developing and administering an organization's workplace violence program. An existing relationship and communication channel between an organization and local law enforcement may also make the response more effective if an emergency arises" (*Workplace Violence Prevention*, 2005, p.38).

Although no two incidents of workplace violence are exactly the same, a general multipronged approach of prevention and control is used as a starting point for most cases. Part of an emergency preparedness effort should include steps to make blueprints or floor plans of the premises available to law enforcement, should an episode of workplace violence turn into a barricaded subject incident or one where hostages are involved.

Officers can work with a company's crisis response team to train staff in how to detect signs of violence and procedures for reporting them to the threat management team. Prescreening programs are also strongly recommended. Because workplace violence can strike anywhere, thorough background checks are a first line of defense.

Other preventive measures include a no-weapons policy, drug and alcohol testing, and alternative dispute resolution (ADR) programs. Access control is another area businesses may consider when addressing the issue of workplace violence. Some companies have developed scripts and step-by-step instructions for on-site security personnel for managing violent employees and visitors, including how to summon and advise law enforcement. In cases where an abuser enters the workplace to victimize an employee, security or another member of the crisis management team must call police immediately.

In taking a community-policing approach to the problem of workplace violence, officers may also educate and inform local businesses of resources available to help employees who are victims of domestic violence.

Preventing Workplace Violence

AN EXAMPLE OF POLICE/ EMPLOYER COOPERATION

The local office of a Fortune 500 company contacted police for advice and help when it was planning a large layoff. Several weeks before the notices were to be issued, police went to the site and met with company officials to prepare for the event, including providing police with the names of the employees to be laid off. The managers also identified 10 employees they thought were most likely to be angry and aggressive when notified. Police ran background checks on them. Some information could not be given to the employer because of the Privacy Act, but could be given to police for the legitimate purpose of preventing violence. Four of the 10 were of concern to the police.

On the day of the layoffs, it was announced to all employees that plainclothes police (five officers) were on site and would remain there for several weeks. The four possible problem workers were notified first, followed by the others to be laid off. The terminations were carried out with no dangerous or disruptive incidents. Police later used the same procedure in assisting other local employers anticipating layoffs.

Source: Eugene A. Rugala and Arnold R. Isaacs. *Workplace Violence; Issues in Response*. Washington, DC: Federal Bureau of Investigation, 2004, p.39.

PROBLEM-ORIENTED POLICING AND VIOLENCE

As noted, violence at home, in school or in the workplace may have its roots in bullying behavior. "The South Euclid School Bullying Project"[1] is one of the 2001 Herman Goldstein Award winners for excellence in problem-oriented policing.

[1]Source: Adapted from "The South Euclid School Bullying Project." In *Excellence in Problem-Oriented Policing: The 2001 Herman Goldstein Award Winners*. Washington, DC: National Institute of Justice, Community Oriented Policing Services and the Police Executive Research Forum, 2001, pp.55–62.

Attention to tailor-made, individual responses in a broader, more holistic fashion is [an] attribute of successful projects. In South Euclid, crime prevention through environmental design (CPTED)–style modifications were paired with better teacher supervision of "hotspots." Role-playing training for teachers in conflict resolution was paired with antibullying education for students and parents. Combining physical prevention with social and managerial prevention strategies is called "2nd Generation CPTED" and represents the most advanced form of crime prevention.

Scanning

Unchecked disorderly behavior of students in South Euclid, Ohio, led the SRO to review school data regarding referrals to the principal's office. He found that the high school reported thousands of referrals a year for bullying, and the junior high school had recently experienced a 30 percent increase in referrals for bullying. Police data showed that juvenile complaints about disturbances, bullying and assaults after school hours had increased 90 percent during the last 10 years.

Analysis

All junior high and high school students were surveyed. Interviews and focus groups were also conducted with students—identified as victims or offenders—teachers and guidance counselors. Finally, the South Euclid Police Department purchased a geographic information system (GIS) to complete crime and incident mapping of hotspots within the schools. The main findings pointed to four main areas of concern: the environmental design of school areas, teachers' knowledge and response to the problem, parents' attitudes and responses, and students' perspectives and behaviors.

Environmental Design Findings

- Locations in the school with less supervision or denser population (primarily the hallways, cafeteria and gymnasium) were more likely to have higher rates of bullying.
- Students avoided certain places at school because of fear of being bullied (for example, students avoid hallways near lockers of students who are not their friends or who are not in their classes).
- Race and ethnicity was not a primary factor in bullying.
- A vast majority of students reported witnessing bullying or being bullied in the classroom during class.

Teacher Issues

- Although bullying occurred frequently, teachers and students infrequently intervened.
- When students were asked what would happen if they told a teacher about an incident of bullying, more than 30 percent said, "nothing."
- In interviews, students said they wouldn't tell teachers about bullying incidents because they were afraid of further retaliation, they expected the

teacher to "do nothing" or were afraid the teacher wouldn't believe or support them, especially if the bully was popular or well liked by the teacher.

Parent Issues

- Students who reported being physically disciplined at home were more likely to report that they had been bullied.
- More than one-third of parents who had talked to their kids about bullying had instructed them to fight back. Students said they would not tell a parent if they are bullied because they believed their parents would "overreact."

Student Issues

- Students who reported that they engaged in bullying typically perceived their own behavior as "playful" or "a normal part of growing up." They said that everyone gets picked on but some "don't know how to take it," "take things too seriously" or "just don't know how to fight back."
- Victims of bullying did not perceive this behavior as "fun" or "normal."
- Victims viewed bullies as "popular."
- Only 23 percent of students were likely to tell their parents they were a victim of bullying.
- Students were more likely to seek adult help for someone else who was bullied than for themselves.
- Students with lower grade point averages were significantly more likely to physically hurt someone else.
- Students who were secure in a peer group were more likely to intervene in bullying and were less fearful of retaliation.
- Students suggested that involvement in school activities helped them to form a niche where they felt safe, supported and free from victimization.

Response

The SRO, collaborating with a social worker and university researchers, coordinated a response planning team to respond to each of the areas identified in the analysis. Environmental changes involved modifying the school bell times and increasing teacher supervision of hotspot areas. Counselors and social workers conducted teacher training courses in conflict resolution and bullying prevention. Parent education included mailings with information about bullying, an explanation of the new school policy, and discussion about what they could do at home to address the problems. Finally, student education focused on classroom discussions with homeroom teachers and students, and assemblies conducted by the SRO. The Ohio Department of Education also contributed by opening a new training center for "at-risk students" to provide a nontraditional setting for specialized help.

Assessment

The results from the various responses were dramatic. School suspensions decreased 40 percent. Bullying incidents dropped 60 percent in the hallways and 80 percent in the gym area. Follow-up surveys indicated there were positive attitudinal changes among students about bullying and more students felt confident teachers would take action.

The overall results suggested that the school environments were safer and that early intervention was helping "at-risk" students succeed in school.

SUMMARY

Wives, husbands, children, elders—in fact, anyone within a family unit—may be at risk of becoming a victim of domestic violence. Police officers responding to a domestic violence call are responsible for investigating it thoroughly as an assault and for making an arrest if probable cause exists. Responding to a domestic violence call is hazardous, but not as hazardous as is often thought. In the Minneapolis experiment, police officers responding to domestic violence calls found that arrest was clearly more effective in reducing future violence than was advice or sending the suspect away. *Thurman v. City of Torrington* (1984) established that domestic violence is an assault rather than simply a family affair. Officers and departments can be sued for "failure to protect."

School violence is of growing concern to law enforcement and almost never occurs without warning. An effective three-pronged approach to school security encompasses crisis planning, security technology and school/law enforcement/community partnerships. Some schools have adopted controversial measures to prevent school violence, including zero-tolerance policies or school security procedures known as lockdowns.

Similarities between school and workplace violence include the perpetrators' profiles, the targets, the means and the motivation. As with school violence, workplace violence rarely occurs without warning.

APPLICATION

With the addition of several new elderly care facilities and homes in your community, you have noticed an increase in elderly related crimes, a crime that has begun to rapidly increase in other jurisdictions as well. Deputies within your agency are not yet well experienced in dealing with these incidents, including the investigation that is required of these cases. As a supervisor, your sheriff has approached you and requested that you draft a policy on dealing with elder abuse in your community. This policy should have guidelines that the deputies responding to these types of incidents can reference. In addition to the policy, you are also tasked with implementing elder abuse training for your deputies. Detail how you would train your deputies and what sources you would use.

INSTRUCTIONS

Write a policy for your sheriff's office detailing deputies' response to elder abuse crimes. The policy should contain the needs statement first. It should also include procedures for domestic violence, resources, and referrals to social services and related agencies. The statement should include the sheriff's office's expectations of deputies in dealing with these types of calls. This policy should also include special needs and considerations toward this demographic in the community.

The training outline should include a goals statement. It should also include what topics and issues should be covered in the training to make it successful for both the elderly community and the sheriff's deputies.

EXERCISES IN CRITICAL THINKING

A. On November 22, Officers David Miller and Peter Kelly were called to investigate a disturbance of the peace at 1131 Selby Avenue, St. Paul, Minnesota, reported by Jeanne McDowell, a neighbor. In the past month, several domestic disturbances had been reported and investigated at this address, which officers knew was the residence of Eddie and Donna Konkler.

While approaching 1131 Selby, the officers heard a loud male voice shouting obscenities, the sound of breaking glass, two loud thumps and the muffled sounds of children crying. Officer Miller knocked loudly on the door and called out to Eddie, who opened the door. He held a revolver in his right hand, and his breath smelled of an alcoholic beverage. Donna was sitting on the floor leaning against a wall. She had a bloody nose and several red marks on her face. Broken glass was scattered around the room.

Officer Miller was successful in talking Eddie into relinquishing the revolver and in quieting him, but for 15 minutes, Eddie and Donna continued shouting and cursing at each other and at the officers. During this time, Officer Kelly assisted Donna in stopping the bleeding, and she became subdued. Eddie continued his verbal abuse, so the officers requested that Eddie leave the house until he became calm. Eddie then told the police he was sorry and would not cause any more trouble. The officers gave suggestions for possible agencies that could help and suggested specific places where Donna could receive assistance if future repetitions of abuse were to occur.

1. What mistake did Officers Miller and Kelly make?
    a. Because of the cold weather in Minnesota, Eddie should not be removed from his residence; a firm warning and threat of arrest would be sufficient.
    b. Police should not approach a domestic disturbance by letting an abusive person know who they are. The abuser should not be given a chance to then draw a dangerous weapon.
    c. Police should not allow the parties to refuse to talk to one another—make the two stop fighting and shouting, and then insist that they talk and think about their situation so that mediation can bring about a solution to their problem.
    d. Repeated domestic abuse and an assault involving the display of a dangerous weapon justifies an arrest for second-degree assault.
    e. The officers should issue a ticket for disturbing the peace, but cases of domestic problems do not involve an arrest for criminal sexual conduct, kidnapping, terroristic threats or second-degree assault.

B. William Mosby, age 34, had known the mother and family of N.D., age 7, for seven years. Immediately before the events in question, Mosby had lived with N.D.'s family for three weeks. At the end of the third week, N.D.'s mother gave permission for N.D. to go grocery shopping with Mosby while she went to work.

After going to the cleaners, grocery store and liquor store, Mosby took her back to the apartment building. There Mosby had N.D. scrub a shower stall. He gave her a robe to change into, saying he would wash her clothes with his laundry. N.D. reported that Mosby, who had been drinking beer, had N.D. sit on his lap. N.D. reported that Mosby said, "I want to have a baby by you." But N.D. said she was not ready for that. After taking a shower, Mosby came and stood naked in front of N.D. He then put on some boxer shorts, sat on the bed and asked N.D. to comb his hair. Mosby then told her to lie down and asked if she "ever had a dicky before." He then put his finger in her vagina and touched her chest. N.D. began crying and Mosby slapped her, telling her to shut up, and tried to get the robe off. When she ran to unlock the door, Mosby told her to lock the door, or he was going to beat her. However, N.D. unlocked the door and ran screaming to the caretaker's apartment.

The caretaker testified that Mosby, wearing only boxer shorts, came running after N.D. and asked the caretaker if he believed N.D. N.D. told the caretaker to look at her, opened the robe, and said, "Look at what I've got on." Mosby kept closing the door to the caretaker's apartment, and the caretaker kept opening it. A next-door tenant came and said she had called the police. Mosby looked excited, jumped up and left the apartment building. The next-door tenant took N.D. to the tenant's apartment. N.D. threw up while there. The police let N.D. go home without being given a medical examination.

2. What is the responsibility of the police who arrive on the scene?
    a. Having made sure that physical violence has ceased, the police are responsible to advise the mother on her rights and responsibilities.

b. Police should require the caretaker to notify them if Mosby returns and again causes trouble.
c. Police must interview all witnesses, determine if there is a substantial basis for finding probable cause for criminal sexual conduct, procure an arrest warrant and go out to search for Mosby.
d. As no probable cause for arrest exists, mediate so that emotions can calm down, and help the mother and N.D. start talking about their situation by suggesting possible solutions and sources of assistance.
e. Instead of letting N.D. go home without being given a medical examination, medical assistance should be sought.

3. Why are cases of domestic violence or criminal sexual conduct difficult to prosecute?
   a. Evidence is usually insufficient to establish beyond a reasonable doubt that one is guilty of domestic violence or criminal sexual conduct in either the first or second degree.
   b. Testimony is insufficient to establish sexual penetration.
   c. Victims have tendencies, due to emotional trauma, to fabricate charges resulting in evidence of dubious credibility that, upon close examination, is filled with discrepancies.
   d. Victims are fearful of future retaliation and continue to hope the offender will change his ways.
   e. Adult males are more believable than children or women.
4. If N.D.'s mother obtains an order for protection (OFP),
   a. The police can arrest Mosby even if he had done nothing to N.D. or her mother *if* he comes to their home after having been ordered to stay away, and N.D.'s mother calls the police.
   b. Mosby can have no further contact with the victim at her home but can make contact only on neutral ground.
   c. Police can and should make an arrest only if additional assault or threat of bodily harm is made.
   d. A police officer will be assigned to protect N.D. for 24 hours.
   e. It will be voided if N.D.'s mother lets the abuser into her home or allows visitation with her children.

DISCUSSION QUESTIONS

1. Before reading this chapter, did you know about the extent of domestic violence? If yes, what have you read, seen or known about the problem?
2. Do you think parents have the right to discipline their teenage children? What do you think about hitting, slapping, yelling, restricting youths to their rooms, or imposing monetary penalties on dependent adolescent children?
3. Much controversy exists in the schools regarding punishing children through the use of physical force. What is your position on allowing school officials to use physical force against students?
4. What do school and workplace violence have in common?
5. Why should law enforcement be knowledgeable about workplace violence?
6. What has been your experience with bullying?
7. Does your local police department have an SRO? If so, in what schools does the officer work and what are some of the typical functions they perform within those schools?

GALE EMERGENCY SERVICES DATABASE ASSIGNMENTS

- Use the Gale Emergency Services database to help answer the Discussion Questions as appropriate.
- Use the Gale Emergency Services database to search one of these topics for an article to review: *stalking psychology*, *intimate partner*

violence, elder abuse, workplace violence, school shootings, bullying. Be prepared to share and discuss your outline with the class.

- Use the Gale Emergency Services database to read and outline one of the following articles:
  - "The School Shooter: One Community's Experience" by William P. Heck
  - "Addressing School Violence: Prevention, Planning and Practice" by Francis Q. Hoang
  - "Safe Harbor" by Steven C. Bahls and Jane Easter Bahls
  - "Murder at Work" by Jane McDonald
  - "Nonfatal Workplace Violence Risk Factors: Data from a Police Contact Sample" by Mario J. Scalora, David O'Neil Washington, Thomas Casady, and Sarah P. Newell
  - "Intimate Partner Violence in Pregnancy" by Tracey Fox-Bartels
  - "A Study on Cyberstalking: Understanding Investigative Hurdles" by Robert D'Ovidio and James Doyle
  - "Stalking-Investigation Strategies" by George E. Wattendorf
  - "Stalking the Stalker: A Profile of Offenders" by Robert A. Wood and Nona L. Wood
  - "Law Enforcement and the Elderly: A Concern for the 21st Century" by Lamar Jordan

REFERENCES

Albrecht, Leslie. "Elder Abuse Investigations: Police Response to Abuse, Neglect, Theft and Scams." *Law Officer Magazine*, April 2008, pp.44–46.

Banda, P. Solomon. "Columbine Changed How Police React in Rampages." *Washington Post*, April 19, 2009.

Baum, Katrina; Catalano, Shannan; Rand, Michael; and Rose, Kristina. *Stalking Victimization in the United States (NCVS).* Washington, DC: Bureau of Justice Statistics Special Report, January 2009. (NCJ 224527)

Beres, Judith. "Ensuring a Safe School Environment." *Community Policing Dispatch*, August 2008.

Burke, Tod W.; Owen, Stephen S.; and Jordan, Michael L. "Law Enforcement and Gay Domestic Violence in the United States and Venezuela." *ACJS Today*, May/June 2001, pp.1, 4–6.

Commission on Accreditation of Law Enforcement Agencies. *Standards for Law Enforcement Agencies*, 5th ed. Fairfax, VA: CALEA, 2006, updated 2008.

Crime in the United States 2007. Washington, DC: Federal Bureau of Investigation, 2007.

Daniels, Rhianna. "Spotlight on Mall Security." *Security Director News*, January 2008, pp.1, 15.

Dinkes, Rachel; Kemp, Jana; Baum, Katrina; and Snyder, Thomas D. *Indicators of School Crime and Safety: 2008.* Washington, DC: Bureau of Justice Statistics, April 2009.

Domestic Violence by Police Officers: A Policy of the IACP Police Response to Violence against Women Project. Arlington, VA: International Association of Chiefs of Police, July 2003.

Donald, Elizabeth. "Ill. Campus Begins Text 'e-lert' System." *PoliceOne.com News*, March 11, 2008.

"Elder Abuse." Washington, DC: National Institute of Justice, November 6, 2007.

"Elder Abuse: Frequently Asked Questions." Washington, DC: National Center on Elder Abuse, August 21, 2007.

Entwistle, Martha. "Security Leaders Turn to Training to Quell Violence." *Security Director News*, July 2008, p.17.

Gallo, Gina. "Airing Law Enforcement's Dirty Laundry." *Law Enforcement Technology*, June 2004, pp.132–137.

Gane, Scott R. "Avoiding Violent Outcomes." *Security Management*, June 2007, pp.138–140.

Golden, Jeffrey S. "De-Escalating Juvenile Aggression." *The Police Chief*, May 2004, pp.30–34.

Green, Ariana. "More States Use GPS to Track Abusers." *New York Times*, May 9, 2009.

Harne, Eric. "Terminations and Violence." *Security Management*, February 2008, pp.101–102.

Hill, Rodney. "Domestic Violence and the Reluctant Victim: Prosecuting without the Victim's Cooperation." *Subject to Debate*, March 2008, pp.3, 6.

Hirschel, David; Buzawa, Eve; Pattavina, April; Faggiani, Don; and Reuland, Melissa. *Explaining the Prevalence, Context, and Consequences of Dual Arrest in Intimate Partner Cases.* Washington, DC: U.S. Department of Justice, May 2007, Document No. 218355.

Howell, Ed. L.; Morin, Paul; Cell, Paul; Rush, Maureen S.; and Stormo, Vicky M. "College and University Policing." *The Police Chief*, March 2008, pp.20–30, 33.

"Intimate Partner Violence." Washington, DC: National Institute of Justice, October 24, 2007.

"Intimate Partner Violence: Definitions." Atlanta, GA: Centers for Disease Control and Prevention, October 21, 2008.

Jackson, Shelly; Feder, Lynette; Forde, David R; Davis, Robert C.; Maxwell, Christopher D.; and Taylor, Bruce G. *Batterer Intervention Programs: Where Do We Go from Here?* Washington, DC: National Institute of Justice, June 2003. (NCJ 195079)

Klein, Andrew R. *Practical Implications of Current Domestic Violence Research.* Washington, DC: U.S. Department of Justice, April 2008.

Labriola, Melissa; Rempel, Michael; and Davis, Robert C. "Do Batterer Programs Reduce Recidivism: Results from a Randomized Trial in the Bronx." *Justice Quarterly*, June 2008, pp.252–282.

Larson, Randall D. "The Shooting at Virginia Tech: The View from the 9-1-1 Center." *9-1-1 Magazine*, January/February 2008, pp.38–55.

Margolis, Gary J., and Healy, Steven J. "Campus Threat Assessment Training: A Multidisciplinary Approach." *Community Policing Dispatch*, April 2009.

McNamee, Catherine C., and Murphy, Mary B. "Elder Abuse in the United States." *NIJ Journal*, November 2006.

Moffitt, Terrie E.; Robins, Richard W.; and Caspi, Avshalom. "A Couples Analysis of Partner Abuse with Implications for Abuse-Prevention Policy." *Criminology and Public Policy*, November 2001, pp.5–36.

Morin, Paul. "Integration of Technology Assists Franklin & Marshall Campus Police." *The Police Chief*, March 2008, pp.20–24.

National Elder Abuse Incidence Study. Prepared by the National Center on Elder Abuse at the American Public Human Services Association in collaboration with Westat, Inc., September 1998. Accessed: http://www.aoa.gov/AoARoot/AoA_Programs/Elder_Rights/Elder_Abuse/docs/ABuseReport_Full.pdf

Neiman, S., and DeVoe, J. F. *Crime, Violence, Discipline, and Safety in U.S. Public Schools: Findings from 2007–08*. Washington, DC: National Center for Education Statistics, Institute of Education Sciences, U.S. Department of Education, 2009.

Noonan, James H., and Vavra, Malissa C. *The CARD Report—Crime in Schools and Colleges: A Study of Offenders and Arrestees Reported via National Incident-Based Reporting System Data*. Washington, DC: Federal Bureau of Investigation, October 2007.

Olweus, Dan. "Bullying among Schoolchildren: Intervention and Prevention." In *Aggression and Violence throughout the Lifespan*, edited by R. Peters, R. McMahon, and V. Quinsey. Newbury Park, CA: Sage Publications, 1992.

"OSHA Standards." Washington, DC: Occupational Safety & Health Administration, July 20, 2007.

Peak, Kenneth J.; Barthe, Emmanuel P.; and Barcia, Adam. "Campus Policing in America: A Twenty-Year Perspective." *Police Quarterly*, June 2008, pp.239–260.

Penrod, Gary S. "Operation CleanSWEEP: The School Safety Program that Earned an A+." *FBI Law Enforcement Bulletin*, October 2001, pp.20–23.

Peterson, Karen S. "When School Hurts." The Law Enforcement Trainer, July/August 2001, pp.17–19.

Petrocelli, Joseph. "Patrol Response to Elder Abuse." *Police*, February 2007a, pp.16–17.

Petrocelli, Joseph. "Patrol Response to Stalking." *Police*, August 2007b. pp.22–23.

Reaves, Brian. *Campus Law Enforcement, 2004–2005*. Washington, DC: Bureau of Justice Statistics Special Report, February 2008. (NCJ 2193740)

"Risk Factors for Elder Abuse." Washington, DC: National Center on Elder Abuse, August 21, 2007.

Rugala, Eugene A., and Isaacs, Arnold R. *Workplace Violence: Issues in Response*. Washington, DC: Federal Bureau of Investigation, 2004.

Sampson, Rana. *Domestic Violence*. Washington, DC: Office of Community Oriented Policing Service, Problem-Oriented Guides for Police, Problem-Specific Guides Series, Guide No. 45, January 2007.

Sampson, Rana. *Bullying in Schools*. Washington, DC: Office of Community Oriented Policing Service, Problem-Oriented Guides for Police, Problem-Specific Guides Series Problem-Oriented Guides for Police, Problem-Specific Guides Series, Guide No.12, January 2009.

Schuster, Beth. "Preventing, Preparing for Critical Incidents in Schools." Washington, DC: National Institute of Justice, March 27, 2009.

Schwartz, Martin D. and DeKeseredy, Walter S. "Interpersonal Violence against Women: The Role of Men." *Journal of Contemporary Criminal Justice*, May 2008, pp.178–185.

Sherman, Lawrence W. "Domestic Violence." In *Crime File Study Guide, National Institute of Justice*. Washington, DC: U.S. Government Printing Office, no date.

Sherman, Lawrence W., and Berk, Richard A. *The Minneapolis Domestic Violence Experiment*. Washington, DC: Police Foundation Reports, 1984.

"Stalking." Washington, DC: National Institute of Justice, October 25, 2007.

Stelter, Leischen. "Standard Brings Together Security and Human Resources to Address Workplace Violence." *Security Director News*, 2009a, p.2.

Stelter, Leischen. "Workplace Violence Tops 2009 Concerns." *Security Director News*, January 2009b, p.2.

The 2004 Survey of State Adult Protective Services: Abuse of Adults 60 Years of Age and Older. Washington, DC: Report to the National Center on Elder Abuse, Administration on Aging, February 2006.

Turner, Nancy, and Rizzo, Michael. "Smaller Agency Executives Benefit from the IACP's National Law Enforcement Leadership Institute on Violence against Women." *Big Ideas*, Winter 2009, pp.5–6.

"Understanding Intimate Partner Violence." Atlanta, GA: Centers for Disease Control and Prevention, Fact Sheet, 2006.

"Understanding Teen Dating Violence." Atlanta, GA: Centers for Disease Control and Prevention, Fact Sheet, 2008.

Velazquez, Sonia E.; Garcia, Michelle; and Joyce, Elizabeth. "Mobilizing a Community Response to Stalking: The Philadelphia Story." *The Police Chief*, January 2009, pp.30–37.

Violence against Women: Identifying Risk Factors. Washington, DC: NIJ Research in Brief, November 2004. (NCJ 197019)

"Workplace Violence." Washington, DC: Occupational Safety & Health Administration, July 20, 2007.

"Workplace Violence." Washington, DC: Occupational Safety & Health Administration, OSHA Fact Sheet, 2002.

Workplace Violence Prevention and Response Guideline. Alexandria, VA: American Society for Industrial Security, International, 2005.

CASE CITED

Thurman v. City of Torrington, 595 F. Supp. 1521 (D. Conn.) (1984)

CHAPTER 8

Emergency Situations

When Disaster Strikes

DO YOU KNOW . . .

- What emergencies a police department should plan for?
- What the four phases of an emergency usually are?
- What should be included in a predisaster plan?
- What FEMA's mission is?
- What two major difficulties police face during disasters?
- What the "pulse" of the government's response to an emergency is?
- What posttraumatic stress disorder is and why it is important to police officers who respond to emergency calls?
- Who should conduct a critical-incident stress debriefing and when, and who should attend?
- What emergency conditions require special considerations and contingency planning?
- What the prime consideration in any emergency is?
- What the two postemergency "killers" may be?
- What other emergencies contingency plans must be made for?
- What the policy of most police departments is regarding the handling of suspected bombs?
- How important the police are during a pandemic?

CAN YOU DEFINE?

critical-incident stress debriefing (CISD)
emergency operations center (EOC)
FEMA
firewall
hazmat incident
pandemic
posttraumatic stress disorder (PTSD)
predisaster plans
swatting (not flies)
triage

INTRODUCTION

Emergencies may be natural or caused by people. Natural emergencies include floods, fires, tornados, hurricanes, typhoons, tidal waves, landslides, avalanches, volcanic eruptions, extreme temperatures, blizzards, leaking natural gas and earthquakes. People-caused emergencies include civil disturbances; industrial and transportation accidents; hazardous-materials spills; water contamination; radiological and arson incidents; explosions; biological, chemical and nuclear attacks; and terrorist attacks. Emergencies may involve individuals, neighborhoods, communities, counties or even larger areas.

After a disaster, things seldom get back to what was normal before the crisis. Emergencies such as school shootings change not only the school, but the entire community. Since September 11, 2001, the United States itself has been forever changed. Terrorism and homeland security are the focus of Chapter 9. The devastation left in 2005 by Hurricane Katrina is still being felt today : "Neither the city nor its police department has yet recovered from the storm. Officers assigned to the three police districts and headquarters that were flooded still work out of trailers and the buildings have not yet been repaired" ("New Orleans Law Enforcement," 2007, p.4). Those departments not prepared to handle emergencies may fail to protect property and life and may face expensive, time-consuming lawsuits as well as adverse political decisions.

Police departments should have predisaster plans for those emergencies likely to occur within their jurisdictions.

This chapter begins with a look at the four phases of an emergency, followed by a discussion of predisaster plans and incident command systems. Next, the guidelines for dealing with emergencies are examined, including how to deal with posttraumatic stress following large-scale disasters and the importance of critical-incident stress debriefings. The chapter then focuses on special considerations in dealing with specific kinds of natural and person-made emergencies. The chapter concludes with a brief look at the relationship between emergency situations and community policing.

THE FOUR PHASES OF AN EMERGENCY

Most emergencies happen in four phases: (1) the *warning* period, (2) the *impact* period, (3) the *immediate reaction* after impact and (4) the period of *delayed response*.

Usually as much *warning* as possible is desirable. Sometimes, however, warnings are impossible, as is the case, for example, with earthquakes and train derailments. In addition, advanced warning might have an adverse effect on some individuals, who may panic and become totally helpless, as though the emergency had already occurred. Their panic may spread to others. For example, this reaction sometimes occurs following the posting of a hurricane warning when the eye of the storm is projected to make landfall over a heavily populated area.

During the *impact period*, when the emergency is actually happening, different people will react differently. Many will react with stunned inactivity, a paralysis of sorts, with people unable to act effectively. Others, fueled by adrenaline, may act with determination, purpose and strength. Some report going "on automatic pilot." The period *immediately following the disaster* is the most crucial from the standpoint of rescue operations. Effective performance can save property and lives. A *delayed response* may occur once the immediate danger is past. Those who were functioning effectively may cease to do so, and vice versa.

PREDISASTER PLANS

Every department should have a carefully formulated, periodically updated emergency plan, the contents of which will depend on the types of emergencies to be anticipated for a jurisdiction. Jurisdictions in the North, for example, would need to include responses for blizzards, while those along the coast would include hurricane responses. *Unanticipated* emergencies should, however, also be included. For example, blizzard-like conditions can paralyze southern states precisely because such weather is not expected there.

predisaster plans
Preparing for anticipated and unanticipated emergencies before they occur.

Predisaster plans should include

- What emergencies to prepare for.
- What needs to be done in advance (supplies on hand, agreements with other agencies, etc.).
- What specific functions must be performed during the emergency and who is responsible for performing them, including outside organizations and agencies that might help.
- How continuity of operations and governance will be maintained.
- How personnel and their families will be protected.
- How to keep the media informed.
- What steps need to be taken to restore order after the emergency is ended.
- How the response is to be evaluated.

The Department of Homeland Security (DHS) *Nationwide Plan Review Phase 2 Report* assessing the emergency plans of all states and territories of the United States found that a significant number of states (59 percent) and urban areas (65 percent) do not have sufficient continuity of operations (COOP) or continuity of government (COG) plans (Cashen, 2008, p.67). A COOP "facilitates the performance of essential functions during an emergency situation that disrupts normal operations, and it provides for the resumption of normal operations once the emergency has ended" (Cashen). A COG refers to preserving, maintaining or reconstituting civil governments' ability to carry out its constitutional responsibilities.

An emergency plan should also identify the levels of emergencies that might occur and the level of response required. Many jurisdictions use a three-level approach, with Level 1 including minor events that can usually be handled by on-duty personnel. A Level 2 event is a moderate-to-severe situation that requires aid from other agencies and perhaps other jurisdictions. A Level 3 event refers to catastrophes in which a state of emergency is proclaimed and county, state and even federal assistance is requested. In such instances, the National Guard is often called for help.

46.1

CALEA STANDARD 46.1 states, "The planning function is vital to the success of the critical incident plan. Preparation of a documented incident action plan is one of the first responsibilities of the planning function. This function is also responsible for collecting and evaluating information about the incident, the status of resources and anticipated equipment and manpower needs. The planning function is typically tasked with assembling information on current and alternative strategies, identifying needs for special resources, providing periodic predictions on incident potential, and preparing recommendations for release of resources." (*Standards for Law Enforcement Agencies*, 5th edition, 2006)

The plan should *not* be developed solely by top management, but also by those who would be involved in implementing it, including government officials, fire department personnel, health care personnel and the like. Including staff and dependent care in emergency plans is of "paramount importance" (Cashen, 2008, pp.69–70). Jurisdictions may seek assistance in developing their predisaster plan from the Federal Emergency Management Agency (FEMA).

The Federal Emergency Management Agency (FEMA)

FEMA

The Federal Emergency Management Agency, an independent federal agency charged with building and supporting the nation's emergency management system. Its mission is to reduce loss of life and property and protect our nation's critical infrastructure from all types of hazards through a comprehensive, risk-based, emergency management program of mitigation, preparedness, response and recovery.

FEMA, a federal agency founded in 1979 and charged with building and supporting the nation's emergency management system, is staffed by more than 2,600 full-time employees and nearly 4,000 standby disaster assistance employees available to help after disasters ("About FEMA," 2008). FEMA has replaced the American Red Cross as the agency in charge of coordinating the provision of shelter, food and first aid to disaster victims. This change in the federal emergency plan was partially the result of criticism regarding the lack of cooperation between FEMA and Red Cross leaders after Hurricane Katrina as well as a new law bolstering FEMA's role in providing emergency housing, human services, case management and financial help (Hsu, 2007, p.A08).

The mission of FEMA is to reduce loss of life and property and protect our nation's critical infrastructure from all types of hazards through a comprehensive, risk-based, emergency management program of mitigation, preparedness, response and recovery.

On March 1, 2003, FEMA became part of the Department of Homeland Security. It has three strategic goals:

1. Protect lives and prevent the loss of property from natural and technological hazards.
2. Reduce human suffering and enhance the recovery of communities after disaster strikes.
3. Ensure that the public is served in a timely and efficient manner (FEMA Web site).

FEMA recommends communities address the following functions in disaster plans: (1) communication, (2) transportation, (3) public works, (4) firefighting, (5) intelligence efforts to assess damage, (6) mass care for those people displaced from their homes, (7) resource support (contracting for the labor needed to assist in a disaster), (8) health and medical, (9) search and rescue, (10) hazardous materials, (11) food or feeding and (12) energy. Communications should be the number one priority.

FEMA has developed a document, *Are You Ready? An In-Depth Guide to Citizen Preparedness* (2008), that provides the public with the most current disaster preparedness information available, including a step-by-step approach on being informed about local emergency plans, identifying hazards that affect their area, and how to develop and maintain an emergency communication plan and disaster supplies kit. The guide also includes evacuation information, how to locate emergency public shelters, what to do about pets and information specific to people with disabilities. For first responders, Bradford (2008, p.24) points out, "If you are going to be comfortable doing your job, you will need to know that they [your family members and neighbors] can take care of themselves during the initial hours of an emergency. You will need a well thought out plan and *they* will have to be able to carry it out! They will need accessible supplies and tools and they will have to know how to utilize them." The FEMA guide is one resource for learning how to accomplish this.

The Emergency Management Assistance Compact (EMAC)

The Emergency Management Assistance Compact (EMAC) is a congressionally ratified organization managed by the National Emergency Managers Association to provide form and structure to interstate mutual aid: "Through EMAC a state affected by disaster can request and receive assistance from other member states quickly and efficiently. . . . In 2005 EMAC transferred over 46,000 resources into the Gulf Coast states after Hurricanes Katrina and Rita" (Henninger and Bullock, 2008, p.42).

Historically, many police departments have placed low priority on emergency management, believing that mass disasters were unlikely to happen in their jurisdictions. However, this is no longer realistic. In our post–9/11 society, every agency should have a plan for responding to an emergency and that plan should be practiced. Agencies with high-risk terrorist attack locations within their jurisdiction additionally need to address emergency preparedness for their own communities and devise specific emergency action plans (EAPs) for possible incidents at such locations and facilities. Federal grants are available to help fund the training and tools needed to properly address emergency response planning in locations that contain high-risk areas.

Lack of communication and coordination are the major problems during disasters.

Communication and Coordination

Whether by voice or through data transmissions, interoperable communications can mean the difference between life and death for citizens and first responders, as discussed in Chapter 2. A key to effective communication and coordination is found in the *National Incident Management System* (2004) developed by the DHS.

The National Incident Management System (NIMS) The *National Incident Management System* (2004, p.2) states,

> While most incidents are generally handled on a daily basis by a single jurisdiction at the local level, there are important instances in which successful domestic incident management operations depend on the involvement of multiple jurisdictions, functional agencies, and emergency responder disciplines. . . . The NIMS uses a systems approach to integrate the best of existing processes and methods into a unified national framework for incident management. This framework forms the basis for interoperability and compatibility that will, in turn, enable a diverse set of public and private organizations to conduct well-integrated and effective incident management operations. . . . The NIMS is based on an appropriate balance of flexibility and standardization.

NIMS, which is linked to the National Response Plan, "provides a vital organizational method for the public and private sectors to coordinate in the event of an emergency, whether manmade or natural" (Moore, 2007, p.28). At the heart of NIMS is the Incident Command System (ICS), which is a vital tool in designating clear roles and responsibilities for any type of disaster (Moore, p.32).

46.1 CALEA STANDARD 46.1, the critical incident section, follows the NIMS, noting, "The Incident Command System (ICS) has proven very effective in federal and fire services emergencies over the past two decades. This system permits a clear point of control and can be expanded or contracted with ease to escalating or diminishing situations. . . . With responders using a common language and standardized procedures, they will all share a common focus, and will be able to place full emphasis on incident management when a critical incident occurs." (*Standards for Law Enforcement Agencies*, 5th edition, 2006)

Mulholland (2007, p.12) explains, "NIMS provides principles to organize incident response in a uniform manner (the Incident Command System), collect and share information during an incident (multiagency coordination systems) and notify the public before and during an incident (public information systems)." The Federal Communications Commission (FCC) is required by the 2006 Warning Alert and Response Network Act to develop ways to alert the public about emergencies. In April 2008, federal regulators approved a plan creating a nationwide emergency alert system using text messages delivered to cell phone, a service that could be in place by 2010 ("Emergency Text Alerts to

Cell Phones Approved," 2009, p.62). Advances are also being made in the ability of agencies to communicate with all those involved in an emergency. One such advance is a versatile communications super-command center.

The NOMAD Incident Command Platform Ross (2009, p.68) asserts, "Cross-breed a Hummer H2 with a top-of-the-line laptop, add a satellite phone, fax machine, digital printer and broadband Internet access, and you can begin to picture the NOMAD's capabilities and ruggedness. This unit is a shining example of the future of crisis communication equipment for first responders." Measuring roughly 22 × 18 × 10 inches and weighing 56 pounds, NOMAD is an expandable kit of critical tools and technology to support mobile communication needs and can be deployed by a single user in less than 5 minutes. Capabilities and features of the NOMAD include the ability to support hundreds of users over a large geographic area; a combination of technology, durability and portability that allows it to be deployed to any part of the country in minutes; being small enough and light enough to haul in fire trucks or in the back of police cruisers; a power supply able to run up to 24 hours of mission support on a single charge; and having passed rigorous field testing (Ross, pp.68–70). The NOMAD is currently deployed to every FEMA region across the country and is used in other countries as well (Ross, p.70). In 2007, NOMADS were deployed to California to help battle the blazing wildfires.

Planning for Evacuation

In any disaster requiring evacuation, traffic control becomes a major challenge. The National Incident Management Coalition (NIMC) is an alliance representing the U.S. government, motorist clubs, the trucking industry and highway safety organizations whose purpose is to spread the "Incident Management" idea throughout the country. Its incident management approach has four parts: detection, response, clearance and recovery.

Planning to Protect Computers

Virus protection software and firewalls should be in place to protect against accidental or intentional sabotage of computers and networks. A **firewall** is a security measure intended to prevent unauthorized Internet users from accessing private networks connected to the Internet.

firewall
A security measure intended to prevent unauthorized Internet users from accessing private networks connected to the Internet.

A good intrusion-detection system can analyze network traffic for intrusions and intrusion attempts as well as examine events and compare them to patterns identified as indicators of misuse. Finally, risks can be reduced by having duplicate back-ups or a fully redundant communications system.

Planning to Interact with the Media

"During a critical incident requiring police action, one of the last things the police think about is public perception. All critical incidents have the potential to be a world-watched event, forcing us to have to rely on the media to help shape the public's perception of our actions. Unfortunately in the media world, perception equals reality" (Donlon-Cotton, 2007, p.24).

Critical incidents can be classified as either expected or unexpected. Officers should know how to anticipate the likely media coverage in these two very different types of situations and how they might respond to media questions (Donlon-Cotton, 2007, pp.24–28). For example, during a planned event such as a rock concert or a sports competition in which things get out of hand, "your agency will be up against the expectation of perfection, which is almost certainly impossible to attain" (Donlon-Cotton). Officers should be prepared to answer "why" questions during the incident: "Why are you taking that young girl into custody?" A possible answer is, "Just because this is an atypical day in our community doesn't mean we stop upholding the laws." "Why are you just standing around and letting these people run amok?" A possible answer is, "At this point, we're concentrating on keeping the law-abiding citizens safe." Also with a planned event that gets out of control, the media and public review will be harsher after the event, so officers should be prepared for the media to be in attack mode. Donlon-Cotton recommends going on the offense and holding a post-event press conference showing what went right as well as acknowledging any shortcomings and how they will be dealt with in the future.

During an unexpected incident such as a natural disaster, the media will be concerned with the quality of the officers' immediate and initial actions. In most disasters, the media are not officially notified and have to "go on the prowl for information. This results in automatically placing the law enforcement agency on the defensive and immediately sets the stage for a media disaster" (Donlon-Cotton, 2007, p.24). First responders need to respond to the media during such incidents rather than referring them to someone else or saying they can't take time to talk. Donlon-Cotton suggests responses such as, "The rescue effort is going well, and all officers are doing their best. Our primary concern is making sure everyone is safe, and then we'll focus on what comes next."

An example of an unexpected incident was the crash of US Air flight 1549 into the Hudson River on January 15, 2009. Rosenthal (2009, p.6) uses the way Doug Parker, the company's CEO, handled the media relations portion of that crisis:

- Rule #1: Deal with the media right now! Never ignore the media or refuse any comment because you don't have all the facts. Do that and you lose control of your story and lose essential credibility as well. You should deliver your first statement to the media within two hours after the crisis hits, and that's exactly what US Airways' Parker did.
- Rule #2: Be empathetic. Express your concern about the incident, your caring for the victims/citizens/community, and your commitment to making things right. Parker expressed his concern for the passengers and announced the airline had already set up a response team and a hotline to help them and their families.
- Rule #3: Always deal in facts and information. Tell what you know, not what you think you know . . . Give the media what you can early on; then follow up with frequent updates. Never speculate. Parker not only refused to speculate, in his first statement he urged the media to avoid speculation, too.[1]

[1]Reprinted with permission of author Rick Rosenthal, President, RAR Communications, Inc.

The needs of officers are met by an efficient and effective emergency operations center. Here officials from various law enforcement agencies work in the New York Police Department Emergency Operations Center preparing for the Republican National Convention held in New York City in August 2004. © Mary Altaffer/Pool/Reuters/CORBIS

Police and media representatives should meet and draw up agreements that respect the presses' First Amendment right to freedom of the press, but also the Sixth Amendment rights of others to privacy and law enforcement's need for safety and successful management of critical incidents. Effective message management must be built on mutual trust that can be built over time for the price of a cup of coffee, an occasional lunch and visits to the local media offices. But remember, it is in the department's best interest to work *with* the media. If you do not provide them with something, they will fill in the gaps themselves. If dealt with correctly, the media can be a great asset to the police.

THE EMERGENCY OPERATIONS OR COMMUNICATIONS CENTER

During times of disaster, it is imperative that government continues to function in a coordinated way. A key to effective emergency management is the emergency operations or communications center (EOC): "The communications center is the heart and soul of an agency's operations" (Moore, 2009, p.10).

The **emergency operations center** (**EOC**), the location from which personnel operate during a natural disaster or other type of emergency, is the "pulse" of the government's response to an emergency and helps reduce the problems of lack of communication and coordination.

emergency operations center (EOC)
The location from which personnel operate during a natural disaster or other type of emergency.

Sometimes the incident will dictate the location of such a center. Often an existing site in a government building works well. Ideally, the center is located close to police, fire and government officials. Mobile EOCs—typically large recreational-type vehicles or buses converted and equipped with the necessary tools and devices—may also be available.

Dispatchers are key people in the communications center, taking calls and sending officers to respond. One problem they face is a phenomenon called **swatting**, an emerging trend by pranksters involving communication centers in which a false report is filed, via Internet, to the emergency dispatch center to deploy SWAT teams to a residence where the occupants are oblivious to the situation (Garrett, 2009, p.31). The potential for violence, injury and death is "huge" with such calls, and some suggest the offense not be treated as a prank, a misdemeanor, but rather that perpetrators be charged with filing a false report as well as what they caused SWAT team members to do: assault with a deadly weapon and false imprisonment of the innocent victims (Garrett, p.27).

swatting
An emerging trend by pranksters involving communication centers in which a false report is filed, via Internet, to the emergency dispatch center in order to deploy SWAT teams to a residence where the occupants are oblivious to the situation.

GUIDELINES FOR DEALING WITH EMERGENCIES

Every emergency will present a unique challenge to responding officers. Nonetheless, several guidelines can help ensure the most effective response possible at each phase of the disaster.

Before the Emergency

- Be prepared. Be proactive. Anticipate the immediate problems and the personnel needed to deal with them.
- Identify the equipment and resources required, and make certain they are either available or immediately accessible. To deal with disasters, departments should have, at minimum, lighted traffic batons, barricades, reflective signs for vehicles, safety vests for traffic officers and special vehicle-mounted lights and sirens. First aid kits, gloves and blankets are also imperative. It is recommended departments have ready access to gas masks and hazardous materials (hazmat) suits, also.
- Establish and maintain good relationships with the media. They are among the first on the scene of emergencies and have a job to do. They can be invaluable in getting messages out to the general public and keeping panic to a minimum. They can also be a terrific liability if a good relationship does not exist.
- Establish a system so that police officers can know that their own families are safe during an emergency. As discussed previously, first responders must be confident their own families—their first priority—are being taken care of before they can fulfill their sense of duty to other citizens and the community at large.

During the Emergency

- Take time to assess the situation. Do not make the situation worse by acting without thinking.
- Make saving lives a top priority. Establish a **triage** area where surviving victims can be separated according to the severity of their injuries. Those with critical medical needs should be tended to immediately and, once

triage
Prioritizing, sorting out by degree of seriousness, as in medical emergencies.

stabilized, transported to medical facilities. A morgue area for those who have died in the crisis should also be established.

- Do not broadcast a general call for help. Carefully but quickly assess what is needed and call for that.
- Keep the channels of communication open and the information flowing as required to those who need it.
- Keep as many options open as possible. Avoid "either/or" thinking that limits problem solving.
- Do not get sidetracked by personal, individual requests for help but, rather, focus on the big picture, routing individual requests to the appropriate source of assistance.
- Accept the fact that the police cannot do everything. The emergency manager must prioritize and delegate responsibilities quickly. Mistakes will probably happen.
- Involve key personnel as rapidly as possible. Do not let other agencies shirk their responsibilities.
- Keep top city officials fully informed of progress and problems.
- Ensure that someone is tending to normal business.

After the Emergency

- Get back to "normal" as soon as possible, but sometimes this just doesn't happen.
- Expect that victims of the disaster or emergency may have very emotional reactions, including posttraumatic stress disorder. This is also true of the officers who have dealt with the disaster or emergency.
- Also expect that lawyers will get into it. *Document* everything that was done.

Evaluate the response after the situation has returned to normal. Look upon "mistakes" as the "least effective alternatives" as well as learning opportunities. Modify emergency-preparedness plans as needed based on what has been learned.

Posttraumatic Stress after Large-Scale Disasters According to the American Psychiatric Association, **posttraumatic stress disorder (PTSD)** refers to the development of characteristic symptoms following a psychologically traumatic event generally outside the range of human experience. The symptoms include

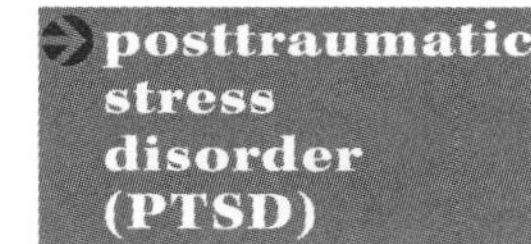

A reaction to a violent event that evokes intense fear, terror and helplessness; a debilitating stressful reaction to a trauma that may last for months or years. It can be experienced not only by victims, but also by those who help the victims.

- Re-experiencing the event, either while awake or in recurrent dreams.
- Detachment and lack of involvement, diminished interest in formerly important activities, detachment from other people.
- At least two other of the following symptoms not present before the event:
    - Hyper-alertness.
    - Sleep disturbance.
    - Guilt about surviving when others did not.
    - Memory impairment or trouble concentrating.
    - Avoiding activities that remind the person of the event.

Many disaster victims experience PTSD, but so do many of those involved in helping them, especially if deaths have been particularly gruesome or have involved children. Police officers *are* susceptible to PTSD and should have support groups available to them.

Posttraumatic stress disorder (PTSD) is a debilitating stressful reaction to a traumatic event; PTSD may last for months or years. It can be experienced by those who help the victims, as well as by the victims.

Jetmore (2008, pp.63–64) cautions, "The emotional exhaustion resulting from continuous exposure to stress related trauma can ultimately cause an officer to change from a positive, service-oriented, care-giving person to one who is uncaring, negative and callous."

The likelihood that PTSD will occur in responding police officers can be reduced by having contingency plans that require them to mentally rehearse probable disaster situations, thus lowering their anxiety. It can be reduced further by practicing these plans, assigning each officer a specific task, maintaining order during the emergency, requiring that officers get some break periods during the emergency if it lasts longer than 10 hours and having a thorough debriefing following the emergency.

The After-Action Report An after-action report (AAR) should detail what happened, why it happened and how it can be done better: "An AAR is about learning, not about finger pointing or even fixing a problem. Conducting AARs should focus on improving a process, policy and/or procedure" (Cashen, 2008, p.71).

The Critical-Incident Stress Debriefing An important consideration following a disaster is to conduct a **critical-incident stress debriefing (CISD)**, proven to be a powerful tool in preventing posttraumatic stress disorder.

critical-incident stress debriefing (CISD)
Officers who experience a critical incident, such as a mass disaster or large accident with multiple deaths, are brought together as a group for psychological debriefing soon after the event.

A CISD should be conducted by a professional mental health practitioner 24 to 48 hours after the incident and should be mandatory for all personnel involved in the incident.

One conducted before 24 hours has passed is likely to be ineffective because the full impact may not yet be felt. These debriefings should be mandatory to avoid anyone's feeling it is not macho to attend. The FEMA search and rescue teams located throughout the country are trained to do debriefing if an agency needs assistance in this area.

Identifying Fatalities A comprehensive disaster plan should include how fatalities will be identified. Help in identifying fatalities is available through the FBI Identification Division's Disaster Squad, which has aided in such disasters as the volcanic eruption of Mount St. Helens, in the 1978 mass murder-suicides at Jonestown, Guyana, and in the 1986 space shuttle

Increasing numbers of police departments are going to new technology, such as push-to-talk cellular phones, to overcome the problem of "dead spots" that hilly terrain and other types of obstructions can pose to the more common 800 MHz police radios. This ability to communicate in locations with spotty radio coverage is especially critical during emergencies.
© AP Images/Chris Gardner

explosion. It also provided assistance during Operation Desert Storm. Its free identification services are available 24 hours per day. In addition to cost-free fatality identification services offered by the Disaster Squad, the FBI provides assistance to law enforcement and civic agencies in formulating emergency response plans.

Restoring Order When emergencies have been controlled and their urgency has diminished, police services are still needed. The constant threat of looting and malicious damage will continue until the area again becomes functional and the residents return to their homes or emergency workers are no longer present. When extra police are required following an incident, supervisors should conduct a gradual phase-out rather than allowing an abrupt return to normal duty.

Also, following any emergency situation, there is usually a steady flow of curiosity seekers that will tend to taper off as interest diminishes and the area returns to normal. This process may take several hours, days or weeks, depending on the emergency's magnitude. Some emergencies are so severe they are declared disasters.

NATURAL DISASTERS

Just as general guidelines can be specified for emergencies, general guidelines and considerations can be made in advance for specific kinds of natural emergencies, reducing the loss of property and lives.

In addition to general predisaster plans, contingency plans should be made for such natural disasters as floods, explosions, fires, cyclones and earthquakes. In all such emergencies, saving lives is top priority.

Floods

A flood, although damaging and usually predictable, demands a coordinated response and implementation of a previously thought-out plan. Normally, police will assist residents and merchants in the affected areas to evacuate their homes and their businesses. As soon as a police department receives notice of an impending flood, the regular and reserve officers are usually called to duty. In some instances, they may be put on alert or on standby in case they are needed.

During an evacuation and while the emergency is in progress, the police must seal off the affected area to prevent looting and vandalism. Special passes can be issued to residents who have legitimate business in the area. All others not living or having business in the flood area should be excluded.

Explosions

Explosions may be accidental or purposeful. Accidental explosions may result from earthquakes, natural fires, plane or train crashes or natural gas leaks. Purposeful explosions include those caused by arsonists, discussed later in the chapter, and by terrorists, discussed in Chapter 9. Department policies and procedures should be developed for dealing with all types of explosions.

Fires

Fires are usually the fire department's primary responsibility, although some police departments have a combined public safety service. Such departments have trained officers to assist firefighters. One police responsibility is to protect firefighters from harassment. Some sections of cities are plagued with spectators who taunt firefighters and try to disrupt firefighting. In these cases, police officers must protect firefighters and also control spectators, protect fire equipment and regulate traffic drawn to the scene.

When the Bandelier National Park Service started a "controlled burn" west of Los Alamos, New Mexico, in 2000, high winds spread the fire eastward, destroying structures in Los Alamos and threatening the Los Alamos National Laboratory. The area's 18,500 residents were evacuated without a single death or serious injury. The police department had long had a plan in place because of the sensitivity of the work at the National Laboratory, which conducts classified nuclear weapons development.

Utility agencies shut off gas and water. A reverse 911 system notified many residents by telephone, delivering instructions on the evacuation. The local radio station switched to 24-hour coverage of the evacuation, and loudspeaker announcements from emergency vehicles reached residents who had not heard the news. To prevent looting, National Guard personnel patrolled the town along with state and local police. In addition, the police held two press briefings a day to accommodate the hundreds of media people on the scene.

Cyclones: Hurricanes and Tornados

In strict meteorological terminology, a cyclone is an area of low atmospheric pressure surrounded by a wind system blowing, in the Northern Hemisphere, in a counterclockwise direction. When this weather system develops over water, it is called a hurricane or, in the western Pacific, a typhoon. A hurricane is a very strong tropical cyclone involving heavy rains and sustained winds stronger than 74 miles per hour (mph). It may also be accompanied by a strong storm surge, with large waves causing extensive damage to coastal property and near-shore structures.

Cyclones occurring over land are tornados—dark, funnel-shaped clouds containing violently rotating air that twists, rises and falls, and, where it reaches the earth, causes great destruction. A tornado's diameter can range from a few feet to over a mile, with winds circulating between 200 and 300 mph. The length of a tornado's path on the ground varies from under a mile to several hundred miles. In an average year in the United States, some 800 tornadoes injure more than a thousand people. Again, preparedness is the key to limiting the amount of destruction. Tornado warning systems are an integral part of preparedness, as is education of the public about steps to take, where to seek shelter and the like.

Many of the emergencies already discussed may also occur during a hurricane or tornado, including flooding, fires and explosions, accompanied by looting and vandalism. In addition to the tragic loss of life and damage to property, those responding to the disaster may face communication and mobility problems. Regular phone lines may be down, two-way radio communications may be unavailable because of damaged repeaters, and cellular communications networks may be overwhelmed by ongoing use. Getting around may be difficult because road signs and other landmarks may be gone, street lights may be out, and many roads may be blocked by such obstacles as fallen trees, live utility wire and other debris. Some low areas may be flooded and impassable. Highways and other main travel arteries may become gridlocked during the evacuation efforts, and debris scattered across roadways may cause numerous flat tires and other traffic mishaps, involving citizens and first responders.

Eventually, things will come under control, but time, and perhaps lives, may be saved if a predisaster plan is in place. Citizens should be educated about the steps to take, such as evacuating if advised to do so, boarding up windows or closing shutters if not evacuating, and having ample potable water and flashlights or candles available.

In the aftermath of such natural disasters, many departments find their most significant problem is not, as might be expected, the cleanup but rather the quick depletion of their yearly overtime budgets and completion of the massive amount of paperwork required by FEMA so the jurisdiction can be reimbursed for expenses resulting from the disaster.

Postemergency "killers" may be overruns in overtime and excessive paperwork.

Earthquakes

Although floods and hurricanes usually can be predicted, earthquakes strike with no warning. Areas in which earthquakes are likely to occur must have preestablished plans to deal with such emergencies. Included within these plans should be measures to deal with collapsed buildings and bridges, downed power lines, fires, explosions, injuries and deaths. As in other kinds of emergencies, traffic problems, vandalism and looting must also be anticipated.

ACCIDENTAL OR INTENTIONAL EMERGENCIES

Jurisdictions must also be prepared for catastrophic accidents and deliberate acts that can lead to loss of life or injury and destruction of property.

Contingency plans also must be made for other emergencies such as bridge collapses, plane crashes, hazardous materials spills, bomb threats, actual bombings and terrorist attacks involving chemical, biological and nuclear weapons of mass destruction. Regardless of the cause, saving lives is the top priority in all such emergencies.

Our country's aging and, in many cases, ailing infrastructure poses a growing danger to the public. For example, a comprehensive assessment of the nation's 600,000 bridges confirmed that many of them are in serious trouble: "In almost all cases, structurally deficient bridges remain operational. They may have reduced weight limits posted, but they generally stay open. The I-35W had a structurally deficient rating, and short-term repairs were being done at the time of the collapse" (Eggers, 2007, p.94).

The collapse of the I-35W bridge over the Mississippi River in Minneapolis, Minnesota, occurred at 6:05 P.M., August 1, 2007, during rush hour, leaving 13 people dead and more than 100 injured, dozens critically. Rich Stanek, born in the Minneapolis area, who had served as the state's commissioner of public safety and director of homeland security previously and, at the time of the collapse, was serving as the county's sheriff, oversaw the crisis, testing his department's personnel and training as well as testing skills derived from NIMS training. Moore (2008, p.9) says, "It would take the full resources of the Hennepin County Sheriff's Office and the resources of 103 additional agencies, most notably the Minneapolis police and fire departments, to complete the rescue and recovery of victims and their vehicles." She (p.10) adds, "It took three weeks and involved multiple agencies, importation of ultra-high-tech equipment, and respectful handling of information for both the press and the families of those killed." The remarkable response of all responding was praised throughout the country.

Stanek said a number of lessons were learned from the tragedy. His number 1 lesson: Expect the unexpected. The second lesson: Plan, train and prepare incessantly. He notes that they had worked and trained with many of the 100-plus law enforcement agencies that came to assist previously ("Minneapolis Area Police Officials," 2007, pp.1, 4–5).

Plane Crashes

Although often accidental, plane crashes may also occur at the hands of terrorists in their effort to cause death and fear, as discussed in the next chapter. Two accidental crashes—the 1996 crash of TWA Flight 800 off Long Island into the Atlantic and the November 2001 crash of American Airlines Flight 587 into a residential neighborhood in Queens, New York—and the terrorist hijacking and subsequent crash of United Flight 93 into a rural Pennsylvania field on September 11, 2001, highlight the extreme destruction and tragedy such an emergency can cause. A plane crash carries very heavy responsibilities because loss of life usually is associated with the crash. Upon notification of a plane crash, the police department must notify the Federal Aviation Administration (FAA), which has jurisdiction over and responsibility for such investigations. The National Transportation Safety Board (NTSB) also has jurisdiction if a death is involved. In the case of a military aircraft, the military service involved must be notified. The security of the aircraft and its scattered parts then become the responsibility of the military police.

The initial responsibility of the police department is to seal off the area surrounding any parts that may have been separated from the plane. Frequently, other jurisdictions may become involved, as parts of the aircraft may be found several blocks or miles away from the main crash site. If large numbers of people are injured, the ambulance services and the fire department rescue units may become overburdened. When this occurs, the hospital may send several of its staff members to the scene to assist. Police officers must provide easy access to and from the scene for those hospital personnel.

Hazardous Materials (Hazmat) Incidents

Some emergencies to which police are called may involve hazardous materials—known as a **hazmat incident**—and other dangerous goods: derailed trains, overturned chemical-laden tank trucks, incidents at industrial plants or other scenes where toxic substances are present. Modes of transportation of hazardous materials include truck, rail, pipeline, water and air, and each mode presents its own unique challenges to hazmat responders.

hazmat incident
An incident involving hazardous materials.

The U.S. Department of Transportation reports that 13,453 hazmat incidents have occurred in the past decade, with 1,274 occurring in 2008 ("Hazardous Materials Safety," 2008). Most hazmat incidents were caused by human error, followed by dropping, improper preparation for transportation and a defective component or device. For the past decade, the vast majority of incidents occurred on a highway, as did the bulk of fatalities and injuries. In addition, the greatest amount of damage sustained occurred on our highways.

An example of an accidental hazmat emergency was the derailment in North Dakota of a train with four cars carrying anhydrous ammonia that leaked following the crash. One person died and hundreds were evacuated, with many requiring hospitalization.

Hazmat events may also be intentional, such as the dispersal of anthrax using the U.S. mail system. The law enforcement response to such deliberate releases involves actions directed toward the hazmat incident itself and toward the follow-up criminal investigation.

Whatever the origin, the increasing number of hazardous materials in commercial use has significantly raised the likelihood of law enforcement officers being called to a spill, and they must be trained to respond appropriately. Some law enforcement agencies have their own hazmat teams, but others have a regional team.

Short of any specialized training, officers should know some basic guidelines for responding to hazmat emergencies. When hazardous cargo is being transported, federal law requires the haulers to carry a manifest specifically detailing what they are carrying, how much and the shipment destination. Many manifests also provide a material safety data sheet (MSDS), with information on handling, containing and neutralizing the hazardous materials or dangerous goods in the event of a spill, leak or other inadvertent release. Haulers are also required to display a colored placard and symbol identifying the hazardous nature of their shipment. The most familiar warnings are the colored placards on the sides and rear of the trailer or shipping container, generally visible from a greater distance than the symbol, thereby, allowing first responders to tailor their approach accordingly. The standard placard colors and what they represent are

- Flammable—red
- Corrosive—black and white
- Explosive—orange
- Poison—black and white
- Nonflammable gas—green
- Oxidizer—yellow

Officers should have binoculars in their vehicles so they can read, from a safe distance, the placards and markings on trucks or railroad cars involved in accidents. Because the danger of explosion, fire or toxic fumes is always present, officers should stay as far away as possible but also try to identify what the truck or railroad car was transporting.

General safety precautions and other basic guidelines for first responders to a hazmat accident scene include

- Respond upwind and upgrade, when possible, and anticipate changes in wind direction.
- Park vehicles heading away from the incident, then approach on foot.
- The first priority is to isolate and secure the scene. Use barrier tape, traffic cones or barricades, *not* flares.
- Keep contaminated, ill or injured people away from others.
- If necessary, initiate an evacuation.
- Do not eat, drink or smoke at any hazardous materials incident.
- Do not touch any container, and avoid contact with liquids or fumes.
- Treat all hazardous materials as if they were toxic or explosive. Always consider the possibility of more than one hazard being present.
- Latex (surgical type) and leather gloves are *not* adequate protection against most hazardous materials.
- Keep your dispatcher informed of any/all actions you take at the scene.
- Be cautious about keying up the microphone on your handheld radio or squad radio because the transmission might ignite chemicals present in the air.

A useful resource is the Chemical Transportation Emergency Center (CHEMTREC), established in 1971 by the chemical industry as a public service hotline for firefighters, law enforcement and other emergency responders. An integral part of the American Chemistry Council, CHEMTREC maintains a state-of-the-art communication center and a high-end MSDS document storage and retrieval system, containing nearly 2.8 million MSDSs. These documents enable CHEMTREC to supply information on a product's known hazards and what to do and not do in case of a spill, a fire or exposure to the substance.

CHEMTREC can also provide immediate advice by telephone for the on-scene commander at a hazmat emergency. Its personnel will promptly contact the shipper of the hazardous material(s) involved in the incident for detailed assistance and relay an appropriate response back to the on-scene incident commander. In some situations, a segment of the chemical industry or even a company may have a hazmat team that will respond. CHEMTREC can alert such teams if they exist. CHEMTREC's 24-hour Emergency Call Center, located in Arlington, Virginia, may be accessed toll-free by first responders.

Bombs and Bomb Threats

Any business or establishment can be the victim of a bomb threat or bombing. Among the most common targets are airlines, banks, educational institutions, government buildings, hospitals, industrial complexes, military installations, office buildings and utilities. According to the Bureau of Alcohol, Tobacco, Firearms and Explosives (ATF), the top three motivating factors for bombings are vandalism, revenge and protest.

The February 26, 1993, bombing of the World Trade Center in New York, which killed six and injured more than a thousand, and the April 19, 1995, bombing of the Alfred P. Murrah Federal Building in Oklahoma City, which left 169 people dead and nearly 500 injured, were not just disasters resulting in loss of life but were also major crime scenes—the sites of the mass murders of innocent civilians.

Although most law enforcement officers will never encounter an actual bomb, it is probable that they will have to deal with suspicious packages and bomb threats. Even though 98 percent of bomb threats are hoaxes, the threats are costly and emotionally charged, and may be dangerous if people panic. Having a well-established procedure to handle a bomb-threat call is imperative. It should be written, kept in plain view of those who answer the phone, and practiced. If a threat is received, the person who receives it should know exactly what to do. Receivers of bomb threats should

- Keep the caller talking as long as possible.
- Try to learn as much as possible about the bomb, especially when it will go off and where it is located.
- Try to determine the caller's sex, age, accent and speech pattern, and whether he or she is drunk or drugged.
- Listen for any background noises.
- Immediately notify the appropriate person(s) of the call.

Some organizations have forms such as that shown in Figure 8.1 to be completed by any individual who receives a telephoned bomb threat. It is critical that individuals who answer telephones know who to report a bomb threat to. This person then determines what action to take. Alternatives include ignoring

BOMB THREAT INSTRUCTIONS

Place this card under your telephone

Questions to ask:
1. *When is the bomb going to explode?*
2. *Where is it right now?*
3. *What does it look like?*
4. *What kind of bomb is it?*
5. *What will cause it to explode?*
6. *Did you place the bomb?*
7. *Why?*
8. *What is your address?*
9. *What is your name?*

Exact wording of the threat:

____
____
____
____
____
____

Sex of caller: __________ Race: __________
Age: __________ Length of call: __________

Additional information on reverse.

Number at which call is received:
Time: __________ Date: __/__/__

Caller's Voice:
☐ Loud ☐ Soft ☐ High ☐ Deep
☐ Intoxicated ☐ Disguised ☐ Calm ☐ Angry
☐ Fast ☐ Slow ☐ Stutter ☐ Nasal
☐ Distinct ☐ Slurred ☐ Accent (*type:* ________)

Other Characteristics: ______________________
____

If voice is familiar, who did it sound like? __________

Background Sounds:
☐ Voices ☐ Quiet ☐ Animals
☐ Street Traffic ☐ Office Machinery ☐ Airplanes
☐ Trains ☐ Factory Machinery ☐ Music
Other: ______________________

Threat Language:
☐ Foul ☐ Well spoken (educated)
☐ Taped ☐ Message read by threat-maker
☐ Irrational ☐ Incoherent

Remarks: ______________________
____
____

Report call immediately to: __________
Phone number: __________

Date: __/__/__
Name: __________
Position: __________
Phone Number: __________

FIGURE 8.1 Sample Bomb Threat Instructions
Source: International Association of Chiefs of Police. *Project Response: The Oklahoma City Tragedy*. Alexandria, VA: IACP, 1995, p.10. Reprinted by permission.

the threat, searching for the possible bomb or evacuating the premises. No matter what alternative is selected, the police should be called.

A command post should be established as soon as the decision is made to treat the bomb threat as real. The entire building should then be diagrammed and areas crossed off as they are searched. A system of communicating among searchers must be established, but it must not involve the use of portable radios because they may detonate the bomb. All searchers should be cautioned not to turn on lights because this might also detonate the bomb. Searchers should move slowly and carefully, listening for any ticking sounds and watching for trip wires.

Sometimes metal detectors are used to assist in the search. Many police departments are using bomb-sniffing dogs with great success. Such dogs are trained to move quietly and to not bark when a bomb is located, but rather to simply "point" to it. Explosives-detecting dogs are especially valuable in searching cluttered or inaccessible areas. Officers who respond to bombs (threatened or actual) should have available bomb suits, hazmat protection and robots.

Remotely operated vehicles have been used for various tasks by SWAT teams and bomb squads for many years (Attariwala, 2008, p.20). A more recent application is using unmanned aerial vehicles (UAVs) for domestic emergency services that operate under the same standards required of remote controlled model aircraft, not operating within three miles of an active airport and only at or below 400 feet above ground level.

Areas that are usually unlocked and unwatched are the most common sites for bombs, for example, restrooms, lobbies, lunch rooms, elevators and stairs. Officers should look for anything out of place or foreign to the area, for example, a briefcase in the restroom. Bombs can be hidden in lunch pails, briefcases, shopping bags, candy boxes and any number of other types of containers.

Bombings with potentially disastrous effects are remarkably simple to perform. Several underground newsletters give detailed instructions on how to make improvised explosive devices (IEDs) using common materials A quick search on the Internet can also reveal easy instructions for making a bomb.

Many indicators should alert law enforcement officers to suspicious packages: lopsidedness, protruding wires, oily stains on the wrapper, a strange odor, no return address, excessive weight, visual distractions, foreign mail, air mail, special delivery, restrictive markings such as confidential or personal, postage not canceled, excessive security tape or string and handwritten or poorly typed addresses. Officers should be suspicious of any plastic bottle emitting a gas or causing the ground around it to discolor.

If a bomb is found, the police should be prepared to deal with it themselves or know who to call to deal with it.

The policy of most police departments when dealing with a suspected bomb is *do not touch*—move the people away from the bomb, not the bomb away from the people. A 300-foot radius is a good general rule to follow.

It is usually not necessary for officers to act immediately other than to evacuate the immediate area and to then call the fire department or a bomb disposal unit, which are better equipped to handle such situations. If a military installation is close by, its bomb demolition team may help. When a suspicious object or bomb is located, doors and windows in the area should be opened, and all fire extinguishers should be readied and in position to combat any fires caused by the explosion. The bomb should be surrounded with sandbags or similar shock-absorbing objects. Valuable and irreplaceable documents, files, computer disks and other items should be removed from the vicinity and, if time allows, so too should highly flammable material.

A recoilless disrupter might also be used. This is a device that uses gunpowder to fire a jet of water or a projectile at a particular component of an explosive to render it safe.

As with other emergency responses, collaboration among many agencies is required during and immediately following an explosion or bombing. This was certainly true on September 11, 2001. Explosive technicians and special investigators worked side by side with clean-up crews, around the clock, seven days a week, sifting through hundreds of tons of debris. The army of response and rescue workers included law enforcement officers, firefighters, sheriff's deputies, dog handlers, emergency medical teams, hospital personnel, engineers, heavy equipment operators, chaplains, National Guard members, Red Cross staff and volunteers and social service workers from across the country.

PANDEMICS

pandemic

An infectious disease that occurs over a large geographic area and affects a significantly high percentage of the population.

A potential crisis that does not fit into either the natural, accidental or man-made crisis but that is gaining increasing attention among law enforcement agencies is the pandemic. A **pandemic** is an infectious disease that occurs over a large geographic area and affects a significantly high percentage of the population. In 1918 to 1919, the "Spanish flu" killed 50 million people worldwide, 650,000 of them in the United States. In 1968 to 1969, the "Hong Kong flu" killed 34,000 people in the United States. The 21st century has raised concerns about the "Avian (bird) flu" and "Swine flu" becoming pandemics. Although a pandemic might seem like a public health problem, it is also a concern to law enforcement:

> Police may be called upon to enforce quarantines, to provide security in hospitals swamped with patients, and to ensure that vaccines—when they become available in limited quantities—could be delivered to those with the greatest need for them.
>
> But perhaps the biggest reason why a flu pandemic would be a police problem lies in the answer to this question: Whenever anything bad happens, whom do people call? The local public health agency? How many people even know the name of their public health agency, much less its phone number?
>
> When bad things happen, people call the police. Public health agencies would take the leading role in dealing with a flu pandemic, but police would be involved from start to finish, if only because the public always looks to the police to answer their questions and solve their problems. (Wexler, 2007, p.ii)

Police are vital in maintaining order and providing services should a pandemic occur. People look to the police first when things go wrong.

The Police Executive Research Forum (PERF) has published *Police Planning for an Influenza Pandemic: Case Studies and Recommendations from the Field* (Luna et al., 2007), which states in its Introduction, "A pandemic flu has the potential to cause more death, illness, and social and economic disruption than most other threats faced by law enforcement." This document (p.8) states, "In every site, plans call for police to maintain public order *and*

- Provide security for vaccine/treatment transport and vaccine distribution sites,
- Be prepared to assist in executing public health orders,
- Provide initial site security as needed at medical facilities and similar venues, and
- Assist with handling mass fatalities."

Because the police are first responders and, as such, have a high likelihood of exposure, it is important that they be among the first to be vaccinated. If officers believe their own safety and the safety of their families are at risk, they may not respond to incidents, regardless of whether their job depends on it.

In a pandemic, as in all the previously discussed emergency situations, an agency that has incorporated the community policing philosophy into its operations is likely to be much more effective than are those agencies that are more reactive.

EMERGENCIES AND COMMUNITY POLICING

One difficulty frequently encountered by departments seeking to implement community policing is that no sense of community exists. This is noted by Miller et al. (2010, p.67): "It is extremely difficult to implement community policing when the values of groups within a given area clash." In times of crisis, such as that following the terrorist attacks of September 11, this "sense of community" may either be strengthened or weakened.

On the "up-side" of emergencies and disasters, be they natural or not, is how the community often pulls together for survival, support and recovery. Walls come down, the circle of trust expands and people look past their differences to focus on their common ground—as Americans in need of help from one another. The other side to this, of course, is that some people may react just the opposite—walls go up, trust in others diminishes, and suspicion and fear grows toward citizens who share any characteristics with those deemed responsible for the crisis.

SUMMARY

Police departments should have predisaster plans for those emergencies likely to occur within their jurisdictions. Such plans should include what emergencies to prepare for; what needs to be done in advance (supplies on hand, agreements with other agencies, etc.); what specific functions must be performed during the emergency and who is responsible for performing them, including organizations and agencies that might help; how to keep the media informed; what steps need to be taken to restore order after the emergency is ended; and how the response is to be evaluated. Most emergencies happen in four phases: (1) the *warning* period, (2) the *impact* period, (3) the *immediate reaction* after impact and (4) the period of *delayed response.*

Jurisdictions may seek assistance in developing their predisaster plan from the Federal Emergency Management Agency, or FEMA, an independent federal agency charged with building and supporting the nation's emergency management system. The mission of FEMA is to reduce loss of life and property and protect our nation's critical infrastructure from all types of hazards through a comprehensive, risk-based, emergency management program of mitigation, preparedness, response and recovery.

Lack of communication and coordination are the major problems during disasters. These problems can be reduced by having an emergency operations center (EOC), which is considered the "pulse" of the government's response to an emergency and helps reduce the problems of lack of communication and coordination by providing a single location from which personnel operate during a natural disaster or other type of emergency. Any particularly devastating event can have long-range emotional effects, including posttraumatic stress disorder (PTSD), a debilitating stressful reaction to a traumatic event. PTSD may last for months or years. It can be experienced by those who help the victims as well as by victims. A powerful tool in preventing posttraumatic stress disorder is the critical-incident stress debriefing (CISD), which should be conducted by a professional mental health practitioner 24 to 48 hours after the incident and should be mandatory for all personnel involved in the incident.

In addition to general predisaster plans, contingency plans should be made for such natural disasters as floods, explosions, fires, cyclones and earthquakes, as well as other person-made emergencies such as bridge collapses, plane crashes, hazardous materials spills, bomb threats, actual bombings and terrorist attacks involving chemical, biological and nuclear weapons of mass destruction. In *all* such emergencies, saving lives is top priority. Common postemergency "killers" include overruns in overtime and excessive paperwork.

The policy of most police departments when dealing with a suspected bomb is *do not touch*—move the people away from the bomb, not the bomb away from the people. A 300-foot radius is a good general rule to follow.

Police are vital in maintaining order and providing services should a pandemic occur. People look to the police first when things go wrong.

APPLICATION

As your department's emergency management officer, you have been directed to establish a policy and procedure to respond to a natural disaster likely to threaten your jurisdiction. Include the roles of local, state and federal agencies in your policy and procedure.

AN EXERCISE IN CRITICAL THINKING

On July 8 at 3:35 A.M., two police officers in separate squad cars received a call reporting a multiple-vehicle crash on the eastbound lanes of Interstate Highway 94 three miles east of Twin Lakes at the crossing of the Kinnickinnic River. There were patches of fog approaching the area, reducing visibility in the location of the collisions to 100 feet. Seven vehicles had collided. Four were in the ditch to the right side of the road; one was on the left shoulder facing toward the ditch; one was on the right shoulder with the front left tire four feet into the right lane; and one vehicle was straddling the two lanes with its front tire in the right lane and its back tires in the left lane.

1. As no headlights of approaching traffic can be seen,
   a. Both officers should leave their squad cars, with lights flashing as warnings, and survey damages to vehicles and personal injuries.
   b. One officer should stop all approaching traffic at a point west of the patches of fog while the other officer surveys the scene to call for the appropriate assistance.
   c. One officer should act as an emergency manager and prioritize and delegate responsibilities.
   d. Immediately broadcast a general call for help—obtain ambulance and medical help, wreckers and clean-up assistance, then stand aside to direct traffic.
   e. The first to arrive on the scene should attempt to give first aid to individuals requesting help, and the second should begin an investigation to see if gross misdemeanors for aggravated driving violations are in order.
2. If one person is observed leaving the scene of the crash,
   a. The officer arriving second should pursue and arrest that individual and place him or her in the back seat of the squad car for later interrogation and sobriety tests.
   b. The first officer to arrive should call for K-9 backup to track down the individual for interrogation.
   c. Both officers should ignore this departure unless the individual appears to pose a threat to others. After the initial traumatic shock, this person will probably recover emotional balance and return without coercion.
   d. Action should be taken only if the emergency manager assesses it to be necessary and timely.

   e. Officers should request an ambulatory survivor who is physically able to chase down this individual and bring him or her back to the scene of the crash.

3. In addition to three injured people who were removed in ambulances and two who were given medical attention but not hospitalized, Reginald Jones was found slumped behind the wheel of the vehicle found in the middle of the highway. Others stated that they had braked and swerved to miss his vehicle, which along with the poor visibility had caused the onset of the multiple-vehicle collision. One officer walked up just as Jones was about to be removed from the vehicle by ambulance attendants. The attendants turned Jones over to the officer, who noticed indications of intoxication. Jones refused to take field sobriety tests, stating the officer had no right to ask him because an acquaintance named "Arel" had been driving the car all evening until it stalled at the spot where police found it. Jones did not request an attorney.
   a. Jones should be arrested for an aggravated driving violation.
   b. Insufficient evidence exists for Jones to be tested or arrested.
   c. Only if other witnesses can corroborate that no other person was in the vehicle with Jones should he be interrogated.
   d. If Jones can give "Arel's" full name and address, then he should be released; otherwise, he should be arrested and interrogated.
   e. As Jones is the prime suspect who has caused the entire emergency, he should be arrested, searched, handcuffed and taken to police headquarters for interrogation.

DISCUSSION QUESTIONS

1. What types of emergencies are most likely to occur in your community? Least likely?
2. Assume that the potential for flooding exists in your community. What type of training would you recommend for the police department?
3. What should be the foremost concern of police officers when dealing with a natural disaster?
4. In dealing with a bomb threat, what are the most important considerations?
5. How might the media be of help during an emergency situation?
6. Have you ever been involved in an emergency situation yourself? How well was it handled? What could have been done differently?
7. Does your local law enforcement agency have an emergency preparedness plan? If so, what does it consist of?

GALE EMERGENCY SERVICES DATABASE ASSIGNMENTS

- Use the Gale Emergency Services database to answer the Discussion Questions as appropriate.
- Find and read the article "The Manageable Future" by Charles S. Heal. Pay special attention to the two figures. Summarize what each figure graphically depicts.
- Find and read the article "Nationwide Application of the Incident Command System" by Michael D. Cardwell and Patrick T. Cooney. Write a brief report explaining what the acronym FIRESCOPE stands for, what it is intended to do and why the authors suggest it should be adopted nationwide.

REFERENCES

"About FEMA." Washington, DC: Federal Emergency Management Agency, November 10, 2008.

Are You Ready? An In-Depth Guide to Citizen Preparedness. Washington, DC: Federal Emergency Management Agency, October 21, 2008.

Attariwala, Joetey S. "Communicating with UAVs: Unmanned Aerial Vehicles for Emergency Services." *9-1-1 Magazine*, September/October 2008, pp.20–22, 55.

Bradford, George R. "Self-Survival." *9-1-1 Magazine*, September/October 2008, pp.24–26, 52.

Cashen, Kevin. "Elements for Continuity of Operations." *Law and Order*, May 2008, pp.67–72.

Commission on Accreditation of Law Enforcement Agencies. *Standards for Law Enforcement Agencies*, 5th ed. Fairfax, VA: CALEA, 2006, updated 2008.

Donlon-Cotton, Cara. "Critical Incidents: Dealing with the Media." *Law and Order*, September 2007, pp.24–28.

Eggers, Ron. "America's Ailing Infrastructure Poses Dangers." *9-1-1 Magazine*, November/December 2007, p.94.

"Emergency Text Alerts to Cell Phones Approved." *Criminal Justice Research Review*, January/February 2009, p.62.

Garrett. Ronnie. "Sighting in Swatting." *Law Enforcement Technology*, May 2009, pp.26–32.

"Hazardous Materials Safety." Washington, DC: U.S. Department of Transportation, 2008.

Henninger, Dwight, and Bullock, Bill. "State and Interstate Mutual Aid: EMAC and FEMA." *The Police Chief*, October 2008, pp.42–43.

Hsu, Spencer. "FEMA to Take Lead Role in Coordinating Disaster Aid." *Washington Post*, April 18, 2007, p.A08.

Jetmore, Larry F. "Post Traumatic Stress Syndrome." *Law Officer Magazine*, May 2008, pp.62–66.

Luna, Andrea M.; Brito, Corina Sole; and Sanberg. Elizabeth A. *Police Planning for an Influenza Pandemic: Case Studies and Recommendations from the Field.* Washington, DC: Police Executive Research Forum, October 2007.

Miller, Linda S.; Hess, Kären Matison; and Orthmann, Christine Hess. *Community Policing: Partnerships for Problem Solving*, 6th ed. Clifton Park, NY: Delmar Publishing Company, 2010.

"Minneapolis Area Police Officials Describe 'Lessons Learned' from Bridge Collapse." *Subject to Debate*, October 2007, pp.1, 4–5.

Moore, Carole. "NIMS Compliance—2007." *Law Enforcement Technology*, September 2007, pp.28–38.

Moore, Carole. "An Accident Waiting to Happen." *Law Enforcement Technology*, January 2008, pp.8–14.

Moore, Carole. "Telling Your Officers Where to Go—and How to Get There." *Law Enforcement Technology*, May 2009, pp.10–16.

Mulholland, David J. "NIMS: Information Sharing for Results." *The Police Chief*, November 2007, p.12.

National Incident Management System. Washington, DC: Department of Homeland Security, March 1, 2004.

"New Orleans Law Enforcement Is Still Reeling from Hurricane." *Criminal Justice Newsletter*, April 16, 2007, pp.4–5.

Rosenthal, Rick. "Media Relations Lessons from Flight 1549." *ILEETA Digest*, January/February/March 2009, p.6.

Ross, David Anthony. "Reliable Communications in Unreliable Conditions." *Law Enforcement Technology*, May 2009, pp.68–70.

Wexler, Chuck. "Foreword." In *Police Planning for an Influenza Pandemic: Case Studies and Recommendations from the Field.* By Luna, Andrea M.; Brito, Corina Sole; and Sanberg. Elizabeth A. Washington, DC: Police Executive Research Forum, October 2007.

CHAPTER 9

Terrorism

Securing Our Homeland

DO YOU KNOW . . .

- What most definitions of terrorism include?
- What three elements are common in terrorism?
- How the FBI classifies terrorist acts?
- What motivates most terrorist attacks?
- What domestic terrorist groups exist in the United States?
- What methods terrorists might use?
- What federal office was established as a result of 9/11?
- What the lead federal agencies in combating terrorism are?
- How the USA PATRIOT Act enhances counterterrorism efforts by the United States?
- What the first line of defense against terrorism in the United States is?
- What the three-tiered model of al Qaeda terrorist attacks consists of?
- What three obstacles to intelligence effectiveness are?
- What a key to successfully combating terrorism is?
- What the Community Protection Act authorizes?
- What two concerns are associated with the current "war on terrorism"?
- What balance law enforcement must maintain in the "war on terrorism"?

CAN YOU DEFINE?

asymmetric war
bioterrorism
contagion effect
cyberterrorism
deconfliction
ecoterrorism
estimative language
fusion center
jihad
sleeper cells
terrorism

INTRODUCTION

"Terrorism is the most significant national security threat our country faces" (*Strategic Plan 2005–2009*, 2004, p.26). The horrific events of September 11, 2001, pulled together and unified the American people in a way most had never seen. Patriotism was immediately popular. Thousands of volunteers helped search for victims and donated blood and money. The American flag flew everywhere. In addressing the nation, President George W. Bush stated, "Tonight we are a country awakened to danger and called to defend freedom. Our grief has turned to anger, and anger to resolution."

In addition to galvanizing the nation, the events of that tragic day had other ramifications, such as changing how our nation viewed its security, with law enforcement working to redefine its role as traditional crime fighters while taking on tremendous new counterterrorism activities. But the threat remains. The Justice Department's top priority is to support law enforcement and intelligence agencies in the fight against terrorism:

> After Sept. 11, our country entered a new era of policing. Departments around the country looked at their mission differently. Think back on some of the major changes:
>
> - Federal agencies were reorganized.
> - Entirely new agencies were established, including the Transportation Security Administration and the Department of Homeland Security.
> - A color-coded security system was established to indicate the terrorism threat level.
> - Billions of dollars have been spent in an effort to better equip and prepare agencies to respond to both natural and man-made disasters.
> - Interoperability in communications and data sharing has not only become a priority but is also the norm in some parts of the country. (Stockton, 2008, p.8)

Many have voiced concern over the increased attention and funding given to terrorism: "The Department of Homeland Security announced $1.9 billion in anti-terrorism grants . . . , stirring a growing debate among state and local officials nationwide over whether such funds are coming at the expense of other law enforcement priorities that some say are more urgent, such as fighting drugs, gangs, and violent crime" (Hsu, 2007, p.A02). The increase in violent crime in recent years has led some to dub homeland security "the monster that ate criminal justice" and has resulted in louder warnings that local police departments cannot be effective homeland security partners if they are overwhelmed by the responsibilities of their core mission (Garrett, 2007, p.10). The need for balancing crime fighting efforts with counterterrorism efforts should be kept in mind while reading this chapter: "For cops, crime fighting and counterterrorism go hand in hand" (Kelling et al., 2007).

Americans, including law enforcement officers, must not become complacent, believing another attack as horrific as that of 9/11 could not happen again: "What form an attack will take, what will trigger it, and where it will happen no one knows. But it's going to happen again. I believe we are in a period of calm before the storm" (Griffith, 2008, p.53).

This chapter begins by defining terrorism, looking at the extent of the problem and classifying terrorism as domestic or international. Next is a look at the various motivations for terrorism, the new type of war that law enforcement is engaged in and the methods used by terrorists. This is followed by a look at the federal response to terrorism, including the formation of the Department of Homeland Security (DHS) and passage of the USA PATRIOT Act. Next is a discussion of the critical role of local law enforcement in responding to terrorism and efforts to detect, prepare for, prevent, protect against, respond to and recover from terrorist attacks. Then initiatives to assist in the fight against terrorism and the role of the media in this fight are discussed, followed by two major concerns related to that war: erosion of civil liberties and retaliation against people of Middle Eastern descent. The chapter concludes with a discussion of community policing and homeland security.

TERRORISM DEFINED

The Terrorism Research Center defines **terrorism** as "the use of force or violence against persons or property in violation of the criminal laws of the United States for purposes of intimidation, coercion or ransom."

terrorism
The use of force or violence against persons or property in violation of U.S. criminal laws for purposes of intimidation, coercion or ransom.

Most definitions of terrorism have common elements, including the systematic use of physical violence, either actual or threatened, against noncombatants to create a climate of fear and to cause some religious, political or social change.

Three elements of terrorism are (1) it is criminal in nature, (2) targets are typically symbolic and (3) the terrorist actions are always aggressive and often violent.

Terrorism is a global problem. The *2008 Report on Terrorism* by the National Counterterrorism Center states, "Approximately 11,800 terrorist attacks against noncombatants occurred in various countries during 2008, resulting in over 54,000 deaths, injuries and kidnappings. Compared to 2007, attacks decreased by 6,700 or 20 percent. As was the case last year, the largest number of reported terrorist attacks occurred in the Near East, but unlike previous years, South Asia had the greater number of fatalities" (2009, p.10).

CLASSIFICATION OF TERRORIST ACTS

The FBI categorizes terrorist acts in the United States as either domestic or international terrorism.

Domestic Terrorism

The 1995 bombing of the Murrah Federal Building in Oklahoma City and the 2009 shooting of a guard at the Holocaust Museum in Washington, DC, highlight the threat of domestic terrorists. They represent extreme right- or left-wing and special interest beliefs. Many are antigovernment and antitaxation and engage in survivalist training to perpetuate a White, Christian nation. The right-wing militia or patriot movement is a law enforcement concern because of the potential for violence and criminal behavior. Some states have passed

A shell of what was once part of the twin towers of New York's World Trade Center rises above the rubble that remains after both towers were destroyed in a terrorist attack September 11, 2001. The 110-story towers collapsed after two hijacked airliners carrying scores of passengers slammed into the symbols of American capitalism.
© David Turnley/CORBIS

legislation limiting militias, including types of training they can undergo. In October 2002, the Washington, DC, area was terrorized by a sniping spree. The sniper mastermind, John Allen Muhammad was sentenced to death and executed on November 10, 2009.

Hill and Fitzgerald (2009) describe the attempted terrorist plot by four Muslims who, fed by a hatred for America and Jews, aimed to blow up synagogues and military planes in the Bronx. The would-be terrorists spent months scouting targets and securing what they thought were powerful explosives, but the Federal Bureau of Investigation (FBI) was watching their every move. They were arrested May 20, 2009, outside a synagogue where they had planted a useless bomb, which was packed with inert explosives supplied by the FBI rather than by the Pakistani terrorist group they had pledged to support. The FBI Web site headline archives of May 22, 2009, quoted New York City Mayor Bloomberg thanking the investigators of the foiled bomb plot: "We know we live in very dangerous times, but thankfully we have an excellent system of defenses to protect us. And in the first line of these defenses are our superb law enforcement officers, including those we honor today" ("New York Says Thanks," 2009). Domestic terrorism is examined in-depth under the discussion of motivation for terrorism.

International Terrorism

International terrorism is foreign-based or directed by countries or groups outside the United States against the United States. The FBI divides international terrorism into three categories: (1) foreign state sponsors of international terrorism using terrorism as a tool of foreign policy, for example Iraq and Afghanistan; (2) formalized terrorist groups such as Osama bin Laden's al Qaeda; and (3) loosely affiliated international radical extremists who have a variety of identities and travel freely in the United States, unknown and undetected by law enforcement or the government.

The FBI's greatest concern is the threat from al Qaeda attack cells, which can inflict serious harm with little or no warning (*Strategic Plan*, pp.26–27). The

This combo image from the FBI Internet site shows "Assam the American" believed to be Adam Gadahn, a missing California man and a follower of Osama bin Laden. Gadahn, now 26, converted to Islam at age 17 and attended a mosque in Orange County, California.

cells maintain strict operational and communications security and minimize contact with militant Islamic groups and mosques in the United States to remain undetected. The plan notes that although al Qaeda is the most lethal terrorist group, Harakat al-Muqawamah al-Islamiyyah (HAMAS) and Hezbollah also have extensive presences in the United States.

The events of 9/11 turned the threat of terrorism into a reality for U.S. citizens. Just how real this threat is has been examined in *National Intelligence Estimate: The Terrorist Threat to the US Homeland* (2007), a report that uses **estimative language**, or language based on analytical assessments and judgments rather than on facts or hard evidence. The report uses terms such as *we assess* and *we judge* synonymously and outlines the following key judgments:

estimative language
Language based on analytical assessments and judgments rather than on facts or hard evidence.

- We judge the U.S. Homeland will face a persistent and evolving terrorist threat over the next three years. The main threat comes from Islamic terrorist groups and cells, especially al-Qaida. We judge that al-Qaida will intensify its efforts to put operatives here.
- As a result, we judge that the United States currently is in a heightened threat environment.
- We assess Lebanese Hezbollah, which has conducted anti-U.S. attacks outside the United States in the past, may be more likely to consider attacking the Homeland over the next three years if it perceives the United States as posing a direct threat to the group or Iran.
- We assess that the spread of radical—especially Salafi—Internet sites, increasingly aggressive anti-U.S. rhetoric and actions, and the growing number of radical, self-generating cells in Western countries indicate that the radical and violent segment of the West's Muslim population is expanding.

Al Qaeda's leadership, once on the run, is thought to have regrouped and, having found a safe haven in Pakistan, might be stronger than ever, retaining its ability to organize complex, mass-casualty attacks and inspiring others to do the same (Whitelaw, 2007, p.33). However, a "perverse 'competition' is now in evidence between the Arabic-dominated al Qaeda terrorists and the Iranian-controlled Hezbollah terrorist group" (Jones, 2007, p.36). These two groups compete for funding as well as recruits.

Dennis Blair (2009, p.6), director of National Intelligence, reports that despite successes in weakening al Qaeda, it and its affiliates remain "dangerous and adaptive enemies." Led by Osama bin Ladin, al Qaeda remains intent on attacking U.S. interests worldwide and is likely to focus on prominent political, economic, and infrastructure targets to produce mass casualties, visually dramatic destruction, significant economic "aftershocks" and fear among the population.

DeYoung (2007, p.A01) believes the next terrorist assault on the United States is likely to consist of relatively unsophisticated, near simultaneous attacks similar to those attempted in Britain in June 2007, meant to cause widespread fear and panic rather than to cause major losses. Counterterrorism officials say the attacks in England and Scotland coincide with U.S. intelligence indicating increased movement of money and people from al Qaeda camps in the ungoverned tribal areas of Pakistan near the Afghan border (DeYoung).

FBI Director Robert Mueller has warned that while the United States continues to face threats from al Qaeda, it must also focus on lesser-known terrorist groups, especially extremists from visa-waver countries, who are "merely an e-ticket away from the United States" (Wyllie, 2009).

The Dual Threat

In fighting terrorism, all law enforcement—local, state and federal—must keep as close an eye on domestic terrorists as they do on the international variety. And sometimes the line between the two is blurred. For example, since 2007 at least 24 young Somali Americans have disappeared from their homes in Minneapolis. According to National Public Radio ("Somali-Minneapolis Terrorist Axis," 2009), "For months, young Somali men and teenagers have been turning up missing from their homes in Minneapolis. Law enforcement officials have traced them to Somalia, where they are believed to have linked up with a Somali group on the U.S. list of terrorist organizations. Now there's word that some of the boys may have returned home."

MOTIVATIONS FOR TERRORISM

One approach to understanding terrorism is to examine the motivations that produce it.

Most terrorist acts result from dissatisfaction with a religious, political or social system or policy and frustration resulting from an inability to change it through acceptable, nonviolent means.

Religious motives are seen in Islamic extremism. Political motives include such elements as the Red Army Faction. Social motives are seen in single-issue groups such as antiabortion groups, animal rights groups and environmentalists.

Terrorist groups within the United States with specific motivations include right-wing extremists (White supremacists, Black supremacists, and militia groups), left-wing extremists, pro-life extremists, animal rights activists and environmental extremists.

Right-Wing Extremists

Right-wing extremism began in the early 1980s and has remained active since then, perhaps motivated by the government's actions at Ruby Ridge and Waco.

The Ruby Ridge incident involved an attempt to arrest Randy Weaver, a White supremacist charged with selling illegal firearms to undercover Bureau of Alcohol, Tobacco, Firearms and Explosives (ATF) agents. A shootout ensued, resulting in the death of a U.S. marshal and Weaver's young son. The FBI laid siege to Weaver's Ruby Ridge cabin and killed his pregnant wife before Weaver surrendered.

The federal siege of the Branch Davidian compound near Waco, Texas, began in 1993 when ATF agents, trying to serve a search warrant, were met with gunfire that killed four agents and wounded several others. After a three-month siege, FBI agents moved in with tear gas, not knowing the compound was laced with gasoline. The compound burned, killing more than 70 people, including several young children.

The FBI's *Strategic Plan* (p.27) notes that right-wing domestic terrorism groups will continue to target law enforcement personnel and minority groups. Militias will seek to disrupt the personal and financial lives of government workers and elected officials by misuse of property claims or liens against personal assets. The most violent right-wing groups, White supremacists, have strengthened their recruiting and rhetoric since 9/11.

White Supremacists include one of the original American terrorist organizations, the Ku Klux Klan, formed following the Civil War to terrorize Blacks and exert political influence over the Reconstruction South. The Klan is still a threat, burning churches and intimidating and harassing minorities and minority advocates. Neo-Nazi groups such as the Skinheads also espouse White supremacy. Among Black Supremacists is the Black Panther Party for Self-Defense, established in 1966 during a time of racial turmoil.

Another right-wing extremist group is the militia movement. Most militia groups are heavily armed and practice shooting. Many militia members are frustrated, overwhelmed and socially unable to cope with the rapid pace of change in the modern world. Militia groups commonly provide the rhetoric for violence.

AN OFFICER'S PERSPECTIVE

During my time working as a police officer in a relatively suburban area of Minnesota, I have conducted traffic stops and made contact with several people who have identified themselves as "Posse Comitatus," an antigovernment militia group that does not believe in the authority of any law enforcement other than the actual sheriff elected by the people for the county. They also do not believe in paying taxes, and I have stopped a few with license plates that they have created on their own. Although these people told me that they did not believe in my power of authority as a law enforcement official, I still held them accountable to the law. Fortunately, the ones that I have had contact with ended up cooperating, but that is not always the case. It is also important to note that these individuals are not only secluded in small rural areas; they are around the suburbs and cities as well.

—Sgt. Henry Lim Cho

Left-Wing Extremists

Left wing extremists take a Pro-Marxist stance, believing the rich must be brought down and the poor raised up. According to the FBI's *Strategic Plan* (pp.27–28), as left-wing terrorist groups regenerate over the coming years, they will continue to pose a threat to economic and law enforcement targets, with violent protests against the perceived effects of trade globalization on human rights, labor rights and the environment continuing and likely escalating. The plan cites as an example of left-wing "anarchist movement" activity the large-scale destructive protests at World Trade Organization and notes that special interest extremism incidents have increased during the last several years.

Pro-Life Extremists

Although many pro-life, antiabortion advocates stay within the law in promoting their beliefs, some groups do not. One such group is an active terrorist organization called the Army of God whose crimes range from arson, to assault, to assassination.

Animal Rights Activists

An active domestic terrorist group is the Animal Liberation Front (ALF), which has claimed credit for attacks on meatpacking plants, furriers and research labs. Founded in England in 1976, ALF's influence spread to the United States in 1982. Since then, the group has caused millions of dollars in damage and medical research setback through its acts of vandalism, arson and freeing of laboratory animals. Leaders of this underground movement often seek free speech protections under the First Amendment while leading criminal lifestyles to maintain both themselves and the group: "The ALF's ultimate objective is to eliminate animal euthanasia and the use of all animals in laboratory testing in universities and science centers. In the pursuit of these objectives, elements of the group have become more violent" (Downing, 2009, p.35).

Environmental Extremists

ecoterrorism Seeks to inflict economic damage to those who profit from the destruction of the natural environment.

Environmental extremists are often referred to as ecoterrorists, with *eco* being derived from *ecology*—the study of the interrelationships of organisms and their environment. **Ecoterrorism** seeks to inflict economic damage to those who profit from the destruction of the natural environment. The FBI considers ecoterrorism to be the No. 1 domestic terror threat in the United States and defines it as "the use or threatened use of violence of a criminal nature against innocent victims or property by an environmentally oriented, subnational group for environmental-political reasons, or aimed at an audience beyond the target, often of a symbolic nature" ("FBI: Eco-Terrorism," 2008).

One ecoterrorist group is the Earth Liberation Front (ELF), which often works with the ALF. Arson is a favorite weapon, responsible for tens of millions of dollars of property damage, including a U.S. Department of Agriculture building, a U.S. Forest Service ranger station and a Colorado ski resort. The group claims responsibility for releasing 5,000 mink from a Michigan fur farm, 600 wild horses from an Oregon corral and burning the Michigan State University's genetic engineering research offices. In 2000, ELF claimed responsibility for torching a $2 million home in Colorado. Ecoterrorists commit many crimes as they fight to save nature, including equipment vandalism, package bombs or pipe bombs, destruction of research data, arson of buildings, obliteration of experimental plants and animals and the like.

A NEW KIND OF WAR—AN ASYMMETRIC WAR

Although motivations for terrorists both within the United States and outside our borders might differ, they have in common the tactics they use, that being an entirely different type of warfare. The Terrorism Research Center declared, "The attack of September 11 will be the precipitating moment of a new kind of war that will define a new century. This war will be fought in shadows, and the adversary will continue to target the innocent and defenseless." This new kind of war has been called an **asymmetric war**, in which a much weaker opponent takes on a stronger opponent by refusing to confront the stronger opponent head on.

asymmetric war
One in which a much weaker opponent takes on a stronger opponent by refusing to confront the stronger opponent head on.

The Dictionary of Military Terms says, "Asymmetric warfare includes threats outside the range of conventional warfare and difficult to respond to in kind" (Phillips, 2006). Banks (2008) notes, "By its definition, asymmetric warfare is the type of battle that is difficult to predict or prepare for. Terrorists do not announce a launch date. Because they are usually smaller and do not have the resources of a well-funded government military, they try to attack with greatest surprise to do the most damage." Although the preceding definition and discussion refers primarily to our military, the concept of this new kind of war must be understood by those on the front lines of this new war—local law enforcement. Attacks on American soil have caused a blurring of war and crime and drawn law enforcement directly into the war on terrorism. Because of this, local law enforcement is expected to be knowledgeable about the various methods terrorists use.

METHODS USED BY TERRORISTS

The *2008 Report on Terrorism* (p.11) reports that, like in 2007, most terrorist attacks in 2008 used fighting methods such as armed attacks, bombings, and kidnappings, but in unconventional ways. They continued their strategy of coordinated attacks, including secondary attacks on first responders at attack sites, and continued to improve on methods to create improvised explosive devices (IEDs). According to this report, worldwide, armed attack was most common (constituting almost 50 percent of attacks), followed by bombings, as shown in Figure 9.1.

Terrorists use arson, explosives and bombs, weapons of mass destruction (biological, chemical or nuclear agents), and technology.

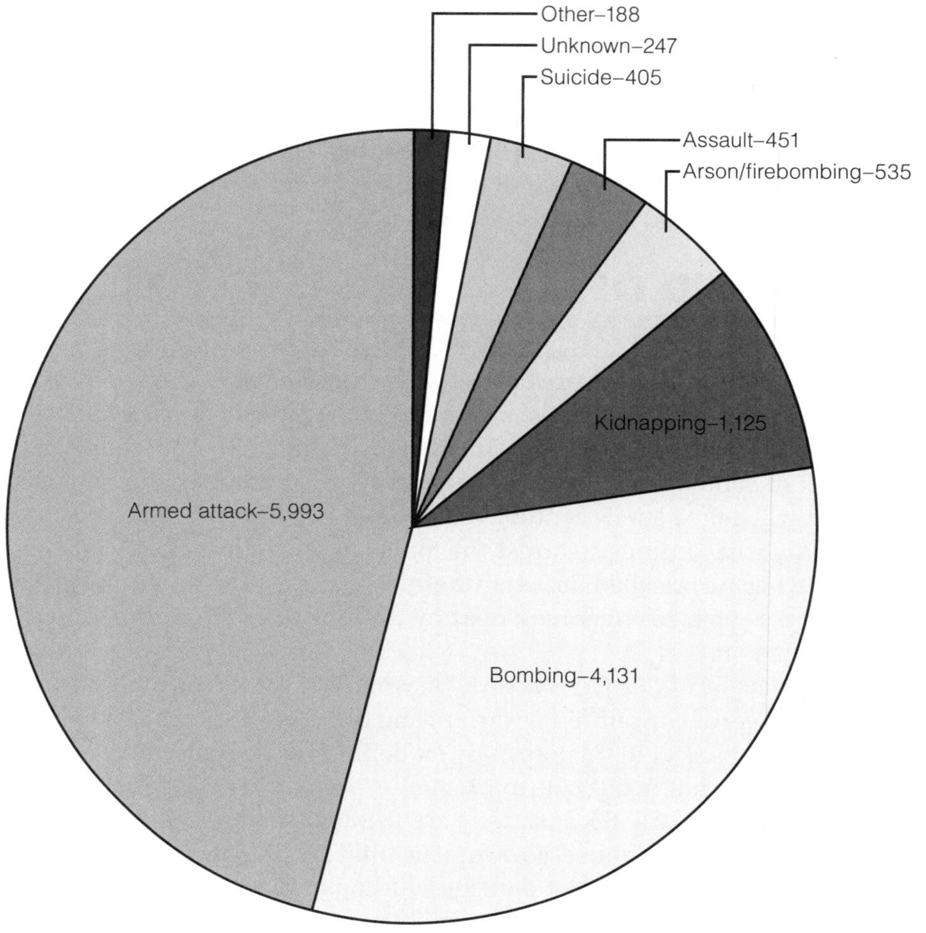

FIGURE 9.1
Primary Methods Used in Attacks
Note: 11,770 attacks, some double counting occurred when multiple methods were used
Source: *2008 Report on Terrorism.* Washington, DC: National Counterterrorism Center. April 30, 2009, p.28.

Explosives and Bombs

Bombs and bomb threats were discussed from the perspective of an emergency in Chapter 8. This discussion looks at explosives as a method of terrorism. From 1978 to 1996, Theodore Kaczynski terrorized the country as the Unabomber, through a string of 16 mail bombings that killed three people apparently in a protest against technology. Ramzi Ahmed Yousef, found guilty of masterminding the first World Trade Center bombing in 1993, declared that he was proud to be a terrorist and that terrorism was the only viable response to what he saw as a Jewish lobby in Washington. The car bomb used to shatter the Murrah Federal Building in 1995 was Timothy McVeigh's way to protest the government and the raid on the Branch Davidians at Waco. In 2002, Lucas Helder terrorized the Midwest by placing 18 pipe bombs, accompanied by antigovernment letters, in mailboxes across five states. Six of the 18 bombs exploded, injuring four letter carriers and two residents. And the most horrific act of terrorism against the United States occurred on September 11, 2001, when two airplanes were used as missiles to explode the Twin Towers of the World Trade Center, and another plane was used as a missile to attack the Pentagon. A fourth plane crashed in a Pennsylvania field before it could reach its intended target.

Suicide Bombers Most terrorists believe sacrificing themselves makes them martyrs and ensures them a place in their version of heaven. Their families are held in reverence and taken care of. Suicide bombers try to kill as many people as possible.

Wexler (2007, p.i) suggests, "The 9/11 hijackers were the ultimate suicide bombers. They used commercial aircraft as bombs rather than devices that fit inside a backpack. But at their core, their motivations were the same—they believed that political or religious ideology justified murdering innocent bystanders and killing themselves in the process." When experts were asked which two types of terrorist attacks are most likely, the most common response was "suicide bombing attacks" closely followed by "attack on major infrastructure" (Wexler).

Potential suicide terrorists come from different backgrounds and age groups, and are male or female, educated or uneducated, upstanding citizens or deviants. Among the warning signs revealing a suicide bomber are unseasonable garb; profuse sweating; obvious disguises (such as a police uniform with a security badge); and a well-dressed, perfumed appearance and demeanor fitting for one who is going to meet his maker.

Priem et al. (2007, p.35) explain the typical phases in a suicide bombing attack:

> The operational cycle for suicide bombing attacks can be viewed as a nine-phase process that begins with identification and recruitment of bombers; continues through their training, target selection, purchase of components, fabrication of devices, final preparation, and movement to the target; and ends with the detonation of the device. . . .
>
> Interdiction during the last two phases is extremely difficult. Law enforcement agencies must be proactive, taking advantage of opportunities for detection and effective interdiction during the initial seven stages. . . .
>
> There is evidence to suggest that recruiting initiatives may be under way in U.S. prison populations and among radicalized extremists—including U.S. citizens in a number of U.S. communities. . . .
>
> Perhaps the best opportunities for detection and successful interdiction occur when terrorist organizations are selecting targets and conducting reconnaissance against them as well as when they are purchasing explosives components and fabricating explosive devices.

The Police Executive Research Forum (PERF) has developed guidelines for a patrol-level response to a suicide bomb threat, stressing that any protocol should be consistent with the agency's policies and procedures for use of force, active shooter situations, and bomb threats.

A suggested tactic for first responders facing a potential suicide bomber is to issue a clear verbal command: "Do not move." Any movement might trigger the explosives (Chudwin, 2007, pp.62–63). Live-fire shooters should stand ready to make a head shot, preferably with a long gun able to deliver a high-velocity round or 12-gauge slug. Officers should not let their guard down with "presumed compliance." Officers should establish a perimeter around the suspected bomber, considering that the blast radius for explosive devices attached to the body can easily cover 100 yards.

Prevention Strategies A significant challenge to law enforcement is stopping the terrorists' low-tech, lethal weapon of choice, the car bomb, whose simplicity and stealth make them complex adversaries. It is impossible to screen all the cars and trucks that drive past critical buildings or other infrastructure. So authorities now use simple tools, such as restricting parking and traffic and putting up concrete median barriers and security checkpoints.

Weapons of Mass Destruction (WMD)

The FBI's *Strategic Plan* (p.32) states, "Recent findings indicate that terrorist organizations are showing an increasing interest in the acquisition and development of weapons of mass destruction (WMD). As proven by the anthrax attacks following the 9/11 terrorist attacks and the plot by Jose Padilla to detonate a radioactive 'dirty bomb,' the use of WMD by terrorists is a very real possibility."

The acronym CBR includes all potential terrorist threats that can have consequences for the health of large numbers of people, including chemical agents (C), biological agents (B) and radiation exposure (R). Nuclear, biological or chemical agents are also referred to as NBC agents. Biological WMDs have been used since the 1300s. The 20th century saw the first use of artificially produced WMDS—or chemical agents—during World War I. Today, the means and recipes for developing nuclear, radiological, biological and chemical weapons are well known and documented.

Some experts suggest that bioterrorism is the third most likely terrorist act to occur. Incendiary devices and explosives are most likely to be used because they are easy to make. Chemical devices are next in likelihood because the raw materials are easy to get and easy to use.

bioterrorism
Involves such biological weapons of mass destruction (WMD) as anthrax, botulism and smallpox.

Biological Agents **Bioterrorism** involves using viruses, toxins or fungi—classes of organism that include anthrax, botulism and smallpox—as weapons of mass destruction. The letters laced with anthrax sent to television news anchor Tom Brokaw (NBC News), Senators Patrick Leahy and Tom Daschle, and the *New York Post* generated hundreds of calls to *America's Most Wanted*. Especially susceptible to bioterrorism are the nation's food and water supply, which might also be attacked using chemical agents.

Chemical Agents The four common types of chemical weapons are nerve agents, blood agents, choking agents and blistering agents. One agent, ricin toxin, is both a biological and a chemical weapon and is 1,000 times more poisonous than cyanide. In its purest form, a particle of ricin no bigger than a grain of table salt can kill an adult. Reportedly, detailed procedures for ricin extraction and use were found in al Qaeda's military manuals seized in safe houses and caves in Afghanistan.

The Aum Shinrikyo attack in the Tokyo subway in 1995 occurred when members of the religious cult released a poisonous gas, sarin, into the crowded subway system. The incident confirmed that a nonstate entity could manufacture a viable chemical agent and deliver it in a public location. Unfortunately, anyone with access to the Internet can obtain the chemical formula for sarin in less than 40 minutes through a Web search and can produce it inexpensively.

One chemical agent receiving increased attention is chlorine gas. Although a chlorine gas attack requires perfect conditions and a poor emergency response to cause heavy casualties, "if properly released in a well-populated area, chlorine gas has the potential to cause tens of thousands of casualties" (Harwood, 2007, p.18).

The DHS has released interim rules to streamline federal security regulations for high-risk chemical facilities nationwide (Edwards, 2007, p.1). Efforts are ongoing to screen more than 15,000 chemical facilities and require those with certain quantities of specified chemicals to complete an assessment to determine a risk level. A company found to pose greater risk will be required to conduct a vulnerability assessment and submit site security plans that meet DHS's performance standards (Daniels, 2007, p.8). Failure to comply could result in penalties as high as $25,000 a day and an order to cease operations.

Nuclear Terrorism A survey conducted for the Sage Foundation found that the top fear of Americans is nuclear terrorism; 74 percent of Americans believe that a successful terrorist attack on U.S. soil is likely to happen, with almost half (49 percent) believing an attack will include some sort of nuclear device ("Survey: Nuclear Terrorism Top Fear," 2008). Goodwyn (2008, p.48) notes, "Terrorists' attraction to nuclear weapons is due to the destructive capability of the weapons, the horrific effects it would have on life and property, and also the economic impact on all U.S. citizens as well as the entire world." According to the U.S. Nuclear Regulatory Commission (NRC), an average of approximately 375 devices of all kinds containing radioactive material are reported lost or stolen (called *orphaned*) each year.

The successful detonation of a low-yield nuclear device or radiological dispersion device (RDD), also called a dirty bomb, would be more devastating than the terrorist attacks on September 11, 2001. It is likely that the most destruction and disruption from such a dirty bomb would be caused by public panic, rather than radiation: "Even though a dirty bomb incident would be unlikely to cause many deaths, its real purpose would be to create instant terror in the form of mass panic, with lingering psychological damage" (Page, 2009, p.50). Such a dirty bomb, if detonated in a crowded sports arena or shopping mall, would make the decontamination and treatment of perhaps thousands of panic-stricken victims a severely daunting, expensive task.

Detecting Radiation and Other Bioterrorism Agents A variety of technologies is available to help investigators detect radioactive and other hazardous agents. Dosimeters are small, lightweight devices that use silicon diode technology to instantaneously detect and display the accumulated radiation exposure dose and dose rate. They can identify the specific radionuclide(s) involved and let investigators calculate how long they can safely remain on the scene.

Another tool used to detect hazardous agents is the *electronic nose*, which is already used to select fragrant wines and diagnose diseases. Electronic nose technology is designed to detect all chemicals within an aroma or fragrance and miss nothing. Some electronic noses use wireless technology, allowing an investigator more than a mile away from the device to use a computer to remotely monitor the vapors, smells, odors, and chemistry of the air. Faherty (2007) describes an application being used to safeguard New York City from nuclear attack: "The goal of the program is to ban nuclear weapons from the city by creating a 50-mile protective perimeter. The detectors decipher between deadly radiation in nuclear weapons and harmless radiation carried by New Yorkers involved in recent medical tests. It tells you precisely what the element is and how much radiation exists, which is 90 percent of the battle. The detectors function by differentiating between harmful and innocuous isotopes in radiation."

Robotic detection and identification technology can warn responders of NBC agents' presence and strength. Global positioning systems (GPS) can be applied to determine the coordinates of an NBC release relative to the position of responders, residential or other civilian centers or other critical location information. GPS can also track vehicles charged with transporting NBC materials to and from the site. Finally, weather data, such as wind direction and speed, barometric pressure, relative humidity, and so forth, is critical to responders at NBC scenes.

Law enforcement officers must be prepared to manage the 21st-century threats of chemical, biological, radiological, nuclear, and explosives (CBRNE) through detection devices, although such devices are relatively new and used mainly by larger metropolitan agencies seen as potential terrorist targets (Trudeau, 2009, p.44). One such detection device, the RadTruck, is equipped with adaptable radiation area monitors (ARAMs) mounted in the back cargo areas of sports utility vehicles (SUVs) (Page, 2009, p.50). The ARAMs can detect a radiation source no larger than a grain of sand and determine, in an instant, if it is a lethal substance or the harmless potassium found in a banana, all while cruising past a person, vehicle, or building at street speed in a police SUV. The ARAMs are built to detect illicit low-energy gamma rays and neutron emissions characteristic of weapons-grade plutonium and highly-enriched uranium. They can provide accurate, positive warning and identification if suspicious materials come within detection range or if a RadTruck comes within the range of the suspicious material.

Of course, law enforcement should not overlook the low-tech options of canines, which are increasingly being trained to detect various scents associated with agents used to make a variety of explosives. Such bomb dogs are commonly used at airports and other mass transit hubs.

RESPONDING TO A WMD INCIDENT

In most instances, patrol officers will be dispatched to a WMD event. Terrorists might attempt to interfere with the emergency response by detonating secondary explosives, creating additional events requiring emergency resources and unauthorized entrance to restricted areas. First responder responsibilities include rescuing the injured and trapped victims and calling for medical assistance if needed: "In a WMD incident, this process must occur, but with strict attention to preserving the health and safety of responders. This implies that emergency responders without protective personal equipment (PPE) should not perform such duties" (Carlson, 2008). Table 9.1 illustrates the level of protection, description, type of protection afforded, and circumstance for use of each level of equipment.

Table 9.1 Personal Protective Equipment

Level	Description	Protection	Circumstance
D	Work uniform	Provides no respiratory protection and minimal skin protection	Should not be worn on any site where respiratory or skin hazards exist
C	Full facepiece, air-purifying, canister-equipped respirator and chemical-resistant clothing	Same skin protection as level B, but a lower level respirator	Worn when airborne substance is known, concentration is measured, criteria for using air-purifying respirators are met, and skin and eye exposures are unlikely
B	Chemical-resistant clothing (overalls and long sleeves) and self-contained breathing apparatus (SCBA)	Provides splash protection	When the highest level of respiratory protection is needed but a lesser level of skin and eye protection is sufficient
A	Fully encapsulating chemical-resistant suit and SCBA Can be worn for only 15 to 30 minutes due to overheating; special training is required	Provides full protection	When the highest level of respiratory, skin, eye, and mucous membrane protection is needed

Source: Melissa Reuland and Heather J. Davies. *Protecting Your Community from Terrorism: Strategies for Local Law Enforcement*, Vol. 3: *Preparing for and Responding to Bioterrorism*. Washington, DC: Community Oriented Policing Services (COPS) and the Police Executive Research Forum, September 2004.

After the injured have been attended to, the responsibilities of first responders turn to containing, protecting, assisting and investigating (Carlson, 2008). Unified command might be achieved by using the National Incident Management System (NIMS) discussed in Chapter 8. The incident command post should establish a joint information center to handle all public and media releases. Carlson concludes, "The possibility of a terrorist attack using weapons of mass destruction poses a challenge unlike any other facing today's law enforcement profession. Beyond dealing with the death and destruction brought about by such an event, agencies must ensure the safety and survival of their personnel and their families."

A major catastrophe might be beyond a police agency's capability to handle and could require assistance from many law enforcement organizations, public safety departments, other government services, and the private sector. Many law enforcement agencies have formed WMD teams to be ready if needed.

A WMD Team In addition to responding to dirty bombs, the toxic dust at Ground Zero or the anthrax-laced letters sent to government building, first responders are also trained to respond to suspected meth labs, all involving situations immediately dangerous to life or health (IDLH). Hazardous materials (hazmat) training, first discussed in Chapter 8, will be of tremendous benefit in such situations. In IDLH situations, federal agencies, including the Occupational Safety and Health Administration (OSHA), have established standards emergency responders must adhere to, which apply to tactical officers as well as to fire department and the hazmat team (Perin, 2009, p.20). Thus, it makes sense for departments to combine hazmat and special weapons and tactics (SWAT) training for tactical operations. Although both entities are first responders and bound by OSHA standards, SWAT team operators' mission differs from that of a hazmat team when responding to potential hazards. Nonetheless, personnel from each team might benefit from training together and learning how to assist each other in numerous situations. "HAZSWAT" teams might be the strategy of the future.

Technological Terrorism

A method of terrorist attack that is much more difficult for law enforcement to recognize and respond to is technological terrorism. The United States is susceptible to two methods of technological terror. The first involves the conversion of an industrial site, such as a chemical plant, into a lethal instrument through sabotage. The second is an attack on a source that supplies technology or energy. Either method could be catastrophic. Any interruption of energy supplies could be a national security threat.

cyberterrorism
Terrorism that initiates, or threatens to initiate, the exploitation of or attack on information systems.

Cyberterrorism is defined by the FBI as "terrorism that initiates, or threatens to initiate, the exploitation of or attack on information systems." Damage to our critical computer systems can put our safety and our national security in jeopardy.

FUNDING TERRORISM

It takes money to carry out terrorism, not only for weapons but for general operating expenses: "If you really want to fight a War on Terror, you need to hit terrorists where it hurts—their pocketbooks" (Garrett, 2008b, p.6). Terrorist groups commonly collaborate with organized criminal groups to deal drugs, arms, and, in some instances, humans. To finance their operations, terrorist groups smuggle stolen goods and contraband, forge documents, profit from the diamond trade, and engage in extortion and protection rackets (White, 2006, pp.68–79). Many terrorist operations are financed by charitable groups and wealthy Arabs sympathetic to the group's cause. To investigate local charities, any interested individual can access the information by contacting the Better Business Bureau or the Wise Giving Alliance.

THE FEDERAL RESPONSE TO TERRORISM

In 1996, the FBI established a Counterterrorism Center to combat terrorism. Also in 1996, the Antiterrorism and Effective Death Penalty Act was passed, including several specific measures aimed at terrorism. It enhanced the federal government's power to deny visas to individuals belonging to terrorist groups and simplified the process for deporting aliens convicted of crimes.

In 1999, the FBI announced the prevention of terrorism as its top priority by adding a new Counterterrorism Division with four subunits: the International Terrorism Section, the Domestic Terrorism Section, the National Infrastructure Protection Center and the National Domestic Preparedness Office. But this was not enough to avert the tragic events of 9/11. It took a disaster of that magnitude to make the war on terrorism truly the first priority of the United States: "September 11, 2001 is a significant day in American history. It should be memorialized as the greatest single day of sacrifice and loss in public safety history" (Garrett, 2008a, p.6). One of the first federal initiatives was the establishment of the Department of Homeland Security.

The Department of Homeland Security

On October 8, 2001, President Bush signed Executive Order 13228 establishing the Department of Homeland Security (DHS).

As a result of 9/11, the Department of Homeland Security was established, reorganizing the departments of the federal government.

How the establishment of this department reorganized the federal government was explained in Chapter 1. The mission of the DHS is "to develop and coordinate the implementation of a comprehensive national strategy to secure the United States from terrorist threats or attacks." Michael Chertoff, U.S. Secretary of Homeland Security, describes five goals he sees as priorities for the DHS ("An Interview," 2007, pp.16–18):

1. Increase our ability to keep bad people out of the country.
2. Keep bad things out of the country, increasing port security.
3. Protect our infrastructure better.
4. Continue to build a response capability with modern computer tools.
5. Promote intelligence sharing, not only horizontally across the federal government but vertically with the local government as well.

At the federal level, the FBI is the lead agency for responding to acts of domestic terrorism. The Federal Emergency Management Agency (FEMA) is the lead agency for consequence management (after an attack). The Department of Homeland Security serves in a broad capacity, facilitating collaboration between local and federal law enforcement to develop a national strategy to detect, prepare for, prevent, protect against, respond to and recover from terrorist attacks within the United States.

The DHS has established a five-level color-coded threat system used to communicate with public safety officials and the public at large: green represents a low level of threat, blue a guarded level, yellow an elevated level, orange a high level and red a severe level.

In addition, the Office for Victims of Crime (OVC) has available the Terrorism and International Victims Unit (TIVU) to help victims of terrorism and mass violence. This organization provides training and technical assistance to first responders. It provided support to Oklahoma City in 1995 following the bombing of the Murrah Federal Building. After the attack on America September 11, 2001, TIVU played a key role in OVC's response to victims and their families in New York. Another effort to enhance national security was passage of the USA PATRIOT Act.

The USA PATRIOT Act

On October 26, 2001, President George W. Bush signed the Uniting and Strengthening America by Providing Appropriate Tools Required to Intercept and Obstruct Terrorism (USA PATRIOT) Act into law, giving police unprecedented ability to search, seize, detain or eavesdrop in their pursuit of possible terrorists. The law expands the FBI's wiretapping and electronic surveillance authority and allows nationwide jurisdiction for search warrants and electronic surveillance devices, including legal expansion of those devices to e-mail and the Internet.

The USA PATRIOT Act significantly improves the nation's counterterrorism efforts by

- Allowing investigators to use the tools already available to investigate organized crime and drug trafficking.
- Facilitating information sharing and cooperation among government agencies so they can better "connect the dots."
- Updating the law to reflect new technologies and new threats.
- Increasing the penalties for those who commit or support terrorist crimes.

Using Tools Already in Use in the War on Drugs The war the United States has waged on illicit drugs can provide lessons in the war against terrorism, as both wars have several commonalties in their delivery and control. For example, drugs and terrorism involve covert illegal activities that use sophisticated undercover operations. Both have a domestic component, but the organized and international component of each is far more devastating. In addition, some terrorist cells and networks have structures similar to those of drug cartels. Finally, both "wars" require coordination among various law enforcement agencies, and cooperation and information sharing with other partner countries and an overall policy weighing global strategies.

Facilitating Information Sharing The importance of this provision of the act can be seen in the case of an al Qaeda cell in Lackawanna, New York:

> This case involved several residents of Lackawanna, who traveled to Afghanistan in 2001 to receive training at an al Qaeda–affiliated camp near Kandahar. The investigation of the "Lackawanna Six" began during the summer of 2001, when the FBI received an anonymous letter indicating that these six individuals and others might be involved in criminal activity and associating with foreign terrorists. The FBI concluded that the existing law required the creation of two separate investigations in order to retain the option of using FISA [Foreign Intelligence Surveillance Act]: a criminal investigation of possible drug crimes and an intelligence investigation related to terrorist threats. Over the ensuing months, two squads carried on these two separate investigations simultaneously, and there were times when the intelligence officers and the law enforcement agents concluded that they could not be in the same room during briefings to discuss their respective investigations with each other.
>
> The USA PATRIOT Act, however, took down the "wall" separating these two investigations by making clear that the sharing of case-sensitive information between these two groups was allowed. As a result of key information shared by intelligence investigators, law enforcement agents were able to learn that an individual mentioned in the anonymous letter was an agent of al Qaeda. Further information shared between intelligence and law enforcement personnel then dramatically expedited the investigation of the Lackawanna Six and

allowed charges to be filed against these individuals. Five of the Lackawanna Six pleaded guilty to providing material support to al Qaeda, the sixth pleaded guilty to conducting transactions unlawfully with al Qaeda. These individuals were then sentenced to prison terms ranging from seven to ten years. (*Report from the Field: The USA PATRIOT Act at Work*, 2004, p.3)

Updating the Law to Reflect New Technologies and New Threats Those who defend the constitutionality of roving wiretaps note that the act is not asking the law to expand, but rather to grow as technology grows. Terrorists are trained to change cell phones frequently and to route e-mail through different Internet computers to defeat detection.

Increasing the Penalties for Terrorism The PATRIOT Act also includes money laundering provisions and sets strong penalties for anyone who harbors or finances terrorists. The 1984 Act to Combat International Terrorism (ACIT) established a monetary reward program for information involving terrorism and increased the amount of money offered or paid to an informant. The PATRIOT Act also established new punishments for possessing biological weapons and made it a federal crime to commit an act of terrorism against a mass transit system.

Controversy over the USA PATRIOT Act

Some members of Congress and civil liberties groups say the act gives federal agents too much power to investigate suspected terrorists, threatening the civil rights and privacy of Americans. Those who defend the law argue that repealing it would endanger American lives and help terrorists achieve their mission. Expanding the powers of federal agents to use wiretaps, surveillance and other investigative methods and to share intelligence has given them the tools they need to adapt and out-think terrorists. Attempts to strip law enforcement agents of their expanded legal powers could open the way to further terrorist attacks.

The PATRIOT Act was passed as an immediate response to the 9/11 attacks to provide *federal* law enforcement with better means to defend against terrorism" (emphasis added). However, federal officials recognized the importance of local officers in defense against terror, and in October 2001, President Bush signed Executive Order 12321, calling for federal agencies to reach out to state and local agencies. The concern about local involvement was later incorporated into the Homeland Security Act (HSA) in November 2002. But again, this act focused on reorganizing 22 agencies to defend against terrorism. Unquestionably, the efforts of local law enforcement agencies are critical in the fight against terrorism.

The Renewal of the USA PATRIOT Act

The renewal of this legislation occurred after a year of contested debate between those who believed our national security depended on its renewal and those who believed that increased government powers were no longer needed after the immediate threat seemed to have passed. Questions were raised about whether the PATRIOT Act needed to be renewed in its entirety. Pike (2006, p.40) notes some of the controversial provisions of the act:

> Among the most criticized (components) were provisions allowing for "sneak and peek" warrants—issued secretly and without notice until after the search is completed—and expansions in the use of National Security Letters (NSLs), which are warrantless demands for certain records. Of most concern to librarians and others in the informational industry was Section 215, which expanded the definition of business records that could be obtained under a secret warrant to include "any tangible things," a broad definition that would include records from libraries and bookstores. These criticisms were countered by the Bush administration and supporters of the act who believed that it was necessary, that it was working, and that the concerns about civil liberties were misplaced.

After an extension from its expiration at the end of 2005, the Senate cleared the renewal on March 2, 2006, by a vote of 29 to 10. The House of Representatives followed suit on March 7, voting 280–13, days before the law was set to expire on March 10 (Greene, 2006, p.6). On March 9, President Bush signed into law the USA PATRIOT Improvement and Reauthorization Act. Proponents assert the law will keep America safe from threats, but opponents fear the real threat is from a nearly unbridled government armed with this law.

When President Bush signed the extension, almost unchanged from the original PATRIOT Act, he stated, "The law allows our intelligence and law enforcement officials to continue to share information. It allows them to continue to use tools against terrorists that they use against drug dealers and other criminals. It will improve our nation's security while we safeguard the civil liberties of our people. The legislation strengthens the Justice Department so it can better detect and disrupt terrorist threats. And the bill gives law enforcement new tools to combat threats to our citizens from international terrorists to local drug dealers." (The reauthorized PATRIOT Act also includes new tools to combat the manufacture and distribution of methamphetamine.)

Other than two provisions, the revised version of the PATRIOT Act will be permanent; it will not expire and will change only if done so through legislation. The sections dealing with business and library records and roving wiretaps will expire at the end of 2009.

Changes in the Federal Bureau of Investigation following 9/11

The FBI's *Strategic Plan 2004–2009* (p.1) states,

> The events of September 11th have forever changed our nation and the FBI. Since that terrible day, the FBI's overriding priority has been protecting America by preventing further attacks. The FBI has made and will continue to make many significant changes in order to protect America. . . .
>
> Working with our partners over the past 28 months, we have conducted numerous counterterrorism investigations, resulting in more than one thousand arrests and hundreds of convictions or pre-trial diversions. We broke up the Lackawanna Six, dismantled the Portland Seven, and put would-be shoe bomber Richard Reid behind bars.

During the past five years, the FBI has "dramatically" strengthened its ability to combat terrorism by realigning resources, shifting agents to counterterrorism, doubling the number of intelligence analysts, and tripling the number of linguists. It has also increased multiagency joint terrorism task forces (JTTFs) from 35 to 101 since 2001 ("Counterterrorism," n.d.).

As laudatory as these efforts are, the FBI's effectiveness in counterterrorism ultimately depends on the vigilance of and information from local law enforcement. In addition, the FBI and Justice Department are getting ready to change the previous system based mainly on clandestine detentions and interrogations to one emphasizing transparent investigations and prosecutions of terrorism suspects (Meyer, 2009). This new approach reverses the overriding thrust of the Bush administration in which counterterrorism was treated primarily as an intelligence and military problem rather than as a law-enforcement one.

THE CRITICAL ROLE OF LOCAL LAW ENFORCEMENT IN HOMELAND SECURITY

Every terrorist act committed in the United States occurs in some local law enforcement agency's jurisdiction. That agency is closer to the activities in its community and has the responsibility and jurisdiction to protect that community. Law enforcement personnel have realized that, in our post–9/11 society, their duties have expanded considerably, and they are no longer looking to federal agencies and the military as the source of our county's protection. Lovette (2008, p.34) echoes, "On 9/11 cops became a vital component of the homeland security mission. And the majority of the responsibility for this additional requirement came to rest squarely on the shoulders of the uniformed patrol officer, America's first line of defense in the war on crime, the war on drugs, the war on gangs, and now, the war on terror."

The first line of defense against terrorism is the patrol officer in the field.

46.3

CALEA STANDARD 46.3 requires, "The agency maintains liaison with other organizations for the exchange of information relating to terrorism. The exchange of information should facilitate information sharing and multijurisdictional preemption of terrorist acts or events. Private agencies should be considered for participation in information sharing as necessary for various situations. (*Standards for Law Enforcement Agencies*, 5th edition, 2006)

Newly appointed (sworn in February 3, 2009) U.S. Attorney General Eric Holder, speaking at the National League of Cities Conference, stressed the importance of cities, particularly their law enforcement agencies: "Our cities are, in a very real sense, on the front lines in our fight against terrorism. Your police officers are often the first to see a threat and the first to report it. And information reported by a cop on the street in Omaha can make a difference in thwarting an attack in San Francisco. We are making a big mistake if we don't find ways to partner with urban law enforcement to multiply our forces in the fight against terrorism" (Holder, 2009).

The local police have the powers of search, seizure of evidence, and arrest; an increasing ability to manage, share, and analyze information; skill in identifying interpreting suspicious behaviors; and skill in carrying out investigations from beginning to end. They also add the "critical elements of speed, resources, and numbers" (Downing, 2009, p.30). The crime-fighting model used to investigate organized crime gangs and drug trafficking organizations can apply equally to investigating terrorist networks: "Police hold the key to mitigating and ultimately defeating terrorism in the United States" (Downing, p.40).

AN OFFICER'S PERSPECTIVE

Post–9/11, all police officers in my agency [a suburban metropolitan department] are required to read and complete several online Homeland Security Courses put out by universities and the federal government. These courses involve several hours of required reading and the completion of several tests at the end of the course. A passing score is required; otherwise you must retake the course. The courses outline what our roles as first responders are if a terrorist attack or a disaster were to occur in our community. One of the benefits of this training, beyond the obvious one of preparedness, is the eligibility to receive federal grants.

In addition to new terrorism/disaster training, there have been other changes implemented at the patrol level. Since 9/11, we have now outfitted each of our squad cars with a "Terrorism/Disaster" bin, placed in the trunk, that includes a bio-hazard protective or hazmat suit, latex gloves, and boot covers. There is also a gas mask that officers are fitted for on an annual basis. There are several other emergency items in this bin, such as a medical kit, flares, cones, blanket, and more.

Responding to calls has changed as well. In the city I work in, there is a refinery that has been identified as a sensitive target for a possible terrorist attack. Before 9/11, if an individual was to stop in the area to photograph the facility on public area, there was no issue. Post 9/11, however, private security along with law enforcement attempt to make contact and identify the suspicious activity. That information is then passed on through a Joint Terrorism Task Force (JTTF) agency that works in cooperation with local law enforcement.

—Sgt. Henry Lim Cho

Savelli (2004, pp.65–66) stresses, "Keep in mind, any law enforcement officer can potentially come in contact with a terrorist at any time, whether investigating an unrelated crime, conducting normal duties or responding as a back-up for another law enforcement officer. Also, keep in mind how many of the 9-11-01 hijackers had contact with law enforcement officers in various parts of the country and how many unsuspecting law enforcement officers, in any capacity, may have such contact with terrorists today or in the future." For example (Savelli, pp.65–66):

- September 9, 2001, Ziad Jarrah, hijacker of the plane that crashed in Shanksville, Pennsylvania, was stopped by police in Maryland for speeding. He was driving 90 mph in a 65-mph zone. He was issued a ticket and released.
- August 2001, Hani Hanjour, who hijacked and piloted the plane that crashed into the Pentagon, killing 289 persons, was stopped by police in Arlington, Virginia. He was issued a ticket for speeding and released. He paid the ticket so he would not have to show up in court.
- April 2001, Mohammed Atta, who hijacked and piloted the plane that crashed into the north tower of the World Trade Center, was stopped in Tamarac, Florida, for driving without a valid license and issued a ticket. He didn't pay the ticket so an arrest warrant was issued. A few weeks later, he was stopped for speeding but let go because police did not know about the warrant.

Agencies and cities across the country have increased security-related spending time. including surveillance cameras, security gates, bulletproof glass, filters for building ventilation systems, security badges, outdoor lighting, gas respirators, concrete planters, body armor, biohazard suits, metal detectors, fences, motion detectors, caller-ID technology, alarms, vehicle-tracking systems, electronic door locks, guardhouses and bomb-sniffing dogs. However, in a poll conducted by the International Association of Chiefs of Police (IACP), 71 percent of the 4,500 agencies that responded to the survey reported being "not at all prepared" or "somewhat unprepared" to prevent terrorism. A mere 1 percent claimed that they were "adequately prepared" (Garrett, 2004, p.6). An important step in preparedness is learning about and understanding the enemy.

Understanding the Enemy

To successfully fight terrorism in the United States, law enforcement must have a clear understanding of the adversary—who the adversaries are, their thinking processes, their tactics and their mind-sets. Local law enforcement must also try to establish good relationships in the Arab and Muslim communities so that they can obtain information about any terrorists or terrorist activity that might be suspected.

The Criminal versus the Terrorist The importance of knowing one's enemy cannot be overemphasized. One critical dimension of this knowledge is differentiating the street criminal from the terrorist. Officers who are trained and equipped to deal with traditional crimes are now expected to apprehend individuals operating with different motivations and who usually use much deadlier weapons than traditional criminals.

It should be recognized, however, that terrorists also engage in criminal behavior.

Crimes Associated with Terrorists The following crimes are commonly associated with terrorists: mail theft, coupon fraud, sale of illegal cigarettes, identity theft, credit card scams, ATM fraud, counterfeit food products and postage stamps, money laundering and video/audio piracy (Savelli, 2004, pp.21–36).

Terrorist Indicators Savelli (2004, p.16) also notes, "Law enforcement officers should be aware of terrorist indicators. Awareness of these indicators will give the law enforcement officer a strong basis to recognize terrorist-related information upon being exposed to it. Such indicators are negative rhetoric, excessive physical training, anti-American literature or a disregard for U.S. laws. Terrorists and their supporters tend to act similar since many of them have trained in the same terrorist training camps and share the same negative ideology."

Identifying Possible Terrorists Identification can be aided by a familiar tool of law enforcement—profiling. Such profiling must hinge on behavioral characteristics, however, because racial profiling is illegal. This is not say, however, that law enforcement should not take appearances into account; it means that appearance cannot be the sole factor in profiling. The typical appearance of an al Qaeda terrorist is a young (20 to 30) Middle-Eastern-appearing male of average height and weight with prominent facial hair and a foreign accent. Few use alcohol or smoke cigarettes, although many terrorists intentionally shave their beards, wear western style clothes, frequent bars and smoke cigarettes to avoid detection.

Behavior pattern recognition (BPR) can also help in identifying terrorists. BPR is based on two activities: observation of irregular behaviors for a given location and targeted conversations with suspects. The community can also be instrumental in providing information, especially those areas in which community policing is used, as discussed later in the chapter.

Local law enforcement officers can improve their ability to detect a potential terrorist attack in their communities by educating themselves—understanding the enemy as already discussed. Officers should also gather intelligence just as they would on any investigative encounter. When making a traffic stop, ask questions such as "Where are you from? Where do you work? Why are you here?" Note that these questions are not specific to profiling possible terrorists but are standard policing methods used by officers attempting to gather information on possible criminal activity, regardless of whether it has to do with homeland security.

Finally, officers should report what they learn. They should know who is gathering intelligence at the local, state and federal level as well as how to obtain needed information (Smith, 2009).

Valuable Targets for a Terrorist Attack Targets include high-occupancy structures or any site where a significant number of lives are affected; a structure containing dangerous substances; any vital, high-use portion of the infrastructure; any item of significant historical, symbolic, strategic, defensive or functional value; and a structure holding highly sensitive, rare, or irreplaceable artifacts, or documents.

The Typical Stages in a Terrorist Attack Terrorist attacks typically have three stages. The first stage is research, including surveillance, stake-outs, and local inquiries. This is the stage during which local law enforcement officers can best serve the counter-terrorism effort because the terrorists are out in public, watching us, studying our habits, discovering our vulnerabilities and reporting back to their handlers with prospective targeting data to begin the planning stage. (Recall the nine-stage process used by suicide bombers, discussed previously, and the need for law enforcement to detect and intervene during the earliest stages possible.)

The second stage is planning, usually conducted behind closed doors. The average planning cycle for international terrorists is 92 days, compared with 14 days for environmental terrorists (Smith, 2008). The third stage is execution, the actual attack, and possible escape.

In addition to the preceding general information regarding terrorists, law enforcement officers should become familiar with the training received by members of al Qaeda and the tactics they use. White (2004, pp.99–101) describes the lessons taught in the al Qaeda manual seized by the Manchester Constabulary in the United Kingdom. The first lesson is a general introduction beginning with a lamentation on the state of the world and ending with a call to holy war (***jihad***). Other lessons focus on the qualities of al Qaeda members; forgery; safe houses and other hiding places, including instructions for establishing a clandestine terrorist network; secret transportation and communication; training and security during training; and weapons, one of the keys to terrorism, including building an arsenal and safely storing explosives. The remaining lessons discuss secrecy and member safety, emphasizing the need to maintain family and neighborhood ties in the operational area; security, emphasizing planning and operations (secrecy is constantly stressed); reconnaissance, including methods for clandestine spying and capturing prisoners; intelligence gathering; tips on handling recruited agents and dealing with counter measures; and instructions about behavior when arrested. Al Qaeda appears to have a working knowledge of the rights of prisoners in Western justice systems.

jihad
A holy war.

White (2004, p.98) also describes the three-tiered model of al Qaeda terrorist attacks, in which **sleeper cells**, groups of terrorists who blend into a community, are used.

sleeper cells
Groups of terrorists who blend into a community.

The three-tiered model of al Qaeda terrorist attacks consists of sleeper cells attacking in conjunction with the group's leaders in Afghanistan and Pakistan, sleeper cells attacking on their own apart from centralized command and individuals supported by small cells.

The challenge, and key to disrupting these cells, is identifying its members.

Lessons Learned from Mumbai Theodore Roosevelt once said, "Americans only learn by disaster." Considering, in retrospect, how much has changed since 9/11, this assessment certainly seems accurate. Our knowledge continues to grow with each event endured, and numerous valuable lessons were learned in the wake of the terrorist attacks in Mumbai in November 2008. The first lesson is to *heed the warning signs*. The United States had warned India's government of a coming attack, probably on luxury hotels, but the message was not communicated from the top down (Chudwin, 2009, pp.51–55).

The second lesson is that *leadership must be proactive, responsive and adaptive*. Law enforcement exists as hierarchical organizations geared toward making the big decisions. But in critical incidents, leaders must be willing to allow line-level decision making: "In attacks like those in Mumbai, patrol supervisors will be the generals of the street, and individual initiative will rule the moment" (Chudwin, 2009, p.51).

Third, the key to stopping terrorist attacks is keeping in touch to have an opportunity at *prevention and deterrence*. The intelligence function is the foundation of this effort.

Fourth, *system capability and officer response* are vital. In Mumbai, the home-field advantage was lost to the terrorists, who had done reconnaissance and knew their target better than the police and follow-on military did. To maintain the home-field advantage, officers should study building plans; do walk-throughs of potential targets; liaison with security directors of hotels, airports, and other likely targets; and plan ahead of an attack what should be done. Officers should be aware of and make use of the intelligence fusions centers around the country and get to know members of the JTTF in the local FBI office.

Last, *stand ready and prepared to fight*. There will be no time to wait for special teams. If terrorists are allowed time to set defenses, blockade entrances and set explosives, it will be Mumbai again. The bottom line is, "Police must be capable and ready to fight. This is the core mission of law enforcement: protect our citizens and residents from threats to their lives. There's a time to talk and a time to fight. Administrators and street officers must know the difference." Chudwin (2009, p.55) suggests that each officer have at-the-ready a "go bag" that contains extra ammunition, radio and flashlight batteries, wound bandages, a tourniquet, binoculars and other combat essentials: "We have skilled men and women in uniform on the street and in command positions. It only takes the willingness to accept that the threat is real, imminent and coming to your hometown. In the end, it's not enough to be willing to fight. There must be a total commitment to win" (p.55).

Intelligence Gathering and Sharing

As has been mentioned throughout the chapter, intelligence gathering and sharing is vital to successful counterterrorism efforts. Many of the day-to-day duties of local law enforcement officers bring them into proximity with sources of information about terrorism. Traffic can track down information related to terrorism if properly trained in what to look for and what questions to ask when interacting with citizens. The intelligence process focuses on knowing what you don't know, asking for what you don't know, finding the answers and then making sure the answers get to the right people (*Strategic Plan,* p.23). Finding intelligence gaps should lead to specific intelligence collection or production tasks. Then information needs to be collected to fill these gaps in intelligence. The information gathered should be used for briefings, reports and studies that are then dissemination to all interested parties and partners. Figure 9.2 illustrates a model to help local police implement their new antiterrorism responsibilities regarding information and intelligence.

Three obstacles to intelligence effectiveness are technological, political and ethical.

The most challenging technological issue, as discussed previously, is *interoperability,* the ability to exchange information seamlessly. Political obstacles

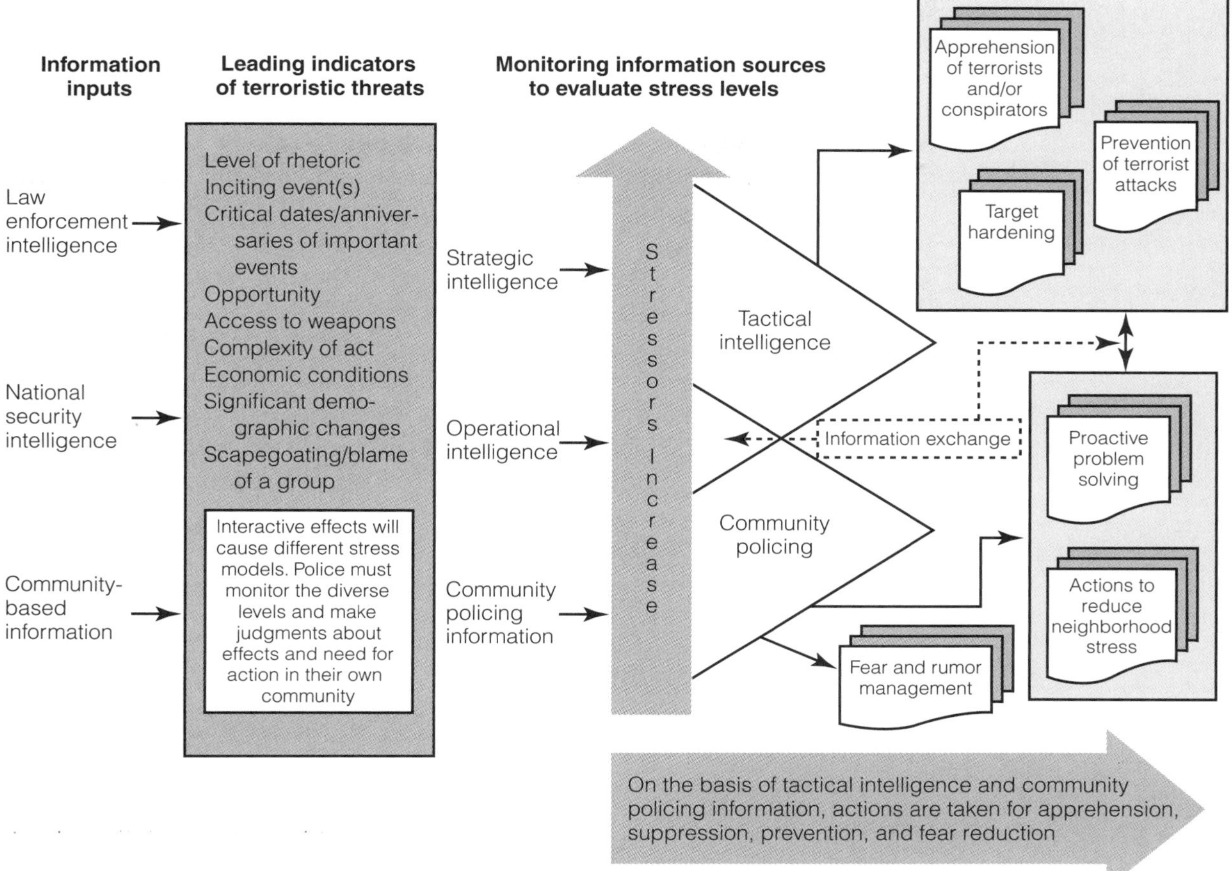

FIGURE 9.2 Implementation Model for Anti-Terrorism Responsibilities
Source: David L. Carter and Richard N. Holden. "Terrorism and Community Security." *Local Government Police Management*, 4th ed. Edited by William A. Geller and Darrel W. Stephens. Washington, DC: International City/County Management Association, 2003, p.307. Reprinted by permission.

include finances (who pays for what) and turf wars, including relationships with the FBI and with the state police. The ethical obstacles include the issues of profiling and open records legislation.

Withholding Information Counterterrorism efforts are made more difficult by the operational style that exists at almost every level of policing and in most agencies—withholding, rather than sharing, information, often referred to as "working in silos": "On the surface it seems simple: Defense and intelligence communities gather information concerning possible terrorist activities in the United States. . . . Under the surface, however, a complex network of interagency rivalries, laws, security clearance issues and turf protection reduces the possibility of shared information" (White, 2004, p.17).

Sometimes information cannot be shared, such as classified information. Rules of federal procedure and grand jury classified material are two other limitations to what or how much information can be shared. Savelli (2004, p.43) observes, "The last thing any law enforcement officer wants to do is compromise a terrorism investigation. The best way to avoid compromising an existing investigation, or conducting conflicting cases, is to develop a local networking module with local, state and federal law enforcement agencies to discuss investigative and enforcement endeavors to combat terrorism. . . . These networking modules should have built-in deconfliction protocol. **Deconfliction**, in essence, means avoiding conflict. Deconfliction can be deployed with declassified and confidential investigations."

deconfliction
Avoiding conflict.

The National Criminal Intelligence Sharing Plan (NCISP) A subtitle of the Homeland Security Act of 2002, called the Homeland Security Information Sharing Act, required the president to develop new procedures for sharing classified information as well as unclassified but otherwise sensitive information with state and local police. This charge was fulfilled in May 2002 when the IACP, the Department of Justice, the FBI, the DHS and other representatives of the federal, state, tribal and local law enforcement communities endorsed the National Criminal Intelligence Sharing Plan (NCISP), which increases cooperation and communication among local, state and federal partners to an unprecedented level, strengthening the abilities of the justice community to detect threats and protect American lives and liberties.

Intelligence Reform and Terrorism Prevention Act of 2004 In December 2004 President Bush signed into law the Intelligence Reform and Terrorism Prevention Act to enhance public safety communication operability at all levels of government. It requires the president to facilitate sharing terrorism information among all appropriate federal, state, local, tribal and private security entities through the use of policy guidelines and technology.

Crucial Collaborations—Partnerships and Communication

The importance of partnerships between law enforcement agencies at all levels cannot be overstated as it applies to the war on terrorism.

A key to combating terrorism lies with the local police and the intelligence they can provide to other jurisdictions as well as state and federal authorities.

As stressed earlier, communication should be the number one priority in any preparedness plan, and it is also number one in collaboration among local, state and federal law, as well as others who can provide helpful information.

INITIATIVES TO ASSIST IN THE FIGHT AGAINST TERRORISM

Several initiatives have been undertaken to help in the fight against terrorism. One such initiative is production of the *FBI Intelligence Bulletin*, a weekly online publication containing information related to terrorism in the United States.

Recipients include duly authorized members of all law enforcement agencies who have registered with a law enforcement network.

Another initiative that indirectly supports the fight against terrorism is passage of the Community Protection Act.

The Community Protection Act gives off-duty as well as qualified retired police officers the right to carry their concealed firearms in all 50 states.

H.R. 218, the Law Enforcement Officer's Safety Act of 2004, amended Title 18, United States Code, to exempt qualified current and former law enforcement officers from state laws prohibiting the carrying of concealed handguns. Other initiatives include increased security at our borders, the Community Vulnerability Assessment Methodology, the Terrorist Center, the National Infrastructure Protection Plan (NIPP), fusion centers, the Memorial Institute for the Prevention of Terrorism (MIPT) , the Center for Food Protection and Defense and the National Incident Management System.

Increased Border Security

The terrorist attacks in Mumbai, India, brought to the forefront the vulnerability of our nation's ports because the United States has no central port authority to oversee security (Taylor and Kaufman, 2009). Approximately 8,000 ships with foreign flags make 51,000 calls on U.S. ports each year, and 90 percent of overseas commerce comes by ship. In addition, more than 6.5 million passengers from cruise ships pass through the nation's ports each year, along with about 9 million cargo containers—about 26,000 cargo containers a day: "If terrorists used a cargo container to conceal a weapon of mass destruction and detonated it upon arrival at a U.S. port, the impact on global trade and the world economy could be immediate and devastating" (Taylor and Kaufman).

Research on security measures currently in place at our nation's ports found that many have created physical barriers, limited access, installed detection equipment, increased law enforcement activity and coordinated strategies among agencies (Taylor and Kaufman, 2009). Some of the best systems combined closed-circuit television (CCTV) and video analysis to analyze video proactively based on observed behavior. One simple strategy used by most of the ports visited stacked empty shipping containers with their doors facing each other to block entry to terrorists, stowaways or smugglers. Other border security programs are aimed at those seeking illegal entry into the United States.

The Department of Homeland Security's program, U.S. Visitor and Immigrant Status Indicator Technology (US-VISIT), seeks "to enhance the security of our citizens and visitors; facilitate legitimate travel and trade; and ensure the integrity of our immigration system." The program requires visitors to submit to inkless finger scans and digital photographs to allow Customs and Border Protection officers to determine whether the person applying for entry is the same one who was issued a visa by the State Department. Biometric and biographic data will also be checked against watch lists of suspected foreign terrorists and databases of sexual predators, criminals wanted by the FBI and people deported previously from the United States.

The stricter identification requirements for entering the country from Canada and Mexico, instituted in June 2009, may help border agents (Sherman, 2009). The land and sea portion of the Western Hemisphere Travel Initiative (WHTI) is intended to standardize the documents required to enter the United States (Burton, 2009). The goal is to facilitate entry for U.S. citizens and legitimate foreign visitors while reducing the possibility of people entering the country using fraudulent documents. Another new development is the electronic passport (e-passport), which is the same as a regular passport but with a small computer chip embedded in the back cover as an upgraded security feature. Since August 2007, the U.S. has issued only e-passports.

Community Vulnerability Assessment Methodology

The Community Vulnerability Assessment Methodology (C-VAM) identifies a community's weaknesses by using a detailed, systematic analysis of the facilities and their relationship to each other. By considering a community as individual structures, a department can focus its resources on the areas where they are most needed.

The Terrorist Screening Center

The Terrorist Screening Center (TSC) maintains the government's Terrorist Watchlist—a single database of identifying information about those known or reasonably suspected of being involved in terrorist activity. According to the FBI, the Terrorist Watchlist is one of the most effective counterterrorism tools for the U.S. government. While distributing information about encounters with known or suspected terrorists, the TSC is also "dedicated to ensuring the data it stores is maintained in a manner consistent with protecting the privacy and civil liberties of Americans" ("Terrorist Screening Center," n.d.).

The National Infrastructure Protection Plan (NIPP)

The NIPP is a comprehensive risk management framework defining critical infrastructure protection roles and responsibilities of federal, state, local, tribal and private security partners. The goal of the NIPP is to "Build a safer, more secure and more resilient America by enhancing protection of the nation's critical infrastructure and key resources (CI/KR) to prevent, deter, neutralize or mitigate the effects of deliberate efforts by terrorists to destroy, incapacitate or exploit them; and to strengthen national preparedness, timely response and rapid recovery in the event of an attack, natural disaster or other emergency" (*National Infrastructure Protection Plan*, 2009).

The cornerstone of the NIPP is the risk management framework, shown in Figure 9.3. This framework establishes the process for combining consequence, vulnerability and threat information to produce a comprehensive, systematic and rational assessment or national or sector-specific risk that drives CI/KR-protection activities.

An updated *National Strategy for the Physical Protection of Critical Infrastructures and Key Assets* (2008) lists the following as critical infrastructures:

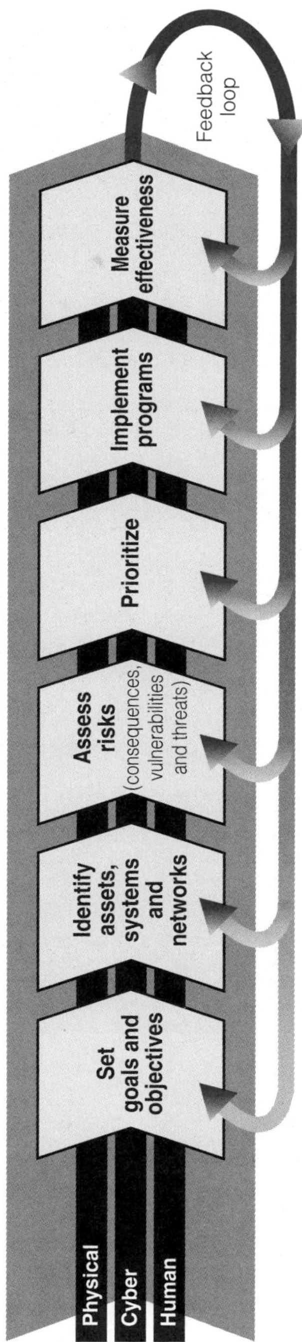

FIGURE 9.3
NIPP Risk Management Framework
Source: *National Infrastructure Protection Plan.* Washington, DC: Department of Homeland Security, 2009, p.4.

agriculture and food, water, public health, emergency services, defense industrial base, telecommunications, energy, transportation, banking and finance, chemical industry and hazardous materials, and postal and shipping facilities. It lists the following as key assets: national monuments and icons, nuclear power plants, dams, government facilities, and commercial key assets.

The NIPP (2009, p.4) describes sector-specific agencies and assigned critical infrastructure and key resources sectors in Table 9.2.

Table 9.2 Sector-Specific Agencies and Assigned CIKR Sectors

Sector-Specific Agency	Critical Infrastructure and Key Resources Sector
Department of Agriculture[a] Department of Health and Human Services[b]	Agriculture and Food
Department of Defense[c]	Defense Industrial Base
Department of Energy	Energy[d]
Department of Health and Human Services	Healthcare and Public Health
Department of the Interior	National Monuments and Icons
Department of the Treasury	Banking and Finance
Environmental Protection Agency	Water[e]
Department of Homeland Security Office of Infrastructure Protection	Chemical Commercial Facilities Critical Manufacturing Dams Emergency Services Nuclear Reactors, Materials, and Waste
Office of Cybersecurity and Communications	Information Technology Communications
Transportation Security Administration	Postal and Shipping
Transportation Security Administration United States Coast Guard[f]	Transportation Systems[g]
Immigration and Customs Enforcement, Federal Protective Service	Government Facilities[h]

[a]The Department of Agriculture is responsible for agriculture and food (meat, poultry, and egg products).
[b]The Department of Health and Human Services is responsible for food other than meat, poultry, and egg products.
[c]Nothing in this plan impairs or otherwise affects the authority of the Secretary of Defense over the Department of Defense (DoD), including the chain of command for military forces from the President as Commander in Chief, to the Secretary of Defense, to the commander of military forces, or military command and control procedures.
[d]The Energy Sector includes the production, refining, storage, and distribution of oil, gas, and electric power, except for commercial nuclear power facilities.
[e]The Water Sector includes drinking water and wastewater systems.
[f]The U.S. Coast Guard is the SSA for the maritime transportation mode.
[g]As stated in HSPD-7, the Department of Transportation and the Department of Homeland Security will collaborate on all matters relating to transportation security and transportation infrastructure protection.
[h]The Department of Education is the SSA for the Education Facilities Subsector of the Government Facilities Sector.
Source: *National Infrastructure Protection Plan*. Washington, DC: Department of Homeland Security, 2009, p.3.

Fusion Centers

An initiative aimed at promoting and facilitating information and intelligence sharing among federal and local law enforcement agencies is the development of fusion centers throughout the country: "Fusion centers combine multiple agencies in one location, pooling resources and personnel in order to share information and develop intelligence" (Johnson and Dorn, 2008, p.34).

fusion center
Manages the flow of information and intelligence across all levels and sectors of government and private industry, turning information and intelligence into actionable knowledge.

Straw (2008, p.68) notes, "While government is notoriously slow to implement change, one post-9-11 reform has bucked the trend: the rapidly growing national network of state, regional, and urban intelligence fusion centers. At the centers, teams of analysts crunch data and produce refined intelligence to help stakeholders address all hazards and all crimes." A **fusion center** manages the flow of information and intelligence across all levels and sectors of government and private industry, turning information and intelligence into actionable knowledge. According to the FBI, in 2009, there were 70 centers around the country—50 state and 20 regional centers ("Fusion Centers," 2009).

The Memorial Institute for the Prevention of Terrorism (MIPT)

The Memorial Institute for the Prevention of Terrorism (MIPT), which originated from the 1995 bombing of the Alfred P. Murrah Federal Building, is a counterterrorism center focused on training, analysis and information sharing in preventing terrorist attacks. Its name and mission are identical—prevent terrorism. Members of the institute do so by delivering training on site or remotely, creating exercises and teaching tools, advising government and private enterprise and sharing knowledge through their library ("About MIPT," n.d.).

In April 2009, the MIPT hosted a round-table discussion with law enforcement officers from the Middle East, including Afghanistan, Bangladesh, Egypt, Kuwait, Maldives, Pakistan, Qatar and the West Bank. The objective was to share lessons learned from fighting terrorism as well as to examine the roles, responsibilities and cooperative efforts of key law enforcement institutions (Manos, 2009).

The Center for Food Protection and Defense

The mission of the National Center for Food Protection and Defense is to safeguard the security of the food system through research and education. Its goals are to reduce the vulnerability of the nation's food system to terrorist attack by contamination with biological, chemical, or radiological agents at any point along the food supply chain; to strengthen the food system's preparedness and resiliency to threats, disruption, and attacks; and to mitigate the potentially catastrophic public health and economic effects of food system attacks (National Center for Food Protection and Defense, 2008). This effort is lead by the University of Minnesota.

The National Incident Management System

In 2004, the National Incident Management System (NIMS) became the country's first standardized management approach unifying federal, state and local governments for incident response. NIMS establishes standardized incident management processes, protocols and procedures that all responders—federal, state, tribal and local—use to coordinate and conduct response action, as discussed in Chapter 8.

THE ROLE OF THE MEDIA IN THE WAR ON TERRORISM

An old saying goes, "The operations that go as planned never get noticed; mistakes make the headlines" (Griffith, 2008, p.46). The Terrorism Research Center suggests, "Terrorism and the media have a symbiotic relationship. Without the media, terrorists would receive no exposure, their cause would go ignored, and no climate of fear would be generated. Terrorism is futile without publicity, and the media generates much of this publicity." This often results in the **contagion effect**, that is, the coverage of terrorism inspires more terrorism. It is, in effect, contagious. For example, an article in *The Police Chief* states, "The media attention and public reaction to the Mumbai attacks could possibly prompt other terrorist incidents" ("Need for Homeland Security,"

contagion effect
Coverage of terrorism inspires more terrorism—it is, in effect, contagious.

2009, p.25). This controversial issue leads to discussions about censorship in the war on terrorism.

CONCERNS RELATED TO THE WAR ON TERRORISM

Two concerns related to the "war on terrorism" are that civil liberties might be jeopardized and that people of Middle Eastern descent might be discriminated against or become victims of hate crimes.

Concern for Civil Rights

The first guiding principle of the DHS is to protect civil rights and civil liberties: "We will defend America while protecting the freedoms that define America. Our strategies and actions will be consistent with the individual rights and liberties enshrined by our Constitution and the Rule of Law. While we seek to improve the way we collect and share information about terrorists, we will nevertheless be vigilant in respecting the confidentiality and protecting the privacy of our citizens. We are committed to securing our nation while protecting civil rights and civil liberties" (*Securing Our Homeland*, n.d, p.6).

Civil libertarians are concerned that valued American freedoms will be sacrificed in the interest of national safety. For example, the Justice Department has issued a new regulation giving itself the authority to monitor inmate-attorney communications if "reasonable suspicion" exists that inmates are using such communications to further or facilitate acts of terrorism. However, criminal defense lawyers and members of the American Civil Liberties Union (ACLU) have protested the regulation, saying it effectively eliminates the Sixth Amendment right to counsel because, under codes of professional responsibility, attorneys cannot communicate with clients if confidentiality is not ensured. The ACLU has vowed to monitor police actions closely to see that freedoms protected under the Constitution are not jeopardized.

A difficult challenge facing law enforcement is balancing the need to enhance security with the need to maintain freedom.

Retaliation or Discrimination against People of Middle Eastern Descent

Another concern is that some Americans might retaliate against innocent people of Middle Eastern descent, many of whom were either born in the United States or are naturalized citizens. We must remember the Japanese internment camps during World War II and make sure we do not repeat that mistake. Henderson et al. (2008) identified four significant obstacles to improved relations between police and Arab Americas communities:

- Distrust between Arab American communities and law enforcement.
- Lack of cultural awareness among law enforcement officers.
- Language barriers.
- Concerns about immigration status and fear of deportation.

Community policing efforts can do much to overcome these obstacles.

Closely related concerns are the rights of citizens detained as enemy combatants and the rights of detained foreign nationals. In *Hamdi v. Rumsfeld* (2004), the Supreme Court ruled that a citizen detained in the United States as an enemy combatant must be afforded the opportunity to rebut such a designation. Petitioner Hamdi was captured in an active combat zone in Afghanistan following the September 11, 2001, attack on America and surrendered an assault rifle. The U.S. District Court found that the declaration from the Defense Department did not support Hamdi's detention and ordered the government to turn over numerous materials for review. The U.S. Court of Appeals for the Fourth Circuit reversed, stressing that, because it was undisputed that Hamdi was captured in an active combat zone, no factual inquiry or evidentiary hearing allowing Hamdi to rebut the government's assertions was necessary. A 6–3 Supreme Court vacated and remanded, concluding that Hamdi should have a meaningful opportunity to offer evidence that he was not an enemy combatant.

In *Rasul v. Bush* (2004), the Supreme Court ruled that U.S. courts have jurisdiction to consider challenges to the legality of the detention of foreign nationals captured in Afghanistan in a military campaign against al Qaeda and the Taliban regime that supported it. The petitioners, 2 Australians and 12 Kuwaitis, were being held in Guantanamo Bay, Cuba, without charges. These and other legal issues regarding civil rights will be debated as the country seeks to balance the need for security with civil rights.

Lively controversy surrounds the future of Guantanamo Bay (aka GITMO), where a detainment facility run by the U.S. military houses "enemy combatants" captured in the war on terrorism. President Barack Obama is committed to closing the facility but is facing criticism and challenges from Congress, the public and other sources for possible ramifications of releasing dangerous individuals who are intent on causing harm to our country and its citizens. Various reports have concluded that a significant proportion of prisoners—as many as 1 out of 7, or 14 percent—released from Guantanamo Bay return to militant activity (Bumiller, 2009, p.A1; Wall, 2009). It is impossible to predict what might result from such a dismantling of this facility, but this will undoubtedly be a topic of discussion for future editions of this text.

COMMUNITY POLICING AND HOMELAND SECURITY

Community policing officers can do much to educate citizens in their jurisdiction on preparedness plans, including a meeting place in case of a terrorist attack. Citizen Corps, a component of the USA Freedom Corps, focuses on opportunities for people across the country to participate in a range of measures to make their families, homes and communities safer from the threats of terrorism, crime and disasters of all kinds. In addition, Citizen Corps brings together a community's first responders, firefighters, emergency health care providers, law enforcement and emergency managers with its volunteer resources.

The CAT Eyes Program, the Community Anti-Terrorism Training Initiative, was designed to enlist community members in the fight against terrorism by educating citizens about how to raise neighborhood security by increasing their powers of observation. The CAT Eyes Program also encourages mutual assistance and concern among neighbors (Giannone and Wilson, 2003, p.37).

Scheider et al. (n.d., p.162) contend, "In the 21st century the community policing philosophy is well positioned to take a central role in preventing and responding to terrorism and in efforts to reduce citizen fear. Law enforcement agencies should realize that community policing is more important than ever in proactively dealing with and responding to terrorism in their jurisdiction." They (p.160) explain, "An officer in a department that fully embraces the community policing philosophy would know of potential terrorist targets in his jurisdiction because he has been assigned a regular patrol area and given the responsibility and authority to protect it."

Vernon (2008, p.57) offers these guidelines for departments wanting to mobilize their community in counterterrorism efforts:

1. Establish a liaison with DHS.
2. Formulate a policy statement that will guide community mobilization efforts.
3. Educate community members about the significant differences between reporting sought-after information (proper) and conducting covert investigations or other quasi-police actions (improper).
4. Emphasize the importance of reporting information without making assumptions about a person's guilt.

Several sources of information in the community include Neighborhood Watches, hotels, real estate agents, storage facilities, religious groups, social and civic clubs, colleges and universities, print shops, business managers, transportation centers, tourist attractions, major industrial enterprises, schools, office building custodians, health care providers, bar and liquor stores and inspectors and code enforcers.

Officers engaged in community policing can do much to educate citizens in their jurisdictions about preparedness plans, including setting a family meeting place in case of a terrorist attack. Citizen Corps is a component of the USA Freedom Corps that focuses on opportunities for people across the country to participate in a range of measures to make their families, homes, and communities safer from the threats of terrorism, crime, and disasters of all kinds. In addition, Citizen Corps brings together a community's first responders, firefighters, emergency health care providers, law enforcement, and emergency managers with its volunteer resources. The Citizen Core program in Kentucky uses a four-pronged strategy to include citizen preparedness, business preparedness, kids' preparedness, and special needs and vulnerable population's preparedness ("Citizen Corps Programs," 2007, pp.8–9). In New York City, police are providing antiterrorism training to building superintendents and door attendants to be the eyes and ears of the department, with plans calling for training 28,000 building employees.

SUMMARY

The threat of terrorism has become a reality in America. Most definitions of terrorism have common elements, including the systematic use of physical violence, either actual or threatened, against noncombatants to create a climate of fear to cause some religious, political or social change. Three elements of terrorism are (1) it is criminal in nature, (2) targets are typically symbolic and (3) the terrorist actions are always aggressive and often violent. The FBI classifies terroristic acts as either domestic or international. Most terrorist acts result from dissatisfaction with a religious, political or social system or policy and frustration resulting from an inability to change it through acceptable, nonviolent means. Terrorist groups within the United States with specific motivations include right-wing extremists (White supremacists, Black supremacists, and militia groups), left-wing extremists, pro-life extremists, animal rights activists and environmental extremists. Terrorists might use arson, explosives and bombs, weapons of mass destruction (biological, chemical or nuclear agents), and technology.

As a result of 9/11, the Department of Homeland Security (DHS) was established, reorganizing the departments of the federal government. At the federal level, the FBI is the lead agency for responding to acts of domestic terrorism. The Federal Emergency Management Agency (FEMA) is the lead agency for consequence management (after an attack). The DHS facilitates collaboration between local and federal law enforcement to develop a national strategy to detect, prepare for, prevent, protect against, respond to and recover from terrorist attacks within the United States.

The USA PATRIOT Act significantly improves the nation's counterterrorism efforts by

- Allowing investigators to use the tools already available to investigate organized crime and drug trafficking.
- Facilitating information sharing and cooperation among government agencies so they can better "connect the dots."
- Updating the law to reflect new technologies and new threats.
- Increasing the penalties for those who commit or support terrorist crimes.

The first line of defense against terrorism is the patrol officer in the field.

The three-tiered model of al Qaeda terrorist attacks consists of sleeper cells attacking in conjunction with the group's leaders in Afghanistan and Pakistan, sleeper cells attacking on their own apart from centralized command and individuals supported by small cells. Three obstacles to intelligence effectiveness are technological, political and ethical. A key to combating terrorism lies with the local police and the intelligence they can provide to other jurisdictions as well as state and federal authorities. The Community Protection Act gives off-duty as well as qualified retired police officers the right to carry their concealed firearms in all 50 states.

Two concerns related to the "war on terrorism" are that civil liberties might be jeopardized and that people of Middle Eastern descent might be discriminated against or become victims of hate crimes. A difficult challenge facing law enforcement is balancing the need to enhance security with the need to maintain freedom.

APPLICATION

You are a public safety administrator with an agency that has several high-risk terrorism target locations, as identified by the FBI, in your city. Among the targets identified are a large oil refinery and a nationally recognized water park that draws hundreds of thousands of tourists and local visitors annually. Your agency is large and well prepared for general public safety; however, it seems that the city does not have the funds to properly outfit your agency with all of the items needed to respond to a terrorist attack or a large-scale disaster. Your agency is eligible to receive grants because of the recognized terrorist targets within your community and the potential for attack is high, and your chief administrator has requested that you research and write some federal or state grants. Your objective is to receive funding to alleviate some of the financial burden on items that need to be purchased to respond to a terrorist incident.

Draft a grant requesting the items you need for your city, and provide a detailed explanation of why you need them. Your application should include the details of your agency, and a purpose statement. Furthermore, research what federal or state agencies might have available grant money for Homeland Security specific funding such as this.

AN EXERCISE IN CRITICAL THINKING

You are a police officer with Big City Police Department who has been assigned to a specialized Terrorism Task Force Unit and Retail Liaison with a large mall that operates in your city. This mall is a major international tourist attraction and has a worldwide reputation that embodies much of what the United States represents in terms of free trade and capitalism. Your assignment includes working closely with the mall's company administration and security, as well as with federal agents from the Department of Homeland Security and the FBI. Your duties include gathering intelligence and investigating suspicious activity that could be terrorism related.

While conducting foot patrol around the mall, you notice a man of Middle Eastern descent walk toward a restricted corridor in the building. You follow him to make contact. When you approach him, you see he has a high quality digital camera and is taking pictures of the inside of the restricted area. When he sees you he appears startled and quickly takes the memory card out of his camera and places it in his pocket. Upon questioning he tells you his name, shows you a state-issued identification document, and states he just got lost because the building was so large. A check comes back to a valid and clear person. He is cooperative until you ask him why he was taking pictures in the restricted area. At that time he becomes nervous and no longer wishes to speak with you.

1. How would you handle the situation?
   a. Arrest the man for suspicious activity and being in a restricted area on private property. Then bring him to an area where you can attempt a detailed interrogation and take his property as a search incident to arrest and trespass him from the property.
   b. Confiscate his camera and memory card on scene and release him since you have already identified who he is.
   c. Accept the man's excuse as reasonable, log his information and pass it on as intelligence. Inform the man that his information is on file and that he is not allowed to take further pictures of restricted areas. Then escort him off the property.
   d. Because he is suspicious, arrest him. Then draft a search warrant and legally retrieve the pictures for intelligence purposes.
2. What follow up would you do as a result of your decision?
   a. Nothing. You have already gained his information and identity.
   b. Ensure that the suspect's information was passed on to mall administration, security, and federal officials.
   c. Post the suspect's information publicly as well as contact the media over the incident.
   d. Attempt to contact the suspect later on, to see what he is up to.

DISCUSSION QUESTIONS

1. Which is the greater threat—domestic or international terrorism? Why?
2. Does your police department have a counterterrorism strategy in place? If so, what?
3. What type of terrorist attack do you fear most? Why?
4. Do you feel Americans have become complacent about terrorism?
5. What provisions of the PATRIOT Act do you think are most important?
6. What barriers to sharing information among the various local, state and federal agencies do you think are most problematic?
7. Does media coverage of terrorist acts lead to more terrorism, that is, do you think the contagion effect is in operation?
8. Should Americans expect to give up some civil liberties to allow law enforcement officers to pursue terrorists?
9. Do you think a terrorist sleeper cell could operate in your community? What signs might indicate that such a cell exists?
10. What means might terrorists use to attack the United States in the future? Are we more or less vulnerable at home or at our interests abroad?

GALE EMERGENCY SERVICES DATABASE ASSIGNMENTS

- Use the Gale Emergency Services database to help answer the Discussion Questions as appropriate.
- Use the Gale Emergency Services database to determine how many countries in the world have been exposed to terrorism and the specific

nature of terrorist acts, if any distinguishing trends are noted.

- Use the Gale Emergency Services database to find and outline one of the following articles:
  - "State and Local Law Enforcement: Contributions to Terrorism Prevention" by William McCormack
  - "The FBI Joint Terrorism Task Force Officer" by Brig Barker and Steve Fowler
  - "One of These Things Is Not Like the Others: Customizing Terrorism Preparedness to Meet L.A. County's Unique Needs" by Linda Spagnoli
  - "Demands on Police Services in a WMD Incident" by Joel A. Carlson
  - "Law Enforcement and Hazmat/WMD Emergency Response: NFPA 472 As a Tool for Compliance" by Ed Allen and Steve Patrick
  - "Countering Violent Islamic Extremism: A Community Responsibility" by Carol Dyer, Ryan E. McCoy, Joel Rodriguez and Donald N. Van Duyn
  - "Words Make Worlds: Terrorism and Language" by Angus Smith

REFERENCES

"About MIPT." Oklahoma City, OK, no date.

Banks, David. "Center for Asymmetric Warfare Teams Up with Naval Graduate School." *Ventura Country Star*, June 22, 2008.

Blair, Dennis C. *Annual Threat Assessment of the Intelligence Community for the Senate Select Committee on Intelligence*, Washington, DC: Office of the Director of National Intelligence, February 12, 2009.

Bumiller, Elisabeth. "Later Terror Link Cited for 1 in 7 Freed Detainees." *New York Times*, May 21, 2009, p.A1.

Burton, Fred. "Practical Implications of the WHTI." *PoliceOne.com News*, June 2, 2009.

Carlson, Joel A. "Demands on Police Services in a WMD Incident." *FBI Law Enforcement Bulletin*, March 2008.

Chudwin, Jeff. "Homicide Bombers: Tactics for First-Responders." *Law Officer Magazine*, January 2007, pp.62–64.

Chudwin, Jeff. "Terror, Again: First-Responder Lessons from the Attacks in India." *Law Officer Magazine*, January 2009, pp.50–55.

"Citizen Corps Programs Ensure Everyone Is Prepared in the Event of a Disaster." *NCJA Justice Bulletin*, March 2007, pp.8–9.

Commission on Accreditation of Law Enforcement Agencies. *Standards for Law Enforcement Agencies*, 5th ed. Fairfax, VA: CALEA, 2006, updated 2008.

"Counterterrorism." Washington, DC: Federal Bureau of Investigation, no date.

Daniels, Rhianna. "Chemical Facilities Secure DHS Standards." *Security Director News*, February 2007, p.8.

DeYoung, Karen. "Attempts Seen as Model for New Attacks on U.S. Soil." *Washington Post*, July 3, 2007, p.A01.

Downing, Michael P. "Policing Terrorism in the United States: The Los Angeles Police Department's Convergence Strategy." *The Police Chief*, February 2009, pp.28–43.

Edwards, Al. "DHS Reveals Chemical Guidelines." *Security Director News*, May 2007, p.1.

Faherty, Christopher. "Police Test Technology to Safeguard City from Nuclear Attacks." *New York Sun*, April 2, 2007.

"FBI: Eco-Terrorism Remains No. 1 Domestic Terror Threat." *Fox News*, March 31, 2008.

"Fusion Centers: Unifying Intelligence to Protect Americans." Washington, DC: Federal Bureau of Investigation Headline Archives, March 12, 2009.

Garrett, Ronnie. "The Wolf Is at the Door: What Are We Waiting For?" *Law Enforcement Technology*, March 2004, p.6.

Garrett, Ronnie. "A Storm Is Brewing. . . ." *Law Enforcement Technology*, October 2007, p.10.

Garrett, Ronnie. "The Numbers Don't Lie." *Law Enforcement Technology*, November 2008a, p.6.

Garrett, Ronnie. "Waging War on Terror." *Law Enforcement Technology*, April 2008b, p.6.

Giannone, Donald, and Wilson, Robert A. "The CAT Eyes Program: Enlisting Community Members in the Fight against Terrorism." *The Police Chief*, Mach 2003, pp.37–38.

Goodwyn, Al. "Minimizing the Nuclear Threat: A Local Law Enforcement Strategy." *The Police Chief*, February 2008, pp.45–59.

Greene, Kevin E. "Congress Reauthorizes Anti-Terrorism Law." *Subject to Debate*, April 2006, p.6.

Griffith, David. "Stopping the Next 9/11." *Police*, September 2008, pp.46–53.

Harwood, Matthew. "Assessing Chlorine Gas Bombs." *Security Management*, June 2007, pp.18–19.

Henderson, Nicole J.; Ortiz, Christopher W.; Sugie, Naomi F.; and Miller, Joel. *Policing in Arab-American Communities*. Washington, DC: National Institute of Justice, July 2008. (NCJ 221706)

Hill, Michael, and Fitzgerald, Jim E. "New York Terror Case Latest of Many Homegrown Plots." *PoliceOne.com News*, May 22, 2009.

Holder, Eric. "Remarks as Prepared for Delivery by Attorney General Eric Holder at the National League of Cities Conference." Public Radio News, March 16, 2009.

Hsu, Spencer S. "Anti-Terror Funds Questioned." *Washington Post*, July 26, 2007, p.A02.

"An Interview with Homeland Security Secretary Michael Chertoff." *The Police Chief*, February 2007, pp.14–18.

Johnson, Bart R., and Dorn, Shelagh. "Fusion Centers: New York State Intelligence Strategy Unifies Law Enforcement." *The Police Chief*, February 2008, pp.34–46.

Jones, Keith. "Terrorism Deterrence, Part I." *Tactical Response*, January/February 2007, pp.34–36.

Kelling, George L.; Eddy, R. P.; and Bratton, William J. "The Blue Front Line in the War on Terror." *City Journal*, September 20, 2007.

Lovette, Ed. "Anti-Terrorism Intel for the Patrol Officer." *Police*, February 2008, pp.32–37.

Manos, Christi. "MIPT Engages in Open Exchange with Law Enforcement Officials from the Middle East." Oklahoma City, OK: Memorial Institute for the Prevention of Terrorism, April 28, 2009.

Meyer, Josh. "New FBI System Brings Terror Operations Out of the Dark." *Chicago Tribune*, May 24, 2009.

National Center for Food Protection and Defense Web site. Accessed August 20, 2008. http://www.ncfpd.umn.edu/

National Infrastructure Protection Plan. Washington, DC: Department of Homeland Security, 2009.

National Intelligence Estimate: The Terrorist Threat to the US Homeland. Washington, DC: National Intelligence Council, July 2007.

The National Strategy for the Physical Protection of Critical Infrastructures and Key Assets. Washington, DC, February 2008. Accessed August 19, 2008. http://www.dhs.gov/xlibrary/assets/Physical_Strategy.pdf

"The Need for Homeland Security: Greater Than Ever." *The Police Chief*, February 2009, pp.24–25.

"New York Says Thanks to Investigators of Foiled Bomb Plot." Washington, DC: Federal Bureau of Investigation Headline Archives, May 22, 2009.

Page, Douglas. "The RadTruck Stops Here." *Law Enforcement Technology*, May 2009, pp.50–55.

Perin, Michelle. "HAZSWAT Changed?" *Law Enforcement Technology*, May 2009, pp.20–25.

Phillips, Joan T. "Asymmetric Warfare." *Dictionary of Military Terms*, July 2006. Fairchild Research Information Center, Maxwell Air Force Base, Alabama. Accessed: http://www.au.af.mil/au/aul/bibs/asw.htm

Pike, George W. "USA PATRIOT Act: What's Next?" *Information Today*, April 2006, pp.33, 40.

Priem, Richard G.; Hunter, Dennis M.; and Polisar, Joseph M. "Terrorists and Suicide Tactics: Preparing for the Challenge." *The Police Chief*, September 2007, pp.32–36.

Report from the Field: The USA PATRIOT Act at Work. Washington, DC: Department of Justice, July 2004.

Savelli, Lou. *A Proactive Law Enforcement Guide for the War on Terrorism.* Flushing, NY: Looseleaf Law Publications, Inc., 2004.

Scheider, Matthew C.; Chapman, Robert E.; and Seelman, Michael E. "Connecting the Dots for a Proactive Approach." *BTS (Border and Transportation Security) America*, no date, pp.158–162.

Securing Our Homeland. Washington, DC: U.S. Department of Homeland Security, no date.

Sherman, Christopher. "Stricter ID Requirements May Help Border Agents."*PoliceOne.com News*, June 2, 2009.

Smith, Betsy. "A Patrol Officer's Guide to Terrorism Prevention." *PoliceOne.com News*, April 2, 2009.

Smith, Brent. "A Look at Terrorist Behavior: How They Prepare, Where They Strike." *NIJ Journal*, July 2008, pp.2–7.

"The Somali-Minneapolis Terrorist Axis." National Public Radio, 2009.

Stockton, Dale. "The End of the Beginning." *Law Officer Magazine*, January 2008, p.8.

Strategic Plan 2004–2009. Washington, DC: Federal Bureau of Investigation, 2004.

Straw, Joseph. "Smashing Intelligence Stovepipes." *Security Management*, March 2008, pp.68–74.

"Survey: Nuclear Terror Is Top Fear of Americans." 1105 Media, Inc., January 3, 2008.

Taylor, Bruce, and Kaufman, Pat. "Protecting America's Ports." *NIJ Journal*, March 2009.

The Terrorism Research Center. www.totalintel.com

"The Terrorist Screening Center." Washington, DC: Federal Bureau of Investigation, no date.

Trudeau, Scott. "Managing 21st-Century Threats with Chemical, Biological, Radiological, Nuclear, and Explosives Detection Devices." *The Police Chief*, February 2009, pp.44–50.

2008 Report on Terrorism. Washington, DC: National Counterterrorism Center, April 30, 2009.

Vernon, Bob. "Reliable Sources: The Right Way to Mobilize Your Community to Increase Security." *Law Officer Magazine*, June 2008, pp.56–57.

Wall, Tara. "Bush Sees Dangers Closing Gitmo." *The Washington Times*, January 16, 2009.

Wexler, Chuck. "Foreword." In *Patrol-Level Response to a Suicide Bomb Threat: Guidelines for Consideration.* By Lisa L. Spahr, Joshua Ederheimer and David Bilson. Washington, DC: Police Executive Research Forum, April 2007.

White, Jonathan R. *Defending the Homeland: Domestic Intelligence, Law Enforcement and Security.* Belmont, CA: Wadsworth Publishing Company, 2004.

White, Jonathan R. *Terrorism and Homeland Security*, 5th ed. Belmont, CA: Wadsworth Publishing Company, 2006.

Whitelaw, Kevin. "A Resurgent Menace." *U.S. News & World Report*, May 14, 2007, pp.32–33.

Wyllie, Doug. "FBI Director Mueller: A Mumbai-Style Attack Can Happen in the U.S." *PoliceOne.com News*, March 3, 2009.

CASES CITED

Hamdi v. Rumsfeld, 542 U.S. 507 (2004)

Rasul v. Bush, 542 U.S. 466 (2004)

USEFUL RESOURCES

Centers for Disease Control and Prevention: www.cdc.gov

The Counterterrorism Training and Resources Web site: http://www.counterterrorismtraining.gov

Federal Emergency Management Agency: http://www.fema.gov/areyouready

Federal Bureau of Investigation: http://www.fbi.gov

U.S. Department of Homeland Security: www.ready.gov

SECTION III

Specialized Police Operations

The previous section described the basic police operations within any law enforcement agency: patrol; traffic; dealing with crime and disorder; dealing with violence at home, in school and on the job; dealing with emergencies; and fighting the war on terrorism—protecting the homeland. In addition to these basic functions, law enforcement agencies also perform highly specialized operations. In smaller departments, the patrol officer performs these specialized operations. In larger departments, they may be assigned to specific officers or even to specialized departments.

This section discusses the specialized operations that may be required of law enforcement agencies, including investigation (Chapter 10), dealing with juveniles (Chapter 11) and dealing with gang and drug problems (Chapter 12). Even when the specialized operations are performed by nonpatrol officers, they still will require patrol officers' input and cooperation and, indeed, that of the entire community for maximum effectiveness.

CHAPTER 10

Criminal Investigation

DO YOU KNOW . . .

- How realistic fictionalized detectives are?
- What the primary goals of a criminal investigation are?
- What the most critical phase in the majority of criminal investigations is?
- What AFIS is and how it helps solve crimes?
- What two forms of positive identification may be available in criminal investigations?
- What the major violent crimes are, their elements and what special considerations might be involved in each?
- What the major property crimes are, their elements and what special considerations might be involved in each?
- What may be involved in computer-related crime?
- What victimless crimes are?
- When surveillance, undercover assignments and raids might be necessary?

CAN YOU DEFINE?

accelerants
Automated Fingerprint Identification System (AFIS)
contamination
covert investigations
CSI effect
DNA fingerprinting
equivocal death investigation
forensics
igniters
overt investigations
parallel proceedings
phishing
premeditation
proxy data
spoofing
victimless crimes

INTRODUCTION

One of the most important functions of law enforcement agencies is criminal investigation. This is largely carried out by detectives, and everyone knows what a detective is because of television programs such as *NYPD Blue, CSI* and *Law & Order.* To the public, detectives and criminal investigation are the "glamour jobs" within law enforcement.

Actually, this same view is held by many officers who, at some point in their careers, want a promotion to the detective division.

The glamorous, exciting, action-packed fictionalized detective presents an exaggerated, unrealistic picture that differs greatly from the reality of detective work.

The criminal investigative function—the process by which officers collect evidence, interview people, and compile facts for the purpose of supporting a prosecution—has always been viewed as the most challenging of all police work (Cronin et al., 2007). This chapter describes the real-life challenges of criminal investigation, an exceedingly complex field that can be only briefly introduced here. The chapter begins by discussing the primary goals, the investigation process, the preliminary investigation and the follow-up. Next is a look at *who* is responsible for investigating crimes, the types of evidence to look for, and the role of forensics and crime analysis in criminal investigations. Then the discussion turns to investigating specific crimes, including the violent and property crimes classified as Index offenses and other serious crimes, as well as the special considerations involved in each type of investigation. This is followed by a quick look at the problem of false reports and the challenges of investigating so-called victimless crimes. Next surveillance, undercover assignments, raids and stings are explored, including the use of informants. The chapter concludes with a look at the relationship between criminal investigation and community policing, including problem solving.

GOALS OF CRIMINAL INVESTIGATION

Hess and Orthmann (2010, p.7) observe, "The goal of criminal investigation would obviously seem to be to solve cases; to discover 'whodunit.' In reality, the goals of criminal investigation are not quite so simple."

The primary goals of criminal investigation are to

- Determine whether a crime has been committed.
- Legally obtain information and evidence to identify the responsible person.
- Arrest the suspect.
- Recover stolen property.
- Present the best possible case to the prosecutor.

Secondary goals of investigation include surveillance, crime prevention, crime scene investigation, background investigations and sexual offender tracking.

An investigation can be considered successful if it follows a logical sequence and legally obtains all available physical evidence and information from witnesses and suspects, if all leads are thoroughly developed and if all details of the case are accurately and completely recorded and reported. The overriding goal in a criminal investigation is to determine the truth regarding a specific crime. Successful investigation involves a balance between scientific knowledge acquired by study and experience and the skills acquired by the artful application of learned techniques.

THE INVESTIGATIVE PROCESS

A criminal investigation is usually initiated by an officer's personal observation of an incident or by information from a citizen through a call for service. In other words, patrol officers may see a suspicious action or person, or a citizen may report suspicious actions or people. Such information is received at police headquarters by telephone, fax, e-mail, radio, or direct report when a person steps up to a police complaint desk. A police dispatcher relays the information to a patrol officer by radio or phone, and the officer responds. However the incident becomes known to police, this reporting of a crime sets the investigative wheels in motion and is the first stage in a criminal investigation. Unless the incident is complicated, dynamic, time-consuming or potentially high-profile, the case is generally not referred to a special criminal investigations unit and the responding patrol officer is typically the one who investigates the matter. The various stages of the investigative process, as well as the personnel involved, the official reports generated, and the victim's role, are described in Table 10.1.

Table 10.1 A Brief Summary of the Investigative Process

Stage of Investigation	Police Role	Stage of Reports	Victim's/ Complainant's Role	Suspect's Role
Initial report	Police dispatched to call for service.	Recording of initial call/ report.	Report the incident, request police response.	Sometimes interferes with the call.
Initial investigation/ police contact	Police arrive on scene and acquire information. May collect evidence.	Incident reports and all applicable forms.	Provide interviews and information about the incident and suspect. May provide evidence.	Provides interviews and information about the incident. May provide evidence.
Incident review	After a review of the case, it is determined if further investigation is required.	Police supervisor reviews the case for approval.	Sometimes informed of case status.	None.
Follow-up investigations	Officers and investigators gather remaining information and evidence required for the case.	Additional reports, additional interviews and evidence.	Verify and confirm information.	Provides additional interviews and interrogations if cooperative and warranted.
Case preparation and approval	Police officer reviews the reports, coordinates the case with prosecution.	Ready to submit for formal charging or court processing.	None.	None.
Prosecution and charging of crime	Police need to be available for court and testimony.	Prosecution and court reports.	Be available for court and testimony.	Are in custody or present for court. If not present, have legal representation.
Conclusion	Officers clear reports, release or purge evidence and close case with a disposition.	File all complete reports into Records.	Retrieve any property used as evidence in the case.	None.

Table created by Henry L. Cho, 2009.

THE PRELIMINARY INVESTIGATION

Most criminal investigations have two phases: the preliminary investigation and the follow-up investigation. Chapter 6 stressed the importance of the preliminary investigation and outlined the duties and responsibilities typically encountered.

The most critical phase in most criminal investigations is the preliminary investigation.

A brief review of the typical steps of a preliminary investigation is warranted:

- Attend to any existing emergencies, such as an injured person or a fleeing suspect.
- Secure the scene.
- Make necessary arrests.
- Measure, photograph, videotape and sketch the scene.
- Search for evidence.
- Identify, collect, examine and process physical evidence.
- Interview victims, witnesses and suspects.
- Record all statements and observations in notes to be later transformed into a report.

The order in which these tasks are performed will depend on the specific circumstances. Questioning witnesses, which is a procedural must, may also include canvassing the neighborhood, which is warranted in certain types of incidents. The last task, recording all information into a pocket notebook or onto a digital recorder, is vital.

Documenting the Scene

Documentation and creating an evidence chain of custody is vital throughout an investigation. Most people who go into law enforcement are amazed at the amount of paperwork and writing that is required—as much as 70 percent of an investigator's job is consumed by these functions. In addition, photography plays an important role in documenting evidence and presenting cases in court.

Start taking notes as soon as possible after receiving a call to respond, and continue recording information as it is received throughout the investigation. Enter general information first: the time and date of the call, location, officer assigned, and arrival time at the scene. Police departments using centrally dispatched message centers may automatically record date, time, and case numbers. Even if this is done, make written notes of this initial information because recorded tapes may not be kept for extended periods or may become unusable. The tapes and notes corroborate each other. Record all information that helps to answer the questions, Who? What? Where? When? How? and Why?

Take notes describing the physical scene, including general weather and lighting conditions. Record everything you observe in the overall scene: all services rendered, including first aid; description of the injured; location of wounds; who transported the victim and how. Record complete, accurate information regarding all photographs taken at the scene. As the search is conducted, record the location and description of evidence and its preservation. Record information to identify the type of crime and what was said and by whom. Include the name, address, and phone number of every person present at the scene and all witnesses.

In addition, investigative photographs and videotapes are essential to proper crime scene documentation. The basic purpose of crime scene photography is to record the scene permanently. Photos and video taken immediately, using proper techniques to reproduce the entire crime scene, provide a factual record of high evidentiary value. The time that elapses between the commission of a crime and when a suspect in that crime is brought to trial can stretch into years, during which time the crime scene will undoubtedly change. Thus, photos and videos are a way to preserve the crime scene.

Finally, sketch all serious crime and crash scenes after photographs are taken and before anything is moved. Sketch the entire scene, the objects, and the evidence. The crime scene sketch accurately portrays the physical facts, establishes the precise location and relationship of objects and evidence at the scene, helps create a mental picture of the scene for those not present and is usually admissible in court. Computer software programs, such as CAD crime scene applications, have become an essential tool for investigators to diagram complex crime scenes.

Many believe that the initial and follow-up reports are the most critical aspects of the investigative process. Exactly *who* is responsible for the preliminary and follow-up investigations varies by department, although most officers are expected to be trained and competent in performing basic investigative operations.

WHO INVESTIGATES?

Most local police departments lack special criminal investigative units, with line personnel bearing responsibility for crime scene duty. However, some departments, particularly those in larger jurisdictions, staff specialized teams of detectives to perform investigative functions. Some agencies also have specialized units within the investigations unit to handle different types of cases, for example, a detective who specializes in sex crimes or crimes against children. Although most detectives are crime scene investigators, many agencies have a separate crime scene unit (CSU) that conducts this portion of the investigation (processing the scene). In these instances, it is important that the investigator is still involved and has open communication with the CSU's findings and reports.

Popular television series such as *CSI, Cold Case,* and *Without a Trace* have brought the role of the crime scene investigator and the importance of forensic evidence into the limelight. One 2006 weekly Nielsen rating showing that 30 million people watched *CSI* on one night and that 70 million watched at least one of the three *CSI* shows (Shelton, 2008, p.2). Forty million people watched

Actors William Petersen (left), Marg Helgenberger and Paul Guifoyle investigate a bombing in the CBS television series *CSI: Crime Scene Investigation,* photographed on January 29, 2001, in Los Angeles, California.
CBS/Landov

two other forensic dramas, *Without a Trace* and *Cold Case*, meaning that 5 of the top 10 television programs that week were about scientific evidence, a topic that amassing more than 100 million viewers. Shelton (p.3) surveyed 1,000 jurors about what forensic evidence they expected the prosecution to present and found that jurors expected in every criminal case to see

- Some kind of scientific evidence (46 percent).
- DNA evidence (22 percent).
- Fingerprint evidence (36 percent).
- Ballistic or other firearms laboratory evidence (32 percent).

Jurors also expect crime lab results and an entire investigation to be completed in a matter of a few hours, followed by a nice graphically designed portrayal of the incident presented on video that ties the entire incident together . . . much like they view on TV. These expectations have been referred to collectively as the ***CSI* effect**, "where unrealistic portrayals of the science have translated to equally unrealistic expectations from not only the public but also other professions that operate within the justice system who now apparently believe in magic" (Fantino, 2007, p.26). These are unrealistic expectations. The basic function of a crime scene investigator (CSI) is to detect, collect, evaluate and preserve crime scene evidence, including taking photographs in most instances.

***CSI* effect**
"Where unrealistic portrayals of the science have translated to equally unrealistic expectations from not only the public but also other professions that operate within the justice system" who have unrealistic expectations about what crime scene investigators can do.

THE FOLLOW-UP INVESTIGATION

In many cases, the preliminary investigation does not yield enough evidence or information to close a case. In such instances a follow-up investigation is needed, again performed either by the patrol officer who responded to the original call or by a detective, depending on the case and the size of the agency. If investigators take over a case begun by patrol officers, coordination is essential.

The follow-up phase builds on what was learned during the preliminary investigation. Investigative leads that may need to be pursued include checking the victim's background; talking to informants; determining who would benefit from the crime and who had sufficient knowledge to plan the crime; tracing

Investigative Lead Sheet

Case number ______ **Lead number** ______

Priority level: ☐ **Low** ☐ **Medium** ☐ **High**

Subject ______ Informant ______

Subject	Informant
Name ______	Name ______
Address ______	Address ______
Race ______ DOB ______ Sex ______	Home telephone ______
Height ______ Weight ______ Eyes ______ Hair ______	Other telephone ______
Identifying features ______	How informant knows subject ______
Employed ______ Occupation ______	______

Telephone numbers Home ______ Work ______

Vehicle make ______ Year ______ Model ______ Color ______ Condition ______ Tag ______

Associates ______

ID confirmed ☐ Yes ☐ No How? ______

Details of lead ______

______

Lead received by ______ Date/Time ______

Lead # assigned ______

Lead status ☐ Good lead ☐ Questionable lead ☐ Suspicious informant ☐ Insufficient information

Lead assigned to ______ Date/Time ______

Findings ______

______

______

☐ Open lead ☐ Additional investigation required ☐ Subject has weak alibi

☐ Could not locate subject ☐ Other

☐ Closed lead ☐ Unfounded ☐ Subject has alibi ☐ Cleared by evidence ☐ Other

Other lead number references ______

Report completed ☐ Yes ☐ No Report# ______

Investigative supervisor ______ Date ______

Lead-room supervisor ______ Date ______

FIGURE 10.1 Investigative Lead Sheet

Source: Stephen E. Steidel, Ed. *Missing and Abducted Children: A Law Enforcement Guide to Case Investigation and Program Management*, 3rd ed. Washington, DC: The National Center for Missing and Exploited Children, 2006.

weapons and stolen property; and searching MO, mug shot, and fingerprint files. Figure 10.1 provides an example of an investigative lead sheet that might be used in the follow up. Specific follow-up procedures for the major offenses are presented later in the chapter.

42.2.2

CALEA STANDARD 42.2.2 requires that a follow-up investigation include at a minimum:

- Reviewing and analyzing all previous reports prepared in the preliminary phase, departmental records, and results from laboratory examinations.
- Conducting additional interviews and interrogations.
- Seeking additional information (from uniformed officers, informants).
- Planning, organizing, conducting searches, and collecting physical evidence.
- Identifying and apprehending suspects.
- Determining involvement of suspects in other crimes.
- Checking suspects' criminal histories.
- Preparing cases for court presentation (*Standards for Law Enforcement Agencies,* 5th edition, 2006).

Regardless of who is charged with conducting a criminal investigation and whether it is preliminary or follow up, the types of evidence to look for remain the same, and maintaining the integrity and subsequent admissibility of such evidence is as vital a role for the line officer as it is for the special crime scene investigator.

EVIDENCE

The successful resolution of a criminal investigation most often hinges on the availability of irrefutable, relevant and admissible evidence. Even when a suspect confesses, evidence is still required because the confession may later turn out to be untrue, it may later be denied, or there may be claims it was coerced or involuntary and is, therefore, inadmissible. A confession is only one part of an investigation. It must be corroborated by independent evidence.

Criminal investigators and forensic scientists work often with proxy data. **Proxy data** are not seen as they are created but are the remnants of an event left behind. This is based on the theory of transfer developed by Edmund Locard, a French forensic microscopist in the early 20th century who posited: When two things come into contact, information is exchanged. The results of such a transfer are proxy data. Once criminal activity stops, any transfers that take place are considered **contamination**, that is, an undesired transfer of information between items of evidence.

proxy data
Evidence not seen as they are created but are only the remnants of an event left behind.

contamination
An undesired transfer of information between items of evidence.

Advances in technologies for detecting and distinguishing evidence hold promise for speeding up evidence collection, limiting contamination and facilitating analysis. Among the advancements are a variety of alternative light sources (ALS) being used to enhance evidence.

Classification of Evidence

Evidence is generally categorized as one of four types: testimonial, documentary, demonstrative or physical. *Testimonial evidence* is information obtained through interviewing and interrogating individuals about what they saw (eyewitness evidence), heard (hearsay evidence) or know (character evidence). *Documentary evidence* typically includes written material, audio recordings and videos. *Demonstrative evidence* includes mockups and scale models of objects or places related to the crime scene and helps juries visualize more clearly what they are unable to view personally. Most commonly, investigators deal with *physical evidence*, that is anything real or tangible—that is, which has substance—that helps to establish the facts of a case. It can be seen, touched, smelled or tasted; is solid, semisolid or liquid; and can be large or tiny. It may be at an immediate crime scene or miles away; it may also be on a suspect or a victim. Hess and Orthmann (2010, pp.122–123) classify physical evidence as follows:

> One common classification is direct and indirect evidence. *Direct evidence* establishes proof of a fact without any other evidence. *Indirect evidence* merely tends to incriminate a person—for instance, a suspect's footprints found near the crime scene. Indirect evidence is also called *circumstantial evidence*, or evidence from which inferences are drawn. Extremely small items, such as hair or fibers, are a subset of direct evidence called *trace evidence*. Evidence established by law is called *prima facie evidence*. For example, 0.8 percent ethanol in the blood is direct or *prima facie* evidence of intoxication in some states. *Associative evidence* links a suspect with a crime. Associative evidence includes fingerprints, footprints, bloodstains, hairs and fibers.
>
> *Corpus delicti evidence* establishes that a crime has been committed. Contrary to popular belief, the corpus delicti ("body of the crime") in a murder case is not the dead body but the fact that death resulted from a criminal act. Corpus delicti evidence supports the elements of the crime. Pry marks on an entry door are corpus delicti evidence in a burglary.
>
> *Probative evidence* is vital to the investigation or prosecution of a case, tending to prove or actually proving guilt or innocence. Also of importance to the investigator is *exculpatory evidence*, which is physical evidence that clears one of blame—for example, having a blood type different from that of blood found at a murder scene. *Best evidence*, in the legal sense, is the original evidence or highest available degree of proof that can be produced.

Kinds of Evidence

Evidence found at crime scenes may include fingerprints; blood, hair, and other DNA-rich substances such as semen, skin and fingernails; digital/electronic evidence; bite marks; shoe and tire impressions; soil; tool fragments; glass; paint; safe insulation; fibers; insects; documents; and firearms.

Fingerprints, the science and study of which is called *dactyloscopy*, are among the most common and useful types of evidence found at crime scenes because they are a positive form of identification (Jetmore, 2008, p.76). If latent prints are found, they can be entered into a city's or state's print database system or into the Federal Bureau of Investigation's (FBI) *Automated Fingerprint Identification System*, which contains millions of prints.

Automated Fingerprint Identification System (AFIS)
Computerized database maintained by the FBI used to identify a limited number of likely matches for a latent fingerprint.

The **Automated Fingerprint Identification System** (**AFIS**) drastically reduces the time needed to identify latent fingerprints by selecting a limited number of likely matches for the latent prints.

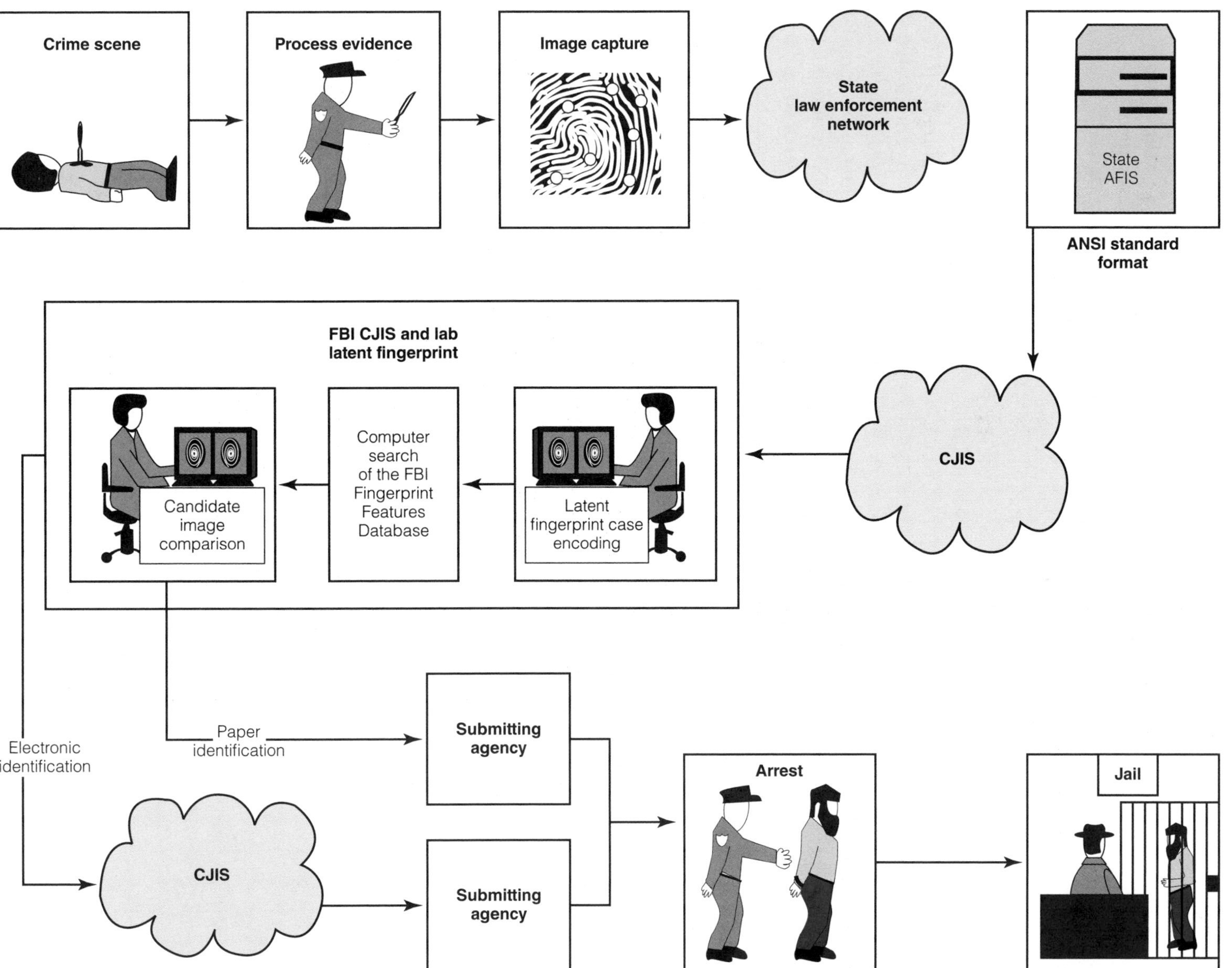

FIGURE 10.2 Electronic Latent Print Submission
Source: http://www.fbi.gov/hq/cjisd/iafis/efts71/section_3.htm

AFIS technology is continuously being enhanced through the introduction of new services and features. For example, the Integrated Automated Fingerprint Identification System (IAFIS) provides to local, state, and federal criminal justice agencies combined, nationwide access to electronic ten-print identification services, latent fingerprint databases, subject search and criminal history databases, document and image services and remote search service. Figure 10.2 illustrates the submission of an electronic ten-print.

Live scan is an advance in fingerprinting technology that reduces the chance that prints will be disqualified because of poor quality. In this method, a computer analyzes the prints in progress and will not allow the process to move forward until it captures a passing print, which is identified from the computer itself. The information is then stored in a digital format, making it easy to send or share the files: "Electronic live-scan capture of fingerprints has eliminated many of the messy problems that irritated officers using ink on paper. . . .The move to optical live-scan devices brought significant benefits. Digital fingerprint files can be stored simply, retrieved accurately, and transmitted rapidly" (Oehler, 2007, p.123).

Mobile AFIS technology also offers several benefits. Because it can process multiple people at once, mobile AFIS is useful in curtailing gang activity. For example, police confronted with breaking up a gang fight have been able to line up the subjects, fingerprint them, and obtain positive identification within minutes (Geoghegan, 2008, p.48). Before mobile AFIS, the subjects would have to have been transported to the station and processed, placing the officers in more danger: "The bottom line is that mobile AFIS protects officers in the field, expedites subject identification during time-critical encounters, and keeps criminals off the street" (Geoghegan, p.49).

In addition to fingerprints, palm print technology is making advances. This is important because many latent impressions at a crime scene are palm prints or partial palm prints. Savvy burglars often use their palms to push open windows, believing the AFIS cannot compare the palm prints. However, advances in biometrics have made it possible for automated palm print systems to complement the standard AFIS, providing a more complete identification solution.

Despite the progress made in sharing data regarding fingerprints, there is still room for improvement. For example, the Department of Homeland Security (DHS) continues to maintain a separate database with prints obtained from many illegal alien offenders. Unless the prints typically submitted to the FBI's AFIS are also submitted to the DHS and cross-checked against that database, which is not commonly known or done, it is likely the search will return "no hits," and the case may stall for lack of possible suspects.

Blood and Hair *Blood* may be valuable as evidence in assaults, homicides, burglaries, hit-and-run cases and rape. Blood is classified as A, B, AB or O. Although blood cannot be used to identify a particular individual's race or sex, it can help *eliminate* suspects.

Hair from victims and suspects can be found on clothing, weapons, blankets, sheets, seat covers and the undercarriage of vehicles. Microscopic examination can identify hair as human or animal, but it cannot be identified as coming from a specific person. Microscopic examination of hair can usually identify the person's race, but not the person's sex or age, except in the case of infants. Microscopic examination can also tell if the hair was pulled out forcibly and

Table 10.2 Location and Sources of DNA Evidence

Evidence	Possible Location of DNA on the Evidence	Source of DNA
Baseball bat	Handle	Skin cells, sweat, blood, tissue
Hat, bandanna or mask	Inside surfaces	Sweat, hair, skin cells, dandruff, saliva
Eyeglasses	Nose or ear piece, lens	Sweat, skin cells
Facial tissue, cotton swab	Surface	Mucus, blood, sweat, semen, ear wax
Dirty laundry	Surface	Blood, sweat, semen, saliva
Toothpick	Surface	Saliva
Used cigarette	Cigarette butt (filter area)	Saliva
Used stamp/envelope seal	Moistened area	Saliva
Tape or ligature	Inside or outside surface	Skin cells, sweat, saliva
Bottle, can or glass	Mouthpiece, rim, outer surface	Saliva, sweat, skin cells
Used condom	Inside/outside surface	Semen, vaginal or rectal cells
Bed linens	Surface	Sweat, hair, semen, saliva, blood
"Through and through" bullet	Outside surface	Blood, tissue
Bite mark	Surface of skin	Saliva
Fingernail/partial fingernail	Scrapings	Blood, sweat, tissue, skin cells

Note: When reviewing evidence, it is important to maintain chain of custody, consult with laboratory personnel, and take all appropriate precautions against contamination, including wearing gloves and changing them between handling of different pieces of evidence.
Source: *Using DNA to Solve Cold Cases*. Washington, DC: NIJ Special Report, July 2002, p.21.

which part of the body it is from. If the root is still attached to the hair, DNA from that portion can be analyzed.

DNA Fingerprinting Blood, hair and other body tissues and fluids, such as semen, saliva, skin and fingernails, can also be used in **DNA fingerprinting**. This technique analyzes the genetic sequence of DNA—the "blueprint of life." Whereas other tests of human tissues and secretions can only eliminate suspects, DNA can positively identify an individual, except for identical twins.

DNA fingerprinting
Use of the unique genetic structure of an individual for identification. Blood, hair and other body tissues and fluids may be used in this process.

A new powerful forensic tool involves "touch" or "trace" DNA, a term describing the collection and analysis of microscopic amounts of cellular material, so small it can't be seen with the naked eye (Spraggs, 2008, p.26).

Prime and Newman (2007, p.35) contend, "DNA analysis will continue to be regarded as the standard of excellence for the development of impartial, unbiased scientific evidence in the support of the justice system." Indicators are that DNA collection will surpass lifting latent fingerprints in the near future. The technology has become advanced enough to extrapolate DNA evidence from fingerprints left behind on evidence. Thus, instead of lifting prints, investigators will eventually just swab the prints for the DNA, and submit the sample for analysis.

Investigators need to know where DNA evidence is likely to be located. Table 10.2 describes the possible location and source of DNA evidence.

Even with no suspect, DNA can be helpful as it can be entered into the FBI's Combined DNA Index System (CODIS), also called the National DNA Index System (NDIS), and searched against an ever-growing collection of DNA profiles. This national database and searching mechanism had more than 7,042,503 offender profiles and 268,404 forensic profiles by May 2009. More than 100 crime laboratories nationwide have installed the CODIS system.

Although DNA fingerprinting has been heralded as a major breakthrough for criminal investigation, some courts still do not accept it. In *California v. Simpson* (1995), DNA played a pivotal role. The defense focused on procedures rather than the scientific validity of DNA analysis to discredit and have thrown out the DNA evidence. In several states, legal challenges have been *unsuccessfully* raised that DNA collection constitutes an invasion of an individual's right to privacy.

The privacy issue relates to the controversy regarding when DNA should be collected and whether those of preconviction status should be exempt: "Law enforcement officials are vastly expanding their collection of DNA to include millions more people who have been arrested or detained, but not yet convicted. The move, intended to help solve more crimes, is raising concerns about the privacy of petty offenders and people who are presumed innocent" (Moore, 2009). The FBI expects its DNA database of more than 7 million profiles to accelerate its growth rate from 80,000 new entries a year to 1.2 million annually by 2012—a 17-fold increase (Moore). This expansion is also likely to contribute to the current backlog problem.

Research is helping counter some of these criticisms, however. A study done in Chicago that followed the criminal histories of eight convicted felons concluded that if officials had collected DNA upon these felons' first felony arrests, officials would have prevented 60 violent crimes, including 30 rapes and 22 murders (Garrett, 2009b, pp.31–32). Using such data to support their actions, 16 states have passed legislation requiring law enforcement to collect DNA for most felony arrests and upload it to the state DNA databank (Garrett, p.31).

Yet another controversial issue related to DNA collection is for what offenses DNA should be sought as evidence. Traditionally, DNA analysis has been reserved for violent crimes such as murder and rape. However, extensive field testing by Roman et al. (2008) on the use of DNA testing in investigating high-volume crimes such as burglary and automobile theft found that DNA can be very helpful in solving property crimes. This randomized study of as many as 500 crimes in each of five sites found that property crimes where DNA evidence is processed have more than twice as many suspects identified, twice as many suspects arrested, and more than twice as many cases accepted for prosecution compared with traditional investigation (p.3). DNA is at least five times as likely to result in a suspect identification compared with fingerprints. And suspects identified by DNA had at least twice as many prior felony arrests and convictions as did those identified by traditional investigations. Critics contend that adding DNA testing for property crimes would completely clog the already critically overburdened laboratories. For example, according to the FBI, there were almost 10 million property crimes brought to the attention of the police in 2007. Nonetheless, the research indicates that this technology greatly assists in clearing property crimes cases.

Physical fingerprints and DNA fingerprinting are the two forms of positive identification available to investigators.

As technology improves, police are turning to older, smaller degraded DNA samples to help solve cases. For example, researchers have used DNA fingerprinting to make identifications from a four-year-old bloodstain and from semen stains that were several weeks old. Also as the result of advances in DNA analysis, many cold cases are being reinvestigated, as discussed later in the chapter.

Digital/Electronic Evidence With the proliferation of electronic devices that hold information, digital evidence has become increasingly important in many investigations. Most investigators are not educated in examining digital evidence, but they should recognize sources for such evidence at a crime scene, including computers, external hard drives, flash drives, cell phones, iPods, PDAs, digital cameras, global positioning systems (GPS) units and game units. Most criminals fail to consider their electronic gadgets as digital storage devices containing potentially incriminating evidence (Garrett, 2009a, p.12). Patrol officers commonly run across cell phones containing a wealth of information. In one case involving a California gang shooting, where rival gangs rolled into a parking lot and fired hundreds of rounds at each other with automatic weapons, responding officers were met with claims by those involved that they hadn't seen anything. However, when officers confiscated and searched the gang members' cell phones, they found photos, text messages and other information about the shootings (Garrett, p.15). Yet in most cases, local departments lack the base knowledge and internal technical capability to analyze every single digital device or computer involved in every investigation, thus requiring such evidence to be submitted to a task force or larger agency that has the requisite resources and training to process it (Garrett, p.15). McNeil (2009, p.30) stresses, "It is important to recognize that managing digital evidence must be done in an integrated manner where SOPs [standard operating procedures], chain of custody, access controls, and security are uniformly applied."

In addition to evidence found on a suspect's electronic gadgets, a wealth of information can be found on the Internet, by performing an Internet search for an area of interest, and on social network sites such as MySpace, Facebook and Twitter.

Other Kinds of Evidence *Bite marks* are sometimes significant in child and adult abuse cases, rape and homicide cases, and assault and battery cases. They may also be left on the perpetrator by the victim. Bite marks have individual characteristics that match the size and configuration of the teeth. Bite marks helped convict Ted Bundy in Florida. The key is successfully preserving the tissue. Marks on the body may last for several weeks. Bite marks can also be found at a crime scene on inanimate objects such as pencils, Styrofoam cups, gum, candy bars, apples, and other partially eaten soft foods (Page, 2007, p.115). Forensic orthodontologists can help investigators analyze tooth-related evidence (Jetmore, 2007, p.22).

Shoe or *tire impressions* often are found where suspects have entered or left a crime scene hastily. Shoe and tire prints are of two types: contamination prints and impressions. Contamination prints are left when a shoe or tire has on it a substance such as dirt or blood, which then leaves a print on a hard surface. Impressions are imprints left in soft surfaces such as mud or sand. Shoe or tire impressions can place a suspect at a crime scene.

Soil is also analyzed in some cases The composition of various soils and other ground substrates can be unique and distinguishable, thus providing evidence that a suspect (or their shoes or tires) crossed over a particular stretch of land at some point in time.

Tool fragments also may be found at a crime scene and later matched to a broken tool in a suspect's possession. *Tool marks* are found most often in burglaries and in malicious-destruction-of-property crimes. Tool marks may be found on windowsills and frames, doors and frames, cash register drawers, file cabinets and cash boxes. Tool marks often are left when windows have been forced open with screwdrivers or pry bars; when locks have been snipped with bolt cutters or when safes have been opened with hammers, chisels or punches. These tools leave marks that often can be identified as definitely as fingerprints.

Glass from windows, automobiles, bottles and other objects often is used as evidence in assaults, burglaries, murders and many other crimes. When a person breaks a window, tiny pieces of glass are usually found in the clothing, pant cuffs or pockets, or on the clothing's surface. Glass is excellent evidence because two different pieces of glass rarely contain the same proportions of sand, metal oxides or carbonates. In addition, police usually can determine whether the glass was broken from inside or outside a building by observing the fracture marks and the location of the fragments.

Paint frequently is transferred from one object to another during the commission of a crime. During burglaries, it may be chipped off surfaces. During hasty getaways, it may flake off automobiles. Paint has provided a strong link in the chain of circumstantial evidence because it can associate an individual with the crime scene. It also can eliminate innocent suspects.

Safe insulation can be identified microscopically by composition, color, mineral content and physical characteristics. Particles of safe insulation or fireproof insulation on a suspect's clothing or shoes are strong indications of guilt.

Fibers from clothing are often found where burglars have crawled through a window or opening. Clothing fibers are also often found adhering to the fenders, grill, door handles or undercarriage of hit-and-run vehicles. Fingernail scrapings and weapons also may contain fiber evidence. Examination of the fibers can identify the type of fabric: wool, cotton, rayon, nylon and so on. Sometimes the type of garment from which the fibers came can be identified.

Insects on a body or present at a scene can provide high evidentiary value, particularly when they are not normally present in such a location. The developmental stage of insects found on a body can provide significant information to investigators regarding a death. Criminal investigators increasingly rely on the field of forensic entomology for assistance in solving crimes.

Documents may contain fingerprint evidence and may be examined for handwriting characteristics or for typewriter or printer characteristics. If a document has been handwritten, experts can do a side-by-side comparison of the document and samples of the suspect's handwriting to determine if both were done by the same person. Testimony of handwriting experts has been accepted in our courts for several years. Documents produced on a typewriter or printer can be examined to determine the manufacturer, make, model and age of the machine.

Firearms left at a crime scene may be traced to their owner through the serial number, the manufacturer's identification or the dealer who sold the gun. Firearms also may contain fingerprints or other marks that could lead to identification. The weapon's make usually is determined by the barrel rifling, spiral grooves cut into the gun barrel in its manufacture. The rifling varies considerably from manufacturer to manufacturer and imparts a "signature" on bullets passing through, which can help investigators link weapons to shootings.

In the 1990s, the Bureau of Alcohol, Tobacco, Firearms and Explosives (ATF) and the FBI had competing systems with the FBI being interested in cartridge cases through its DrugFire program and the ATF being interested in bullets through its Integrated Ballistics Information System (IBIS). In 1999, however, the directors of the ATF and the FBI signed a memorandum of understanding to create a unified ballistics evidence system, using the basic technology of the IBIS machine and combining it with functions specific to the DrugFire system, creating the National Integrated Ballistics Information Network (NIBIN).

An innovative new gun identification technology is called *microstamping*: "The fledgling microstamping technology, considered by some the next generation in ballistics information, is a relatively recent development that utilizes lasers to make distinct microscopic engravings on the breech face and firing pin of a gun. As the gun is fired, the weapon's serial number is stamped onto the cartridge, giving police some chance of determining from which weapon the shell was fired" (Page, 2008, p.54).

An often overlooked tool in discovering ballistic evidence is the metal detector. Investigators using standard search pattern with a metal detector can ensure that the crime scene is completely covered.

The Chain of Custody

Whatever evidence investigators deal with, they must be certain to document the chain of custody. The importance of the chain of custody is evidenced in the CALEA standards.

83

CALEA STANDARD 83 states, "For physical evidence to be accepted by the court at time of trial, it is essential that the chain of evidence be maintained. The initial step in this process is marking or labeling the item at the time it is collected, seized, or received. Items should be marked so as not to damage or contaminate the evidence. Items that cannot be marked should be placed in an appropriate container, sealed, and the container labeled.

For all items of evidence gathered at a crime scene, the investigator and/or processor should prepare a list containing a description of the item collected, the source (person or location obtained from), and the name of the person collecting the item.

If the evidence is transferred to another person prior to being logged in with the agency, documenting the transfer is critical to maintaining the chain of custody. The record of transfer of evidence should include the following: date and time of transfer, receiving person's name and functional responsibility; reason for the transfer; name and location of the laboratory; synopsis of the event; examinations desired; and date of transfer to a laboratory not within the agency" (*Standards for Law Enforcement Agencies*, 5th edition, 2006).

FORENSICS

forensics
The application of scientific processes to solve legal problems, most notably within the context of the criminal justice system.

Law enforcement has benefited greatly from the many advances in **forensics**—the application of scientific processes to solve legal problems, most notably within the context of the criminal justice system (Fantino, 2007, p.26). However, television programs have given the viewing public the mistaken notion that crime laboratories can provide results quickly when, in truth, most crime laboratories have large case backlogs ("Increasing Efficiency in Crime Laboratories," 2008, p.1).

On February 18, 2009, the National Academy of Sciences (NAS) released a report citing serious deficiencies in the United States' forensic science system. The nationally mandated report, *Strengthening Forensic Science in the United States: A Path Forward*, found serious deficiencies in the nation's forensic science system and calls for major reforms and new research. Mandatory certification programs for forensic scientists are currently lacking, as are strong standards and protocols for analyzing and reporting on evidence. There is also a scarcity of peer-reviewed studies establishing the scientific bases and reliability of many forensic methods.

The report noted that, with the exception of DNA analysis, "no forensic method has been rigorously shown able to consistently, and with a high degree of certainty, demonstrate a connection between evidence and a specific individual or source" (Feigin, 2009, p.3). This despite the ruling in *Daubert v. Merrell Dow Pharmaceuticals* (1993), which established the essential factors in scientific testimony, including empirical testing, peer review, error rate, and acceptability in the scientific community.

The University of Tennessee's National Forensic Academy (NFA) provides one possible approach to improving the country's forensic system (Blakely, 2009, p.75). This 7,000-square-foot space includes an interactive classroom, a laboratory, photography lab and specially designed clean experiment rooms where CSIs can learn to better evaluate blood evidence and practice casting tire and footwear impressions. This 10-week, in-residence training program holds three sessions each year, each involving 170 hours of classroom instruction and 230 hours of field practice. The instructors are nationally known experts, both academically and as practitioners. An investigator from Georgia who attended the academy said, "NFA provided me with new techniques and skills that at best, would have taken years to learn on my own, and may have, at worst, never learned if not for the NFA" (Blakely, p.78).

The FBI is also engaged in improving our country's forensic capabilities. They now have nine Regional Computer Forensics Laboratories (RCFL), which provides accreditation to computer forensic laboratories: "The accreditation process is an intensive assessment which evaluates the qualifications of all laboratory personnel; the laboratory's operational and technical policies, practices, and procedures; and the laboratory's quality management system" ("FBI's Regional Computer Forensics Laboratory Network Increases Number of Accredited Labs," 2009).

In addition to well-trained computer forensic examiners and CSIs, criminal investigation is greatly enhanced by experts in crime analysis, as discussed in Chapter 6.

CRIME ANALYSIS

"The invention of the personal computer and crime-mapping software launched crime analysis as a profession" (Osborne, 2008, p.36). Before computers, investigators relied on pin maps, wall charts and other such devices to analyze facts related to a crime. This has changed considerably with the advent of the computer. Chapter 6 discussed several computerized crime mapping tools, including geographic information systems (GIS), regional crime analysis program (ReCAP) and CompStat.

Osborne (2009) makes the interesting observation that we in the United States put more thought and effort into analyzing sports than in analyzing crime. He advocates better utilization of existing technology to analyze our criminal opponents and plan more effective offensive and defensive strategies. White (2008, pp.1–2) stresses the importance of enhancing the problem-solving capacity of crime analysis units:

> The theoretical framework of problem-oriented policing has evolved steadily over the past few decades, and it has become increasingly clear how much the approach depends for its success on the careful analysis of data about crime problems. Indeed, problem-oriented policing and data analysis are highly interdependent. A framework for problem-oriented policing is of little use if good data are not available and, similarly, complex data about crime problems require a meaningful framework for analysis. . . .
>
> Whatever they [crime analysts] are called, their responsibilities—collecting, collating, distilling, interpreting and presenting data and information—are similar. They are typically tasked with a long list of duties, such as diagnosing emerging crime trends, creating administrative reports, and identifying likely suspects.

For crime analysis to be useful to the patrol officer, it must be actionable; that is, it must provide information directing police personnel to a particular response in a particular time and place: "The officer does not just receive the information but actually performs his or her tasks differently according to the information received. It is important to spend the limited resources of crime analysis units on producing reports that are relevant and useful to patrol officer" (Scalisi, 2009). Crime analysis supports the patrol function by focusing on short-term activity while providing command structure with responses to long-term problem areas such as hot spots (Scalisi).

Computers are being used to determine where to focus investigative resources. Artificial intelligence (AI) programs being used in several police departments help structure investigations by using software to help determine which cases are most likely to be cleared by arrest.

Geographic Profiling

Chapter 6 introduced crime mapping as a way to identify hot spots of crime. Geographic profiling takes crime mapping techniques and turns them inside out. Geographic profiling can help prioritize suspect lists, direct patrol saturation and stakeouts and conduct neighborhood canvasses. In March 2008, the Office of Community Oriented Policing Services (COPS) and the National

Institute of Justice (NIJ) launched the first issue of *Geography and Public Safety*, dealing with applied geography for the study of crime and public safety. The first article explains how crime mapping has evolved from pushpins to advanced spatial statistics to understand and analyze crime: "In the coming years, crime analysts will be able to use applied geography to assess why crime occurs, where it does and the characteristics of high-crime environments" (Wilson and Smith, 2008, p.1).

Regardless of the highly sophisticated technologies available to criminal investigators, to respond effectively and appropriately to a crime, officers must first know what defines the crime.

INVESTIGATING SPECIFIC CRIMES

Some actions and activities may seem "wrong" and unjust but are not technically criminal. Someone took something? Was it robbery, burglary, larceny/theft or simply a misunderstood "borrowing"? Following is a brief examination of some specific crimes and how they are generally investigated. This section begins with the FBI's eight Index offenses and their general definitions, including the specific elements of each offense that must be proven during a criminal investigation. Then investigating other serious crimes is discussed, including crimes against children, bias/hate crimes, computer-related crimes and environmental crimes.

VIOLENT CRIMES

Investigating violent crimes is difficult because of the emotionalism usually encountered, not only from the victim and the victim's family, but also from the public and, at times, the officer. Generally, however, investigating crimes against persons results in more and better information and evidence than does investigating property crimes because, in violent crimes, the victim is often an eyewitness, an important source of information and a key to identifying the suspect. The victim and other witnesses can often provide important information about how and by what means the attack was made; what the attacker's intent or motive was; descriptive information about the attacker, weapon and any getaway vehicle; and what words may have been spoken. Weapons may provide physical evidence, as may any injuries suffered by the victim. Typically, violent crimes yield much physical evidence, with the type of evidence to anticipate directly related to the type of crime committed. Officers could expect to find such evidence as a weapon, blood, hair, fibers, fingerprints, footprints and the like, depending on the specific crime. Therefore, the arrest rate for violent crimes is high.

Violent crime investigations have been enhanced by the establishment of the Violent Criminal Apprehension Program (VICAP) at the FBI National Police Academy in Quantico, Virginia. The goal of this program is to coordinate major violent crime cases, regardless of their location, in the United States. Information considered viable is published in the FBI's *Law Enforcement Bulletin*. If the case merits interagency cooperation, a major case investigation team of investigators from all involved agencies may be formed.

The major violent crimes are homicide, rape, assault, and robbery.

Keep in mind that entire books and courses are devoted to criminal investigation and, because of space and time limitations, what follows is necessarily only a cursory look at what is involved in investigating criminal offenses.

Homicide

Homicide is the killing of one person by another. Homicide receives extensive public attention as well as intensive police attention. Unfortunately, the homicide clearance rate has declined steadily, dropping from 92 percent in 1961 to 61 percent in 2005 (Mentel, 2008). This decrease may be attributed to an increase in the more difficult to solve "stranger-to-stranger" homicides, reduced cooperation from witnesses, the release of 650,000 inmates yearly, and increases in illegal immigrants who fear police and thus, make poor sources of information as crime victims or witnesses.

Homicide investigations frequently require all investigative techniques and skills. A primary requirement is to establish that death was caused by a criminal action. The four basic types of death are death by natural causes, accidental death, suicide and homicide. Although technically officers are concerned only with homicide, frequently they do not know at the start of an investigation what type of death has occurred. Therefore, any of the four types of death may require investigation.

Homicide is classified as criminal (felonious) or noncriminal. The various degrees of murder and manslaughter are criminal homicide, noncriminal homicide (which includes excusable homicide, the unintentional, truly accidental killing of another person) and justifiable homicide (killing another person under authorization of law).

The elements present in a criminal homicide determine whether the act is charged as murder in the first, second or third degree, or as voluntary or involuntary manslaughter. The "weapon" used also influences the charge, as in the case of criminal vehicular homicide, a.k.a. vehicular manslaughter. All states except Alaska, Montana and Arizona have vehicular homicide statutes, and most statutes state this crime involves the death of an individual from the negligent operation of a vehicle (including DWI), which is generally a lesser charge than manslaughter. The Model Penal Code has no specific category for vehicular homicide, and the offense is generally categorized under negligent homicide. In those states without specific vehicular homicide statutes, offenders can still be charged with murder or manslaughter depending on the circumstances.

A common element in every charge is "causing the death of another human being." Other elements in homicide include premeditation, malicious intent, adequately provoked intent resulting in heat of passion, while committing or attempting to commit a crime that is not a felony, when forced or threatened, culpable negligence or depravity or simple negligence. **Premeditation**, the deliberate, precalculated plan to cause death, is the essential element of first-degree murder, distinguishing it from all other murder classifications.

premeditation
The deliberate, precalculated plan to act; the essential element of first-degree murder, distinguishing it from all other murder classifications.

Heat of passion homicides are often the culmination of intimate partner violence. In addition, "An overwhelming proportion of intimate partner homicide perpetrators are under the influence of substances when the crime occurs, and alcohol consumption is a strong indicator of intimate terrorism of women" (Roberts, 2009, p.67).

The first priority in a preliminary homicide investigation is to determine that death has occurred—provided the suspect is not at the scene. Signs of death include lack of breathing, lack of heartbeat, lack of flushing of the fingernail bed when pressure is applied and then released and failure of the eyelids to close after being gently lifted. In some instances, police can enter a premise without a warrant if they believe a person is in need of medical assistance or if they believe the premises may contain a victim or a killer, as established in *Flippo v. West Virginia* (1999). The Supreme Court "acknowledged that police may make warrantless entries onto premises if they reasonably believe that a person is in need of immediate aid or may make a prompt warrantless search of a homicide scene for other victims or a killer on the premises."

After priority matters are completed, the focus of the homicide investigation is to identify the victim, establish the time of death, establish the cause of death and the method used to produce it and to develop a suspect.

Homicide victims are identified by their relatives, friends or acquaintances; by personal effects, fingerprints, DNA analysis, skeletal studies including teeth and dental records, clothing and laundry marks; or through missing-persons files.

Determining the time of death is one important part of any homicide investigation. General factors used to estimate time of death are body temperature, rigor mortis, postmortem lividity, appearance of the eyes, stomach contents, stage of decomposition and evidence suggesting a change in the victim's normal routine.

Currently, if a body is found within a day, investigators can determine the time of death quite accurately based on lividity, appearance of the eyes, rigor mortis and the like. After a day has passed, it becomes much more difficult to determine time of death. A project at the Oak Ridge National Laboratory is developing a device to wave over a body to determine how long a person has been dead. The project is based on the fact that as a body decomposes, proteins break down into amino acids and progressively smaller molecules. By studying whether there is a constant rate at which the large molecules of the body break down, researchers can correlate the percentage of larger molecules to small ones within a number of days.

Another aid in homicide investigations comes from forensic entomology. Insects, particularly flies, are attracted to the nose, eyes, ears and mouth of dead bodies and lay eggs, which emerge or "hatch" into maggots. Interpreting entomological evidence at a crime scene can help establish time of death, season of death, geographic location of death, movement or storage of the remains following death, specific sites of trauma on the body, sexual molestation and even the drug use.

A medical examination or autopsy provides legal evidence as to the cause and time of death and corroborates information obtained during the investigation.

It may also reveal evidence that may otherwise have gone undetected and that may link the victim to a suspect. Suspects are developed by determining a motive for the killing and by circumstantial evidence.

Physical evidence in a homicide includes a weapon, a body, blood, hairs and fibers. The type of evidence available will depend on the nature of the homicide and the type of scene involved. For example, a hit-and-run crime scene may have numerous kinds of physical evidence, including hairs, fibers, blood and other biological fluids, and materials from the vehicle, including broken plastic or glass from lights.

The initial police response to a homicide call and their subsequent degree of involvement and thoroughness in the follow-up investigation directly affect the outcome of the case and whether it is cleared. Some homicide investigations are relatively straightforward and free of complication. Others, however, pose one or more challenges.

Special problems in homicide investigations include pressure by the public and the media; difficulty in establishing that it is homicide, rather than suicide or an accidental or natural death; handling serial murders; and, in some cases, reopening cold cases.

Among the most common causes of unnatural death are gunshot wounds; stabbing and cutting wounds; blows from blunt instruments; asphyxia induced by choking, drowning, hanging, smothering, strangulation, gases or poisons; poisoning and drug overdoses; burning; explosions; electric shock; and lightning. An **equivocal death investigation** may have two or more meanings and may be presented as either a homicide or a suicide, depending on the circumstances. The facts may be purposefully vague or misleading or appear suspicious or questionable. Any weapon tightly clutched in the victim's hand as the result of cadaveric spasm indicates suicide rather than murder, but this cannot always be assumed. The victim's background also provides information about whether the death was accidental, suicide or homicide. This background and evidence on the victim's body often provide leads to a suspect.

equivocal death investigation
May have two or more meanings and may be presented as either a homicide or a suicide, depending on the circumstances.

One type of equivocal death is autoerotic asphyxia, the intentional cutting off of oxygen to the brain for sexual arousal. An estimated 500 to 1,000 Americans die from asphyxiophilia each year (Fritsche, 2009). The difficulty in investigating such cases is determining if the death is accidental or suicide. In rare instances, murder might be suspected.

Occasionally, investigators find themselves handling multiple homicide cases with key similarities. Such cases may be linked merely by coincidence or may be the signature of a serial killer. The FBI held a four-day symposium attended by 135 experts on serial murder (*Serial Murder*, 2008). The report on the symposium cited the following myths and facts about serial killers. First, serial killers are not all dysfunctional loners: "The majority of serial killers are not reclusive, social misfits who live alone" (p.3). The Green River Killer, Gary Ridgeway, who killed 48 women over a 20-year period, was married, employed and attended church. A second myth is that all serial killers travel interstate when, in fact, most operate in a defined geographic area, staying within their comfort zone. Those who do travel are either itinerants, homeless, or have jobs that involve interstate travel (p.4).

A third myth is that all serial killers are White males when the reality is that they span all racial groups, reflecting the racial makeup of the country, and have included women (*Serial Murder*, 2008, p.4). Fourth, a widely believed myth is that all serial killers are motivated by sex, when many are actually motivated by anger, thrill, financial gain or attention seeking. The Washington, DC, snipers killed primarily out of anger and for the thrill. In the end, they sought financial gain (p.4).

A fifth myth is that serial killers cannot stop killing. BTK killer Dennis Rader murdered 10 victims from 1974 to 1991 but did not kill again. He was captured in 2005, stating that he used autoerotic activities as a substitute (*Serial Murder*, 2008, pp.4–5). A sixth myth is that all serial killers are insane or are evil geniuses: "As a group, serial killers suffer from a variety of personality disorders.... Most, however are not adjudicated insane. Their intelligence ranges from borderline to above average levels" (p.6). A final myth is that serial killers want to get caught: "As serial killers continue to offend without being captured, they can become empowered, feeling they will never be identified" (p.6).

The experts agree that there is no generic profile of a serial killer, but some traits are commonly observed, including sensation-seeking, lack of remorse or guilt, impulsivity, the need for control and predatory behavior.

The FBI has launched a new initiative focused on highway serial killings, with the bodies of murdered women being dumped along the Interstate 40 corridor in Oklahoma, Texas, Arkansas, and Mississippi ("Highway Serial Killings," 2009). Most victims lived high-risk, transient lifestyles, often involving substance abuse and prostitution, and were picked up at truck stops or service stations, predominantly by long-haul truck drivers.

Commonly, cases involving serial killers have been put on hold because of lack of evidence. The National Institute of Justice defines a cold case as a case whose probative investigative leads have been exhausted. A case that is only a few months old may be classified as "cold." More attention has been focused on cold cases because of the popular televisions series and the increased involvement and public visibility of family members as well as recent advances in DNA technology (Heurich, 2008, p.21).

In other instances, the perpetrator may be known but his or her whereabouts is unknown. The FBI acknowledges the contribution of *America's Most Wanted* (AMW) in helping the FBI with unsolved fugitive cases since the show's debut in 1988: "To date, the show has helped catch more than 1,000 fugitives worldwide, including a dozen criminals from our Ten Most Wanted Fugitives list" ("Hitting the Airwaves," 2009).

Sexual Assault

Sexual assault (rape) is sexual intercourse with a person against the person's will. It is classified as forcible (by use or threats of force) or statutory (with a minor, with or without consent).

Most states have in common the following elements for the crime of rape or sexual assault: (1) an act of sexual intercourse, (2) committed without the victim's consent, (3) against the victim's will and by force.

All sexual assault reports should be considered valid unless evidence indicates otherwise because strong sexual assault cases require strong, thorough written reports with a high level of detail (Kurash, 2009, p.12). Failing to adhere to this principle opens an agency up to liability and can result in offenders avoiding accountability for their crimes.

Special problems in investigating rape include the sensitive nature of the offense, social attitudes and the victim's embarrassment and feelings of shame. The victim's age can also present a challenge, and there is typically special training given to those who investigate sexual assaults on children and young juveniles. Culture can also be a hindrance, as can language barriers. A rape investigation requires great tact. A sexual assault response team (SART) consisting of an investigator, a rape crisis advocate, and a nurse examiner can provide victims with information about their medical, legal and psychological options.

Modus operandi factors important in investigating sex offenses include type of offense, words spoken, use of a weapon, method of attack, time of day, type of location and the victim's age. Physical evidence commonly found in rape cases includes stained or torn clothing; scratches, bruises and cuts; evidence of a struggle; and pubic hairs, semen and bloodstains.

A particular challenge to law enforcement is drug-facilitated sexual assault, with the most common date rape drugs being Rohypnol (also called "roofies" or "ruphees") and gamma hydroxybutyrate or GHB. A timely response is necessary because such drugs may, in only a few hours, be metabolized and rendered undetectable in the victim's bloodstream, or eliminated in the victim's urine.

Other tools in dealing with sexual assault are sex offender registration and community notification programs. After Jacob Wetterling was abducted in October 1989 and never found, Congress passed the Jacob Wetterling Crimes against Children and Sexually Violent Offender Registration Act in 1994. The act required states to create sex offender registries within three years or lose 10 percent of their funding. The act also gave states the option of releasing information about registered sex offenders to the public, but did not require it.

Although registries gave police valuable information to identify, monitor and track sex offenders, they did little to protect the public. Then, in 1994, seven-year-old Megan Kanka was raped and murdered by a paroled sex offender living across the street. In 1996, Congress amended the Wetterling Act to require states to disclose information about registered sex offenders.

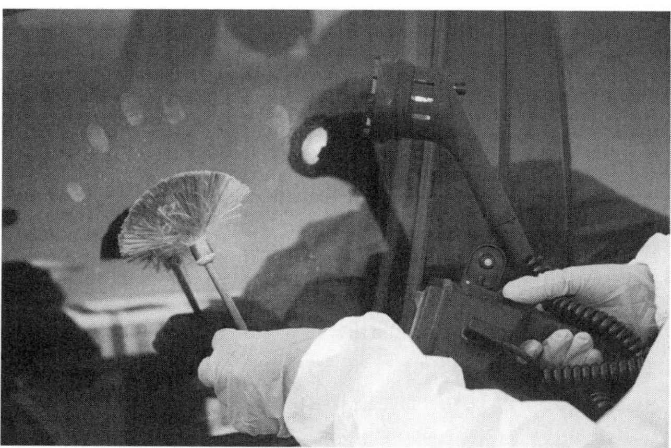

A forensics officer collects evidence by dusting a car window for fingerprints at a crime scene. The officer is using a powerful ultraviolet (UV) lamp to reveal the fingerprints.

Given that each year about 24,000 sex offenders are released to the community after serving an average six-year prison sentence, a registration and notification system seems logical and necessary. It would also seem to strike a balance between the public's right to be informed and the offender's right to privacy. However, not everyone agrees. A federal court in the District of Columbia struck down that district's "Megan's Law," saying it deprived sex offenders of their Fifth Amendment due process rights without giving them a hearing.

Adding to the challenge of handling sex offenders is that laws vary from state to state, including the level of offense a person is charged with and whether that is a trackable level. Typically, a public notification is only required on the highest level of offenders. This means there are many more mid- and lower-level sex offenders living next door to the general public without the community's knowledge.

Assault

Assault is unlawfully threatening to harm another person, actually harming another person or attempting unsuccessfully to do so. Simple assault is intentionally causing another to fear immediate bodily harm or death or intentionally inflicting or attempting to inflict bodily harm on another. It is usually a misdemeanor. Aggravated assault is an unlawful attack by one person on another to inflict *severe* bodily injury. It often involves use of a dangerous weapon and is a felony. In specified instances, teachers, people operating public conveyances and law enforcement officers use physical force legally.

The elements of the crime of simple assault are (1) intent to do bodily harm to another, (2) present ability to commit the act and (3) commission of an overt act toward carrying out the intent. An additional element in the crime of aggravated assault is that the intentionally inflicted bodily injury results in (1) a high probability of death; (2) serious, permanent disfigurement; or (3) permanent or protracted loss or impairment of the function of any body member or organ or other severe bodily harm. Attempted assault requires proof of intent and an overt act toward committing the crime.

Special problems in investigating assaults include distinguishing the victim from the suspect, determining if the matter is civil or criminal, and determining if the act was intentional or accidental. Obtaining a complaint against simple assault also is sometimes difficult.

Proving the elements of the offense of assault requires establishing the intent to cause injury, the severity of the injury inflicted and whether a dangerous weapon was used. Physical evidence in an assault includes photographs of injuries, clothing of the victim or suspect, weapons, broken objects, bloodstains, hairs, fibers and other signs of an altercation.

Domestic abuse, stalking and elder abuse all are candidates for categorization as separate crimes, rather than being lumped in the general category of assault for reporting—and thus research—purposes. These offenses were discussed in Chapter 7.

Robbery

Robbery is the felonious taking of another's property from his or her person or in his or her presence through force or intimidation. Robberies are classified as either residential, commercial, street or vehicle-driver robberies or carjacking, the taking of a motor vehicle by force or threat of force. A relatively new type of residential robber is the home invader. Many home invaders are young Asian gang members who travel across the country robbing Asian families, especially business owners.

The elements of the crime of robbery are (1) the wrongful taking of personal property, (2) from the person or in the person's presence, (3) against the person's will by force or threat of force.

The rapidity of a robbery, its potential for violence and the taking of hostages, and the usual lack of evidence at the scene pose special problems in robbery investigations. Officers responding to a robbery-in-progress call should proceed rapidly but cautiously. They should assume the robber is at the scene unless otherwise advised, and be prepared for gunfire; look for and immobilize any getaway vehicle discovered; avoid a hostage situation if possible; and make an immediate arrest if the situation warrants.

Each element of robbery must be proven separately. To prove that personal property was wrongfully taken, the legal owner of the property must be identified and the property and its value described completely. To prove that property was taken from the person or in the person's presence, the exact words, gestures, motions or actions the robber used to gain control of the property must be recorded. To prove the property was removed against the victim's will by force or threat of force, a complete description of the robber's words, actions and any weapon used or threatened to be used must be obtained.

Convenience stores robberies pose a special problem because, as the name implies, they are convenient for robbers as well as for customers. Most convenience stores lack security and have poorly trained, inexperienced employees who are encouraged to comply with a robber's demands (Petrocelli, 2008b, p.21). These stores should maximize natural surveillance, limit the amount of cash in the register and post a notice to this effect, put a height strip near the door to help employees get an accurate height reading with a glance, and set aside a visible area in the store equipped with a table and chair where officers can come to write their reports (Petrocelli, 2008b, pp.22–23).

Commercial bank robberies are jointly investigated by the FBI, state and local law enforcement personnel: "The average bank robbery takes less than three minutes, oftentimes occurring so quickly that other customers are not aware of anything happening. About 25 percent of bank robberies occur on Fridays and most occur during the day shift between 9 A.M. and noon" (Petrocelli, 2008a, p.16). Suggested strategies to reduce bank robberies include enlisting the support of banks, focusing on high-risk branches and specific types of bank robbery, limiting cash access, using dye packs, using tracking devices and bait money, banning hats and sunglasses, employing greeters and hiring security guards, offering rewards, upgrading electronic surveillance and installing bullet-resistant glass barriers between tellers and customers (Weisel, 2007, pp.36–46).

Information about the suspect's general appearance, clothing and disguises, weapon(s) and vehicle(s) used should be obtained. Important modus operandi information includes type of robbery, time (day and hour), method of attack (threatened or real), weapon, object sought, number of robbers, voice and words, vehicle used and any peculiarities. Physical evidence that can connect the suspect with the robbery includes fingerprints, shoe prints, tire prints, restraining devices used, discarded garments, fibers and hairs, a note and the stolen property.

PROPERTY CRIMES

Many property crimes are difficult to investigate because they typically have little evidence and no eyewitnesses. Physical evidence in property crimes is often similar to that found in violent crimes: fingerprints, footprints, tire impressions, hair, fibers, broken glass and personal objects left at the crime scene. Other important evidence in property crimes includes tools, tool fragments, tool marks, safe insulation, disturbance of paint and evidence of forcible entry. The modus operandi of a property crime often takes on added importance because other significant leads are absent. Further, property crimes tend to occur in series, so solving one crime may lead to solving an entire series of similar crimes.

The major property crimes are burglary, larceny/theft, motor vehicle theft and arson.

Burglary

Burglary is the unlawful entry of a structure to commit a crime. It differs from robbery in that burglars are covert, trying to remain unseen, whereas robbers confront their victims directly. Burglary is a crime against property; robbery is a violent crime against a person. Burglaries are classified as residential or commercial

The elements of the crime of burglary include (1) entering a structure (2) without the consent of the person in possession (3) with the intent to commit a crime therein. Additional elements of burglary that may be required include (1) breaking into (2) the dwelling of another (3) during the nighttime. A burglary's severity is determined by the presence of dangerous devices in the burglar's possession, by the value of the property stolen, and whether the property or residence was occupied at the time of the offense. Attempted burglary and possession of burglary tools are also felonies. The elements of the crime of possessing burglary tools include (1) possessing any device, explosive or other instrumentality (2) with intent to use or permit their use to commit burglary.

Officers responding to a burglary call should proceed to the scene tactically, being observant and cautious. They should search the premises inside and outside for the burglar.

Special considerations in investigating burglary include the problem of false alarms, determining the means of entry into a structure, as well as into such objects as safes or vaults and recovering the stolen property. Jimmying is the most common method to enter a structure to commit burglary. Attacks on safes and vaults include punching, peeling, pulling or dragging, blowing, burning, chopping and, for safes, hauling them away.

Physical evidence at a burglary scene often includes fingerprints, DNA, footprints, tire prints, tools, tool marks, broken glass, safe insulation, paint chips and personal possessions. Important modus operandi factors include the time, the types of premises, the type of victim, point and means of entry, type of property taken and any peculiarities of the offense.

Mapping can be especially effective in dealing with burglaries, given that burglars often live or work within a two-mile residential radius. Mapping plus modus operandi information can often effectively zero in on suspects. Burglarized houses are likely to be burglarized again. Therefore, the most important use of data is to facilitate preventive measures such as target hardening after an initial victimization.

Fences, pawnshops, secondhand stores, flea markets and informants should be checked for leads in recovering stolen property.

Larceny/Theft

Larceny/theft is the unlawful taking, carrying, leading or riding away of property from another's possession. It is synonymous with theft. Both larceny and burglary are crimes against property, but larceny, unlike burglary, does not involve illegally entering a structure. Larceny differs from robbery in that no force or threat of force is involved. The two major categories of larceny/theft are grand larceny, a felony based on the value of stolen property (usually over $100), and petty larceny, a misdemeanor based on the value of the property (usually under $100).

The elements of the crime of larceny/theft are (1) the felonious stealing, taking, carrying, leading or driving away of (2) another's personal goods or property (3) valued above or below a specified amount (4) with the intent to permanently deprive the owner of the property or goods. In most states, taking found property with the intent to keep or sell it is also a crime.

Among the common types of larceny are purse-snatching, picking pockets, theft from coin machines, theft from motor vehicles, theft from buildings, jewelry theft, bicycle theft and shoplifting (including altering the price of an item). (See Figure 10.3.) Closed circuit television (CCTV) is one effective way to detect shoplifters as well as dishonest employees.

One of the most frequent thefts is that of bicycles. More than 1 million U.S. residents have their bicycles stolen each year. Bicycle theft is usually seen as a low police priority, but when viewed in the aggregate, bicycle theft represents

FIGURE 10.3
Larceny/Theft Distribution
Source: *Crime in the United States 2007.* Washington, DC: Federal Bureau of Investigation, September 2008.

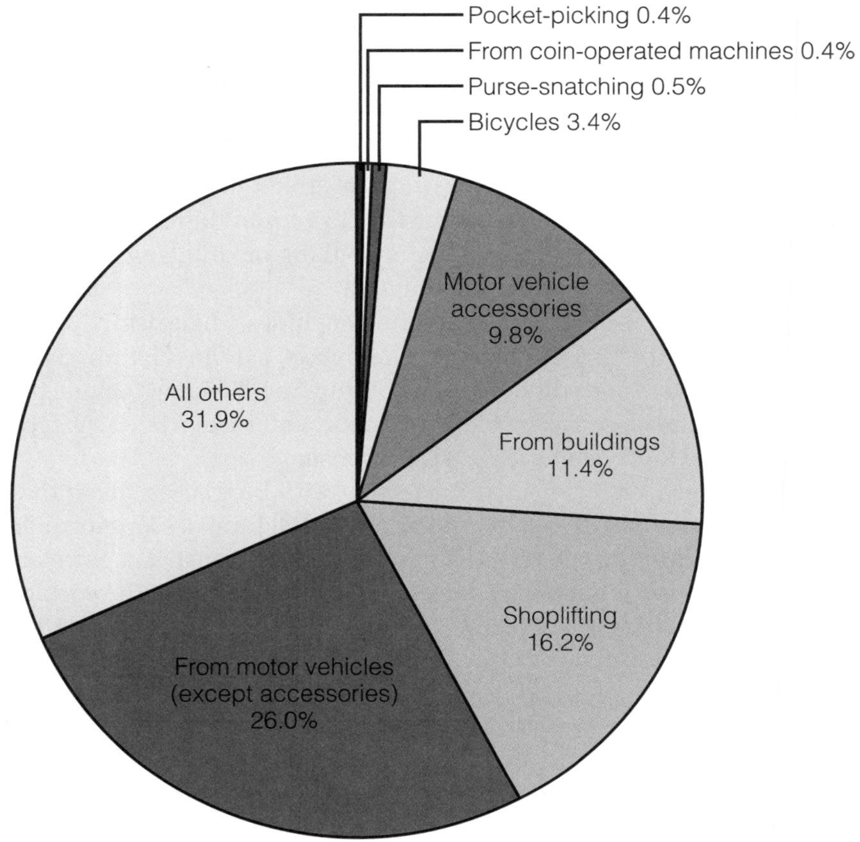

a large problem with harmful economic and societal effects (Johnson et al., 2008, p.2). The FBI Uniform Crime Reports (UCR) puts the annual cost of bicycle theft at between $800 million and $1 billion. Although police nationwide recover nearly 50 percent of lost and stolen bikes, less than 5 percent ever make it back to their rightful owners. This could be rectified if bike owners would register with the National Bike Registry. A top priority in reducing bicycle theft is educating the public about using effective bicycle locks and locking practices (Johnson et al., p.34).

Of increasing concern is the theft of copper, which, according to the FBI, threatens the U.S. infrastructure ("Precious Metal," 2008). An example of this threat was an incident in which vandals removed 300 feet of copper wire from a Federal Aviation Administration tower in Ohio, threatening to interrupt communications between in-flight aircraft and air traffic controllers. According to the FBI, the demand for copper from developing nations such as China and India has created a "robust" international copper trade; from 2001 until 2008, the price of copper has increased more than 500 percent. The thieves, many of whom are drug addicts or gang members, act individually or as part of organized groups. Their targets include electrical substations, railroads, security and emergency services, construction sites and new home developments, and other sensitive sites.

Although jewelry and art theft may be committed by those merely acting on opportunity, professional thieves or organized rings may also be responsible for these crimes. Given the enhanced security usually afforded such items of great monetary value, those who commit jewel or art theft have typically invested more time in planning their heist and may go to greater extremes to protect themselves and their loot, including being heavily armed. The FBI and Interpol are commonly involved in thefts of fine art. Officers investigating jewelry theft should also inform the FBI of the theft, even without immediate evidence of interstate operations.

As with burglary investigations, officers investigating cases of larceny/theft should check with fences, pawnshops, secondhand stores, flea markets and informants for leads in recovering stolen property.

The elements of the offense of receiving stolen goods are (1) receiving, buying or concealing stolen or illegally obtained goods (2) knowing them to be stolen or illegally obtained.

Fraud is intentional deception applied to cause a person to give up property or some lawful right. It differs from theft in that fraud uses deceit rather than stealth to obtain goods illegally. Fraud is committed in many ways, including the use of checks, credit cards, confidence games and embezzlement. Perpetrators of fraud are rarely prosecuted because the courts often regard fraud cases as civil rather than criminal. An additional challenge lies in establishing the criminal intent required for conviction. Furthermore, most current fraud cases are tied to the Internet and the perpetrators are difficult to trace, many times being located outside the jurisdiction of the United States. Such inter-jurisdictional cases are difficult to investigate and to prosecute.

Closely related to the preceding types of fraud are debit and credit-card fraud. Retailers and credit card companies incur tens of millions of dollars in losses each year because of credit-card fraud.

Elements of the crime of larceny by debit or credit card include (1) possessing cards obtained by theft or fraud (2) by which services or goods are obtained (3) through unauthorized signing of the cardholder's name. Bank embezzlements are investigated jointly by the local police and the FBI.

White-collar crime was coined in 1939 by criminologist Edwin Sutherland to describe an offense "committed by a person of respectability and high social status in the course of his occupation" (Sutherland, 1983). Later definitions focused more on the offense than the offender and included such elements as illegal acts committed by nonphysical means through deception and concealment during legitimate business activity. Over the years, the term has become synonymous with the full range of frauds committed by business and government professionals, both individuals and corporations.

White-collar or business-related crime includes securities theft and fraud; environmental crime; insurance fraud; credit-card and check fraud; consumer fraud; mortgage fraud; insurance fraud; health care fraud; telemarketing fraud; illegal competition and deceptive practices; bankruptcy fraud; computer-related fraud; embezzlement and pilferage; bribes, kickbacks and payoffs; and receiving stolen property.

Research by Piquero et al. (2008, pp.305–306) found that in four of six comparisons, white-collar crimes were perceived to be more serious than street crimes. Most individuals in the study also perceived that white-collar crimes were as serious—if not more so—than street crimes. Indeed, the economic costs of "suite" crime far exceed the costs of traditional street crime: "We cannot afford to neglect the capacity of corporations, the most powerful actors in the nation, to victimize society. Although corporate crime is usually less spectacular than the usual homicide or robbery, it still does significant harm, and in many respects this harm may far exceed the damage wrought by more traditional modes of criminality" (Cullen et al., 2006, p.18).

Detecting fraud and other forms of white-collar crime can be extremely challenging because many of the offenses involve spatial separation between victims and offenders, meaning they never come face-to-face, and many of the crimes are non-self-revealing, such as when a shady auto mechanic claims to have conducted a repair or performed a service and the vehicle owner lacks the expertise to know anything different. "Unlike most so-called traditional street crimes, such as robbery, burglary, auto theft, and assault, white-collar crimes are not obvious. They often do not leave visible traces of their occurrence. Even the victims may not be aware that a crime has taken place, let alone law enforcers" (Benson and Simpson, 2009, p.207). Without detection, investigation becomes impossible.

White-collar crime has been in the headlines for several decades, with the insider trading scandals of the 1980s, the saving and loan scandals of the 1990s, and the more recent financial and accounting fraud scandals involving Enron, Qwest, Tyco, WorldCom, Adelphia Communications and others. The FBI has refocused its efforts on white-collar crime, seeking to convict criminals who helped to create or are now exploiting the financial crisis occurring in this country (Kingsbury, 2009). For example, in March 2009, the FBI opened more than 200 mortgage-fraud cases and 36 corporate-financial investigations and the number is expected to grow exponentially: "Congress is already weighing an increase to the FBI's budget to address the spike in frauds related to the economic crisis" (Kingsbury).

Some of the white-collar crimes have gained national attention. One such investigation involves Tom Petters, who, in December 2009, was convicted on all 20 fraud, conspiracy and money laundering counts in his multibillion-dollar Ponzi scheme trial. In another recent scandal, in March 2009, Bernard Madoff pled guilty to securities fraud, perjury and other crimes committed during a 30-year span in what some have called the largest fraud in history. The 71-year-old former NASDAQ chairman was accused of bilking investors out of $64.8 billion. There was no plea bargain, and Madoff was sentenced to 150 years in prison in June 2009. Indeed, studies show that Americans seem to support such drastic punishments for those convicted of white-collar crime, generally favoring the same "get-tough" approach on corporate illegality as is commonly held for violent crime (Unnever et al., 2008, p.163).

Ponzi schemes are not the only white-collar crime grabbing headlines. Internet crime increased by 33 percent in 2008, with 275,284 complaints received that involved $265 million in dollar losses compared with 2007 when 206,884 complaints involving $239 million in dollar losses ("FBI/National White Collar Crime Center," 2009). Some Internet sites are becoming venues for criminals to seek unsuspecting victims. For example, Craigslist, an online bazaar used by about 30 million people every month, may be "edging toward infamy as a digital haven for hucksters looking to defraud the unwitting, or sell stolen goods and sex" (Pulkkinen, 2008).

A problem of increasing concern is *identity theft*, the unlawful use of another's personal identifying information, Historically, higher fraud rates occur when the economy worsens. In 2008, 9.9 million Americans were identity theft victims, a 22 percent increase over 2007 (Kanable, 2009, p.28). One reason identity theft has increased so dramatically is that there are more than 200 valid forms of ID or drivers' licenses issued in the United States. The increasingly sophisticated computer equipment and photocopying and imaging methods available to the public makes it easy to alter or counterfeit almost any document. The Internet has hundreds of Web sites that sell fake driver's licenses, ID cards, police IDs and birth certificates on CDs.

Identity theft became a federal crime in 1998 when President Bill Clinton signed the Identity Theft and Assumption Deterrence Act. Although this act looks good on paper, it does not cover thefts less than the $50,000 to $100,000 threshold most attorneys use to determine if federal prosecution should occur.

The rising threat of terrorism makes identity theft an even greater concern. As an example, all 19 of the September 11 hijackers had social security numbers, including several that were stolen. In July 2004, President George W. Bush signed into law a sentence imposing mandatory prison terms for criminals who use identity theft to commit terrorist acts and other offenses.

As with computer-related crime and digital/electronic evidence, many local police departments are ill equipped to deal with white-collar crime and other nontraditional forms of larceny/theft.

Motor Vehicle Theft

Motor vehicle thefts include cars, trucks, buses, motorcycles, motor scooters, mopeds, snowmobiles, vans, self-propelled watercraft, and aircraft. Although motor vehicle theft investigations take much investigative time, they can provide important information on other crimes under investigation. The vehicle identification number (VIN), critical in motor vehicle thefts, identifies the specific vehicle in question and is the primary nonduplicated, serialized number assigned by the manufacturer to each vehicle.

Categories for motor vehicle theft based on the offender's motive include (1) joyriding, (2) transportation, (3) stripping for parts and accessories, (4) use in committing another crime and (5) reselling for profit.

Although referred to as "motor vehicle theft," most cases are prosecuted as "unauthorized use of a motor vehicle" because a charge of theft requires proof that the thief intended to deprive the owner of the vehicle permanently, which is often difficult or impossible to establish.

The elements of the crime of unauthorized use of a motor vehicle are (1) intentionally taking or driving (2) a motor vehicle (3) without the consent of the owner or the owner's authorized agent. Embezzlement of a motor vehicle occurs if the person who took the vehicle had consent initially and then exceeded the terms of that consent.

False motor vehicle theft reports are often filed because a car has been taken by a family member or misplaced in a parking lot, to cover up for an accident or a crime committed with the vehicle or to provide an alibi for being late. The FBI and the National Auto Theft Bureau provide valuable help in investigating motor vehicle theft.

To apprehend car thieves, many departments are using bait cars, specially outfitted cars placed in areas where they are likely to be stolen, based on trends in the community. A computer monitors the cars' locations and sounds an alarm if anyone gets in. Fairfax County, Washington, uses bait cars equipped with GPS devices, hidden video cameras and technology that allows the police to remotely shut down the cars' engines or blow their horns loudly (Jackman, 2009). During the first quarter of 2009, 13 percent fewer cars were stolen in that jurisdiction than in the same quarter in 2008.

To improve the ability to recognize stolen vehicles, officers should keep a list of stolen vehicles in their cars, develop a checking system for rapidly determining if a suspicious vehicle is stolen, learn the common characteristics of stolen vehicles and car thieves, take time to check suspicious people and vehicles and learn how to question suspicious drivers and occupants. Numerous motor vehicle thefts can be prevented by effective educational campaigns and by manufacturer-installed security devices. The Dyer Act made interstate transportation of a stolen motor vehicle a federal crime and allowed for federal help in prosecuting such cases.

Arson

Arson is the malicious, willful burning of a building or property. Fires are classified as natural, accidental, criminal (arson), suspicious or of unknown origin. They are presumed natural or accidental unless proven otherwise.

The elements of the crime of arson include (1) the willful, malicious burning of a building or property (2) of another, or of one's own to defraud (3) or causing to be burned, or aiding, counseling or procuring such burning. Attempted arson is also a crime. Some states categorize arson as either aggravated or simple. Aggravated arson is intentionally destroying or damaging a dwelling or other property by means of fire or explosives, creating an imminent danger to life or great bodily harm, which risk was known or reasonably foreseeable to the suspect. Simple arson is intentional destruction by fire or explosives that does not create imminent danger to life or risk of great bodily harm. Other states use the Model Arson Law, which divides arson into four degrees: first-degree involves the burning of dwellings; second-degree involves the burning of buildings other than dwellings; third-degree involves the burning of other property; and fourth-degree involves attempts to burn buildings or property.

Logic suggests that the fire department should work to *detect* arson and determine the point of origin and probable cause, whereas the police department should *investigate* arson and prepare the case for prosecution. Special problems in investigating arson include coordinating efforts with the fire department and others, determining if a crime has been committed, finding physical evidence and witnesses and determining if the victim is a suspect.

An administrative warrant is issued when it is necessary for the agent to search the premises to determine the cause and origin of the fire. A criminal warrant is issued on probable cause when evidence of a crime is found on the premises. Entry to fight a fire requires no warrant. Once in the building, fire officials may remain a reasonable time to investigate the cause of the blaze. After this time, an administrative warrant is needed, as established in *Michigan v. Tyler* (1978).

Although the fire department is responsible for establishing when arson has occurred, law enforcement investigators must be able to verify such findings. To do so requires understanding what distinguishes an accidental fire from arson. Basic to this understanding is the concept of the fire triangle, which consists of three elements necessary for a substance to burn: air, fuel and heat. In arson, at least one of these elements is usually present in abnormal amounts for the structure. Evidence of **accelerants**, substances that promote burning, is a primary form of evidence at an arson scene. The most common accelerant used is gasoline. Also important as evidence are **igniters**, articles used to light a fire. These include matches; candles; cigars and cigarettes; cigarette lighters; electrical, mechanical and chemical devices; and explosives.

accelerants

Substances that promote burning; are a primary form of evidence at an arson scene; the most common accelerant used is gasoline.

igniters

Articles used to light a fire.

Burn indicators that provide important information include alligatoring (blistering), crazing, depth of char, lines of demarcation, sagged furniture springs and spalling. The point of origin is established by finding the area with the deepest char, alligatoring and (usually) the greatest destruction. Fires normally burn upward, are drawn toward ventilation and follow fuel. Arson is likely in fires that

- Have more than one point of origin.
- Deviate from normal burning patterns.
- Show evidence of trailers.
- Show evidence of having been accelerated.
- Produce odors or smoke of a color associated with substances not normally present at the scene.
- Indicate that an abnormal amount of air, fuel or heat was present.
- Reveal evidence of incendiary igniters at the point of origin.

Officers investigating vehicle fires should look for evidence of accelerants and determine whether the vehicle was insured. It is seldom arson if there is no insurance. Officers investigating explosions and bombings should pay special attention to any fragments of the explosive device as well as to any powder present at the scene and attempt to determine a motive. If a computer is found at an arson scene, it is likely that the data on the hard drive is intact, surviving the heat and flames as well as the water and steam from the firefighting efforts.

Arson investigations might also be made more effective and efficient if police officers are cross-trained with firefighters.

OTHER CRIMES

Beyond the eight Index crimes, officers commonly investigate other offenses, such as crimes against children (discussed in detail in Chapter 11), hate or bias crimes, environmental crimes and computer-related crimes. Many of these offenses involve one or more elements of one or more of the Index crimes. For example, crimes against children may include assault, rape or murder. Bias crimes may be directed at a person (assault, homicide) or property (arson). Environmental crimes may involve theft of a commodity (for example, lumber) or, in some instances, homicide, as was the case when lethal acid was left on the street with the regular garbage and someone exposed to the chemical died. Finally, computer-related crimes may involve various forms of theft, including identity theft, and computers have been increasingly used to perpetrate crimes against children and distribute pornography.

Bias/Hate Crimes

A *hate crime*, according to the FBI, is "a criminal offense committed against a person, property or society which is motivated, in whole or in part, by the offender's bias against a race, religion, disability, sexual orientation or ethnicity/national origin." The FBI's *Hate Crime Statistics* (2007) reports 7,624 single-bias incidents in 2007, with race being the most frequent motivation of hate crime (50.8 percent) followed by religion (18.4 percent), sexual orientation (16.6 percent), ethnicity (13.2 percent), and disability (1.0 percent) (See Figure 10.4.) Most hate crimes are not reported to the police. The International Association of Chiefs of Police (IACP) has developed a hate crime continuum depicting what can happen if a community ignores racial epithets or hate symbols, whereby relatively nonsevere acts can escalate into assault, arson and even murder. Graffiti, epithets and symbols should be photographed and then be removed quickly.

Hate crimes differ from nonhate-based crimes in several other important ways, as summarized in Table 10.3.

The Anti-Defamation League has launched a Web site to serve as a database for law enforcement officers investigating hate groups. The site identifies and monitors extremist groups and allows police to search for symbols they might find on literature or tattoos. It also tracks hate group meetings and rallies on a state-by-state calendar.

Environmental Crime

Environmental crimes range from people littering to those illegally disposing of used tires, used oil, biohazardous waste and other hazardous substances. In some states, property owners can be civilly fined up to $500 a day if the cleanup is not completed within the required time.

When both civil and criminal proceedings are instituted against a violator; a frequent occurrence in environmental crimes.

When both civil and criminal proceedings are instituted against a violator, it is known as **parallel proceedings**. The courts have ruled that taking both criminal and civil actions against a violator is not considered double jeopardy. Unfortunately, many law enforcement agencies consider polluting the environment a civil matter and do not devote resources to finding and prosecuting those who break the laws concerning protecting the environment.

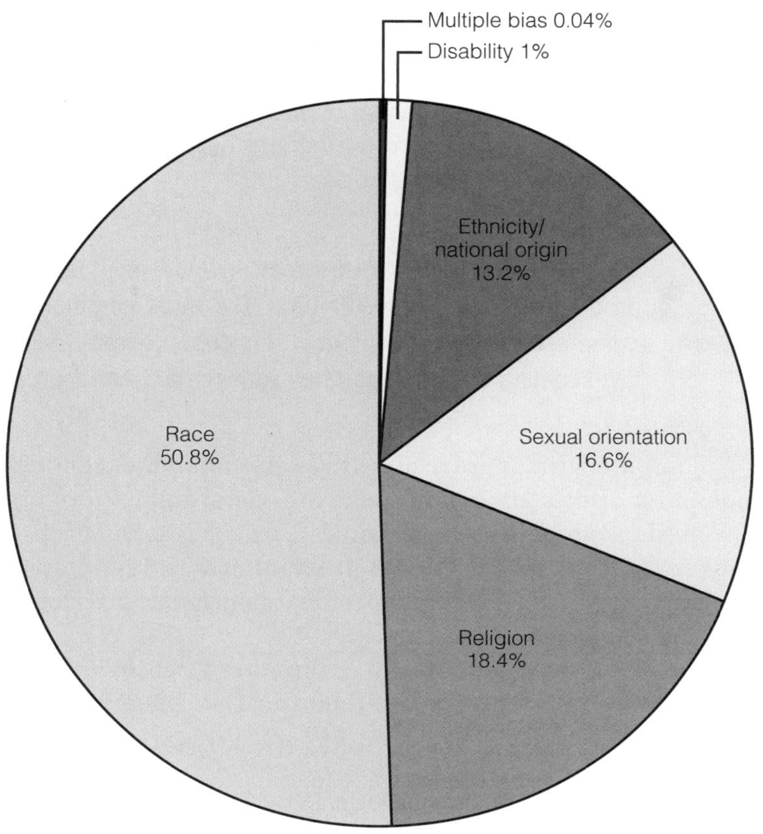

FIGURE 10.4 Bias-Motivated Offenses
Source: *Hate Crime Statistics*, 2007. Washington, DC: Federal Bureau of Investigation, October 2008.

Table 10.3 Hate-Based Crime versus Nonhate-Based Crime

Characteristics	Nonhate-Based Incidents	Hate-Based Incidents
Relationship of victim to perpetrator	Most assaults involve two people who know each other	Assaults tend to be "stranger" crimes
Number of perpetrators	Most assaults have one perpetrator and one victim	Involve an average of four assailants for each victim
Nature of the conflict	Tends to be even	Tends to be uneven—hate crime perpetrators often attack younger or weaker victims, or arm themselves and attack unarmed victims
Amount of physical damage inflicted	Not typically "excessive"	Extremely violent, with victims being three times more likely to require hospitalization than "normal" assault victims
Treatment of property	In most property crimes, something of value is taken	More likely that valuable property will be damaged or destroyed
Perpetrator's personal gain	Attacker settles a score or profits from the crime	In most, no personal score is settled and no profit is made
Location of crime	No place with any symbolic significance	Frequently occur in churches, synagogues, mosques, cemeteries, monuments, schools, camps, and in or around the victim's home

Source: Adapted from Christina Bodinger-deUriarte. "Hate Crime: The Rise of Hate Crime on School Campuses." Research Bulletin No. 10 of Phi Delta Kappa, Center for Evaluation, Development, and Research, December 1991, p.2. Reprinted with permission of Phi Delta Kappa International.

Computer-Related Crimes

Computer-related crimes are often very technically complex; thus, an in-depth discussion on their investigation is far beyond the scope of this chapter. It is important, however, for patrol officers to be familiar with some of the basic facets and features of these offenses.

Computer-related crimes may involve input data, output data, the program itself or computer time. The most common types of computer crime are misuse of computer services, program abuse and data abuse. Investigating such crimes often requires a team approach.

Computer crimes are relatively easy to commit and difficult to detect. Most computer crimes are committed by insiders, and few are prosecuted. People involved in computer-related crimes are usually technical people such as data entry clerks, machine operators, programmers and systems analysts. Common motivators for such crimes are personal gain, ignorance, misguided playfulness and maliciousness or revenge.

The four common phases of a computer forensic investigation are collection, examination, analysis and reporting (Jacobia, 2004, p.30):

> The collection phase involves the search for, recognition, collection and documentation of electronic evidence. This phase would normally be accomplished by the first responder.
>
> The examination phase helps make the evidence visible and explains its origin and significance. It should document the content and state of the evidence in its totality. Also included in this phase is the search for any information that may be hidden or obscured.
>
> The analysis phase looks at the results of the examination for its significance and probative value to the case.
>
> The report phase results in a written report that outlines the examination process and pertinent data recovered. Examination notes must be preserved for discovery or testimony.

Evidence in computer-related crimes is often contained on tapes or disks, not readily discernible and highly susceptible to destruction. In addition to information on tapes and disks, evidence may take the form of data reports, programming or other printed materials based on information from computer files.

Investigators who handle computer tapes and disks should avoid contact with the recording surfaces. They should never write on affixed computer disk labels and should never use paper clips on or rubber bands around computer disks. To do so may destroy the data they contain. Computer tapes and disks taken as evidence should be stored vertically, at approximately 70°F and away from bright light, dust and magnetic fields.

The FBI and the Department of Justice have created the Internet Fraud Complaint Center (IFCC), which, in its first three-and-a-half days, logged 3,700 complaints. The site allows consumers and small businesses nationwide to file Internet fraud complaints online.

A relatively recent form of computer crime is **phishing**, using fraudulent e-mails and Web sites to fool recipients into divulging personal information. **Spoofing**, which is often associated with phishing, is another newer trend in computer-related crime and involves senders who alter or change the origin or source of an e-mail so that the origin of the e-mail is unknown. Many fraudulent scams use spoofed Internet protocol (IP) addresses. A variety of programs are available to make spoofing easy to do, and criminals are capitalizing on the anonymity afforded by the Internet along with the difficulty of tracing the source when using this technology.

phishing
Use of fraudulent e-mails and Web sites to fool recipients into divulging personal information.

spoofing
A newer trend in computer-related crime involving senders who alter or change the origin or source of an e-mail so that the origin of the e-mail is unknown. Many fraudulent scams use spoofed Internet protocol (IP) addresses.

Spoofing has been used to make prank phone calls, an offense called "telephone spoofing." Since services such as Skype, which allow people to use their Internet connection as a phone line as well, have been developed, there have been reported incidents where prank phone call spoofing has occurred. This seemingly harmless idea creates a headache for law enforcement, however, when incidents escalate to a dangerous level. One such incident, first mentioned in Chapter 8, involved a prank 911 call from a spoofed source that resulted in a police SWAT team being dispatched to a house where innocent people were confronted and arrested in a high-risk style. The perpetrator turned out to be a young teen from across the country who, through computer technology, was able to make it appear as though he was actually calling from the innocent people's residence with a gruesome, albeit fraudulent, report. This new trend is called "swatting," a term based on spoofing. Beside the fact that it is very difficult and time consuming to trace such spoofed calls, there are also jurisdictional issues because this crime can be committed from far distances, much like Internet fraud. In addition, spoofing itself is currently not illegal in the United States.

FALSE REPORTS

Whether officers are investigating violent crimes or property crimes, they should always be aware of the possibility of a false report. People may claim to have been burglarized to collect money for the stolen items from their insurance companies. Or they may set a friend up to "rob" them while they are at work alone and in control of a large amount of cash.

VICTIMLESS CRIMES

A great amount of investigative time is spent on the so-called **victimless crimes**, such as prostitution, gambling, pornography and dealing/doing drugs. Such crimes are sometimes assigned to a division called *vice investigations*.

victimless crimes
Offenses in which there are no complainants; includes prostitution, pornography, gaming and drug dealing/using.

Victimless crimes include prostitution, pornography, gaming and drug dealing/using.

Opinion polls indicate that most of the public is not all that upset about victimless crimes. However, a crime is a crime, even if the victim does not recognize or acknowledge it. This section addresses the "victimless" crimes of prostitution, gambling and pornography. Chapter 12 discusses investigating crimes involving drugs.

Prostitution and Pornography

How aggressively police deal with prostitution depends greatly on public expectations. According to Parker (n.d.), "Prostitution, pornography and other forms of commercial sex are a multibillion dollar industry. They enrich a small minority of predators, while the larger community is left to pay for the damages." He further notes, "People used in the sex industry often need medical care as a result of the ever-present violence. They may need treatment for infectious diseases, including AIDS. Survivors frequently need mental health care for posttraumatic stress disorder, psychotic episodes and suicide attempts. About a third end up chronically disabled and on social security." Further problems are that the sex trade plays an active role in promoting alcohol and drug abuse and that pimps also may use their prostitutes in forgery and credit-card fraud. In addition, more 80 percent of suspected human trafficking incidents in 2007 and 2008 involved forced prostitution (Kyckelhahn et al., 2009, p.1).

Although streetwalking prostitutes are the most visible sign of a problem, escort services should not be overlooked. Because escort services advertise in local newspapers, telephone directories and online Web sites, these sources can be reviewed to reveal their presence. Many prostitutes are homeless, have limited education and very few social or professional ties with the community. For most, prostitution is not a chosen career but rather a matter of survival, often as the result of a drug habit, combined with the lack of skills or resources.

One common strategy to address prostitution is to focus on the "johns," exposing them to public humiliation. Undercover operations may also be successful in breaking up organized prostitution. In some instances, officers wait outside suspected establishments and talk with exiting customers.

Pornography presents its own unique challenges because of the subjective nature of what is considered "offensive" and the various interpretations allowed of the First Amendment right to freedom of expression. Defining what is *pornographic* is problematic—given the graphic sex scenes on television and in movies, what are the standards today? Most citizens cannot agree. The Internet has also added a new dimension to pornography. Some countries are banning American online services, claiming they are pornographic.

Gaming

The term *gaming* has replaced the older term *gambling* among those who are involved in this activity. In years past, gaming was a focus of law enforcement, with raids on gaming establishments making headlines. Legal gaming includes charitable gaming, paramutual betting, casino gaming and lotteries. Illegal gaming may attract other vices, such as prostitution, pornography, loan-sharking and extortion. A NIJ study found that arrestees had significantly more problems gambling than in the general population and had high levels of criminal activity related to their pathological gambling. Nearly one-third of the arrestees identified as pathological gamblers admitted having committed robbery in the previous year, and about 13 percent had assaulted someone for money. In addition, pathological gamblers were much more likely to have sold drugs than were other arrestees (McCorkle, 2004).

The most significant forms of illegal gaming are numbers, betting with bookmakers or bookies and sports pools or sports cards. The Internet is responsible for a large growth in gaming, with more than 300 gaming-related sites, some of which have set up operations offshore.

Many investigations, including those of victimless crimes, make use of surveillance, undercover assignments and raids.

SURVEILLANCE, UNDERCOVER ASSIGNMENTS, RAIDS AND STINGS

"Follow that car!" "Don't lose her." "I've been made." "My cover's blown." "It's a raid." "We gotcha." Fictionalized detective work frequently portrays the glamorous side of surveillance, undercover assignments, raids, and stings. In reality, however, such assignments often involve days, weeks, even months of tedious yet dangerous watchfulness.

Surveillance, undercover assignments, raids, and stings should be used only when all other investigative alternatives have failed.

Because they are expensive and potentially dangerous, these investigative techniques are not routinely used. When they are used, it is often by specialized units such as drug task forces, gang strike forces, vice squads, and so on.

Surveillance

The purpose of surveillance is to gather information about people, their activities and associates that may help solve a crime or protect a witness. Surveillance can be designed to serve several functions (Hess and Orthmann, 2010, pp.220–221):

- Gain information required for building a criminal complaint.
- Determine an informant's loyalty and degree of trustworthiness and credibility.
- Verify a witness' statement about a crime.
- Gain information required for obtaining a search or arrest warrant.
- Gain information necessary for interrogating a suspect.
- Identify a suspect's associates.
- Observe members of terrorist organizations.
- Find a person wanted for a crime.
- Observe criminal activities in progress.
- Make a legal arrest.
- Apprehend a criminal in the act of committing a crime.
- Prevent a crime.
- Recover stolen property.
- Protect witnesses.

A common type of surveillance is the stakeout, a stationary surveillance in which officers set up an observation post and monitor it continuously. Other forms of surveillance include aerial surveillance and audio surveillance, or wiretapping. Before a judge will approve an application for electronic surveillance, those requesting it must show why surveillance is necessary, for example, standard techniques have been tried and failed or standard investigative techniques are too dangerous to try.

Using closed-circuit television (CCTV) cameras to monitor public spaces is increasing, both in the United States and abroad. Despite people's concern about the government watching and recording them as they pass through parks, streets and other public areas, CCTV use by criminal justice personnel in the United States seems to be increasing: "When implemented with a well-thought plan and used properly, CCTV can potentially be a real force multiplier for law enforcement agencies of any size" (Kanable, 2008, p.30). Balancing legal electronic surveillance and an individual's right to privacy is a challenge to the criminal justice system.

Undercover Assignments

Those conducted openly, usually with officers in uniform or introducing themselves as police officers.

Those done secretively, for example, using surveillance and undercover personnel.

An investigation can be overt or covert. **Overt investigations** are conducted openly, usually with officers either in uniform or introducing themselves as officers. **Covert investigations**, in contrast, are done secretively, for example, using surveillance and undercover personnel. Most people are aware of undercover (UC) operations from the television programs and movies in which detectives take on false identities and infiltrate groups engaged in illegal activity. However, undercover operations have been criticized by some as having no place in a free society such as ours.

Undercover operations can offer information not otherwise available. The police cannot be everywhere. They must rely on inside information or tips where highly skilled criminal activities are involved, particularly lacking identifiable victims or witnesses. Audio recording or video filming a crime is often feasible in undercover operations. This is a surer form of evidence and is more difficult to manipulate than verbal testimony. Undercover practices are costly and susceptible to abuse and unintended consequences. Therefore, they should be used only for serious offenses when alternative means are not available, and then only under careful monitoring.

Undercover assignments are used to obtain information and evidence about illegal activity when it can be obtained in no other way.

Undercover work can be used to capture fugitives, to establish probable cause to arrest or search, (3) to serve a warrant without use of force, or (4) to interview an uncooperative subject. Undercover operations may even extend into cyberspace. The undercover work itself may be light or deep.

Light cover involves deception, but the officer usually goes home at night. While on assignment the officer may pose as a utility worker or phone company repair person to obtain access to a suspect's home or workplace. Other covers may include that of a writer or member of the news media or a phony photographer.

Deep cover is much more dangerous but can be very effective. The officer lives an assumed identity in an attempt to infiltrate a group or organization.

No identification other than the cover identification is carried. Communication with the police department is risky and carefully planned. Plans also are made for what the undercover officer is to do if the criminal operation is "busted" and for how the officer will end the relationship. Officers can risk much working deep under cover, including their own lives. When the operation is completed, they may have to go under witness protection. The officer's family may also be at risk. The deep investigation typically engulfs an individual's entire life, so these officers are usually separated from their families for the duration of a long investigation, which creates tension in their personal lives. Undercover officers may also become close to those they are investigating, which can create severe internal turmoil and identity conflict.

The nature of undercover work can lead to "nightmarish situations because, by definition, undercover officers are supposed to melt into their surroundings. Snap decisions—when to back off, when to make arrests, certainly when to shoot—are rarely uncomplicated or without peril" (Haberman, 2007, p.1). Grossi (2009, p.24) asserts that undercover work requires a "carefully crafted persona and unrelenting self-discipline." He notes that the DEA recommends that undercover officers keep their real first names in case they are greeted by someone on the street who does not know they are working undercover. It is also advisable to keep their real birth date so it comes naturally if asked for it.

One danger of using undercover operations is that officers may become what they start out only pretending to be. Another danger of using undercover operations is the potential for a charge of entrapment, discussed in Chapter 14. Also controversial is the use of informants.

Informants Because of the information informants can provide, many crimes have been solved that would not have been without their assistance. Sometimes police informers, also referred to as "CIs" for "criminal informants," are paid, but more often their motives for assisting the police are to receive a reduced sentence for a pending criminal matter. Other common motives include concern for the public safety and revenge.

Informants who operate in undercover roles may be involved only in passive observation. They can be used to vouch for and introduce sworn police undercover agents to a suspected person or group and then should be dropped from the investigation. Informants may also play an active role in the criminal activities of those on whom they are informing. Only a small fraction of informers ever testify in court, although the information they provide may be offered to the judge to obtain warrants for arrests, searches, wiretaps or electronic surveillances.

Some informers go beyond giving information obtained in their natural environment and use disguises and infiltrations. The environment is deceptively shaped to elicit information. For example, an informant is placed in a suspect's cell as a cellmate in the hope that confidences will be transmitted. Other examples are an agent posing as an employee to infiltrate a factory in response to problems such as employee thefts or the police posing as reporters seeking comments from political and social activists.

Known tactics whose legality is questionable include planting informers in a group organized for the legal defense of an activist facing serious criminal charges or having a police officer dressed as a clergyman visit an arrested person in jail. Another common, and often significant, tactic is the "front," such as a cocktail lounge or a neighborhood used-property store set up for a sting operation or specifically created by the police for intelligence purposes.

Once a person has begun to inform, the threat of exposure becomes a factor. Allegiances may shift or become more intense. A criminal who becomes overzealous and tries to play the role of super cop may jeopardize a whole operation. Or, informants may become double agents—that is, clever informants experienced in deception who manipulate and control their police contact, rather than the reverse. Such individuals can also become double informants, having several different police contacts who do not know of each other. This situation may arise more often in cross-jurisdictional investigations. Double informers may share the same information and be reimbursed several times over for the same information.

Because undercover work is complex, it has both positive and negative aspects. Assessing them is difficult. Little research can be done because of the work's covert nature and the courts' and civil rights advocates' suspiciousness.

Raids

The errors involved in the raid in Waco in 1993 underscore the criticality of planning and timing. Although the planners of the raid knew that they had probably lost the element of surprise, rather than rethinking the plan for the raid, they speeded up their activities, and the result was a deadly blaze on April 19 and much public criticism. Raids are discussed in greater detail in Chapter 12.

Stings

Sting operations cover a wide variety of crimes, but most have four basic elements (Newman and Socia, 2007, p.3):

1. An opportunity or enticement to commit a crime created or exploited by police
2. A targeted likely offender or group of offenders for a particular crime type
3. An undercover or hidden police officer or surrogate, or some form of deception
4. A "Gotcha" climax when the operation ends with arrests

Sting operations may involve offering a bribe to a politician suspected of corruption, purchasing illegal drugs in an open-air drug market, buying liquor by a minor, or hiding in an area where drivers are known to exceed the speed limit: "The clearest, defining feature of sting operations nowadays is that there is a point that ends the operations with a 'gotcha,' when police suddenly reveal themselves and catch the offender 'in the act'" (Newman and Socia, 2007, p.3).

Although surveillance, undercover work, raids, and stings are specialized forms of investigation, a much more common and often relied upon source of information is the citizenry of a community, people who can be additional eyes and ears for a department.

INVESTIGATION AND COMMUNITY POLICING

Shifting investigation work from a reactive to a proactive model is in keeping with the community policing philosophy. A new investigative structure might center around developing integrated major crime problem-solving task forces, with detectives developing stronger ties with the community. Citizens become allies in investigations, providing information to the police.

A shift to community-oriented investigations acknowledges that crime is complex and requires a balanced response, with detectives collaborating among themselves and with community stakeholders.

PROBLEM-ORIENTED POLICING AND INVESTIGATION

The use of problem solving in investigation may seem to be a stretch. Criminal investigation is, by its nature, concerned with solving crimes that have already occurred. Following is the 2003 Goldstein Award Winner for excellence in problem-oriented policing, "The Oakland Airport Motel Program"—The Oakland Police Department Beat Health Unit.

Scanning

In September 2000, the recurring nuisance and criminal activity at a major motel, which is part of an international chain, located near the Oakland International Airport, came to the attention of Officer Brad Gardiner of the Oakland Police Department's Beat Health Unit. Problems included inordinate calls for police service, prostitution, illegal drug activity, abandoned cars, illegal auto repair business in the motel parking lot and renting of rooms to minors.

Analysis

Data checks, site visits, interviews, undercover surveillance and comparisons of management practices to other nearby motels led police to conclude that it was the poor management practices at the motel that allowed crime and nuisances to flourish at this motel.

Response

After meetings with on-site motel managers and corporate executives failed to result in improvements at the motel, Beat Health Unit officers and city attorneys filed a drug nuisance abatement lawsuit against the parent corporation. Eventually, through intense negotiations, the parent corporation agreed to improve its management practices and to post a $250,000 performance bond covering a two-year monitoring period to guarantee reductions in crime and nuisance at the motel. It further agreed to pay the City of Oakland about $35,000 to cover the costs of its investigation. Numerous specific improvements were made to the physical environment and management practices at the motel.

Assessment

Two years after the agreement was signed, there have been few calls for police service at the motel and the property has been returned to productive use. The stipulated two-year monitoring period concluded in March 2003.

Judge's Commentary

The Oakland Airport Motel project exemplifies the practice of problem- oriented policing in several significant ways. First, it illustrates the importance of careful documentation of the conditions that give rise to a problem. Particularly when dealing with sophisticated corporate executives, the Oakland police officials and city attorneys took great care to compile irrefutable evidence that a significant amount of crime and nuisance activity was occurring at the motel, that the amount of such activity was greatly disproportionate to that experienced by similarly situated motels, and that the poor management practices at the motel were largely to blame for the problems. Second, the project exemplifies the value of a systematic approach to addressing problems. The Beat Health Unit carefully followed its own step-by-step procedure for building a case against a problem property. This deliberate approach ensured that the investigating officers gathered the necessary information and drew the right conclusions from it before settling on a course of action. Third, and perhaps most significantly, this project exemplifies how police can, with proper documented evidence and careful analysis, shift the ownership of crime and disorder problems away from the police and local government alone, back to those individuals and groups whose actions create the problems and who have the capacity to address them. (Source: "The Oakland Airport Motel Program." *Excellence in Problem-Oriented Policing: The 2003 Herman Goldstein Award Winner and Finalists.* Washington, DC: The Office of Community Oriented Policing Services and the Police Executive Research Forum, November 2003.)

SUMMARY

The glamorous, exciting, action-packed fictionalized detective presents an exaggerated, unrealistic picture that differs greatly from the reality of detective work. The goals of criminal investigation are to determine if a crime has been committed, legally obtain information and evidence to identify the person(s) responsible, arrest the suspect(s), recover stolen property and present the best possible case to the prosecutor. The most critical phase in most criminal investigations is the preliminary investigation.

The successful resolution of a criminal investigation most often hinges on the availability of irrefutable, relevant and admissible evidence. The Automated Fingerprint Identification System, AFIS, drastically reduces the time needed to identify latent fingerprints by selecting a limited number of likely matches for the latent prints. Physical fingerprints and DNA fingerprinting are the two forms of positive identification available to investigators.

Detectives must be familiar with techniques to investigate specific crimes. The major violent crimes are homicide, rape, assault and robbery. Homicide is classified as criminal (felonious) or noncriminal. The various degrees of murder and manslaughter are criminal homicide, noncriminal homicide (which includes excusable homicide, the unintentional, truly accidental killing of another person) and justifiable homicide (killing another person under authorization of law). A common element in every charge is "causing the death of another human being." Other elements in homicide include premeditation, malicious intent, adequately provoked intent resulting in heat of passion, while committing or attempting to commit a crime that is not a felony, when forced or threatened, culpable negligence or depravity or simple negligence. Premeditation, the deliberate, precalculated plan to cause death, is the essential element of first-degree murder, distinguishing it from all other murder classifications. After priority matters are completed, the focus of the homicide investigation is to identify the victim, establish the time of death, establish the cause of death and the method used to produce it and to develop a suspect. Special problems in homicide investigations include pressure by the public and the media; difficulty in establishing that it is homicide, rather than suicide or an accidental or natural death; handling serial murders; and, in some cases, reopening cold cases.

Most states have in common the following elements for the crime of rape or sexual assault: (1) an act of sexual intercourse, (2) committed without the victim's consent, (3) against the victim's will and by force.

The elements of the crime of simple assault are (1) intent to do bodily harm to another, (2) present ability to commit the act and (3) commission of an overt act toward carrying out the intent. An additional element in the crime of aggravated assault is that the intentionally inflicted bodily injury results in (1) a high probability of death, (2) serious, permanent disfigurement or (3) permanent or protracted loss or impairment of the function of any body member or organ or other severe bodily harm. Attempted assault requires proof of intent and an overt act toward committing the crime.

The elements of the crime of robbery are (1) the wrongful taking of personal property, (2) from the person or in the person's presence, (3) against the person's will by force or threat of force.

The major property crimes are burglary, larceny/theft, motor vehicle theft and arson. Burglaries are classified as residential or commercial. The elements of the crime of burglary include (1) entering a structure (2) without the consent of the person in possession (3) with the intent to commit a crime therein. Additional elements of burglary that may be required include (1) breaking into (2) the dwelling of another (3) during the nighttime. A burglary's severity is determined by the presence of dangerous devices in the burglar's possession, by the value of the property stolen and whether the property or residence was occupied at the time of the crime. Attempted burglary and possession of burglary tools are also felonies. The elements of the crime of possessing burglary tools include (1) possessing any device, explosive or other instrumentality (2) with intent to use or permit their use to commit burglary.

The elements of the crime of larceny/theft are (1) the felonious stealing, taking, carrying, leading or driving away of (2) another's personal goods or property (3) valued above or below a specified amount (4) with the intent to permanently deprive the owner of the property or goods. In most states, taking found property with the intent to keep or sell it is also a crime. The elements of the offense of receiving stolen goods are (1) receiving, buying or concealing stolen or illegally obtained goods (2) knowing them to be stolen or illegally obtained. Elements of the crime of larceny by debit or credit card include (1) possessing cards obtained by theft or fraud (2) by which services or goods are obtained (3) through unauthorized signing of the cardholder's name. Bank embezzlements are investigated jointly by the local police and the FBI.

Categories for motor vehicle theft based on the offender's motive include (1) joyriding, (2) transportation, (3) stripping for parts and accessories, (4) use in committing another crime and (5) reselling for profit. The elements of the crime of unauthorized use of a motor vehicle are (1) intentionally taking or driving (2) a motor vehicle (3) without the consent of the owner or the owner's authorized agent. Embezzlement of a motor vehicle occurs if the person who took the vehicle had consent initially and then exceeded the terms of that consent.

The elements of the crime of arson include (1) the willful, malicious burning of a building or property (2) of another, or of one's own to defraud (3) or causing to be burned, or aiding, counseling or procuring such burning. Attempted arson is also a crime. Some states categorize arson as either aggravated or simple. Aggravated arson is intentionally destroying or damaging a dwelling or other property by means of fire or explosives, creating an imminent danger to life or great bodily harm, which risk was known or reasonably foreseeable to the suspect. Simple arson is intentional destruction by fire or explosives that does not create imminent danger to life or risk of great bodily harm. Other states use the Model Arson Law, which divides arson into four degrees: first-degree involves the burning of dwellings; second-degree involves the burning of buildings other than dwellings; third-degree involves the burning of other property; and fourth-degree involves attempts to burn buildings or property.

Other crimes officers must investigate include crimes against children, bias/hate crimes, environmental crimes and computer-related crimes. Computer-related crimes may involve input data, output data, the program itself or computer time. The most common types of computer crime are misuse of computer services, program abuse and data abuse. Investigating such crimes often requires a team approach. Investigations may also involve so-called victimless crimes, such as prostitution, pornography, gaming and drug dealing/using.

Many investigations, including those of victimless crimes, make use of surveillance, undercover assignments, raids, and stings. These methods should be used only when all other investigative alternatives have failed.

APPLICATION

To provide better service to the community, the department has decided to add a detective division to its organization. The chief has asked you to develop a policy and procedure for turning cases over to this division, after a patrol officer has conducted the preliminary investigation.

INSTRUCTIONS

Using the form in the Appendix, write a policy on what specific types of cases will be assigned to the detective division. Then write the procedure(s) for assigning cases to this division. Be sure to consider a smooth transition in the investigation from the patrol officer who conducted the preliminary investigation to the detective assigned to handle the case.

EXERCISES IN CRITICAL THINKING

A. Mary Jones, an 18-year-old high school girl, quarreled with her boyfriend, Thomas Smith. At 3 A.M. following the evening of their quarrel, Mary went to Smith's home to return his picture. Smith stated that after receiving the picture, he went to his room, went to bed and awoke about 8 A.M. When he looked out his window, he saw Mary's car parked out front. Looking into the car, he discovered Mary sitting erect behind the steering wheel, shot through the chest, a .22 revolver lying beside her on the front seat. She was dead—apparently a suicide. The revolver had been a gift to Mary from her father. Smith called the police to report the shooting.

Mary had been shot once. The bullet entered just below the right breast, traveled across the front of her body and lodged near her heart. The medical examiner theorized that she did not die immediately. When found, she was sitting upright in the car, her head tilted slightly backward, her right hand high on the steering wheel, her left hand hanging limp at her left side.

When questioned, Smith steadfastly denied any knowledge of the shooting. Mary's clothing, the bullet from her body and the gun were sent to the FBI Laboratory for examination. An examination of her blouse where the bullet entered failed to reveal any powder residues. The bullet removed from her body was identified as having been fired from the gun found beside her body.

1. Is the shooting likely to be a suicide or a homicide? What facts support this?
2. How should the investigation proceed?

B. Ten-year-old Denise was playing in a school parking lot with her nine-year-old stepbrother, Jerry. A car pulled up to the curb next to the lot, and the man driving the car motioned for Denise and Jerry to come over. When the man asked where they lived, Denise described their house. The man then asked Denise to take him to the house, saying he would bring her right back to the lot afterward. Denise got into the car with the man, and they drove away. When they did not return after an hour, Jerry went into the school and told a teacher what had happened. Denise did not return home that evening. The next day the police received a report that a body had been found near a lover's lane. It was Denise, who had been stabbed to death with a pocketknife.

1. What steps should be taken immediately?
2. Where would you expect to find leads?
3. What evidence would you expect to find?
4. Specifically, how would you investigate this murder?

DISCUSSION QUESTIONS

1. What are some motivations for citizens to become informants?
2. How might officers arriving at a crime scene contaminate evidence?
3. What was the purpose of establishing the Violent Crime Apprehension Program (VICAP) at the National Police Academy in Quantico, Virginia?
4. Is the expense involved in testing DNA from crime such as burglary justified?
5. What are some dangers of undercover operations?
6. What are some purposes of a surveillance? When would a surveillance be useful?
7. How does the general public view the police detective? Where do these images come from?

GALE EMERGENCY SERVICES DATABASE ASSIGNMENTS

- Use the Gale Emergency Services database to help answer the Discussion Questions as appropriate.
- Use the Gale Emergency Services database to locate and outline one of the following articles to share with the class:
  - "Electronic Surveillance: A Matter of Necessity" by Thomas D. Coldbridge
  - "Working with Informants: Operational Recommendations" by James E. Hight
  - "Best Practices of a Hate/Bias Crime Investigation" by Walter Bouman
  - "Computer Forensics: Characteristics and Preservation of Digital Evidence" by Loren D. Mercer
  - "Conducting Surveillance Operations: How to Get the Most Out of Them" by John T. Nason
  - "The Hate Model" by John R. Schafer and Joe Navarro
  - "Major Case Management: Key Components" by Brian P. Carroll

REFERENCES

Benson, Michael L., and Simpson, Sally S. *White-Collar Crime: An Opportunity Perspective.* New York: Routledge, 2009.

Blakely, Amy. "University of Tennessee's National Forensic Academy." *Law and Order*, May 2009, pp.75–78.

Cronin, James M.; Murphy, Gerard R.; Spahr, Lisa L.; Toliver, Jessica I.; and Weger, Richard E. *Promoting Effective Homicide Investigations.* Washington, DC: Police Executive Research Forum, August 2007. (NCJ 221792)

Commission on Accreditation of Law Enforcement Agencies. *Standards for Law Enforcement Agencies*, 5th ed. Fairfax, VA: CALEA, 2006, updated 2008.

Cullen, Francis T.; Cavender, Gray; Maakestad, William J.; and Benson, Michael L. *Corporate Crime under Attack: The Fight to Criminalize Business Violence*, 2nd ed. Albany, NY: Matthew Bender & Co., Inc. (LexisNexis), 2006.

Fantino, Julian. "Forensic Science: A Fundamental Perspective." *The Police Chief*, November 2007, pp.26–28.

"FBI/National White Collar Crime Center (NW3C) Release Annual Report on Internet Crime." Washington, DC: Federal Bureau of Investigation, Press Release, March 30, 2009.

"FBI's Regional Computer Forensics Laboratory Network Increases Number of Accredited Labs." Washington, DC: Federal Bureau of Investigation, Press Release, April 7, 2009.

Feigin, Matthew. "Landmark NAS Report Questions Basis of Forensic Sciences in U.S." *Subject to Debate*, April 2009, pp.3–5.

Fritsche, Volitta. "Investigating Autoerotic Fatalities." *LawOfficer.com*, March 23, 2009.

Garrett, Ronnie. "The Byte Stuff." *Law Enforcement Technology*, April 2009a, pp.10–16.

Garrett, Ronnie. "DNA Saves." *Law Enforcement Technology*, February, 2009b, pp.28–37.

Geoghegan, Susan. "The Latest in Mobile AFIS." *Law and Order*, June 2008, pp.46–49.

Grossi, Dave. "Going Under." *Law Officer Magazine*, April 2009, pp.24–28.

Haberman, Clyde. "Plain Clothes, Perilous Choices." *Subject to Debate*, January 2007, pp.1, 5.

Hate Crime Statistics. Washington, DC: Federal Bureau of Investigation, 2007.

Hess, Kären Matison, and Orthmann, Christine Hess. *Criminal Investigation*, 9th ed. Clifton Park, NY: Delmar Publishing Company, 2010.

Heurich, Charles, "Cold Cases: Resources for Agencies; Resolution for Families." *NIJ Journal*, July 2008, pp.20–23.

"Highway Serial Killings: New Initiative on an Emerging Trend." Washington, DC: Federal Bureau of Investigation Headline Archives, April 6, 2009.

"Hitting the Airwaves: Help Solve Cold Cases." Washington, DC: Federal Bureau of Investigation Headline Archives, April 14, 2009.

"Increasing Efficiency in Crime Laboratories." *NIJ in Short: Toward Criminal Justice Solutions*, January 2008.

Jackman, Tom. "Hoping Thieves Take the Bait Car." *The Washington Post*, May 14, 2009.

Jacobia, Jack. "Computer Forensics: Duties of the First Responder." *Law Enforcement Technology*, April 2004, pp.28–30.

Jetmore, Larry F. "The Truth's in the Teeth: Using Forensic Dentistry to Solve Crimes." *Law Officer Magazine*, July 2007, pp.22–25.

Jetmore, Larry F. "Dactyloscopy: The Science of Fingerprints." *Law Officer Magazine*, April 2008, pp.76–79.

Johnson, Shane D.; Sidebottom, Aiden; and Thorpe, Adam. *Bicycle Theft*. Washington, DC: Community Oriented Policing Services Office, June 2008.

Kanable, Rebecca. "Setting Up Surveillance Downtown." *Law Enforcement Technology*, February 2008, pp.30–39.

Kanable, Rebecca. "The Face of Identity Theft." *Law Enforcement Technology*, April 2009, pp.28–33.

Kingsbury, Alex. "Amid Recession, FBI Makes New Push on Financial Crimes: In the Age of Bernie Madoff, Agents Are Scrambling to focus on White-Collar Criminals." *U.S. News and World Report*, April 2, 2009.

Kurash, Aviva. "New Tools for Sexual Assault Investigations." *Big Ideas*, Spring 2009, pp.12–13.

Kyckelhahn, Tracey; Beck, Allen J.; and Cohen, Thomas H. *Characteristics of Suspected Human Trafficking Incidents, 2007–08*. Washington, DC: Bureau of Justice Statistics Special Report, January 2009. (NCJ 224526)

McCorkle, Richard C. *Gambling and Crime among Arrestees: Exploring the Link*. Washington, DC: National Institute of Justice, July 2004.

McNeil. TiTi. "Managing Digital Evidence." *Law Enforcement Technology*, January 2009, pp.30–37.

Mentel, Zoe. "The Rising Trend of Unsolved Homicides: Understanding the Problem." *Community Policing Dispatch*, March 2008.

Moore, Solomon. "Study Calls for Oversight of Forensics in Crime Labs." *The New York Times*, February 19, 2009.

Newman, Graeme R., and Socia, Kelly. *Sting Operations*. Washington, DC: Community Oriented Policing Services Office, October 2007.

"The Oakland Airport Motel Program." In *Excellence in Problem-Oriented Policing: The 2003 Herman Goldstein Award Winner and Finalists*. Washington, DC: The Community Oriented Policing Services Office and the Police Executive Research Forum, November 2003.

Oehler, Michael. "Better Fingerprints from Same Fingers." *Law and Order*, September 2007, pp.123–128.

Osborne, Deborah. "Crime Analysis: Best Practices from 6 Agencies." *Law Officer Magazine*, September 2008, pp.36–42.

Osborne, Deborah. "Play to Win: Analysis Is Your Ally." *LawOfficer.com*, June 2, 2009.

Page, Douglas. "The Bite Stuff?" *Law Enforcement Technology*, February 2007, pp.112–119.

Page, Douglas. "Microstamping Calls the Shots." *Law Enforcement Technology*, January 2008, pp.54–59.

Parker, Joe. "How Prostitution Works." *Prostitution Research and Education*, no date.

Petrocelli, Joseph. "Patrol Response to Bank Robberies." *Police*, January 2008a, pp.16–17.

Petrocelli, Joseph. "Patrol Response to Convenience Store Robberies." *Police*, 2008b, pp.20–23.

Piquero, Nicole Leeper; Carmichael, Stephanie; and Piquero, Alex R. "Assessing the Perceived Seriousness of White-Collar and Street Crimes." *Crime & Delinquency*, April 2008, pp.291–312.

"Precious Metal: Copper Theft Threatens U.S. Infrastructure." Washington, DC: Federal Bureau of Investigation Headline Archives, January 3, 2008.

Prime, Raymond J., and Newman, Jonathan. "The Impact of DNA on Policing: Past, Present, and Future." *The Police Chief*, November 2007, pp.30–35.

Pulkkinen, Levi. "Free and Friendly Craigslist Has Its Dark Side." *Seattle Post-Intelligencer*, April 25, 2008.

Roberts, Darryl W. "Intimate Partner Homicide: Relationships to Alcohol and Firearms." *Journal of Contemporary Criminal Justice*, February 2009, pp.67–88.

Roman, John K.; Reid, Shannon; Reid, Jay; Chalfin, Aaron; Adams, William; and Knight, Carly. *The DNA Field Experiment:*

Cost-Effectiveness Analysis of the Use of DNA in the Investigation of High-Volume Crimes. Washington, DC: U.S. Department of Justice, April 2008. (NCJ 222318)

Scalisi, Nicole J. "The Role of Crime Analysis in Patrol Work: New Developments." *Community Policing Dispatch*, June 2009.

Serial Murder: Multi-Disciplinary Perspectives for Investigators. Washington, DC: Federal Bureau of Investigation, 2008.

Shelton, Donald E. "The CSI Effect: Does It Really Exist?" *NIJ Journal*, March 2008, pp.1–8.

Spraggs, David. "Just a Touch." *Police*, December 2008, pp.26–29.

Strengthening Forensic Science in the United States: A Path Forward. Washington, DC: The National Academies Press, 2009.

Sutherland, Edwin H. *White-Collar Crime: The Uncut Version.* New Haven, CT: Yale University Press, 1983.

Unnever, James D.; Benson, Michael L.; and Cullen, Francis T. "Public Support for Getting Tough on Corporate Crime: Racial and Political Divides." *Journal of Research in Crime and Delinquency*, May 2008, pp.163–190.

Weisel, Deborah Lamm. *Bank Robbery.* Washington, DC: Community Oriented Policing Services Office, March 2007.

White, Matthew B. *Enhancing the Problem-Solving Capacity of Crime Analysis Units.* Washington, DC: Community Oriented Policing Services Office, February 2008.

Wilson, Ron, and Smith, Kurt. "What Is Applied Geography for the Study of Crime and Public Safety?" *Geography & Public Safety*, March 2008, pp.1–3.

CASES CITED

California v. Simpson, No. BA097211 (Cal. Super Ct. 1995)
Daubert v. Merrell Dow Pharmaceuticals, 509 U.S. 579 (1993)
Flippo v. West Virginia, 528 U.S. 11 (1999)
Michigan v. Tyler, 436 U.S. 499 (1978)

HELPFUL RESOURCES

- The National Institute of Justice has published *Fire and Arson Scene Evidence: A Guide for Public Safety Personnel*, available online at www.ojp.usdoj.gov/nij/pubs-sum/181584.htm
- The Department of Justice has published "Searching and Seizing Computers and Obtaining Electronic Evidence in Criminal Investigations," available at www.cybercrime.gov/s&smanual2002.htm
- The International Association of Chiefs of Police (IACP) also has a guide, *Best Practices for Seizing Electronic Evidence*, available on the Internet at www.theiacp.org
- Another valuable Web site is www.cybercrime.gov, maintained by the Computer Crime and Intellectual Property Section of the U.S. Department of Justice. The site is a collection of documents and links to other sites and agencies that may assist in preventing, detecting, investigating and prosecuting computer-related crime.
- The FBI's *Handbook of Forensic Services*, revised in 2007, provides information on crime scene searches as well as the kinds of evidence that might be found.
- Former ATF Special Agent William Queen wrote an excellent book called *Under and Alone*, detailing his accounts of infiltrating one of the most notorious motorcycle gangs, the Mongols. William Queen, *Under and Alone.* Random House, 2005. ISBN 978-1400060849.
- The Anti-Defamation League has launched a Web site to serve as a database for law enforcement officers investigating hate groups: http://www.adl.org/learn.

CHAPTER 11

Responding to Children and Juveniles

Our Nation's Future

DO YOU KNOW . . .

- What greatly influences youths' attitudes toward law and law enforcement?
- Below what age most states consider a person a juvenile?
- What the primary difference between the adult criminal justice and the juvenile justice system is?
- What reforms have been proposed for the juvenile justice system?
- What categories of children are included in the juvenile justice system's jurisdiction?
- What predelinquent indicator often goes unnoticed?
- What special challenge is posed by a missing child report?
- What conduct is included in status offenses?
- What factors enter into the disposition of status offenders?
- How much discretion officers have with status offenders?
- What dispositions are available to officers when dealing with status offenders and what the most common disposition is?
- Who usually enters juveniles into the justice system?
- What rights *In re Gault* guarantees juveniles involved with the juvenile justice system?
- What two programs are widely used throughout the United States to combat the drug and gang problem?

CAN YOU DEFINE?

AMBER Alert
child maltreatment
child welfare model
D.A.R.E.
decriminalization
diversion
8% problem
G.R.E.A.T.
juvenile
juvenile delinquents
juvenile justice model
Munchausen syndrome by proxy (MSBP)
one-pot jurisdictional approach
osteogenesis imperfecta
parens patriae
raves
status offenses
street justice
thrownaways
truancy

INTRODUCTION

"Each professional working with children must understand children, their behavioral patterns and psychological development, and their changing emotional needs as they mature, seek independence, and acquire sexual appetites," says Juvenile Judge Emeritus Lindsay G. Arthur (2010, p.xv). Police are some of the most important professionals who work with children and juveniles. Law enforcement is commonly the first contact young victims and victimizers have with the juvenile justice system, and serve as the gatekeeper to the rest of the system. The police are charged with protecting youths, both victims and offenders, and dealing fairly with them. A balance is sought between what is in the best interest of the youth and what is best for the community. Also, the crime-fighting philosophy must be balanced with the service ideal.

The importance of the officer on the street cannot be overlooked. Every law enforcement officer, no matter at what level, has an opportunity to be a positive influence on youths. Ultimately, youths' perceptions about the law and law enforcement will be based on one-on-one interactions with law enforcement officers.

Youths' attitudes toward law and law enforcement are tremendously influenced by personal contacts with law enforcement officers. Positive interactions are critical to delinquency prevention.

This chapter begins with an explanation of who is a juvenile and a brief overview of our juvenile justice system. This is followed by a discussion of law enforcement's response to children in need of help and protection, including victims of child abuse and neglect and those who are runaways, thrownaways or otherwise missing. Next, status offenders and the law enforcement response to them as well as violent juvenile offenders are presented. This is followed by an explanation of legal procedures when dealing with youths. The chapter concludes with a discussion of programs aimed at youths and a problem-oriented approach to dealing with a juvenile problem.

WHO IS A JUVENILE?

Just who is a juvenile is determined by the legal age set in state statutes. All states have specified an age below which individuals are subject to the juvenile justice system. This age varies from state to state and even within parts of the justice system itself in some states. For example, some state statutes specify that their juvenile courts have jurisdiction over all individuals under age 18, but that the juvenile correctional facilities have jurisdiction over all those under age 21 who were committed to a correctional facility before their 18th birthdays.

The youngest age for juvenile court jurisdiction in delinquency matters ranges from age 6 to age 10. The oldest age for juvenile court jurisdiction in delinquency matters ranges from 15 to 18, with 17 being the most common age. Previously, the age range was from 16 to 19, with the most common age being 18. This lowering of the oldest age reflects the current tendency to "get tough" on youth in trouble with the law, discussed later in the chapter.

A **juvenile** is a person not yet of legal age. In three-fourths of the states, juveniles are defined as youths under age 18.

juvenile
A person not yet of legal age, usually under the age of 18.

In 2007, there were 73.9 million children under age 18 in the United States, making up 24.5 percent of the population (*America's Children*, 2008).

AN OVERVIEW OF OUR JUVENILE JUSTICE SYSTEM

The dual role of protecting both children and the public and investigating behavioral facts is a great challenge facing juvenile officers and any police officer who interacts with youth in any way. The aspect of protection in dealings with juveniles has its roots in the common law of England.

In English common law, the king, through his chancellor, was a substitute parent for abandoned, neglected and dependent children under a doctrine called ***parens patriae***. In the United States, each individual state replaced the king in this responsibility. The doctrine of *parens patriae* allows the state to assume guardianship of abandoned, neglected and "wayward" children.

parens patriae
A doctrine allowing the state to assume guardianship of abandoned, neglected and "wayward" children.

Under this doctrine, the state is to act toward the children entrusted to its care as a loving parent would. This is very different from the punitive thrust behind the adult justice system, which removed youths from homes and placed them in lockups and jails. To return to the principle of *parens patriae*, the Illinois Juvenile Court Act of 1899 established the first juvenile court in the United States. This court's primary purpose was to "save" children from becoming criminals.

Historically the juvenile justice system has been an informal, confidential, nonadversarial system that stresses rehabilitation rather than punishment of youth. This directly contrasts with the punitive nature of the criminal justice system and is reflected in the terminology used in the juvenile justice system, which underscores its emphasis on protecting youth from harmful labels and their stigmatizing effects. For example, youth are not *arrested;* they are *taken into custody.* If the allegations against the youth are true, the youth is called a *delinquent* rather than a *criminal.* Youth sentenced to custodial care upon release receive *aftercare* rather than *parole.*

The juvenile justice system, under *parens patriae*, has historically taken a rehabilitative approach in handling children, rather than the punitive approach taken in the adult criminal justice system.

Although treatment and rehabilitation have been the traditional goals of the juvenile justice system, a trend to "get tough" on young violent offenders has led to increased debate about the mission of this system and a reevaluation regarding the underlying philosophy of the system.

The Welfare Model versus the Justice Model

child welfare model
Society's attempt to help youths who come in conflict with the law.

The concept of "helping" youths who are members of violent gangs and who engage in heinous crimes is very difficult for police officers and others within the juvenile justice system to accept. This has led to a call for reform of the juvenile justice system, revising state statutes to make juvenile court operate under a justice model rather than a welfare model. In a **child welfare model**,

Law enforcement may come in contact with youths who are accused of heinous offenses but who, because of their age, are handled as delinquents instead of criminals. Here, a teenager and two 10-year-old boys walk to a waiting van after their first judicial appearance. The three boys, accused of attacking a homeless day laborer on a street and smashing a concrete block into his face, were each charged by police with aggravated battery.

the courts operate with the best interests of the youths as the main consideration. In a **juvenile justice model**, the courts hold youths responsible and accountable for their behavior. To adopt a justice model is not to rule out or diminish the importance of rehabilitative measures employed by juvenile courts. Disapproval of, and punishment for, the wrongful act is probably the single most important rehabilitative measure available to the court.

juvenile justice model

A judicial process in which young people who come in conflict with the law are held responsible and accountable for their behavior.

Our current juvenile system is treatment or welfare focused. Some argue it should be replaced with a juvenile justice system whereby youths who commit serious crimes are held accountable and punished for those acts.

In many states, the justice model has replaced the welfare model. This is not the only aspect of the juvenile justice system being challenged. Another problematic area is the juvenile justice system's jurisdiction.

The "One-Pot" Jurisdictional Approach

Our juvenile justice system's evolution, from the beginning, was designed to deal not only with "wayward" children—that is, **juvenile delinquents**, whose "crimes" could range from talking back to their parents to murder—but also with children who were abandoned, abused or neglected. Early laws, in effect, equated being poor with being criminal.

juvenile delinquents

Young people who violate the law.

one-pot jurisdictional approach

Use of the same system to deal with youths who are neglected or abused, those who are status offenders and those who commit serious crimes.

The juvenile justice system includes children who are neglected or abused, those who are status offenders and those who commit serious crimes, in what is called the **one-pot jurisdictional approach**.

CHILD MALTREATMENT: ABUSE AND NEGLECT

Not all youths that police officers deal with are breaking the law. A great many are victims who need help or protection. Crimes against children were introduced in Chapter 7 and include abuse and neglect (maltreatment), abandonment, exploitation, and kidnapping. Runaways, though technically classified as status offenders, commonly become victims as well.

Child abuse involves causing physical, emotional or sexual trauma to a child, and *neglect* includes failing to provide proper care and attention to a child's needs. Parents who deny their children the food, clothing, nurturing or any other basic need they require are guilty of neglect, which can be just as damaging to the child as physical abuse. Frequently, child abuse and neglect occur together, although either one alone constitutes **child maltreatment**, a broader term that encompasses all variations of abuse (physical, emotional, sexual) and neglect (physical, emotional, educational). According to the Centers for Disease Control and Prevention (CDC), "Child maltreatment is any act or series of acts of commission or omission by a parent or other caregiver that results in harm, potential for harm, or threat of harm to a child" ("Child Maltreatment: Definitions," 2009).

child maltreatment

A broad term that encompasses all variations of child abuse (physical, emotional, sexual) and neglect (physical, emotional, educational). According to the CDC, "Child maltreatment is any act or series of acts of commission or omission by a parent or other caregiver that results in harm, potential for harm, or threat of harm to a child."

In 2006, state and local child protective services (CPS) investigated 3.6 million reports of children being abused or neglected in the United States; 905,000 children were victims of maltreatment (*Child Maltreatment 2006*, 2008). In addition, 1,540 children died in the United States in 2006 from abuse and neglect. The younger the child, the more likely it is he or she will become a victim; 78 percent or more deaths occurred among children younger than age 4. The same is true of maltreatment victims, with the rate of 24.4 per 1,000 for 0- to 1-year-olds, decreasing to 14.2 per 1,000 for 1- to 3-year-olds, and continuing to decrease to 6.3 per 1,000 for 16- to 17-year-olds.

Why parents abuse their children is perplexing. Sometimes it is out of frustration. Sometimes it is from unrealistic expectations. Often abusing parents feel their children "have it coming" because of words or actions. And sometimes it is simply, and sadly, the only way parents know to treat their children, having been raised in abusive homes themselves.

Millions of children have been witness to or victims of violence in their homes or communities. Such a history may send these youths down a future course of repeated and increasingly serious run-ins with law enforcement. Even when children are not themselves the direct targets of abuse, they may become "invisible victims" through continued exposure to other abusive relationships.

Intergenerational Cycle of Abuse

Violence is learned behavior that often is self-perpetuating. When adults teach children by example that those who are bigger and stronger can use violence to force their wishes on others who are smaller and weaker, children remember the lesson. Children who witness domestic abuse learn that it is okay to hurt the people you care about and that it is acceptable to use violence to get what you want. Children who are abused or neglected may grow up with poor self-images and view the world as hostile and violent, tending to perpetuate dysfunctional behavior in the relationships and families they form as adults.

The connection between children's histories of neglect or abuse and subsequent delinquency, crime and other problems has been largely ignored by our juvenile justice and social service systems. However, a growing body of empirical evidence shows that those who experience violent, abusive childhoods are more likely to become child or spouse abusers themselves or to display other forms of adult criminal behavior: "Abused and neglected children are 4.8 times more likely to be arrested as [a] juvenile, 2 times more likely to be arrested as an adult and 3.1 times more likely to be arrested for a violent crime than matched controls" (English et al., 2002, p.iii). These findings replicate earlier studies.

Karmen (2007, p.6) describes a cycle of violence in which victims are transformed into victimizers over time: "A group of picked-upon students may band together to ambush their bullying tormentors; a battered wife may launch a vengeful attack against her brutal husband; or a child subjected to periodic beatings might grow up to parent his sons in the same excessively punitive way he was raised. A study that tracked the fortunes of boys and girls known to have been physically and sexually abused over a follow-up period of several decades concluded that being harmed at an early age substantially increased the odds of future delinquency and criminality."

Receiving Reports of Child Maltreatment

Educators are the most common source of reports of abuse and neglect to child protective service agencies. Reports may also come from a variety of other sources such as doctors, neighbors, or even the victims themselves, although that is rare. Professionals in all states, and even citizens in some states, are mandated to report child abuse to responsible authorities. Child welfare investigations substantiate or confirm about one-third of all child maltreatment reports. In some states, investigations are conducted jointly by child welfare and police; in a few jurisdictions, law enforcement has the sole responsibility for investigation, and is increasingly involved in child abuse cases.

The Police Response to Child Maltreatment

Historically, as with spousal abuse, law enforcement agencies were reluctant to pursue reports of child abuse with the same vigor as calls involving other, more traditional offenses. Today, however, the responsibility of the police in regard to abused children is clear. When police are called about child abuse, their first responsibility is to the child. In many states, if it appears the child is in danger, police may take the child into protective custody.

It is good practice for police officers to speak to children as they are responding to the call because, if the incident is in progress or has just occurred, children have not yet had time to be "coached" by the parents or to otherwise have had their statements biased. Young children tend to be blunt and truthful about what they observed. In communities with large immigrant populations, it is not uncommon to speak with the children about the incident anyway because they may be the only ones in the home who speak English. It is important, however, to separate the children from the suspected offender during this interview, to reduce the likelihood of the child being intimidated by the alleged offender, even if the suspect is one of the parents.

In addition, officers responding to a domestic call involving adults must remain aware of the "invisible victimization" suffered by children who witness violence in the home and tend to these young victims as well. Often, when adults are arrested for domestic violence, additional charges of *endangering children* should be made if children were present during the abuse, and those children should also be taken into protective custody. Social Services should be contacted immediately to find placements for the children. In some instances, placement can be made with other family members.

The decision to remove a child from the home commonly depends on who the alleged suspect is. If the abuse suspect is a family member, the child may be removed and placed in protective custody by police and social services while the incident is being investigated, and a social worker will be assigned to the family. If the child is assaulted by a neighbor or other "outsider," the child is considered safe with his or her own family and may not be placed.

Officers' next responsibility is to thoroughly investigate the situation. Interviews with family members, medical records, reports from social workers and interviews with neighbors can all help determine if a charge of child abuse is warranted. Bear in mind that, without consent, medical records are protected and need to be obtained by a search warrant. Police must be especially careful when charges of child sexual abuse are involved because such allegations can do much damage and destroy reputations, even if unfounded. The interviews also can provide information about whether the child can be returned to the home or should be placed in a foster home.

Interviewing child victims and witnesses requires much sensitivity and adherence to certain protocol. In most child abuse cases, children tell the truth to the best of their abilities. Investigators should listen carefully to children and should look at indicators of neglect or abuse. These indicators may be physical or behavioral or both.

Handling child abuse cases is a highly specialized field because children have a different form of communication than adults and they can easily be led in an interview. Although police generally have basic training and can develop interview techniques through field experience, specialized child interviewing training is still not standard among law enforcement. Several types of certifications exist for interviewing children in specific situations, such as alleged maltreatment incidents, sexual abuse cases, and so on.

Two Supreme Court decisions affect children's testimony in abuse and neglect cases. The Court held in *Maryland v. Craig* (1990) that the Sixth Amendment "right to confront witnesses" does not always mandate face-to-face confrontation between a defendant and a child abuse victim-witness at trial, if the child victim-witness will be emotionally traumatized by testifying in the defendant's presence. In *Idaho v. Wright* (1990), the Court ruled that an out-of-court statement by an alleged child sexual abuse victim is not automatically deemed trustworthy nor guaranteed to be admitted at trial, but also ruled that an out-of-court statement may be admitted if it is determined the child making the statement is likely to be telling the truth.

States vary in the standard of proof required to substantiate allegations of child abuse and neglect, ranging from a caseworker's judgment, to some credible evidence, or a preponderance of evidence. However, some cases of abuse are obvious. For example, in a well-publicized 1996 case, a Chicago couple faced multiple charges of child abuse after their four children told authorities their parents had fed them a "regular diet" of boiled rats and cockroaches and had repeatedly raped and drugged them for the previous four years. And in 1999, 2½-year-old Miguel Arias-Baca spent the final moments of his short life getting slammed against the floor. He died slowly and painfully, his brain swelling with blood and his face smeared with his own feces, after his drunken foster father returned home from a Super Bowl party to find the toddler with a dirty diaper.

Sometimes these fatal tragedies result from a single violent episode. Most often, however, they are the culmination of months, even years, of abuse that somehow went unnoticed or fell through the cracks of the child protective and criminal justice services.

Special Challenges Related to Child Abuse Investigations

Problems in investigating crimes against children include the need to protect the child from further harm, the possibility of parental involvement, the difficulty in interviewing children and the potential need to involve other agencies. Some cases of child abuse present special challenges to responding officers, such as those involving "brittle bone disease" or Munchausen syndrome by proxy and child sexual abuse cases.

Osteogenesis Imperfecta (OI) A challenge related to investigations of child abuse is when a medical condition mimics the signs of physical abuse, as in cases involving **osteogenesis imperfecta**, commonly known as "brittle bone disease," a condition characterized by bones that break easily. Because child abuse is also characterized by broken bones, false accusations of child abuse may occur in families with children who suffer from OI. Similarly, birthmarks or other naturally occurring skin spots may be mistaken for bruising caused by abuse.

osteogenesis imperfecta
A medical condition characterized by bones that break easily; also called *brittle bone disease*.

Unfortunately, when false accusations of child abuse occur, families become victimized. Consequently, it is critical for responding officers to be aware of such conditions and to not automatically discount a parent's denial of child abuse. A thorough investigation will include interviews with social services staff and medical professionals.

Cases in which parents are found to have a history of often changing the hospitals or physicians who treat their children *may* indicate an attempt to hide child abuse. In other instances, children who are frequently admitted to the hospital may be the victims of a form of abuse known as Munchausen syndrome by proxy.

Munchausen Syndrome by Proxy **Munchausen syndrome by proxy (MSBP)** is a psychiatric ailment that causes a person to fabricate a child's illnesses to fulfill the adult's own needs for attention and sympathy. Subjecting a child to unnecessary, even dangerous, medical procedures and treatments certainly constitutes maltreatment.

Munchausen's syndrome by proxy (MSBP)
A psychiatric ailment that leads a person to fabricate a child's illnesses to fulfill his or her own needs for attention and sympathy.

Child Sexual Abuse Cases As with other forms of neglect or abuse, the sexual victimization of children can have devastating effects on the victims and can lead to an intergenerational cycle of violence and abuse. Although media reports of child sexual abuse tend to sensationalize these crimes, statistics show a decline in child sexual abuse cases.

Investigators should be aware of pedophiles, adults who have either heterosexual or homosexual preferences for young boys or girls of a specific, limited age range. Pedophiles' reactions to being discovered usually begin with complete denial and progress through minimizing the acts, justifying the acts and blaming the victims. If all else fails, pedophiles may claim to be sick.

Many pedophiles are members of sex rings, and many have moved from prowling the playgrounds to searching for their victims in cyberspace.

Child Pornography on the Internet The Child Protection Act of 1984 prohibits child pornography and greatly increases the penalties for adults who engage in it. The advent of the World Wide Web has greatly facilitated the sharing of child pornography, as well as a range of other Internet crimes against children. Because Internet sex crimes against minors include a diverse range of offenses, cases sharing crucial common elements relative to challenges posed for law enforcement investigators should be grouped into categories such as those shown in Figure 11.1.

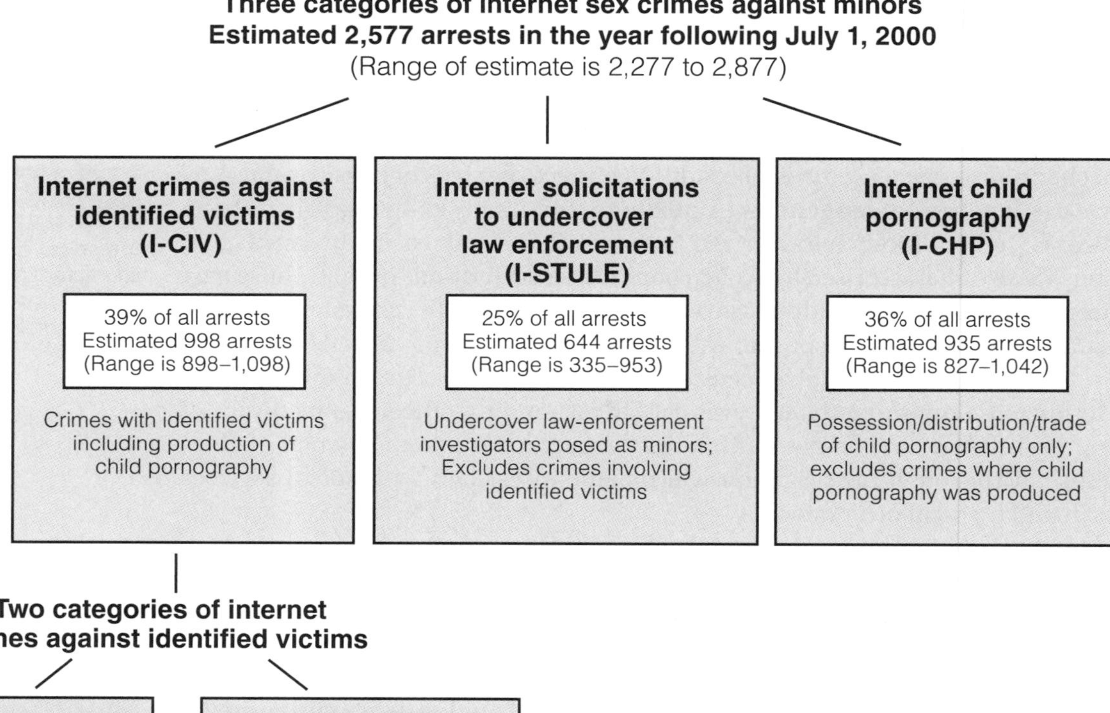

FIGURE 11.1 Three Categories of Internet Sex Crimes against Minors

Source: Janis Wolak, Kimberly Mitchell and David Finkelhor. *Internet Sex Crimes against Minors: The Response of Law Enforcement*. Washington, DC: National Center for Missing and Exploited Children, 2003. Reprinted by permission.

The second category involved undercover operations in which officers went on Internet chat rooms posing as minors, usually in the age range of 13 to 15, and waited to be contacted by adults seeking sexual encounters. The undercover officers were careful not to initiate any conversations about sexual topics, and they kept logs of all their online conversations to be used as evidence in court. The online relationships culminated in face-to-face meetings where the offenders were arrested and charged with attempted sexual assault or other offenses.

One federal initiative to combat child pornography on the Internet is the Innocent Images National Initiative (IINI), a component of FBI's Cyber Crimes Program:

> Innocent Images is an intelligence driven, proactive, multi-agency investigative operation to combat the proliferation of child pornography/child sexual exploitation (CP/CSE) facilitated by an online computer. The IINI provides centralized coordination and analysis of case information that by its very nature is national and international in scope, requiring unprecedented coordination with state, local, and international governments and among FBI field offices and legal attachés.
>
> Today, computer telecommunications have become one of the most prevalent techniques used by pedophiles to share illegal photographic images of minors and to lure children into illicit sexual relationships. The Internet has dramatically increased the access of the preferential sex offenders to the population they seek to victimize and provides them greater access to a community of people who validate their sexual preferences.
>
> The mission of the IINI is to reduce the vulnerability of children to acts of sexual exploitation and abuse which are facilitated through the use of computers; to identify and rescue child victims; to investigate and prosecute sexual predators who use the Internet and other online services to sexually exploit children for personal or financial gain; and to strengthen the capabilities of federal, state, local, and international law enforcement through training programs and investigative assistance.
>
> The FBI and the Department of Justice review all files and select the most egregious subjects for prosecution. In addition, the IINI works to identify child victims and obtain appropriate services/assistance for them and to establish a law enforcement presence on the Internet that will act as a deterrent to those who seek to sexually exploit children.
>
> Online child pornography/child sexual exploitation investigations, which are worked under the FBI's Innocent Images National Initiative, accounted for 39 percent of all investigations worked under the FBI's Cyber Division in fiscal year 2007.
>
> Between fiscal years 1996–2007, the Innocent Images National Initiative has recorded the following statistical accomplishments:
>
> - Number of cases opened: 20,134
> - Number of informations & indictments: 6,844
> - Number of arrests, locates & summons: 9,469
> - Number of convictions & pretrial diversions: 6,863 ("Online Child Pornography/Child Sexual Exploitation Investigations," 2009)

CHILDREN WHO ARE THROWNAWAYS, RUNAWAYS OR OTHERWISE MISSING

Sexual abuse and other types of abuse and neglect are common reasons why youth sometimes run away from home. The National Incidence Studies of Missing, Abducted, Runaway, and Thrownaway Children in America (NISMART) has five categories of missing children: (1) thrownaways, (2) runaways, (3) nonfamily abducted children, (4) family abducted children and (5) lost, injured or otherwise missing children.

Thrownaways

thrownaways
Youths who were either told to leave, were not allowed back after having left, ran away and no one tried to recover them, or were abandoned or deserted.

A **thrownaway** is a child who was told to leave home, who was not allowed back after having left, who ran away and no one tried to recover the child, or who was abandoned or deserted (Hess and Orthmann, 2010, p.155). Runaway/thrownaway children may band together and join other youths who are just "hanging out." Such youths may also pose a problem for law enforcement if they become disorderly.

Runaways

Running away is leaving home without parental permission. Usually, however, police are more interested in locating and returning the runaway than in entering the youth into the juvenile justice system. Often, no police investigation, social service inquiry or school inquiry is conducted to determine why these children left home, were truant because of this absence or why they continue to run away.

Running away is a predelinquent indicator, but its importance often is not recognized by the parents, police, school, social agencies or the courts.

AN OFFICER'S PERSPECTIVE
Handling Runaways

When I take a report of a juvenile runaway and enter it into the statewide system, it remains there until the juvenile is reported found. Often times, however, juveniles come back home, and the parents or guardians neglect to notify the police. This becomes a problem when the juveniles have contact with the police later on and, although they may not actually be a runaway at that later time, they are in the system as though they are. The officer then has to follow up on this, which is an extremely inefficient use of time.

I have also had calls where the parents are aware of their child's location but, for a variety of reasons, do not want to pick the child up themselves. They believe the police have the responsibility to retrieve the child and can report the child as a runaway as long as the juvenile refuses to come home. In these instances, we inform parents to retrieve their children themselves. If, however, there are people who are preventing the parent from picking up the child, then the situation does become a police issue.

—Sgt. Henry Lim Cho

If police dispositions are to be effective, the family must recognize the early signs of maladjustment in children. Running away is the most visible indicator of a possible future victim (assaulted, murdered) or involvement in criminal activity to support individual needs (prostitution, pornography, burglary, theft, robbery).

Missing and Abducted Children

When police are called to deal with a missing-child report, their responsibility is less clear. Many departments lack specific procedures to deal with missing-children calls. In addition, significant variation exists in the initial response to such calls. Officers might obtain a physical description, description of clothing and jewelry, amount of money carried, possible destination and places frequented and why the person filing the report thinks the child is missing. A picture should also be obtained. Many jurisdictions also have policies about when the information must be entered into the National Crime Information Center (NCIC) system. In California, for example, the law requires that a child's name be entered into the NCIC system within four hours if the child is under age 12.

A special challenge in cases where a child is reported missing is determining if the child has run away (a status offense) or has been abducted.

In some cases, one parent believes, correctly or incorrectly, that the other parent is physically or sexually abusing or neglecting the child. The risk of abduction increases if the parent making the accusation was a victim of abuse or neglect as a child. The risk also increases if the suspecting parent has a network of family members or friends who help the abducting parent obtain a new identity and find a new home.

Time is especially crucial in abduction cases: "Most abductions are short term and involve sexual assault; 44 percent of abducted children who are killed are killed in less than one hour of being abducted; 75 percent are killed within 3 hours of being abducted; 91 percent are killed within 24 hours of being abducted; 99 percent of those murdered are killed within 7 days of being abducted" (Swager, 2007, p.137). Although data shows that sex-related child abduction homicides are statistically rare (100 to 200 cases annually), they are particularly horrific crimes: "Delays in reporting missing children become critical. . . . Any delay can make a difference in whether the victim is found alive" (Geberth, 2004, p.33).

Because of the time-sensitive nature of child abductions, many police departments have a child abduction response team (CART) in place. The mission of a CART is to bring expert resources to child abduction cases quickly. Such a team typically consists of seasoned, experienced officers from around the region, each with a preplanned response related to that officer's field of expertise, and may include mounted patrol, all-terrain vehicles (ATVs), helicopters, and K-9s—whatever resources are readily available. A CART might also include coordinators for the family, the media, the crime scene, the search party and other agencies involved.

Fingerprints of a child are taken by a police officer in a campaign against child kidnapping. Of all children kidnapped in the USA each year, approximately half of them are murdered. The remainder are generally the object of parental kidnapping (by father or mother), and the act is often a by-product of divorce.
© Sophie Elbaz/Sygma/Corbis

AMBER Alert
Voluntary partnerships between law enforcement agencies and public broadcasters to notify the public when a child has been abducted.

A valuable resource in abduction cases is the America's Missing: Broadcast Emergency Response (AMBER) alert program. **AMBER Alert** is a voluntary partnership between law enforcement agencies and public broadcasters as an early warning system to notify the public when a child has been abducted. It originated in the Dallas–Fort Worth region after the murder of Amber Hagerman, a nine-year-old girl who was abducted from her home.

All 50 states now have statewide AMBER Alert plans. These alerts may be put on television and radio stations, electronic message systems on highways and other media. In most departments, the public information officer (PIO) is the communication cornerstone of this network and the primary point of contact for the media, meaning the PIO is responsible for conveying all information from the law enforcement agency to the public via the media and for fielding inquiries from journalists. According to a Department of Justice press release ("Department of Justice Conference," 2008), 426 children have been safely recovered since the AMBER Alert program began, with 96 percent of the recoveries occurring since the program became a nationally coordinated effort in 2002. The program has undertaken a secondary distribution effort in partnership with wireless companies, online service providers, and other private and public entities allowing AMBER Alerts to be sent directly to the public. In addition, tribal nations are working to develop their own plans tailored to their specific needs. According to the press release: "Anecdotal evidence demonstrates that perpetrators are well aware of the power of AMBER Alert, and in many cases have released an abducted child upon hearing the alert."

Before an alert is sent law enforcement should meet the following criteria: (1) confirm that a child 17 or under has been abducted; (2) believe that the circumstances indicate the child is in danger of serious bodily harm or death; (3) have enough descriptive evidence about the child, abductor or vehicle to believe an immediate broadcast alert will help and (4) have entered the child's name and other critical data elements, including the Child Abduction flag, into the NCIC system ("Guidelines for Issuing AMBER Alerts," n.d.).

Yet another resource for law enforcement is a telephone notification system called A Child Is Missing (ACIM). Based in Fort Lauderdale, Florida, ACIM can mobilize an entire community to help search for a missing person. Once an officer at the scene verifies the child is missing, he immediately calls ACIM's toll-free number and gives basic descriptive information to the ACIM technician—name, age, physical and clothing details, and address with zip code where the child was last seen. This is the information that ACIM will give to the public. A technician at ACIM's offices in Florida enters the information into a database and discusses with the officer the radius surrounding the child's last known location to determine what size geographic area should be alerted. Using a unique phone system, ACIM's recorded message can be delivered to a thousand phones in 60 seconds. The message ACIM sends out describes the missing person, and asks recipients to look out their windows or step outside and check the vicinity in case the missing person is nearby.

Another valuable resource in missing children cases is the National Center for Missing and Exploited Children (NCMEC), which provides two services to law enforcement agencies investigating missing children cases. The first is an age progression program that creates photographs of a child that approximate what the child would look like at the present time. The greatest age difference they have created is from age 6 to age 31. The second service is called Project KidCare, provided in collaboration with Polaroid Corporation. This service consists of an educational packet and a high-quality photo in a form the NCMEC and law enforcement consider ideal.

If the body of an abducted child is found, the case becomes a homicide investigation. Officers should conduct a neighborhood canvass in the area of the victim's last known location, the victim/killer contact site, the body recovery site and any other site determined to be important to the investigation. Developing a suspect can be challenging if the offender was transient to the area, rather than someone residing in the community. According to Geberth (2004, p.36), "The majority of suspects in these cases are White males, averaging 27 years old, single, living with someone else, unemployed or under employed if working, considered strange by others, with a history of past violent crimes against children."

In addition to dealing with child victims, police commonly encounter youth engaged in status offenses.

STATUS OFFENDERS

A special category of offenses has been established for juveniles, designating certain actions as illegal for any person under the age specified by the state.

status offenses

Violations of the law applying only to those under legal age; includes curfew violations, drinking alcoholic beverages, incorrigibility, smoking cigarettes, running away from home and truancy.

decriminalization

Making status offenses noncriminal matters.

Status offenses are violations of the law applying only to those under legal age, including curfew violations, drinking alcoholic beverages, incorrigibility, smoking cigarettes, running away from home and truancy.

Frequently, status offenses bring young people into contact with police officers, often in a very negative manner. Sometimes the consequences of negative labeling and perhaps confinement with more criminally inclined youths can result in status offenders becoming involved in crime. Several states and the American Bar Association (ABA) have made a case for the **decriminalization** of status offenses, that is, for not treating them as criminal offenses.

Whether states decriminalize status offenses or not, police officers dealing with juveniles should clearly differentiate between simple delinquent behavior (status offenses) and criminal delinquent behavior (crimes regardless of age). One of the most frequent encounters police have with juveniles is dealing with disorderly youths who are just “hanging out,” those who violate curfew laws and those who are truant.

Disorderly Youths Who Are “Hanging Out”

“Hanging out” behavior is well known to most police officers and is a common part of youths’ development. To most adolescents, peers become all-important. Parents, teachers and other authority figures have less influence on adoles-

“Hanging out” is a popular teen activity and is not, in itself, illegal. The challenge occurs when such activity becomes a public nuisance or deters customers from entering a commercial establishment.
© Michael Newman/PhotoEdit

cents' development and behavior. "Hanging out" is often an indication of lack of direction or purpose and may lead to delinquent behavior, which may be seen as offering excitement. If youths congregate in large numbers inside or outside business establishments, business people and their customers may complain to the police. Some communities have enacted antiloitering laws to discourage groups of youths from "hanging out."

Sometimes the youths have been drinking and are belligerent and unreasonable, making the problem even more difficult. How police officers deal with such situations can make the difference between a peaceful resolution of the problem or a violent confrontation.

Curfew Violators

When youths' behavior is such that the community wants them off the streets at night, a curfew may be established for the public good. The 1990s popularity of curfews as a response to youth crime is simply the most recent revival of a delinquency control measure that has waxed and waned across urban America several times during the last century. Curfew ordinances must demonstrate a compelling state interest and be narrow in interpretation to meet constitutional standards. For example: "The curfew applies to youths under age 17 and between 11 P.M. and 6 A.M., Sunday through Thursday, and midnight to 6 A.M. on Friday and Saturday. Exemptions include juveniles accompanied by an adult, traveling to or from work, responding to an emergency, married, or attending a supervised activity."

Curfews may face resistance from police officers, who see them as babysitting detail and an infringement on crime fighting efforts. Further, many agencies lack adequate personnel to enforce a curfew law. If an officer picks up a child and transports him or her to the station, waits for a parent and does the necessary paperwork, it could take several hours, taking the officer off the street. Curfew programs should include such strategies as

- Creating a dedicated curfew center or using recreation centers and churches to house curfew violators.
- Staffing these centers with social service professionals and community volunteers.
- Offering referrals to social service providers and counseling classes for juvenile violators and their families.
- Establishing procedures—such as fines, counseling or community service—for repeat offenders.
- Developing recreation, employment, antidrug and antigang programs.
- Providing hot lines for follow-up services and intervention.

In some instances, daytime curfews have been implemented to curb truancy.

Truants

Truancy is a major problem in many school districts. **Truancy**, which is loosely defined as habitual unexcused absence from school, is considered a status offense because, although compulsory attendance laws vary some-

truancy
Loosely defined as habitual unexcused absence from school, considered a status offense because, although compulsory attendance laws vary somewhat from state to state, every state requires children between certain ages to be in school during the academic year absent a valid excuse.

what from state to state, every state requires children between certain ages to be in school during the academic year absent a valid excuse. If a child is not in school, he or she is not learning or gaining the knowledge and problem-solving skills required to move successfully into the adult world of employment and self-sufficiency. Furthermore, youths who are skipping school are very likely to be engaged in proscribed activities such as drug use, property crimes or even more serious offenses: "In several jurisdictions, law enforcement officials have linked high rates of truancy to daytime burglary and vandalism" (Baker et al., 2001, p.2). Research has clearly identified truancy as a precursor to myriad negative outcomes: "A lack of commitment to school has been established by several studies as a risk factor for substance abuse, delinquency, teen pregnancy, and school dropout" (Gonzales et al., 2002, p.3).

Underage Drinking

Underage drinking is an especially serious status offense because youths who are drinking (or doing drugs) may commit illegal acts while under the influence of drugs or alcohol. A growing body of evidence links alcohol with adolescent violence. Although studies demonstrating a relationship between alcohol use by juveniles and adolescent violence are not new, recent data has confirmed that youth who often engage in underage drinking are significantly more likely to commit violence while sober than are nondrinking youth (Felson et al., 2008, p.119).

Underage drinking causes a wide range of alcohol-related health, social, criminal justice and academic problems, including drunken driving, disorderly conduct, assaults, acquaintance rape and vandalism. However, as with curfews, some officers see underage drinking as a low priority because of the perceived legal obstacles in processing juveniles; unpleasant, tedious paperwork; special detention procedures required for minors; lack of juvenile detention facilities or centers that are already above capacity; lack of significant punishment for underage drinking; and personal disagreements regarding underage drinking laws, particularly as they apply to people age 18 to 20. Despite the objections officers may have, serious and valid reasons exist for making the enforcement of underage drinking laws a higher priority.

In conjunction with the Harvard study of binge drinking on college campuses, a survey at Louisiana State University (LSU) was taken regarding alcohol policies at LSU (Campus-Community Coalition for Change, 2006, p.9). Support or strong support was indicated for making alcohol rules clearer (94 percent), offering alcohol-free dorms (89 percent) and providing more alcohol-free recreational and cultural opportunities such as movies, dances, sports and lectures (86 percent).

raves

A form of dance and recreation held in a clandestine location with fast-paced, high-volume music, a variety of high-tech entertainment and often the use of drugs.

Rave Parties

A problem closely related problem to underage drinking is that of rave parties. **Raves** are dance parties held in clandestine locations; featuring fast-paced, repetitive electronic music and light shows; and often promising sex, illicit drugs and alcohol. Drug use is intended to enhance ravers' sensations and boost their energy, so they can dance for extended periods. Ecstasy (also called X) is commonly associated with the rave scene, as is methamphetamine (meth). The principal rave-related concerns for police are drug overdoses, drug trafficking and the associated potential for violence with it, noise (from music, crowds and traffic), DUIs, traffic control and parking congestion.

Approaches law enforcement might use when faced with a rave problem include using nuisance abatement laws, prosecuting rave operators or property owners for drug-related offenses and educating ravers about the dangers of drug use and overexertion. Currently, raves do not seem to be as prevalent as they were during the 1990s, partially because youth are being better educated about the dangers of meth and X, and because that trend in music has passed.

POLICE DISPOSITIONS OF STATUS OFFENSES

Police dispositions range from taking no action to referring the children to social service agencies or to the juvenile court. For status offenses, the police have many alternatives that are guided by the community, the local juvenile justice system and individual officer discretion.

In the disposition of matters related to status offenders, how police resolve cases often depends on the officers' discretion, the specific incident and the backup available.

Whether the police actually arrest a juvenile usually depends on several factors, the most important being the seriousness of the offense. Other factors affecting the decision include character, age, gender, race, prior record, family situation and the youth's attitude.

The decision may also be influenced by public opinion, the media, available referral agencies and the officer's experience. Officers' actions usually reflect community interests. For example, conflict could occur between the public's demand for order and a group of young people wanting to "hang out." How police respond to such hanging out is influenced by the officer's attitude and the standards of the neighborhood or community, rather than by rules of the state. Each neighborhood or community and the officer's own feelings dictate how the police perform in such matters.

Sometimes police may "roust" and "hassle" youths who engage in undesirable social conduct, but they probably will not report the incident; in this case, street justice is the police disposition. **Street justice** occurs when police decide to deal with a status offense in their own way—usually by ignoring it.

street justice
Decision of police officers to deal with an offense in their own way—usually by ignoring it.

Police Discretion and the Initial Contact

Between 80 and 90 percent of youths commit some offense for which they could be arrested, yet only about 3 percent of them are. This is largely because they do not get caught. Further, those who are caught have usually engaged in some minor status offense that can, in many instances, be better handled by counseling and releasing. This approach allows youths an opportunity to learn from their mistakes without having to officially enter "the system." The result is more desirable for the juveniles and parents involved, and it saves the officer time in dealing with minor status offenses, leaving them available for more serious calls. Although the "counsel and dismiss" alternative may be criticized as being "soft" on juveniles, this approach is often all that is needed to turn a youth around.

Police officers have considerable discretionary power when dealing with juveniles.

Law enforcement officers have a range of alternatives to take:

- Release the child, with or without a warning, but without making an official record or taking further action.
- Release the child, but write up a brief contact or field report to juvenile authorities, describing the contact.
- Release the child, but file a more formal report referring the matter to a juvenile bureau or an intake unit, for possible action.
- Turn the youth over to juvenile authorities immediately.
- Refer the case directly to the court, through the district or county attorney.

Police officers who deal with juveniles may warn them, with or without an official report; turn them over to their parents, with or without an official report; refer them to a social agency; or refer them to juvenile court.

In some instances, youths engaging in delinquent acts are simply counseled. In other instances they are returned to their families, who are expected to deal with their child's deviant behavior. Sometimes they are referred to social services agencies for help. And sometimes they are charged and processed by the juvenile justice system.

The most common procedure is to release the child, with or without a warning, but without making an official record or taking further action.

diversion
Referring a juvenile out of the justice system and to some other agency or program.

If police officers refer youths to a community agency, this is known as **diversion**. Whether a youth is diverted will depend on department policy, the availability of appropriate programs and police awareness of community resources. Typical police referrals are to youth service bureaus, special school programs, boys clubs, the YMCA, community mental health agencies and drug programs. Typically, if the juvenile successfully completes the program, the charge is eliminated from his or her record.

Most youth referrals to court are from law enforcement.

Remaining referrals to court come from parents, relatives, schools, probation officers, other courts, social services and other services. The options open to police officers when it comes to serious, violent juvenile offenders are much more limited.

44.2.1

CALEA STANDARD 44.2.1 states, "In keeping with the doctrine of *parens patriae*, e.g., that the state plays the role of parent to the child rather than adversary, agencies should seek the least forceful alternative when disposing of cases involving juveniles. Agency referral of alleged juveniles for formal legal proceedings should be restricted to those cases involving serious criminal conduct or repeated criminal violations. In general, delinquent acts requiring referral to the juvenile justice system would include all delinquent acts that, if committed by an adult, would be felonies; all delinquent acts involving weapons; all serious gang-related delinquent acts; all delinquent acts involving aggravated assault and battery; all delinquent acts committed by juveniles on probation or parole or by those with a case pending; and all repeated delinquent acts within the preceding 12 months." (*Standards for Law Enforcement Agencies*, 5th edition, 2006)

VIOLENT OFFENDERS

One problem behavior associated with youth violence is animal abuse. The relationship between cruelty to animals and serious violent behavior, especially among young offenders, is strong. In a study of nine school shootings in the United States, 5 of the 11 perpetrators, or 45 percent, had histories of animal abuse.

Other factors are also associated with serious delinquent offending. Youths coming to the street from backgrounds where violence was used as discipline learn that violence is an appropriate way to settle disputes. Brutality in the home may lead to running away and the accompanying homelessness and poverty as well as a predisposition to anger. Such youths seek each other out and spend significant time together, reinforcing each other's violent behavior as socially accepted.

Other family and social variables were also found to be predictive of recidivism. Juveniles who had been physically or sexually abused, were raised in a single-parent family, had siblings involved in delinquent or criminal activity, had a higher number of out-of-home placements or had experienced significant family problems were at higher risk of recidivism. Juveniles who did not use their leisure time effectively and those with delinquent peers were also at higher risk (recall the discussion of "hanging out"). A history of being in special education classes or having lower standardized achievement test scores, lower full-scale IQ scores and lower verbal IQ scores also predicted reoffending. Race was not a significant predictor.

The classic long-term studies of delinquent youths conducted by Marvin E. Wolfgang found that a relatively small group—6 to 8 percent—of male juveniles accounted for the majority—more than 60 percent—of serious offenses committed by juveniles and that by the third arrest, a juvenile delinquent was virtually guaranteed to continue in a life of crime.

Similar conclusions were reported in *The 8% Solution* (2001). The Orange County (California) Probation Department tracked a small group of first-time offenders for three years and found that a small percentage (8 percent) of the juveniles were arrested repeatedly (a minimum of four times within a three-year period) and were responsible for 55 percent of repeat cases. According to the report (p.1),

8% problem
50–60 percent of juvenile crime is committed by 8 percent of juveniles.

> The characteristics of this group of repeat offenders (referred to as "the **8% problem**") were dramatically different from those who were arrested only once. These differences did not develop after exposure to the juvenile justice system, as some might expect; they were evident at first arrest and referral to juvenile court, and they worsened if nothing was done to alleviate the youth's problems. Unfortunately, in wanting to "give a break" to first-time offenders, the juvenile justice system often pays scant attention to those at greatest risk of becoming chronic offenders until they have established a record of repeated serious offending [emphasis added].
>
> The good news is that most of the small group of potentially serious, chronic offenders can be identified reliably at first contact with the juvenile justice system. The 8% offenders enter the system with a complex set of problems or risk factors, which the study identified as (1) involvement in crime at an early age and (2) a multiproblem profile including significant family problems (abuse, neglect, criminal family members, and/or a lack of parental supervision and control), problems at school (truancy, failing more than one course or a recent suspension or expulsion), drug and alcohol abuse, and behaviors such as gang involvement, running away and stealing.

LEGAL PROCEDURES WHEN DEALING WITH YOUTHS

In re Gault (1967) established that juveniles have the right to counsel, the right to be notified of the charges against them, the right to confront and examine witnesses and the privilege against self-incrimination.

These rights must be respected as police officers interact with children and youths.

Custody and Detention

Police can take children into custody by court order if they have reasonable grounds to believe that the child is suffering from illness or injury or is in immediate danger from his surroundings or believe the child has run away or because he has no parent, guardian, custodian or other person able to supervise and care for him and return him to the court when required.

A landmark Supreme Court case affecting law enforcement is *Schall v. Martin* (1984), which upheld the state's right to place juveniles in preventive detention. Writing for the majority, Justice William Rehnquist cited two reasons for upholding the New York statute for preventive detention. The first was that of "protecting a juvenile from the consequences of his criminal activity." The

Being taken into custody and locked up can be a turning point for many youths. Is this young girl headed for a lifetime of crime, or can she be rehabilitated?
© Fogstock LLC/SuperStock

second was protecting the public. In other words, preventive detention fulfills the legitimate state interest of protecting society and juveniles by temporarily detaining those who might be dangerous to society or to themselves.

After police have taken juveniles into custody, they should either release the juveniles to their parents or guardians, take them before a judge, take them to a detention home or shelter or take them to a medical facility if needed. The parent or guardian and the court are to be notified in writing with all reasonable speed. Delinquents are *not* to be put into a jail or other adult detention facility unless no other option is available. They are put into a room separate from the adults when their detention in an adult facility is necessary for their own safety or that of the public.

An Implementation Guide for Juvenile Holdover Programs (2001, p.1) explains, "A juvenile holdover program (JHP) is both an old and a new concept. The old concept—the creativity of law enforcement officers, social workers and probation officers has always been called upon to decide what to do with a juvenile in need of a safe, and perhaps secure, place to wait until a parent can be located or while the system mobilizes to respond to the needs of a child or youth. . . . The new concept—communities have developed a variety of different responses to meet the need for a short-term, temporary holding program for juveniles that can be called upon when the need arises." Among the key elements of a JHP are that it is integrated into a network of services for youths, is a short-term alternative, is easily accessible and has a trained staff. It should also be able to respond to a youth's immediate needs, to provide comfortable facilities with minimum services for an overnight stay and can respond to and de-escalate the immediate situation if necessary. It should have screening and assessment capacity and referral expertise and be able to coordinate postrelease services to the youth and family.

Interviewing Juveniles and Custodial Issues

Interviewing in-custody juveniles is different than interviewing in-custody adults. There are occasions when it is appropriate to have parents present when interviewing youths, which can be an added hurdle for law enforcement.

Additional issues are posed when school resource/liaison officers (SROs) conduct interviews with juveniles while in school for incidents that have occurred both inside and outside of school. For example, a criminal defense attorney could argue that juveniles may have felt that they were in custody, even if they were in a school setting. Furthermore, juveniles may not be aware that admitting to school administrators or police officers their involvement in incidents that occurred in school may also carry criminal repercussions outside of school. Parents might also take issue with their children being interviewed for possible criminal incidents at a place of learning, where the expectation is for the student to learn and be safe while the parents are not present.

SROs have the additional challenges of working with school administration and school reprimands in these matters. Additionally, there have been cases where school administration has recommended that a juvenile be charged for an incident. It is important to remember that it is not at the discretion of the principal or head administrator of the school in regard to criminal matters; it is ultimately the discretion of the law enforcement officer. In some communities, the relationship between school administration and law enforcement has become such a negative issue that the schools do not have an SRO or liaison officer on the grounds.

Fingerprinting and Photographing Children

In most jurisdictions, law enforcement officers can take fingerprints of children 14 years and older involved in the crimes of murder, nonnegligent manslaughter, forcible rape, robbery, aggravated assault, burglary, housebreaking, purse snatching and automobile theft. However, children's fingerprint files usually must be kept separate from adult files. The fingerprints are to be removed from the file and destroyed if the youth is adjudicated not delinquent or if the youth reaches age 21 and has not committed a criminal offense after becoming 16.

If police officers find latent fingerprints during a criminal investigation and have probable cause to believe a particular youth committed the crime, they may fingerprint the youth, regardless of the youth's age. If the comparison is negative, the youth's fingerprint card should be destroyed immediately.

Police Records and Files

Law enforcement records and files concerning a child should be kept separate from those of adults. Unless a charge of delinquency is transferred for criminal prosecution, the interest of national security requires, or the court otherwise orders in the interest of the child, the records and files should not be open to public inspection or their contents disclosed to the public. Juvenile records may be sealed in these cases:

- Two years have elapsed since the final discharge of the person.
- Since the final discharge, the juvenile has not been convicted of a felony, or of a misdemeanor involving moral turpitude, or adjudicated a delinquent or unruly child, and no proceeding is pending seeking conviction or adjudication.
- The juvenile has been rehabilitated.

Confidentiality versus Openness

Many states have begun to de-emphasize traditional confidentiality concerns while emphasizing information sharing. During the early 1990s, states made significant changes in how the juvenile justice system treats information about juvenile offenders, particularly violent juvenile offenders. As juvenile crime became more serious, community protection, the public's right to know and service providers' need to share information displaced the desire to protect minors from the stigma of youthful indiscretions. Legislatures throughout the country have increasingly called for a presumption of open hearings and records, at least for some juvenile offenders.

LAW ENFORCEMENT PROGRAMS AIMED AT YOUTHS

Most children and youths are *not* in trouble with the law. Programs should be provided that foster positive relations between such individuals and the juvenile justice community so that these youths continue to stay out of trouble. Law enforcement programs aimed at youths take varied approaches. Some approach delinquency with aggressive enforcement and sometimes referrals. Some provide volunteer opportunities through Explorer Posts, described shortly. Some are educational school-based programs aimed at preventing drug abuse and gang involvement, two major problems discussed in Chapter 12. Some are aimed at specific problems. And some are aimed at youths who have gotten into trouble.

Aggressive Enforcement

The North Miami Beach Police Department took aim at the status offense of truancy. Its Police Eliminating Truancy (PET) project is intended to tackle the underlying causes of truancy and, at the same time, reduce the criminal behavior that resulted when juveniles spent their day on the street instead of in school. About 20 percent of the students admitted to committing crimes while truant.

Crime analysis identifies "hot spots" where a high number of Index crimes took place. The PET project assigns two officers to patrol in those hot spots during regular school hours. Truants are taken by officers to the Truancy Evaluation Center (TEC) located in an off-campus classroom. TEC shares space with the department's Alternate to Suspension Program (ASP), whose intensive learning environment and disciplined approach helps many students rededicate themselves to school. A counselor evaluates the truants and then one of three things usually happens. If students have no history of truancy, PET officers take them back to school. Suspended students take part in ASP. Students who seem to be making truancy a habit meet with their parents and the counselor to discuss possible solutions to the problem.

Another positive aspect of aggressive enforcement programs is that youths who are not seriously delinquent can be referred to other programs for help in staying out of trouble in the future.

Referrals/Diversion

Social services agencies, community-based organizations and schools can all play a role in helping a young person to develop and keep from entering the juvenile justice system. Although each community will have different resources available, ideally they will have a youth services center knowledgeable of programs available to help children and youths. Prevention programs and early intervention programs can lessen the need for judicial programs, allowing those programs to concentrate on the more serious problem offenders. Figure 11.2 illustrates the Strategic Home Intervention and Early Leadership Development (SHIELD) process, developed by the City of Westminster (Orange County, California) Police Department, for making referrals to the appropriate program. The referral process usually begins with a police officer encountering an at-risk youth.

Explorer Posts

As the name *Police Explorer Post* suggests, this program provides an opportunity for youths to explore police work. Explorer Posts are extensions of the Boy Scouts of America and allow young men and women a chance to volunteer their services to their local police departments. The minimum age for most programs is 14. Explorers typically participate in numerous ride-alongs with licensed police officers to get a "front row" view of the day-to-day activities of an officer, and explorers usually undergo three to six months of intensive training covering such areas as first aid, traffic control, firearms safety, fingerprinting, community relations and the like. After thorough training they work with sworn officers in numerous capacities. Some agencies allow their explorers to conduct park patrol and may even grant them the authority to cite individuals under city ordinance violations. Every year, there is a National Explorer competition where Explorer Posts throughout the nation come together to compete in various contests, including scenarios such as burglary response, domestics and traffic stops along with skills competitions in categories such as shooting.

The Portsmouth (New Hampshire) Police Department created a special project for its explorers, helping with cutting down speeders and other traffic problems: Cadets Assisting Neighborhoods to Identify Driving Violations (CAN ID). The explorer cadets are trained in traffic monitoring practices, including using handheld digital radar detectors. The cadets take to the streets in pairs to watch for moving violations such as speeding, rolling through stop signs and ignoring pedestrians in crosswalks. One cadet calls out the violation, license

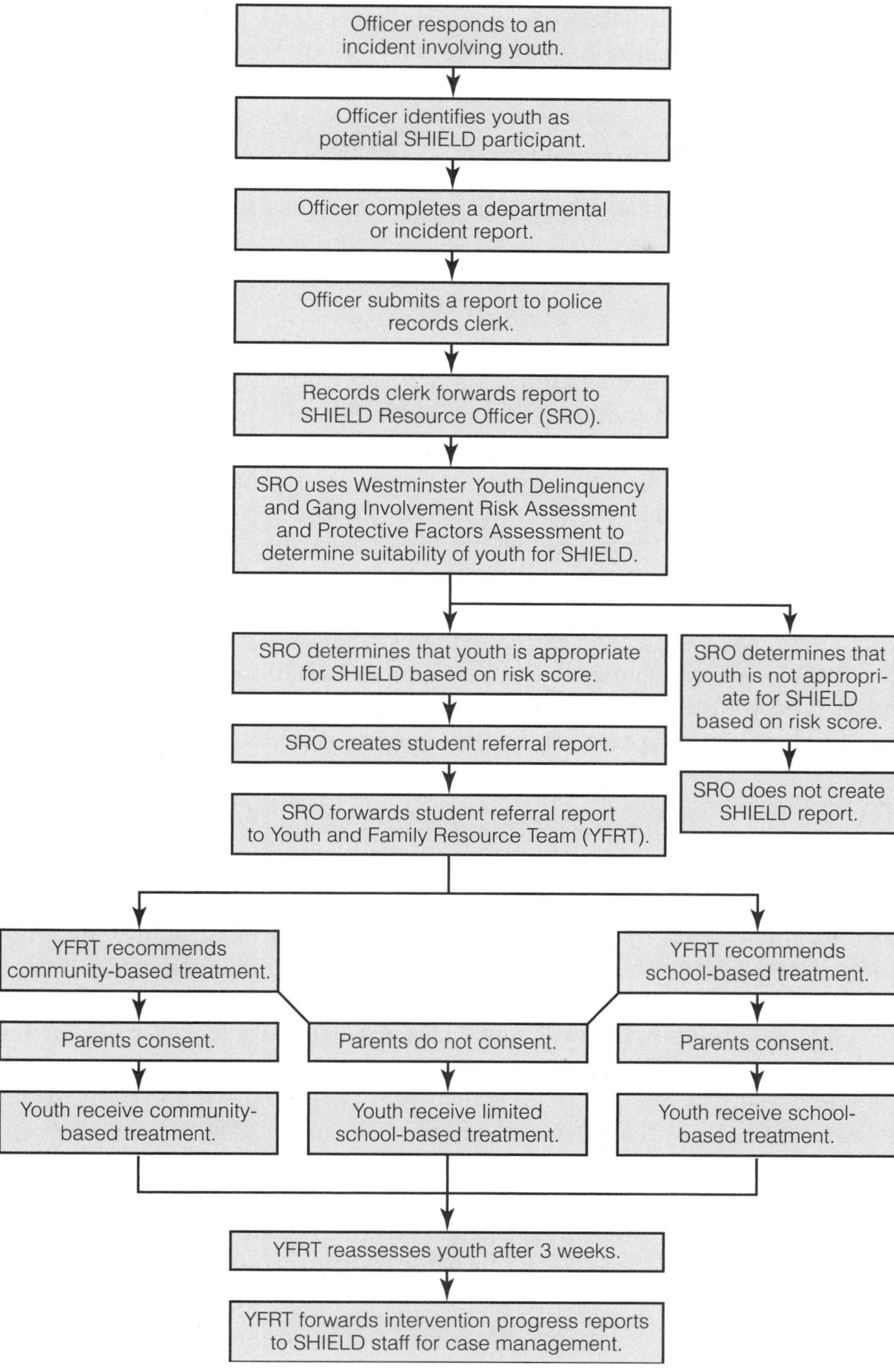

FIGURE 11.2 The SHIELD Program Model
Source: Phelan A. Wyrick, "Law Enforcement Referral of At-Risk Youth: The SHIELD Program." *Juvenile Justice Bulletin.* Washington DC: Office of Juvenile Justice and Delinquency Prevention, November 2000, p.4. www.ncjrs.gov/pdffiles1/ojjdp/184579.pdf

number and make of the car, and the other cadet records the information in a logbook, which they take back to the department and, with the help of an officer, run the license to identify the drivers. These drivers are sent warning letters that future violations will likely result in a ticket.

The New Britain (Connecticut) Police Department came up with a solution regarding what to do with the recovered bicycles piling up, many of which needed repair. They decided to set up a bike shop, teach volunteers to repair the recovered bikes and then distribute them to various organizations, including their Police Explorers Post.

Educational Programs

Two educational programs widely used across the country to combat drugs and gangs are Drug Abuse Resistance Education (D.A.R.E.) and Gang Resistance Education and Training (G.R.E.A.T.).

D.A.R.E.
Drug Abuse Resistance Education, a school program aimed at teaching fourth- and fifth-grade students to say no to peer pressure to use drugs.

Probably the best-known school-based educational program is **D.A.R.E.**, the Drug Abuse Resistance Education program. A study by the University of Illinois tracked 1,800 students for six years and found that by the end of high school any impact of the program had worn off. In fact, evaluations conducted at the end of the 1990s and beginning of the new millennium were resoundingly critical of this effort: "D.A.R.E. has been the subject of 30 other studies over the past several years and all of them have arrived at the same conclusion—any effect that the program has to deterring drug use disappears by the time students are seniors in high school" (Brown, 2001, p.76). In response, the curriculum was revised and tested in high schools and middle schools across the nation. One key change in the new version is that police officers are used more as facilitators and less as instructors. Preliminary evaluations of this revised curriculum indicate there has been an improvement in the effectiveness of D.A.R.E. (Perin, 2008).

G.R.E.A.T.
The Gang Resistance Education and Training program.

Another school-based education program is **G.R.E.A.T.**, the Gang Resistance Education and Training program. This is a proactive approach to deter violence before it begins. The program builds a foundation focused on teaching children the life skills needed to avoid violence and gang membership. Research on the benefits of this program conducted by Esbensen et al. (2001) found that the program was beneficial: "Beneficial program effects emerged gradually over time so that there was, on average, more pro-social change in the attitudes of G.R.E.A.T. students than the non–G.R.E.A.T. students four years following program exposure."

A five-year study by the National Institute of Justice also found the program to have modest positive effects on youths (Esbensen, 2004). A small percent had lower levels of victimization, more negative attitudes toward gangs, more positive attitudes toward police, had less involvement in risk-seeking behaviors and were involved in more prosocial activities with their peers. The study also found, however, that the G.R.E.A.T. program did not reduce gang membership.

Camps

Many police departments sponsor camps for youths, some for at-risk youths and some for youths who have gotten into trouble with the law.

Respect and Responsibility (R&R) is a camp sponsored by the Winnooski (Vermont) Police Department and the National Guard. Its emphasis is on building self-esteem and enhancing young people's ability to work as a team. Activities at the one-week camp include land navigation, wilderness survival, first aid and CPR certification and a rope course.

Camp Turning Point, as the name implies, is for first-time juvenile offenders to have a second chance to turn around their situations. Campers, young men ages 13 to 16, must be enrolled in school or a general education development (GED) program, attend group or individual counseling, perform at least 20 hours of community service and pay any court-ordered restitution in full. The camp has the usual activities of swimming, fishing and horseback riding and teaches campers to work as a team.

Other Programs

Several other programs whose orientations are less educational also have been instituted by police departments to help deal with problem youths. One of the most common programs is a SRO program, described in Chapter 7. Other well-known programs found throughout the country are the Officer Friendly program and the McGruff police dog ("Take a bite out of crime") program. The McGruff program focuses on crime prevention and safety and helps youths contribute positively to the community.

JUVENILE JUSTICE AND PROBLEM-ORIENTED POLICING

A finalist in the Excellence in Problem-Oriented Policing Awards in 2003 was the "Underage Drinking: More than a Minor Issue" project of the Plano Police Department.

Scanning

Officer Richard L. Glenn had noticed that an increasing number of calls for service in his area involved minors in possession of or consuming alcohol. These calls included juvenile problems, noise, party disturbances and other incidents. The minors involved commonly stated that they could easily walk into a beer store in Plano and purchase alcohol.

Analysis

Officer Glenn noted numerous participants in this problem: the minors that he caught in violation, the store clerks who sold the alcohol, the police department, and the residents of the City of Plano. The harm caused to Plano residents was demonstrated in police calls for service involving juvenile problems, party disturbances, noise complaints and alcohol-related traffic accidents. Officer Glenn's goal was to reduce the number of stores in Plano selling alcohol to minors.

Response

Officer Glenn implemented a plan to conduct special enforcement details to increase enforcement, gather specific data on which stores were selling alcohol to minors and educate violators. He used confidential informants under the age of 18 to purchase alcohol under very controlled circumstances. Finding that the problem was pervasive throughout the City of Plano, Officer Glenn identified four main reasons that store clerks sell alcohol to minors and then used this information to educate the community and violators about this problem.

Assessment

Officer Glenn has continued to conduct special enforcement details, and the number of stores selling alcohol to minors in Plano has significantly decreased during the time that he has been working on this project.

Judge's Commentary

Several features of Plano's underage drinking project deserve note. The city is surrounded by dry jurisdictions, making its 159 package stores magnets for an entire region. The problem of underage drinking was particularly significant in Plano because the city prides itself on its quality of life, especially for children. After a beat officer sensed an increasing problem of minors in possession of and consuming alcohol, he was stymied in his attempt to gather conclusive data about the problem. This turned out to be one of those problems that fell through the police department's data system's cracks. Specific cases of underage possession were often handled informally, resulting in no reports and no data. Underage drinking was not a specific code on police reports, so he had no way of determining what proportion of loud parties, noise complaints, juvenile problems, or traffic accidents involved minors in possession. The officer persevered, however, eventually creating his own database to document the scope and seriousness of the problem.

After receiving clearance to address the problem citywide, the officer implemented a systematic enforcement campaign of multiple attempted underage buys at every package store in Plano. This served both as a response to the problem and as a continuation of problem analysis. Offending clerks and their managers were interviewed to determine why underage purchases could be made in their stores. This line of inquiry yielded valuable information that led to additional responses of a nonenforcement nature. The data issues that limited initial problem analysis also made it difficult to demonstrate that this project reduced the impact of underage drinking on noise, disorder or traffic accidents in Plano. However, the officer's careful and systematic efforts did clearly affect the behavior of store clerks and managers, making it harder for minors to purchase alcoholic beverages in the city.

SUMMARY

Youths' attitudes toward law and law enforcement are tremendously influenced by personal contacts with law enforcement officers. Positive interactions are critical to delinquency prevention. A juvenile is a person not yet of legal age. In three-fourths of the states, juveniles are defined as youths under age 18. The doctrine of *parens patriae* allows the state to assume guardianship of abandoned, neglected and "wayward" children. The juvenile justice system, under *parens patriae,* has historically taken a rehabilitative approach in handling children, rather than the punitive approach taken in the adult criminal justice system. Our current juvenile system is treatment or welfare focused. Some argue it should be replaced with a juvenile justice system whereby youths who commit serious crimes are held accountable and punished for those acts. The juvenile justice system is responsible for children who are neglected or abused, those who are status offenders and those who commit serious crimes, in what is called the "one-pot" jurisdictional approach.

Running away is a predelinquent indicator, but its importance often is not recognized by the parents, police, school, social agencies or the courts. A special challenge in cases where a child is reported missing is determining if the child has run away (a status offense) or has been abducted.

Some youths get into trouble with the law for minor status offenses. Status offenses are violations of the law applying only to those under legal age, including curfew violations, drinking alcoholic beverages, incorrigibility, smoking cigarettes, running away from home and truancy. In the disposition of matters related to status offenders, how police resolve cases often depends on the officers' discretion, the specific incident and the backup available. Police officers have considerable discretionary power when dealing with juveniles.

Police officers who deal with juveniles may warn them, with or without an official report; turn them over to their parents, with or without an official report; refer them to a social agency; or refer them to juvenile court. The most common procedure is to release the child, with or without a warning, but without making an official record or taking further action. Of all youth referrals to court, the great majority are from law enforcement.

In re Gault (1967) established that juveniles have the right to counsel, the right to be notified of the charges against them, the right to confront and examine witnesses and the privilege against self-incrimination. Two educational programs widely used across the country to combat drugs and gangs are Drug Abuse Resistance Education (D.A.R.E.) and Gang Resistance Education and Training (G.R.E.A.T.).

APPLICATION

As an officer with the Mytown Juvenile Bureau, you have noted some inconsistent handling of juvenile offenders that has caused the juvenile court authorities to worry about youngsters not receiving due process when taken into police custody. You call together a group, including citizens and youths, to rectify the situation by making a statement of need for juveniles and the ultimate purpose in their apprehension. Based on that group discussion, establish a policy to standardize procedures for handling juveniles.

INSTRUCTIONS

Use the form in the Appendix to formulate a policy that provides guidelines to police officers in handling juveniles. Include in the policy those guidelines necessary for processing juveniles taken into custody for various reasons. The policy and procedure should include searching, questioning and transporting juveniles, as well as public release of information. Necessary reports should be highlighted and dispositions clearly specified. A visit to the local police department or sheriff's office may help determine what to include in the policy and procedure.

AN EXERCISE IN CRITICAL THINKING

D.F.B.'s parents and two younger siblings were killed with an axe on February 18. D.F.B., age 16, was a sophomore in high school and had discussed killing his family with friends. D.F.B. and several friends also had prepared a "hit list" of others to be terminated. Several friends testified, however, that this list was merely a joke.

D.F.B. had no history of delinquent behavior. He had, however, been depressed for several years. D.F.B. expressed fear of his father, but masked the depression with jokes and quick wit at school. Some school reports indicate D.F.B. was depressed when his brother left home (or was ousted) in the fall. Two good friends moved away in the same year. D.F.B. twice attempted suicide, once in June and again in September.

There were 22 wounds on D.F.B.'s father's body, 19 on his mother's body, 8 on his sister's body and 9 on his brother's body. After his family was killed (sometime around 3:00 A.M. on February 18), D.F.B. obtained cash and purchased groceries. He cut and dyed his hair and then slept in a culvert. He was arrested the following day at the post office while talking on the telephone with a friend. D.F.B. was placed in the custody of the county sheriff.

1. Should D.F.B. be referred for adult prosecution?
   a. Yes, for there is probable cause to believe D.F.B. committed first-degree murder, and there is evidence that D.F.B. is not amenable to treatment.
   b. No, because D.F.B. is only 16 years old.
   c. No, because D.F.B. has no history of prior delinquent acts.
   d. No, because although these acts were criminal, they were actions that came from extreme emotional disturbance during puberty when a body is not matured, and such acts will not be repeated as D.F.B. has now run out of family (which was the singular focus of his anger).
   e. No, because police should always use the least restrictive alternative for dealing with any type of juvenile problem.
2. If the county sheriff had known of D.F.B.'s disturbed emotional state of mind before the murders, what action might the police have taken?
   a. Initiate a treatment program (patterned along the lines of informal probation).
   b. Attempt a deterrence program (athletic, recreational and club activities).
   c. Make a voluntary referral to appropriate community agencies.
   d. Establish a counseling service to give one-on-one talks to youths.
   e. Only deal with mandatory referral to mental or public health agencies under statutory authorization to make such referrals (e.g., to detoxification programs).
3. Because of the vulnerability of juveniles, greater safeguards are needed, such as these:
   a. Greater intrusions than are normally allowed under the Fourth Amendment for adults should be allowed to protect juveniles from damaging home environments.
   b. Stronger mandates must be allowed for juvenile treatment programs.
   c. Juveniles should not be permitted to waive constitutional rights on their own.
   d. More restrictive means should be allowed to protect juveniles from themselves (in the instance of suicide).
   e. Juveniles should receive a set of safeguards completely different from those of adults in preliminary investigations (e.g., stop and frisk), questioning, search and seizure and the arrest process.

DISCUSSION QUESTIONS

1. What are the advantages and disadvantages of a separate system of justice for juveniles?
2. A major principle of English common law is *parens patriae*. Is this philosophy viable in today's society?
3. Should the police be responsible for status offenses, or should some other agency such as the welfare department be given the options of dealing with youths who commit these offenses?
4. Would our society be better off if we treated juveniles like adults in the justice system? Explain. Should a child's criminal record follow him or her into adulthood?
5. Is the status offender similar to or different from the delinquent? Do status offenders "get worse"; that is, do their offenses escalate into more serious offenses?
6. Should juvenile offenders be subjected to capital punishment?
7. Does your department have a juvenile division? If so, how many officers are involved?

GALE EMERGENCY SERVICES DATABASE ASSIGNMENTS

- Use the Gale Emergency Services database to help answer the Discussion Questions as appropriate.
- Use the Gale Emergency Services database to read and outline one of the following articles:
  - "Violent Crimes among Juveniles: Behavioral Aspects" by William Andrew Corbitt
  - "Drug-Endangered Children" by Jerry Harris
  - "Idle Hands: What Factors Have Led Adolescence Into a Pharm Frenzy?" by Tabitha Wethal

- "Return to D.A.R.E.: Armed with Scientific Credibility, the New D.A.R.E. Program Makes a Comeback" by Michelle Perin
- "Police Eliminating Truancy: A PET Project" by William B. Berger and Susan Wind
- "Operation Linebacker: Using Status Offenders to Reduce Crime in Communities" by Robert J. Girot
- "Runaway or Abduction? Assessment Tools for the First Responder" by Andre B. Simons and Jeannine Willie

REFERENCES

America's Children: Key National Indicators of Well-Being, 2008. Federal Interagency Forum on Child and Family Statistics. http://www.childstats.gov/americaschildren/index.asp

Arthur, Lindsay G. "Foreword." pp.xiv–xv. In *Juvenile Justice*, 5th ed., by Kären M. Hess. Belmont, CA: Wadsworth Publishing Company, 2010.

Baker, Myriam L.; Sigmon, Jane Nady; and Nugent, M. Elaine. *Truancy Reduction: Keeping Students in School.* Washington, DC: Office of Juvenile Justice and Delinquency Prevention, Juvenile Justice Bulletin, September 2001. (NCJ 188947)

Brown, Cynthia. "DARE Officials Responding to Critics, Come Up with New Program." *American Police Beat*, April 2001, p.76.

Campus-Community Coalition for Change. *Alcohol and Other Drug Use by LSU Undergraduates in Three Residential Types.* Louisiana State University, June 2006.

Child Maltreatment 2006. Washington, DC: Department of Health and Human Services, 2008.

"Child Maltreatment: Definitions." Atlanta, GA: Centers for Disease Control and Prevention, April 20, 2009.

Commission on Accreditation of Law Enforcement Agencies. *Standards for Law Enforcement Agencies*, 5th ed. Fairfax, VA: CALEA, 2006, updated 2008.

"Department of Justice Conference Highlights AMBER Alert System Success, Finds Way to Enhance Program." Washington, DC: Department of Justice press release, October 14, 2008.

The 8% Solution. Washington, DC: OJJDP Fact Sheet #39, November 2001. (FS 200139)

English, Diana J.; Widom, Cathy Spatz; and Ford, Carol Brand. *Childhood Victimization and Delinquency, Adult Criminality and Violent Criminal Behavior: A Replication and Extension.* Washington, DC: National Institute of Justice, 2002. (NIJ 192291)

Esbensen, Finn-Aage. *Evaluating G.R.E.A.T.: A School-Based Gang Prevention Program.* Washington, DC: National Institute of Justice, June 2004. (NCJ 198604)

Esbensen, Finn-Aage; Osgood, D. Wayne; Taylor, Terrance J.; Peterson, Dana; and Freng, Adrienne. "How Great Is G.R.E.A.T? Results from a Longitudinal Quasi-Experimental Design." *Criminology and Public Policy*, November 2001, pp.87–118.

Felson, Richard B.; Teasdale, Brent; and Burchfield, Keri B. "The Influence of Being Under the Influence: Alcohol Effects on Adolescent Violence." *Journal of Research in Crime and Delinquency*, May 2008, pp.119–141.

Geberth, Vernon. "Sex-Related Child Abduction Homicides." *Law and Order*, March 2004, pp.32–38.

Gonzales, Ramona; Richards, Kinette; and Seeley, Ken. *Youth Out of School: Linking Absence to Delinquency*, 2nd ed. Denver: Colorado Foundation for Families and Children, 2002.

"Guidelines for Issuing AMBER Alerts." Washington, DC: Office of Justice Programs: AMBER Alert, no date.

Hess, Kären M., and Orthmann, Christine Hess. *Juvenile Justice*, 5th ed. Belmont, CA: Wadsworth Publishing Company, 2010.

An Implementation Guide for Juvenile Holdover Programs. Washington, DC: National Highway Traffic Safety Administration, Office of Juvenile Justice and Delinquency Prevention and American Probation and Parole Association, June 2001. (DOT HS 809260)

Karmen, Andrew. *Crime Victims: An Introduction to Victimology*, 5th ed. Belmont, CA: Wadsworth Publishing Company, 2007.

"Online Child Pornography/Child Sexual Exploitation Investigations." Washington, DC: Federal Bureau of Investigation, 2009.

Perin, Michelle. "Return to D.A.R.E." *Law Enforcement Technology*, October 2008.

Swager, Brent. "Tampa's Child Abduction Response Team." *Law and Order*, September 2007, pp.134–138.

"Underage Drinking: More than a Minor Issue." *Excellence in Problem-Oriented Policing: The 2003 Herman Goldstein Aware Winner and Finalists.* Washington, DC: Office of Community Oriented Policing Services and the Police Executive Research Forum, 2003, pp.37–44.

CASES CITED

Idaho v. Wright, 497 U.S. 805 (1990)
In re Gault, 387 U.S. 1 (1967)
Maryland v. Craig, 497 U.S. 836 (1990)
Schall v. Martin, 467 U.S. 253 (1984)

CHAPTER 12

Gangs and Drugs

Two National Threats

DO YOU KNOW . . .

- Whether the gang problem is increasing or decreasing?
- How the National Gang Threat Assessment classifies gangs?
- What activities gang members frequently engage in?
- What the first step in dealing with a gang problem usually is?
- How gang members might be identified?
- How gang problems might be dealt with?
- If drugs and crime have been proven to be related?
- What approaches have been suggested to address the drug problem?
- What three stages are involved in a drug buy?
- What the critical elements in an illegal drug buy are?
- Why the sale and use of illegal drugs is difficult for police to investigate and prosecute?
- How to avoid a charge of entrapment?
- What the predominant approach to the drug problem in the 1980s was? In the 1990s? Currently?
- What drug abatement statutes do?

CAN YOU DEFINE?

entrapment
flashroll
gang
graffiti
horizontal prosecution
moniker
nystagmus
pulling levers
street gang
turf
vertical prosecution

INTRODUCTION

People often talk about getting their "gang" together. Belonging to a gang is certainly not a crime. Most people belong to groups or organizations. But when a gang engages in violence or crime, it becomes an issue for law enforcement.

The gang problem is exceedingly complex and is often intertwined with other social and criminal justice problems, including drugs and firearms. However, not all gangs deal with drugs, and not all who use drugs commit other crimes. Law enforcement officers must maintain objectivity and refrain from stereotyping gang members and drug users and pushers, realizing that gang members are also at risk for victimization: "Given the link between gang membership and violent victimization, it is important that gang members be viewed not only as offenders by criminal justice practitioners and researchers. Violent victimization is intertwined with gang membership before, during and after youths are gang-involved" (Taylor, 2008, p.133). The same can be said of those involved in using or dealing drugs. Nonetheless, law enforcement must know how to deal with gangs effectively and how to do their part in the war on drugs. Keep in mind, however, that many gangs are not involved in drugs, either using or selling.

The chapter first focuses on the gang problem, beginning with some definitions of gangs and a description of the current gang problem. This is followed by a look at of the types of gangs in the United States, their characteristics and activities. Next is an explanation of why people join gangs and their characteristics and activities, followed by discussions of how to recognize a gang problem, how to identify gang members and how to investigate illegal activities of gangs. The exploration of gangs concludes with an examination of approaches to the gang problem other than investigation, including community policing.

The chapter then turns to the drug problem in the United States and some of the specific drugs involved. This is followed by a description of approaches to combating the drug problem and combating street-level narcotics sales. Next, recognizing people on drugs is discussed, followed by a discussion of legislation as a tool in the war on drugs. The chapter concludes with a description of prevention efforts and on how community policing and problem-oriented policing can enhance efforts to deal with both the gang and the drug problems.

[*A note*: Because the topics of gangs and drugs are both very detailed and complex, with entire texts, courses and, indeed, careers, devoted to addressing these challenges, this chapter cannot possibly cover all of the pertinent information necessary for an effective police response. The companion Web site contains several useful Web resources relating to this chapter.]

GANGS DEFINED

One of the most basic challenges surrounding the issue of gangs is how to define such groups. The Chicago Police Department (*Gang Awareness*, n.d., p.1) defines a gang as "a group which has an organizational structure, leadership and . . . exists or benefits substantially from the criminal activity of its members." A definition commonly accepted by law enforcement is that a gang is any group gathering continuously to commit antisocial behavior. For the purposes of this discussion, we will define a ***gang*** as a group of individuals with a recognized name and symbols who form an allegiance for a common purpose and engage in unlawful activity.

gang
A group of individuals with a recognized name and symbols who form an allegiance for a common purpose and engage in unlawful activity.

Table 12.1 Definitional Characteristics of Gangs

	Average Rank (1 = Least Important, 6 = Most Important)			
Definitional Characteristics	**Larger Cities**	**Suburban Counties**	**Smaller Cities**	**Rural Counties**
Commits Crimes Together	4.8	4.9	4.7	4.5
Has a Name	3.9	3.7	3.3	3.5
Displays Colors or Other Symbols	3.3	3.2	3.3	3.2
Hangs Out Together	3.1	3.0	3.6	3.3
Claims Turf or Territory	3.3	3.1	3.0	2.9
Has a Leader(s)	2.6	3.1	3.0	3.5

Source: National Youth Gang Center (2009). National Youth Gang Analysis.

street gang
"Any durable, street-oriented youth group whose own identity includes involvement in illegal activity."

A broadly applicable definition of street gangs has evolved from intense discussions among working groups of American and European gang researchers over six years in an assembly that has come to be known as the *Eurogang program.* The Eurogang consensus nominal definition of a **street gang** is "any durable, street-oriented youth group whose own identity includes involvement in illegal activity" (Klein, 2007, p.18).

The definition used greatly affects the perceived magnitude of gang problem and may result in over- or underestimation of the nature and extent of the local gang problem. Having a uniform definition would benefit the law enforcement community in several ways. According to the "National Youth Gang Survey Analysis" (2009),

- In general, law enforcement agencies report that group criminality is of greatest importance and the presence of leadership is of least importance in defining a gang.
- Additionally, law enforcement agencies tend to emphasize the same definitional characteristics in defining a gang irrespective of year of gang onset.

Table 12.1 identifies the defining characteristics of a gang.

In addition to differing definitions for gangs, understanding the threat of gangs is made more complex because of the numerous categories that have been established, to be discussed shortly. First, consider the extent of the gang problem.

THE EXTENT OF THE GANG PROBLEM

The *gang* label has been applied to various groups, from the "Spanky and Our Gang" little rascals of the 1920s to the leather-clad, violent, drug-using outlaw motorcycle gangs of the 1950s and 1960s. The last quarter of the 20th century saw significant growth in gang problems across the country. In the 1970s, less than half the states reported youth gang problems, but by the late 1990s, every state and the District of Columbia reported gang activity. During that same period, the number of cities reporting youth gang problems mushroomed nearly tenfold.

According to the *2006 National Youth Gang Survey* (NYGS), published by the Office of Juvenile Justice and Delinquency Prevention (OJJDP), the percentage of law enforcement agencies reporting gang problems *decreased* from 2002 to 2006 (Egley and O'Donnell, 2008). However, the *2007 National Youth Gang Survey* reports, "Following a marked decline from the mid-1990s to the early 2000s, a steady resurgence of gang problems has occurred in recent years" (Egley and O'Donnell, 2009). It seems the downward trend was short-lived because gang activity appears to be on the rise again.

The youth gang problem appears to be increasing.

These findings are supported by the results of the *National Gang Threat Assessment 2009*, which was developed by the National Gang Intelligence Center and the National Drug Intelligence Center, both agencies of the Justice Department: "Most regions in the United States will experience increased gang membership, continued migration of gangs to suburban and rural areas, and increased gang-related criminal activity" (p.13).

It is unclear exactly how many gangs and gang members actively exist in the United States, perhaps because of differing definitions used to identify such activity and membership. For example, Pistole (2008) estimates 30,000 gangs are actively operating within the country, with a total membership of 800,000. The *National Gang Threat Assessment* (2009, p.2), however, reports, "Approximately 1 million gang members belonging to more than 20,000 gangs were criminally active within all 50 states and the District of Columbia as of September 2008." The *Assessment* also presents these key findings (p.2):

- Local street gangs, or neighborhood-based street gangs, remain a significant threat because they continue to account for the largest number of gangs nationwide. Most engage in violence in conjunction with a variety of crimes, including retail-level drug distribution.
- According to NDTS [National Drug Threat Survey] data, 58 percent of state and local law enforcement agencies reported that criminal gangs were active in their jurisdictions in 2008 compared with 45 percent of state and local agencies in 2004.

A Los Angeles Crips member flashes his gang's sign.
© Daniel Lainé/CORBIS

- Gang members are migrating from urban areas to suburban and rural communities, expanding the gangs' influence in most regions; they are doing so for a variety of reasons, including expanding drug distribution territories, increasing illicit revenue, recruiting new members, hiding from law enforcement, and escaping other gangs. Many suburban and rural communities are experiencing increasing gang-related crime and violence because of expanding gang influence.
- Criminal gangs commit as much as 80 percent of the crime in many communities, according to law enforcement officials throughout the nation. Typical gang-related crimes include alien smuggling, armed robbery, assault, auto theft, drug trafficking, extortion, fraud, home invasions, identity theft, murder, and weapons trafficking.
- Gang members are the primary retail-level distributors of most illicit drugs. They also are increasingly distributing wholesale-level quantities of marijuana and cocaine in most urban and suburban communities.
- Some gangs traffic illicit drugs at the regional and national levels; several are capable of competing with U.S.–based Mexican DTOs [drug trafficking organizations].
- U.S.-based gang members illegally cross the U.S.-Mexico border for the express purpose of smuggling illicit drugs and illegal aliens from Mexico into the United States.
- Many gangs actively use the Internet to recruit new members and to communicate with members in other areas of the United States and in foreign countries.
- Street gangs and outlaw motorcycle gangs pose a growing threat to law enforcement along the U.S.–Canada border. They frequently associate with Canadian-based gangs and criminal organizations to facilitate various criminal activities, including drug smuggling into the United States.

TYPES OF GANGS

Just as there are many ways to define gangs, there are many ways to classify or "type" gangs, such as by ethnicity or region of origin (e.g., Asian gangs, African American gangs, Hispanic gangs, etc.), criminal activity (e.g., drug gangs, auto theft gangs), and location of activity (e.g., street, prison, etc.). According to Klein (pp.54–55),

> There is no *one* form of street gang. Gangs can be large or small, long term or short term, more or less territorial, more or less criminally involved, and so on. If one treats all gangs as being the same, then the treatment will often be wrong, perhaps even making things worse. . . . It is the fact of gang diversity itself that should make us cautious about generalizing too quickly about their nature. . . .
>
> "Compressed" gangs, primarily adolescent groups of 50 to 100 members and less then ten years' duration, are the most common, found in both large and small cities. Least common are "collective" gangs, rather amorphous, but large collections with little internal structure, sometimes held together by loose

neighborhood ties and extensive drug dealing. The smallest in size of our five types, but the most tightly structured, is the "specialty" gang, which is not versatile like the other four types, but rather manifests a narrow pattern of criminal behavior. Drug gangs, robbery or burglary gangs, car theft gangs and skinheads are common examples.

The *National Gang Threat Assessment* notes that gangs vary extensively in membership, structure, age and ethnicity, but three basic types of gangs have been identified by gang investigators: street gangs, prison gangs, and outlaw motorcycle gangs (OMGs) (2009, pp.6–8).

The *National Gang Threat Assessment* classifies gangs as street gangs, prison gangs and outlaw motorcycle gangs.

The *Assessment* states that *street gangs* are the largest and control the greatest geographical area, with the threat becoming magnified as national- and regional-level street gangs migrate from urban areas to suburban and rural communities. National street gangs typically have several hundred to several thousand members nationwide. Regional-level street gangs typically have several hundred to several thousand members. Local street gangs usually range in membership from three to several hundred.

Prison gangs are a serious domestic threat, especially those affiliated with Mexican DTOs, and maintain substantial influence over street gangs in the communities in which they operate. They also operate in local communities through members who have been released from prison and resume their former street gang affiliations.

Outlaw motorcycle gangs (OMGs) are a threat because of their wide-ranging criminal activity, propensity to use violence and ability to counter law enforcement efforts. As of June 2008, state and local law enforcement agencies estimate that between 280 and 520 OMGs are operating at the national, regional and local levels, with more than 20,000 validated OMG members residing in the United States.

Criminal activity is one of the distinguishing characteristics of a gang and a way to distinguish gangs by "type." Table 12.2 summarizes the major types of criminal organizations, most of which are gangs, listing their names and the types of criminal activity they commonly engage in.

Criminal activities of gangs are discussed in greater depth later in the chapter. A note about street gangs versus drug gangs: Not all street gangs are involved in drug dealing. Although many street gangs do engage in the drug business to a degree, some gangs are formed expressly to deal drugs.

Female Gangs

According to the *National Gang Threat Assessment* (2009, p.12), "Female involvement in gangs continues to increase and evolve as females assume greater responsibility in gang activities and grow more independent from their male counterparts. Though gangs are still male-dominated, research indicates that female gang membership is on the rise." The report also states that although

Table 12.2 Criminal Organizations

Type of Group	Subtype of Group	Specific Groups and Distinct Gangs	Criminal Activity
Asian Gangs	Chinese street gangs, Triads, Tongs	Flying Dragons, Fuk Ching, Ghost Shadows, Ping On, Taiwan Brotherhood, United Bamboo, Wah Ching, White Tigers	Extortion of Chinese businesses, gambling, heroin distribution, exploitation of recent immigrants; smuggling of humans
	Japanese gangs (Boryokudan or Yakuza)	Kumlai, Sumiyoshi Rengo, Yamaguchi Gumi	Gambling, prostitution and sex trade, money laundering, trafficking in weapons and drugs
	Korean gangs	American Burger (AB), Flying Dragons, Junior Korean Power, Korean Killers (KK), Korean Power	Prostitution, massage parlors, gambling, loan-sharking, extortion of Korean businesses (particularly produce markets and restaurants)
	Laotian/Cambodian/ Vietnamese gangs	Born to Kill (BTK), Laotian Bloods (LBs), Richtown Crips, Tiny Oriental Crips, Tiny Rascal Gang (TRG)[1]	Strong arm and violent crimes related to business extortion; home invasion for theft of gold, jewelry, and money coupled with rape to deter reporting; street crimes; prostitution; drug trafficking; assault; murder
	Hmong gangs	Cobra gang, Menace of Destruction (MOD), Oriental Ruthless Boys, Totally Gangster Crips, Totally Mafia Crips, True Asian Crips, True Crip Gangsters, True Lady Crips (female Hmongs), True Local Crips, Westside Crips, White Tigers	Gang rape, prostitution, burglary, auto theft, vandalism, home invasion, street crimes, strong arm robbery of businesses, drug trafficking, assault, murder
Latin American gangs	Mexican	18th Street gang, Sureños-Mexican Mafia, Norteños-Nuestra Family, Tijuana Cartel-ArellanoFelix organization, Colima Cartel-Amazcua Contreras brothers, Juarez Cartel-Amado Carillo Fuentes group, Sonora Cartel-Miguel Caro Quintero organization, Sinaloa Cartel-Guzman/Leora organization, Guadalajara Cartel-Rafael Caro Quintero/ Miguel Angel Felix Gallardo, Gulf Cartel	Drug trafficking (cocaine, crack, heroin, marijuana), counterfeiting, pickpocketing money laundering, murder
	Cuban	Cuban Mafia	Drug trafficking (cocaine, crack, heroin, marijuana), counterfeiting, pickpocketing money laundering, murder
	Puerto Rican	Latin Kings, Puerto Rican Stones	Street crimes, drug trafficking, burglary, assault, rape, murder
	Columbian gangs and cartels	Cali Cartel, Medellin Cartel, Norte Del Valle Cartel, North Coast Cartel, Bogota Cartel, Santander DeQuilichao Cartel, Black Eagles, AUC, ELN, FARC	Drug trafficking (cocaine, crack, heroin, marijuana), counterfeiting, pickpocketing money laundering, murder
	El Salvadoran gangs	Mara Salvatrucha 13 (MS-13)	Street crimes, strong arming businesses, assault, drug trafficking, rape, murder
	Peruvian gangs	Shining Path—guerilla organization with a mission for Maoist government	Vandalism and other property damage, assault, rape, murder
Jamaican posses		Shower posse, Spangler posse	Drug trafficking (cocaine, crack, marijuana), weapons trafficking, trafficking green cards
Nigerian gangs		Nigerian Criminal Enterprise (NCE)	Heroin smuggling (via mules) and heroin dealing, credit card fraud, infiltration of private security, planned bankruptcy of companies, exploitation of other Africans

(continued)

Table 12.2 Criminal Organizations (*continued*)

Type of Group	Subtype of Group	Specific Groups and Distinct Gangs	Criminal Activity
Somali gangs		Somali Outlaws, Somalian Hot Boyz, Murda Gang, Somali Mafia, Ma Thug Boys, Ruff Tuff Somali Crips[2]	Street crimes, strong arming businesses, drug trafficking, assault, rape, murder
Russian (**or Soviet**) **gangs**		Evangelical Russian Mafia, Malina/Organizatsiya, Odessa Mafia, Gypsy gangs	Theft (diamonds, furs, gold) and fencing stolen goods, export and sale of stolen Russian religious art and gold, extortion, insurance fraud, money laundering, counterfeiting, daisy chain tax evasion schemes, credit card scams and fraud, smuggling illegal immigrants, drug trafficking
Street gangs	African American, Caucasian, Hispanic, and others	Disciples, Latin Kings, Vice Lords, Dog Pound, and many others, including variants of Bloods/Crips (e.g., Westside Crips or Rolling Crips)	Motor vehicle theft, drug sales (especially crack and marijuana), weapons trafficking, assaults, drive-by shootings, robbery, theft and fencing stolen property, vandalism, graffiti
Drug-trafficking gangs	Traditional street gangs	Bloods, Crips, Gangster Disciples, Latin Kings, and many others	Drug trafficking (heroin, cocaine, crack, and other drugs), violence, arson, indirect prostitution, vandalism, property crime, strong-arm robbery. African American gangs known for crack; Chicano gangs known for heroin and crack
	International drug cartels	Medellin cartel, Cali cartel	Drug trafficking (cocaine, crack, heroin, marijuana)
Graffiti or tagger crews (also tagger posses, mobs, tribes, and piecers)		Known by three-letter monikers such as NBT (Nothing But Trouble) or ETC (Elite Tagger Crew)	Graffiti vandalism, tag-banging in which violence occurs
Prison gangs		Aryan Brotherhood, Black Guerilla Family, Consolidated Crip Organization, Mexican Mafia, Nuestra Familia, Texas Syndicate	Drug trafficking, prostitution, extortion, protection, murder for hire
Outlaw motorcycle gangs (**OMGs**)		Hell's Angels, Outlaws, Pagans, Bandidos	Drug trafficking (methamphetamine/crank, speed, ice, PCP, LSD, angel dust), weapons trafficking, chop shops, massage parlors, strip bars, prostitution, arson
Hate groups (including militias and terrorist groups, which also share a focus on ideology)		Aryan Nation, Ku Klux Klan (KKK), skinheads (White Aryan Resistance or WAR), American Nazi Party, Christian Defense League	Bombings, counterfeiting, loan fraud, armored car and bank robberies, theft rings
La Cosa Nostra (**aka the Mafia**)		Families such as Bonnano, Columbo, Gambino, Genovese, and Lucchese	Gambling; loan-sharking; corruption of public officials and institutions; extortion; money laundering; theft of precious metals, food, and clothing; fencing stolen property; labor racketeering; stock manipulation; securities fraud; weapons trafficking; drug trafficking (particularly heroin distribution); systemic use of violence as a tool in business transactions; murder

Note: Although nationality and ethnicity are often unifying characteristics of criminal organizations and used to identify them, this view is overly narrow and promotes ethnic stereotypes. The organization of criminal groups by nationality and ethnicity in this table is not intended to suggest that criminal behavior is characteristic of any group; ethnicity, however, is often a marker to police.

[1]TRG's originated as a Cambodian gang but now allow Laotian members.

[2]Somali gangs often change their name, colors and signs every few months. For example, the Somali Outlaws, Hot Boys, and Murda Gang are all one gang that has changed its identity. Somali Mafia and Ma Thugs are break-offs of these gangs.

Source: Table data based partly on Deborah Lamm Weisel. "Criminal Investigation." *In Local Government Police Management*, edited by William A. Geller and Darrel W. Stephens. Washington, DC: International City/County Management Association, 2003, p.270. Modified and updated by Kären M. Hess, Christine H. Orthmann, and Henry L. Cho.

predominantly female gangs continue to be rare, they are infrequently the focus of law enforcement, which is less likely to recognize or stop female gang members.

Hybrid Gangs

A new breed of increasingly violent street gangs appearing throughout the country are hybrid gangs, in which several small groups, some of them rivals, band together into one larger gang (Ortega and Calderoni, 2007). Members of hybrid gangs are generally young and particularly profit-driven. These gangs thrive in areas with relatively new gang problems and often include gangbangers who have migrated from larger cities. These gangs represent a "sea of change in gang culture" and bear little resemblance to traditional gangs. Unlike older gangs based on race or neighborhood loyalty, this new generation is singularly focused on making money from drugs, robbery and prostitution.

WHY PEOPLE JOIN GANGS

Many factors contribute to the development of delinquent gangs, including dropping out of school, unemployment, family disorganization, cultural transition, neighborhood traditions of gang delinquency and ethnic status. Gangs provide acceptance and protection to inner-city youth, a sense of belonging and being nurtured, and a sort of surrogate family for those who lack a stable, functional traditional family. For some, gangs provide structure—rules to live by and a code of conduct. Often, gangs provide economic opportunity through criminal activity. Others are drawn to a gang simply for the excitement. Table 12.3 lists numerous factors placing an individual at risk for becoming a gang member.

Research by Bell (2009, p.363) found few differences between boys and girls in risk factors associated with gang membership and outcomes associated with gang involvement: "The results indicate that parental social control, attachment and involvement; school safety; peer fighting; age; and race similarly influence boys' and girls' gang involvement."

GANG CULTURE AND ORGANIZATION

Some gang experts talk about the three Rs of the gang culture: reputation, respect and revenge. Reputation is of prime concern to the gang members, both individually and collectively. They expect, indeed demand, respect. And they are required to show disrespect for rival gang members, called a *dis* in gang slang. Disrespect inevitably leads to the third R—revenge. Every challenge must be answered, often in the form of a drive-by shooting. Noted criminologist David Kennedy is quoted as saying: "The code of the street has reached a point where not responding to a slight can destroy a reputation, while violence is a sure way to enhance it" (Straub, 2008, p.1).

Gang members have differing levels of commitment and involvement in gang activities. Most gang members are either hard-core, associate, or

Table 12.3 Risk Factors for Youth Gang Membership

Domain	Risk Factors
Community	Social disorganization, including poverty and residential mobility Organized lower-class communities Underclass communities Presence of gangs in the neighborhood Availability of drugs in the neighborhood Availability of firearms Barriers to and lack of social and economic opportunities Lack of social capital Cultural norms supporting gang behavior Feeling unsafe in neighborhood: high crime Conflict with social control institutions
Family	Family disorganization, including broken homes and parental drug/alcohol abuse Troubled families, including incest, family violence and drug addiction Family members in a gang Lack of adult male role models Lack of parental role models Low socioeconomic status Extreme economic deprivation, family management problems, parents with violent attitudes, sibling antisocial behavior
School	Academic failure Low educational aspirations, especially among females Negative labeling by teachers Trouble at school Few teacher role models Educational frustration Low commitment to school, low school attachment, high levels of antisocial behavior in school, low achievement test scores and identification as being learning disabled
Peer group	High commitment to delinquent peers Low commitment to positive peers Street socialization Gang members in class Friends who use drugs or who are gang members Friends who are drug distributors Interaction with delinquent peers
Individual	Prior delinquency Deviant attitudes Street smartness: toughness Defiant and individualistic character Fatalistic view of the world Aggression Proclivity for excitement and trouble *Locura* (acting in a daring, courageous, and especially crazy fashion in the face of adversity) Higher levels of normlessness in the context of family, peer group and school Social disabilities Illegal gun ownership Early or precocious sexual activity, especially among females Alcohol and drug use Drug trafficking Desire for group rewards, such as status, identity, self-esteem, companionship and protection Problem behaviors, hyperactivity, externalizing behaviors, drinking, lack of refusal skills and early sexual activity Victimization

Source: James C. Howell. *Youth Gangs: An Overview.* Washington, DC: Office of Juvenile Justice and Delinquency Prevention, August 1998, pp.6–7. (NCJ 167249)

peripheral members. The hard-core members are those most dedicated to the gang. Knowing how a gang is organized and what level of involvement a member has can be of great assistance to investigators. The hard-core member is least likely to cooperate with the police; the peripheral members are most likely to be cooperative.

A gang's degree of organization influences the behavior observed among its members, with even low levels of organization having important implications regarding criminality: "Indeed, even incremental increases in gang organization are related to increased involvement in offending and victimization" (Decker et al., 2008, p.153).

CRIMINAL ACTIVITIES OF GANGS

Street gang members engage in a wide variety of illegal activities, from underage drinking and vandalism, to drug use and drug selling, petty theft, auto theft, assault, robbery and homicide. And although most gang crime consists of relatively minor offenses, such as property damage, theft, and the like, the more serious, albeit infrequent, crimes, such as robbery, assault and murder, garner more publicity: "It is these more serious offenses that capture media attention, create fear in some communities, and end up

Table 12.4 Criminal Activity by Gang Type

Crime	Percent of Police Who Report That Violent Gangs Commit the Offense Very Often or Often (n = 223)	Percent of Police Who Report That Drug-Dealing Gangs Commit the Offense Very Often or Often (n = 148)	Percent of Police Who Report That Entrepreneurial Gangs Commit the Offense Very Often or Often (n = 75)
Motor Vehicle Theft	25	25	44
Arson	1	1	1
Assault	87	69	57
Burglary	36	25	37
Drive-by Shooting	42	49	32
Crack Sale	55	80	39
Powder Cocaine Sale	23	46	29
Marijuana Sale	35	54	33
Other Drug Sale	17	26	25
Graffiti	67	50	38
Home Invasion	10	11	27
Intimidation	81	72	74
Rape	7	4	8
Robbery	33	30	36
Shooting	37	41	38
Theft	49	37	52
Vandalism	57	38	37

Note: Reflects aggregation of police estimates of participation in criminal activity by a gang of that type in the jurisdiction.
Source: Deborah Lamm Weisel. "The Evolution of Street Gangs: An Examination of Form and Variation." In *Responding to Gangs: Evaluation and Research*, edited by Winifred L. Reed and Scott H. Decker. Washington, DC: National Institute of Justice, July 2002, p.36. (NCJ 190351)

receiving the most concentrated attention of the police and the courts" (Klein, 2007, p.37).

Disagreement exists over "which comes first," so to speak: gang involvement or criminal activity. Some contend that joining a gang leads youths into criminal activity, but others assert criminally minded youth are more likely to become gang-involved. Several studies have shown that although most youths were delinquent before joining a gang, their delinquency increased as a result of joining. Tita and Ridgeway (2007, p.208) report, "Research has demonstrated that even after controlling for individual level attributes, individuals who join gangs commit more crimes than do nongang members. Furthermore, the offending level of gang members is higher when they report being active members of the gang. Therefore, gang membership clearly facilitates offending above and beyond individual level characteristics." Table 12.4 compares gang and nongang criminal behavior by gang type.

Gang members often engage in vandalism, drug dealings, larceny/theft, burglary/breaking and entering, aggravated assault, motor vehicle theft and drive-by shootings.

RECOGNIZING A GANG PROBLEM

Many communities are blind to local gang activity. However, gang members usually make their presence known, thriving on attention and recognition. They go unseen only when law enforcement officers, educators and parents fail to recognize the signs of gang activity. Such failure to recognize or acknowledge the existence of gang activity, whether willingly or through the lack of gang identification training, dramatically increases a gang's ability to thrive and develop a power base.

The first step in dealing with a gang problem is to recognize it.

Gang graffiti marks the gang's turf.
Stephen Wilkes/The Image Bank/Getty Images

Identifying specific gangs can be challenging, but a school or community can be aware of warning signs of a gang problem: graffiti, obvious colors of clothing, tattoos, initiations, hand signals or handshakes, uncommon terms or phrases and a sudden change in behavior.

IDENTIFYING GANGS AND GANG MEMBERS

Gang members take pride in belonging to their specific gangs and will make their membership known in various ways.

Gang members identify themselves by their names, clothing, tattoos, sign language, slang and graffiti.

moniker
A gang member's street name.

Many gang members have a street name, called a **moniker**. Often, more than one gang member has the same moniker. The color and type of clothing can also indicate gang membership. For example, Bloods are identified by red or green colors. Crips are associated with blue or purple bandanas or scarves. Many have tattoos, and they frequently flash hand signs or use sign language for quick communication.

Gang members speak a distinct language, and knowing street slang can help officers identify persons as gang members and facilitate communication with these individuals during interviews or interrogations. In the field, police officers are likely to hear gang-related street lingo, such as *set, mix, trey-eight, five-oh*, and infinitely more. Because of space limitations, we cannot possibly list all of the slang officers might find useful. However, many online resources are available to familiarize the reader with some of the more common gang slang (see the list at the end of this chapter). For example, the Gangs OR Us Web site provides an index for gang and hip-hop slang, as well as a link for conducting safe and effective field contacts with gang-involved parolees, relying heavily on the knowledge of gang language.

turf
The territory claimed by a gang, often marked by graffiti.

graffiti
Symbols and slogans written on walls and sides of buildings, often by gang members to mark their turf.

Most gangs establish a specific area, their **turf**, which they mark with **graffiti** (symbols and slogans written on walls and sides of buildings) and will defend to the death. They control their turf through intimidation and violence. Police officers can learn much about gang activity if graffiti appears in their jurisdiction. Graffiti may list gang members' names, often in order of authority. The most graffiti will appear in the center of the turf area. Graffiti crossed out or overwritten is often the challenge of a rival gang. If gang symbols are written upside down, this graffiti is usually written by a rival gang and is a great insult to the gang it depicts. Gang members caught crossing out a rival's graffiti are usually severely beaten or even killed. (See Figure 12.1).

Weisel (2007, p.1) reports, "As with most forms of vandalism, graffiti is not routinely reported to police. Many people think that graffiti is not a police or 'real crime' problem, or that the police can do little about it. Because graffiti is not routinely reported to police or other agencies, its true scope is unknown. But graffiti has become a major concern, and the mass media, including movies and Web sites glamorizing or promoting graffiti as an acceptable form of urban street art, have contributed to its spread."

M.O.B. Member of Bloods

CK Crip Killa

Dog paw made up of three dots

The number **5** and five-point star signify alliance with People Nation

Refer to each other as "dawgs" and "Crip Killers"

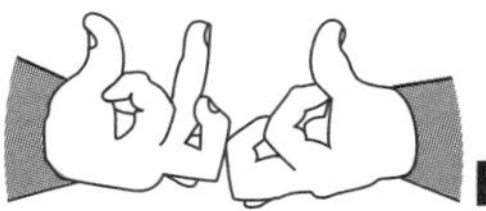

M.O.B.

Bloods

BK Blood Killer

The number **6** and six-point star signify alliance with Folk Nation

Refer to each other as "cuz" (cousin) and "Blood Killers"

Crips

Set of People Nation, allied with Bloods

The number **5** and five-point star signify alliance with Bloods

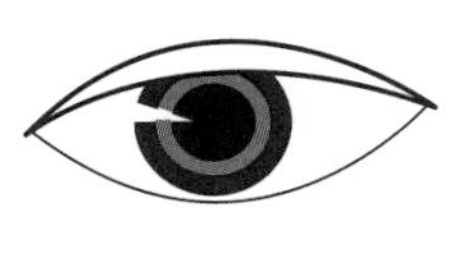

Vice Lords (People Nation)

GD Gangster Disciples, set of Folk Nation, allied with Crips

The number **74** signifying **G**, the 7th letter of the alphabet, **D** the 4th.

Gangster Disciples (Folk Nation)

13 means *Sureño*

Three- or five-point crown signifies Latin Kings

ADR *Amor de rey* (Love of the king)

13

A.D.R.

MS - 13

Mi Vida Loca (My crazy life)

Three- or five-point crown signifies Latin Kings

Latino Gangs: Latin Kings, Sureños 13, MS-13

Asian Boyz

Tien	Money
Tinh	Love
Tu	Prison
Toi	Crime
Thu	Revenge

Asian Gangs

Aryan Brotherhood

G27

Group 27

Mexican Mafia

Nuestra Familia

Prison

Nickname

Position

Outlaw patch

Top rocker (gang/club)

Logo

Bottom rocker (city/state)

B = Bandidos = **2**

O = Outlaws = **15**

P = Pagans = **16**

HA = Hell's Angels = **81**

Outlaw Motorcycle

FIGURE 12.1 A sampling of gang symbols, including graffiti and hand signs.

Source: From HESS/ORTHMANN. *Criminal Investigation*, 9E. © 2010 Delmar Learning, a part of Cengage Learning, Inc. Reproduced by permission. www.cengage.com/permissions.

Graffiti complainants are rising in the United States, with some cities reporting a doubling in calls about defaced property (Schrader, 2009). In the broken windows crime model, graffiti is a foothold crime leading to a neighborhood's decay: "Neighborhoods plagued with graffiti often become breading grounds for loitering, littering, loud music, and public urination. . . . As 'good' citizens begin to avoid 'that side of town,' the criminal element becomes more comfortable and these small public disorder crimes snowball into more serious criminal behaviors. When these more serious crimes flourish, it becomes difficult to assess the true cost of the graffiti offense: expenses mount in terms of prevention, arrests, incarceration, and lost revenue" (Petrocelli, 2008, p.18).

Some agencies and regions have devised checklists to help law enforcement identify gang members, and some states have created databases to track known gang members that have had police contact.

In Practice

GANG POINTER FILE

In Minnesota, the Bureau of Criminal Apprehension (BCA) was tasked in 1997 to create a tracking system as a part of a legislative antigang initiative. The system is called Gang Pointer File, and it is used as a law enforcement tool. To be entered into the system, a person must have been found guilty of a felony or gross misdemeanor and be at least 14 years of age.

Additionally, a 10-point criteria must be met: The person

1. Admits gang membership or association.
2. Is observed to associate on a regular basis with known gang members.
3. Has tattoos indicating gang membership.
4. Wears gang symbols to identify with a specific gang.
5. Is in a photo with known gang members or using gang-related hand signs.
6. Has name on a gang document, hit list, or gang related graffiti.
7. Is identified as a gang member by a reliable source.
8. Is arrested in the company of identified gang members or associates.
9. Corresponds with known gang members or writes and/or receives correspondence about gang activities.
10. Writes about gangs (graffiti) on walls, books and paper.

The "National Youth Gang Survey Analysis" reports how respondents identified individuals as gang members:

- For larger and smaller cities and suburban counties, a clear majority of agencies emphasize the use of the self-nomination technique compared with other criteria (e.g., arrested or associates with known gang members; tattoos, colors, or other symbols; identified by a reliable source) in identifying and documenting individuals as gang members in their jurisdictions.
- The previous pattern is similar for rural counties but with a noticeably greater emphasis on the display of tattoos, colors, or other symbols as a means for designating gang membership.

INVESTIGATING GANGS' ILLEGAL ACTIVITIES

The same procedures used in investigating any other kind of illegal activity apply to investigating gangs' illegal activities. Information and evidence must support the elements of specific offenses and link gang members to those offenses.

It is often difficult to obtain information about a gang's illegal activities because the gang members stick together and will intimidate the people living and working within their turf. Businesspeople and residents alike are usually fearful of telling the police anything, believing the gang will harm them if they do. Furthermore, many immigrant communities, who may be easy targets for gang victimization, have a basic distrust of law enforcement because of the government corruption in their home countries. Many of the same gang members who commit crimes against these immigrants may be related in some way or be the children of family friends. Other challenges faced in dealing with victimized immigrant populations, which can seriously thwart effective police investigation of gang activity, are the language and cultural barriers.

If a neighborhood canvass is conducted and information is received, it is important that the canvass not stop at that point. This would implicate the house or business at which the canvass was terminated as the source of information. In addition, more information might be available from a source not yet contacted during the canvass.

Crime scenes that involve gangs are unique. Often, the crime scene is part of a chain of events. When a gang assault occurs, for example, often a chase precedes the assault, considerably widening the crime scene. If vehicles are involved, the assault is probably by a rival gang. If no vehicles appear to have been involved, the suspects are probably local, perhaps even members of the same gang as the victim. This frequently occurs when narcotics, girlfriends or family disputes are involved. Evidence obtained in gang investigations is processed in the same way as evidence related to any other crime.

Reading Graffiti

Savelli (2004, p.9) suggests, "The key to understanding gang graffiti is being able to analyze the symbols, indicators and terminology used by gangs. Simply, gangs use graffiti to send messages." The purposes of these messages are

- To mark the gang's turf (territory).
- To disrespect a rival gang or gang member.
- To memorialize a deceased gang member.
- To make a statement.
- To conduct business.
- To serve as artistic expression.

Savelli (2004, p.15) notes, "While it is important to read the writing on the walls, it is equally important to cover it over as soon as possible. Don't give the gang a chance to claim your community as their turf by allowing their graffiti to stay intact. . . . When dealing with graffiti, it is recommended to:

- Photograph it (the whole piece and in sections).
- Analyze it while it is intact.
- Remove it (paint over it, sandblast it, etc.).
- Keep an archive of the photo.
- Document the colors used.

Table 12.5 Methods Used for Gathering Information on Gangs, Ranked by "Often Used" Category

	Never Used	Sometimes Used	Often Used
Internal contacts with patrol officers and detectives	1	22	64
Internal departmental records and computerized files	4	22	62
Review of offense reports	2	25	60
Interviews with gang members	5	26	56
Information obtained from other local police agencies	1	35	51
Surveillance activities	6	37	44
Use of unpaid informants	2	44	42
Information obtained from other criminal justice agencies	3	43	42
Information obtained from other governmental agencies	3	47	37
Provision of information by schools	2	50	35
Reports from state agencies	11	63	14
Use of paid informants	28	46	13
Reports from federal agencies	16	62	9
Information obtained from private organizations	27	51	9
Infiltration of police officers into gangs or related groups	75	11	2

Source: James W. Stevens. "Youth Gangs' Dimensions." *The Encyclopedia of Police Science*, 2nd ed., edited by William G. Bailey. New York: Garland, 1995, p.832. Reprinted by permission.

- Document the gang 'Tag' names.
- Document the indicators of 'beef' or violence.
- Get involved in, or create, an antigraffiti program to cover over all graffiti. Get the youths involved!"

Obtaining and Recording Information

The most common way to gather information about gangs is internal contacts with patrol officers and detectives, followed by internal departmental records and computerized files and then by review of offense reports.

An effective records system is critical in dealing with any gang problem. Information is an essential tool for law enforcement and should include the following: type of gang (street, motorcycle, etc.), ethnic composition, number of active and associate members, territory, hideouts, types of crimes usually committed and method of operation, leadership and members known to be violent. Table 12.5 shows the methods used for gathering information on gangs.

Departments can use improving technology by combining the efforts of sworn officers and the capabilities of the information technology (IT) staff with its computer-aid dispatch (CAD) and records management system (RMS) to deliver accurate, timely information on gang activity directly to patrol officers who need it, thus maximizing their effectiveness when dealing with known gang members (Posey, 2008, p.39).

Geographic information system (GIS) technology has been used to create computerized maps that analyze the spatial and temporal distribution of gang activity.

A total community effort is needed to combat gangs and drugs. Public service announcements placed throughout a community help remind citizens of the vital role they play in making their neighborhoods safer.
© alam/Alamy

APPROACHES TO THE GANG PROBLEM

Four general strategies are being used to deal with gang problems: (1) suppression or law-enforcement efforts, (2) social intervention, (3) opportunities to prevent gang involvement and (4) community organization.

The most effective approach is probably a combination of prevention, intervention and suppression strategies. More specific strategies might include not tolerating graffiti, targeting hard-core gang leaders and consolidating major gang-control functions. Table 12.6 shows the law enforcement strategies being used, with what frequency and with what perceived effectiveness if used.

Although in-state information exchange was the most used strategy, it was also among those judged least effective. Street sweeps and other suppression tactics were used by less than half the departments, but their effectiveness was judged high.

Suppression

As might be expected, law enforcement agencies view suppression tactics, such as street sweeps, intensified surveillance and hotspot targeting; crime prevention activities; and community collaboration—in that order—as most effective in preventing and controlling gang crime. "In response to the surge in violent crime, and the public's demand for quick, impressive action, many police departments have moved away from community policing, relying instead

Table 12.6 Law Enforcement Strategies and Perceived Effectiveness*

Strategy	Used (Percent)	Judged Effective (If Used) (Percent)
Some or a lot of use		
Targeting entry points	14	17
Gang laws	40	19
Selected violations	76	42
Out-of-state information exchange	53	16
In-state information exchange	90	17
In-city information exchange	55	18
Federal agency operational coordination	40	16
State agency operational coordination	50	13
Local agency operational coordination	78	16
Community collaboration	64	54
Any use		
Street sweeps	40	62
Other suppression tactics	44	63
Crime prevention activities	15	56

*Percentage of cities $n = 211$. The number of cities responding to each question varied slightly.
Source: James C. Howell. *Youth Gang Programs and Strategies.* Washington, DC: OJJDP, August 2000, p.46. (NCJ 171154)

on traditional law enforcement strategies to fight crime. Tactical enforcement teams, 'stop and frisk' initiatives, neighborhood sweeps, gang injunctions, and public housing 'bar out' (a 'no-trespass' policy used by public housing authorities to reduce drug activity and other crimes) have been used to target and reduce violent crime" (Straub, 2008, p.1).

pulling levers

Cracking down on any type of criminal activity and telling gang members that the crackdown will continue until the violence stops.

One of the most successful suppression responses is **pulling levers**, a deterrence response targeting gang members with chronic involvement in serious crime and setting clear expectations for their behavior: If expectations are not met by even one individual, all members of the gang are subjected to intensified supervision and other forms of enhanced enforcement (Dedel, 2007, p.23). Levers might include arrest for even the slightest infraction such as jaywalking, restricting property (vehicle, housing) ownership, vehicle licensure, enforcing child support payments, asset forfeiture and warrants. At the same time, prosocial alternatives for compliance such as education and employment opportunities, drug treatment, tattoo removal and the like are offered, resulting in a carrot-and-stick approach.

Very similar to the pulling levers approach is the "focused deterrence" approach, also referred to as the High Point (North Carolina) Intervention. This approach puts offenders on notice that their community wants them to stop dealing drugs, that help is available, and that their particular criminal actions will bring heightened law enforcement attention. Kennedy (2009) describes how the High Point Intervention works:

> A particular drug market is identified; violent dealers are arrested; and the nonviolent dealers are brought to a "call-in" where they face a roomful of law enforcement officers, social service providers, community figures, ex-offenders

> and "influentials"—parents, relatives and others with close, important relationships with particular dealers. The drug dealers are told that (1) they are valuable to the community, and (2) the dealing must stop. They are offered social services. They are informed that local law enforcement has worked up cases on them, but that these cases will be "banked" (temporarily suspended). Then they are given an ultimatum: If you continue to deal, the banked cases against you will be activated.

Federal agents are using immigration violations to arrest and deport scores of gang members across the country (Leinwand, 2007). Gang member arrests have increased 73 percent since 2006.

Gang Units and Task Forces

Much like vice and narcotics, gang units are highly specialized in the area of crime enforcement with a focus on gangs. Gang units typically use criminal informants and often are proactive in creating investigations in enforcing laws on gang members. The units also use many of the same methods of enforcement as vice or narcotics, such as surveillance, undercover operations, and so on. This assignment is considered a highly dangerous, as well as respected, aspect of law enforcement.

The National Youth Gang Survey defines a *gang unit* as "a specialized unit with at least two officers primarily assigned to handle matters related to youth gangs." Respondents to the 2006 survey provided the following information regarding the operation of a gang unit in their agencies ("National Youth Gang Survey Analysis," 2009):

- Approximately four in ten law enforcement agencies with a gang problem operated a gang unit in 2006, including 54 percent of larger cities.
- With the exception of smaller cities, the percentage of agencies operating a gang unit increased yearly and was highest in 2006.
- In 2006, 31 percent of law enforcement agencies with a gang problem that did not operate a gang unit reported that one or more officers were assigned to handle gang problems exclusively.

Gang units typically engage in one or more of five main functions: intelligence, enforcement/suppression, investigations, intervention and prevention. The intelligence component gathers information about gangs, analyzes it for trends and manages other data related to gang activity. The suppression component involves collaboration between police, probation and prosecution, targeting the most active gang members and leaders. The investigations component focuses on building cases involving gang-related crime. The intervention component includes giving gang members the chance to finish high school or obtain a GED, to have tattoos removed, to obtain gainful employment and legal assistance. The prevention component includes conflict resolution skills and peer counseling.

In some states with statewide agencies, a gang task force comprises law enforcement officers in multiple jurisdictions. Collaboration among law enforcement agencies can greatly enhance efforts to cope with the gang problem: "Fighting gang-related crime with traditional methods is a lot like putting out a forest fire with a measuring cup—something's being done, but in the long run it's a futile gesture" (Moore, 2007b, p.52). Multiagency task forces bring together differing perspectives and focus manpower and resources on a common goal, providing a more effective response to the issue of gangs.

Gang-Related Legislation, Injunctions, and Ordinances

"Highlights of Gang-Related Legislation" (2008) reports the following:

- 46 states and the District of Columbia (DC) have enacted some form of legislation relating to gangs.
- Gang prevention legislation is gaining momentum, with nearly one-fourth of all states having passed gang prevention laws.
- One-half of the states have laws that provide for enhanced penalties for gang-related criminal acts.
- Over half of the states have laws against graffiti.
- 22 states' public nuisance laws count gang activity among the factors in determining a nuisance. Indiana has defined real estate/dwellings as "psychologically affected property" if they are the locations of criminal gang activity. By law, this factor must be disclosed in real estate transactions.
- 36 states and DC have legislation that defines "gang."
- 21 states define "gang crime/activity."
- 21 states have legislation relating to gangs and schools.
- Only 10 percent of the states have enacted laws that address gangs within correctional facilities.

Some states have also passed laws that automatically increase the severity level of a crime if it is gang-associated in any way.

Civil gang injunctions (CGIs) are neighborhood-level interventions intended to disrupt a gang's routine activities. The injunction targets specific individuals as well as unnamed gang members who intimidate residents by restricting their activities within the boundaries of a defined geographic area.

Another approach to the gang problem in some cities is to pass an antigang ordinance. Such an ordinance was passed in Sunnyside, Washington, to allow police to aggressively pursue individuals who engage in peripheral gang activities. The ordinance makes joining a gang illegal and prohibits hand signals, wearing gang-related clothes and other typical gang activities. This ordinance, however, is being opposed by the Washington ACLU, which claims that it could lead to racial profiling, a finding many gang experts find "baffling," given that race is paramount in gang activity (Moore, 2007a, p.98).

Injunctions and ordinances may be challenged as unconstitutional violations of the freedom of speech, the right of association and due process rights if they do not clearly delineate how officers may apply such orders. For example, Chicago passed a gang congregation ordinance to combat the problems created by the city's street gangs. During the three years following passage of the ordinance, Chicago police officers issued more than 89,000 dispersal orders and arrested more than 42,000 people. But in *Chicago v. Morales* (1999), the Supreme Court struck down the ordinance as unconstitutional because its vague wording failed to provide adequate standards to guide police discretion.

Vertical Prosecution and Special Prosecution Units

Vertical prosecution and using special prosecution units are methods thought to increase the efficiency and effectiveness of bringing gang-related cases before the court. **Vertical prosecution** involves having one assistant prosecutor or a small group of assistant prosecutors handle a criminal complaint from start to finish through the entire court process. This is in contrast to **horizontal prosecution**, where different assistant prosecutors are responsible for specific phases of the court proceedings. In some jurisdictions, a few assistant prosecutors specialize in gang-related cases.

vertical prosecution
Where one assistant prosecutor or small group of assistant prosecutors handle the criminal complaint from start to finish through the entire court process.

horizontal prosecution
Different assistant prosecutors are responsible for specific phases of the court proceedings.

The other strategies, social intervention, opportunities provision and community organization can be seen in the OJJDP five-pronged approach to gang reduction.

THE OJJDP'S COMPREHENSIVE GANG MODEL AND GANG REDUCTION PROGRAM

The OJJDP's Comprehensive Gang Model is based on years of experimentation and research on gang prevention ("Addressing Community Gang Problems," 2009). The model is based on five strategies: (1) community mobilization, (2) social intervention, (3) opportunities provision, (4) suppression, and (5) organizational change and development. The model's key distinguishing feature is a strategic planning process that empowers communities to assess their own gang problems and fashion a complement of antigang strategies and program activities. Their report, *Best Practices to Address Community Gang Problems* (2008), presents the best practices for the Comprehensive Gang Model and highlights results of a National Youth Gang Center Survey and a meeting of practitioners regarding their experiences in implementing the model. Another valuable resource available to all communities is the National Gang Crime Research Center.

The OJJDP's gang reduction program (GRP) uses a five-pronged approach:

1. *Primary prevention* targets the entire population in high-crime, high-risk communities. The key component is a one-stop resource center that makes services accessible and visible to community members. Services include prenatal and infant care, afterschool activities, truancy and dropout prevention, and job programs.
2. *Secondary prevention* identifies young children (ages 7 to 14) at high risk and, drawing on the resources of schools, community-based organizations and faith-based groups, intervenes with appropriate services before early problem behaviors turn into serious delinquency and gang involvement.
3. *Intervention* targets active gang members, close associates and gang members returning from confinement and involves aggressive outreach and recruitment activity. Support services for gang-involved youths and their families help youths make positive choices.
4. *Suppression* focuses on identifying the most dangerous and influential gang members and removing them from the community.

5. *Reentry* targets serious offenders who are returning to the community after confinement and provides appropriate services and monitoring. Of particular interest are "displaced" gang members who may cause conflict by attempting to reassert their former gang roles.

The first two prongs of this program focus on prevention, which is also the objective of the G.R.E.A.T. Program.

THE G.R.E.A.T. PROGRAM

The Gang Resistance Education and Training (G.R.E.A.T.) program is a nationally proven approach aimed at stopping gang membership. Its proactive approach seeks to deter violence before it begins. This school-based, law enforcement officer–instructed classroom curriculum was developed in partnership with nationally recognized organizations such as the Boys & Girls Clubs of America and the National Association of Police Athletic Leagues and is intended as an immunization against delinquency, youth violence and gang membership. The program builds a foundation focused on teaching children the life skills they need to avoid violence and gang membership ("Welcome to the G.R.E.A.T. Web Site," 2009).

A study supported by the National Institute of Justice (NIJ) documented that students who graduated from the G.R.E.A.T. course showed lower levels of delinquency, impulsive behavior, risk-taking behavior and approval of violence. The study also found that students demonstrated higher levels of self-esteem, parental attachment, commitment to positive peers, antigang attitudes, perceived educational opportunities and positive school environments.

In 2006, the NIJ awarded a five-year grant to the University of Missouri at St. Louis to evaluate the revised G.R.E.A.T. program outcomes. The preliminary findings indicate that G.R.E.A.T. students, when compared with non-G.R.E.A.T. students, had more positive attitudes toward police, fewer positive attitudes about gangs, more use of refusal skills, more resistance to peer pressure, lower rates of gang membership and lower rates of self-reported delinquency ("NYGC Research Update," 2009).

GANGS AND COMMUNITY POLICING

A gang problem is not just a law enforcement problem. A community must provide its young people with meaningful alternatives to draw them away from gangs, such as educational programs, social interaction, recreational activities, and employment opportunities. Providing these services will require cooperation among parents and families, schools, social services, businesses, religious organizations and other neighborhood resources. As noted gang expert Richard Valdemar points out, "The biggest cause of gangs is we do nothing for the 90 percent who aren't gang members. If all the attention and respect goes to the gang members, then what happens to the kids who aren't getting that attention and are getting beaten up by gang members?" (Basich, 2009, p.21).

One valuable resource available to all communities is the National Gang Crime Research Center Web site. The community and other law enforcement agencies are also now becoming more involved in dealing with the drug problem, often closely associated with gang problems.

Combating the "Stop Snitching Code of Silence"

The Police Executive Research Forum (PERF) and the Community Oriented Policing Services (COPS) Office have collaborated on a report, *The Stop Snitching Phenomenon: Breaking the Code of Silence*, 2009), aimed at encouraging community members to share vital information and participate in partnership-enhancing activities with their local law enforcement agencies. This stop snitching culture is promoted by drug dealers, gang members and other criminals who threaten violence against people who provide information to or cooperate in any way with the police. The stop snitching message intimidates witnesses and erodes trust between communities and police, threatening police agencies' ability to prevent and solve crime by impeding investigations, arrests and convictions, which could severely erode the criminal justice system ("Combating the Stop Snitching Code of Silence," 2009).

THE LINK AMONG GANGS, VICE, ORGANIZED CRIME AND DRUGS

The CALEA Standards include the control of vice, drugs and organized crime in one standard, acknowledging that some departments may have three separate divisions dealing with these challenges. Because organized crime is often heavily into drugs and some departments consider both groups as gangs, the three areas are combined into one standard. The following standard has been adapted to refer to only drugs and organized crime.

43.1.2 **CALEA Standard 43.1.2** states, "The nature of drug and/or organized crime offenses and the considerable amount of undercover work involved in controlling these offenses contribute to the sensitivity of related records. The agency should keep them secure and limit access to authorized persons only. . . . The nature of the operations of these functions often requires frequent and sometimes large expenditures of money. This can include paying informants, purchasing contraband as evidence, and incurring expenses for surveillance activities and equipment." (*Standards for Law Enforcement Agencies*, 5th edition, 2006)

THE DRUG PROBLEM

Gangs are not the only faction involved in dealing drugs. Organized crime is also heavily into this area, as are some "reputable" businesspeople. Drugs and drug-using behavior have been linked to crime in many ways.

Research supports the link between street-level drug hot spot activity, disorder and serious crime.

In addition, the use of illicit drugs is a major cause of the soaring rate of incarceration, with an estimated two-thirds of federal and state prisoners and probationers characterized as drug involved.

THE SERIOUSNESS AND EXTENT OF THE PROBLEM

The *National Drug Threat Assessment 2009* (2008, p.1) states, "The trafficking and abuse of illicit drugs inflict tremendous harm upon individuals, families, and communities throughout the country." The following demonstrates the extent of the threat (*National Drug Threat Assessment 2009*):

- More than 35 million individuals used illicit drugs or abused prescription drugs in 2007.
- In 2006, individuals entered public drug treatment facilities more than 1 million times seeking assistance in ending their addiction to illicit or prescription drugs.
- More than 1,100 children were injured at, killed at, or removed from methamphetamine laboratory sites from 2007 through September 2008.
- For 2009, the federal government has allocated more than $14 billion for drug treatment and prevention, counterdrug law enforcement, drug interdiction, and international counterdrug assistance.
- In September 2008, there were nearly 100,000 inmates in federal prisons convicted and sentenced for drug offenses, representing more than 52 percent of all federal prisoners.
- Mexican and Colombian DTOs generate, remove, and launder between $18 billion and $39 billion in wholesale drug proceeds annually.
- Diversion of controlled prescription drugs costs insurance companies up to $72.5 billion annually, nearly two-thirds of which is paid by public insurers.

The Growing Threat of Mexican Drug Trafficking Organizations (DTOs) Crossing Our Borders

Laine (2009, p.6) reports, "Over the last several years, we have witnessed a remarkable, and horrific, increase in the level of drug-related violence in Mexico. In 2008 more than 6,200 people died as a result of drug-related violence. So far [in 2009], more than 1,000 people, including police officers, judges, prosecutors, soldiers, journalists, politicians, and innocent bystanders have been killed." Laine also reports that Mexican drug cartels are now present in at least 230 U.S. cities, an increase from about 50 cities in 2006.

> Last year, more than 60 officers were killed and more than 1,350 civilians were murdered in Juarez, a city that shares the international border with El Paso. Such horrific violence has occurred along several areas of the border and has included decapitations, bodies hung from overpasses, corpses dissolved in vats of acid and attacks on anyone with the audacity to confront the narcoterrorists. A group of very well organized and equipped Mexican drug trafficking organizations have become increasingly ruthless as they seek to control the lucrative business of exporting drugs into the United States
>
> Although much of the violence has stayed on the southern side of the border, there are some indications the violence may be spilling over. The American cities of Las Vegas, Phoenix and San Diego have all documented kidnappings related to the violence. Phoenix experienced an unbelievable number of kidnappings last

year—almost 400—and this makes it second only to Mexico City for all cities in North America. (Stockton, 2009, p.8)

Many of the incidents involve narco-on-narco crime, where one band of criminals rips off a second one and the situation deteriorates into chaos (Marizco, 2009, pp.42–43). The dealers are mostly loosely knit freelancers, recruiting in bars, swap meets, even day labor sites. But there are also powerful, highly organized drug cartels fighting one another, threatening to destabilize Mexico. Griffith (2009, p.14) notes, "Drug cartels and gangs like Los Zetas have transformed the country into a battlefield. Last year, the drug war officially claimed the lives of 5,000 people and who knows how many people just disappeared, victims of unspeakable horrors after they were kidnapped." He suggests that drug-related kidnapping and brutality, the "signature activities" of the Mexican drug cartels, are on the rise in the United States, noting that in 2008, Phoenix, now the "kidnapping capital of America," had 370 kidnappings. Phoenix Police Chief Anders is quoted as saying, "We're in the eye of the storm. If it doesn't stop here, if we're not able to fix it here and get it turned around, it will go across the nation" (Griffith).

The United States is taking the threat seriously. Attorney General Eric Holder has called Mexican drug trafficking organizations a "national security threat," and explains that federal authorities have mounted their biggest assault against the Sinaloa organization, one of Mexico's oldest cartels and blamed for a large share of the spiraling violence in the country (Archibold, 2009). For example, in an investigation known as Operation Xcellerator, more than 750 people nationwide were arrested and tons of cocaine and marijuana were seized, disrupting drug distribution through a series of raids and arrests.

Another federal initiative is the building of a "virtual fence" along 53 miles of Arizona's border with Mexico (Rotstein, 2009). Permanent towers holding sensors, cameras and communications gear will detect drug smuggling along this portion of the border. The towers, most as high as 120 feet tall and spaced miles apart, will be built on the remaining 320 miles of the state's southern border, followed by towers in New Mexico, California and most of Texas.

In addition, the U.S. intelligence community is using satellites to track activities of drug cartels along the U.S.–Mexican border, adding one more tool to an ever-expanding technological arsenal aimed at defending the border ("Satellites Take on Crime," 2009).

Further, in April 2009, President Barack Obama added three Mexican cartels—Sinaloa, Los Zetas and La Familia Michoacana—to the list of banned foreign "drug kingpins," empowering the federal government to seize their assets, estimated in the billions of dollars, and allowing the government to seek criminal penalties against U.S. firms or individuals who provide weapons, launder money or transport drugs or cash for the cartels (Hsu, 2009).

Eventually the drugs transported over the border find their way across the country, posing a huge challenge to local law enforcement.

THE DRUGS INVOLVED

According to the *National Drug Threat Assessment 2009* report (2008, p.iv), cocaine is the leading drug threat to society. Methamphetamine is the second leading drug threat, followed by marijuana, heroin, pharmaceutical drugs and MDMA (or Ecstasy). The report notes that the level of domestic outdoor cannabis cultivation is very high and possibly increasing and that marijuana potency has increased to the highest level ever recorded.

Marijuana is the most controversial of the illicit drugs, and a wide spectrum of opinion exists regarding its harmfulness and whether it should be legalized or not. Marijuana, the illicit drug that has previously and pervasively been the most popular drug with teens, has lately taken a backseat to the nonmedical use of pain relievers, with surveys showing more initiates (first-time users) in recent years using these pain relievers than marijuana (Wethal, 2008, p.88).

Field Testing of Drugs

Street drugs can be identified with a narcotics field-test kit. Identification via field testing, however, can be tricky: "Most of [these drugs] are pills or powders that could be pure, uncut dope or baking soda, marijuana or oregano, and the people that market them aren't widely known for their reverence of truth in labeling" (Dees, 2008, p.74). Several brands of self-contained, single-use test kits are available that reduce the likelihood of user error and require very small samples: "Between the variations of similar-looking drugs and the quantity of fake or 'bunk' drugs found by street officers, it's unwise to rely solely on appearance or packaging to form probable cause for an arrest. These tests are reliable and inexpensive" (Dees, 2008, p.79).

Officers must understand that field testing cannot be used to *establish* probable cause, only *confirm* it. Probable cause, through observation and evaluation of other factors, must already exist before a substance can be field-tested. For example, an undercover officer who buys a small bag of white powder from a suspected cocaine dealer has established probable cause and may run a substance-specific field test for cocaine.

Kanable (2008, p.48) recommends that agencies train their own field investigation drug officers (FIDOs). After thorough training and passing an extensive examination, these officers become certified and can conduct chemical color tests for the most common drugs in their jurisdiction. Having the most simple felony possession cases handled in the field allows forensic labs time to spend on more difficult cases (Kanable, p.48). In addition to saving time, these officers can save the agency money; one field test kit costs between $1 and $2, but lab analysis costs $50 or more. As an example, since Utah agencies started doing presumptive screening in the field, they've eliminated about 50 to 60 percent of cases submitted to the lab (Kanable, p.52).

INVESTIGATIVE AIDS

One tool to help law enforcement agencies investigate drug trafficking is the Drug Enforcement Administration (DEA)'s National Drug Pointer Index (NDPIX), a nationwide database that became operational across the United States in 1997. The NDPIX is intended to enhance agent/officer safety, eliminate duplication, increase information sharing and coordination, and minimize costs by using existing technology and 24-hour access to information through an effective, secure law enforcement telecommunications system.

Some investigative aids are not so high-tech. For example, using dogs to detect drugs has been common for decades because their keen sense of smell enables them to detect minute traces of illicit drugs. Canines are effective force multipliers. Law enforcement agencies depend on their K-9s and handlers for many tasks essential to police work, with drug detection topping the list. Ninety percent of surveyed agencies reported they use dogs for this purpose ("Almost 50% of Agencies," 2008, p.14). For example, in one investigation, the Middlesex (Massachusetts) Sheriff's Department's K-9 unit seized 8,000 grams of cocaine, 2,000 grams of heroin, 80 pounds of marijuana, and $2.5 million in drug-smeared cash (Redmond, 2008).

The Supreme Court has ruled that a canine sniff in a public area or during a lawful traffic stop is not a Fourth Amendment "search." However, use of a narcotics-detection dog to sniff at the door of an apartment or a home has been ruled a search within the meaning of the Fourth Amendment and therefore requires a warrant.

Another assist for investigators is a special high-accuracy laser rangefinder developed for the U.S. Customs Service. Investigators use the unit to measure the interior dimensions of cargo containers in their search for hidden compartments in which drugs may be smuggled. The small laser beam allows measurements of loaded containers in which physical access to the rear wall is limited. The handheld, battery-operated laser rangefinder measures distances from 6 to 85 feet with an accuracy of 1 inch.

Flying drones are being used by the U.S. Forest Service to battle pot growers operating in remote California woodlands. The pilotless, camera-equipped aircraft allows law enforcement to pinpoint marijuana fields and size up potential dangers before agents attempt arrests. More than 2.3 million marijuana plants were eradicated from Forest Service lands nationwide in 2007. In California's 18 national forests, an estimated 6 million plants have been removed since 2000 (Brown, 2008).

APPROACHES TO THE DRUG PROBLEM

A summary of the findings from all rigorous academic studies evaluating a range of street-level drug law enforcement interventions found that strategic crime-control partnerships with a range of third parties are more effective at disrupting drug problems than are law-enforcement-only approaches (Mazerolle et al., 2007a).

Approaches that have been suggested to address the drug problem include

- Crime control.
- Punishment.
- Rehabilitation.
- Prevention.
- Legalization.

Figure 12.2 provides an overview of drug-control strategies.

The approaches being suggested should help support the three priorities of the *National Drug Control Strategy* (2009): (1) stopping use before it starts—education and community action, (2) healing America's drug users—getting treatment resources where they are needed and (3) disrupting the market—attacking the economic basis of the drug trade.

The first priority, prevention through education and community action, is discussed at length later in the chapter. The second priority, treatment, is likely to be the focus of the Obama administration, dealing with drugs as a matter of public health rather than criminal justice alone, with treatment's role growing relative to incarceration (Fields, 2009). The third priority, disrupting the flow of drugs, is a vital challenge for local law enforcement.

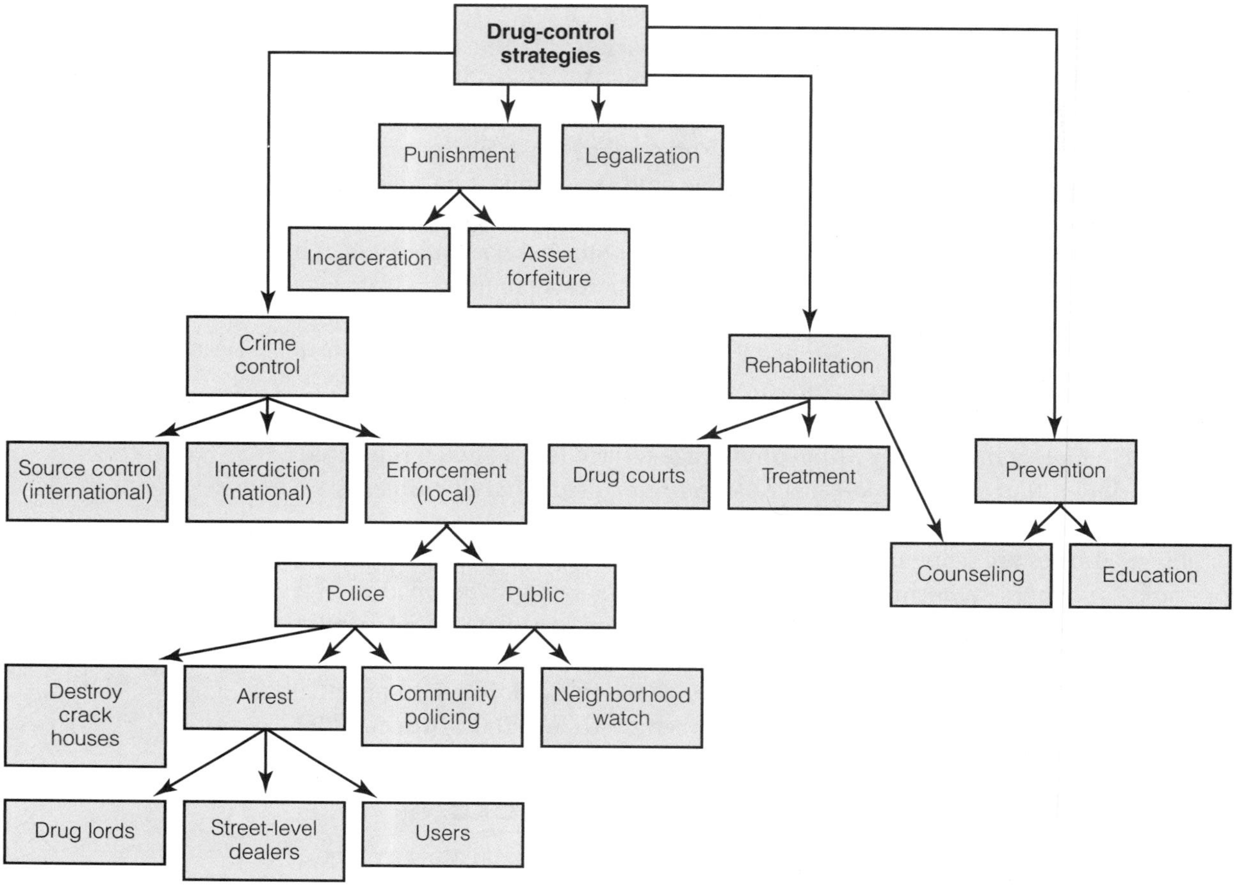

- **Drug-control strategies**
  - Punishment
    - Incarceration
    - Asset forfeiture
  - Legalization
  - Crime control
    - Source control (international)
    - Interdiction (national)
    - Enforcement (local)
      - Police
        - Destroy crack houses
        - Arrest
          - Drug lords
          - Street-level dealers
          - Users
        - Community policing
      - Public
        - Community policing
        - Neighborhood watch
  - Rehabilitation
    - Drug courts
    - Treatment
    - Counseling
  - Prevention
    - Counseling
    - Education

FIGURE 12.2 Overview of Drug-Control Strategies.

Efforts at international source control and national interdiction are beyond the scope of this text. However, local enforcement efforts are of great importance in the efforts to address the drug problem. These efforts often involve drug buys, undercover operations and raids.

The Drug Buy

Many police departments use criminal informants (CIs) or plainclothes police officers who are part of a drug unit or other specialized team to make drug buys, which are watched by a surveillance team. Often, these buys are taped to provide further evidence of illegal activity. In addition, the surveillance team can step in if trouble develops and the plainclothes officer or informant needs help. Such buys are also useful because they can provide leads to the suspect's other customers and associates, as well as to where the supply is coming from. Often, it is best to simply watch and wait, continuing to make buys and to gather information, rather than to make an immediate arrest.

Buy operations occur in three well-defined stages: preparations for the buy, the buy itself and actions needed after the buy to process evidence and information.

AN OFFICER'S EXPERIENCE
Using Informants

Because a CI is often involved, the operation can be highly dynamic and change at any given moment. Keep in mind that CIs are usually petty criminals themselves trying to work off their own charges. In one investigation where a CI was used to buy drugs from a known gang member, the CI decided to go into the dealer's residence and do drugs with him. The CI got high, and the transaction lasted an hour. What should have been a quick buy lasted a long time, consuming the resources of the investigating officers who were also on scene. It is important to consider that, when involved in these investigations, you are not dealing with the most reliable people.

—Sgt. Henry Lim Cho

Preparations for the Buy Officers need to learn all they can about the entire situation. Security is vital. The slightest leak can ruin the operation and endanger the agent. All bills to be used for the buy should be recorded. A backup surveillance team is highly desirable to protect the agent and secure additional evidence. A plan needs to be devised that attempts to cover every contingency. Thorough briefing is essential, but only on a need-to-know basis. When a surveillance team is involved, a set of signals must be arranged. Just before the buy, the officer or informant and vehicle should be searched.

The Actual Buy During the buy, any deviation from the plan increases the risk and decreases the chance of obtaining admissible evidence. The agent should control the situation and refuse to accept suggestions made by the seller, although this is not always possible if the buy occurs on a street corner or a known drug house. Buy location influences the level of control an agent can maintain. Also, the agent should make the buy himself rather than let the informant do it unless, for the purposes of developing intelligence on a certain target, it makes better sense to have a CI do the deal. Sellers should be advised of their rights as soon as they are arrested. They should then be searched to recover the buy money and any other evidence.

After the Buy The drugs should be weighed and tested. Every precaution should be taken to protect their integrity and to maintain the chain of custody as they are checked into the evidence room. All participants should be debriefed. An operational report should be written. Sometimes drug buys are much more sophisticated and complex. Such buys often involve carefully planned undercover operations.

Undercover Operations

One primary approach to dealing with the drug problem is through undercover operations. In such operations, police officers assume a fictitious identity and attempt to infiltrate a drug ring or a drug-dealing gang or to pose as a buyer of drugs. According to Logue (2008, pp.94–95),

Many police departments use plainclothes police officers or informants to make drug buys, which are watched by a surveillance team. Such buys are useful because they can provide leads to the suspect's other customers and associates, as well as to where the supply of drugs comes from. A series of successful drug buys can eventually lead to the arrest of dealers.
© Steve Starr/Corbis

> U/C [undercover work] has changed dramatically over the past 10 to 20 years. The days of the Lone Ranger going out with a pocketful of money and being a bad guy are over for the most part. Advances in technology, increased liability and budget constraints have caused many smaller agencies to steer away from U/C operations and, in turn, these causes have put a once common practice on the endangered species list. . . . The old Playstation 2 slogan "Live in your world, play in ours" adequately sums up the life of the U/C operative. It is American policing at its best but no one ever said being the best would be easy.

Undercover investigations are used more routinely in drug cases than perhaps any other type of criminal investigation. The downside to this common tactic is that drug dealers also know it is routinely used, and they have become fairly adept at sniffing out "narcs." Street dealers are also aware of the restrictions imposed on undercover agents, such as the fact that law enforcement cannot smoke marijuana legally. As a result, undercover narcotics officers have had to develop more convincing ways to fit into the drug culture.

An undercover agent might dress a certain way, use certain slang and talk with an accent, or even gargle with beer or hard liquor just before meeting with a dealer. The negotiations conducted by an undercover narcotics officer are similar to those used by a hostage negotiator and require similar communication skills. In the case of the undercover agent, however, the innocent victim whose life may be saved is the agent. To successfully negotiate, undercover agents need as much *information* as possible about the sellers and their needs. Agents often consider that money is the main objective of drug dealers, but security is often even more important. This can be seen in drug dealers' insistence on controlling all aspects of the transaction, especially the location.

Another critical factor in undercover negotiations is *time.* Most drug dealers want to conduct their business as rapidly as possible, keeping the amount of time they have the drugs in their possession to a minimum. Undercover agents also can give the impression of being in a hurry to conduct business, perhaps by having an airline ticket with an impending departure time printed on the envelope jutting from a pocket. Despite the time press to conduct the transaction, it must also be remembered that the passage of time builds trust.

Information and time are critical elements in an illegal drug buy.

Another crucial aspect of the buy is how the **flashroll**, the buy money, is managed. Many undercover narcotics officers who are injured or killed while on assignment usually have mismanaged the flashroll. The most dangerous time is when the drugs and money are in the same place. Grave risks also occur when the flashroll is *not* present. In such instances, undercover agents may not be as guarded as they should be because they feel they are not at that much risk.

flashroll
Buy money in a drug deal.

If the flashroll is present, agents should allow the dealer to count the money. There is little point in having it on hand if this is not part of the plan. If the agent cannot come up with the full amount requested, it is sometimes a good tactic to simply explain to the dealer that cash is temporarily short. Such an admission can do much to strengthen the agent's cover.

The sale and use of illegal drugs is difficult to investigate and prosecute because sellers and buyers are willing participants.

Entrapment Whether a sophisticated undercover operation or a simple drug buy is involved, care must be taken to avoid a charge of **entrapment**, which occurs when a police officer (or other government official or person acting on behalf of the police or government) entices someone to commit a crime the person would not normally commit. Repeated requests to buy drugs are sometimes considered entrapment.

entrapment
An action by the police (or a government agent) persuading a person to commit a crime that the person would not otherwise have committed.

In *Hampton v. United States* (1976), Hampton was convicted of selling heroin to DEA agents. The question before the Supreme Court was, If a government informant supplies heroin to a person who then sells it to government agents, is this entrapment? The Court said No; Hampton was "predisposed" to deal in drugs. This view agrees with the majority opinion on entrapment, focusing on the defendant's behavior rather than on that of the officers involved. States vary, however, in whether they support the majority or the minority view. The minority view focuses on how officers or their agents conduct themselves.

To avoid charges of entrapment, those making the buy—be they plainclothes officers, informants or undercover agents—should make more than one buy. The more buys made, the weaker the entrapment defense.

Making several drug buys will protect against a claim of entrapment.

Among the other actions to be avoided are pressures such as badgering or coaxing, creating an unusual motive such as sympathy or making the crime unusually attractive. For example, it might be entrapment if officers said the crime would not be detected or that it was not illegal. Police may create an opportunity for someone to commit crime. It is presumed a law-abiding person would resist the temptation. Agents may also originate the criminal plan.

As the California Supreme Court said, "We are not concerned with who first conceived or who willingly, or reluctantly, acquiesced in a criminal project." It is also not entrapment for an officer to take reasonable steps to gain the suspects' confidence.

Proving Guilty Knowledge

Another area police officers involved in drug investigations must consider is the need to prove the person in possession of a package containing illegal substances knew of their presence. This frequently arises in vehicle courier and package delivery cases. Among the facts the courts have found relevant to proving knowledge are (1) inconsistent statements, (2) implausible stories, (3) a large quantity of valuable contraband, (4) nervousness, (5) failure to ask any questions regarding the nature of a trip, (6) more contraband or drug paraphernalia found in the subject's possession, (7) lack of surprise upon discovery of the contraband, (8) scanning for police surveillance, (9) accepting a package without question or surprise, (10) hiding a package once it is delivered and (11) inquiring about the status of a package in anticipation of its delivery.

Drug Raids

During the 1980s, drug raids made frequent headlines. Tanklike vehicles, SWAT teams and sophisticated weaponry all have been involved in drug raids. During such raids, communication is usually critical. It is also advisable to have a narcotic K-9 on standby. Such raids can be highly successful.

In combating the drug problem, law enforcement in the 1980s focused on undercover operations and sophisticated raids. In the 1990s, law enforcement focused on enlisting and educating the public and targeting street-level sales. That emphasis continues into the 21st century.

Combating Prescription Drug Diversion

Two organizations have been formed to help law enforcement tackle the problem of the abuse and diversion of prescription drugs: Prescription Pattern Analysis Tracking Robberies and Other Losses (RxPATROL) and the National Association of Drug Diversion Investigation (NADDI). RxPATROL helps law enforcement solve pharmacy robberies, burglaries and other major crimes committed in health care facilities through its national computer database. NADDI is a nonprofit organization that provides prescription drug abuse education to law enforcement, regulatory agents and health care professionals.

Dealing with Meth Labs

There are two main types of methamphetamine (meth) labs: the super labs, which are highly organized and sophisticated labs using highly trained "cooks" and quality equipment, and "Mom and Pop" labs, generally run by meth users who produce a little extra to sell (Petrocelli, 2009, p.14). Approximately 90 percent of the labs are considered small-scale, and they exist throughout the country. However, most meth found on the street—more than 80 percent—is produced by super labs, which are concentrated in Southern California and Mexico (Petrocelli). The toxic nature of the smaller labs is a major concern for police and local communities, particularly because of the hazardous waste produced.

Common signs indicative of a meth lab include chemical odors (especially ammonia ether); coffee grinders and blenders with white residue; large quantities of matches, acetone, lithium batteries, antifreeze, plastic baggies and glass jars; continuously running exhaust fans; thermoses and plastic liter pop bottles; and constant foot traffic, at all hours, with short stays.

Surveillances and raids are options for law enforcement. However, a more proactive approach to shutting down meth labs is to educate retailers about the ingredients and hardware needed for manufacturing methamphetamine. Several states have approached the meth problem by restricting the sale of cold tablets containing pseudoephedrine, a key ingredient in methamphetamine. Such cold tablets must be locked up, and their sale requires identification and a signature.

Important sources of information include postal carriers, sanitation workers, utility workers, and resident managers and rental property managers. Such individuals should be trained to identify suspicious odors associated with production of meth, including garlic, rotten eggs, cat urine, nail polish remover, and a hospital smell.

Because meth labs pose a high risk of explosion and fire, use of autonomous robots can enhance officers' safety in investigating a suspected meth lab and be an important force multiplier (Weiss, 2007, pp.66–73):

> Imagine if "thinking" robots made the first entry into these hazardous surroundings [meth labs], while responding officers watched their activities from a safe distance away.
>
> By using autonomous robots, law enforcement could gather intelligence in a stakeout and have the robots enter the area before sending in a SWAT team. . . .
>
> As robots enter a lab's vicinity, they use sensor arrays to determine if any humans are present, and whether the individuals are armed or extremely agitated, and potentially dangerous. The robots also can determine whether chemical or dry cooking is taking place, and if poisonous gases are present in the air. The robots use efficient algorithms to search each room—having a plan for every type of contingency. In some situations they would be programmed to alert and acquire the assistance of officers. . . .
>
> Arming autonomous robots with lethal or less-lethal weapons, allowing them to use force or be allowed to move at-will could help protect the officer.

COMBATING STREET-LEVEL NARCOTICS SALES

Street drug dealing can be attacked in one of three ways: (1) Attack the demand (scare off buyers), (2) attack the supply (slow the dealer's business), and (3) alter the environment (make the area "too hot" for dealers and buyers): "The greatest deterrent to drug dealing is officer presence. Just being in the area in a marked unit will scare off drug dealers and drug buyers" (Petrocelli, 2007, p.20).

Citizens know where drug dealing is going on and, if they can be encouraged to report such events, police can concentrate their efforts on those locations receiving the most complaints. Often, police officers want to go higher than the street pusher but should avoid this temptation. If information regarding someone higher up is obtained, it should be given to the narcotics unit for follow-up. The main purpose of the street-level raid is to respond to citizen complaints and to let them see their complaints being acted on—arrests being made. Officers should know where to search a person being detained on suspicion of possession of drugs.

The variety of hiding places for illegal drugs is limited only by the violators' ingenuity. Common hiding places include body orifices, boots, chewing gum packages, cigarettes, coat linings, cuffs, false heels, hair, hatbands, inside ties, lighters, pants, pens and pencils, seams, shoes, shoulder pads, sleeves and waistbands.

Police-led crackdowns and cleanups such as "Weed and Seed" initiatives have been effective in some communities. These programs target drug hot spots, and during and after the crackdown, the targeted areas receive other services aimed at enhancing the quality of life, including code enforcement, litter removal and street light repair.

Public Housing and the Drug Problem

To deal with the drug problem in public housing projects, police officers need to understand the workings of their local public housing authorities or agencies (PHAs) managing these complexes. Officers need to work at establishing a relationship with the PHAs and at overcoming the occasional disbelief of management and residents that the police truly want to help. Once this is accomplished, a fact-finding mission should identify key players, provide information about each organization and determine what programs exist and the participation level. Next the problem should be identified: What is the problem and for whom? Police, residents, housing personnel, the mayor? Does one problem mask another problem? Then a dialogue should be undertaken with key players to enlist support and mobilize the housing project's residents. After that, a strategy should be developed, including goals, objectives and tactics that might be used. Next the strategy should be implemented, coordinating all available resources, specifying roles for each key player and determining a time frame. The final step is to evaluate progress. Was the problem improved or changed?

Various specific strategies have been used to tackle the drug problem in public housing. Some jurisdictions assign liaison officers to high crime public housing areas and may even place a substation in these areas, many of which are grant funded. Other common strategies focus on improving the physical environment: limiting entrances, improving lighting, erecting fences, requiring a pass card to gain entrance to the housing and keeping trash collected.

Efforts may focus on removing offenders, strengthening enforcement and prosecution efforts, enforcing lease requirements and seizing assets. The setting and enforcement of strict housing policies in addition to criminal law enforcement often helps—for instance, informing tenants that any drug-related offenses are grounds for automatic eviction.

Efforts may also focus on reducing the demand, focusing on the buyers of the drugs rather than the sellers either through sting operations or through educational programs, youth diversion programs or treatment programs. Another strategy is to work on improving communications by using community surveys and tip lines and by improving communications between narcotics investigators and patrol officers.

In addition to being concerned with those who deal in drugs, police officers need to be prepared to manage those who use them.

RECOGNIZING INDIVIDUALS USING ILLEGAL DRUGS

Police officers must be able to recognize when a person is probably under the influence of drugs and must be aware of the dangers the person might present. Table 12.7 summarizes the primary physical symptoms, what to look for and the dangers involved in the most commonly used drugs, including alcohol.

Police officers must be able to recognize individuals who might be on phencyclidine (PC), or angel dust. One symptom always present in an individual high on PCP is **nystagmus**, the involuntary jerking or bouncing of the eye, a possible cause of which is intoxication (recall the discussion in Chapter 5 regarding drunk drivers). Individuals on PCP may display superhuman strength.

nystagmus
The involuntary jerking or bouncing of the eye, a possible cause of which is intoxication.

Some agencies have drug recognition experts (DREs) who are specially trained to detect and recognize drug-impaired drivers.

LEGISLATION AS A TOOL IN THE WAR ON DRUGS

The government has the power to finance the war on drugs by seizing the drug traffickers' illegally obtained assets. This includes cars and weapons as well as cash. Among items that have been seized are airplanes, vehicles, radio transmitters with scanners, telephone scramblers, paper shredders, electronic currency counters, assault rifles and electronic stun guns. Asset forfeiture is another form of punishment.

Asset Forfeiture

The U.S. Marshals Service administers the Department of Justice's Asset Forfeiture program, managing and disposing of properties seized and forfeited by federal law enforcement agencies and U.S. attorneys nationwide. The three goals of the program are (1) enforcing the law, (2) improving law enforcement cooperation, and (3) enhancing law enforcement through revenue sharing. Commonly seized assets include real property, vehicles, vessels, aircraft, businesses, financial instruments and jewelry. Under the Equitable Sharing program, proceeds from the sale of forfeited assets are often shared with the state and local enforcement agencies that participated in the investigation leading to the seizure, enhancing cooperation between state/local agencies and federal agencies ("Asset Forfeiture Program," n.d.). In 2006, 385 seizures were made, with total value of $6,040,000 ("Asset Forfeiture Funds Reports," 2006).

Table 12.7 Drugs of Abuse/Uses and Effects

Drugs	CSA Schedules	Trade or Other Names	Medical Uses	Dependence		Tolerance	Duration (Hours)	Usual Method	Possible Effects	Effects of Overdose	Withdrawal Syndrome
				Physical	Psycho-logical						
Narcotics											
Heroin	Substance I	Diamorphine, Horse, Smack, Black tar, *Chiva, Negra* (*black tar*)	None in U.S., analgesic, antitussive	High	High	Yes	3–4	Injected, snorted, smoked	Euphoria, drowsiness, respiratory depression, constricted pupils, nausea	Slow and shallow breathing, clammy skin, convulsions, coma, possible death	Watery eyes, runny nose, yawning, loss of appetite, irritability, tremors, panic, cramps, nausea, chills and sweating
Morphine	Substance II	MS-Contin, Roxanol, Oramorph SR, MSIR	Analgesic	High	High	Yes	3–12	Oral, injected			
Hydrocodone	Substance II, Product III, V	Hydrocodone w/Acetaminophen, Vicodin, Vicoprofen, Tussionex, Lortab	Analgesic, antitussive	High	High	Yes	3–6	Oral			
Hydro-morphone	Substance II	Dilaudid	Analgesic	High	High	Yes	3–4	Oral, injected			
Oxycodone	Substance II	Roxicet, Oxycodone w/Acetaminophen, OxyContin, Endocet, Percocet, Percodan	Analgesic	High	High	Yes	3–12	Oral			
Codeine	Substance II, Products III, V	Acetaminophen, Guaifenesin or Promethazine w/Codeine, Fiorinal, Fioricet or Tylenol w/Codeine	Analgesic, antitussive	Moderate	Moderate	Yes	3–4	Oral, injected			

Other Narcotics	Substance II, III, IV	Fentanyl, Demerol, Methadone, Darvon, Stadol, Talwin, Paregoric, Buprenex	Analgesic, antidiarrheal, antitussive	High-Low	High-Low	Yes	Variable	Oral, injected, snorted, smoked			
Depressants											
gamma Hydroxybutyric Acid	Substance I, Product III	GHB, Liquid Ecstasy, Liquid X, Sodium Oxybate, Xyrem®	None in U.S., anesthetic	Moderate	Moderate	Yes	3–6	Oral	Slurred speech, disorientation, drunken behavior without odor of alcohol, impaired memory of events, interacts with alcohol	Shallow respiration, clammy skin, dilated pupils, weak and rapid pulse, coma, possible death	Anxiety, insomnia, tremors, delirium, convulsions, possible death
Benzodiazepines	Substance IV	Valium, Xanax, Halcion, Ativan, Restoril, Rohypnol (Roofies, R-2), Klonopin	Antianxiety, sedative, anticonvulsant, hypnotic, muscle relaxant	Moderate	Moderate	Yes	1–8	Oral, injected			
Other Depressants	Substance I, II, III, IV	Ambien, Sonata, Meprobamate, Chloral Hydrate, Barbiturates, Methaqualone (Quaalude)	Antianxiety, sedative, hypnotic	Moderate	Moderate	Yes	2–6	Oral			

(continued)

Table 12.7 Drugs of Abuse/Uses and Effects (*continued*)

				Dependence							
Drugs	**CSA Schedules**	**Trade or Other Names**	**Medical Uses**	**Physical**	**Psychological**	**Tolerance**	**Duration (Hours)**	**Usual Method**	**Possible Effects**	**Effects of Overdose**	**Withdrawal Syndrome**
Stimulants											
Cocaine	Substance II	Coke, Flake, Snow, Crack, *Coca*, *Blanca*, *Perico*, *Nieve*, Soda	Local anesthetic	Possible	High	Yes	1–2	Snorted, smoked, injected	Increased alertness, excitation, euphoria, increased pulse rate and blood pressure, insomnia, loss of appetite	Agitation, increased body temperature, hallucinations, convulsions, possible death	Apathy, long periods of sleep, irritability, depression, disorientation
Amphetamine/ Methamphetamine	Substance II	Crank, Ice, Cristal, Krystal Meth, Speed, Adderall, Dexedrine, Desoxyn	Attention deficit/ hyperactivity disorder, narcolepsy, weight control	Possible	High	Yes	2–4	Oral, injected, smoked			
Methylphenidate	Substance II	Ritalin (Illy's), Concerta, Focalin, Metadate	Attention deficit/ hyperactivity disorder	Possible	High	Yes	2–4	Oral, injected, snorted, smoked			
Other Stimulants	Substance III, IV	Adipex P, Ionamin, Prelu-2, Didrex, Provigil	Vasoconstriction	Possible	Moderate	Yes	2–4	Oral			
Hallucinogens											
MDMA and Analogs	Substance I	(Ecstasy, XTC, Adam), MDA (Love Drug), MDEA (Eve), MBDB	None	None	Moderate	Yes	4–6	Oral, snorted, smoked	Heightened senses, teeth grinding and dehydration	Increased body temperature, electrolyte imbalance, cardiac arrest	Muscle aches, drowsiness, depression, acne

LSD	Substance I	Acid, Microdot, Sunshine, Boomers	None	None	Unknown	Yes	8–12	Oral	Illusions and hallucinations, altered perception of time and distance	(LSD) Longer, more intense "trip" episodes	None
Phencyclidine and Analogs	Substance I, II, III	PCP, Angel Dust, Hog, Loveboat, Ketamine (Special K), PCE, PCPy, TCP	Anesthetic (Ketamine)	Possible	High	Yes	1–12	Smoked, oral, injected, snorted		Unable to direct movement, feel pain, or remember	Drug seeking behavior *Not regulated
Other Hallucinogens	Substance I	Psilocybe mushrooms, Mescaline, Peyote Cactus, Ayahausca, DMT, Dextromethorphan* (DXM)	None	None	None	Possible	4–8	Oral			
Cannabis											
Marijuana	Substance I	Pot, grass, Sinsemilla, Blunts, *Mota*, *Yerba*, *Grifa*	None	Unknown	Moderate	Yes	2–4	Smoked, oral	Euphoria, relaxed inhibitions, increased appetite, disorientation	Fatigue, paranoia, possible psychosis	Occasional reports of insomnia, hyperactivity, decreased appetite
Tetrahydrocannabinol	Substance I, Product III	THC, Marinol	Antinauseant, appetite stimulant	Yes	Moderate	Yes	2–4	Smoked, oral			
Hashish and Hashish Oil	Substance I	Hash, Hash oil	None	Unknown	Moderate	Yes	2–4	Smoked, oral			

(*continued*)

Table 12.7 Drugs of Abuse/Uses and Effects (*continued*)

Drugs	CSA Schedules	Trade or Other Names	Medical Uses	Dependence: Physical	Dependence: Psycho-logical	Dependence: Tolerance	Duration (Hours)	Usual Method	Possible Effects	Effects of Overdose	Withdrawal Syndrome
Anabolic Steroids											
Testosterone	Substance III	Depo Testos-terone, Sus-tanon, Sten, Cypt	Hypogonad-ism	Unknown	Unknown	Unknown	14–28 days	Injected	Virilization, edema, test-icular atrophy, gyneco-mastia, acne, aggres-sive behavior	Unknown	Possible de-pression
Other Anabolic Steroids	Substance III	Parabolan, Winstrol, Equi-pose, Anadrol, Dianabol, Primabolin-Depo, D-Ball	Anemia, breast can-cer	Unknown	Yes	Unknown	Variable	Oral, injected			
Inhalants											
Amyl and Butyl Nitrite		Pearls, Pop-pers, Rush, Locker Room	Angina (Amyl)	Unknown	Unknown	No	1	Inhaled	Flushing, hypotension, headache	Methemo-globinemia	Agitation
Nitrous Oxide		Laughing gas, balloons, Whippets	Anesthetic	Unknown	Low	No	0.5	Inhaled	Impaired memory, slurred speech, drunken behavior, slow onset vitamin deficiency, organ damage	Vomiting, respiratory depression, loss of con-sciousness, possible death	Trembling, anxiety, insomnia, vitamin deficiency, confusion, hallucinations, convulsions
Other Inhalants		Adhesives, spray paint, hair spray, dry cleaning fluid, spot remover, lighter fluid	None	Unknown	High	No	0.5–2	Inhaled			
Alcohol		Beer, wine, liquor	None	High	High	Yes	1–3	Oral			

Source: *Drugs of Abuse, 2005 Edition*. Washington, DC: Drug Enforcement Administration, 2005. Accessed November 5, 2009: http://www.justice.gov/dea/pubs/abuse/chart.htm.

COPS office has published a guide, *Asset Forfeiture* (Worrall, 2008), that describes applying asset forfeiture to specific crimes, examines legal arrangements for its use, discusses the benefits and consequences to its use, and provides recommendations for launching an asset forfeiture program.

Drug Abatement Statutes

Similar to legislation aimed at the gang problem, recent legislation, such as drug abatement statutes, is also helping in the war on drugs. Such legislation makes it much easier to shut down crack houses and clandestine drug laboratories.

Drug abatement statutes declare any property where illegal drugs are used or sold to be a public nuisance.

Areas in which new legislation would help include drive-by shootings, witness protection programs, lowering age on juvenile offenses, continuing criminal enterprise, loitering, and pointing a weapon from a vehicle.

PREVENTION

Just as it is always preferable to prevent physical illness rather than treating it when it occurs, so it is always preferable to prevent a drug problem rather than treating it after the fact. One problem associated with drug abuse is the transmission of human immunodeficiency virus (HIV) infections when drug addicts share needles. Needle exchange programs (NEPs) have been found to significantly decrease the spread of HIV infections among intravenous drug users.

One effective way to approach prevention is to focus on known risks. The same factors placing youths at risk for joining gangs can also make them at risk for using drugs or alcohol. *Community risk factors* include extreme economic deprivation; low neighborhood attachment and community disorganization; transitions and mobility; community laws and norms favorable toward drug use, firearms and crime; availability of firearms; and media portrayals of violence. *School risk factors* include early and persistent antisocial behavior, academic failure beginning in elementary school and lack of commitment to school. *Family risk factors* include family history of problem behaviors, family management problems, family conflict and unfavorable parental attitudes and involvement. *Individual and peer risk factors* include alienation and rebelliousness, early initiation of problem behaviors, friends who engage in problem behaviors and favorable attitudes toward problem behaviors.

It is not enough to simply identify risks, however. Programs must also be put into place to keep youths from abusing drugs.

Educational Programs

Educational programs such as D.A.R.E. were discussed previously. A booklet, *The Coach's Playbook against Drugs* (n.d.), published by the OJJDP, is aimed at the coaches in youth athletic programs. Most coaches have special relationships with their athletes and can influence their thinking and behavior. The booklet provides a list of "do's and don'ts," as well as how the game will be affected and how team spirit will suffer.

Another approach might be to address what many see as flaws in current drug education programs. One such flaw is to equate drug use with drug abuse, using the terms interchangeably. But teenagers know the difference. Another flaw is the "gateway" theory, a mainstay of drug education, that use of marijuana leads to use of harder drugs such as cocaine. There is no research evidence to support this. These flaws conflict with what students observe and experience. Many prevention programs involve community partnerships.

WHAT RESEARCH SAYS

Limited research has been done on what works and what doesn't. A review of the evaluation literature on drug law enforcement revealed five categories of intervention: (1) international/national interventions (e.g., interdiction and drug seizure), (2) reactive/directed interventions (e.g., crackdowns, raids, buy-busts, saturation patrol, etc.), (3) proactive/partnership interventions (e.g., third-party policing, problem-oriented policing, drug nuisance abatement, etc.), (4) individualized interventions (e.g., arrest referral and diversion), and (5) interventions that used a combination of reactive/directed and proactive/partnership strategies (Mazerolle et al., 2007b). This review found that "proactive interventions involving partnerships between the police and third parties and/or community entities appear to be more effective at reducing both drug and nondrug problems in drug problem places than are reactive/directed approaches" (Mazerolle et al., 2007b, p.115).

McCabe (2008, p.289) studied the relationship between serious crime, drug arrests and nuisance abatement using data from New York City between 1995 and 2001, a period in which the city experienced a dramatic decrease in crime. One common explanation for this crime decrease is a version of Wilson and Kelling's broken windows theory. McCabe tested this theory using drug arrest and nuisance abatement closings as an approach to the drug problem. His research showed that the rate of marijuana arrests and the closing of drug locations through nuisance abatement statutes are inversely related to the crime rate, and that the rate of controlled substance arrest is directly related to the crime rate.

As has been seen throughout this chapter, gangs and drug are often a dual problem for communities. Following is an example of how problem-oriented policing has been used to address this dual challenge.

PROBLEM-ORIENTED POLICING, GANGS AND DRUGS

Public housing often poses a problem for both gangs and drugs. The SARA model has been successfully used to address such problems, as illustrated in the following case study from "Ridding Public Housing of Organized Drug Gangs" by Ron W. Glensor.[1]

---

[1]Source: *Problem-Oriented Drug Enforcement: A Community-Based Approach for Effective Policing*. Washington, DC: Bureau of Justice Assistance, October 1993, pp.38–40.

Case Study

Scanning John Hope Homes and University Homes are two large Atlanta public housing complexes adjacent to one another and to the Clark-Atlanta University Center that essentially constitute one community of more than 1,200 units and house about 2,100 residents. The Atlanta Police Department, the Atlanta Housing Authority and the residents identified the community as a problem site for drug trafficking because street gangs were selling drugs in and around the housing units. Drug-related violence also increased, including reports of gunfire.

Police believed most of these incidents resulted from turf battles between rival drug gangs. Although shootings had usually ceased by the time police arrived, spent shell casings collected by officers at the scene indicated that semiautomatic and automatic weapons were being used. Questioning of residents and suspects helped police identify three groups involved—locals operating independently, a local gang known as the Terry White Boys and a third group known as the Miami Boys.

The Miami Boys were quickly identified as the most dangerous of the three groups because, unlike neighborhood-based gangs, the Miami Boys' operation appeared similar to that of organized crime. They ran a citywide criminal enterprise composed of several different factions, which operated essentially independently of one another but were loosely linked and known to cooperate on occasion. Seven factions of the gang were identified as operating in the Atlanta area.

Intelligence data provided by Atlanta narcotics officers revealed that each faction was organized in a hierarchical, military fashion. A captain served as the liaison between each faction and the supply source, which was presumed to be in south Florida. Two lieutenants were responsible for distributing drugs and collecting monies. Each lieutenant controlled two sergeants, who in turn controlled street workers who fell into one of four categories—lookouts, couriers, enforcers or dealers. Members were recruited from neighborhoods in southern Florida and relocated to Atlanta.

The Miami Boys were considered particularly violent—weapons of choice were the Ingram MAC 11 machine pistol and the Intratec automatic rifle. Within a short time, they had come to dominate the drug market at John Hope and University Homes. Their success was achieved by intimidating competitive drug dealers, including murder if necessary. Murders were usually carried out by members of one of the factions not operating out of the John Hope and University Homes complexes. Because the shooters did not originate from the neighborhood, they were almost impossible to identify.

Analysis Officer T., assigned to the neighborhood evening watch, began gathering information on the Miami Boys. He talked with area residents; questioned arrestees and suspected dealers; and conducted surveillance by hiding in bushes, trees or vacant apartments and videotaping his suspects. Officer T. discovered that the gang openly displayed firearms (including machine guns) to intimidate residents and other rival narcotics dealers while they conducted sales of crack cocaine, 24 hours a day in 12-hour shifts. Gang members gained access to apartments to sell and stash their wares through several methods—by supplying users living in the buildings with cocaine, through romantic liaisons with tenants and by force. Higher-level gang members even paid residents to let the group store large amounts of cocaine in their apartments.

Because the gang was a tightly knit group, it was difficult to gather information about its inner workings, particularly about higher-ranking members. In addition, the gang controlled area residents, who became visibly nervous when officers approached them. Residents were threatened and often too frightened to even come out of their apartments because they feared gang retaliation. As a result, they rarely provided any information about the gang.

Response In response to increased street-level drug dealing and associated violence, the Atlanta commissioner of public safety established a new street-level strike force, the Red Dog Squad. Officer T. was assigned to the squad, where he continued to work on the Miami Boys' case. Based on his analysis of the gang's operations, he devised a two-part plan to break them up. The first part of his plan called for gathering information. Officer T. and the Red Dog Squad wanted to determine who was controlling the Miami Boys' operation at the complex. Because they hoped this information could be secured from the gang's underlings and from those residents whose apartments the gang used, they decided to make strategic arrests of gang members and collaborating tenants. The plan's second phase involved seizing control of the community from the drug dealers through numerous arrests. By disrupting the drug dealing and ridding the complex of some of the dealers, he hoped to send a message to the gang that they did not own the community. Even more importantly, visible police presence in the area would show residents that the Miami Boys were not as fearsome as they appeared.

Officer T. and his partner conducted military-type reconnaissance missions in the community. At times they would lie in the bushes for hours, waiting for an opportunity to move into an abandoned apartment to conduct direct surveillance of the group. When it rained, they would take advantage of the weather to move undetected around the area and position themselves to observe the dealer's operation and literally "appear from nowhere" to make surprise arrests of group members. These tactics accounted for some attrition among group members and psychologically demoralized gang members because they were unaccustomed to losing members through arrest.

Arrests and seizures also resulted from undercover buys, informant buys and search warrants. Most low-level dealers arrested could not make bail and consequently remained off the street. Others returned to Florida as part of a plea agreement. Officer T.'s tactics were depleting the Miami Boys' Florida-born labor pool.

A break came when a dealer identified as G.P. was arrested for narcotics violations. Originally thought to be a low-level dealer, interrogations of Miami Boys and local suspects revealed that G.P. was, in fact, the Miami Boys' leader. Local suspects revealed that G.P. had been selling only because of the arrests of his street workers. Officer T. also learned through a Florida records check that G.P. had only recently been released from prison.

The apartment in John Hope Homes where G.P. stored his crack cocaine shipments was identified through surveillance and intelligence. G.P. paid the resident $75 a day for use of the apartment. After a search warrant was issued, police seized a large amount of money and more than two ounces of narcotics. Faced with a long jail sentence, the tenant provided information that confirmed that G.P. was an upper-level member of the Miami Boys and enabled prosecutors to obtain a grand jury indictment against him for trafficking in cocaine. Out on bond, G.P. and the few left in his operation moved their business from John Hope Homes into two other apartment complexes in northwest Atlanta. However, G.P. was followed by police and later arrested on the indictment warrant while he was transporting 15 bags of crack cocaine.

Assessment Because of successful enforcement activities, the Miami Boys gang in John Hope and University Homes was completely shut down. Residents, housing authority staff and police officers noted a subsequent decline in street-level drug dealing at the complex.

Resident fear was also substantially reduced. Tenants began to walk through the complex at night, and children began to play in the playgrounds during the day, unheard of occurrences when the Miami Boys were in charge.

During the latter part of the Miami Boys' crackdown, residents began to demonstrate visible support for the police. For example, during police raids, residents came outside and praised the officers and offered words of encouragement. They also began providing information about the drug situation in their area, which surfaced initially in the form of whispers and confidential telephone calls. Eventually, as trust grew, residents began to openly volunteer information and gave their names freely.

Partially because area residents began to understand their role in ridding the area of drug dealers, no other Miami Boys factions or other organized drug gangs were able to establish a foothold. Officer T. and his partner continued to monitor the situation at the complex.

SUMMARY

The youth gang problem appears to be increasing. The *National Gang Threat Assessment* classifies gangs as street gangs, prison gangs and outlaw motorcycle gangs. Gang members often engage in vandalism, drug dealings, larceny/theft, burglary/breaking and entering, aggravated assault, motor vehicle theft and drive-by shootings. The first step in dealing with a gang problem is to recognize it. Once the problem is recognized, police need to identify gangs and their members. This is not difficult as most gang members identify themselves by their names, clothing, tattoos, sign language, slang and graffiti.

Four general strategies are being used to deal with gang problems: (1) suppression or law enforcement efforts, (2) social intervention, (3) opportunities provision to prevent gang involvement and (4) community organization.

Frequently, gangs and drugs are integrally related. Research supports the link between street-level drug hot spot activity, disorder and serious crime. Approaches that have been suggested to address the drug problem include crime control, punishment, rehabilitation, prevention and legalization.

Police often use simple drug buys, undercover operations and raids to combat the drug problem. Buy operations occur in three well-defined stages: preparations for the buy, the buy itself and actions needed after the buy to process evidence and information. Information and time are critical elements in an illegal drug buy. The sale and use of illegal drugs is difficult to investigate and prosecute because sellers and buyers are willing participants. Making several drug buys will protect against a claim of entrapment.

In the 1980s, law enforcement focused its efforts in dealing with the drug problem on undercover operations and sophisticated raids. Law enforcement's focus in the 1990s was on enlisting and educating the public and targeting street-level sales. That emphasis continues into the 21st century.

Legislation may also help, such as drug abatement statutes, which declare any property where illegal drugs are used or sold to be a public nuisance.

APPLICATION

The chief wants you, the new commander of the narcotics squad, to establish some policies and procedures regarding drug buys. The present guidelines are obsolete. He instructs you to look at the previous general orders, policy and procedure bulletins, and to upgrade the operations.

INSTRUCTIONS

Use the form in the Appendix. Identify the problems and needs. Specify what the policy is, why it is needed and what the police department's responsibility is. In this set of policies and procedures, concentrate on only drug *buy* procedures. Include the preparation, intelligence, surveillance, the buy money procedures, what to do during and after the buy, what to do when making arrests and processing evidence, and what the report should contain.

AN EXERCISE IN CRITICAL THINKING

On July 8, Mike O'Brien came to an apartment building with five minors to purchase marijuana from a minor who lived in the complex. A group of minors (gang members) was also present in the parking lot for the same purpose. A number of the youths congregated around O'Brien's car, a classic 1966 Chevrolet Impala that O'Brien was in the process of restoring.

Fred Fidel (a member of a rival neighborhood gang) pulled into the parking lot and attempted to pull his vehicle partway into the limited space next to O'Brien's car, almost hitting it. Although none of the building's tenants were assigned designated parking spaces, Fidel habitually parked in the spot directly adjacent to the spot in which O'Brien had parked and in which many of the youths were standing. Although other parking spaces were available, Fidel pulled up to the spot where the youths were standing and repeatedly honked his horn. At that time, O'Brien told Fidel, "If you scratch my car, I'll kick your ass."

Fidel got out of his car, entered into an altercation with O'Brien, and pulled out a knife, brandishing it back and forth in front of O'Brien. O'Brien initially backed away as Fidel walked toward him. Fidel got back into his car and attempted to pull further into the parking space. Fidel then got out of his car, leaving it in such a position that O'Brien would be unable to move his car to leave.

As Fidel walked toward the building, O'Brien went toward him, advising Fidel that he was blocking O'Brien's car and offering to move it for him. During this second confrontation, Fidel again pulled out his knife. O'Brien told him to "back off; everything is cool." Fidel, however, grabbed O'Brien by the shirt with one hand as O'Brien tried to remove himself from Fidel's grasp and thrust the knife into O'Brien's chest with his other hand.

O'Brien was interviewed by police on the scene, but he bled to death before medical care could be administered. When Fidel was questioned by police, he at first denied possessing a knife or knowing anything about the stabbing. After a few minutes, he changed his account of the event and claimed self-defense.

1. Given the conflicting testimony between the members of the gang and Fidel, is there sufficient evidence to arrest Fidel for second-degree felony murder?
   a. Numerous witnesses give probable cause to believe that Fidel committed felony murder, and therefore, Fidel should be arrested.
   b. Because the only witnesses are juvenile gang members whose testimony is suspect, prosecution will be nearly impossible; therefore, Fidel's testimony should be recorded, but he should not be arrested.
   c. As Fidel clearly was outnumbered and likely felt insecure, he probably wanted only to intimidate O'Brien; so there is insufficient cause to arrest Fidel for second-degree felony murder.
   d. Because of the intended purchase of drugs, Fidel can be arrested for first-degree intentional murder.
   e. Because it is Fidel's word against the gang's, both negate each other, leaving insufficient evidence for arresting and convicting Fidel of second-degree felony murder.

DISCUSSION QUESTIONS

1. How might possible changes in the juvenile justice system be a deterrent to juveniles joining gangs?
2. Does your community have a gang problem? If so, describe it.
3. What role can citizens and community groups usefully play in coping with the drug problem?
4. What must officers consider when establishing a fictitious past for a cover story as an undercover agent?
5. As an undercover agent, if someone asks you if you are a "narc," how do you respond? What attitude will protect your safety?
6. Is drug dealing a problem in your educational institution? Your community?
7. What are some unobtrusive signals surveillance team members can use to cover such various situations as when the buy has been completed, when help is needed and so on?

GALE EMERGENCY SERVICES DATABASE ASSIGNMENTS

- Use the Gale Emergency Services database to answer the Discussion Questions as appropriate.
- Using the Gale Emergency Services database, find and outline one of the following articles:
    - "The Life Development of Gang Members: Interventions at Various Stages" by Mike Meacham and Tony Stokes
    - "Street Gangs: Lessons from a Task Force" by Carole Moore
    - "Street Gang Mentality: A Mosaic of Remorseless Violence and Relentless Loyalty" by Anthony J. Pinizzotto, Edward F. Davis, and Charles E. Miller III
    - "Gangs in Indian Country: The Growing Phenomenon of Native American Gangs" by Liz Martinez
    - "Understanding and Tackling Gang Violence" by Karen Bullock and Nick Tilley
    - "Return to D.A.R.E.: Armed with Scientific Credibility, the New D.A.R.E. Program Makes a Comeback" by Michelle Perin
    - "Jesus Malverde's Significance to Mexican Drug Traffickers" by Robert J. Botsch
    - "An Analysis of Clandestine Methamphetamine Laboratory Seizures in Oklahoma" by Rashi K. Shukla and E. Elaine Bartgis
    - "Assembling Recidivism: The Promise and Contingencies of Post-Release Life" by Mark Halsey
    - "Implementing an Asset Forfeiture Program" by Victor E. Hartman
    - "Connecting Drug Paraphernalia to Drug Gangs" by Robert D. Sheehy and Efrain A. Rosario

REFERENCES

"Addressing Community Gang Problems." Washington, DC: National Youth Gang Center, 2009.

"Almost 50% of Agencies Routinely Use K-9s." *Police*, March 2008, p.14.

Archibold, Randal C. "U.S. Moves against Top Mexican Drug Cartel." *The New York Times*, February 26, 2009.

"Asset Forfeiture Funds Report." Washington, DC: U.S. Marshals Service, 2006.

"Asset Forfeiture Program." Washington, DC: U.S. Marshals Service, no date.

Basich, Melanie. "Are Gang Members Hopeless Cases?" *Police Magazine*, May 2009, pp.21–22.

Bell, Kerryn E. "Gender and Gangs: A Quantitative Comparison." *Crime & Delinquency*, July 2009, pp.363–387.

Best Practices to Address Community Gang Problems. Washington, DC: Office of Juvenile Justice and Delinquency Prevention, 2008. (NCJ 222799)

Brown, Matthew. "Flying Drones to Battle Pot Growers." *Police One.com News*, April 4, 2008.

The Coach's Playbook against Drugs. Washington, DC: Office of Juvenile Justice and Delinquency Prevention, no date. (NCJ 173393)

"Combating the Stop Snitching Code of Silence." *Community Policing Dispatch*, July 2009.

Commission on Accreditation of Law Enforcement Agencies. *Standards for Law Enforcement Agencies*, 5th ed. Fairfax, VA: CALEA, 2006, updated 2008.

Decker, Scott H.; Katz, Charles M.; and Webb, Vincent J. "Understanding the Black Box of Gang Organization." *Crime & Delinquency*, January 2008, pp.153–172.

Dedel, Kelly. *Drive-By Shootings*. Washington, DC: Community Oriented Policing Services Office, March 2007.

Dees, Tim. "Field Narcotics Testing." *Law Officer Magazine*, June 2008, pp.74–79.

Egley, Arlen, Jr., and O'Donnell, Christina E. *Highlights of the 2006 National Youth Gang Survey*. Washington, DC: Office of Juvenile Justice Delinquency Prevention, July 2008.

Egley, Arlen, Jr., and O'Donnell, Christina E. *Highlights of the 2007 National Youth Gang Survey*. Washington,

DC: Office of Juvenile Justice Delinquency Prevention, April 2009.

Fields, Gary. "White House Czar Calls for End to 'War on Drugs.'" *The Wall Street Journal*, May 14, 2009.

Gang Awareness. Chicago: City of Chicago, Department of Human Services, no date.

Griffith, David. "Finding a Cure for a Cancer." *Police*, March 2009, p.14.

"Highlights of Gang-Related Legislation Spring 2008." Washington, DC: Institute for Intergovernmental Research, 2009.

Hsu, Spencer. "Obama Targets Mexican Cartels." *The Washington Post*, April 18, 2009.

Kanable, Rebecca. "Returning Results with FICO Programs." *Law Enforcement Technology*, November 2008, pp.48–55.

Kennedy, David. "Drugs, Race and Common Ground: Reflections on the High Point Intervention." *NIJ Journal*, March 2009.

Klein, Malcolm W. *Chasing after Street Gangs: A Forty-Year Journey*. Upper Saddle River, NJ: Pearson/Prentice Hall, 2007.

Laine, Russell B. "A Crisis We Must Confront." *The Police Chief*, April 2009, p.6.

Leinwand, Donna. "Immigration Charges Used to Crack Down on Gangs." *USA Today*, October 8, 2007.

Logue, Darin. "The Hidden Badge: The Undercover Narcotics Operation." *Law Enforcement Technology*, February 2008, pp.94–100.

Marizco, Michel. "Border Epidemic?" *Law Enforcement Technology*, February 2009, pp.40–47.

Mazerolle, Lorraine; Soole, David W.; and Rombouts, Sacha. *Crime Prevention Research Reviews No. 1: Disrupting Street-Level Drug Markets.* Washington, DC: Office of Community Oriented Policing Services, July 22, 2007a.

Mazerolle, Lorraine; Soole, David; and Rombouts, Sacha. "Drug Law Enforcement: A Review of the Evaluation Literature." *Police Quarterly*, June 2007b, pp.115–153.

McCabe, James E. "What Works in Policing? The Relationship between Drug Enforcement and Serious Crime." *Police Quarterly*, September 2008, pp.289–313.

Moore, Carole. "The ACLU Plays 'Go Fish.'" *Law Enforcement Technology*, November 2007a, p.98.

Moore, Carole. "Street Gangs." *Law Enforcement Technology*, January 2007b, pp.52–57.

National Drug Control Strategy 2009 Annual Report. Washington, DC: Office of National Drug Control Policy, January 2009.

National Drug Threat Assessment 2009. Washington, DC: National Drug Intelligence Center, December 2008.

National Gang Threat Assessment 2009. Washington, DC: U.S. Department of Justice, 2009.

"NYGC [National Gang Youth Center] Research Update." 2009. Accessed: http://www.nationalgangcenter.gov/Content/Documents/Evaluation-Updates.pdf

"National Youth Gang Survey Analysis." Washington, DC: Institute for Intergovernmental Research, 2009.

Ortega, Francisca, and Calderoni, Valeria. "Gangs Unite as 'Hybrids,' Increasing Violence." *Police One*, October 1, 2007.

Petrocelli, Joseph. "Patrol Response to Street Corner Drug Dealing." *Police*, January 2007, pp.20–22.

Petrocelli, Joseph. "Patrol Response to Graffiti." *Police*, March 2008, pp.18–19.

Petrocelli, Joseph. "Patrol Response to Clandestine Meth Labs." *Police*, January 2009, pp.14–17.

Pistole, John S. "Major Executive Speeches." Washington, DC: Federal Bureau of Investigation, March 3, 2008.

Posey, Ed. "Using Existing Records to Keep a Closer Eye on Sex Offenders and Gang Members in the Community." *The Police Chief*, June 2008, pp.38–47.

Redmond, Lisa. "'Sophisticated' K-9 Units Help Mass. Cops." *The Lowell Sun*, June 23, 2008.

Rotstein, Arthur H. "Feds Ready to Build 'Virtual Fence' along Border." *PoliceOne.com News*, May 11, 2009.

"Satellites Take on Crime Busting along the Border." *U.S. News & World Report*, May 18, 2009.

Savelli, Lou. *Gangs across America and Their Symbols.* Flushing, NY: Looseleaf Law Publications, Inc., 2004.

Schrader, Jordan. "Graffiti Complaints, Cleanup Efforts on Rise." *USA Today*, May 11, 2009.

Stockton. Dale. "A Clear & Present Danger: Violence South of the Border Poses a Serious Threat." *Law Officer Magazine*, June 2009, p.8.

The Stop Snitching Phenomenon: Breaking the Code of Silence. Washington, DC: Community Oriented Policing Services Office, June 15, 2009.

Straub, Frank G. "Commissioner Frank Straub Testifies on Reducing Gang and Youth Violence." *Subject to Debate*, June 2008, pp.1, 4, 5.

Taylor, Terrance J. "The Boulevard Ain't Safe for Your Kids . . . Youth Gang Membership and Violent Victimization." *Journal of Contemporary Criminal Justice*, 2008, pp.125–136.

Tita, George, and Ridgeway, Greg. "The Impact of Gang Formation on Local Patterns of Crime." *Journal of Research in Crime and Delinquency*, May 2007, pp.208–237.

Weisel, Deborah Lamm. *Graffiti.* Washington, DC: Problem Oriented Policing Services Office, June 12, 2007.

Weiss, Joseph. "Autonomous Robotics for Law Enforcement." *Law Enforcement Technology*, February 2007, pp.66–73.

"Welcome to the G.R.E.A.T. Web Site," 2009. Accessed: http://www.great-online.org/

Wethal, Tabatha. "Idle Hands." *Law Enforcement Technology*, July 2008, pp.86–94.

Worrall, John L. *Asset Forfeiture.* Washington, DC: Office of Community Oriented Policing Services, November 2008.

CASES CITED

Chicago v. Morales, 527 U.S. 41 (1999)

Hampton v. United States, 425 U.S. 484 (1976)

HELPFUL WEB RESOURCES

Florida Department of Corrections: Street Gangs: http://www.dc.state.fl.us/pub/gangs/sets.html

Know Gangs: www.KnowGangs.com

National Gang Crime Research Center: http://www.ngcrc.com

Robert Walker's *Gangs OR Us*: www.gangsorus.com

SECTION IV

The Personal Side of Police Operations

Section I described the basic skills needed to perform the functions of today's law enforcement agencies legally and in the context of a changing society, while using discretion wisely. The need to protect the constitutional rights of all citizens, including those who commit crimes, was emphasized throughout Section I, as was the need to act professionally.

Sections II and III examined the basic police operations as well as specialized functions of police, still emphasizing the importance of respecting individual rights, of acting within the law and of using discretion professionally.

This section examines the personal side of police operations even as it continues to stress the needs for protecting the rights of others and for acting professionally. Today's officers face more stresses than ever before, so it is incumbent on them to be physically and mentally fit. The stresses of the job can be every bit as hazardous as a gun-wielding

criminal (Chapter 13). The text concludes with two critical areas in law enforcement, avoiding civil liabilities and doing what is moral and right. Given the great amount of discretion officers have, it is crucial that they select alternatives that are legally and morally acceptable to themselves, their colleagues and the public they serve (Chapter 14).

CHAPTER 13

Physical and Mental Health Issues

Keeping Fit for Duty

DO YOU KNOW . . .

- What the prime factor in physical fitness is?
- What police-specific physical skills are important?
- What job-related factors detract from police officers' physical fitness?
- What constitutes an effective fitness program?
- What bloodborne pathogens police officers should protect against?
- What the concept of universal precaution recommends?
- What the greatest threat to officers' mental fitness is?
- What the major categories of stressors for police officers are?
- What the effects of stress might include?
- What the awareness spectrum is and where in that spectrum police officers should try to be?
- What the three sides of the border patrol's survival triangle are?
- What the five Cs of basic tactics for survival are?

CAN YOU DEFINE?

acute stress
aerobic training
anaerobic training
awareness spectrum
burnout
burst stress
chronic stress
cross-training
depression
mental fitness
physical fitness
split-second syndrome
survival triangle
universal precaution

INTRODUCTION

Police work has been characterized as long periods of devastating boredom punctuated by sporadic, relatively brief periods of utter terror. Quigley (2008, p.62) notes, "Making split-second, life saving decisions; facing inherent dangers; working shift work and long hours; and constantly interacting with people who are upset, angry, or uncooperative all take a toll on individuals." Much about the job, unfortunately, allows officers to become less physically and mentally fit than they were when they passed the rigorous preemployment screening. Murray (2007, p.48) stresses, "Total preparation, in mind and body, prepares officers for physical encounters."

Physical and mental fitness are fundamentally related: mental discipline is needed to maintain or improve physical fitness, and mental alertness requires physical fitness. Physical and mental fitness also affect stress levels and officers' responses to stress. Furthermore, physical fitness, mental fitness and adaptability to the stresses of police work are all correlated with officers' safety on the job—in effect, their very lives may depend on such physical and mental preparedness.

Although this chapter discusses physical fitness, mental fitness, stress and officer safety as separate topics, their interrelationship must be kept in mind. The chapter begins with a discussion of physical fitness. This is followed by discussions of physical fitness training programs and the threats posed by bloodborne pathogens and biological and chemical agents. Next, mental fitness is explored, including an explanation of stress, sources of stress, the effects of stress, reducing stress and mental fitness programs. The chapter concludes with a discussion of officer safety.

PHYSICAL FITNESS

The United States has become fitness conscious. Visit almost any city and you can see joggers and runners, bikers and rollerbladers. Health clubs do a brisk business. Weight-loss programs have proliferated. Even fast food chains are now offering reduced-fat and fat-free items. People strive to be fit. **Physical fitness** is the body's general capacity to adapt and respond favorably to physical effort.

The general capacity to adapt and respond favorably to physical effort.

The demands of police work require officers to be in top physical condition. Physical fitness may make the difference between success and failure on the job and sometimes may even make the difference between life and death. Furthermore, officers who are not physically fit are not prepared to adequately discharge their duties and may, as a result, be sued. In *Parker v. District of Columbia* (1988), the jury awarded nearly half a million dollars to a man shot twice by a DC police officer during an arrest. The jury reasoned, "Had the officer been physically fit, . . . he might have overpowered the suspect instead of reaching for his gun. The officer 'simply was not in adequate physical shape' to do his job." This is not an isolated case.

Grossi (2007, p.26) notes, "Many studies reveal that fit cops are not only more productive, but use force less often, live a lot longer and are more likely to survive a high-risk (or deadly) encounter." The FBI considers physical fitness so important that its National Academy at Quantico, Virginia, has made CJ340, "Fitness in Law Enforcement," the only required course for all police students attending (Grossi). Fitness is also considered an ethical obligation to one's coworkers: "The uniformed officer simply must be fit enough to offer backup assistance to a fellow officer. If not, it is like showing up at a gunfight without a gun" (Sanow, 2009, p.95).

Consider the following definition of being *fit for duty*: "If an officer can safely perform his or her duties in an effective manner without jeopardizing his or her life or the lives of others, including other officers, bystanders, even subject and suspect, the officer is fit for duty" (Young, 2008, p.48). Agencies are encouraged to adopt a fit-for-duty statement supporting officer safety first and foremost: "Being fit for duty is not only an officer safety issue. It is the mark of a professional who is ready to fight to protect him- or herself, fellow officers, and the public" (Young, p.49). A study conducted in North Carolina showed impressive results among agencies that implemented fitness programs (Quigley, 2008, p.63): "The data show improvements across the board in overall fitness. Significant cardiovascular and strength improvements were noted, and several participants were even able to stop taking medication for diabetes and hypertension because of their weight loss. The participating agencies reported a 25 percent increase in productivity through a variety of factors: reduced absenteeism, reduced turnover rate, reduced accidents, and reduced worker's compensation claims. Research has shown that for every one dollar invested into fitness and wellness programs, the return ranges from two to five dollars."

Another important benefit of being physically fit is that, often, the mere appearance of fitness might deter an attack: "Offenders, especially desperate ones, size us up. A fit officer's appearance sends an unspoken message that challenging this officer might not be a good life choice" (Johnson, 2009, p.18).

Many people evaluate fitness on the basis of appearance alone. Although personal appearance can give certain indications of fitness levels, what is going on inside is more important. The prime indicators of physical fitness are endurance, balance, agility, flexibility, strength, power and body composition.

Although many factors contribute to a well-conditioned body, the prime factor is the condition of the circulatory (cardiovascular) system, upon which endurance or stamina depends.

Many agencies require active law enforcement officers to pass annual physical fitness tests to continue working in that capacity. Failure to pass may be grounds for dismissal from employment. The requirements of such tests are often similar to those used by the military and set different standards based on age and sex.

Many police departments are also now using body composition rather than height/weight charts in setting their physical standards. Excessive body fat not only hinders physical motion; it is also a serious risk factor for heart disease, diabetes and stroke. In addition to the preceding factors involved in physical fitness, several other physical factors are related specifically to how well police officers perform.

Motor skills important to police officers include coordination, speed and accuracy.

Myths about Physical Fitness

People hold many misconceptions about physical fitness, sometimes as excuses to avoid getting back into shape.

Physical fitness may make the difference between success and failure on the job and may even make the difference between life and death.
© Michael Newman/ PhotoEdit

Too Far Gone Many people feel they either are too old or have physically deteriorated to such a degree it is impossible to get back into good physical shape. This is not true. Regardless of age or how "far gone" a person is, if the person is generally healthy and free of serious disease, he or she can become fit through a well-structured physical training program.

Hard Work Will Kill You A rather common misconception is that the harder you work, the quicker you die. Not only is this false, but just the opposite is true. People need to exercise regularly or they deteriorate. People "rust out" from inactivity far more than they "wear out" from hard physical work.

Any Kind of Exercise Is Good Again, this is not true. Different exercises and activities have varying degrees of value depending on their intensity, duration and frequency. Short-duration exercising such as stretching or isometrics offers limited benefits. Likewise, an hour of racquetball, tennis or softball every few weeks by a usually sedentary person offers only limited benefits, and can be extremely dangerous. The most beneficial programs are those done regularly for at least 20 to 30 minutes and directed toward all aspects of total fitness.

No Pain, No Gain When people first begin exercise programs they often experience some stiffness and soreness, but such programs usually should not cause pain. This is not to imply, however, that getting and keeping physically fit is not hard work.

The Quick and Easy Way to Fitness Despite hordes of advertisements to the contrary, getting and keeping physically fit is hard work and requires commitment and discipline. It also takes time—weeks or months—to get into shape. Unfortunately, it takes much less time to get out of shape.

Police work is often sedentary, boring, involves irregular hours and rotating shifts, and may promote poor diets, excessive cigarette smoking and consumption of alcohol, and great amounts of stress.

Because of these factors, it is important that police officers engage in some sort of physical fitness training program.

PHYSICAL FITNESS TRAINING PROGRAMS

Because police officers often face situations involving physical restraint, self-defense or foot pursuit, many police departments have set up both mandatory and voluntary physical fitness programs for officers. "A total fitness program," says Quigley (2008, p.64), "incorporates the development of good lifestyle habits, including regular exercise, good nutrition, weight management, stress management, and substance abuse prevention."

Some agencies provide a "work out on duty" program that allows officers to exercise several times a week while on their regular shifts, if time permits. This is a benefit organizations use to recruit officers and to promote a healthy force. Many of the agencies that have on-site gyms also staff full-time registered dieticians and physical trainers for their officers. Other departments are able to arrange for discounted or fully paid memberships to local health and fitness center. Law enforcement officers who are required to pass annual physical fitness standards can generally write off most exercise related expenses for tax purposes. Furthermore, many agencies reward officers for exceeding physical fitness standards.

The kind of program instituted varies from department to department but should include **aerobic training** aimed at the cardiovascular system. This can be biking, cross-country skiing, rowing, swimming or walking. It also can include treadmills, stationary cycles and rowing machines. Aerobic training should be done at least three times a week for a minimum of 15 to 20 minutes. It should be preceded by a light warm-up and followed by a brief cool down. Aerobic training can also incorporate **cross-training**, with an officer biking one day, running one day and swimming one day.

aerobic training
Physical training aimed at strengthening the cardiovascular system.

cross-training
Alternating between different forms of exercise.

Speed training should be incorporated into the aerobic portion of the exercise. Police officers are often older than the suspects they chase and are further hindered by the 20 or more pounds of weight added by their gun belt and accessories. Although speed is usually needed in a foot chase, agility is often even more important. Agility can be practiced on an obstacle course or through drills such as those football players use. Jumping rope is another way to improve agility. Eye-hand coordination can be improved through racquetball, tennis, basketball and softball. Martial arts training can improve an officer's power, flexibility, speed and balance.

Another important part of an exercise program is *strength training,* or **anaerobic training**. Strength training helps maintain muscle tissue. Strength exercises can also help reduce low-back problems. Aerobic activities do little in this area.

anaerobic training
Physical training aimed at strengthening the muscles of the body.

In addition, an officer's physical abilities are frequently tested in such activities as restraining a violent suspect, pushing a disabled vehicle and lifting an injured person. Among the methods available for building strength are free weights and machines, which usually rely on "progressive resistance," and resistance against one's own body weight, which usually relies on "progressive repetition." Exercises using resistance against one's own body weight include push-ups, pull-ups, dips and sit-ups.

Flexibility training is also important. This can be done as stretching in the warm-up and cool down portions of aerobic or strength training. Stretching reduces muscle tension, improves coordination and can prevent injuries. Each stretch should be held for approximately 10 seconds. Breathing should be normal, and no bouncing should be done. It should *not* be painful. If a muscle is stretched to the point of pain, it is being stretched too far.

An effective physical fitness training program that is varied and of interest to the officer should include aerobic, strength and flexibility training. It should be engaged in regularly for 20 to 30 minutes a day, at least three days a week.

Besides the obvious benefits to individual officers, physical fitness programs tend to foster more positive attitudes and reduce absenteeism, use of sick time, job-related injuries, use-of-force issues and early retirement. Insurance premiums may go down, and productivity often goes up.

Collingwood et al. (2004) researched physical fitness assessments for 15 years, with validation studies performed on more than 5,500 incumbent officers representing 75 federal, state and local law enforcement agencies. Their study was designed to assess the accuracy of a physical fitness test as a predictor of an officer's ability to perform physical job tasks. The researchers (p.33) identified three basic events containing critical and frequent tasks:

1. Roadway clearance, involving lifting, carrying and dragging debris, and pushing a car
2. Victim extraction, involving sprinting to a disabled vehicle and lifting and dragging a dummy to safety
3. Sustained foot pursuit, involving running up stairs, dodging, jumping, climbing a fence, crawling, vaulting obstacles, striking and moving a dummy, and simulated cutting using resistance bands.

The researchers then isolated fitness factors and tests that might measure them. For example, a 1.5-mile run could be used to test the fitness factor of endurance and aerobic power; the vertical jump can test explosive leg strength; and the sit-and-reach test can test extent flexibility (Collingwood et al., 2004, p.34).

Other Aspects of Physical Fitness

Nutrition plays an important role in a person's overall fitness. Low-cholesterol, low-fat foods can reduce the risks of coronary artery disease (CAD), sometimes called coronary heart disease (CHD) or cardiovascular disease. Cardiovascular disease is the number one killer of law enforcement officers, but making healthy nutrition choices can add years and quality of life well beyond retirement

(Vonk, 2009a, p.30). Although carbohydrates have been given a bad rap, they are the most important food group for emergency service professionals and athletes alike (Vonk, 2009b, p.14). They allow officers to fight longer, deliver more powerful strikes, and think and respond more rapidly. Carbohydrates include fruits, vegetables, pasta, bread, rice and potatoes.

Just as officers get ready for their tour of duty by checking their weapons and other equipment, they should also stock their squad with appropriate snacks, as they might not get a chance to actually eat a meal. Recommended items include bottles of water, energy bars, trail mix and bananas (Schreiber, 2008, p.14). A detailed discussion of what constitutes proper nutrition is beyond the scope of this text. Hundreds, probably thousands, of books are available on the subject for those interested in learning more.

HEALTH HAZARDS

Garrett (2008, p.46) reminds us of the obvious: "Police work is a high-risk occupation that often involves physical contact to subdue violent suspects or prisoners. But today's criminals bring more than a potential for violence to the streets, some also carry the silent and less obvious risk of unknown infections. Likewise, once officers restrain a subject, the danger is far from over. The infectious material these individuals transmit may continue to contaminate booking stations, holding cells or incarceration facilities for some time to come."

Bloodborne pathogens police officers should protect against include HIV infections and AIDS, hepatitis B, and hepatitis C.

HIV Infection and AIDS

Human immunodeficiency virus (HIV) is typically transmitted from one person to another, usually during unprotected sex or by sharing needles during IV drug abuse. HIV may also be transmitted through blood transfusions. Acquired immune deficiency syndrome (AIDS) is the end stage of HIV infection.

The potential for exposure to HIV/AIDS in police work remains minimal. However, civil liability may result when officers deal with suspects who have AIDS. A police department can be vulnerable both to internal and external civil claims. For example, in *Jane Doe v. Borough of Barrington* (1990), a city was held responsible for failing to adequately train its officers about AIDS, resulting in privacy right violations to the family of an HIV-positive arrestee. Likewise, in *Woods v. White* (1990), the court ruled that individuals have a constitutional right to privacy in information relating to AIDS. Another issue is whether offenders with HIV should be isolated.

The main concerns involve including HIV information in police reports and having officers disclose their own HIV status to coworkers and supervisors. Including a suspect's HIV status in a police report may violate medical information laws, but not including it may raise issues of why an officer acted in a certain way.

Hepatitis B Viral Infection

Hepatitis B viral infection affects the liver and poses a much greater risk than HIV. It can progress to chronic liver disease or liver cancer and death. Symptoms range from fever, aching muscles and loss of appetite to prolonged nausea and vomiting and yellowing of the skin (jaundice).

Fortunately, a vaccine is available whose protection lasts for nine years. Since 1992, the Occupational Safety and Health Administration (OSHA) has required law enforcement agencies to offer at no cost the vaccination against hepatitis B to all officers who may have contact with body fluids while on the job.

Hepatitis C Viral Infection

Hepatitis C virus also attacks the liver and is much more treacherous than hepatitis B. Unfortunately, there is no effective treatment or protective vaccine for this disease.

How Bloodborne Pathogens Are Spread

Hepatitis B, hepatitis C and HIV infection are spread in the same way—through contact with blood, semen, vaginal secretions (sexual contact) and any other body fluid or tissue that contains visible blood. Infection can also occur through contact with the fluid that surrounds an unborn child and the fluid around the heart, lungs or joints. Body fluids such as sweat, tears, saliva, urine, stool, vomit, nasal secretions and spit have not been shown to transmit bloodborne diseases, unless they contain visible blood.

These viruses are not spread through the air like cold and flu germs, so contamination will not occur simply from working alongside someone who is infected, from touching them, or by being coughed or sneezed on by them, nor will infection occur from sharing telephones, bathrooms, eating utensils, gym equipment, swimming pools or water fountains with an infected person.

Other Diseases

Tuberculosis (TB) is transmitted through the air by people who are coughing, hacking and wheezing. Officers may encounter TB when dealing with people from other cultures, such as immigrants from African regions. *Meningitis* is also spread by airborne transmission. It causes inflammation of the membranes that surround the brain and can result in headaches, fever, vomiting, stiff neck, light sensitivity and death.

A particularly worrisome and growing health hazard is *methicillin-resistant staphylococcus aureus (MRSA) infection*: "MRSA . . . pronounced 'mersa,' is an epidemic plaguing all law enforcement agencies and correctional facilities in the United States. The bacteria causes a drug resistant infection that is as effective as a bullet in wreaking pain, suffering, and even death, killing more than 100,000 people in U.S. hospitals alone every year" (Schneider, 2007, p.18). Although previously found primarily in hospitals, and still a threat to police officers who may spend their shifts in a hospital setting, guarding a hospitalized suspect or prisoner, the "superbug" is now also found in every area of law enforcement: "MRSA is a type of staph (bacteria) that may cause skin infections that often look like pimples, boils, a spider or other insect bites. These may be red, swollen, painful, and could have pus or other drainage. The infected area may also be warm to the touch and accompanied with a fever. What makes the MRSA type of staph so alarming is its resistance to detection and treatment, earning the moniker "superbug" (Haughton, 2009, pp.39–40).

Protecting Oneself

OSHA has developed standards on bloodborne pathogens that require employers to address employee protection in a written exposure control plan describing precautions employees can take to prevent exposures as well as steps to take if exposure does occur. Precautions against bloodborne disease include getting the hepatitis B vaccine, treating all body fluids as infectious (a practice referred to as *universal precaution*), wearing appropriate personal protection equipment (PPE), thoroughly washing your hands and other exposed parts of your body after every personal contact, following department protocol after every exposure [e.g., get tested], and documenting and reporting all exposures.

The concept of **universal precaution** recommends that all blood and potentially infectious materials other than blood must be treated as if infected.

universal precaution
All blood and potentially infectious materials other than blood must be treated as if infected.

Proper personal hygiene is important, including effective hand washing, showering before leaving work, and having uniforms cleaned at work instead of at home. In addition, the property room and vehicles should be sterilized and disinfected. Numerous sterilizing and disinfecting technologies are now available.

Cuts, scrapes and puncture wounds can all become infected and should be thoroughly washed and bandaged as soon as possible. Several self-sealing cut closure strips, bandages and similar products are available for wound care and should be included in an officer's first-aid kit. Avoid sharing personal items, such as towels, washcloths, razors, clothing or uniforms that may have had contact with an infected wound or bandage (Schneider, 2007, p.23).

Officers can also become infected from human bites. An officer who is bitten by a human should wash the wound immediately and then see a doctor for the appropriate antibiotics. An officer who is bitten by an animal should impound the animal if possible and have it tested for rabies.

The *tetanus shot* is an important safeguard against infections and should be repeated every 10 years. If, however, a deep or dirty wound is sustained, a tetanus shot should have been given within the last five years.

Biological and Chemical Threats

The potential threat of chemical, biological and other unconventional weapons has increased on the local, state and federal levels and should be prepared for. Responding to hazardous materials (hazmat) incidents was discussed in Chapter 5.

Keys to Preventing Infections and Other Health Hazards

The FBI's *Handbook of Forensic Services* (Waggoner, 2007, pp.150–152) begins its discussion of protective measures by noting that the concept of following universal precautions is the primary mechanism for infection control. Other protective measures include the following:

- Use barrier protection—such as disposable gloves, coveralls, and shoe covers—if contact with potentially infectious materials may occur. Change gloves when torn or punctured or when their ability to function as a barrier is compromised. Wear appropriate eye and face protection to protect against splashes, sprays, and spatters of potentially infectious materials.
- Wash hands after removing gloves or other personal protective equipment. Remove gloves and other personal protective equipment in a manner that will not result in contaminating unprotected skin or clothing.
- Prohibit eating, drinking, smoking, or applying cosmetics where human blood, body fluids, or other potential infectious materials are present, regardless of personal protection that may be worn.
- Place contaminated sharps in appropriate closable, leakproof, puncture-resistant containers when transported or discarded. Label the containers with a BIOHAZARD warning label.
- Do not bend, re-cap, remove, or otherwise handle contaminated needles or other sharps.
- After use, decontaminate equipment with a daily prepared solution of household bleach diluted 1:10 or with 70 percent isopropyl alcohol or other appropriate disinfectant. Noncorrosive disinfectants are commercially available. It is important to allow sufficient contact time for complete disinfection.
- In addition to universal precautions, engineering controls and prudent work practices can reduce or eliminate exposure to potential infectious materials. Examples of engineering controls include long-handled mirrors used to locate and retrieve evidence in confined or hidden spaces and puncture-resistant containers used to store and dispose of sharps and paint stirrers.

Specialized, easily donned protective gear is also available for certain high-risk situations. For example, police-grade Kevlar-lined gloves may be used when searching suspects, especially in drug related incidents.

The ever-present threat of physical injury and infection goes hand-in-hand with the police profession and can cause significant stress and anxiety in officers. A crucial strategy to effectively handle this stress and the physical demands of the job is to pay adequate attention to mental fitness.

mental fitness
A person's emotional well-being, the ability to feel fear, anger, compassion and other emotions and to express them appropriately; also refers to a person's alertness and ability to make decisions quickly.

MENTAL FITNESS

Mental fitness is not as easily perceived or analyzed, but it is equally as important as physical fitness. **Mental fitness** refers to a person's emotional well-being, the ability to feel fear, anger, compassion and other emotions and to express them appropriately. It also refers to a person's alertness and ability to make decisions quickly.

The greatest threat to officers' mental fitness is negative stress.

STRESS

Most people have a general idea of what stress is. Most people also perceive stress as negative, but this is not necessarily true. A certain amount of stress keeps people alert and functioning. Too much stress, or *distress,* however, can be incapacitating. In ancient China, the symbol for stress included two characters—one symbolizing danger, the other opportunity.

Stress may be acute or chronic. **Acute stress** is temporary and may result in peak performance. Adrenaline rushes through the body; heart rate increases; blood pressure, brain activity, breathing rates and metabolic rates increase—adapting the body for fight or flight. Thousands of years before we became "civilized," our bodies were faced with simple survival, for which either a "fight or flight" response was appropriate.

acute stress
Temporary stress that may result in peak performance; body adapts for fight or flight.

Chronic stress, in contrast, is ongoing, like being under a state of constant siege. This can lead to severe psychological problems. In his classic work *The Stress of Life* (1956), Dr. Hans Selye suggested that humans subjected to excessive stress undergo a "general adaptation syndrome" consisting of three distinct stages: alarm reaction, resistance and exhaustion. In the first stage, *alarm reaction,* individuals perceive a threat to their safety or happiness. They recognize their inability to reach their personal/professional goals. The body releases stress hormones. In the second stage, *resistance,* individuals try to cope with the problem. The amount of resistance to the stressors increases, and bodily defense mechanisms are activated. In the third stage, *exhaustion,* individuals feel helpless and hopeless. Bodily resources are also exhausted, and people cannot adequately defend against the stressors.

chronic stress
Ongoing, continuous stress; like being under a state of constant siege; can lead to severe psychological problems.

SOURCES OF STRESS

Many lists of stressors have been generated, including stressors specific to the police profession. Most of the stressors fall into four main categories, although some overlap exists.

Sources of stress for police officers include

- Internal, individual stressors.
- Stressors inherent to the police job.
- Administrative and organizational stressors.
- External stressors from the criminal justice system and the citizens it serves.

Internal, Individual Stressors

Internal stressors vary greatly and can include officers' worries about their competency to handle assignments as well as feelings of helplessness and vulnerability. Mandatory training, court duty, shift work and overtime can leave police officers feeling trapped in a profession that does not allow room for family and recreational pursuits. Duty-related tasks can occupy so much time that an officer's home life suffers. Shift work may cause officers to routinely miss anniversary or birthday celebrations; their children's concerts, sports activities and school open houses; and other important family functions. This dearth of time for personal development can translate into divorce, suicide, alcoholism or burn-out.

Vernon (2009, p.48) identifies what he calls perhaps the most dangerous condition in law enforcement: the "Knights of the Roundtable Syndrome." Noting that many officers refer to police work as "The Job," Vernon describes how, as part of the syndrome, The Job takes central priority in an officer's life, providing a sense of purpose, significance and fulfillment, to the detriment of everything else: "We can neglect other very important responsibilities and relationships—*even with our own families*." He cautions, "It's possible for an officer to finish their career with no family, no friends—other than a few other cops—and no outside interests. And when The Job ends, as it must, there's nothing."

To avoid this situation Vernon recommends officers recognize the hazard and actively consider the impact being a police officer has on friends and family. For example, officers might arrange a shift change with a cooperative partner so as to be able to attend a family function (if department policy allows): "The key is balance. We should do our best in this most significant responsibility, but it should not consume one's life" (Vernon, 2009, p.48).

Stress Related to Police Work

The police role itself is often vague and contradictory. Many people become police officers to fight crime, not to do social work or spend hours writing reports. They are surprised to see how much "service" is actually involved in police work and how much time is spent documenting incidents and actions. They are also surprised to learn that their efforts are often not appreciated and that, in fact, their uniform is an object of scorn and derision.

The media often presents a distorted view of police work and police officers, resulting in unrealistic expectations by many citizens. Further, the distorted image is displayed over and over. Approximately one-third of regular television programming deals with some aspect of the criminal justice system. Citizens come to wonder: If a TV cop can solve three major crimes in an hour, why can't the local police at least keep prostitutes off the street or find the person who vandalized the school?

burst stress

Having to go from relative calm to high intensity, sometimes life-threatening, activity.

split-second syndrome

In some circumstances, officers have very little time to think through decisions. A high percentage of inappropriate decisions should be expected and accepted because the officer must act quickly.

The police badge may weigh only a few ounces, but it carries a heavy weight to those who wear it. They need to be in constant emotional control. And they experience what is referred to as **burst stress**, that is, having to go from relative calm to high intensity, sometimes life-threatening activity. This is closely related to what Fyfe (1986) refers to in his classic **split-second syndrome** that affects police-decision making in crisis. In such situations, all that can reasonably be asked is that officers respond quickly and that a high percentage of inappropriate decisions should be expected and accepted. The split-second syndrome asserts that if a person has intentionally or unintentionally provoked or threatened a police officer, at that instant the provoker rather than the police should be viewed as the cause of any resulting injuries or damages.

Every day officers are ready for the dangers and rigors of the job. When they go off duty, their bodies need downtime, yet day-to-day activities require them to continue pushing their bodies. A common result is fatigue.

Fatigue Fatigue is a dangerous and costly hazard of police work: "Sleep-loss related fatigue degrades performance, productivity and safety as well as health and well-being. Fatigue costs the U.S. economy $136 billion per year in health-related lost productivity alone" (Vila, 2009). Research has found that more than 90 percent of officers surveyed reported being routinely fatigued, and 85 percent reported driving while drowsy (Vila). One study has shown that officers on six or seven hours of sleep are twice as likely to be involved in a collision as those getting the recommended eight hours of sleep, and those on five hours of sleep have five times the likelihood (Yates, 2008).

Other research has attempted to quantitatively assess the dangerousness of sleep deprivation by comparing with drunk driving. One study found that being awake for 19 hours produces impairments comparable to having a blood alcohol concentration (BAC) of 0.05 percent; being awake for 24 hours is comparable to having a BAC of roughly 0.10 percent (Vila, 2009). It is a crime to drive with a BAC of 0.08 percent or above in all 50 states.

Several practices that contribute to the problem of line officer fatigue include secondary employment, overtime, court appearances and commuting. Although research has documented the reality of a tired workforce, it has also revealed a low-level desire among agency chiefs to have fatigue reduction policies (Senjo and Dhungana, 2009, p.123).

Agencies should review their policies that might contribute to fatigue, including how shifts are scheduled, the rotation of shift, the consecutive hours and days allowed to work and how many hours of extra jobs in a week an officer can work (Yates, 2008). One of the most popular policies is the "16-8 rule," which states that for every 16 hours of work, department must provide 8 hours of rest time (Yates). Regulating the amount of work time and rest time is standard practice for airline pilots and over-the-road truck drivers.

Additional Stressors Associated with the Police Job In addition to fatigue, shift work is associated with other complicating factors. Shift work may contribute to isolation from family and friends as previously noted, as well as contribute to the "blue wall" and "code of silence" perceptions some have. Monthly shift rotations necessitate physical adaptations such as getting used to sleeping different hours, as well as adaptations in officers' social and personal lives. Other stressors inherent in police work include constant threats to safety, entering dark buildings in which armed suspects are believed to be hiding, high-speed pursuits, continual exposure to victims in pain as well as unsavory criminals, the immense responsibilities of the job; the authorization to take a life; the ability to save a life, and the need to remain detached yet be empathetic.

Administrative and Organizational Stressors

Many management practices and organizational factors can cause stress specific to law enforcement. Stress frequently arises from having to operate from a set of policies and procedures drawn up by individuals who do not have to carry them out. Seldom is the on-the-line officer's opinion on operational policies and procedures sought, even though the individual officer must carry out these policies and procedures.

Researchers have found that the bureaucratic and organizational aspects of police work are actually more stressful than critical incidents are (Best, 2009, p.9). A PoliceOne poll ("P1Poll," 2009) revealed that the biggest pet peeve about police work was the bureaucracy (51 percent), followed by lack of funds (28 percent). Other sources of administrative and organizational stress include lack of support from administration when a questionable action is taken, the unavailability of needed resources or the poor condition of equipment. Additional stressors include excessive paperwork, adverse work schedules, unfair discipline, and lack of training and promotional opportunities. The Commission on Accreditation of Law Enforcement Agencies (CALEA) Standard 33 addresses training and career development.

33 CALEA STANDARD 33 states, "Training has often been cited as one of the most important responsibilities in any law enforcement agency. Training serves three broad purposes. First, well-trained officers are generally better prepared to act decisively and correctly in a broad spectrum of situations. Second, training results in greater productivity and effectiveness. Third, training fosters cooperation and unity of purpose. . . .

Career development is a structured process that is utilized by an agency to provide opportunities for individual growth and development at all levels. It is designed to promote productive, efficient, and effective job performance and to improve the overall level of individual job satisfaction." (*Standards for Law Enforcement Agencies*, 5th edition, 2006)

If an agency does not provide effective training and opportunities for growth and development that might lead to promotion, this can certainly cause additional stress for individual officers.

Stressors Related to the Criminal Justice System and Society

The criminal justice system and society at large also can induce stress in police officers. Officers are often faced with the court's scheduling of police officers for appearances, prosecutors' decisions not to prosecute a case, defendants "getting off" because of a loophole in the law, the court's perceived leniency, the early release of offenders on bail or parole, corrections' failures to rehabilitate criminals resulting in "revolving door" justice, the exclusion of police officers when plea bargaining is used and the perceived lack of appreciation for the role of law enforcement. One officer put it this way: "I think the crowning blow was to see that it's almost futile to go out there and do anything about it. You keep putting 'em away, and they keep letting 'em out. And then new people come along, and it just doesn't stop, and it will never stop."

EFFECTS OF STRESS

Chronic stress can result in high blood pressure, heart disease, chronic headaches and gastric ulcers. Other physical effects of stress are chronic back pain, tension headaches, neck pain, gastrointestinal distress, chest pain, skin rashes and hives. Some disorders such as constipation, heartburn, irritable bowel syndrome and stomach ulcers can be made worse by stress. Stress can also lead to severe depression, alcohol and drug abuse, aggression and suicide.

Police officers tend to have high rates of alcoholism, divorce, posttraumatic stress disorder, burnout, depression and suicide, often related to the stress of the job.

Whether police divorce and alcoholism rates are higher than such rates for people in other professions is open to question. It is known, however, that the police job does seriously interfere with officers' social and home lives, that many officers take their jobs home with them, that spouses worry about the officers' safety and that rotating shifts make normal social life difficult. Some authorities feel that police suicides are underreported because fellow officers are usually the first on the scene and may cover up the suicide to save the family further pain or embarrassment or for insurance purposes. Police suicide is discussed shortly. It is also clear that stress usually results in other forms of behavior changes.

Devastating psychological effects of stress include posttraumatic stress disorder, burnout, depression and suicide.

Posttraumatic Stress Disorder (PTSD)

Posttraumatic stress disorder (PTSD) may occur when an individual's life or the life of someone close to him or her has been threatened or from any event that is truly traumatic to the individual. PTSD may cause officers to miss work or lose their jobs entirely. It can ruin marriages and other relationships. This condition was initially discussed in Chapter 8, but one aspect of PTSD that was not covered was how survival stress can affect post-event memory. Officers need to be educated that after a deadly force encounter, their statements may be only a "best guess," as they fill in the blanks in their memory with how they think they must have acted: "In most traumatic and stressful situations, there is usually a sensory overload during which law enforcement officers will experience memory loss; the greater the stress, the greater the potential for memory problems. . . . Immediately after the incident, there will be post-incident amnesia, with most of the observed information forgotten. The best memory recovery will take place after a healthy night's sleep" (Weiss and Davis, 2009, p.70).

burnout
Condition experienced by a person who is "used up or consumed by a job," made listless through overwork and stress; the person lacks energy or has little interest in work.

Burnout

When stress continues unremittingly for prolonged periods, it can result in the debilitating condition referred to as *burnout.* **Burnout** has occurred in a person who is "used up," showing a persistent lack of energy or interest in his or her job caused by overwork and stress: "Job burnout is a physical and mental state caused by severe strain placed on the body until all resources are consumed" (Carlton, 2009, p.66). Strategies to prevent burnout, or to fight it off should it begin to show signs of occurring, include keeping the body healthy, staying fit, watching work hours, talking about it, varying assignments, taking time off and accentuating the positive aspects of the job (Carlton, pp.68–69).

Unfortunately, burnout generally happens only to those who are initially "on fire"—that is, to enthusiastic, highly productive workers. As one officer said, "I just couldn't go on. It seemed that there was nothing inside of me to keep me going. I couldn't look at one more dead body, one more abused child, or handle one more domestic fight. I'd just had it." Officers who are burned out are at extremely high risk of being injured or killed on duty because they are usually not safety conscious. They are also at risk for depression or suicide.

Depression

depression
A serious and life-threatening medical illness.

Depression is a serious, life-threatening medical illness. Anyone can be affected, and police officers are no exception. Unfortunately some in our society stigmatize having depression or seeking help for it.

Because depression is a medical illness, an imbalance of chemicals in the brain, medication can often be prescribed to treat it. But frequently people do not recognize the symptoms, which can include significant changes in appetite and sleep patterns, irritability, anger, worry, loss of energy, persistent lethargy, feelings of worthlessness or hopelessness, indecisiveness, lack of interest in hobbies, indifference, excessive consumption of alcohol or drugs, and recurring thoughts of death or suicide. The difficulty lies in getting people to recognize the symptoms and to seek treatment. Depression must be treated because it is one of the leading causes of suicide.

Officer Suicide

Alcohol, family problems, the breakup of relationships and stress all contribute to the high rate of police suicide, about 30 percent higher than what is found in the general population. The stigma attached to suicide can be so great that friends and family members of the person who committed suicide are embarrassed or ashamed to discuss it. Thus, suicide isn't talked about, but every law enforcement officer, supervisor and administrator needs to know about it.

Help for those at risk of suicide within the department includes counseling units, peer counseling groups and police chaplains. Outside the department, help might be sought from physicians, priests, ministers, rabbis, attorneys, family and friends. The Police Suicide Prevention Center's Web site features information about suicide, suicide prevention and related subjects, as well as links to suicide prevention and mental health cites.

REDUCING STRESS

Many books and articles deal with stress reduction. Good nutrition and exercise can help. So can taking time for oneself, relaxing, meditating, going for a walk or finding a hobby. Perhaps the most important step to take for reducing law enforcement-related stress is to have something outside of policing. Leave the stress at work. Have friends outside of the job; regularly spend time with family away from work. Too often law enforcement becomes an individual's identity, and officers live the lifestyle in its entirety. This can be dangerous for those officers because they will not receive certain basic needs from the job alone.

Officers should anticipate the stressors involved in police work and, when possible, avoid them. They should prepare in advance for those that may be unavoidable. They should also be physically fit and active and get adequate sleep. Stress management is taking care of yourself. You can't take care of others unless you take care of yourself first!

MENTAL FITNESS PROGRAMS

Although seldom called *mental fitness programs,* many police departments have established programs geared to helping their officers combat emotional problems. Such programs are absolutely essential. The following problems are often included in stress programs: postshooting trauma, alcoholism, drug abuse, marital or other family difficulties, difficult relationships with fellow officers or supervisors, trauma associated with the catastrophic death of a child or spouse, debt management, gambling, issues associated with layoffs because of budget cuts and adjustment to retirement.

Law enforcement departments should be as concerned with their officers' mental health as with their physical health and should offer employee assistance programs for those officers needing help in this area. Professional counseling, peer counseling, police-spouse support groups and the like can do much to improve the mental fitness of a law enforcement agency. A physically and mentally fit officer is a much safer officer. However, officers can do even more to ensure their safety on the job.

OFFICER SAFETY AND SURVIVAL

A physically and mentally fit officer is in a much better position to perform effectively and to stay alive, but another aspect of officer safety sometimes comes into play. After being in police work for a few years, officers often come to feel invincible, having what is called the "it won't happen to me" syndrome. This is known as the *complacency period,* and it usually happens when officers are 4 to 6 years into their policing career. Statistically, most law enforcement officer deaths occur during this time frame. Although they see people all around them being victimized, such police officers refuse to believe they can become victims themselves. This attitude lulls them into a false sense of security.

Most officers injured or killed in the line of duty could have either avoided the confrontation or minimized the injury had they been mentally prepared for the danger, alert and trained in the proper survival techniques.

The **awareness spectrum** describes an officer's level of awareness, ranging from environmental unawareness, to panicked/blacked out/ perhaps dead. Ideally, officers will be between these two stages, alert but relaxed.

awareness spectrum
Framework for describing officer's level of awareness, ranging from condition white, environmental unawareness, to condition black, panicked/blacked out/ perhaps dead. Ideally, officers will be at condition yellow: alert but relaxed.

In assessing personal threat levels, the analogy of a traffic light may be used. Condition green exists when everything is OK and the environment is assessed as safe. In contrast, condition red means a threat has been identified and the officer is prepared to deal with it. Between conditions green and red is the yellow light: "Understand that condition yellow is not a state of paranoia. It is a state of awareness. In condition yellow, you are prepared for what could happen. You are prepared for when that light might turn red" (Rayburn, 2004, p.62).

Recognizing Indicators of Aggression

Among officers' survival skills is the ability to recognize the indicators of aggression—to be prepared for an attack before it happens. Among the common indicators of aggression are the folded arm stance, hands on hips, an invasion of personal space, finger pointing, wandering attention, ignoring verbal commands, pacing, standing with fists clenched and talking through clenched teeth: "Pre-fight tensions will cause jaw muscles to bulge, fists to close and facial muscles to contract" (Glennon, 2008). Other "telegraphed" indicators of hostile intent include

- *Scanning*, where the subject is paying attention to the surrounding area rather than the interviewer, looking for the officer's back-up, witnesses, escape routes or even his own buddies.
- The *target glance*, which refers to the obvious preoccupation an offender has with a particular area of an officer's body or with any of the officer's weapons. One of the most common target glances involves the suspect eyeing an officer's gun, perhaps considering a "gun-grab."
- *Eye blinks*, as under stress, people will either blink very rapidly or very slowly.
- The *pugilistic stance*, or fighting stance, where one leg and side of the body (usually the strong side) is dropped behind the other. Any shifting of the weight or stance may be a significant indicator of an impending attack.

Paying attention to such indicators is critical to officer safety, indeed, sometimes to officer survival (Glennon, 2008).

Part of being alert is being aware of objects that can pose a danger to police officers. A crucial axiom among officers is "hands kill." Be sure you can always see a subject's hands and anything they may be holding. Many everyday items can be used as dangerous weapons, for example, a ball point pen or a plastic straw can serve as a knife; a tightly rolled newspaper or magazine can serve as a baton; a set of keys firmly locked between the fingers and raked across exposed skin can serve as brass knuckles.

Safe Driving

Vehicle-related fatalities held rank in 2008 as the primary cause of line-of-duty deaths, accounting for nearly 50 percent of officer deaths (Kanable, 2009, p.22). One common-sense approach to reducing these statistics is to insist that officers wear their seat belts, but many agencies do not have such a policy. Examination of pursuit policies might be another approach to reducing vehicle-related fatalities.

Countering a Canine Attack

According to one report, in nearly 25 percent of the incidents where officers fire their weapons, they are taking aim at dogs (Baker and Warren, 2009). It is not uncommon for offenders to keep dogs for protection and train them to attack on command. Rayburn (2003, p.64) recommends that, to stop an attacking dog, officers should

- Lower their center of gravity by bending their knees.
- Yell at the dog.
- Spray it with OC.
- If they can do so safely, shoot the dog before it bites them.
- When they can't shoot the dog before it bites them, control the attack by making the dog bite their weak side arm.
- Do everything they can to stay on their feet.
- Shoot the dog in the chest or shoulder until it releases them.

If the decision is made to shoot a dog, especially one who has locked onto an officer's arm, the shot should be to the chest area as the dog's head is protected by a lot of thick bones (Grossi, 2008, p.27).

The Border Patrol's Survival Triangle

Another approach to officer safety and survival is suggested by the Border Patrol's "survival triangle," illustrated in Figure 13.1.

survival triangle
Model for police survival; consists of mental and physical preparedness, sound tactics and weapon control.

The border patrol's **survival triangle** consists of these components:

- Mental and physical preparedness.
- Sound tactics.
- Weapon control.

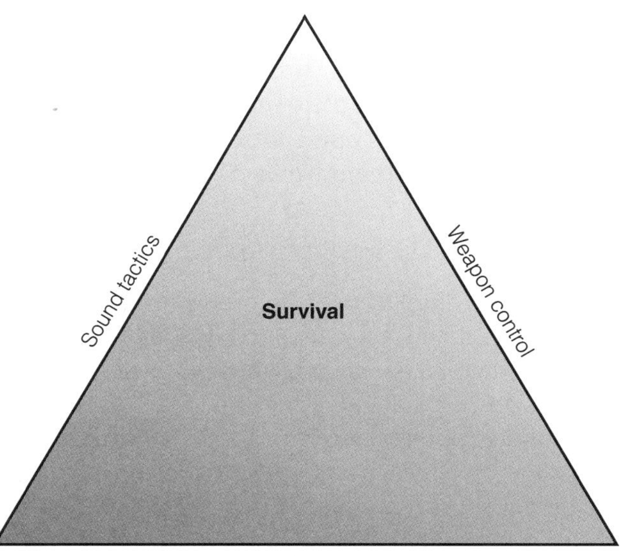

FIGURE 13.1
Survival Triangle

The Other Two Sides of the Survival Triangle

The focus of this chapter has been on the base of the survival triangle, physical and mental preparedness. The second side of the survival triangle is sound tactics, which consist of the five "Cs": cover, concealment, control, containment and communications. Effective, constant communications is the single thread that stitches all the pieces together.

The five Cs for survival tactics are cover, concealment, control, containment and communications.

The third side of the survival triangle is weapons control. This is addressed in the following checklist:

1. Do you know the capabilities and limitations of yourself and each of your weapons?
2. Are your weapons clean and functional?
3. Are they loaded? How are they loaded? What type of ammunition are they loaded with? Does your partner know the answers to these questions?
4. Are your weapons immediately accessible to you? Or are they on the seat next to you where they might slide out of reach under your leg, or in the trunk, or the back seat? Close to you is not the same as accessible in a dynamic confrontation!
5. Do you practice constant forearm contact with your sidearm? (This is an excellent habit to acquire.)
6. Have you mastered a good technique for weapon retention?
7. Can you practice fire discipline?
8. Have you mentally prepared yourself to use your weapons? Lag time is a killer.

Witness reports of officers who were shot indicated some made no attempt to draw or use their weapons once they were down. Other reports stated that officers were shot by assailants while lying on the ground pleading, with arms raised to deflect gunshots. Even though they had full use of their arms and hands, they made no attempt to use their weapon for protection. Officers should also take safety precautions for keeping their service revolvers at home as well as carrying them when off duty.

Avoiding 10 Fatal Errors

According to the FBI ("FBI Releases Preliminary Statistics," 2009), 41 law enforcement officers were feloniously killed in the line of duty in 2008. Of these felonious deaths, 10 occurred during arrest situations, 8 during traffic pursuits/stops, 7 during tactical situations, 6 while investigation suspicious persons/circumstances, 6 resulted from ambush situations, 2 officers were conducting investigations, 1 was responding to a disturbance call, and 1 was transporting a prisoner. Unfortunately, after reaching a nearly 50-year low in 2008, the number of law enforcement officers killed in the line of duty jumped 20 percent during the first six months of 2009 ("Law Enforcement Line-of-Duty Deaths," 2009).

The Central Florida Police Stress Unit considered these harsh realities and compiled a list of 10 fatal errors that have killed experienced police officers and suggests that all "boots on the ground" officers review the list periodically ("Avoiding the 10 Fatal Errors," n.d.):

1. *Attitude*—If you fail to keep your mind on the job or you carry personal problems into the field you will make errors. It can cost you or fellow officers their lives.
2. *Tombstone Courage*—No one doubts that you have courage. But in any situation where time allows—*wait* for the backup. There are few instances where alone, unaided you should try and make a dangerous apprehension.
3. *Not enough rest*—To do your job you must be alert. Being sleepy or asleep on the job is not only against regulations, but you endanger yourself, the community and all your fellow officers.
4. *Taking a bad position*—Never let anyone you are questioning or detaining manipulate you into a position of disadvantage. Always be aware of position. Maintain the advantage. There is no such thing as a routine arrest or stop.
5. *Danger signs*—As an officer you should recognize "danger signs." Fast movement and strange cars are warnings that should alert you to watch and approach with caution. Know your community and watch for what looks to be "out of place."
6. *Failure to watch the hands of a suspect*—Is he reaching for a weapon or getting ready to strike you? How else can a potential killer strike but with his hands?
7. *Relaxing too soon*—Observe carefully. Are you certain the crisis is over? Don't be quick to relax simply because the immediate and apparent threat has been neutralized.
8. *Improper use or no handcuffs*—See that the hand that can kill is safely cuffed. Once you have made an arrest, handcuff the prisoner immediately and properly.
9. *No search or poor search*—There are so many places to hide weapons that your failure to search is a crime against fellow officers. Many criminals carry several weapons and are prepared to use them against you.
10. *Dirty or inoperative weapon*—Are your weapons clean? Will they fire? How about the ammunition? When did you last fire so that you can hit a target in combat conditions? What's the sense of carrying any firearm that may not work when you need it the most?

    The lesson behind these 10 errors is think . . . and please wear your body armor [and seatbelt].

The Warrior Attitude

Survival is a constant theme in American law enforcement, but survival isn't enough. To survive simply means to remain in existence: "I want law enforcement personnel to go home the same way they left—unharmed, unscathed and ready for duty; no wheelchairs, medical aids, crutches or coffins. I want officers to *prevail*" (Spaulding, 2009, p.46). To prevail, officers need a *combative mind-set*, which Spaulding defines as "a previous decision based on reason and intellect to be ready and willing to fight back."

In our society today, it is mandatory that officers maintain their weapons skills through continuous training. Here a police sergeant fires a bean bag round at a paper target during Special Response Team training. Officers on the team all qualify with submachine gun shooting as well as with hand guns. They then practice with the less-lethal bean bag rounds, fired by a shotgun, which are designed to incapacitate an individual while reducing the chance of killing the subject.
© AP Images/Dan Dalstra

SUMMARY

Physical fitness is the body's general capacity to adapt and respond favorably to physical effort. Although many factors contribute to a well-conditioned body, the prime factor is the condition of the circulatory (cardiovascular) system, upon which endurance or stamina depends. Motor skills important to police officers include coordination, speed and accuracy.

Police work is often sedentary, boring, involves irregular hours and rotating shifts and may promote poor diets, excessive cigarette smoking and consumption of alcohol, and great amounts of stress. These factors can be offset by physical fitness training programs. An effective physical fitness training program that is varied and of interest to the officer should include aerobic, strength and flexibility training. It should be engaged in regularly for 20 to 30 minutes a day, at least three days a week.

Bloodborne pathogens that present a risk to police officers and that they should protect against include HIV infections and AIDS, hepatitis B and hepatitis C. The concept of universal precaution recommends that all blood and potentially infectious materials other than blood must be treated as if infected.

Mental fitness is as important as physical fitness. The greatest threat to officers' mental fitness is negative stress. Sources of stress for police officers include internal, individual stressors; stressors inherent to the police job; administrative and organizational stressors; and external stressors from the criminal justice system and the citizens it serves. The effects of stress may include high rates of alcoholism and divorce, posttraumatic stress disorder, burnout, depression and suicide. Devastating psychological effects of stress include posttraumatic stress disorder, burnout, depression and suicide.

Officer safety is another important aspect of keeping prepared for duty. The awareness spectrum describes an officer's level of awareness, ranging from environmental unawareness, to panicked/blacked out/perhaps dead. Ideally, officers will be somewhere in between these two extremes, alert but relaxed. The border patrol's survival triangle, useful for all police officers, consists of mental and physical preparedness, sound tactics and weapon control. The five Cs for survival tactics are cover, concealment, control, containment and communications.

APPLICATION

You have noticed that many of your fellow officers are stressed out, and the department has no program to assist them. You approach your supervisor and offer to discuss this with your colleagues and then develop a policy dealing with stress management. The policy should point out various types of stressors officers must cope with and various services available to help officers. It also should bring employee assistance programs to the attention of the officers. It should include how to contact an individual or a group for help. Consider such programs as Alcoholics Anonymous, marriage counseling, financial advisors, psychological counseling and any other services locally available. It should stress that officers may keep their contacts confidential and that no department interference will be generated that might impair or threaten an officer's job because that officer seeks assistance.

AN EXERCISE IN CRITICAL THINKING

You are a five-year veteran of the State Police Department and take pride in remaining physically fit for duty. Your agency requires that you pass an annual physical fitness test to continue to work out on patrol. You work hard every year to not only meet these standards but to exceed them. When you first started on the force, you were partnered with Officer Bailey. Officer Bailey and you graduated from the academy together and have worked the streets together ever since. Initially, Officer Bailey was in good physical shape and passed all of the standards that are required by your agency. However, in the last few years you have noticed that Officer Bailey has continued to gain a significant amount of weight and developed poor eating habits while you have worked together. You have made a point to bring this up on several occasions, only to be told to mind your own business. You are not only concerned with Officer Bailey's welfare, but with your own safety as well as the public's safety when performing your duties. You rely heavily on Officer Bailey as your partner in day-to-day operations. The gradual weight gain has caused you to pick up Officer Bailey's slack in your normal duties. In the most recent annual fitness test, you observe Officer Bailey intentionally miss a few of the obstacles when not observed by the proctor and claim that he passed them. You know for a fact that he did not.

Recently you responded to a domestic violence incident where a husband was actively assaulting his wife upon your arrival. When the husband saw both of you, he ran from the scene. As you began to chase after him along with Officer Bailey, Officer Bailey stops after a few feet, bends over and cannot catch his breath and yells for you to help him. You stop to make sure your partner is okay, which results in the assailant getting away. After a few minutes Officer Bailey is fine and states that he is just out of shape. The following day you are both called to your sergeant's office to explain what happened and why the suspect was not arrested. You are aware that the victim has also generated a complaint.

1. What would your response be to your supervisor?
   a. Protect your partner; he has been with you since day one and there is the "Code of Silence." You will just have to continue picking up his slack until you can convince him to change his ways.
   b. Tell your supervisor that the suspect was just too fast and that neither of you could catch him, even though you both tried.
   c. Tell your supervisor that you believe Officer Bailey has some health issues that may have contributed to the escape and that are affecting his work performance as well. However, do not go into further detail; leave it for Officer Bailey to explain.

d. Tell your supervisor of the ongoing health issues you have observed with Officer Bailey, express your concerns for safety, and also advise him that you know Officer Bailey did not successfully pass the recent annual physical fitness test however made his way through anyway by cheating.

1. How would you address the issue with Officer Bailey after the incident?
   a. Express your concerns over his safety, your own safety and the safety of others in light of his recent inability to perform some of his duties.
   b. Tell him that you will notify your supervisors of him cheating on the annual fitness test.
   c. Since he has been with you since day one, get together with Officer Bailey to come up with plan on what to say to supervisors. Then work out a deal about how you will be responding to calls together in the future because he is no longer physically able to do some things.
   d. Do not address it with him. Leave it alone, pick up his slack and hope that he realizes it and eventually does something about it on his own.

DISCUSSION QUESTIONS

1. Is peer counseling—"cops working with cops"—better for helping troubled officers than outside professional counseling? Is it better for short-term or long-term impact?
2. Is there one best way to handle officers who have drinking problems? Explain.
3. One reason police officers are reluctant to seek therapeutic services is that they fear their careers will be jeopardized. How can this obstacle be overcome?
4. Is it a good idea for every police department to have its own police psychologist? What are the advantages of in-house versus outside psychological assistance?
5. Are police officers confronted with the same stressful problems faced by everyone in society, such as firefighters, construction workers, business people and military personnel?
6. Do the media create unnecessary stress for police officers in your community? If so, how?
7. How do police administrations contribute to the stresses of police officers? What role does the department play in dealing with the stress faced by an officer's spouse/family? Why should it become (or not become) involved?

GALE EMERGENCY SERVICES DATABASE ASSIGNMENTS

- Use the Gale Emergency Services database to help answer the Discussion Questions as appropriate.
- Use the Gale Emergency Services database to find and outline one of the following articles:
  - "The Effects of Sleep Deprivation" by Glory Cochrane
  - "HIV/AIDS in Law Enforcement: 'What-If' Scenarios" by John Cooley
  - "Surviving Assaults: After the Physical Battle Ends, the Psychological Battle Begins" by Arthur W. Kureczka
  - "Police Trauma and Addiction: Coping with the Dangers of the Job" by Chad L. Cross and Larry Ashley
  - "The 'Modern Warrior': A Study in Survival" by Richard H. Norcross
  - "Physical Fitness in Law Enforcement: Follow the Yellow Brick Road" by Patti Ebling
  - "Fit for Duty: How to Train for the Real Deal" by Carole Moore

REFERENCES

"Avoiding the 10 Fatal Errors." Central Florida Police Stress Unit, no date. http://policestress.org/ten.htm

Baker, Al and Warren, Matthew R. "Shooting Highlights the Risks Dogs Pose to Police, and Vice Versa." *The New York Times*, July 10, 2009.

Best, Suzanne. "Proactive Stress Management for Police Executives." *Big Ideas*, Spring 2009, pp.9–10.

Carlton, Jerry. "Preventing the Long and Lonely Ride to Officer Burnout." *Law Enforcement Technology*, March 2009, pp.64–70.

Collingwood, Thomas R.; Hoffman, Robert; and Smith, Jay. "Underlying Physical Fitness Factors for Performing Police Officer Physical Tasks." *The Police Chief,* March 2004, pp.32–37.

Commission on Accreditation of Law Enforcement Agencies. *Standards for Law Enforcement Agencies*, 5th ed. Fairfax, VA: CALEA, 2006, updated 2008.

"FBI Releases Preliminary Statistics for Law Enforcement Officers Killed in 2008." Washington, DC: Federal Bureau of Investigation press release, May 11, 2009.

Fyfe, James J. "The Split-Second Syndrome and Other Determinants of Police Violence." In *Violent Transactions,* edited by Anne Campbell and John Gibbs. New York: Basic Blackwell, 1986.

Garrett, Ronnie. "Super Bugs: Coming to a Department Near You." *Law Enforcement Technology*, March 2008, pp.46–51.

Glennon, Jim. "Pre-Attack Indicators: Conscious Recognition of Telegraphed Cues." *PoliceOne.com News*, February 12, 2008.

Grossi, Dave. "Tactical Wellness." *Law Officer Magazine*, October 2007, p.26–27.

Grossi, Dave. "Surviving Dog Attacks." *Law Officer Magazine*, November 2008, pp.26–28.

Haughton, Brian P. "The MRSA Menace." *Tactical Response*, March–April 2009, pp.38–44.

Johnson, Robert Roy. "Officer Fitness." *Law and Order*, January 2009, p.18.

Kanable, Rebecca. "Going Home at Night." *Law Enforcement Technology*, January 2009, pp.22–27.

"Law Enforcement Line-of-Duty Deaths Rose 20 Percent during First Half of 2009." Washington, DC: National Law Enforcement Officers Memorial Fund, January 12, 2009.

Murray, Ken. "The Seven Survivals." *Law Officer Magazine*, December 2007, pp.48–49.

"P1Poll: What Is Your Biggest Pet Peeve about Police Work?" *PoliceOne Member News*, March 16, 2009

Quigley, Adrienne. "Fit for Duty." *The Police Chief,* June 2008, pp.62–64.

Rayburn, Michael T. "Countering Canine Attacks." *Police*, March 2003, pp.64–69.

Rayburn, Michael T. "Personal Threat Levels." *Police*, February 2004, pp.62–63.

Sanow, Ed. "Fitness Is an Ethical Obligation." *Tactical Response*, January–February 2009, pp.95–96.

Schneider, Jason. "MRSA Infections: Tougher Than Kelvar." *Law Enforcement Technology*, September 2007, pp.18–23.

Schreiber, Sara. "Healthy Choices: Training for Firearms, Fugitives and . . . Trans-Fat?" *Law Enforcement Technology*, September 2008, pp.10–16.

Selye, Hans. *The Stress of Life.* New York: McGraw-Hill, 1956.

Senjo, Scott R., and Dhungana, Karla. "Field Data Examination of Policy Constructs Related to Fatigue Conditions in Law Enforcement Personnel." *Police Quarterly*, June 2009, pp.123–136.

Spaulding, Dave. "Mindset Matters." *Law Officer Magazine*, April 2009, pp.46–47.

Vernon, Bob. "Knights of the Roundtable" *Law Officer Magazine*, June 2009, p.48.

Vila, Bryan. "Sleep Deprivation: What Does It Mean for Public Safety Officers?" *National Institute of Justice Journal*, March 27, 2009.

Vonk, Kathleen. "Law Enforcement and Nutrition." *Tactical Response*, January–February 2009a, pp.30–33.

Vonk, Kathleen. "The Nitty-Gritty of Proper Nutrition." *Law and Order*, February 2009b, pp.14–17.

Waggoner, Kim, editor. *Handbook of Forensic Services.* Quantico, VA: An FBI Laboratory Publication, 2007.

Weiss, Jim, and Davis, Mickey. "Survival Stress Research and Post-Event Memory." *Tactical Response*, March–June 2009, pp.66–70.

Yates, Travis. "Police Driver Fatigue: 'Our Dirty Little Secret.'" *PoliceOne.com News*, March 28, 2008.

Young, Dave. "Redefining Fit for Duty." *Police*, August 2008, pp.42–49.

CASES CITED

Jane Doe v. Borough of Barrington, 729 F.Supp. 376 (D.N.J.) (1990)

Parker v. District of Columbia, 850 F.2d 708 (D.C. Cir. 1988), cert. denied, 489 U.S. 1065, 109 S.Ct. 1339, 103 L.Ed.2d 809 (1989)

Woods v. White, 899 F.2d 17 (7 Cir.) (1990)

HELPFUL RESOURCES

Police Suicide Prevention Center: www.policesuicide.com

CHAPTER 14

Liability and Ethics

Is It Legal? Is It Moral?

DO YOU KNOW . . .

- Under what three types of state liability (tort) law officers may be sued?
- On what basis most civil lawsuits against police are brought?
- What the most common civil actions brought against the police involve? What the most common defenses used against civil liability police officers are?
- What can protect against civil liability?
- How to minimize lawsuits?
- Whether officers can countersue?
- Whether ethical issues are usually absolute or relative?
- According to conventional wisdom, what the defining characteristics of the police culture are and what the result is?
- What three areas in discussions of law enforcement ethics are controversial?
- What the key elements in corrupt behavior are?
- What the most important factor in police officers becoming corrupt is?
- What other factors may cause officers to become corrupt?
- If scandals are caused by "bad apples" or "bad barrels"?
- What basic ethics tests can be used to assess behavior?
- What maxim should guide ethical decisions?
- Who is most responsible for the ethics of a law enforcement agency?

CAN YOU DEFINE?

absolute issue
blue lie
civil actions
Civil Rights Act
collective deep pocket
discretionary acts
intentional tort
libel
litigious
malfeasance
malicious prosecution
ministerial acts
negligence
nonfeasance
police placebo
relative issue
Section 1983
slander
slippery slope
strict liability
tort
vicarious liability

INTRODUCTION

Law enforcement officers must act within the law. If they do not, they may be found criminally liable for misconduct under Title 18, U.S.C., Section 242, as well as under state criminal law. Most lawsuits against law enforcement officers, however, deal with civil matters and are filed under Title 42, U.S.C., Section 1983. In carrying out their official duties, law enforcement officers must protect the constitutional rights of their public. The consequences of violating such rights in a criminal investigation were discussed in Chapter 3. Actions in violation of a suspect's constitutional rights can cost a favorable decision. In addition, the suspect can sue the police.

Police operations also involve considerable discretion, and discretion is central in the debate regarding the "letter of the law" versus the "spirit of the law." Very simply, a "letter of the law" approach tends to be quite rigid and take a "black-and-white," right-or-wrong stance in assessing situations, whereas a "spirit of the law" philosophy generally takes into account contextual factors, recognizing the various shades of gray that often accompany specific incidents. This variable application of discretion, too, can result in actions viewed as conduct "not becoming a police officer" and thereby subject officers to civil lawsuits. The United States has been called a **litigious** society—that is, its citizens are very likely to sue over any perceived wrong.

litigious
Highly likely to sue.

AN OFFICER'S PERSPECTIVE
Getting Sued

In law enforcement culture, there is a saying, "If you haven't been sued, you are not doing your job." This hints at the reality that at some point during your career, *you will be sued*, regardless of whether it is a frivolous accusation. It is not uncommon for a veteran officer to have been sued several times throughout his or her career. This affects all demographics of law enforcement.

—Sgt. Henry Lim Cho

Law enforcement officers must act legally, and they must act ethically. *Ethics* refers to standards of fair and honest conduct. It involves *integrity*, doing what is considered just, honest and proper. Ethics looks at human conduct in the light of *moral principles*, that is, set ideas of right and wrong. Moral principles can be established by individuals, set forth by a particular society or culture, laid down by a religious body or doctrine or established by a given subculture. In most instances, an individual's moral principles derive from a combination of all of these. Further, in our pluralistic country, many differences exist in what is considered right and wrong.

This chapter begins with an overview of civil liability and Section 1983, the Civil Rights Act. This is followed by common charges brought against police officers. Next is a discussion of defenses in civil lawsuits, of ways to reduce their occurrence and of the possibility of countersuits. The discussion of legal liability ends with a look at legal liability and community policing.

The chapter then changes its focus from what is legal to what is moral or ethical. This discussion begins with an overview of ethics and of ethics in law enforcement. This is followed by a discussion of the police culture and of how this culture might encourage unethical conduct, including some gray areas in police ethics and outright unethical behavior. Next, corruption in policing is discussed and basic ethics tests are presented. The chapter concludes with the role of the police department in fostering ethical behavior and problem solving.

CIVIL LIABILITY: AN OVERVIEW

civil actions
Lawsuits for perceived wrongs against individuals for which restitution is sought in civil court.

tort
A civil wrong, the equivalent to a crime in criminal law.

A person who feels wronged by someone, even though the action may not be a crime, can sue. Such lawsuits are called **civil actions**. In civil law, the wrongdoing itself is called a **tort**. Sometimes an action is considered both a tort and a crime. For example, a person who strikes someone could be charged with assault (a crime) and sued for the assault (a tort). An individual found guilty of a crime is *punished* by paying a fine, serving a jail or prison sentence or both. An individual found guilty of a tort is made to make *restitution*, usually in the form of a monetary payment.

An estimated 30,000 civil actions are filed against the police every year, with between 4 and 8 percent resulting in an unfavorable verdict. The threat of a lawsuit may influence officer decisions such as to arrest or to use force and how much. There have been instances when an officer did not fire on a suspect who was pointing a gun at him. Uncertain as to whether the gun was real, the officer hesitated and was shot to death, more fearful of a lawsuit than of being killed. Officers may find themselves in a "Catch 22"—sued if they take action or sued if they don't.

AN OFFICER'S PERSPECTIVE
Which is Worse: Death or a Lawsuit?

In officer survival training, trainers commonly reference the quote, "It is better to be judged by 12 than carried by 6." Translation: You may have to deal with the most negative of repercussions in a courtroom but you will still be alive, which matters most. This is as opposed to being wrong, and dead.

Because of America's litigious culture, officers are forced to continue their education and training to properly do their jobs. The increasing standards foster more educated officers, which is not a bad thing, but education cannot teach reactionary instinct. You either have it or you don't.

—Sgt. Henry Lim Cho

Law enforcement officers can be sued in just about every phase of police operations. Each time officers are sued, it exposes them to personal embarrassment in the community and on the job. It may result in possible job loss. It may mean financial ruin. Equally damaging is the undermining of respect for the rule of law when officers are found guilty. Although the increase in lawsuits is alarming, it is still true that few lawsuits against police officers can be traced to extremely poor judgment or malicious acts by one or more officers. The responsible behavior of officers is a definite deterrent to any action against them.

Officers may be sued under three types of state liability (tort) laws: strict liability, intentional tort and negligence.

Strict liability refers to an act where the injury or damage is so severe and the harm should have been foreseen so that intent or mental state need not be proven, for example, reckless operation of a vehicle. **Intentional tort** refers to an act where the officer's intent to engage in the behavior must be proven, for example, wrongful death or false arrest. **Negligence** refers to an act where intent or mental state does not matter. What must be proven is if some inadvertent act or failure to act created an unreasonable risk to another person, for example, speeding resulting in a traffic accident or not responding to a 911 call.

strict liability
Refers to an act where the injury or damage is so severe and the harm should have been foreseen so that intent or mental state need not be proven.

intentional tort
An act where the officer's intent to engage in the behavior must be proven, for example, wrongful death or false arrest.

negligence
An act where intent or mental state does not matter; what must be proven is if some inadvertent act or failure to act created an unreasonable risk to another person, for example, speeding resulting in a traffic crash or not responding to a 911 call.

SECTION 1983, THE CIVIL RIGHTS ACT

Most civil lawsuits brought against law enforcement officers are based on Statute 42 of the U.S. Code, **Section 1983**, also called the **Civil Rights Act**.

This act, passed in 1871 after the Civil War, was originally part of the Ku Klux Klan Act of 1871, one part of which is now called the Civil Rights Act of 1871. The act was designed to prevent the abuse of constitutional rights by officers who "under color of state law" deny defendants those rights. The act states, "Every person who, under color of any statute, ordinance, regulation, custom, or usage, of any State or Territory, subjects, or causes to be subjected any citizen of the United States or other person within the jurisdiction thereof to the deprivation of any rights, privileges, or immunities secured by the Constitution and laws, shall be liable to the party injured in an action at law, suit in equity, or other proper proceeding for redress."

In other words, Section 1983 says that anyone acting under the authority of the law who violates another person's constitutional rights can be sued. This includes law enforcement officers. It now may also include their supervisors, their departments and even their municipalities. Such lawsuits may involve First Amendment issues such as freedom of speech, religion and association; Fourth Amendment matters such as arrest and detention, search and seizure, and use of force; Fifth Amendment issues in interrogation and confessions; Sixth Amendment concerns regarding the right to counsel; and Fourteenth Amendment claims of due process violations. It is important for law enforcement officers to understand Section 1983 because it is often the basis for a civil action against police.

Section 1983
The Civil Rights Act; it states that anyone acting under the authority of the law who violates another person's constitutional rights can be sued; the legal authority for most lawsuits against law enforcement officers and agencies.

Civil Rights Act
States that anyone acting under the authority of the law who violates another person's constitutional rights can be sued. See also *Section 1983*.

Vicarious Liability

Vicarious liability makes others specifically associated with a person also responsible for that person's actions. Most lawsuits naming supervisory officers are attempts to get to more, wealthier and better-insured defendants through

vicarious liability
Responsibility for a person's actions or others specifically associated with that person.

collective deep pocket

A pool of defendants from which astronomical financial judgments can be collected; created by suing every possible individual and agency involved in an incident.

vicarious liability. Suing every possible individual and agency involved creates a **collective deep pocket** from which astronomical judgments can be collected.

COMMON CHARGES BROUGHT AGAINST POLICE OFFICERS

As noted, most cases being tried are based on Section 1983, alleging police violation of constitutional rights. More recently, several lawsuits have been brought for failure to protect or investigate. Two important distinctions determine personal liability of city officers and employees for acts committed while on duty: discretionary versus ministerial acts and malfeasance versus nonfeasance.

discretionary acts

Those actions officers perform using their own judgment; policies and procedures for the acts leave decisions up to the officers.

ministerial acts

Duties prescribed by law as some of the tasks of an administrative office.

Discretionary acts are those actions officers perform using their own judgment. Policies and procedures for the acts leave decisions up to the officers. If police officers are carrying out a duty requiring judgment, they cannot be liable for damages unless they are willfully or grossly negligent. Making an arrest is an example of a discretionary act. **Ministerial acts** have to do with the way the duty is to be performed. If officers fail to perform the duty as prescribed, they can be sued. If, for example, a department has a policy against shooting a gun from a moving squad car and an officer does so and injures someone, the officer can be sued.

malfeasance

Acts of misconduct or wrongdoing.

nonfeasance

Failure to take action, with the result being injury or damage to another person.

Malfeasance refers to acts of misconduct or wrongdoing, while **nonfeasance** refers to failure to take action. In the infamous Rodney King incident, officers participating in the beating might be charged with malfeasance in civil proceedings. Those who stood by and did nothing to interfere might be charged with nonfeasance.

The most frequent civil lawsuits against police involve false arrest or imprisonment, malicious prosecution, use of unnecessary or excessive force, brutality, wrongful death, negligent service and failure to protect.

False Arrest or Imprisonment

The largest number of lawsuits, accounting for about 50 percent of all lawsuits filed, is for false arrest and imprisonment. False arrest and false imprisonment are exceptionally vulnerable to lawsuits because such suits are filed with ease and can be filed as group actions. False arrest and false imprisonment are almost synonymous under the law. Both are usually alleged against the officer.

Arrest is broadly defined as taking an individual into custody by physical or constructive restraint with the intention of charging the individual in a court of law. Physical force need not be used to accomplish arrest or imprisonment. The assertion that would be brought to the court's attention in such a lawsuit is that the officer lacked probable cause to arrest. An absolute defense in such a case is that probable cause *did* exist. The courts look at two important factors when examining liability for false arrest: (1) the information known to the police officer at the time the arrest was made and (2) the reasonableness of the officer's action given all the circumstances at the time of the arrest.

A common problem occurs when police officers respond to retail stores' calls for assistance in arresting people suspected of shoplifting. Most agencies have standardized procedures requiring the apprehending store employee to make a formal citizen's arrest. In this case, a claim of false imprisonment may be filed against both the store and the police officer.

Many other false-arrest suits result from drunk and disorderly arrests and from warrantless arrests under pro-arrest domestic violence statutes.

Malicious Prosecution

An area of liability closely associated with false arrest and imprisonment is malicious prosecution. **Malicious prosecution** is a proceeding instituted in bad faith without any probable cause in the belief that the charges against the defendant can be sustained. The cause of action in the civil suit is usually for damages suffered. This type of civil action arises most frequently when one citizen formally charges another citizen and the defendant is not successfully prosecuted.

malicious prosecution
A proceeding instituted in bad faith without any probable cause, in the belief that the charges against the defendant can be sustained.

Excessive Force or Brutality

The second largest numbers of civil actions against police officers are filed in the areas of excessive force or brutality. Such a suit can be the result of lawful or allegedly unlawful arrest and will usually name a supervisor as a defendant along with the officer(s) actually involved.

The specific allegations may be civil assault and battery. *Assault* refers to conduct that may result from a well-founded fear of imminent peril. *Battery* is the unlawful, hostile touching or shoving of another, no matter how slight. Some states have combined the two into a single charge of assault. In some instances, criminal charges may be brought as well. For example, if a police officer were to strike a handcuffed prisoner with a nightstick hard enough to shatter the bones in the prisoner's face, the prisoner could bring a civil action *and* press criminal charges against the officer.

Courts have held an officer liable for assault and battery if that officer strikes a suspect or uses an aerosol irritant on the suspect for talking back, or if an officer continues to beat a defendant who has stopped resisting. Almost every state now has statutes that define the extent to which police officers can use physical force in specific situations. All officers should become thoroughly familiar with their states' statutes in this area.

Most states allow officers to use some physical force short of deadly force to make an arrest or prevent an escape. Officers may also use physical force, short of deadly force, to defend themselves. Recall that *Graham v. Connor* (1989) established that police officers could be held liable for using excessive force, with the test for liability being "objective reasonableness."

Lawsuits are also likely when use of deadly force is involved. As stated in Chapter 3, the use of *deadly force* to make an arrest or prevent an escape is generally permitted only when

- The crime committed was a felony involving the use or threatened use of imminent physical force against a person.
- The crime committed was an inherently dangerous felony such as kidnapping, arson or burglary in a dwelling, and the officer felt that the escape of the felon would contribute to the possible death or harm of others if not

stopped (having known the felon has already committed one of those severe felonies).

- The officer's life or personal safety, or the safety of others, was endangered in the particular circumstances involved.
- The person was an escapee from a correctional facility.

The Commission on Accreditation of Law Enforcement Agencies (CALEA) Standards address use of force in its first standard dealing with law and authority.

> 1
>
> CALEA STANDARD 1 states, "Few issues outweigh the concern raised in a community when it is perceived that members of a law enforcement agency use an inappropriate levels of force. A community rightfully expects that its law enforcement agency will issue weapons only to those agency members legally authorized to carry same as a condition of their duties, and that weapons and tactics are only utilized in conformance with sound policies, procedures, and training.
>
> Policies, procedures, and training on topics such as use of force and officer discretion have typically touched upon the legal aspects of these issues; in some jurisdictions this may even be mandated. Accredited agencies look beyond simply what might be legal, providing sound written guidance consistent with agency values that often conveys a sense of responsibility and compassion that transcends all laws." (*Standards for Law Enforcement Agencies*, 5th edition, 2006)

It is doubtful the court would uphold the use of deadly physical force in cases involving property crimes unless there was imminent danger to the officer or other individuals.

The use of physical force by police officers to prevent destruction of evidence is controversial. Generally, the force used must be reasonable under all circumstances. Deadly physical force is *never* permitted in preventing the destruction of evidence. The swallowing of drugs in an arrest is an issue for which courts have not given police any guidelines. Cases have included everything from officers sticking their fingers down suspects' throats to officers taking suspects to hospitals to have emergency personnel give them enemas. Handcuffing an arrested person who is resisting arrest also has been deemed excessive force in some instances, as discussed in Chapter 3.

Wrongful Death

Closely related to excessive force and brutality complaints is the area of wrongful death actions. Wrongful deaths can be caused either by intentional or negligent acts or by omissions of police officers. Intentionally inflicting fatal injuries causes the greatest number of wrongful death actions. Circumstances that lead to wrongful death suits include shooting an unarmed, fleeing misdemeanant; a fleeing felon when the felon could have been subdued without deadly force; any misdemeanant to effect an arrest; excited delirium deaths; cases where

TASERs or oleoresin capsicum (OC) pepper spray were used; and shooting in self-defense of an actual or threatened attack when the attacker did not use great bodily force.

Negligent killings account for a much smaller number of deaths and usually arise in the following situations:

- Shooting to halt a motor vehicle and striking a passenger. (Most police departments have regulated this practice by forbidding firing at a moving vehicle.)
- Accidentally shooting a bystander.
- Reckless firing of warning shots. (Many police departments forbid the firing of warning shots.)
- Poor aim when shooting to wound a suspect. (This includes accidentally striking a hostage or accidentally discharging a firearm, wounding or killing an innocent person.)

Officers participating in raiding parties, such as those making drug arrests, must act reasonably. Any lawsuits that may emanate from their actions will encompass all officers participating in the raid. The lawsuit can extend to the supervisors, the department and the city itself. Some wrongful death suits arise from police pursuits or negligent operation of squad cars.

Negligent Operation of a Vehicle

Another area of specific liability is the operation of a police vehicle. Liability in this particular area has increased dramatically in recent years. Police officers are charged with the same standard of care as the general public and are found liable under a straight negligence theory for the negligent operation of vehicles. Statutes allowing police officers to disregard stop signs and other traffic laws and cautions are now being interpreted by the courts to require officers to use reasonable care under existing circumstances. The requirement of reasonable care is particularly critical when "hot pursuit" is involved and the police vehicle is unmarked and lacks a siren and red lights. Liability concerns have led many departments to adopt "no pursuit" policies.

Failure to Protect

Another broad area of officer liability involves lawsuits alleging "failure to protect." This can take several forms, including failure to answer calls for help, failure to respond in a reasonable amount of time, failure to arrest, failure to investigate and so on. Some "special relationships" have been found to exist in certain circumstances, and failure to protect can involve several types of situations.

General Failure to Protect One of the most common situations occurs when a victim assumes the police will provide protection and then relies on that assumption. Publishing a 911 number, according to some courts, implies that the police will protect those who call that number.

Failure to protect also occurs when the police tell a victim they will let the victim know when someone is released from custody or from prison and fail to do so. Failure to protect witnesses who have cooperated with police and whose cooperation brings them into contact with the suspects also has resulted in lawsuits.

Failure to Arrest or Restrain People Committing or About to Commit Violent Crimes This is usually classed as an act of negligence. For example, an officer failed to get a drunken motorist off the road before the motorist caused a serious accident. Failure to arrest a person known to be dangerous when probable cause exists can also lead to suits for damages subsequently done by that person.

Failure to Respond to Calls for Assistance If police officers have reason to believe someone is in imminent danger, they must take action or face the possibility of a lawsuit. In *Thurman v. City of Torrington* (1984) the victim, an estranged wife who was stabbed by her husband, received a $2.3 million award because the police had refused to act on her complaints.

Failure to Identify

At times, failure to identify oneself as a police officer before making an arrest can lead to liability on negligence theory. The liability would be for incurred damages or injuries that might have been avoided if the officer had given proper identification.

Negligent Service

The past decades have seen an increase in civil lawsuits claiming negligence by police officers, departments and municipalities in providing traffic services. Police officers or agencies may be liable if they know of a potentially dangerous condition and fail to take reasonable action to correct the existing hazard. They may also be liable if they fail to warn oncoming traffic of an existing hazard.

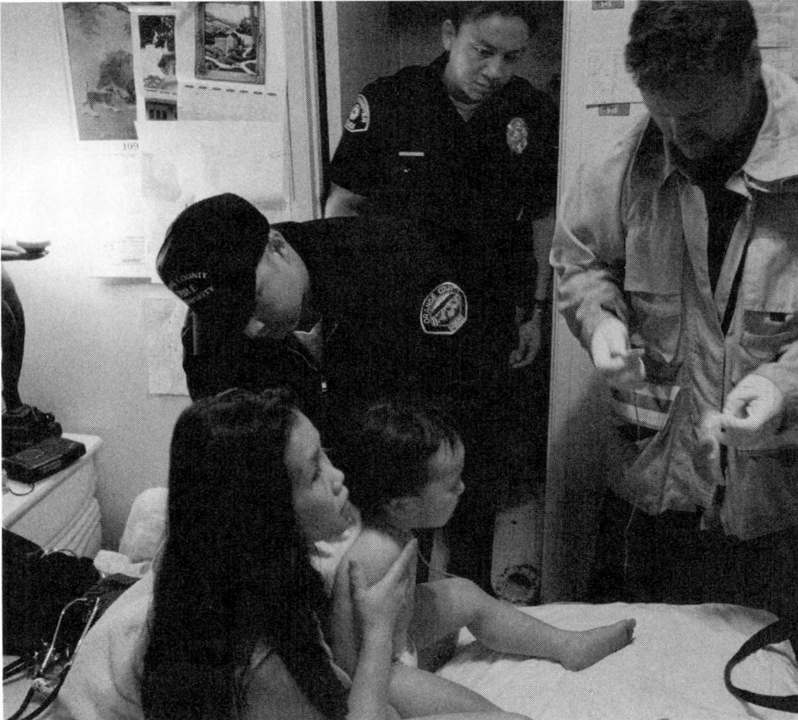

One of the main responsibilities of a police officer is to administer first aid to victims.
© David Butow/CORBIS SABA

Some courts do hold police officers responsible for providing assistance at a crash scene. Other courts, however, contend that although the police have a duty to help at a crash scene, officers become liable only after establishing a special relationship with the victim.

Traffic-related incidents are not the only area in which charges of negligent service can be made. Some cases suggest that the negligent administration of first aid by police officers can be the basis for an action in negligence in which an officer's act or omission becomes the cause for complaint. In addition, some lawsuits have been filed in attempts to make officers liable for not recognizing existing medical impairments. Though these cases are rare, officers should be aware of them. Most have not been successful, and many have centered around individuals who appeared to be drunk and were treated as being drunk, but who in actuality were suffering heart attacks or having epileptic seizures.

Other Areas of Civil Liability

Although the next areas to be discussed have produced limited litigation against police officers to date, officers should be aware of these possibilities for lawsuits.

Libel and Slander An action in this area usually is based on written (**libel**) or spoken (**slander**) false statements that tend to humiliate and degrade a person in the esteem of others. These usually are known as *defamation of character* suits. These suits often pivot around statements made during arrests because much of the court process and testimony are privileged communications and should not be repeated by the police officers. Proving the statement's truth is a defense to such actions.

libel
Written defamation of another's character; false statements that tend to humiliate a person and degrade that person in the esteem of others.

slander
Spoken defamation of another's character; false oral statements that tend to humiliate a person and degrade that person in the esteem of others.

The normal defenses used by police officers, departments and municipalities being sued are that

- They did not intend to deprive the plaintiff of constitutional rights.
- They acted in good faith.
- They acted with what was considered reasonable judgment at the time and with valid authority.

REDUCING THE OCCURRENCE OF CIVIL LAWSUITS

According to Means (2007, p.33), "Nothing whatsoever reduces legal problems and liability risks in law enforcement like good interpersonal communication skill. We all know officers who can go in a biker bar, make an arrest, and leave with a friend. Other officers could start a fight in a Quaker Friends meeting." The critical need for effective communication spills into every aspect of police work and will not be discussed further here even though it is one vital way to avoid lawsuits.

Police officers and agencies can expect more rather than fewer lawsuits unless specific steps are taken. Ultimately, the risk of civil liability rests on the individual actions of each police officer. Police departments can develop extensive policies and procedures to help ensure that their officers act in a way that will deter civil lawsuits.

Protection against lawsuits includes

- Effective policies and procedures clearly communicated to all.
- Thorough and continuous training.
- Proper supervision and discipline.
- Accurate, thorough police reports.

At the heart of protecting against lawsuits are the department's *policies and procedures.* A department's procedures manual should clearly state that a fundamental mission of the department is to protect everyone's civil rights and that officers and supervisory personnel have an affirmative duty to intervene if they witness the violation of civil rights by anyone, including fellow officers

As Scoville (2008, p.56) explains, "By definition, policy is a course of action, a guiding principle or procedure considered expedient, prudent, or advantageous. By practice, the policies of a law enforcement agency dictate the protocol by which officers are expected to conduct their duties, often carrying with it the added responsibility of mitigating potential liability resulting from those duties. By all accounts, it is often more restrictive than what the law requires, than what cops desire, and more than what their employers would want in an ideal world." In many areas requiring police discretion, policies seek to prevent abuses of authority, minimize threats to the community, mitigate the need for civil redress, and generally keep the employing agency out of the headlines, rather than guiding officers in what is expected under general circumstances: "Policies are formal declarations of what agency is expected and willing to do. They have import. They have purpose. Perhaps one day, they will allow greater leeway for officers to exercise their authority and greater latitude for the men and women who evaluate their discretions so that if they can't temper justice with mercy, then perhaps with a little common sense. . . . For some the writing is on the wall: 'To err is human. To forgive is against department policy'" (Scoville, 2008, p.63).

CALEA's Web site notes, "In today's litigious environment, state and local governments are increasingly being sued and held liable for acts committed by public employees. Activities involving public safety personnel are the source of a significant percentage of these lawsuits. This can be particularly worrisome for public safety agencies that are operating under outdated or nonexistent policies and procedures" ("Risk Management, Liability Insurance, and CALEA Accreditation"). Adopting performance standards such as CALEA's internationally accepted accreditation program can go far in reducing the risk of being sued. In addition, many insurance companies provide lower insurance rates for those who meet these standards or local or state standards that have been validated.

Burch (2008, p.69) asks, "How do you train officers to balance doing what they are told with using some common sense? How do you train them to sort out following the letter of the policy or they will be in trouble versus following the spirit of the law or they will be in trouble?" This is a true training challenge.

Training should include the basic rookie training as well as ongoing in-service training and specialized training. Training must include the policies and procedures of the department. It also must include continual updating on changes in laws that affect police operations, as discussed earlier in the text.

Proper supervision and discipline are also vital to avoiding lawsuits. Discipline can be viewed both positively and negatively. On the positive side, police departments should foster professional discipline within their officers; that is, they should encourage an atmosphere in which officers act according to established policies and procedures. They should be able to say of their personnel that they are well-disciplined officers. On the negative side, officers who do not act according to established policies and procedures should be reprimanded (disciplined).

Another key area in preventing lawsuits is *thorough, accurate police reports* establishing the reasonableness of officers' actions, especially important in use-of-force reports. Grossi (2008, p.30) prefers to call these documents *subject management reports*, focusing on something the subject did (or failed to do) that caused the officer to have to use some level of force to control them and take them into custody. Indeed, increasing numbers of agencies are changing the names of these reports to such titles as "Response to Resistance" reports, to reflect the shift in focus from the force used by an officer to the resistance used by a subject.

Effective subject management reports serve numerous purposes. They can be used by the training unit to document what is and is not working on the street and highlight where more training is needed. They can be used by the crime analysis team to identify crime hot spots. They can also give a judge, jury or hearing officer a clear understanding of who and what an officer was up against (Grossi, 2008).

As many as one in every 60 officers in the United States is currently being sued for a use of force incident: "To successfully combat a use of force lawsuit, an officer must do two things. First, and most importantly, the officer needs to be right (i.e., reasonable) in the use of force. Second, the officer must carefully and clearly document why he or she was right and reasonable. Any inaccuracy or omission in the report will be used to attack the officer's integrity and professionalism" (Joyner, 2009).

Officers tend not to see their own writing errors because they are familiar with what they have just written. In a hurry to submit a report and move on to a new activity, too many officers turn in error-filled documents before effectively reviewing them. A brief separation from the report, in both time and space, is often enough to overcome this problem. Set the report aside for 10 minutes and then go back to review it, using these three steps (Bowden, 2009):

- First, check for completeness in the information blocks and in the narrative. Is all necessary information included?
- Second, check the content. Read the narrative to make sure it flows well, makes sense and speaks clearly.
- Third, check for spelling and capitalization. Reading it backward forces you to look at every word separately.

The importance of documentation cannot be emphasized enough. Comprehensive, well-written incident reports are vital to defenses against civil suits.

Videotaping traffic stops also provides officers with documentation of their actions, especially in cases involving DWI arrests. Griffith (2009a, p.8) suggests that all officers remember this dictum: "There is always a camera watching you, and it would be better if you had one too." Data from the International Association of Chiefs of Police (IACP) shows "93 percent of officers charged with misconduct are exonerated when video evidence is available" (Griffith, 2009b, p.38). This statistic provides strong incentive to heed the advice. Griffith (2009b, p.38) envisions the day when agents who want to reduce nuisance lawsuits will be equipped with body-worn video systems comparable with what they now have in their squads.

To minimize lawsuits at a more personal level, law enforcement officers should

- Know and follow their department's policies and procedures.
- Stay in the scope of their duties.
- Always act professionally.
- Know and respect their constituents' rights.
- Seek advice if in doubt.
- Carefully document their activities in their reports.
- Maintain good community relations.
- Keep current on civil and criminal liability cases and know the laws.

COUNTERSUITS

In many instances, civil suits brought against law enforcement officers either have no basis or are frivolous. Some people consider the best defense to be a good offense and, therefore, sue the officer who arrested them, thinking it might put them in a better bargaining position.

Law enforcement officers and agencies can countersue if they are falsely accused of a civil offense.

In one case, a deputy sheriff responded to a public drunkenness complaint at a convenience store. When he arrived, the deputy approached the suspect and asked that he come outside with him to discuss the problem. The suspect filed a brutality complaint against the deputy, claiming the deputy grabbed him by the throat and physically dragged him out of the store. The evidence obtained from the convenience store security camera showed that the deputy did not grab the suspect by the throat, and even held the door open for him when they left the store. The trial judge awarded the deputy sheriff $25,000 in damages as a result of the false accusations.

Law enforcement officers also can sue even if they have not been sued. Prosecutors, police and sheriff's deputies are entitled to the same right to recover for wrongful injury as any other citizen.

LEGAL LIABILITY AND COMMUNITY POLICING

If community policing becomes a reality in a jurisdiction, citizens will better understand why the police do what they do. Citizens should also be less likely to bring suit against officers if they view them as partners. Likewise, police officers operating under a community policing philosophy will have a service orientation and will be less likely to infringe on the constitutional rights of those with whom they work. This may also lead to officers policing in a more ethical manner.

ETHICS: AN OVERVIEW

Ethics usually involves what is often referred to as the *conscience*, the ability to recognize right from wrong and to follow one's own sense of what is right. Some believe conscience is an innate moral sense; people are either born with it or not. Others believe it is a power acquired by experience—that is, it can be taught or consciously ignored.

A complexity in ethical behavior is whether the issues addressed by ethics are absolute or relative. For example, is killing a human being always "bad" (absolute) or is it even "good" at times (relative)?

An **absolute issue** is one with only two sides; the decision is between "black" and "white." A **relative issue** is one with a multitude of sides, that is, varying shades of "gray" between the two absolute positions. Ethical issues are usually relative.

absolute issue
An issue with only two sides, viewed as either/or, black or white.

relative issue
An issue with a range of morally acceptable options, which are of several shades of gray rather than either black or white.

Ethics involves looking at moral rules recognized by individuals with a conscience and held to be either absolute or relative. What one individual considers ethical behavior may be considered highly unethical behavior by another individual. An example of this is the Hmong practice in which adult males marry very young girls. To Hmong people, this is moral and right. To many Americans, this is immoral and wrong.

Ethics *is* complex and presents serious challenges to those who seek to behave ethically. Consider, for example, which of the following ethical principles are behind your behavior:

- Do unto others as you would have them do unto you.
- Do what will accomplish your goal/vision in the most efficient manner.
- Do whatever you please so long as it does not cause harm to anyone else.
- Might makes right.

Ethics includes integrity, that is, doing right when no one is watching. Ethical integrity is paramount in a profession endowed with power, authority and discretion, and thus, it is the most important value a law enforcement officer can

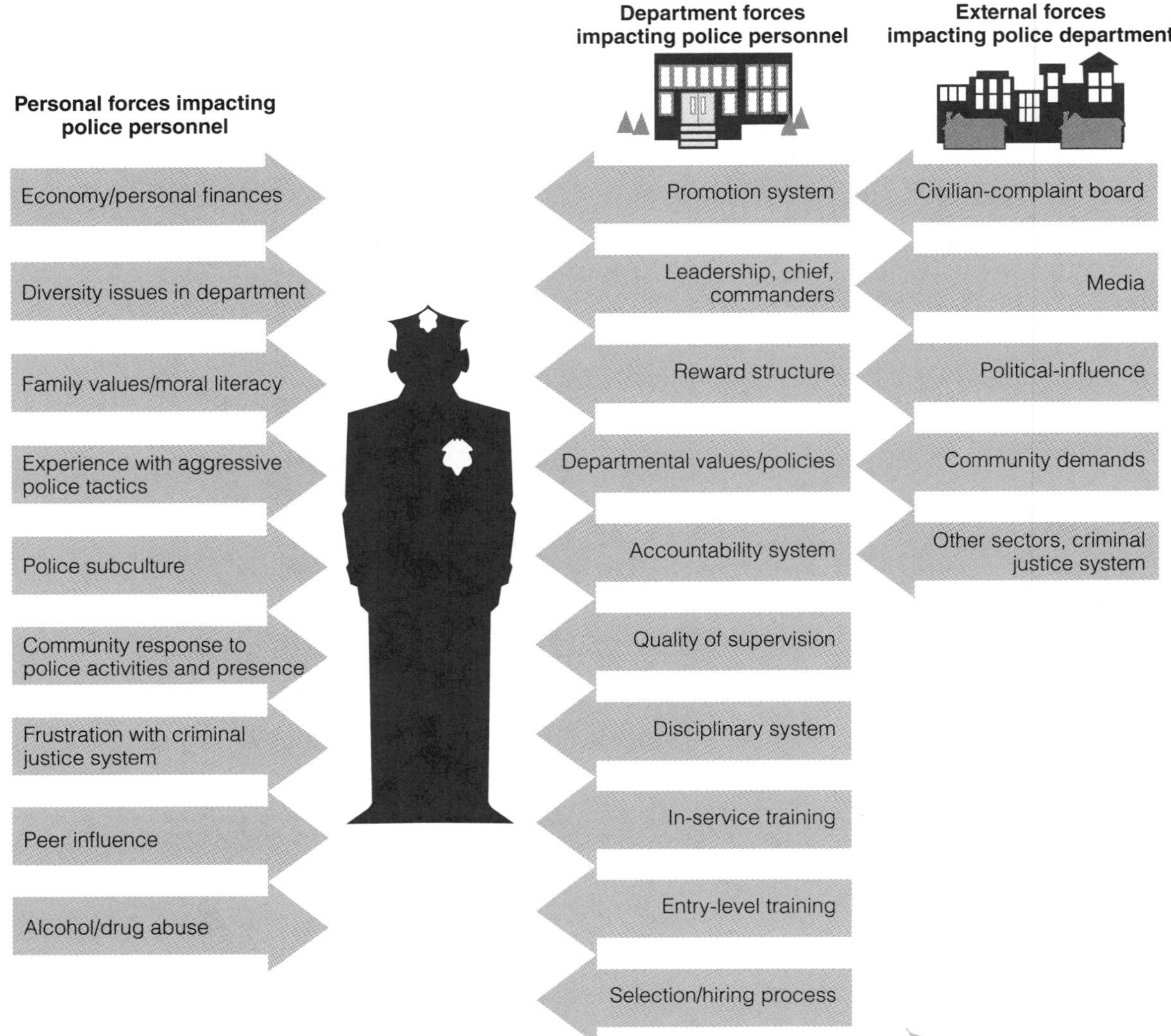

FIGURE 14.1 Dynamics of Police Integrity
Source: *Police Integrity: Public Service with Honor.* Washington, DC: National Institute of Justice, January 1997, p.92.

have. Figure 14.1 illustrates the dynamics of integrity in a police career, including the personal, departmental and external forces affecting an officer's behavior.

Jetmore (2008a, p.104) points out, "Deciding what's right or wrong is a large part of what police officer do, and state statute books are full of laws, so why is it tough to figure out the right thing? It's because our society entrusts the police to decide under what circumstances to enforce the law. Simply because an officer has the legal power to do something doesn't make it the right thing to do." He (p.106) explains that improper conduct can be rationalized because of the disparity that exists between official policy and the reality of what occurs on the street and because of the nature of police discretion in making decisions. Jetmore (2008b, p.68) also notes the sharp difference between the philosophical definition of *ethics* used in the academic world and that of the real-life definition facing officers confronting the "claw and the fang" world of "drive-by shootings, murders, the affects of drugs, suicide, widespread homeless, AIDS, domestic violence, poverty, child abuse, etc."

The Law Enforcement Oath of Honor

1.12 CALEA STANDARD 1.12 states, "A written directive requires all personnel, prior to assuming sworn status, to take and subsequently abide by an oath of office to enforce the law and uphold the nation's Constitution or basic law of the land, and, where applicable, those of governmental subdivisions." (*Standards for Law Enforcement Agencies*, 5th edition, 2006)

On October 21, 1988, the IACP passed the following resolution (Bennett et al., 1999, pp.24–29):

> WHEREAS, integrity is acknowledged by the International Association of Chiefs of Police to be one of the most significant needs throughout the world and for virtually all professions, and because the International Association of Chiefs of Police seeks to demonstrate worldwide leadership in the advancement of professional honor, integrity, and ethics, and
>
> WHEREAS, an oath is universally recognized to be a solemn pledge someone makes when they sincerely intend to commit to what they advocate and affirm,
>
> WHEREAS, sincere commitment to an oath can provide vital guidance during a life's most crucial decisions, a moral anchoring that can endure the test of time and a solid emotional foundation for officer's facing their most difficult moments; now, therefore be it
>
> RESOLVED that the International Association of Chiefs of Police does adopt the Law Enforcement Oath of Honor.
>
> On my honor I will never betray my badge, my integrity, my character, or the public trust. I will always have the courage to hold myself and others accountable for our actions. I will always uphold the Constitution and the community I serve.

In most police departments, new officers recite the oath of honor, which stresses integrity. The indoctrination of an individual into policing through the recital of the oath is often marked with ceremony and witnessed by one's family, friends, peers and colleagues. It is a proud rite of passage into a profession steeped in tradition. The newcomers soon become part of the police culture.

Codes of Ethics

Another focus in most departments is a code of ethics, which further define what is expected of officers. One departmental force influencing police officers is often a *code of ethics* that sets forth accepted standards of behavior for a profession. The code of ethics is often framed and hanging on the wall. Such codes usually have at least three important themes:

- Justice or fairness is the single most dominant theme. Officers are not to take advantage of people or accept gratuities.
- The importance of the law and the police as tools of the Constitution is a second theme. Police behavior must be totally within the bounds set by the law.

- The third theme is that police must at all times uphold a standard of behavior consistent with their public position.

Often, however, the police department's formal code of ethics and its informal code of ethics are entirely different. The informal code of ethics results from what is commonly referred to as the police culture.

THE POLICE CULTURE

This culture has been studied for more than 40 years and may include some of the following beliefs unique to the profession and that may promote unethical behavior: The police are the only real crime fighters. Loyalty counts more than anything. It is impossible to win the war on crime without bending the rules. The public is demanding and nonsupportive.

Conventional wisdom holds that the defining characteristics of the police culture are social isolation and group loyalty, resulting in a code of silence. This phenomenon is also called the *thin blue line*.

Officers have to decide where their *first loyalty* lies—to fellow officers or to enforcing the law. The answer is in the oath of honor every officer takes upon accepting the call to the badge. The officer promises to support, protect and defend the Constitution of the United States, the constitution and laws of his state and possibly the laws and ordinances of his county or city. Fellow officers, the chief or the sheriff are not mentioned. Nonetheless, many officers will put loyalty to their colleagues above loyalty to the public or even to the department, often by abiding by the code of silence.

The Code of Silence Neal Trautman (2000), head of the National Institute of Ethics (NIE), reports on what he considers the most extensive research ever conducted on the police code of silence by the National Institute of Ethics between February 1999 and June 2000, participated in by 3,714 officers and recruits. Their findings:

- 79 percent said that a law enforcement code of silence exists and is fairly common throughout the nation.
- 52 percent said that the fact a code of silence exists does not really bother them.
- 24 percent said the code of silence is more justified when excessive force involves a citizen who is abusive.
- 46 percent said they would not tell on another cop for regularly smoking marijuana off duty.

Another survey by the NIE, with 1,116 officers participating, found that 46 percent of the officers stated they had witnessed misconduct by another employee but had not taken action (Trautman, 2001, p.68). Of those officers, 47 percent said they had felt pressure to take part in the code of silence from the officers who committed the misconduct. According to Trautman (p.69), "Anger was the most frequent incident for which the code of silence was used; 41 percent were excessive use of force circumstances." A code of silence breeds, supports and nourishes other forms of unethical actions. Furthermore, "The 'Us vs. Them' mentality is usually present within the minds of those who participate in the Code of Silence" (Trautman, p.71).

The code of silence and the Us vs. Them mentality often bond. Loyalty becomes more important than integrity.

Developing loyalty and the code of silence is an understandable phenomenon among people who spend significant time together. This intimate bond is unique to professions such as law enforcement where officers may have to sacrifice their lives for their partners, and the partners are willing to do the same for them. Quinn (2004) cautions,

> As terrible as it is, there is no escaping the Code. It is as inevitable as your childhood diseases and just as necessary. Each stinging battle with the Code will be either an inoculation of the spirit and an opportunity to grow stronger or a crippling injury to your integrity. Regardless of the outcome there will be vivid images you can't erase from your memory. There will always be the mental and physical scars to remind you of your battles. (pp.24–25)
>
> But, each encounter can leave you better prepared both physically and mentally for the tough challenges ahead, if you are willing to admit you're not superman, and you recognize your "dark side" for what it is. Because only when we know the Code of Silence for what it is can we gain some control over it. Either way, you won't escape unscathed because at some point in time you are going to "Walk with the Devil" in order to get the job done. (p.25)
>
> Every day is a new challenge and ethical police conduct is often an uphill battle. Even the best of cops have days when they want to give up and do whatever it takes to put a child molester, baby murderer, or other lowlife in prison. When you sit inches away from these scum and they brag about the truly horrific things they have done to an innocent it's easy to abide by the Code—if that's what it takes. When the evidence isn't perfect, you just use a little creative report writing and this guy will never harm another person again. Illegal searches, physical abuse, or even perjury, you know you will be in the company of many good cops who have done the same. But are they really good cops? (pp.13–14)
>
> The choice of being a "Peace Officer" means there will be many battles in solitary combat with other cops and with yourself. You will not win them all—you cannot—the cards are stacked against you. There will be no medals, awards ceremonies or cheering crowds for the battles you do win. But there will be honor and integrity—in your life and in your work. (p.18)

Using the code of silence to "cover" for a colleague is usually clearly unethical. But many areas of policing are not so clear.

GRAY AREAS IN POLICE ETHICS

Three areas in discussions of law enforcement ethics are controversial: police use of deception, police acceptance of gratuities and professional courtesy.

Police Use of Deception

As Klockars (1995, p.552) comments, "At the core of the ethical life of the officer is a profound moral dilemma. On the one hand, the officer's obligations to the values of civilized society oblige him or her to coerce people effectively. On the other hand, the officer's obligation to coerce people effectively requires that he or she suspend the very values that civilized society treasures."

police placebo

A lie told by the police when the lie benefits the person lied to and when no more effective means of dealing with the problem is available. Also known as a *white lie*.

Klockars (1995, p.552) describes two types of lies commonly used by police officers in doing their duties. The first is the **police placebo** (sometimes referred to as the "little white lie"): "Police officers find it ethically defensible to lie when the lie is told to benefit the person lied to and no more effective means of dealing with the problem is available." Klockars gives as an example two mentally ill brothers well known to police who believed they were being pursued by invisible agents from outer space. The officers told the brothers that they had reported the so-called invasion to Washington and were sending out a squad of equally invisible investigators to protect them.

blue lie

A lie told not to help or comfort the person lied to but, rather, to exert control.

The second type of lie is the **blue lie** (Klockars, 1995, p.553): "'Blue lies' are different from police placebos in that they are not told to help or comfort the person lied to but, rather, to exert control." Klockars gives as an example a police officer attempting to remove an abortion protestor from an abortion clinic waiting room. She insisted they'd have to carry her out. The officer told her he had just had a hernia repaired and was afraid if he lifted her he would tear out his stitches. He even offered to show her, but his lie was sufficient to get her to leave peacefully.

In some circumstances, lies may be justified by investigative necessity. While performing their duties, officers may engage in a significant amount of deceptive conduct essential to public safety. Consider lying to suspects, conducting undercover operations and even deploying unmarked cars. Presenting a suspect with false evidence, a false confession of a crime partner or a false claim that the suspect was identified in a lineup are but a few of the deceptive practices police officers have used for years during interrogations. These investigatory deceptive practices are necessary when no other means would be effective, when they are lawful, and when they are aimed at obtaining the truth.

Alpert and Noble (2009, p.237) agree that police often use the preceding practices in interrogation, but note, "Although they are allowed to be dishonest in certain circumstances, they are also required to be trustworthy, honest, and maintain the highest level of integrity." Some deceptive practices may lead to unintended consequences such as false confessions. One such contested practice is entrapment, introduced in Chapter 12.

Sorrells v. United States (1932) was the first time the Supreme Court recognized the entrapment defense. In this case, a federal prohibition agent, undercover as a tourist, engaged Sorrells in conversation. After gaining the defendant's confidence by sharing common war experiences, the agent asked for some liquor and was twice refused. The third time he asked, however, Sorrells gave in and was then arrested and subsequently prosecuted for violating the National Prohibition Act. Speaking for the Court, Chief Justice Hughes said the defendant should have had the defense of entrapment available. This defense prohibits law enforcement officers from instigating a criminal act by those "otherwise innocent in order to lure them to its commission and to punish them."

According to Rutledge (2007, p.59), "Sometimes you have to resort to trickery to get confessions from suspects." However, as the Supreme Court has repeatedly acknowledged, "Criminal activity is such that stealth and strategy are necessary weapons in the arsenal of the police officer" (*Sorrells v. United States*, 1932). "Nor will the mere fact of deceit defeat a prosecution, for there are circumstances when the use of deceit is the only practicable law enforcement technique available" (*United States v. Russell*, 1973).

Moore (2007, p.146) contends, "It's a fact of life in law enforcement; criminals don't often go quietly into the night. Many times police are forced to use deceptive means to corral suspects who continue to elude arrest. And as long as the means are legal, then as far as I'm concerned whatever it takes to get the job done is fine." She gives as an example an officer who posed as a reporter to lure a suspect with outstanding warrants into a position to be arrested. The media cried foul, claiming entrapment. It simply was not.

Other deceptive practices used by police are clearly unethical, for example, a police officer may testify falsely to imprison a criminal. Although the officer's intent—removing a criminal from society—may be laudable, and the officer may truly believe he is engaging in a greater good, this lie (perjury) violates a standard of reasonableness and appropriateness under the circumstances, considering the status obligations of the person engaging in the lie. Although the intent may be legitimate, the actions are unethical. This malice is the motive by which any sense of limits or constraint or fidelity to law and policy is destroyed. Motive or intentions can be mixed, so a person may deceive to pursue some worthwhile, utilitarian goal (such as public safety) and at the same time have a total disregard for the rights of the suspect and for the laws, policies, and limits that apply to policing.

Accepting gratuities such as free coffee can be the first step toward becoming corrupt.

Behavior might be viewed on a continuum with intentional, unethical, deceptive conduct on one end and lies justified by necessity and based on circumstances at the other end. Lies of the latter variety might be excused, even if not accepted. Lies of the former type, however, can cause great harm and often leave no option other than the termination of officer's employment. Unethical deception might include falsely testifying in court ("testilying"), failing to reveal exculpatory evidence or creating false evidence implicating someone in a criminal act.

Gratuities

Another gray area of ethics includes the acceptance of gratuities. The formal law enforcement code of ethics disapproves of *gratuities*, material favors or gifts given in return for a service. However, many citizens feel there is nothing wrong with a business giving freebies, such as gifts or free admission, to a police officer. Many officers believe these are small rewards for the difficulties they endure in police work.

The question becomes, What gratuities are acceptable and under what circumstances, if any? Certainly gratuities are acceptable in many other professions. But in a profession involving great discretion, gratuities can be extremely problematic. They can give the appearance of preferential treatment, even if such preferential treatment does not exist. As O.W. Wilson was fond of saying, "Nobody ever gave a cop something for nothing." Figure 14.2 summarizes the arguments for and against accepting gratuities.

Allowing Gratuities

- They help create a friendly bond between officers and the public, thus fostering community-policing goals.
- They represent a nonwritten form of appreciation and usually are given with no expectation of anything in return.
- Most gratuities are too small to be a significant motivator of actions.
- The practice is so deeply entrenched that efforts to root it out will be ineffective and cause unnecessary violations of the rules.
- A complete ban makes officers appear as though they cannot distinguish between a friendly gesture and a bribe.
- Some businesses and restaurants insist on the practice.

Banning Gratuities

- The acceptance violates most departments' policies and the law enforcement code of ethics.
- Even the smallest gifts create a sense of obligation.
- Even if nothing is expected in return, the gratuity may create an appearance of impropriety.
- Although most officers can discern between friendly gestures and bribes, some may not.
- They create an unfair distribution of services to those who can afford gratuities, voluntary taxing, or private funding of a public service.
- It is unprofessional.

FIGURE 14.2 Arguments For and Against Gratuities
Source: Mike White. "The Problem with Gratuities." *FBI Law Enforcement Bulletin*, July 2002. p.21.

AN OFFICER'S PERSPECTIVE
Gratuities: To Accept or Not to Accept?

Many people who support the police and want to show gratitude may do something like bake them cookies. In one community, some citizens wanted to thank their public safety professionals, so they baked cookies for the local firefighters and police officers. The firefighters accepted them with thankfulness. The police, however, had to turn them away saying they could not accept gratuities, which offended the citizens.

The argument behind the difference between the firefighters being able to accept the cookies and the police being unable to do so is that the police have the influence of authority over individuals.

In jurisdictions with such absolute policies regarding gratuities, it is still hard to turn away the small child who made cookies for the police simply because she wants to someday become a police officer. She clearly has no expectation of anything in return—it is a pure gesture of gratitude.

—Sgt. Henry Lim Cho

An example of a questionable ethical situation would be a gas station that offers complimentary coffee to the police. Although this not an expensive item, there are certain possible expectations that may occur from accepting the coffee. Perhaps the owner expects to get out of a speeding ticket if stopped by the local police he gives free coffee to. Even if there are no expectations such as this, perhaps the fact that officers know that this establishment offers them free coffee results in them frequenting the business more often than other local business. Another business that does not offer this complimentary service might argue that it is not being protected or frequented as equally as the business that does.

Accepting gratuities may be the first small step on the road to more unethical behaviors and eventually to corruption.

Professional Courtesy

Professional courtesy has existed in the medical profession for centuries, physicians taking care of each other and their families, lawyers representing each other and their families, usually for no fee. However, the situation in law enforcement is different. Wolfe (2009) describes how, in his one-squad-car town, with him the only officer under the chief, the chief explained how cops need to help other cops when they were in trouble. This is certainly true in the case where one officer's home is devastated by a hurricane or tornado, but this is not what the chief was talking about. He used the example of an off-duty cop who crashed his car while driving drunk. If there were no witnesses, he would have no problem "looking the other way," giving the officer a ride home, and cleaning up the accident scene. He stressed that cops had to watch out for one another, to take care of each other, to extend them *professional courtesy*.

Sometimes off-duty officers who are pulled over for speeding will be sure to make their badge visible to the officer who stopped them, in what may be an attempt to get out of a ticket. In many cases, this tactic works. However, many—citizens and officers alike—consider this to be an abuse of the badge.

Wolfe suggests that how each officer handles the matter is up to the individual officer. Consider the offender's attitude. Might a verbal warning solve the problem? And remember, anyone can order a badge. A call to the supervisor to verify the ID might be in order. Nonetheless, the safest and most ethical practice is to treat off-duty officers as you would treat any citizen.

Professional courtesy should not mean that one officer lets another officer go simply because he or she carries a badge. To Wolfe, it means that when another officer is in his jurisdiction, that officer will behave so as to not require contact with him. In other words, officers who come into his jurisdiction must act professionally and he, in turn, will do likewise. He, like many, does not condone using the badge as a "get out of jail free" card.

UNETHICAL BEHAVIOR

Police misconduct involves a broad spectrum of behavior including mistreatment of offenders, discrimination, illegal searching and seizures, violation of suspects' constitutional rights, perjury, evidence planting and other forms of corruption. Concern has always existed about controlling the powers granted by the government to the police to use force. Where power exists, the potential to abuse that power also exists. Unethical behavior, which in its extreme form results in corruption, is an exceedingly complex problem.

Police routinely deal with the seamier side of society, not only drug addicts and muggers, but middle-class people involved in dishonesty and corruption. The constant displays of lying, hiding, cheating and theft create cynicism and threaten even the strongest code of ethics, especially when these behaviors are carried out by judges, prosecutors, superiors and politicians. The following are some rationales police might easily use to justify unethical behavior:

- The money is there—if I don't take it, someone else will.
- I'm only taking what's rightfully mine; if I got a decent wage, I wouldn't have to get it on my own.
- I need it—it's a good cause—my wife needs an operation.
- I put my life on the line every day—I deserve it.

One way to help officers facing ethical decision making is to help them understand what might be tempting to them. The FBI has a formula to explain temptation:

$$\text{Attraction} + \text{Proximity} + \text{Perceived Availability} = \text{Temptation}$$

For example, if a person who likes money is placed in situations where money is readily available and there is little chance of being caught, temptation is high. But even in high temptation situations, most officers do not act unethically. Why? This is explained by another formula delineating consequences:

$$\text{Temptation} - \text{Perceived Consequences} = \text{Action}$$

Without any perceived consequences, unethical behavior is much more likely to occur. The FBI defines perceived consequences by yet another formula:

Perceived Consequences = Rules, Enforcement of Consequences, Reality

To avoid unethical behavior, officers need to know what might be tempting to them. If the proximity or availability of the desired object cannot be changed, thus removing or reducing temptation, the consequences must be equally high or greater.

CORRUPTION

Corruption is not a 21st-century police problem. Much police corruption is drug related, for example, stealing money or drugs from drug dealers, selling stolen drugs, planting drugs on suspects and protecting drug operations. A police officer making a modest salary may be greatly tempted by easily gaining the equivalent of two years' salary by making one "favorable" decision for the drug trafficker. Other corrupt behaviors may or may not be drug related, such as conducting unconstitutional searches and seizures, providing false testimony and submitting false crime reports. Although examples of police corruption vary, they all have key elements in common.

The key elements in corrupt behavior are (1) conduct prohibited by law (2) involving misuse of position (3) resulting in a reward or personal gain for the officer.

Why Do Officers Become Corrupt?

Several factors contribute to becoming corrupt, such as ego, greed, sex or the exercise of power; tolerance of the behavior by the community; socialization from peers or the organization; inadequate supervision and monitoring of behavior; lack of clear accountability of employees' behavior; and no real threat of discipline or sanctions.

Perhaps the most important factor in police officers becoming corrupt is the extraordinary amount of discretion they have.

Chief Justice Warren Burger stated, "The officer working the beat makes more decisions and exercises broader discretion affecting the daily lives of people everyday and to a greater extent than a judge will exercise in a week." This discretion in ethical decision making connects strongly with the ends versus means dilemma.

The Ends versus Means Dilemma The "ends" of policing are noble: keep the peace, bring criminals to justice, serve and protect the public. Some officers come to believe that the ends justify the means by which they are accomplished. They resort to unlawful behavior in the name of justice. Police officers on television and in the movies frequently behave in a way that would get them fired in the real world, but they usually get away with it because they are seen as an officer who does bad things to bad people and for good reasons.

slippery slope
One small indiscretion can lead to more serious misbehavior and finally to actual corruption.

The Slippery Slope Another theory on why good cops turn bad is that something seemingly insignificant, such as accepting free coffee or meals, can put an officer on a **slippery slope**, leading to major crimes. According to Trautman (2001, p.68), "Research repeatedly confirms that most scandals start with one employee doing relatively small unethical acts and grow to whatever level the leadership allows." He calls this the *corruption continuum.*

Being above the Law Another explanation for police officers becoming corrupt is that they are taught in the academy that in many areas they may break the law; for example, they can exceed speed limits, go through red lights and carry concealed weapons.

Violating the law may impair crime control by alienating the public, lessening their willingness to assist the police. In addition, when police violate the law, they forfeit the cooperation they need and increase the likelihood that encounters with the public will generate hostility and violence, placing police officers at risk:

In addition to the existence of discretion, officers may become corrupt because they believe the ends justify the means, they begin with accepting gratuities and progress to larger indiscretions, they believe they are above the law or they engage in the code of silence.

Rotten Apples versus Rotten Barrels

Although corruption begins with individual officers, controversy exists about whether a rotten apple spoils the barrel or the other way around. It is commonly thought that a few "bad apples" can cause a whole department's reputation to suffer when a scandal is uncovered. Some scandals, such as the Rodney King incident, can cause the whole profession's reputation to suffer.

The culture of the police department (the barrel) can allow or eliminate corrupt behavior (bad apples).

Fortunately, only a small percentage of officers are corrupt. As noted, most corrupt behaviors begin with unethical behavior rather than outright corruption.

WHY OFFICERS ACT UNETHICALLY

Trautman (2009) offers four primary reasons good cops do unethical things:

1. They lie to themselves with excuses.
2. They experience momentary selfishness.
3. They just make a bad decision.
4. They are afraid of "being ostracized" for doing the right thing.

Trautman suggests three steps to take when thinking about an ethical decision: (1) clearly understand the issues, (2) evaluate the facts, and (3) make the decision by applying objective standards to the dilemma. He says officers should ask themselves,

- What would I do if my family was behind me?
- Is it worth my job and career?
- How will I feel about myself 20 years from now?
- Would those who love me be proud or ashamed?

The following basic ethics tests might also be of help.

BASIC ETHICS TESTS

Some questions, such as the question of gratuities, might appear to be black-and-white (absolute) issues to most, but many other ethical decisions police officers must make are not black and white at all, but are instead varying shades of gray (relative issues). To arrest or not? To inform on someone or not? To lie to suspects to build a case or not? In such instances, the answer is seldom obvious. How do police officers decide what is and is not ethical behavior?

Some basic ethics tests include asking oneself, Am I doing the right thing? At the right time? In the right way? For the right reason? How would I feel if it were to be made public?

Many people believe all behavior should be guided by the Golden Rule, Do unto others as you would have them do unto you. Other, less positive people have coined the Silver Rule, Do unto others before they do unto you. A simple maxim might guide police officers when they wrestle with ethical decisions:

There is no right way to do a wrong thing.

Police officers have awesome powers over other people's lives. They must act legally and ethically to be true professionals and to be true to themselves as individuals. It has been said that there is no pillow so soft as a clear conscience.

Ethical behavior within a law enforcement agency is ultimately the responsibility of each individual officer within that agency.

A BRIEF WORD ABOUT INTERNAL AFFAIRS INVESTIGATIONS

When police corruption or unethical behavior is suspected or alleged, a department is obligated to respond and investigate, often by initiating an internal affairs (IA) investigation. Policing the police is a difficult job, and many such investigators are referred to as "the rat squad" by officers outside the IA division (Griffith, 2003, p.76).

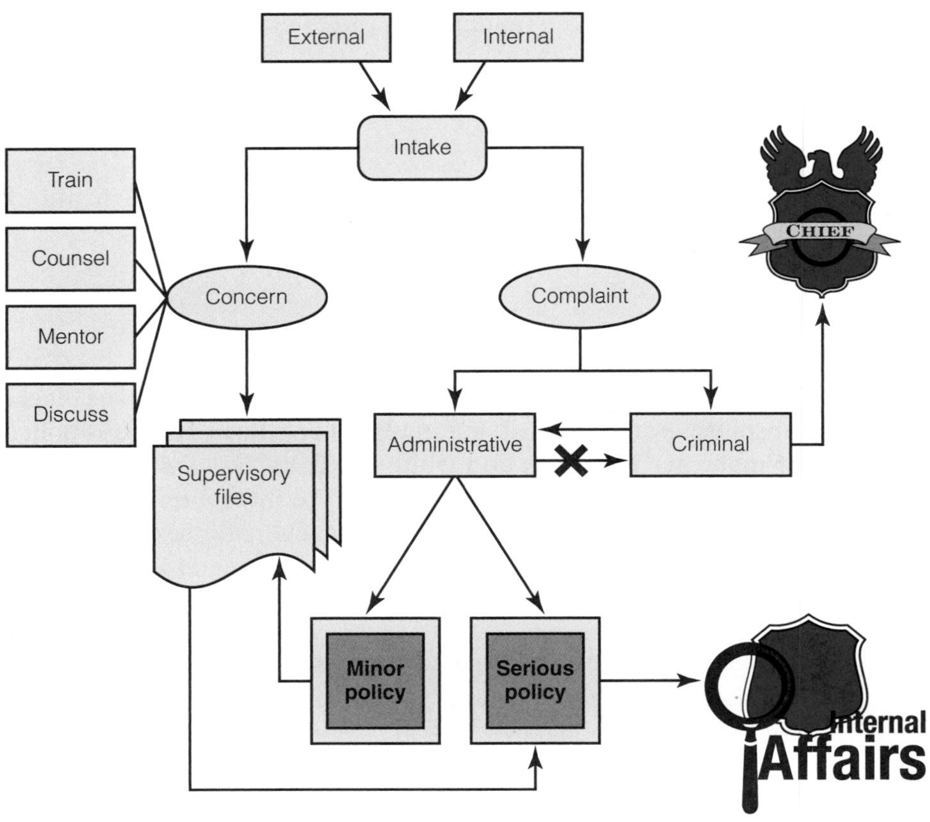

FIGURE 14.3
Sorting Chart: How a Case Gets to Internal Affairs
Source: Deputy Chief Todd Sandell, Richfield (Minnesota) Police Department. 2009. Reprinted by permission. Use of this chart without expressed written consent of its originator is strictly prohibited.

Internal affairs sections traditionally are reactive, responding to citizen complaints and reports of misconduct and policy violations from other department members (Dees, 2003, p.88). Although IA investigators protect the public from abusive or unethical police, they also work to protect individual officers from unfounded allegations. Five functions of the IA process are (1) protecting the public, (2) protecting the department, (3) protecting the employee, (4) removing unfit personnel and (5) correcting procedural problems (Kelly, 2003, p.5).

Figure 14.3 illustrates how an issue can flow through the system to become an internal affairs investigation. As shown, issues come to the attention of the department at the *intake* stage from internal (other officers) and external (the public) sources. At intake, a first-line supervisor, usually a sergeant, determines if the issue is a concern or a complaint. Complaints are further sorted as minor, serious or criminal, with the cases involving serious administrative policy concerns being those processed into the internal affairs division.

Colaprete (2005, p.112) emphasizes, "Police administrators are constantly faced with political pressure, media attention, the requirements of legal and collective bargaining agreements, and the protection of the community in the conduct of all internal investigations." If there is even a hint of criminal behavior by the officer, the matter should be separated into both a criminal and an administrative investigation. The criminal investigation should be conducted first, including the *Miranda* warning if applicable. This is followed by the administrative investigation, including a *Garrity* warning if applicable.[1]

The first step is to review all evidence. Next, obtain copies of all associated elements of the case. These can include a copy of the crime or arrest report, a computer printout of the call-for-service, a copy of radio transmissions and any other retrievable items. A fundamental component of most investigations is interviewing all involved parties.

ETHICS AND COMMUNITY POLICING AND PROBLEM SOLVING

The roots of community policing can be found in Sir Robert Peel's instructions to the Metropolitan Police in 1829: "The primary objective of an efficient police department is prevention of crime: the next that of detection and punishment of offenders if crime is committed. . . . In attaining these objectives, much depends on the approval and cooperation of the public, and these have always been determined by the degree of the esteem and respect in which the police are held."

As police officers get involved with the community and work together to solve problems, they may change the way they think and, more importantly, the way they behave.

Integrating Ethics into the SARA Model

Trautman (2009) asserts, "Law enforcement does a shameful job of preparing cops to make difficult ethical decisions. This is particularly tragic considering the fact that virtually every time an officer is justifiably fired or arrested it resulted from a bad ethical decision." Agencies are duty-bound to train about the moments most likely to destroy an officer's career.

The Boston Police Department has done just this by establishing a task force to integrate ethics analysis into the SARA problem-solving model by using the dilemmas-options-consequences (DOC) method as well: "The DOC method puts moral decision making in the day-to-day realm of an officer's professional and personal life. The DOC method challenges officers to carefully consider their decisions, as well as the short- and long-term consequences of those decisions" (Romano et al., 2000, p.98).

---

[1]The Supreme Court ruled in *Garrity v. New Jersey* (1967) that a violation of the Fourteenth Amendment occurs when the government uses a police officer's statement in a criminal trial against that officer. Officers accused of misconduct can be threatened with loss of their jobs if they do not cooperate with an internal investigation. *In other words, anything used in a criminal trial may be used in an administrative trial, but the reverse is not true.*

Under the *Garrity* rule, "An employer has the right to require employees to answer questions regarding their conduct as long as those questions are narrowly drawn and directly related to the duties they were hired to perform. The employer may use these statements in disciplinary actions involving the employee which could result in termination of employment." However, if the employer uses Garrity to compel an officer to answer questions, employers are prohibited from giving this information to police or having it used during a criminal trial. The officer must request *Garrity* protection. Officers can protect themselves by getting in writing a *Garrity protection*, a written notification that they are making their statement or report involuntarily.

Romano et al. (2009, p.99) say if a decision maker is facing a dilemma that "feels" wrong, he or she should ask questions such as

- What feels unsatisfactory? What feels wrong?
- Who or what is presenting a choice to me?
- Is there a moral or ethical threat to me or someone else?
- Will I, or someone in the community, be affected or hurt physically or emotionally?
- Will I, or someone in the community, be treated disrespectfully or without dignity?
- Is my quality of life, or the quality of life of someone in the community threatened?

Once the dilemma is defined, the action or response phase involves the following questions:

- What are my options?
- What are the extreme options?
- Am I considering all options?
- Am I being open-minded and creative about my options?
- Do my options rely only on me, or could I use a resource or someone's help? What are those resources? Whose help could I use?

For each option, the consequences must be assessed by asking questions such as the following:

- What happens because of my choice? What happens if I do nothing?
- Who is affected by what I do? How will they be affected? How will I be affected?
- Will I be preserving and protecting the quality of life and the dignity of others?
- Will I be preserving my moral and ethical integrity? Will I be preserving the moral and ethical integrity of my organization?
- What are the short-term effects? What are the long-term effects?

As Romano et al. (2009, p.102) suggest, "Ethical problem solving incorporates values, human dignity and respect into the problem-solving process. It encourages officers to include stakeholders, rather than exclude stakeholders. This method raises the standards in the community and will ultimately positively affect the qualify of life in that community."

SUMMARY

Officers may be sued under three types of state liability (tort) laws: strict liability, intentional tort and negligence. Most civil lawsuits brought against law enforcement officers are based on Statute 42 of the U.S. Code, Section 1983, also called the Civil Rights Act. This act says that anyone acting under the authority of the law who violates another person's constitutional rights can be sued. The most frequent civil lawsuits against police involve false arrest or imprisonment, malicious prosecution, use of unnecessary or excessive force, brutality, wrongful death, negligent service and failure to protect.

The normal defenses used by police officers, departments and municipalities being sued are that they did not intend to deprive the plaintiff of constitutional rights, that they acted in good faith and that they acted with what was considered reasonable judgment at the time and with valid authority. Protection against lawsuits includes effective policies and procedures clearly communicated to all, thorough and continuous training, proper supervision and discipline, and accurate, thorough police reports. The importance of documentation cannot be emphasized enough. Comprehensive, well-written incident reports are vital to defenses against civil suits.

To minimize lawsuits at a more personal level, law enforcement officers should know and follow their department's guidelines; stay in the scope of their duties; always act professionally; know and respect their constituents' rights; seek advice if in doubt; carefully document their activities in their reports; maintain good community relations; keep current on civil and criminal liability cases; and know the laws. Law enforcement officers and agencies can countersue if they are falsely accused of a civil offense.

Police officers should be concerned with acting legally to avoid civil lawsuits, as well as with acting ethically. Ethics deals with standards of honesty, fairness and integrity in behavior. An absolute issue is one with only two sides—the decision is between black and white. A relative issue is one with many sides, that is, varying shades of gray between the two absolute positions. Ethical issues are usually relative and are affected by the police culture. Conventional wisdom holds that the defining characteristics of the police culture are social isolation and group loyalty, resulting in a code of silence. The code of silence and the attitude of Us versus Them often bond. Loyalty becomes more important than integrity. This phenomenon is also called the *thin blue line*.

Three areas in discussions of law enforcement ethics are controversial: police use of deception, police acceptance of gratuities and professional courtesy. Accepting gratuities may be the first step on the way to corrupt behavior. The key elements in corrupt behavior are (1) conduct prohibited by law (2) involving misuse of position (3) resulting in a reward or personal gain for the officer. Perhaps the most important factor in police officers becoming corrupt is the extraordinary amount of discretion they have. In addition to the existence of discretion, officers may become corrupt because they believe the ends justify the means, they begin with accepting gratuities and progress to larger indiscretions, they believe they are above the law, or they engage in the code of silence. The culture of the police department (the barrel) can allow or eliminate corrupt behavior (bad apples).

Basic ethics tests include asking oneself, Am I doing the right thing? At the right time? In the right way? For the right reason? How would I feel if it were made public? There is no right way to do a wrong thing. Ethical behavior within a law enforcement agency is ultimately the responsibility of each officer within that agency.

APPLICATION

The chief of police has been concerned about officers coming to him wanting advice about what to do when business people give them gratuities such as boxes of candy, children's toys, bottles of liquor and other items useful to an officer and the officer's family. The officers are concerned as to how much they can take, when they can take it and whether they should report to the administration upon receipt. The chief asks a committee, of which you are chair, to develop a policy and procedure to clarify how officers are to respond to such offers.

INSTRUCTIONS

Write a policy and procedure specifying the need for uniformity in accepting gratuities and gifts and if they are to be accepted at all. Include what can be accepted and under what circumstances.

EXERCISES IN CRITICAL THINKING

A. In the early morning hours, Jacqueline McKone stepped outside her apartment and witnessed what she said was the uncalled-for arrest and beating of a young Black man, 21-year-old Dennis Cherry. McKone was a legal assistant in an attorney's office, completing course work to become a court reporter. She reported that four police officers held Cherry, and one, whom she identified as Ed Nelson, hit him. Cherry, she reported, had done nothing to attract the police or to resist their efforts to arrest him. The incident occurred more than a block away from the Convention Center to which police had come to close down a dance.

Several officers, including Ed Nelson, tried to intimidate McKone as she stood watching the scene. She said this to herself, however: I can't stop it, but I will watch this whole thing and report it. When Lieutenant Bruce Jones arrived on the scene, she approached him to report what she had witnessed.

1. When Lieutenant Bruce Jones arrived at the scene, what should have been his treatment of McKone?
   a. To tell McKone that the police were simply following arrest procedure and that because she was not present at the beginning of the incident or close enough to hear all that Cherry said to police, she could not be expected to understand what actually happened.
   b. First, to ask if she had been harmed, second, to apologize for what she had witnessed and then, to provide her with the information needed to contact civilian review.
   c. First, to interview the police officers who conducted the arrest, then to interview McKone and then to explain to McKone that although Cherry denied it, the police said he tried to hit them, which justified their treatment of Cherry.
   d. To ignore McKone other than to tell her that she could bring her views and testimony to the Police Civilian Review Authority.
   e. To gently remind McKone that it was not wise to offend local police, especially well-liked officers such as Ed Nelson, and to point out that if she called the news media and filed a complaint, she would get a series of hateful, racist responses accusing her of having a Black boyfriend or of being a "nigger lover."

B. In June, a police officer received information from a confidential, reliable informant. He had observed a film depicting a 16-year-old girl engaging in sex with a Rottweiler dog while at the home of Robert Bonynge. The officer applied for a search warrant for Bonynge's residence. The affidavit accompanying the application reiterated the information received from the informant and stated that the officer sought the search warrant "to seize any film involving child pornography and bestiality." The warrant permitted seizure of the following:

> Pornography films involving female juveniles and a Rottweiler dog and any contraband that would violate the state statute governing the pornography laws. Any filming equipment and duplicating equipment.

The affidavit was attached to the warrant. The police executed the search warrant at Bonynge's residence. A police lieutenant observed the Rottweiler dog on the premises and numerous videocassettes, 8-millimeter movies, photographs and magazines depicting sexual scenes involving young females, possibly juveniles. The officers seized hundreds of films and photographs including several commercial videotapes of popular motion pictures. The officer stated that it was his experience that "obscene material is planted in the middle of what appears to be a commercial tape to make it difficult to locate."

2. Were the videotapes seized in violation of Bonynge's Fourth Amendment rights?
   a. Yes, because the Fourth Amendment gives individuals the right to be free from unreasonable search and seizure and declares that warrants shall particularly describe the place to be searched and the person or things to be seized, and not

all the videotapes were of pornographic subjects.

b. Yes, because a warrant limits the discretion of the executing officers as well as gives notice to the party searched, and the materials seized were not described with sufficient particularity.

c. No, because a warrant to search a residence gives rights to search all parts of that residence and seize any evidence found.

d. Yes, because pornography is an ethical issue that must be left to individual discretion—no law or police action is appropriate.

e. No, because the officers who swore out the affidavit also executed the search; they had the benefit of the more specific language of the affidavit.

3. Which of the following would be unethical?
   a. The temporary seizure of constitutionally protected material (in this case, of every film and videotape regardless of content).
   b. Providing a prior adversary hearing before authorizing the seizure of allegedly obscene material for the purpose of destroying it.
   c. Accepting gratuities from bookstores or commercial theaters involved in the distribution or exhibition of pornographic materials and being loyal to fellow officers who accept gratuities.
   d. Varying the times when you take breaks, eating meals at different times and places, filling out reports at irregular times and places to protect yourself from temptation and blowing the whistle on colleagues who routinely bend rules.
   e. Exercising discretion while extending due process to criminal suspects and victims alike (such as withholding the identity of the 16-year-old girl).

DISCUSSION QUESTIONS

1. Have any misconduct lawsuits been filed against local police officers? Check with your police department to see what their history of civil lawsuits has been.
2. How much training is enough to avoid lawsuits under Section 1983? Explain your reasoning in the areas of firearms, search and seizure, and laws of arrest.
3. How could a Section 1983 action be brought where an officer in the locker room preparing for duty accidentally discharged his revolver, striking a custodian? What would be the justification for a lawsuit in this case?
4. In what areas of law enforcement should police officers be exempt from lawsuits, if any?
5. What are some temptations that lead to police misconduct or corruption?
6. Can ethical standards that apply to police officers be circumvented when it comes to apprehending drug dealers? If so, to what extent?
7. Do you feel there is value in civilian review boards?

GALE EMERGENCY SERVICES DATABASE

- Use the Gale Emergency Services database to answer the Discussion Questions as appropriate.
- Use the Gale Emergency Services database to find and outline one of the following assignments:
  - "Getting Along with Citizen Oversight" by Peter Finn
  - "Managing for Ethics: A Mandate for Administrators" by Timothy J. O'Malley
  - "Organizational Ethics through Effective Leadership" by Brandon V. Zuidema and H. Wayne Duff
  - "Above Reproach" by Brian Parsi Boetig
  - "Law Enforcement Ethics Do Not Begin When You Pin On the Badge" by Norman Stephens
  - "To Arrest or Not Arrest" by Carole Moore
  - "Crime Scene Ethics: Take It or Leave It" by Douglas Page
  - "Ethics and Law Enforcement" by J. Kevin Grant
  - Institutional Integrity: The Four Elements of Self-Policing" by John H. Conditt, Jr. List and briefly explain what the four elements of self-policing are according to Conditt.

REFERENCES

Alpert, Geoffrey P., and Noble, Jeffrey J. "Lies, True Lies, and Conscious Deception: Police Officers and the Truth." *Police Quarterly*, June 2009, pp.237–254.

Bennett, Charles; Bushey, Keith; Cummings, Patrick; Doherty, Ann Marie; Hesser, Larry; Jahn, Mike; and Melton, Richard. "The Law Enforcement Oath of Honor." *The Police Chief*, October 1999, pp.24–29.

Bowden, John. "On Language, Communication, and Leadership." *P! Exclusive: Police Report Writing*, January 30, 2009.

Burch, Jay. "The Loss of Common Sense in Policing?" *Law and Order*, 2008, pp.69–74.

Chudwin, Jeff. "Lawsuits, Training and Officer Safety." *Tactical Response*, Spring 2003, p.10.

Colaprete, Frank. "Internal Affairs Interviews." *Law and Order*, June 2005, pp.112–115.

Commission on Accreditation of Law Enforcement Agencies. *Standards for Law Enforcement Agencies*, 5th ed. Fairfax, VA: CALEA, 2006, updated 2008.

Dees, Tim. "Internal Affairs: Management Software." *Law and Order*, May 2003, pp.88–95.

Griffith, David. "Policing the Police." *Police*, October 2003, pp.76–79.

Griffith, David. "The All Seeing Eye." *Police*, June 2009a, p.8.

Griffith, David. "Turning Cops into Cameras." *Police*, June 2009b, pp.38–41.

Grossi, Dave. "Tactics for Survival Writing." *Law Officer Magazine*, October 2008, pp.30–33.

Jetmore, Larry R. "Investigative Ethics." *Law Officer Magazine*, August 2008a, pp.104–108.

Jetmore, Larry R. "Investigative Ethics: Part 2." *Law Officer Magazine*, September 2008b, pp.68–69.

Joyner, Chuck. "A Proper Use of Force Report—Protection against Liability." *PoliceOne.com News*, May 20, 2009.

Kelly, Sean F. "Internal Affairs Issues for Small Police Departments." *FBI Law Enforcement Bulletin*, July 2003, pp.1–6.

Klockars, Carl B. "Police Ethics." In *The Encyclopedia of Police Science*, 2nd ed., edited by William G. Bailey, New York: Garland, 1995, pp.549–553.

Means, Randy. "The Greatest Liability Reduction Tool." *Law and Order*, December 2007, pp.32–33.

Moore, Carole. "Deceptive Techniques." *Law Enforcement Technology*, August 2007, p.146.

Quinn, Michael W. *Walking with the Devil: The Police Code of Silence (What Bad Cops Don't Want You to Know and Good Cops Won't Tell You)*. Minneapolis, MN: Quinn and Associates, 2004.

"Risk Management, Liability Insurance and CALEA Accreditation." CALEA Online. Accessed March 1, 2009. http://www.calea.org/Online/CALEAPrograms/LawEnforcement/lawenfprogram.htm

Romano, Linda J.; McDevitt, Jack; Jones, Jimmie; and Johnson, William. "Combined Problem-Solving Models Incorporate Ethics Analysis." *The Police Chief*, August 2000, pp.98–102.

Rutledge, Devallis. "The Lawful Use of Deception." *Police*, January 2007, pp.59–62.

Scoville, Dean. "Rules of Engagement." *Police*, October 2008, pp.56–63.

Trautman, Neal. *Police Code of Silence*. Arlington, VA: International Association of Chiefs of Police, 2000.

Trautman, Neal. "Truth about Police Code of Silence Revealed." *Law and Order*, January 2001, pp.68–76.

Trautman, Neal "Overcoming the Moments Most Likely to End Your Career." *LawOfficer.com*. June 15, 2009.

Wolfe, Duane. "Defining 'Professional Courtesy.'" *PoliceOne.com News*, June 5, 2009.

CASES CITED

Garrity v. New Jersey, 385 U.S. 493 (1967)

Graham v. Connor, 490 U.S. 386 (1989)

Sorrells v. United States, 287 U.S. 435 (1932)

Thurman v. City of Torrington, 595 F. Supp. 1521 (D. Conn. 1984)

United States v. Russell, 411 U.S. 423 (1973)

APPENDIX

Policies and Procedures Sample Form

Name of agency: Date issued:

Procedure directive no.: Page ______ of ______

Effective date:

Subject:

Goal:

Policy:

Policy no.: Page ______ of ______

Procedures:

____

Chief of Police

GLOSSARY

Numbers in (parentheses) indicate the chapter in which the term can be found.

A

absolute issue—An issue with only two sides, viewed as either/or, black or white. (14)
absolute privilege—Information or testimony that cannot be received; there are no exceptions (see *privileged information*). (2)
accelerants—Substances that promote burning; are a primary form of evidence at an arson scene; the most common accelerant used is gasoline. (10)
acute stress—Temporary stress that may result in peak performance; body adapts for fight or flight. (13)
admission—Statement containing some information concerning the elements of a crime, but falling short of a full confession. (2)
aerobic training—Physical training aimed at strengthening the cardiovascular system. (13)
AMBER Alert—Voluntary partnerships between law enforcement agencies and public broadcasters to notify the public when a child has been abducted. (11)
anaerobic training—Physical training aimed at strengthening the muscles of the body. (13)
arrest—The official taking of a person into custody to answer criminal charges; involves at least temporarily depriving the person of liberty and may involve the use of force. (3)
asymmetric war—One in which a much weaker opponent takes on a stronger opponent by refusing to confront the stronger opponent head on. (9)
Automated Fingerprint Identification System (AFIS)—Computerized database maintained by the FBI used to identify a limited number of likely matches for a latent fingerprint. (10)
awareness spectrum—Framework for describing officer's level of awareness, ranging from condition white, environmental unawareness, to condition black, panicked/blacked out/perhaps dead. Ideally, officers will be at condition yellow: alert but relaxed. (13)

B

battered woman syndrome—Defense used by women who have been beaten by their husbands and who then kill those husbands, apparently while completely sane and in control. (7)
battering—The use of physical, emotional, economic or sexual force to control another person. (7)
beachheading— Deliberate questioning first and then *Mirandizing* and requestioning, an unconstitutional interrogation strategy. (2)
bifurcated society—Divided into two distinct socioeconomic groups, upper and lower. (1)
bioterrorism—Involves such biological weapons of mass destruction (WMD) as anthrax, botulism and smallpox. (9)
blood-alcohol concentration (BAC)—The weight of alcohol in grams per milliliter of blood. (5)
blue lie—A lie told not to help or comfort the person lied to but, rather, to exert control. (14)
broken windows metaphor—Broken windows in a neighborhood make a statement that no one cares enough about the quality of life in the neighborhood to bother fixing little things that need repair. (1)
bullying—Intentional, repeated hurtful acts, words or behavior. (7)
burnout—Condition experienced by a person who is "used up or consumed by a job," made listless through overwork and stress; the person lacks energy or has little interest in work. (13)
burst stress—Having to go from relative calm to high intensity, sometimes life-threatening, activity. (13)

C

chain of custody—Documented account of who has had control of evidence from the time it is discovered until it is presented in court. Also called *chain of possession.* (6)
chain of possession—See *chain of custody.* (6)
child maltreatment— A broad term that encompasses all variations of child abuse (physical, emotional, sexual) and neglect (physical, emotional, educational). According to the CDC, "Child maltreatment is any act or series of acts of commission or omission by a parent or other caregiver that results in harm, potential for harm, or threat of harm to a child." (11)
child welfare model—Society's attempt to help youths who come in conflict with the law. (11)
chronic stress—Ongoing, continuous stress; like being under a state of constant siege; can lead to severe psychological problems. (13)
civil actions—Lawsuits for perceived wrongs against individuals for which restitution is sought in civil court. (14)
civil disobedience—Intentional breaking of a law to prove a point or to protest something. (6)
Civil Rights Act—States that anyone acting under the authority of the law who violates another person's constitutional rights can be sued. See also *Section 1983.* (14)
closed question—Limits the amount or scope of information that a person can provide, for example, "What color was the car?" (the opposite of an open-ended question). (2)
cognitive interview—Interviewing method that puts witnesses mentally back at the scene of an incident and encourages them to tell the whole story without interruption. (2)
collective deep pocket—A pool of defendants from which astronomical financial judgments can be collected; created by suing every possible individual and agency involved in an incident. (14)
collective efficacy—Cohesion among neighborhood residents combined with shared expectations for informal social control of public space that inhibits both crime and disorder. (6)
community policing—Involves empowering citizens to help local law enforcement provide safer neighborhoods; usually includes an emphasis on foot patrol, partnerships and problem solving. (1)
compliance—A complete lack of physical resistance. (3)
conditional privilege—The official information privilege; that is, the information can be received but the source of the information can be protected. (2)

confession—Information supporting the elements of a crime that is provided and attested to by any person involved in committing the crime; can be oral or written. (2)
contagion effect—Coverage of terrorism inspires more terrorism—it is, in effect, contagious. (9)
contamination—An undesired transfer of information between items of evidence. (10)
continuum of contacts—Almost limitless variations of contacts between the public and the police, ranging from no contact to incarceration or even the death penalty. (3)
covert investigations—Those done secretively, for example, using surveillance and undercover personnel. (10)
Crime Index—Term identifying the FBI's Uniform Crime Report program (UCR); includes the violent crimes and the property crimes. (6)
critical-incident stress debriefing (CISD)—Officers who experience a critical incident, such as a mass disaster or large accident with multiple deaths, are brought together as a group for psychological debriefing soon after the event. (8)
cross-training—Alternating between different forms of exercise. (13)
cruising—Driving around and around a predetermined, popular route, usually through the heart of a town or city; a social activity of teenagers. (5)
***CSI* effect**—"Where unrealistic portrayals of the science have translated to equally unrealistic expectations from not only the public but also other professions that operate within the justice system" who have unrealistic expectations about what crime scene investigators can do. (10)
curtilage—A house and the area immediately surrounding it. (3)
cyberterrorism—Terrorism that initiates, or threatens to initiate, the exploitation of or attack on information systems. (9)

D

D.A.R.E.—Drug Abuse Resistance Education, a school program aimed at teaching fourth- and fifth-grade students to say no to peer pressure to use drugs. (11)
de facto arrest—A detention without probable cause that is factually indistinguishable from an arrest. (3)
deconfliction—Avoiding conflict. (9)
decriminalization—Making status offenses noncriminal matters. (11)
depression—A serious and life-threatening medical illness. (13)
differential police response strategies—Practice of varying the rapidity of response as well as the responder, based on the type of incident and the time of occurrence. (4)
directed patrol—Use of officers' discretionary patrol time to focus on specific department goals. (4)
discovery crimes—Offenses that have been completed and whose scenes have been abandoned before the crimes are noticed. In contrast to *involvement crimes.* (4)
discretion—The freedom to act or decide a matter on one's own. (1)
discretionary acts—Those actions officers perform using their own judgment; policies and procedures for the acts leave decisions up to the officers. (14)
diversion—Referring a juvenile out of the justice system and to some other agency or program. (11)
DNA fingerprinting—Use of the unique genetic structure of an individual for identification. Blood, hair and other body tissues and fluids may be used in this process. (10)
dog shift—Typically the shift from 11 P.M. to 7 A.M. (1)
drug recognition expert (DRE)—Specially trained individual who can determine if someone is under the influence of drugs. Also called *drug recognition technician.* (5)
drug recognition technician (DRT)—See *drug recognition expert.* (5)
dual motive stop—A stop in which the officer is stopping a vehicle to investigate a traffic violation and because the driver looks suspicious. Also called a *pretext stop.* (5)
due process of law—The fundamental principle of American justice. It requires notice of a hearing or trial that is timely and that adequately informs the accused persons of the charges; it also gives the defendant an opportunity to present evidence in self-defense before an impartial judge or jury and to be presumed innocent until proven guilty by legally obtained evidence. (3)

E

ecoterrorism—Seeks to inflict economic damage to those who profit from the destruction of the natural environment. (9)
8% problem—50–60 percent of juvenile crime is committed by 8 percent of juveniles. (11)
elder abuse—The physical and emotional trauma, financial exploitation and general neglect of individuals over 65 years of age. (7)
emergency operations center (EOC)—The location from which personnel operate during a natural disaster or other type of emergency. (8)
enforcement index—Standard suggesting that for each fatal and personal injury crash, between 20 and 25 convictions for hazardous moving violations indicates effective traffic enforcement. (5)
entrapment—An action by the police (or a government agent) persuading a person to commit a crime that the person would not otherwise have committed. (12)
equivocal death investigation—May have two or more meanings and may be presented as either a homicide or a suicide, depending on the circumstances. (10)
estimative language—Language based on analytical assessments and judgments rather than on facts or hard evidence. (9)
Exclusionary Rule—Courts cannot accept evidence obtained in illegal searches and seizures, regardless of how relevant the evidence is to the case (*Weeks v. United States,* 1914). (3)
exigent circumstances—Conditions surrounding an emergency situation in which no time is available to secure an arrest or search warrant. (3)
expressive violence—That resulting from hurt feelings, anger or rage. (7)

F

felony syndrome—Obtaining complete information on only felony cases, deeming them to be the only "real" police work. (2)
FEMA—The Federal Emergency Management Agency, an independent federal agency charged with building and supporting the nation's emergency management system. Its mission is to reduce loss of life and property and protect our nation's critical infrastructure from all types of hazards through a comprehensive, risk-based, emergency management program of mitigation, preparedness, response and recovery. (8)
field inquiry—The unplanned questioning of a person who has aroused a police officer's suspicions. (2)
firewall—A security measure intended to prevent unauthorized Internet users from accessing private networks connected to the Internet. (8)
flashbangs—Devices that explode with a loud bang and emit brilliant light; used by police as a diversion. (6)
flashroll—Buy money in a drug deal. (12)
forensics—The application of scientific processes to solve legal problems, most notably within the context of the criminal justice system. (10)
frisk—A brief patdown following a stop to determine if a person is armed. (3)
functional equivalent—Refers to places other than actual borders where travelers frequently enter or exit the country, such as international airports. (3)

fusion center—Manages the flow of information and intelligence across all levels and sectors of government and private industry, turning information and intelligence into actionable knowledge. (9)

G

gang—A group of individuals with a recognized name and symbols who form an allegiance for a common purpose and engage in unlawful activity. (12)
geographic information systems (GIS)—Creating, updating and analyzing computerized maps. (6)
goals—Broad, general purposes. (1)
good faith—Belief that one's actions are just and legal. (3)
graffiti—Symbols and slogans written on walls and sides of buildings, often by gang members to mark their turf. (12)
grapevine—A network of informal, internal channels of communication. Also called the *rumor mill.* (2)
G.R.E.A.T.—The Gang Resistance Education and Training program. (11)

H

hazmat incident—An incident involving hazardous materials. (8)
horizontal prosecution—Different assistant prosecutors are responsible for specific phases of the court proceedings. (12)
hot spots—Clusters of crime in certain geographic areas. (6)

I

igniters—Articles used to light a fire. (10)
impact evaluation—Assessment that determines if a problem declined. (4)
implied consent law—A law stating that those who request and receive driver's licenses agree to take tests to determine their ability to drive; refusal will result in revocation of the license. (5)
incivilities—Subtle signs of a community not caring about disorder, including rowdiness, drunkenness, fighting, prostitution and abandoned buildings. (6)
informant—A human source of information in a criminal action whose identity must be protected. (2)
instrumental violence—That used to exert control. (7)
intentional tort—An act where the officer's intent to engage in the behavior must be proven, for example, wrongful death or false arrest. (14)
interoperability—The ability of public safety officials to communicate with each other seamlessly in real time over their wireless communications network either by voice or through data transmissions. (2)
interrogation—The questioning of suspects from whom officers try to obtain facts related to a crime as well as admissions or confessions related to the crime. (2)
interview—The planned questioning of a witness, victim, informant or other person with information related to an incident or a case. (2)
"in the presence"—Perceived by an officer through the senses (does not refer to proximity). (3)
involvement crimes—Offenses in which the victim and the suspect confront each other. In contrast to *discovery crimes.* (4)

J

jihad—A holy war. (9)
juvenile—A person not yet of legal age, usually under the age of 18. (11)
juvenile delinquents—Young people who violate the law. (11)
juvenile justice model—A judicial process in which young people who come in conflict with the law are held responsible and accountable for their behavior. (11)

L

leading question—One that suggests an answer, for example, "You wanted your boss dead, isn't that correct?" (2)
libel—Written defamation of another's character; false statements that tend to humiliate a person and degrade that person in the esteem of others. (14)
litigious—Highly likely to sue. (14)
lockdowns—Periods when students are detained in classrooms while police and dogs scour the building searching for contraband or any danger to a safe educational environment. (7)

M

malfeasance—Acts of misconduct or wrongdoing. (14)
malicious prosecution—A proceeding instituted in bad faith without any probable cause, in the belief that the charges against the defendant can be sustained. (14)
mental fitness—A person's emotional well-being, the ability to feel fear, anger, compassion and other emotions and to express them appropriately; also refers to a person's alertness and ability to make decisions quickly. (13)
mere handcuff rule—A policy stating that in the interest of officer safety, all persons arrested and transported shall be handcuffed. It disregards the fact that handcuffing is a form of force and should be used only if the situation warrants. (3)
ministerial acts—Duties prescribed by law as some of the tasks of an administrative office. (14)
***Miranda* warning**—A statement of a suspect's rights when that suspect is being questioned: the rights to remain silent, to talk to an attorney and to have an attorney present during questioning, the attorney to be provided free if a suspect cannot afford one. (2)
mission—An organization's reason for existence, its purpose. (1)
mission statement—Written statement of an organization's reasons for existence or purpose. (1)
moniker—A gang member's street name. (12)
Munchausen's syndrome by proxy (MSBP)—A psychiatric ailment that leads a person to fabricate a child's illnesses to fulfill his or her own needs for attention and sympathy. (11)

N

negligence—An act where intent or mental state does not matter; what must be proven is if some inadvertent act or failure to act created an unreasonable risk to another person, for example, speeding resulting in a traffic crash or not responding to a 911 call. (14)
nonfeasance—Failure to take action, with the result being injury or damage to another person. (14)
nystagmus—The involuntary jerking or bouncing of the eye, a possible cause of which is intoxication. (5, 12)

O

objectives—Specific activities to accomplish a goal. (1)
one-pot jurisdictional approach—Use of the same system to deal with youths who are neglected or abused, those who are status offenders and those who commit serious crimes. (11)
open question—One that allows for an unlimited response from the witness in his/her own words, for example, "What can you tell me about the car?" (the opposite of a closed-ended question). (2)
osteogenesis imperfecta—A medical condition characterized by bones that break easily; also called *brittle bone disease.* (11)
overt investigations—Those conducted openly, usually with officers in uniform or introducing themselves as police officers. (10)

P

pandemic—an infectious disease that occurs over a large geographic area and affects a significantly high percentage of the population. (8)

parallel proceedings—When both civil and criminal proceedings are instituted against a violator; a frequent occurrence in environmental crimes. (10)

parens patriae—A doctrine allowing the state to assume guardianship of abandoned, neglected and "wayward" children. (11)

participatory leadership—Allows officers to influence decisions affecting them and seeks to form a cohesive team. (1)

patdown—A brief feeling of a person's outer clothing to determine if a weapon is present. Also called a *frisk*. (3)

phishing—Use of fraudulent e-mails and Web sites to fool recipients into divulging personal information. (10)

physical fitness—The general capacity to adapt and respond favorably to physical effort. (13)

plain view—Term describing evidence that is not concealed, that is easily seen by officers while performing their legal duties. (3)

police operations—Those activities conducted in the field by law enforcement officers as they "serve and protect." They usually include patrol, traffic, investigation and general calls for service. (1)

police placebo—A lie told by the police when the lie benefits the person lied to and when no more effective means of dealing with the problem is available. Also known as a *white lie*. (14)

policy—A guiding principle or course of action. (1)

positional asphyxia—A type of strangulation that results if a person's body position interferes with breathing. (3)

posttraumatic stress disorder (PTSD)—A reaction to a violent event that evokes intense fear, terror and helplessness; a debilitating stressful reaction to a trauma that may last for months or years; can be experienced by those who help the victims as well as by victims. (8)

predisaster plans—Preparing for anticipated and unanticipated emergencies before they occur. (8)

preliminary investigation—The on-the-scene interviews of victims and witnesses, interrogations of suspects and search of the crime scene itself. (6)

premeditation—The deliberate, precalculated plan to act; the essential element of first-degree murder, distinguishing it from all other murder classifications. (10)

pretext stop—A stop in which the officer is stopping a vehicle to investigate not only a traffic violation but because the driver looks suspicious. Also called a *dual motive stop*. (5)

primary victim—One who actually is harmed. (2)

privileged information—Data that does not need to be divulged to the police or the courts because of the existence of a special relationship, such as that between spouses or between lawyers and their clients. (2)

probable cause—The fact that it is more likely than not that a crime has been committed by the person whom a law enforcement officer seeks to arrest. An officer's probable cause to conduct an arrest depends on what the officer knew *before* taking action. (3)

problem-oriented policing (POP)—A proactive approach to patrol and policing that focuses on problems to be solved rather than incidents to be responded to. (4)

procedural law—Deals with process, or how the law is applied. (3)

procedures—Step-by-step instructions for carrying out department policies. (1)

process evaluation—Assessment that determines if a response was implemented as planned. (4)

property crimes—Offenses in which no physical contact with the victim occurs, including arson, auto theft, burglary and larceny/theft. (6)

proportionate assignment—Determination of area assignments by requests for service based on available data. No area is larger than the time it takes a car to respond in three minutes or less. (4)

proximate—Closely related in space, time or order; very near. (4)

proxy data—Evidence not seen as they are created but are only the remnants of an event left behind. (10)

pulling levers—Cracking down on any type of criminal activity and telling gang members that the crackdown will continue until the violence stops. (12)

pursuit—An active attempt by a law enforcement officer on duty in a patrol car to apprehend one or more occupants of a moving motor vehicle, providing the driver is aware of the attempt and is resisting apprehension by maintaining or increasing his speed or by ignoring the law enforcement officer's attempt to stop him. Can also refer to a foot chase. (5)

R

racial profiling—Inconsistent, discriminatory enforcement of the law; an officer uses a person's race to assess the likelihood of criminal conduct or wrongdoing. (1, 5)

rapport— A relationship of mutual trust, conformity, accord and respect; a sense between two people that they can communicate comfortably and openly. (2)

raves—A form of dance and recreation held in a clandestine location with fast-paced, high-volume music, a variety of high-tech entertainment and often the use of drugs. (11)

reader-friendly writing—Avoids police jargon and communicates in plain, simple language; it is written as it would be spoken, and it considers who the audience is. (2)

regulations—Rules governing the actions of employees of the city, including police department personnel. (1)

relative issue—An issue with a range of morally acceptable options, which are of several shades of gray rather than either black or white. (14)

response time—The time elapsed from when the need for police arises and when they arrive on the scene. (4)

road rage—An assault with a motor vehicle or other dangerous weapon by the operator or passenger(s) of one motor vehicle on the operator or passenger(s) of another motor vehicle and is caused by an incident that occurred on the roadway. (5)

S

scofflaws—Persistent lawbreakers. (5)

secondary victim—One who is not actually harmed but who suffers along with the victim—a spouse or parent, for example. (2)

Section 1983—The Civil Rights Act; it states that anyone acting under the authority of the law who violates another person's constitutional rights can be sued; the legal authority for most lawsuits against law enforcement officers and agencies. (14)

selective enforcement—The ability to decide when to impose legal sanctions on those who violate the law, whether issuing traffic tickets or arresting someone. (1, 5)

slander—Spoken defamation of another's character; false oral statements that tend to humiliate a person and degrade that person in the esteem of others. (14)

sleeper cells—Groups of terrorists who blend into a community. (9)

slippery slope—One small indiscretion can lead to more serious misbehavior and finally to actual corruption. (14)

split-second syndrome—In some circumstances, officers have very little time to think through decisions. A high percentage of inappropriate decisions should be expected and accepted because the officer must act quickly. (13)

spoofing— A newer trend in computer-related crime involving senders who alter or change the origin or source of an e-mail so that the origin of the e-mail is unknown. Many fraudulent scams use spoofed Internet protocol (IP) addresses. (10)

stake-in-conformity variables—Include marital status, employment, residential stability and age—all variables offenders might lose if convicted for a repeat offense. (7)
statement—A legal narrative description of events related to a crime. (2)
status offenses—Violations of the law applying only to those under legal age; includes curfew violations, drinking alcoholic beverages, incorrigibility, smoking cigarettes, running away from home and truancy. (11)
Stockholm syndrome—In a hostage situation, the process of transference, with the hostages feeling positive toward their captors (and negative toward the police) and the captors returning these positive feelings. (6)
stop—Brief detention of a suspicious person by law enforcement officers for questioning. (3)
stop-and-frisk situation—One in which law enforcement officers briefly detain a suspicious person for questioning and pat the person's outer clothing to ensure that they are not armed. (3)
street gang—Any durable, street-oriented youth group whose own identity includes involvement in illegal activity. (11)
street justice—Decision of police officers to deal with an offense in their own way—usually by ignoring it. (11)
strict liability—Refers to an act where the injury or damage is so severe and the harm should have been foreseen so that intent or mental state need not be proven. (14)
substantive law—Deals with the content of what behaviors are considered crimes; defines the elements of crimes and the punishments for them. (3)
survival triangle—Model for police survival; consists of mental and physical preparedness, sound tactics and weapon control. (13)
swatting—An emerging trend by pranksters involving communication centers in which a false report is filed, via Internet, to the emergency dispatch center to deploy SWAT teams to a residence where the occupants are oblivious to the situation. (8)

T

terrorism—The use of force or violence against persons or property in violation of U.S. criminal laws for purposes of intimidation, coercion or ransom. (9)
thrownaways—Youths who were either told to leave, were not allowed back after having left, ran away and no one tried to recover them, or were abandoned or deserted. (11)
tort—A civil wrong, the equivalent to a crime in criminal law. (14)
totality of circumstances—All relevant variables in an arrest, including an individual's age, mentality, education, nationality and criminal experience, as well as the reason for the arrest and how it was explained to the individual being arrested. During an interrogation, it also includes whether basic necessities were provided and the methods used during the interrogation. (2)
traffic calming—Describes a wide range of road and environment design changes that either make it more difficult for a vehicle to speed or make drivers believe they should slow down for safety. (5)
triage—Prioritizing, sorting out by degree of seriousness, as in medical emergencies. (8)
truancy—Loosely defined as habitual unexcused absence from school, considered a status offense because, although compulsory attendance laws vary somewhat from state to state, every state requires children between certain ages to be in school during the academic year absent a valid excuse. (11)
turf—The territory claimed by a gang, often marked by graffiti. (12)

U

Uniform Crime Reports (UCRs)—The FBI's national crime reporting system, published annually as *Crime in the United States.* (6)
universal precaution—All blood and potentially infectious materials other than blood must be treated as if infected. (13)

V

vertical prosecution—Where one assistant prosecutor or small group of assistant prosecutors handle the criminal complaint from start to finish through the entire court process. (12)
vicarious liability—Responsibility for a person's actions or others specifically associated with that person. (14)
victimless crimes—Offenses in which there are no complainants; includes prostitution, pornography, gaming and drug dealing/using. (10)
violent crimes—Offenses in which physical contact with the victim occurs, including assault, murder, rape and robbery; sometimes called *crimes against persons.* (6)

Z

zero-tolerance policies—School policies that mandate predetermined consequences or punishments for specific offenses, for example, suspension or expulsion for possession of drugs or a weapon. (7)

INDEX

O

P